France
and the Coming of the
Second World War
1936-1939

France
and the Coming of the
Second World War
1936-1939

ANTHONY ADAMTHWAITE

FRANK CASS

73848

First published in 1977 in Great Britain by
FRANK CASS AND COMPANY LIMITED
Gainsborough House, Gainsborough Road,
London E11 1RS, England

and in the United States of America by
FRANK CASS AND COMPANY LIMITED
c/o Biblio Distribution Center
81 Adams Drive, Totowa, New Jersey 07512

ISBN 0 7146 3035 7

Printed in Great Britain by
Chapel River Press, Andover, Hants

TO GERALDINE

Contents

Acknowledgements   ix
Introduction   xi
Chronological list of major events, 1933-39   xvii
Maps: 1. European Frontiers after the First World War   xxi
       2. Europe, 1938-1939   xxii

Part One: The Setting

  1. Dilemma   3
  2. Quest for Security   17
  3. Wit's End   37
  4. Wait and See   58
  5. Retreat   77

Part Two: Personnel and Machinery of Policy-Making

  6. Enter Daladier and Bonnet   95
  7. The Cabinet   111
  8. Parliament   125
  9. Quai d'Orsay   137
10. The Armed Forces   159

Part Three: Undeclared War

11. 'Czechoslovakia 1938'   175
12. 'Better late than never'   200
13. Strategy and Diplomacy   226
14. 'L' effort du sang'   245
15. A free hand in the east?   264
16. Penguins and Porpoises   280
17. A Change of course   300
18. Calm before the storm   317
19. Last days   335

Conclusions   353

Abbreviations   359

Notes to Chapters   360

Appendices   397

Bibliography   414

Index   427

Appendices

A. A note on the French sources   397
B. Biographical note on French personalities   403
C. Principal holders of office, 1936-39   409
D. French Governments, 1936-39   410
E. Organisation of the French Foreign Ministry, 1938-39   412

Illustrations

Following page 42 and page 74. By courtesy of
Radio Times Hulton Picture Library

Acknowledgements

My chief debt is to the late Prof. Pierre Renouvin, chairman of the commission which is engaged in publishing the series *Documents Diplomatiques Français*. The commission kindly allowed me to consult the documents collected for publication in volumes VIII, IX, X, XI of the series for the period January to October 1938. I was also given access to material which was being assembled for inclusion in later volumes covering the period October 1938 to September 1939.

For permission to see and quote from documents in privately held collections, I am indebted to Lady Liddell Hart, Lady Frances Phipps, Lord Simon, the late M Lucien Lamoureux, the late M Francois Piétri, and MM Jean Montigny, Henri Noguères, Michel Soulié.

My thanks are also due to the following institutions which permitted me to consult documents in their collections: British Library of Economics and Political Science, Foreign Office Library, University of Birmingham Library, Scottish Record Office, Edinburgh, Bibliothèque de Documentation Internationale Contemporaine, Paris, Fondation Nationale des Sciences Politiques, Paris, Service des Archives of the French National Assembly, Service Historique de l'Armée de l'Air, General Sikorksi Historical Institute, London. Crown copyright documents are reproduced by permission of the Controller of Her Majesty's Stationery Office.

In studying the period I was greatly helped by the assistance in correspondence and conversation of former French ministers and officials, many of whom are now sadly deceased. The late MM Paul Baudouin, Gaston Bergery, Paul Marchandeau, were especially helpful. For explaining to me the workings of the Quai d'Orsay and clarifying aspects of French diplomacy I am most grateful to MM Pierre Bressy, René Massigli, Roland de Margerie, the late M Pierre Comert, the late M Charles Corbin. M Guy la Chambre talked to me about his work as Air Minister in 1938-39 and kindly allowed me to see some of his papers. The role of *Le Temps* was described to me by M Jacques Chastenet, its editor in the 1930s.

On the British side, the late Mr Alexander Werth was a mine of information about French politics in the 1930s and, in particular about relations between the Quai d'Orsay and the foreign press corps in Paris. The late Sir Reginald Leeper, the late Sir Frederick Leith-Ross, and the late

Sir Horace Wilson generously answered questions and discussed their activity at the time.

For their assistance in correspondence, I am most grateful to the following: the late Mr Thomas Barman, MM Jean Chautemps, Alfred Fabre-Luce, Eugène Frot, Roger Genebrier, Léon Noel, Charles Pomaret, the late M Emile Mireaux, M Roger Peyrefitte, the late M Paul Reynaud, the late M Jules Romains.

Special mention must be made of the former French foreign minister, the late M Georges Bonnet. He gave unstintingly of his time in correspondence and in conversation and was unfailingly courteous and patient in answering my many queries.

I am grateful to Professor Stephen Holt of the University of Bradford for his encouragement, and to the Trustees of the Twenty Seven Foundation for their assistance towards the expenses of writing and research.

My ultimate expression of gratitude is to my wife, Geraldine, for her unsparing help and advice, a debt which is inadequately repaid in the dedication of this book.

Introduction

The French Foreign Minister in 1938-39, the late Georges Bonnet, entitled his two volumes of memoirs 'Defence of Peace'. A later volume of recollections was called 'In the Tempest'.[1] The titles aptly convey the flavour of the period. The years 1936 to 1939 were ones of 'undeclared war' in which Hitler waged a diplomatic *Blitzkrieg* against Britain and France. It was a war which France lost. Capitulations followed in swift succession: the Rhineland in 1936, *Anschluss* and Munich in 1938, Prague in 1939. By 15 March 1939, without firing a shot, Germany had regained the hegemony lost in 1918. Within nine months of the outbreak of the Second World War in September 1939 France had been occupied and turned into a vassal state.

The dénouement of 1940 was not an inevitable one. In September 1939 France remained a great military power on paper but the ambushes of the preceding three years had robbed her of major strategic advantages. Until March 1936 the demilitarised Rhineland zone had constituted an open door through which French troops could, in theory at least, have gone to the aid of their eastern allies, Czechoslovakia and Poland. After closing the door in March 1936 Germany proceeded to bolt and bar it with fortifications. The Munich agreement of September 1938 dissolved the Franco-Czech alliance and deprived France of the support of 35 Czech divisions. After 15 March 1939 Czechoslovakia and central Europe fell completely under German control.

Thus the conditions in which France declared war on Germany on 3 September 1939 could hardly have been worse. The possibility of imposing a two front war on Germany had gone. Poland alone was no match for Germany in the east. In contrast to 1914, France had no major ally in eastern Europe. Hitler and Stalin came to terms in the German-Soviet pact of 23 August 1939. In addition, the intolerable strain under which Ministers and diplomats worked during the last eighteen months of peace took its toll of morale, private and public. France's heart was not in the war. 'Nothing has been better prepared in the war plans than the evacuation of the Ministries', wrote the French Minister of Public Works, Anatole de Monzie.[2]

All the so-called 'men of Munich' have gone; Edouard Daladier, prime minister in 1938-39, died in 1970; Georges Bonnet, his Foreign Minister, died in 1973. Yet very little has been written about their leadership of France in the approach to war. English-speaking historians have naturally concentrated on the dissection of British diplomacy, giving no more than a sideways glance at the French. Why has the French record for so long remained obscure and unexplained? Primarily because of the problem of evidence—an abundance of memoirs and a dearth of official documents.*

Of the men who guided France in the 1930s only a very few resisted the temptation to put pen to paper. At the top of the list for the years 1938-39 are the memoirs of the foreign minister, Bonnet. Next in importance are the reflections of General Gamelin, Chief of the General Staff from 1931 to 1940.[3] Although Paul Reynaud did not become prime minister until March 1940, he was minister of finance in 1938-39 and his memoirs for the pre-war period are full and detailed.[4] Missing alas from the list of memorialists is the prime minister, Edouard Daladier. However, memoirs were no substitute for documents. The versions of events given by different participants often conflicted: *obscurum per obscurius*.

Until the French government began the publication of the series *Documents Diplomatiques Français* in 1963 there was next to nothing for the pre-war crises, apart from the French Yellow Book of December 1939 which, like all the coloured books published by the belligerents, was little more than a propaganda exercise. Over the last decade the documentary picture has changed for the better. The publication of diplomatic documents is well advanced and the archives of the French Ministry of Foreign Affairs will soon be open to general inspection.

Another reason why French historians shunned a close look at the pre-war period was because the events had such profound and far-reaching consequences. The defeat of 1940 was the greatest in French history, more complete and final than Sedan in 1870 or Waterloo in 1815. The cataclysm of 1940 exposed deep and violent hatreds in French society comparable, though less intense, to the passions aroused by the Dreyfus affair in the 1890s. Four years of enemy occupation deepened and hardened these divisions. Not surprisingly, French historians preferred to leave the war of words to the memorialists and publicists.

This book, then, breaks new ground because it is the first full study of French foreign policy in the crucial three years preceding the outbreak of war. Moreover, it is based on new evidence from the French diplomatic, military and parliamentary archives. Reinforcing and illuminating the official record of cables, reports and assessments are the private papers of ministers, including hitherto unpublished notes of cabinet deliberations. At last, therefore, the clash of personalities and the conflict of policies can be adequately scrutinised.

The subject of the book is French policy in Europe from Hitler's reoccupation of the Rhineland in March 1936 to his invasion of Poland in September 1939. The three and a half years which spanned these events were some of the most momentous in recent European history, marking as they did the final dissolution of the peace settlement of 1919 and the

*See Note on the French sources, Appendix A.

recovery of German primacy. The war that followed destroyed both France and Germany as leading military powers. Divided after 1945 Germany could never hope to regain the influence she had possessed from 1936 to 1939. France, though re-established as an independent state in 1944-45, soon found herself relegated along with Britain to the ranks of the second-class powers.

The work focusses on France's position in Europe, in particular her relations with Britain, Germany and Italy. This approach mirrors France's own choice of priorities. The horizon of French ministers was almost completely bounded by Europe, the Mediterranean and the Near East. Here was a major difference between British and French policies on the eve of war. Britain was acutely conscious of her world role and her strategy was strongly shaped by imperial and overseas commitments. By contrast, France saw herself primarily as a European and Mediterranean power.

The French story makes little sense without reference to the domestic setting. French diplomacy was crippled by internal divisions. From 1936 to 1939 France was in the throes of two conflicts: abroad a war of nerves with Nazi Germany and Fascist Italy, at home a class struggle which was at its most intense during Léon Blum's Popular Front government of 1936-37. The interaction of the two conflicts was summed up succinctly in the slogan: 'Better Hitler than Blum'.

The attrition of the period left its scars on politicians and diplomats. Many of the propertied classes went in fear of their lives. Pierre Bressy, Bonnet's private secretary in 1938-39, told the author how in June 1936 workmen erected a gallows outside the main entrance to the Foreign Ministry. Talking to the author in 1963, Pierre Comert, head of the Quai d'Orsay press and news department in the 1930s, recalled that the ideological quarrels of the period had often made him physically ill.

While Left and Right took to the barricades, ministers wrestled with the effects of the Great Depression. Though the British economy slowly picked up in the years after 1934, the French economy remained sluggish. The key to the rapid erosion of French power in the 1930s lay not in inept diplomacy nor, as some believed, in the machinations of a Germanophile Fifth Column but in the domestic storms which buffeted the French leadership. The simple, physical fact was that the energies of French statesmen were almost wholly absorbed by the fight to save the franc and the search for economic recovery. This interplay of foreign and domestic perils is a principal theme of the book.

With fresh perspectives from new evidence it is possible to understand more fully France's failure to oppose German ambitions. Although Germany was certainly recognised as the ultimate enemy, the documents reveal that French statesmen were preoccupied with Italy and her Mediterranean designs. The loss of Italian friendship after the Ethiopian crisis of 1935-36 and Italy's involvement in the Spanish civil war forced the French government and its military counsellors to give priority to the Mediterranean theatre. The defence of French interests in central and eastern Europe had to take second place. From February 1939 onwards France girded herself for a war against Italy in the Alps and in North Africa. The assumption was that on the Rhine there would be a military deadlock. The Maginot line was believed to be virtually impregnable and the German Siegfried line provided a conclusive argument in favour of the defensive. However, it is not fair to label the French as entirely defensive-minded. They were only too ready in the spring of 1939 to take the offensive against Italy. Such bellicosity was embarrassing for the British Prime Minister, Neville Chamberlain, and his Foreign Secretary, Lord Halifax, who believed that the *Duce* could exercise a restraining influence on Hitler.

The story of Czechoslovakia in 1938, though well-known, has been told largely from a British vantage point. Here are revealed for the first time the full details of French pressure on her Czech ally in the summer of 1938, the use of unofficial intermediaries between Paris and Prague, the French 'ultimatum' to President Benes on 20-21 September, and the frantic behind-the-scenes moves by the French foreign minister and his sympathisers to prevent France going to war.

The records also make possible a reassessment of French appeasement. Some commentators have drawn a sharp contrast between British idealism and French realism in the approaches to Germany. In truth, French appeasement, like its British counterpart, was an amalgam of many influences. French Ministers must be given credit for considerable idealism in their advances to Germany. Undeniably, fear was the dominant motive, but Blum in 1936 and Bonnet in 1938 genuinely wanted a Franco-German understanding for its own sake.

Moreover some analysts have adopted a rather simplistic approach to French appeasement. Ministers and diplomats have been divided into sheep and goats; resisters and appeasers. In reality, such sharp, clear-cut differences did not exist. For example, in September 1938 the majority of Ministers and diplomats favoured some agreement with Germany at the expense of Czechoslovakia. This is not to say that they were prepared to abandon Czechoslovakia to Hitler's mercies. It was agreed, however, that Prague would have to make substantial territorial concessions to Berlin. A clear distinction can be made between the two minority groups of ministers in the Cabinet: the Reynaud-Mandel group who wanted to defend France's interests in central and eastern Europe and the Bonnet-Monzie group who were prepared to abandon Czechoslovakia rather than fight Germany. Yet it must be stressed that at no point did the Reynaud-Mandel group consider going to war without an unequivocal pledge of British support.

Another feature of the book is that it analyses the relationship between French strategy and diplomacy. In September 1938, German troops were poised to attack Czechoslovakia. Although the French army was still a formidable force with more trained reserves than the German army and the Maginot line was superior to the then unfinished Siegfried line, Daladier chose not to fight and attended the conference in Munich. French apologias have emphasised the uncertainty of British support and its exiguous character when conceded at the eleventh hour on 26 September. Also, French and British writers have stressed the weakness of the French air force. Much has also been written about the dichotomy between France's essentially defensive war doctrine and her eastern pacts.

What emerges from this study is that at least six months before Munich the political and military leadership had decided that France could not effectively assist her Czech ally and must seek a peaceful outcome to the crisis. The decision was primarily a political one. The search for agreement with Germany and a European detente precluded the active defence of central Europe. Not that military considerations were unimportant. As Hitler shrewdly realised, the possibility of a Mediterranean conflict with Italy was enough to make the French extremely cautious towards Czechoslovakia.

The dichotomy between French strategy and alliances can be overstated. Only the Polish pact of 1921 qualified as a full military alliance. By the end of the first post-war decade France was already having second thoughts about her eastern pacts, and after 1936 French leaders had tacitly agreed that some degree of disengagement from the east was desirable and unavoidable.

The documents make it possible to explode such myths as British culpability for France's failure to resist Germany's reoccupation of the Rhineland in March 1936, or the long-held belief that British pressure in July-August 1936 led Blum to adopt the policy of non-intervention in the Spanish civil war. Again, there is no documentary evidence for the widely-held view that Bonnet gave the German foreign minister, Ribbentrop, a free hand in eastern Europe in their conversations in Paris on 6-7 December 1938. Lastly, it can be shown that Bonnet has been unjustly blamed for the fact that the British and French declarations of war on Germany were delayed until 3 September 1939, two days after the attack on Poland.

Perhaps the saddest part of the story is the weakness of the Franco-British entente. Axis solidarity could only have been countered by a solid Franco-British alliance. If a military alliance had been constructed in 1936, instead of in 1939, a European war might have been averted. It is depressing to record the opinions which the two allies had of each other. British ministers and their advisers were scathing in their judgements of French personalities. Their greatest opprobrium was reserved for the Foreign Minister. By April 1939 Bonnet was regarded as the rallying point for defeatism. He was 'a public danger to his own country and to ours', minuted Halifax's private secretary.[5] But the French could give as good as they got. Here is Daladier talking to the American Ambassador on 6 February 1939:

> he considered Chamberlain a desiccated stick; the King a moron; and the Queen an excessively ambitious woman who would be ready to sacrifice every other country in the world in order that she might remain Queen Elizabeth of England . . . he considered Eden a young idiot . . . He felt that England had become so feeble and senile that the British would give away every possession of their friends rather than stand up to Germany and Italy.[6]

Some secrets of the Franco-British partnership are disclosed after 35 years. In April 1938, for instance, the intervention of the British

Ambassador in Paris was probably decisive in preventing the re-appointment of Paul Boncour as Foreign Minister in the new Daladier government. In March-April 1938 the Foreign Office proposed taking measures to bring about the downfall of Blum's second Popular Front ministry. Again, in September 1939, the Foreign Office suggested steps to secure the removal of Bonnet from the Quai d'Orsay. Whether measures were actually implemented is not clear, but what a pity more thought was not given to the unseating of the dictators.

Chronological Table

1933	January	Hitler becomes Chancellor of Germany
	February	Japan leaves the League of Nations
	October	Germany leaves the League of Nations and Disarmament Conference
1934	January	German-Polish pact
		Beginning of Stavisky scandal in France
	6 February	Riots in Paris
	July	Abortive Nazi putsch in Austria; murder of Dollfuss
	October	Murder of Alexander of Yugoslavia and of Louis Barthou
1935	6 January	Franco-Italian agreements in Rome
	13 January	Saar plebiscite
	14 March	Hitler announces conscription and a military air force
	14 April	Stresa agreements between France, Britain and Italy
	2 May	Franco-Soviet pact
	16 May	Czech-Soviet pact
	18 June	Anglo-German naval agreement
	27 June	Franco-Italian military convention
	July	Popular Front demonstrations in Paris
	August	American Neutrality Act
	October	Italy invades Ethiopia
1936	7 March	Hitler repudiates Locarno agreements and reoccupies the Rhineland
	26 April–	
	3 May	Popular Front elections in France; strikes and occupations of factories
	4 June	Blum government
	11 July	Austro-German agreement
	17 July	Spanish civil war begins
	25 September	France leaves gold standard; devaluation of franc
1937	3 January	Signing of Anglo-Italian 'Gentleman's Agreement'

	16 March	Clichy incident
	24 April	Anglo-French declaration recognising Belgium's return to neutrality
	26 April	Bombing of Guernica
	24 May	Opening of Paris International Exhibition
	31 May	Neville Chamberlain becomes Prime Minister
	21 June	Blum government falls
	30 June	Second devaluation of franc
	July	Japanese begin advance into China
	24-29 September	Mussolini visits Germany
	6 November	Italy joins Germany and Japan in Anti-Comintern Pact
	19 November	Halifax visits Hitler
	29-30 November	Chautemps and Delbos in London
	11 December	Italy leaves the League of Nations
1938	13 January	Chautemps government falls
	17 January	New Chautemps Ministry
	4 February	Ribbentrop replaces Neurath as Foreign Minister
	12 February	Austrian Chancellor visits Hitler
	10 March	Resignation of Chautemps Ministry
	12 March	German occupation of Austria
	13 March	Annexation of Austria proclaimed
		Formation of second Blum cabinet
	10 April	Daladier forms new government
	28-29 April	Daladier and Bonnet in London
	4 May	Third devaluation of franc
	3-9 May	Hitler in Rome
	20-22 May	Scare over Czechoslovakia
	19 July	Royal visit to France
	23 July	Lord Runciman 'invited' to Czechoslovakia
	12 August	Financial crisis in France; Daladier asks Chamberlain for help; dockers' strike at Marseilles
	17 August	Chamberlain says he cannot help in any material way
	18 August	Communist party calls for recall of French parliament
	21 August	Daladier announces changes in forty hour week; two of his ministers, Frossard and Ramadier, resign
	15 September	Chamberlain-Hitler meeting at Berchtesgaden
	18 September	Daladier and Bonnet in London
	19 September	Anglo-French plan for cession of Sudetenland to Germany
	20 September	Czechs refuse Anglo-French plan
	21 September	Anglo-French ultimatum to Benes accepted

	22-23 September	Chamberlain-Hitler meeting at Godesberg
	25-26 September	Daladier and Bonnet in London
	29-30 September	Munich conference and agreement
	October	Break-up of Popular Front in France
	30 November	Failure of general strike in France
	6 December	Franco-German declaration signed in Paris
	22 December	Italy denounces Rome agreements of 6 January 1935
1939	26 January	General Franco takes Barcelona
	14 March	Slovak Diet votes for independence
	15 March	Germany occupies Bohemia and Moravia
		Hungary occupies Ruthenia
	19 March	Britain rejects Soviet proposal for five-power talks on Rumania
	21-24 March	President Lebrun and Bonnet in London
	23 March	Lithuania cedes Memel to Germany
	29 March	Full Franco-British staff talks begin
	31 March	Provisional Franco-British guarantee of Poland
	28 March	Surrender of Madrid
	7 April	Italy invades Albania
	13 April	Franco-British guarantees of Greece and Rumania
	14 April	Franco-British negotiations with Soviet Union recommence
	26 April	Chamberlain announces conscription
	28 April	Hitler denounces Anglo-German naval agreement and German-Polish pact
	15-21 May	Franco-Polish military and political talks
	22 May	Pact of Steel signed in Berlin
	1-2 July	Scare over Danzig
	12 August	British and French military missions begin talks in Moscow
	21 August	Anglo-Franco-Soviet military talks suspended
	23 August	German-Soviet pact signed in Moscow
	25 August	Anglo-Polish agreement signed
		Mussolini tells Hitler he cannot join in a general conflict
		German invasion of Poland, ordered for 26th, postponed
	26 August	Daladier's personal appeal to Hitler
	28 August	German attack fixed for 1 September
	31 August	Mussolini proposes a conference to discuss Versailles problems
	1 September	Germany invades Poland
		Britain and France send warnings to Berlin

	2 September	French parliament recalled
		Franco-British disagreement over timing of ultimatums to Germany
		Bonnet seeks support for Italian conference proposal
	3 September	Britain and France declare war
1940	20 March	Resignation of Daladier government
	21 March	Formation of Reynaud ministry
	10 May	Germany invades Holland and Belgium
	13 May	German attack in the Ardennes: crossing of Meuse
	16 May	Burning of Quai d'Orsay archives
	10 June	Italy enters the war
	16 June	Reynaud resigns; Marshal Pétain forms new government
	22 June	Franco-German armistice
	24 June	Franco-Italian armistice
	10 July	National Assembly Meeting at Vichy votes Marshal Pétain full powers to promulgate a new constitution

1. European Frontiers after the First World War

By permission of Messrs Edward Arnold (Publishers) Ltd., based on
R. R. Sellmann, *A Student's Atlas of Modern History*.

2. Europe, 1938-1939

By permission of Messrs Hamish Hamilton Ltd., based on
A. J. P. Taylor, *The Origins of the Second World War*, 1961.

PART ONE
The Setting

Chapter 1

Dilemma

French institutions and foreign policy in the interwar years generally received much more criticism than sympathy from British ministers. Up or down, France always seemed to be in the wrong. 'France is full of the idea that she is going to control, overwhelm and keep under Germany . . . It is only France who could give us trouble now', Lloyd George told his Cabinet on 30 June 1920.[1] Eighteen years later all the talk in the British government was about the defects of the French who had 'no Government, no aeroplanes and no guts'.[2] Even the fall of France and passing of the Third Republic was greeted with some satisfaction. 'The third French Republic', wrote Henry Channon, R. A. Butler's Private Secretary, on 10 July 1940, 'has ceased to exist and I don't care; it was graft-ridden, incompetent, Communistic and corrupt and had outlived its day'.[3]

Such verdicts showed little appreciation of the limitations which circumstances placed on French statesmen. The shrinking of French power was as well-established as the decline of British influence. French predominance in the 1920s masked a deep, underlying predicament. France, like Great Britain, was not a power from her intrinsic strength, as the United States and the Soviet Union were fast becoming between the two world wars. Many of the trials and tribulations which plagued France were caused by her endeavour to sustain a role for which she was unfitted. The First World War overtaxed her strength and the peace that followed confirmed her weakness.

The constraints of circumstance with which French leaders had to contend after 1918 were of two kinds: external pressures imposed by the changing international situation, and internal restrictions stemming from the inherent weaknesses and peculiarities of French society. The chief external constraint was the destruction of the balance of power between 1870 and 1914. By her victory of 1870 Germany replaced France as the leading continental power and much of the international history of the next forty years was a direct result of the consequences of this supremacy. However until the 1880s there was an equilibrium in the sense that no one of the five great powers — Austria-Hungary, France, Germany, Great Britain and Russia — could hope to vanquish all the others combined. By 1914, as the First World War showed, Germany, with only a little help from Austria-Hungary, was able to take on a coalition of four great powers — France, Great Britain, Russia—and, from 1915, Italy.

The war of 1914-18, by completing the destruction of the international system, greatly increased the limitations of French power. France owed her victory to the intervention of the United States in 1917, but American withdrawal from Europe after 1919 left a vacuum which a resurgent Germany would sooner or later fill. The survival of Germany as a great power and the withdrawal of the United States marked a fundamental deterioration of France's position. There were no counterbalancing allies. The Russian revolution of 1917 deprived France of a major ally. The Franco-Soviet pact of May 1935 never compensated for the loss of the Franco-Russian military alliance of 1894. Although diplomatic relations with Russia were restored in 1924, the Bolshevik revolution left a legacy of mistrust. The antipathy of French conservatives for the new Soviet regime was compounded by the Bolshevik repudiation of Tsarist debts. Eighty per cent of Russia's pre-1914 state debt was owed to Frenchmen and there was hardly a middle class family which did not hold some Russian bonds.

In the race towards industrialization and military strength France was held back by the poverty of her natural resources. In 1850 Great Britain and France were the only industrial powers of any consequence; by 1880 Germany had outstripped France in coal, iron and steel output and France had slipped to fourth place in the production of these materials. Her coal output in 1913 was 41 million tons, compared with Germany's 279 million tons and Britain's 292 million tons. By 1935-39 the disparity between France and Germany was even more marked: France was producing 47 million tons of coal against Germany's total of 351 millions. In 1938 the French government estimated that in war France would have to import 48 million tons of fuel, including 23 million tons of coal. Of course, Germany herself was overshadowed before 1914 by the meteoric rise of the United States. By 1914 the United States was producing 474 million tons of coal. Moreover French industries were, on the whole, comparatively small and major industries were confined to five departments in the north, the edges of the Massif Centrale, and a few cities such as Paris, Lyons and Marseilles.

Equally as important as France's industrial weakness was her demographic inferiority. In an age of conscript armies the key test of a great power was the number of men she could put into the field. In 1850 France with a population of 35.5 millions was still the most populous country in western Europe. In 1880 she had 15.7 per cent of the European population; in 1900 she had only 9.7 per cent. The rate of increase of the French people between 1880 and 1910 was 5 per cent, for Germany it was 43 per cent, and for Britain 26 per cent. In 1940 France's total population was 41.9 millions; this compared with 45.9 in Great Britain, 43.8 in Italy, and with 69.8 in Germany. The fall in French natality had established itself in the early years of the nineteenth century. Given the lack of population growth, the manpower losses of the war of 1914-18 were disastrous. Of the belligerents, France suffered most in relation to her active male population, losing over 10 per cent of her active males; this compared to 9.8 per cent in Germany, and 5.1 per cent in Great Britain.[4]

The First World War, by testing the fundamental economic resources of the belligerents, demonstrated the inability of France to maintain herself unaided in a major conflict. France was dependent for manufactures and armaments on imports, especially coal. Geography imposed an extra handicap since much of her heavy industry was concentrated in the northern and eastern departments, close to the frontier with Germany. German occupation of large areas of northern France represented 53 per cent of coal production, 64 per cent of iron, 62 per cent of steel, and 60 per cent of cotton and other manufactures. Agriculture was also seriously affected. The territory occupied from 1914 to 1918 accounted for one fifth of the country's wheat supply.

The alliance with Great Britain, indispensable though it was during the war, offered no security for the future. The entente had withstood the test of war but British Ministers shunned a peacetime military pact and a full military alliance was not re-created until the spring of 1939. All that the British Prime Minister, Neville Chamberlain, could promise France in 1938 was two divisions, with the proviso that their despatch would be subject to the decision of the government of the day. Great Britain had her own problems in the postwar decade. She was no longer the self-confident nation of 1914. A sense of diminished power and a growing preoccupation with Imperial interests strengthened the determination of British statesmen to steer clear of continental entanglements.

The changing relationship between Europe and other continents was another adverse circumstance for France's leadership. In a world dominated by the European powers, France had appeared to be stronger than she was. In the Far East, Japan emerged as a great power of formidable naval strength. The war of 1914-18 speeded up the political and economic forces which were undermining Europe's primacy. One indicator of change was the loss of French overseas investments. In 1914, French investments abroad totalled 8,686 millions of United States dollars, by 1938 the sum had shrunk to 3,859 millions. Half of the French portfolio was sold to pay for the war but, unlike the British who rebuilt their foreign investments, the French allowed their holdings to decline.

Another external restriction on France's freedom was the onset of the Great Depression. The effects of the world economic crisis did more to undermine French power than the material losses of the First World War. Without the Depression, the economic recovery of the 1920s might have been maintained. The chief effect of the Depression was to bring to the surface the latent tensions and weaknesses in political and economic life. The timing of the crisis was decisive. As social and economic strife engulfed France, Germany began rearming and the conjunction of foreign and domestic perils presented the political leadership with well-nigh insoluble problems.

In 1932 the major industrial nations were in the trough of the Depression but France did not experience the worst of the crisis until the mid-1930s — by which date Great Britain, Germany and the United States were showing strong signs of recovery. While her competitors recovered France remained in the doldrums and did not show any evidence of renewal until 1939. Between 1929 and 1938 industrial production increased by 20% in Great Britain and 16% in Germany, while in France in the same period it fell by 24%. In terms of unemployment France was not as hard hit as Germany and Great Britain. Unemployment in France never totalled more than half a million but the protracted stagnation was extremely demoralising. Despite the poor economic performance from 1932 to 1938, the end of the decade brought a glimmer of light. Between October 1938 and June 1939 industrial production returned for the first time to the level of 1928. This economic upswing, equalling the rate of growth of the 1920s, came too late in the day to be of any real help. However the renewed vigour of French diplomacy in the spring and early summer owed much to the gold reserves amassed by Paul Reynaud, Minister of Finance.[5]

In addition to these pressures France's rulers were cramped by a number of internal handicaps. The financial burden of the First World War and material devastation caused by the fighting imposed a powerful constraint. The damage was immense. Ten *départements* had been occupied or laid waste. German troops carted away industrial equipment and economic life had to be restarted virtually *de novo*. Also, there was the double burden of paying both for the war and for the cost of raising France from the ruins. This was a mammoth task, coming so soon after the strain of the pre-war armaments race. The weight of armaments had fallen heavily on France and she had set aside for defence nearly the same proportion of her national income as Germany had done. The cost of the war was met almost wholly by borrowing. French insistence on the payment of reparations has sometimes been seen as heartless legalism. In reality, reparations, as the French Foreign Minister, Aristide Briand, reminded British Ministers, were a necessity since his country faced 'ruin and bankruptcy'.[6]

The war, by aggravating underlying defects in French society, contributed to the decline of France as a great power. Without the war, the archaic fiscal system, practically unchanged since 1789, might have held together longer. In the event the cost of the war brought about its collapse. Unlike Great Britain and Germany, who adopted a modern system of direct taxation in the nineteenth century, France did not accept the principle of such a tax until 1914 and income tax was not introduced until 1920. Consequently very little revenue was raised by direct taxation and it was estimated that while 55 milliards of francs were spent on the war in 1918, only 7 milliards of this sum were raised in taxes. With the advent of peace Germany was expected to pay for the war and French opinion was in no mood to welcome a comprehensive scheme of direct taxation.

All the belligerents were confronted with the problem of inflation and the phenomenon was particularly bewildering for the French who had come to consider the stability of the *franc de germinal* of 1803 as part of the natural order. During the war, the value of the franc had been maintained by Anglo-American support and when this was withdrawn in 1919 its value fell rapidly. The depreciation of an hitherto stable currency, coupled with the problems of adjustment to a peacetime economy, sharpened social and economic distress. By 1920 the prices of 1914 had quadrupled, though the value of real wages declined. Economic mobilisation and the need to establish new centres of industry behind the front accelerated the long-term drift of population from the country to the towns. The influx of labour brought new strains and stresses, especially in housing. The fiscal system added to the difficulties. Although the principle of a general income-tax was approved in 1914, its implementation was delayed until 1920. The new tax created considerable injustices and inequalities, which fell largely on the lower paid. Generally, the wealthy escaped the net of income-tax and have retained their privileged position to the present day. Even Prime Ministers might not always pay income-tax. Under the Fifth Republic, M Chaban-Delmas, Prime Minister from 1969 to 1972, was discredited by disclosures that he had paid no taxes for several years. The state might be bankrupt but the rich remained rich. The selfishness of the well-to-do classes threw the burden of taxation, in the form of indirect taxes, on those least able to pay. Successive administrations, loath to incur disfavour, refused to apply an equitable and comprehensive income-tax and resorted to indirect taxes and public loans. Naturally the vast extent of government borrowing added inflation.

The distress caused by postwar inflation was not alleviated by an adequate system of social security. France had nothing to compare with the social insurance which Bismarck gave Germany in the 1880s. A bill for old age pensions had been passed in 1910 but the *Court of Cassation* judged its terms ambiguous and decided that contributions were not obligatory. In 1918 barely 20% of the 8 million originally registered in the scheme were still contributing. In 1919 the dread of social revolution obliged the employers and government to make two belated concessions—legal recognition of trade union contracts with employées, and the granting of an eight hour day. With these measures reform came to a full stop. As the danger of unrest receded enraged conservatives demanded reprisals. And under various pretexts the full application of the eight hour day was delayed until 1925. New schemes for sickness benefits and old age pensions, announced in 1928, had to wait until 1930 for parliamentary approval. Even so, provision for old age pensions was still inadequate. A member of the government scheme had to pay contributions for 30 years (until 1960) before entitlement to a reasonable pension. Further social reform was delayed until the end of the decade. Edouard Daladier's *Code de la Famille* of July 1939 extended and improved family allowances, though old age pensions were not included, and the reforms were not implemented until after 1940.[7]

On the credit side it must be said that the material damage of the war was repaired with surprising speed and success. The ravaged regions were reconstructed and regained their pre-war prosperity by the end of the post-war decade. *Les métèques*, as the immigrant workers from southern and central Europe were known, greatly eased the shortage of manpower. By 1938 there were three million foreign workers in France. The years 1926 to 1931 witnessed considerable economic expansion, notably in the chemical, electrical and motor car industries. In 1930-1 the economy reached a peak which it was not to equal again until the early 1950s. Prosperity was greater than at any time since the Second Empire. The output of coal, iron and steel reached record levels for the interwar years. Moreover the decline of the franc was partly halted by Raymond Poincaré, Prime Minister from 1926 to 1929. He devalued the franc in

June 1928 and the old franc of *germinal* was renamed the Poincaré franc, at a fifth of its 1914 value. The devaluation, or stabilisation as it was officially termed, combined with the economic surge, gave France, for a brief spell, a leading monetary position. Bank of France holdings in gold rose to 83,017 millions of francs in 1932, four times the total for 1925-1927.

Much more significant than the material damage of the war was the huge toll in young life—25% of those under thirty years of age. The enormous loss of life created a most powerful psychological restraint on French thinking. Almost every family had lost one or more of its members in the carnage. The profound pacifism of the peasantry between the wars sprang directly from the trenches and supplied a political constant which no statesman could neglect. The four years of slaughter permanently scarred France and the resolution to avoid a repetition of the holocaust was one of the main determinants of French diplomacy in the 1920s and 1930s. Nothing short of a sudden and spectacular increase in natality could have restored confidence. 'The Treaty means nothing', declared Georges Clemenceau, Prime Minister in 1919, 'if France does not agree to have many children . . . for if France renounces large families, we will have taken all the guns from Germany for nothing'.[8] In the first year or so of peace the birth rate revived slightly only to decline again. Economic changes hastened demographic decline. The migrant labour which moved into the towns during the war found contraceptives both tolerated and more readily obtainable. Families of two children became the norm.

The psychological restraint induced by the casualties of 1914-18 dictated a defensive diplomacy and strategy. Several reasons have been advanced for the defensive-mindedness of the military chiefs. It is said that they were 'misled by the experience of the recent war' attaching too much importance to infantry and artillery, and too little to tanks, aircraft and the possibilities of armoured warfare.[9] Again, the army has been criticised for being too bureaucratic. It is argued that the military establishment stifled the initiatives of younger officers such as Charles de Gaulle. All these strictures are not without some truth but the basic reason for the early adoption of a defensive strategy was the obvious and inescapable fact of German superiority in men and industrial power. French statesmen believed that Germany's resurgence was only a matter of time. The fall in the birth rate and the losses of war meant that the military initiative could not be retained indefinitely. In any future conflict France would not be able to mobilise the same number of men as in 1914. In particular it was known that the years from 1935 to 1940 would be lean years when the number of conscripts for military service would fall because of the slump in the birth rate during the First World War. The certainty of German dominance—60 millions against 40 millions—gave France no alternative but to plan a defensive system which would, it was hoped, by its very strength deter a German attack. When Hitler remilitarised the Rhineland in 1936 the dread of another Franco-German duel effectively bridled the French.

The defects and peculiarities of the political system imposed additional limitations on the freedom of action of French governments. The political leaders were ill-equipped to meet the growing dangers of the 1930s. A variety of circumstances: the practical working out of the constitutional laws of 1875, the narrow social basis of the political élite, the electoral system, the inveterate conservatism of a predominantly peasant society, all combined to encourage an inflexible and myopic approach to the troubles of the time.

The political system had serious shortcomings. The Third Republic had lasted longer than any previous regime since the Revolution of 1789 but the price paid for survival was a high one. The division of opinion and the general dislike of a powerful executive made for compromise and moderation. Administrations were coalitions of conflicting interests and outlooks, encouraging indecisive and muddled leadership. No firm initiative was forthcoming from the presidency which never recovered from the failure of President MacMahon's attempt of 1877 to be an effective head of state. Georges Clemenceau's advice on the occasion of Carnot's election to the Presidency in 1887: 'vote for the stupidest', was elevated into a constitutional maxim. President Albert Lebrun, the last President of the Third Republic, elected in 1932 and re-elected in 1939, though not without some firm opinions on the Popular Front and the Spanish civil war, exercised relatively little influence on events. Nor did the Premiership provide a strong executive.[10] With few exceptions, prime ministers refused to be leaders and concentrated their skill on controlling a restless team of individualists. Since power resided in the Chamber of Deputies prime ministers aimed at being middlemen and conciliators, building their cabinets around a nucleus of prominent personalities of varying political persuasions and varying degrees of loyalty. In short, the Prime Minister regarded himself as *primus inter pares* and to buttress what was often little more than a nominal authority he would take one or more portfolios for himself. In 1938 Edouard Daladier was at once Minister of National Defence and Minister of War, and he added foreign affairs to his responsibilities in September 1939.

Another disability of the political leadership was its social composition. Such stables of the governing class as the *Ecole des Sciences politiques* and the *Ecole polytechnique* recruited their students almost exclusively from the upper ranks of society.[11] The result was often a lack of understanding and sympathy for the problems of those less well off. Electorally, the *scrutin d'arrondissement* tended to put a premium on a candidate's personal following in his constituency and discouraged the growth of stable, disciplined parties. The elections for the Senate in which each commune had equal representation gave a preponderant voice to the rural areas. But the ministerial instability for which the Republic became a byword in its last years was not as damaging as sometimes supposed. Ministerial crisis was a technique of government, concealing a basic continuity of personnel.[12] Clemenceau, criticised for overthrowing so many administrations, retorted that they were all the same. The regime in itself was not unstable but too rigid and even inert. This hardening of the political arteries meant that governments adapted themselves too slowly and sluggishly to social and economic change. Hence the growth of discontent which manifested itself in extra-parliamentary forms—the political leagues and street demonstrations of the mid-1930s.

The lack of a strong governing party with a clear programme and a parliamentary majority was a grave disadvantage. 'Ah, if only there were political parties in France and if these parties had an organisation and a doctrine', declared Léon Blum.[13] The notion of organised parties was disliked and parties were not formally recognised in parliament until 1910; the official report of parliamentary debates still omits to mention them. The absence of disciplined parties, apart from the Communists, resulted in politics being pivoted very much on personalities, with only loose and shifting allegiances to the groups and parties of which they were members. Despite or perhaps because of the highly centralised Napoleonic state, local issues exerted great influence. Possession of a local power base was all important in national politics. Edouard Herriot, for example, was Radical Socialist Deputy for the Rhone from 1919 to 1940 and mayor of Lyons for fifty years. Daladier was Radical Socialist Deputy for Vaucluse from 1919 to 1940 and again from 1946 to 1958. The Gaullists in the Fifth Republic were the first majority party with a genuinely national basis.

The Radical Socialists, mostly Socialists in name only, were the traditional governing party but they were neither reformers nor revolutionaries. There was little dogma and barely any organisation. 'The radical party', as one of its members said, had 'friendships not definitions'[14] The philosopher, Emile Chartier, better known by his *nom de plume* of Alain, was widely regarded as the prophet of Radicalism, though it seems that few Radicals read his *Eléments d'une doctrine radicale* (1925) and Edouard Herriot's *Pourquoi je suis radical socialiste* (1928) was much more popular.[15] Radicalism, in Herriot's opinion, was a 'state of mind'. Such woolliness offered a safe haven to all moderates who found that recommending 'moderation with extreme vehemence' satisfied their zeal.[16] To a party drawing its support from peasant proprietors, small businessmen and shopkeepers, moderation meant steering clear of social reform and other controversial issues. Radicalism was in decline. In 1919, for instance, in the *département* of Saone and Loire the party was a formidable left wing body; by 1939 it was reduced to a rump of notables in alliance with right wing leaders.[17] The *juste milieu* ideal of Radicalism was ill-suited to the extremism generated by the ideologies and upheaval of the 1930s.

The Right was a medley of factions ranging from the rabid royalism of *Action française* to more moderate parliamentary combinations such as the *Union républicaine démocratique* of Louis Marin, the *Alliance démocratique,* the party of Pierre Etienne Flandin, Raymond Poincaré, Paul Reynaud, and André Tardieu. Until the mid-1930s the Right was united on resistance to social reform and in calling for a staunchly nationalist foreign policy. After 1935 opposition to social reform continued but the Right gradually abandoned its traditional Germanophobia. In its opposition to the Left the Right did not shrink from physical violence. In February 1936 *Camelots du Roi* dragged the Socialist leader Léon Blum from his car and beat him savagely. Nor was Bonapartism dead. In 1935 an emissary of 'important political groups of the right and centre' tried to enlist Sir Austen Chamberlain's blessing for a Bonapartist restoration.[18] The former prime minister, Pierre Laval, was alleged to be 'not unfavourable to the idea'. The two men who were to rule France after the collapse of 1940, Marshal Philippe Pétain and Pierre Laval, had Right wing associations and their names were already linked together. Laval, though only semi-active in politics from 1936 to 1939, entertained ideas of a dictatorship. His opinions were much of a piece with those of Pétain. In March 1938 Laval talked of the need for a committee of public governing safety under Pétain, governing by decree, with himself as foreign minister or minister of the interior.[19] But there is no evidence to suggest that the two men ever hatched plots against the regime. They talked and bided their time.[20]

Another manifestation of the violence of the extreme Right was the secret terrorist organisation called the *Cagoule* which was virulently anti-Communist and had close links with certain army officers. The *Cagoule* network in the army was controlled by Loustanau-Lacau, an officer attached to Pétain's personal staff. In the autumn of 1937 bomb explosions near the *Etoile* led to the trial and imprisonment of *Cagoule* leaders. While the *Cagoulards* and ultra right sympathisers were too small a minority to present a real threat to the Republic in the climate of the period they were a divisive influence and their existence lent substance to Left wing fears of a conspiracy to overthrow the government.

After the military defeat of 1940, Right wing writers tended to make the Popular Front the scapegoat for France's collapse. However it is arguable that if the Left had held office for a reasonable period in the 1920s, much of the strife aroused by the Popular Front movement of 1935-36 might have been avoided. Unfortunately, except for the three years of the Popular Front alliance from 1935 to 1938, the Left was in disarray throughout the interwar years and each of the legislatures elected with a Left wing majority—in 1924, 1932 and 1936—abdicated within two years to centre and Right wing governments. The *Cartel des Gauches* administration formed by Edouard Herriot in 1924 lasted less than a year. The Left never recovered from the Congress of Tours in December 1920 when a Communist majority led by Marcel Cachin and L. G. Frossard broke away from the Socialist party to set up a Communist party adhering to the Comintern. Despite a large initial membership the Communist party did not transform the electoral fortunes of the Left. Torn asunder by internal quarrels and secessions, membership fell steeply and massive subsidies from Moscow were required to keep the party afloat. Only after 1934, under the leadership of Maurice Thorez, did the party begin to regain lost ground.

After the Tours schism the Socialists were reduced to a rump of 40-50,000 members, with few resources and no newspaper—*L'Humanité* having passed to the Communists. Under new leaders, especially Léon Blum, who helped found *Le Populaire,* the party made a remarkable recovery. With 132 seats in the Chamber of 1932 on paper, the Socialists were a powerful force, but their effective influence was less than it might have been.[21] Fratricidal battles dissipated the energies of party leaders. Splinter groups on the extreme left of the party led by Marceau Pivert and Jean Zyromski, including the semi-fascist 'Neos' grouped around Marcel Déat and Pierre Renaudel, testified to the deep doctrinal divisions. In the 1930s the party was strongly pacifist and in 1938 Paul Faure, secretary general of the party, together with a large following, parted company from Blum on the issue of Munich. For Faure and his followers conciliation could not be carried too far. 'We desire', he announced, 'a pact with the devil if necessary'.[22] The Popular Front alliance of Socialists, Communists and Radicals was a very uneasy affair. Blum's Popular Front government of June 1936 faced continual sniping from Radicals and Communists. The link with Communists was enough to damn the Socialists in the eyes of conservative Frenchmen. The Popular Front alliance soon disintegrated and left such a legacy of recrimination that it was not until 1972 that Socialists and Communists dared to join forces again in an electoral pact.

While Germany rearmed, France was almost wholly distracted by internal troubles. Political scandal, a recurring sub-theme of the Republic's history, had discredited the parliamentary system. The Stavisky affair of January 1934 had far-reaching repercussions. The fact that Stavisky, a financial swindler, had had his trial postponed no less than nineteen times led to the not unreasonable conclusion of corruption in high places. Right wing indignation exploded in the riots of 6 February 1934 which toppled the Daladier government. Feelings ran so high that the Radical leader, Herriot, on leaving the Chamber of Deputies, narrowly escaped a ducking in the Seine. Others were less fortunate. Seventeen people died and over two thousand were injured in the rioting. The post-1945 parliamentary investigation concluded that the riots were an attempt to overthrow the Republic. Yet it seems unlikely, to say the least, that there was such a plot. The Third Republic had weathered worse storms but such scandals left their mark. In June 1940 an officer noted: 'Literally I have never met a single one of my *poilus* who has not expressed his disgust for the parliamentary regime'.[23]

But political failings of one kind or another were only part of the story. French statesmen were also hampered by their country's economic backwardness. The Depression might have been shaken off sooner but for the problem of under-industrialisation. Though France lacked the stamina to sustain herself as a first rate power, her decline might have been more gradual and controllable if existing economic resources had been exploited to the full.

According to the economist, Alfred Sauvy, two factors — economic Malthusianism and ignorance of economic facts — prevented a greater degree of industrialisation.[24] Economic Malthusianism, inspired by fear of technological change, was a deliberate effort to restrict production by means of protection. French writers of the time sang the praises of a balanced economy in which resources were almost equally divided between town and country. In 1936 out of a total population of 41,907,000, the urban population was 21,972,000, and the rural 19,735,000. In no other industrial country was the margin between town and country so small as in France. This balance between agriculture and urban industry was exalted into a doctrine, as firm and unquestioned as the gold standard.

Government economic intervention was aimed at perpetuating the world of the small, independent peasant. Underlying this policy was an antipathy to technology and modern industrial society which were seen as a perversion of the natural order. The true stock and heritage of France was the peasant proprietor. Conventional wisdom affirmed that 'the land' created 'the most reliable and most responsible' people[25] and 'the land', as Marshal Pétain put it, did not 'lie'.

In comparison with Great Britain, Germany and the United States, France was economically backward and her full industrial transformation was delayed until the 1950s.[26] French wheat yields were among the lowest in Europe. In 1890, a French farmer fed four of his countrymen, his American counterpart seven; by 1940 the Frenchman was feeding five people and the American twenty. In the 1920s the modernization of industry was an uneven and haphazard process. Charles Spinasse, Minister of National Production in the Popular Front government of 1936, complained of the existence of 'industries organised and equipped as they were in the Middle Ages'.[27] The average age of machine tools at the end of the Second World War was said to be twenty five years in France, six to seven in the United States, seven to nine in Great Britain. Although the immediate result of protectionism and under-industrialisation was to shield France from the worst consequences of the economic crisis, over a longer period protectionist tariffs encouraged economic inefficiency and stagnation. Farmers, insulated from foreign competition and world markets, saw no reason to change their ways. Fear of further industrialisation was widespread. Incredible as it may seem, a former prime minister, Joseph Caillaux, called for a heavy tax on industrial inventions.

The economic crisis did not lead to a paralysis of will, nor were the governments of the day reluctant to interfere with the working of the economy. On the contrary, between 1932 and 1935 fourteen plans for economic recovery were announced and the economic debate dominated the attention of the ephemeral administrations of the 1930s, leaving scant time for discussion of foreign affairs. Why, then, was so little achieved? The reasons are many and complex and require further investigation.

Of great importance were the assumptions of the policy makers. Chief of these was the complacent acceptance of the doctrine of a balance between the land and urban industrial development. If opinion had been less resistant to the idea of technological change, some attempt to modernise a backward industrial structure might have been made. Other considerations were the attachment to the dogma of the balanced budget and the opposition to devaluation. The ups and downs of the franc and the problem of budgetary disequilibrium mesmerised rulers and ruled to the neglect of the problems of the economy as a whole. In 1929, parliament rejected the proposal by the Prime Minister, André Tardieu, for 'national retooling', a scheme to invest the budgetary surpluses of 1929-30 in better transport and communications. The argument used to defeat the plan was that the surpluses should go to reduce the national debt.

Another factor was education. The governing elite received, of course, the usual classical and literary education of their time and class. France was traditionally the country of barristers and peasants. Economists

were few and far between. The teaching of economics was controlled
by the law faculties and was of a low standard. Keynes was little read and
a translation of *The General Theory of Employment, Interest and Money*
(1936) did not appear until 1942. Alfred Sauvy censures the politicians
for their ignorance of economic data. But perhaps it is unrealistic to
criticise Blum or Daladier for not showing more awareness of economic
statistics. A politician like Paul Reynaud, a specialist in financial and
economic affairs, who was prepared to break with orthodox opinion in
advocating devaluation, was head and shoulders above his contemporaries. Also, it is worth recalling the other side of the coin. Daladier,
Prime Minister in 1932, when asked if he would devalue, is said to have
replied: 'my advisers are firm. Some tell me "Above all no inflation or
you are lost", and the others: "Above all no deflation or you are finished."
There you have it. If you know two economists who are in agreement
send them to me.'[28]

Closely linked to the economic crisis was another internal limitation
on French foreign policy — the ideological conflict between Left and
Right and its impact on international attitudes. The ideological conflict
centred on the Popular Front. From June 1936 to June 1937 a Popular
Front government was in power under Léon Blum, a largely Socialist
ministry with some Radical participation and Communist support in the
Chamber. Of this period, General Gamelin, Chief of the General Staff,
wrote:

> The crisis of May-June 1936 terrorised a great section of the French bour-
> geoisie. It made many of us lose sight of the dangers of Hitlerism and fascism
> . . . because behind the Popular Front one saw the spectre of Bolshevism.
> Therein lies the origin of the slogans that disfigured the soul of the nation:
> 'Better Hitler than Stalin' and 'Why die for Danzig?'[29]

The Blum experiment, though it barely lasted a year, was a well-
meaning attempt to heal one of the chief fissures in French society, the
growing alienation of the working class from the state.[30] The programme
of social and economic reform won popular support, though Blum was
probably driven further in reform than he at first intended. The interval
between Blum's electoral victory in early May and the formation of a
government on 4 June was filled by a revolutionary ferment that was not
seen again until the troubles of May 1968. Factories were occupied and
it was plain that many of the sit-in strikers expected a new Revolution.
The slogan of 'Everything is possible', coined by the Socialist Marceau
Pivert, voiced the millennial aspirations of the Left. Alas, all was not possible and the sum total of reform was not impressive. Yet it would be
wrong to stress the failure of the experiment. What was significant was
that reform took place at all in such a climate of conflict. After five
years of deflationary policies, the Socialists set about the reflation of
the economy. By the Matignon Agreements of 7 June 1936, government
and employers agreed on wage increases of up to 12%, as well as a forty
hour week. Other gains followed: holidays with pay, semi-nationalisation
of the Bank of France, nationalisation of the armaments industry.
Curiously the reforms did not include old age pensions or unemploy-

ment insurance. The decision to launch a four year programme of re-armament in the autumn of 1936 was a courageous one in the circumstances.

Blum took office in the aftermath of Hitler's Rhineland coup of 7 March, the most damaging blow to French interests since the peace treaties. Within six weeks of the Popular Front's advent to power the outbreak of the Spanish civil war injected fresh venom into the body politic. The attempt to cure social and economic ills could not have taken place in more adverse circumstances. The devaluation of the franc in September 1936, though economically desirable, was politically disastrous because frightened capital holders closed ranks against the government. The flight of capital abroad brought renewed pressure on the franc. France's prestige was lower than at any other period in the interwar years. Henry Morgenthau, Secretary to the United States Treasury, considered that lending to France was 'just flowing money into the Atlantic . . . someone had to tell the French that they were a bankrupt, fourth class power'.[31]

The poet, Paul Eluard, pictured the proletariat banging its head in vain against the 'wall of money'.[32] A financial and industrial oligarchy— the two hundred families as it was polemically described—was accused of thwarting the well-intentioned reforms of Left wing and moderate ministries. That there was a close connection between big business, the leading banks and the press is undeniable but there is nothing to suggest a conspiracy of the rich.[33] Blum in fact was his own worst enemy. Social and economic policies were at odds. The rigid and undiscriminating application of the forty hour week hindered economic revival, since in terms of production it was the equivalent of two months of extra holiday in addition to the fortnight already granted. The September devaluation, by making French prices more competitive, gave a slight boost to the economy but only an immediate and substantial devaluation in June could have significantly affected the situation. Finally, Blum was no revolutionary. I do not know if I have the qualities of a leader . . . it's a test that you are going to make on me and I am going to make on myself', he is reported to have said in May 1936.[34]

The post-mortems that followed the collapse of 1940 showed an understandable preoccupation with the responsibility of individuals and social classes. The Left lambasted the machinations of the 'two hundred families' allegedly in league with a fascist Fifth Column. The Right conjured up a conspiracy of Jews, Freemasons and Communists. Other commentators delivered sweeping diatribes of political and social elites. The journalist Pertinax (André Geraud) entitled his study of the fall of France *The Gravediggers of France* for, as he put it, 'those words tell everything'.[35] Léon Blum indicted the middle classes because they had shown 'no reserves of energy'.[36] Some blame must obviously be assigned to the political and military leadership but an audit of French policy should also take account of the basic constraints and conditions which governed policy-making. The changed circumstances of Europe after 1918 placed France in an increasingly exposed and vulnerable position and her leaders were less and less in charge of the national destiny. Hitler's expansionist designs reduced her freedom of action still further. The French seemed trapped. Acquiescence in German demands portended national humiliation and second class power status; resistance promised at best a pyrrhic victory, at worst annihilation. Whatever France did, a loss of power was inevitable. This was the dilemma that confronted French ministers in the years immediately preceding the Second World War.

Chapter 2

Quest for Security

In Paris during the Peace Conference the saying went that 'the French army had won the war but Clemenceau had lost the peace'. In truth, the diplomatic disasters of the 1930s flowed logically from the inconclusive nature of the victory of 1918. The contribution of the United States and Great Britain had been decisive. The promise of an Anglo-American guarantee was not fulfilled and when in October 1919 the United States Senate rejected the Treaty of Versailles, France lost the guarantee. The Peace of Paris, shorn of the Anglo-American guarantee, was the first of many diplomatic defeats. The new states of eastern Europe could not compensate for the eclipse of Russia. The preservation of Germany's political unity and economic potential gave little hope of permanent peace. 'This is not peace', declared Marshal Foch, allied generalissimo, 'it is an Armistice for twenty years'.[1]

One lesson of the conflict was the need for allies. Clemenceau, the French Prime Minister, made an understanding with Great Britain and the United States the 'essential basis' of his policy at the peace conference.[2] A second conclusion which French statesmen drew from the war was that France, even if supported by allies, would be unlikely to survive another such holocaust. Hence the primary, overriding, instinctive aim of French foreign policy was a search for security, inspired by an intense fear of Germany. It was assumed that Germany would seek revenge for her defeat.

France sought security in three ways: enforcement of the peace treaties and payment of reparations; support for the League of Nations and collective security; the creation of alliances in central and eastern Europe. French behaviour in the postwar decade gave rise to much criticism. Foreign observers, especially British, censured the French for trying to keep Germany down. In January 1923, during the French occupation of the Ruhr, the British prime minister's secretary wrote: 'They (*French*) do not care what happens to Germany or to Europe provided they are able to carry out a semi-military policy'.[3] More recently, historians have indicted the French for vacillation and indecision:

> The French could not avoid facing the choice: conciliation or firmness...the result was the usual outcome: to compromise on a little of each. In retrospect it is clear that this policy made certain the ruin of France . . . France failed

effectively to resist German demands. Equally France failed to give advocates of German moderation the chance to argue that moderation might pay.[4]

Such strictures do not take account of the fundamental defect which flawed French policy. The hesitations and wobbling were rooted in the basic uncertainty of France's international position. The war had given her an artificial predominance in Europe which she lacked the strength to sustain. Dominated as she was by Germany, France did not have a real choice between firmness and conciliation. Firmness towards Germany, as Raymond Poincaré, Prime Minister, discovered was not a practical policy because it meant diplomatic isolation. Nor was total conciliation a feasible alternative. The elections of November 1919 returned the most Right wing legislature since 1876 and opinion would not tolerate any arrangement which might shatter the illusion of victory. The only broadly acceptable and workable policy was the amalgam of moderation and firmness introduced by Aristide Briand, Foreign Minister, in 1924. This *apaisement,* as Briand called it, in contrast to the appeasement which his successors pursued in the 1930s, was a policy of limited concessions made from a position of strength. No French statesman entertained for a moment the idea of sacrificing military superiority or essential treaty rights.

A measure of the importance which the German problem assumed for France after 1919 was the concentration of attention on Europe and a major difference between British and French policies was the weight given by the two governments to their respective overseas commitments. While the French empire in south-east Asia was large, rich and important, it did not give rise to the same strategic preoccupations as Great Britain's Asian possessions. 'The position of France in Europe', explained the French Ambassador in London, 'made it a primary object of French policy to avoid if possible entanglements and commitments elsewhere'.[5] In contrast, Great Britain's awareness of her world interests led her to shun liabilities in Europe. The Dominions, India, the Far East, all impinged heavily on British policy making. As late as November 1933 it was assumed that the chief danger to Britain was in the Far East.[6]

As the weaknesses of France's eastern allies became apparent in the late 1920s, the French public began to take a greater interest in the colonial territories. The Colonial Exhibition of 1931 set out to show that France could count on help from her overseas subjects. There was little interest in events outside the empire. Before the Second World War, no French newspaper thought it worthwhile to station a permanent representative in Moscow and only one paper had a special correspondent in the United States. In the French foreign ministry, the section dealing with political and economic relations with North, South and Central America had a staff of three, while the European section had a staff of ten.

The two leading exponents of French policy in the postwar decade were Aristide Briand and Raymond Poincaré. The two men are often seen as pursuing different policies: Poincaré trying to bludgeon Germany into submission, insisting on the full execution of the treaties, lock, stock and barrel, while Briand sought by sweet reasonableness to conciliate the former enemy, drawing her into the League of Nations. Of differences in temperament and methods of working, there was no question. Briand, with his hunched, shambling gait, large, untidy walrus moustache, a cigarette permanently in his mouth, exuded a relaxed bohemian air. His solution to the deluge of papers which swamped a minister's desk was simple — he never read them. For information and appreciations he preferred to talk to his advisers. By contrast, Poincaré seemed stiff and starchy, a 'human machine...unadaptable, cold and inhuman'.[7] But the obvious differences in personality and techniques have obscured the common purpose which informed their diplomacy. Both statesmen sought security in the containment of Germany and their diplomacy rested on the supremacy of French arms. Briand was capable of defending French treaty rights as tenaciously as Poincaré.[8] Admittedly Poincaré was willing to use force to implement the treaties but Briand might have acted similarly in the early 1920s. The quandary of French policy, implicit in the armistice and peace settlement, only gradually became explicit. The seizure of Frankfurt, Darmstadt and three smaller towns in April 1920 set a precedent for the Ruhr occupation of 1923.

The tantalising limits of French power were demonstrated in 1923 when France, assisted by Belgium, sent troops into the Ruhr to enforce payment of reparations. In reply the Weimar government called for passive resistance from German workers. Then and later it was widely believed that Poincaré, French prime minister since January 1922, was intent on the destruction of German unity or, at the very least, the annexation of the left bank of the Rhine which France had been denied at the Paris peace conference. But though some encouragement was given to separatist movements in the Rhineland there is no evidence that Poincaré had such designs. In the short-run, coercion brought some success. By the summer of 1923 Germany was on the verge of financial and political collapse and in September the government officially abandoned passive resistance. In November Poincaré's proposal that a committee of experts should examine the reparations issue was accepted. An international committee led by the American General Dawes produced the Dawes Plan which Germany, Great Britain and France accepted in April 1924. The reparations issue was settled for the following five years, though French troops remained in the Ruhr until 1925.

Yet the Dawes Plan was a defeat for France's original claims because it reduced Germany's total reparations debts. The proposal for a committee of experts had been put to Poincaré before and during the crisis and rejected. Why, then, did Poincaré accept a compromise proposal which gave France much less than her claims? Several considerations were at work. One point which is often overlooked is that the proposal finally accepted by France in November 1923 was not the same as previous proposals. What France accepted was the creation of two committees of experts, one to study Germany's capacity for payment, and the other to study Germany's monetary difficulties. The creation of the second committee was a shrewd move because it frightened the German leaders into taking the unpopular measures needed to reform the currency. No one wanted an international committee meddling in German domestic affairs. Yet without the restoration of the German currency France had no hope of regular payments. Another factor was Anglo-American criticism of the Ruhr occupation. This displeasure may even have taken the form of strong pressure on the French franc. The French government's reliance on borrowing rather than on direct taxation, coupled with its postwar indebtedness of over 30 billion francs to Great Britain and the United States, gave London and Washington levers on French policy. The franc which was worth 15 to the dollar in January 1923 dropped to 26 to the dollar in March 1924. This pressure could easily have been countered by raising additional revenue but only at the cost of alienating French taxpayers, convinced that Germany must pay for the war. With a general election fixed for May 1924 the Poincaré administration was loath to raise taxes. Another consideration which weighed with Poincaré was the state of Germany in the autumn of 1923. After the partial economic and political paralysis of the summer Germany showed signs of recovery. The government had handed over powers to the army. The French government may have feared the establishment of a military dictatorship, making a final settlement all the more difficult. Lastly, the Dawes Plan of April 1924 offered firm advantages. Though Germany's total debts were reduced, the new arrangements were internationally acceptable and France therefore settled for what she could get. Another attraction of the Dawes plan was that it seemed to strengthen the government's hand in the run-up to the May elections. Criticism within France of the Ruhr occupation was muted but the radicals were known to have strong doubts about the operation. In the event Poincaré's Right wing administration was defeated and replaced by Edouard Herriot's Left wing 'Cartel des Gauches'.

Nevertheless the limited gains of the Ruhr action were vastly outweighed by the damage done to France's international position. The Dawes solution could have been achieved by negotiation without all the expense and ill-will of military occupation. France sacrificed Anglo-American goodwill. The Ruhr episode confirmed British suspicions that France wanted to keep Germany down indefinitely. The resort to force increased the internal tensions in German democracy and provided ammunition for ultra-nationalists and anti-republicans. For a while in 1923 it had looked as if the young Republic would be destroyed. Government encouragement of passive resistance by strike subsidies led to hyperinflation. Arguably France was her own worst enemy. Germany soon recovered her prosperity but the memories of the humiliations of 1923 — hyperinflation, loss of savings, French colonial troops on German soil — all contributed to the collapse of Weimar democracy in the depression years after 1929.

The entente with Great Britain was the sheet anchor of French foreign policy and despite many misunderstandings the French never considered cutting adrift from their ally. In 1921 Poincaré, then president of the Reparations Commission, though condemning Britain for depriving his country of the fruits of victory, stressed that Franco-British solidarity was a cardinal principle of French policy. Equally, the British recognised that the entente was 'of supreme importance'.[9] Yet a vague sense of solidarity and common interest was not enough to save the peace settlement and the structure of 1919 foundered on the rock of Franco-British disunity. The sharp variance of aims and outlook between the two allies allowed Germany to displace France as the leading continental power. Desperately the French tried to resurrect the wartime alliance, proposing on four separate occasions in 1921 a defensive pact. Negotiations for an accord were shipwrecked by the British refusal to guarantee France's eastern allies. The British attitude, as expressed by Lloyd George, Prime Minister, in 1921 remained unchanged until March 1939: '

> So far as the western frontier of Germany was concerned, it would be possible to give France complete guarantee against invasion. The British people were not very much interested in what happened on the eastern frontier...there was general reluctance to get mixed up in these questions in any way.[10]

Poincaré, baulked of the defensive alliance which he wanted, reassured himself with the thought that 'if circumstances arose such as had occurred in 1914...England, in her own interests, will be obliged to take the same action as then'.[11] In practice, France was never confident enough to take the calculated risk of acting without a prior assurance of British support.

The Locarno agreements of October 1925 confirmed what one historian has called 'the deadlock' of French policy.[12] France received guarantees for her own frontiers but not for her eastern allies. Consequently, offensive action against Germany in order to help the allies would have deprived France of the Locarno guarantee. The 'deadlock' could only have been ended in two ways: by a British decision to underwrite the peace settlement in the east, or by a French decision to act offensively on the assumption that Great Britain would willy-nilly support her. The mistake of British ministers was to think that the continental commitment could be limited to the soil of France, whereas maintenance of a European balance of power involved support for France's allies. There was no half-way house between isolation and full alliance. The policy of 'aloofness from the affairs of central Europe' was, in the words of its proponent, Sir Maurice Hankey, Secretary to the Cabinet, 'a selfish policy, perhaps, but the cheapest and best'.[13] In the long run it proved the most expensive.

Several reasons have been suggested to explain Franco-British disunity. A simple, and unconvincing hypothesis, often voiced at the time, was national character. Differences of opinion tended to be explained as the product of differences in national character. In 1926 the Foreign Office asserted that 'given the great gulf . . . between Anglo-Saxon and French mentality there will continue probably for ever to be differences of opinion and friction in almost every question which arises'.[14] Sir Austin Chamberlain, Foreign Secretary in the Baldwin government of 1924-29, told a French visitor:

> The Latin mind was more logical than ours and was always inclined to try and press arguments and situations to their logical conclusions. It was our nature to shun these logical conclusions.[15]

Much more plausible was the view that post-1918 tensions were part of the legacy of ancient antagonism. The rivalry of the seventeenth and eighteenth centuries was reinforced in the nineteenth century in a number of ways: the Mehemet Ali crises of the 1830s, disputes over the Siam border in 1893, the Fashoda incident in 1898 and French unfriendliness in the Boer War.

The alliance of 1914-18 did not always improve relations. Serving in the Pas de Calais the poet Robert Graves wrote home:

> I find it very difficult to like the French here... It is worse than inhospitality here, for after all we are fighting for their dirty little lives...[16]

Later in the war he was to find the peasants of Picardy much more likeable than the Pas de Calais folk. Nevertheless, opinions of the French were permanently shaped by war memories. 'The soldiers thought the Germans were good fellows and hated the French like poison', declares one of George Orwell's heroes.[17]

After the war the old rancours reappeared. The two countries competed fiercely in the Middle East and the French complained that the Treaty of Lausanne of 1923 had despoiled France of her traditional influence in the Levant.[18] 'In almost every quarter of the globe', wrote Lord Curzon, Foreign Secretary, 'the representatives of France were pursuing a policy... unfriendly to British Interests'.[19]

The lack of personal accord between British and French statesmen was common knowledge and persisted through the interwar years. Curzon walked out of one conference with Poincaré in a huff. In 1923, Bonar Law, Prime Minister, had a querulous meeting with the French Prime Minister. At the end of the visit, as the train was waiting to leave the *Gare du Nord*, Bonar Law said to Poincaré through the closed window: 'And you can go to hell', smiling the while at the French minister.[20] Stanley Baldwin was convinced that Pierre Laval was paid by Mussolini,[21] and comforted himself with the thought that in retirement he would not have to meet French statesmen.

Whatever the differences in temperament and national character, the prime cause of discord lay in divergent approaches to the German problem. As Sir Maurice Hankey, Secretary to the Cabinet, put it in 1920:

> The fact is that they (*French*) wanted a stiffer treaty and we wanted an easier one. Moreover, from the first we always intended to ease up the execution of the treaty if the Germans played the game.[22]

Geography imposed a simple, harsh logic on French thinking. The greatest single external threat was Germany and after two wars in living memory the French could not be other than firm in their insistence on security. Strict enforcement of the peace treaties and a defensive alliance with Great Britain were, in French eyes, the essentials of security.

Two motives in particular influenced British policy towards France and Germany. One was war weariness. After four years of fighting, the mood was one of 'never again' and a doctrine of minimum involvement on the continent was a natural reaction to the slaughter of the

Somme. Another motive was economic. In 1921, Great Britain experienced a severe economic setback which reinforced the argument of John Maynard Keynes in *Economic Consequences of the Peace* (1919) that the economic recovery of Europe was dependent on the restoration of Germany. Great Britain's 'real desire', Lloyd George told Briand, 'was to get on with business'.[23] In September 1923 Poincaré was told that 'England wanted a settlement of the Ruhr dispute because rightly or wrongly, she attributed the greater part of her unemployment to the present disorganisation of the world'.[24]

The upshot of these domestic and strategic preoccupations was that Great Britain assumed a mediatory role, seeking a general European understanding but eschewing hard and fast commitments. Austen Chamberlain, Foreign Secretary, modelled his treatment of Germany on Castlereagh's handling of France after 1815. The Foreign Secretary told the German Ambassador that he wanted a Europe in which Germany 'could take her place as an equal'.[25] France was warned that she could not 'count in perpetuity on a combination of powers to hold Germany down in a position of abject inferiority'.[26] The goal of British policy was the revival of a European concert which would maintain and regulate itself with only a minimum of British involvement.

In the 1920s France forged a chain of alliances in central and eastern Europe, gathering under her wing Czechoslovakia, Poland, Rumania, and Yugoslavia. Historians have stressed the disparity or contradiction between French diplomacy and French strategy. France's 'traditional policy of alliances', it is said, clashed with her increasingly defensive war plans.[27] About the eastern pacts there are two things to be said. Firstly the pacts, with the exception of the Polish alliance of 1921, were not military alliances in the full sense of the term. Secondly, when the pacts were negotiated in the early 1920s, French strategy had not yet hardened into a defensive mould. It is misleading, therefore, to judge the pacts by the defensive yardstick of the 1930s.

The Little Entente was a French sponsored alliance, between Czechoslovakia, Rumania and Yugoslavia, based on three bilateral treaties of 1920-21 which were directed against Hungary alone. France was not linked to the Little Entente by a pact of mutual assistance, though she did have bilateral pacts with the members of the Entente.[28] The only full military and political alliance was with Poland. Both countries signed a defensive pact on 19 February 1921, followed by a second treaty of 16 October 1925 based on League of Nations principles. Under the Rambouillet agreement of 6 September 1936, France provided financial help for Poland's armaments and railways. But until Franco-Polish staff talks were held in May 1939, no attempt was made to define and implement the principle of military assistance embodied in a secret military convention of 19 February 1921.

France and Czechoslovakia were linked by treaties of 25 January 1924 and 16 October 1925, pledging consultation and assistance in the event of a threat to common interests. In 1924 an exchange of letters between the two governments provided for co-operation between the general staffs but only one meeting of staffs seems to have taken place. Even in 1938 there

were no formal Franco-Czech staff talks. On 10 June 1926 an accord with
Rumania was signed, promising consultation. The pact included a secret
military protocol affirming the principle of military collaboration. A
similar treaty followed with Yugoslavia in 1927. Arms were sent to
Rumania but there were no staff talks. When in July 1926 the French
envoy at Bucharest suggested that a close watch be kept on the state
of Rumanian defences, the Quai d'Orsay reminded him that the military
protocol did not imply staff talks and these would only take place if
events required. In 1928 Yugoslavia took the initiative and asked for
staff talks, only to be told that military matters could be handled through
the normal attaché channels. Completing these pacts was the Franco-
Soviet alliance of 2 May 1935 and the Czechoslovak-Soviet accord of
16 May 1935, treaties of mutual assistance framed on League principles.
Both pacts were interdependent. The obligation of assistance between
Czechoslovakia and the Soviet Union was made conditional upon the
operation of the Franco-Czechoslovak alliance. The staff talks which
might have given life to the Franco-Soviet pact were studiously evaded
by the French.

The distinctive feature of the eastern pacts, apart from the Polish
treaty of 1921, was that they were constructed in accordance with the
principles and procedures of the League of Nations. The definition of
a *casus foederis* depended on the interpretation of the articles of the
League Covenant. The pacts were therefore much more circumscribed
than traditional military alliances. And in her relations with Poland France
increasingly stressed the treaty of 1925, which was inspired by League
principles, in preference to the 1921 treaty.

It is not true to say that the French army had no offensive plans against
Germany. Until 1926 military planning provided for a strong attack
against Germany, using the Rhineland as a springboard.[29] The decision
to build fortifications was not taken until the end of 1927. Even in the
1930s traces of offensive thinking persisted. In the event of a German
attempt to seize the Saar, placed under League administration in 1919
the French High Command planned to send in troops.[30] Nor did the
army plan to leave its men permanently immured in the Maginot line.
The theory of French strategy was that after troops had been mobilised
and concentrated behind the screen of fortifications offensives would be
launched.[31]

The evolution by the end of the postwar decade of a fully defensive
strategy impelled the French to seek a revision of the Polish treaty of
1921.[32] The Poles, who had been thoroughly alarmed by the Locarno
agreements of 1925, had serious doubts about the efficacy of the French
alliance. In 1927 Paris suggested that the 1921 alliance should be
revised and harmonised with the Locarno and the League Covenant.
Marshal Pilsudski, who had seized power in Poland in 1926, rejected
this move to dilute the military alliance. In the summer of 1928 Pilsudski
sent a general to Paris with instructions to investigate the French
attitude. The Polish emissary met the Chief of the General Staff, General
Debeney, and declared that if France was attacked by Germany, Poland
would at once take military action in accordance with the 1921 pact.

When the Polish general asked what France would do in the event of a German attack on Poland he was told that in such a case the decision would depend 'in the first place' on the attitude of the British government. A year later, René Massigli, a senior official of the Quai d'Orsay, informed Warsaw that the French government would consult London before implementing the pact. In 1934 Pilsudski blocked Barthou's attempts to revise the alliance and military convention.

Disillusionment with the dissensions of the successor states and disappointment over the British refusal to guarantee the settlement in the east produced a slackening of French interest. The eastern allies brought little comfort to France. They were divided by antipathies and rivalries. Czechoslovakia and Poland had little in common and Poland contested Czechoslovakia's possession of Teschen. The Czechs in turn looked askance at the friendly exchanges between Poland and Hungary, and the Poles resented what seemed pro-Soviet tendencies in Czech policy.

Some French politicians and publicists had always disliked the peace settlement in the east. As early as 1922 the Right wing journalist Wladimir d'Ormesson counselled his countrymen that Czechoslovakia was not a viable entity.[33] Paul Deschanel, Anatole de Monzie, and Louis Marin lamented the dissolution of the Hapsburg empire. Many on the Left campaigned for the revision of the Versailles treaties. Emile Roche, Political Director of *La Republique*, an organ rumoured to be the mouthpiece of the Radical leader Edouard Daladier, published articles calling for the revision of the treaties. The articles came from the pens of Pierre Dominique, Alfred Fabre Luce and Jean Montigny, all prominent appeasers in 1938-39. In December 1932, Jacques Kayser, Vice-President of the Radical party and an adviser to Daladier, condemned the peace settlement.[34]

The quest for security was conditioned by a number of interlocking internal pressures and forces: pacifist feeling, ideological conflict, financial weakness and governmental instability. France, in Winston Churchill's phrase, was armed to the teeth and pacifist to the core. Detestation of war was a conviction shared by all sections of the political spectrum. When on 16 March 1935 Hitler announced the introduction of conscription, the Right wing Wladimir d'Ormesson, foreign editor of *Figaro*, spoke of his 'anguish' at the news. Hitler and his henchmen were 'gangsters' who were 'capable of anything'. However a war to stop Hitler was too appalling to contemplate. It would be 'the end of civilisation, the end of the Christian era'.[35] The Left accepted the new dispensation of Geneva and anathematized any suggestion that Europe could return to the arms race and alliances of 1914. Pacifism permeated the literary and intellectual climate. In 1932, the novelist Romain Rolland, an apostle of internationalism and Franco-German friendship, published a manifesto, signed by André Gide among others, calling on intellectuals to promise resistance to war. In 1935, Jean Giraudoux in his play 'Tiger at the Gates' used the classical legend of Troy as a vehicle for a protest against the stupidity of war. The Radical Socialist weekly, *Marianne,* edited by Emmanuel Berl, preached a pacifist message throughout the 1930s. The pacifism of opinion made the pursuit of disarmament and conciliation through the League the only widely acceptable policy.

Although ideological conflict did not reach a climax until the 1930s, anti-Bolshevism was a central plank in the Right wing platform in the immediate aftermath of war. One of the assumptions which informed the peacemaking in 1919 was the need to contain Bolshevism and in the 1920s much moderate, as well as Right wing opinion, believed Communists were a serious threat to the state. Communists were active in spreading anti-colonialist and anti-militarist propaganda. They opposed the Ruhr occupation and the Riff war of 1925-26. In April 1927, the Radical Albert Sarraut, Minister of the Interior, proclaimed 'Communism is the enemy' and while the Chamber was on holiday Communist deputies were proscribed and arrested.[36] In the same year, the Socialist Fernand Buisson, President of the Chamber of Deputies, spoke of Communist activity 'as a perpetual menace to civilisation...in any country where Communism should win the day it would be the end of everything'.[37]

After 1932 political differences were exacerbated by the social and economic effects of the depression. The first objective of Socialists and Communists was to fight fascism in France and it was thought that to envisage even the possibility of war would be playing straight into the hands of the Right. In 1935 the Flandin government's proposal for the extension of military service from one to two years was vehemently denounced by the Socialists and many Radicals. The Flandin proposal was a reply to Hitler's reintroduction of conscription on 16 March. Léon Blum, speaking for the Socialists, said that the Maginot Line had been built in order to allow for a reduction in the strength of the army. Against the background of strident anti-parliamentary agitation, the Left feared the thin end of a militarist wedge.

The years 1935 to 1938 witnessed a fundamental shift in Right and Left wing thinking on foreign affairs. Until the end of 1934 the Right was on the whole united on the necessity of resisting German rearmament, while the Left called for disarmament and collective security. Over the next four years the Left lost much of its faith in the League and disarmament. It was Blum's Popular Front government which took the decision to rearm in the autumn of 1936. In the Czech crisis of 1938, the Socialists, though divided, showed more enthusiasm for the defence of Czechoslovakia than the Right did. This reorientation of Right and Left wing attitudes was largely the outcome of the interplay between foreign and domestic crises. In the Ethiopian conflict of 1935-36 the Right was infuriated by the extent to which the Left, in urging sanctions, was prepared to alienate Italy. Conservative opinion viewed fascist Italy as a valuable counterweight to Germany and as an attractive experiment in authoritarian rule.

The outbreak of the Spanish civil war on 18 July 1936, coming so soon after the formation of the Popular Front government, raised political temperatures to fever pitch. In an outburst of irrational fury against the *Front Populaire* and *Frente Popular* the Right relinquished its traditional thinking on international affairs. By the autumn of 1936, the obsession with Bolshevism at home and abroad had almost replaced the old dread of German nationalism. The changed attitude of the Right towards the Franco-Soviet pact exemplified the evolution of opinion. In May 1935, in the shadow of German rearmament, the mass of Right wing deputies supported the pact, partly because it was the work of the conservative Flandin ministry, partly because the pact itself seemed innocuous. Nine months later, 164 Right wing deputies voted against parliamentary ratification of the pact. The impending general elections and the likelihood of a Popular Front victory completely changed Right wing views. Hitler's noisy beating of the anti-Communist drum drew a sympathetic response from conservatives. Distance, too, lent enchantment and the dynamic, purposeful facade of fascism offered an attractive contrast to what seemed a moribund political system.

The franc was the Achilles heel of French policy. When Great Britain left the gold standard in September 1931 the position of the franc began to deteriorate and the decline was accelerated by the devaluation of the United States dollar in April 1933. The Popular Front devaluation of September 1936 was greatly helped by Anglo-American co-operation in the Tripartite Stabilization Agreement of 25 September. International agreement on the maintenance of exchange rates for the pound sterling, dollar and French franc was welcome but the monetary accord cabined and confined French governments. The franc remained weak but governments were loath to impose exchange controls for fear of offending Britain and the United States. In February 1937, Léon Blum rejected controls to stop the outflow of gold on the grounds of maintaining good relations with Washington and London.[38] The depreciation of the currency imposed additional curbs on French policy. And reliance on extensive borrowing added to the financial pressures. In January 1937, the French government secured a loan of £250 millions on the London money market in order to finance their railways. Neville Chamberlain, Chancellor of the Exchequer, told the Bank of England that the money would have to come from private sources because the government did not wish to make an official loan.[39]

The task of defending the franc and stemming the gold rush from France swallowed up the energies of successive administrations and induced a cautious, conciliatory approach to international affairs. Only a European détente, it was believed, would enable France to recover her financial and economic strength. Expenditure on armaments was seen as an intolerable burden for an ailing economy. As Minister of Finance in the autumn of 1937 Georges Bonnet lopped three milliards of francs off the rearmament programme of fourteen milliards approved in September 1936, although the full programme was restored a few months later.[40] In February 1938, Jacques Rueff, then *Directeur du Mouvement Général des Fonds,* and financial adviser to the governments of the Fourth and Fifth Republics, urged the government to postpone all other expenditure until the 'unprecedented rearmament effort to which we are condemned can be lightened'.[41] The 'spirit of parsimony' was required everywhere and Rueff censured the Paris City Council for spending money on improved street lighting. In August, Georges Bonnet, now Foreign Minister, expressed the fear that 'if France should have to continue to arm at the present rate it would be necessary to regiment the entire population placing the civilian population on soldiers' wages and soldiers' rations. In no other way could the present level of the franc be maintained and the essential military expenditures made'.[42]

After the Stavisky riots of 6 February 1934, France was widely regarded as the sick woman of Europe. In November 1937 Hitler thought a civil war was a strong possibility. And the governmental instability of the last decade of the Republic — 24 changes of ministry in the period 1930 to 1940 — seemed sufficient testimony of decline. In assessing the effect of governmental changes on foreign policy it should be noted that the continuity of men in pivotal ministries such as war and foreign affairs — Briand was at the Quai d'Orsay continuously from 1925 to 1932 and Daladier at the war ministry from 1936 to 1940 — supplied a strong, steadying influence. Also, the close of the decade brought a much greater measure of stability. The Daladier administration of April 1938 lasted nearly two years, an achievement which in the interwar years was only surpassed by Poincaré's governments of 1922 and 1926. Indeed, the extensive use of *pleins pouvoirs,* a device by which parliament authorised the government to rule by decree laws, freed the Daladier ministry from day to day dependence on the legislature.

Arguably, however, by April 1938 the damage had been done. In foreign affairs France's reputation for political instability, though exaggerated, undermined her credibility as a great power. Observers noted the absence of a secure government in two of the great international crises: the re-militarization of the Rhineland on 7 March 1936 and the *Anschluss* on 11 March 1938. While the precise effect on the conduct of foreign policy of the numerous changes of government is debatable, it is certain that the urgency of internal issues, combined with the rituals of the 'dance of the portfolios', left little time for the sustained study of external problems. In the four months from October 1933, when Germany left the League and Disarmament conference, to the Stavisky riots of February 1934 France had four prime ministers. In mid-February 1934 Eden, then Under-Secretary of State at the Foreign Office, visited Paris and was told by the French Foreign Minister, Barthou, that the government was so preoccupied with internal problems that it had not been able to hold a Cabinet to decide its attitude on disarmament. When he returned on 1 March the French 'were in no better position to state their view'.[43]

As Foreign Minister from 1925 to 1932 Briand presided over an Indian summer of French greatness. The Treaty of Locarno, formally signed in London on 1 December 1925, was seen as heralding a fresh start in international relations. Germany, France and Belgium agreed to recognise their existing frontiers as permanent, including the demilitarised Rhineland zone; Great Britain and Italy guaranteed this arrangement and the treaty provided for the settlement of all disputes through the League. Briand's goodwill won praise from the British Foreign Secretary, Sir Austen Chamberlain, who wrote: 'Briand has almost taken my breath away by his liberality, his conciliatoriness, his strong and manifest desire to promote peace'.[44] The German attitude had been the contrary: 'niggling, provocative, crooked'.

Events soon belied the Locarno mood.[45] The treaty was a mixed blessing for France since although Germany had freely recognised the territorial settlement in western Europe she had not abandoned her opposition to the peace settlement in the east. Moreover, in binding her former enemy France also bound herself. She lost the freedom to take unilateral action in defence of treaty rights. A repetition of the Ruhr adventure of 1923 would jeopardise the Locarno guarantees. Détente soon led to deadlock. The private conversation between Briand and the German Foreign Minister Stresemann, at Thoiry in September 1926 led to nothing. The Young Plan of 1929 established a new reparations settlement in return for French evacuation of the Rhineland. The Plan was approved at the second Hague conference in January 1930. However, within just over two years reparations were cancelled *de facto* at the Lausanne conference of June and July 1932.

In 1931, after the financial collapse of Germany, France was at her zenith: 'the Bank of England was shocked to find itself dependent on the Bank of France' and even the Federal Reserve Bank of the United States was 'not altogether independent of French goodwill'.[46] If there was a turning point for France it was in the two years from 1932 to 1934, between Germany's demand for equality of rights in the disarmament talks in the summer of 1932 and the French note of 17 April 1934, refusing to participate in further disarmament discussions until the needs of her security had been met, Curiously French leaders, instead of taking the diplomatic initiative in the assurance of military hegemony, seemed bewildered, floundering in all directions; expressing interest in a bilateral accord with Germany, taking up negotiations for a Franco-Soviet pact, continuing disarmament talks, making efforts to improve relations with Great Britain and Italy. The Four Power Pact of July 1933 between France, Germany, Great Britain and Italy, with its theme of peaceful revision of frontiers, caused consternation among the eastern allies.

The chief cause of these hesitations was the fact that German rearmament brought the French face to face with the dilemma inherent in France's international position since the end of the war. In accepting German rearmament, France seemed to be signing her own death warrant, but there was no effective way of preventing it save by war. In October 1932 the French Prime Minister, Edouard Herriot, told his advisers:

> I have no illusions. I am convinced that Germany wishes to rearm . . . We are at a turning point in history. Until now Germany has practised a policy of submission . . . now she is beginning a positive policy. Tomorrow it will be a policy of territorial demands.[47]

What could France do? It is sometimes said that France should have waged a preventive war and there were rumours that Marshal Pilsudski of Poland invited her to join in such a war and received a refusal. General Weygand, Inspector General of the Army, was reported as saying: 'Why not a preventive war? Today France still has military superiority. Soon she will have lost it'.[48] But there is no evidence to show that Weygand or anyone else translated such ideas into action. The elections of 1932 returned a Left wing majority and the attachment of the Left to pacifism and the League precluded preventive war. French diplomats and ministers rejected the idea of a preventive war. In September 1933 Alexis Léger, Secretary General of the foreign ministry, said that no responsible Frenchman would dare to think of a preventive war. France would remain true to the League and collective security.[49] In December of the same year, Camille

Chautemps, Prime Minister, and his Foreign Minister, Paul-Boncour, 'vigorously' opposed any suggestion of forcible action against Germany.[50] Even if French opinion had favoured such a course the diplomatic restraints were powerful. At a meeting in October 1932 Herriot reminded the military chiefs that if France abandoned disarmament talks she would compromise herself and lose allied support. 'The government's great fear', he said, 'was that one day France would find herself alone facing Germany'.[51] A return to traditional alliances was out of the question. Pierre Viénot, French delegate to the Disarmament Conference, excluded *a priori* 'a return to the pre-war international system'—military alliances, an arms race, spheres of influence.[52]

The rejection of military action left no alternative but to continue talking to Germany in the hope of reaching some agreement. The Military Attaché at Berlin wrote to Daladier, Minister of War, on 13 December 1933:

> it seems that there is no other way for us than to reach an understanding which will contain...at least for a while, Germany's military development...If Hitler is sincere in proclaiming his desire for peace, we will be able to congratulate ourselves on having reached agreement; if he has other designs or if he has to give way one day to some fanatic we will at least have postponed the outbreak of a war and that is indeed a gain.[53]

Such counsel was not calculated to inspire confidence in the future and the fruitless negotiations of 1932-34 induced in the French leadership a profound pessimism. In *Les Hommes de Bonne Volonté* the novelist Jules Romains, who was on close terms with the statesmen of the 1930s, depicts the despair which overwhelmed them. Through the fictitious characters of the Radical Foreign Minister, Jerphanion, and of Grenier, a close collaborator of Daladier, Romains describes the French dilemma. 'For men like us', Jerphanion tells Grenier, 'I mean like Daladier, like Paul-Boncour, like myself, there is no longer anything to be done'.[54] France, it seemed, could only be the loser.

At this critical juncture policy making was bedevilled by the mistrust which soured relations between soldiers and politicians. In tracing the origins of the army's intervention in politics after 1945, historians have stressed the disharmony of civil-military relations under the Third Republic. Marshal MacMahon and General Boulanger were thrust aside and the Dreyfus affair had left a legacy of distrust. The army was considered to have grown too powerful in the war of 1914-18 and there was a fear on the Left that the generals might usurp civil authority. After the fall of Herriot's *Cartel des Gauches* 'a military coup d'etat' was 'quite openly talked about'.[55] This dread of a coup d'etat explains the suspicion with which deputiés received the army reforms proposed by Paul Reynaud and Charles de Gaulle in 1935-36. It was believed that de Gaulle's elite armoured divisions might easily become the shock troops of a Fascist *coup*. At times distrust of the army was expressed in no uncertain manner. In September 1938 the Socialist deputy, Grumbach, told British Labour party leaders to be sceptical about all estimates of military strength 'because if the truth were told many high officers of the General Staff should be immediately court-martialled and shot'.[56] However the distrust which characterised the 1930s was not so strongly marked in the first postwar decade. A recent study of the 1920s suggests that the 'dominant note' was the agreement of civil and military chiefs over large areas of policy.[57]

The main factor in the disputes of the early 1930s was the intransigent personality of General Weygand, Chief of the General Staff until 1931 and then Inspector General of the Army until 1935. Weygand's implacable opposition to disarmament brought him into sharp conflict with the Radical Socialist governments of 1932-34. Not that the general was a blind reactionary, on the contrary, he was well aware of the need for a reappraisal of defence and foreign policies. In January 1933, for example, he called for a review of diplomatic commitments and military planning.[58] However his conservative outlook and associations with the Right prejudiced opinion against him and his plea for a re-thinking of policy went unheeded.

Under the inspiration of Louis Barthou, Foreign Minister in the Doumergue government of February 1934, French diplomacy recovered some of its former balance and sense of purpose. Although Barthou tried to shore up the crumbling defences, he was not an uncompromising opponent of Germany. Contrary to what used to be thought, he was not the chief author of the note of 17 April which rejected further disarmament talks with Germany. The note in fact reflected not so much the Foreign minister's views as those of his colleagues, notably Herriot and Tardieu. Weygand, too, had a hand in the making of the note.[59] At a meeting of the Cabinet on 17 April the Minister for the Navy, François Piétri, drew the obvious conclusion from the note: 'we are initiating a policy of force . . . we must have a defence policy which supports our diplomacy'.[60] Nothing happened. The note was an empty gesture of defiance and exasperation.

The stiffly worded note, by closing the door to disarmament talks, created the worst possible atmosphere for Barthou's bid to regain the initiative. This enterprise took two forms: first the strengthening of the eastern alliances and a plan for their incorporation in a regional security pact linked to the Soviet Union, second the cultivation of Italy as a makeweight to Germany. The problem which baffled French ministers was how to make the eastern pacts coherent and credible. Barthou's solution was an eastern Locarno, a mutual assistance pact between the Soviet Union, Germany, Poland, Czechoslovakia, the Baltic states and Finland. The pact would be linked to the League Covenant. Reactions to the proposal were negative and disheartening. In January 1934 Poland had signed a non-aggression treaty with Germany and showed no interest in a scheme which would link her to the Soviet Union.

The reassertion of the eastern pacts was accompanied by an effort to get on better terms with Italy. On taking office, Barthou promptly sent Mussolini a warm personal message, expressing the hope of close co-operation.[61] This wooing of Italy met with the approval of the General Staff.[62] Italy, it was thought, was the key to France's problems. The military and political advantages of an Italian alliance were indisputable. France urgently needed a major continental ally. Although the Soviet Union was an obvious candidate, the political mistrust which French conservatives felt for Moscow—a mistrust shared by Poland and Rumania—seemed an insuperable obstacle to a full Franco-Soviet pact. Moreover in the absence of a common land frontier between Germany and the Soviet Union France could not expect direct Soviet help in the event of a war with Germany. Such Soviet help as might be given would depend on the goodwill of the Polish and Rumanian governments. By contrast, Italy, it was argued, would serve as a bridge, spanning regional security pacts in western and eastern Europe. An Italian alliance would protect France's vulnerable Mediterranean flank, enabling her to concentrate forces on the Rhine. Italian interests in the Danubian area lent support to these arguments. However Barthou had no immediate success and the *Duce* seemed more concerned with his own designs in central Europe than with acting as a long-stop for French interests in the area. On 9 October 1934 Barthou's diplomacy was abruptly terminated at Marseilles, with the assassination of King Alexander of Yugoslavia. The king, who was paying a state visit to France, was shot by a Croat terrorist, and Barthou at his side was killed.

Pierre Laval, who succeeded Barthou at the Quai d'Orsay and formed an administration of his own in June 1935, was one of the ablest of France's interwar statesmen. Lesser men like the radical Georges Bonnet marvelled at his success. A self-made man, of a peasant family in the Auvergne, he began his political career as a Socialist; by 1934 he was of the Right and had amassed a considerable fortune. With his swarthy, squat figure and white tie he came to personify for many Englishmen all that seemed tricky and suspect in French politics. His attitude towards the Italo-Ethiopian war of 1935-36 earned him a bad name in London and events in 1940 confirmed British suspicions of double-dealing. Yet there is much more to be said in defence of Laval's diplomacy in 1935-36 than critics have conceded.

The Italian invasion of Ethiopia in October 1935 was not a bolt from the blue. For over 50 years Italy had nursed African ambitions. France and Italy had negotiated over the fate of Ethiopia during Laval's first premiership in 1931-32. In Rome plans for an invasion of Ethiopia had been discussed since 1932. On 20 December 1934 Mussolini drew up a directive for war against Ethiopia but did not send it to his chiefs of staff. The event which finally decided Mussolini in favour of war was the conclusion of a political alliance with France—the Rome Agreements of 7 January 1935. Laval had continued the course charted by Barthou. Of the eight agreements concluded in Rome on 7 January four were public, four secret. France and Italy promised to consult together in the case of a threat to Austrian independence. They also promised to consult if Germany should 'modify by unilateral actions her obligations in the matter of armaments'. Of the accords the most controversial was the one on Ethiopia.[63] With only minor exceptions, France handed over to Italy her economic interests in Ethiopia. In a private conversation with Mussolini Laval used the phrase a 'free hand'.[64] Whereas the Italian dictator assumed that this meant France would turn a blind eye to his military plans for Ethiopia, Laval probably assumed Italy would stop short of military conquest. Nothing was put in writing and the ambiguity was doubtless intentional. On 23 January 1935 Mussolini ordered preparations for war against Ethiopia and in February a military build-up began in the Italian colonies of Eritrea and Somalia.

By the spring of 1935 Italy's intentions were not in doubt. Instead of delivering an unequivocal warning the British and French governments chose an admixture of warnings and conciliation, with the emphasis on the latter. Conciliation seemed all the more urgent because on 16 March Hitler announced the re-introduction of conscription. Meeting at Stresa on 11-14 April Great Britain, France and Italy reaffirmed their Locarno obligations and agreed to consult together in the event of a threat to Austrian independence. The three governments declared their determination to oppose 'by all practicable means any unilateral repudiation of treaties which may engender the peace of Europe'. Solidarity on the need to preserve Austrian independence against Germany was obtained at the price of saying nothing to the *Duce* about his obvious designs on Ethiopia.

All the omens seemed favourable for Mussolini. Though Laval journeyed to Moscow for the signing of the Franco-Soviet pact on 2 May 1935 he side-stepped Stalin's proposal for staff talks. The focus of his diplomacy was still Italy. British diplomacy was also reassuring. The Anglo-German Naval Agreement of 18 June 1935 permitting German naval rearmament up to 35% of British tonnage showed the concessions which Great Britain was prepared to make in accommodating Germany. It also illustrated the divergent approaches of Great Britain and France to German rearmament. Great Britain's attitude was pragmatic. She felt that Germany was going to increase her naval strength whatever happened and that an accommodation was necessary in order to keep this increase as low as possible. Great Britain seemed saved from her nightmare of having to confront simultaneously the limitless naval ambitions of Germany and Japan. But France resented British recognition of Germany's violation of Versailles, convinced that without agreements on ground and air forces and a commitment by Hitler to a peaceful policy in eastern Europe Germany would not be restrained. Shortly after the Anglo-German Naval Agreement the Franco-Italian union was consummated. On 27 June 1935 General Gamelin, chief of the French general staff, and Marshal Badoglio, Italian chief of staff, signed a military convention, providing for concerted action in the event of a threat to Austria. The possibility was considered of sending an Italian contingent to the Rhine and also of French forces crossing Italy *en route* to central Europe.[65]

Reassured by these moves Mussolini continued his military preparations against Ethiopia.[66] London and Paris had no intention of going to war with Italy. On 1 September the British Foreign Secretary, Sir Samuel Hoare, and Laval agreed that the issue of war must be avoided. The Italian invasion of Ethiopia on 3 October brought swift condemnation from the League, backed by the imposition of economic sanctions on 18 November. None the less British and French ministers were unremitting in their efforts to buy off Mussolini. Their labours culminated in the Hoare-Laval plan of 8 December 1935, by which two-thirds of Ethiopia would have been ceded to Italy. Ethiopia would have retained a strip of territory as access to the sea. When the details were leaked in the press British opinion was shocked and angry. The British cabinet was compelled to disavow the plan and Hoare resigned. No further compromise plans were prepared. In the meantime the Italian conquest proceeded unhindered. On 2 May 1936 the Emperor Haile Selassie fled his country and on 9 May the King of Italy was proclaimed Emperor of Ethiopia.

Why did Great Britain and France allow Italy to overrun Ethiopia? Three reasons were uppermost: the desire to retain Italy as a makeweight against Germany; military considerations; and thirdly the divisions of opinion in both countries. Neither London nor Paris saw any intrinsic evil in Italian expansion in Ethiopia. Germany, not Italy, was regarded as the main threat to peace. Italy was a Locarno power and a potential ally against Germany. It followed that Mussolini had to be cosseted and wooed. Reinforcing the political argument were military considerations. In London naval anxieties were decisive in influencing the actions of the government.[67] The burden of acting against Italy would fall on the Royal Navy and the chiefs of staff believed that the fleet had to be kept intact for use against Japan. For France military factors were no less decisive.[68] Italy was the only major continental power with whom France had a military understanding. General Gamelin, chief of the general staff, told the *Haut Comité Militaire* on 3 October that in the event of war with Germany Italian neutrality would be worth seventeen French divisions. If these divisions had to be kept in the Alps and in North Africa as a precaution against Italy it would be difficult to help the eastern allies by an offensive across the Rhine.

The divisions of opinion on both sides of the Channel imposed a cautious diplomacy. Although British ministers had no wish to go to war against Italy, they had to reckon with popular attachment to the League and collective security. The Italian attack on Ethiopia, a League member, seemed an open and shut case of aggression. The results of the British Peace Ballot, announced on 28 June 1935, attested the strength of League sentiment. Of eleven million replies, ten million supported the application of economic and non-military sanctions to stop one nation attacking another. With a general election planned for the autumn the British government followed a 'double line', seeking to conciliate Mussolini while pleasing the League lobby. The election of 14 November seemed a vindication of Baldwin's electoral slogan 'all sanctions short of war', with 492 supporters of the National government and only 154 Labour men returned.

In Paris internal preoccupations were equally important. The Italo-Ethiopian crisis coincided with mounting domestic upheaval. The increasing strength of the ultra-nationalist Leagues was countered by the Popular Front alliance of communists, socialists and radicals. Since the Stavisky scandal of February 1934 Right wing governments had held office. In June 1935 the Flandin cabinet fell and was replaced by the Laval administration. However, unlike Baldwin's National government, Laval's ministry had a precarious parliamentary life. Laval was dependent on radical support in the Chamber. France, like Great Britain, was in a pre-election period, with elections due in April-May 1936. Political realities presented Laval with an impossible choice. The Right supported the Italian alliance and would not hear of sanctions, whilst the radicals were on the whole

sympathetic to the League and collective security. Wholehearted enforcement of sanctions would alienate the Right and destroy Laval's cabinet.
Yet to neglect the League would offend the radicals and invite retribu-
tion in the forthcoming elections. The retention of radical support was
worth while because many radicals were far from enthusiastic about the
Popular Front. Herriot, in particular, had strong reservations. However if
Laval failed to support the League he would certainly drive the radicals
into the arms of the socialists and communists. No Peace Ballot was held
in France but three manifestoes were issued which showed the divided
state of opinion. The first, the *Manifesto of French Intellectuals for the
Defence of the West and Peace in Europe,* appeared on 4 October and
was opposed to sanctions against Italy. Within a few days two other manifestoes were published, calling for collective security. Significantly though
the second and third manifestoes were extremely cautious in their references to sanctions, stressing that 'another European war would be an
irreparable disaster'.

The French government was in a quandary: consistent and effective
support for the League was incompatible with the preservation of the
newly formed Italian alliance. British policy in the crisis added to Laval's
difficulties. For political and military reasons British ministers demanded
a clear-cut decision from Paris. Unequivocal French support for the
League, it was thought, might suffice to secure an Italian withdrawal.
Alternatively, French refusal to back the League would provide an excuse
for British inaction. Effective enforcement of sanctions depended on
French naval cooperation. The British chiefs of staff informed the government that French military help was indispensable. As fears grew in November of a mad-dog act by Mussolini French help was judged all the more
important. A British request on 24 September for the assistance of the
French fleet in the Mediterranean placed Laval in a dilemma. Naval action
against Italy would certainly destroy the alliance. None the less the alternative was nightmarish. France needed British naval help in the event of
war with Germany. In a personal letter of 1 September to Laval Piétri,
minister of marine, stressed that in a war with Germany France could not
survive without British sea power, concluding: 'the least unpleasant
solution is the one which does not separate us from England'.[69]

Laval was between the devil and the deep blue sea. Nevertheless his
tightrope diplomacy was not without some success. On 4 November 1935
Badoglio, Italian chief of staff, assured the French military attaché in
Rome that the recent military accord was still valid. And, but for the reactions of British opinion, the Hoare-Laval plan of December 1935 would
almost certainly have been acceptable both to the British cabinet and to
Mussolini. The tone of the letters which the French prime minister and
the Italian leader exchanged in December 1935 and January 1936 was
warm and friendly. On 22 December Laval promised Mussolini that he
would do his utmost to bring about a peaceful settlement of the war.[70]
Although six days later the *Duce* refused to ratify the Rome Agreements,
nothing was said of the Gamelin-Badoglio convention.

Would sanctions have sufficed to stop Mussolini? The sanctions imposed by the League in November 1935 did not include an oil embargo.

We now know that if the oil sanction had been imposed. Mussolini, according to his own statement, would have made peace within 24 hours. Even the limited sanctions applied caused Italy considerable economic distress. Admittedly much of Italy's oil needs were being met by hundreds of small American operators who took advantage of higher prices for oil to charter tankers to Italy and Red Sea ports. Yet determined Anglo-French naval action could have quickly cut off these supplies.

The failure to restrain Mussolini did not make a European war inevitable but it did make war highly probable. 'Us today, you tomorrow', were the Emperor Haile Selassie's last words at Geneva. The Ethiopian crisis, Mussolini wrote to Laval on 16 October 1935, was 'a decisive turning point' in international affairs.[71] Instead of cementing Anglo-French unity, the Italo-Ethiopian war deeply estranged the two countries. Henri Béraud's cry in the extreme Right wing *Gringoire* in October—'England must be reduced to slavery'—echoed the Anglophobia of the ultra-right. Anglo-French naval contacts were far from cordial. One French admiral, who usually spoke perfect English, insisted on speaking quite rude French to British officers.[72] Much more alarming was the general climate of criticism. The Ambassador at Paris, Sir George Clerk, reported:

> an atmosphere here of hysteria and wilful misunderstanding, largely induced by Italian liras and internal politics, that is not only deplorable in itself but is creating a division between the two countries which, if not soon healed, will have tragic consequences for . . . the peace of Europe.[73]

Reassuringly Herriot wrote on 19 October:

> . . . We have just witnessed a Right wing reaction, stupid and almost criminal. I am ashamed of it for my country . . . But the mass of the French people, faithful to its memories, to its good sense . . . rejects with horror the provocations. . .[74]

But the wounds never quite healed. Laval was pilloried as the evil genius of French policy, playing fast and loose with all and sundry. In British eyes, France had proved an unreliable ally and the chiefs of staff desscribed the naval contacts with France as 'profoundly unsatisfactory'.[75] On the French side, the British disavowal of the Hoare-Laval plan confirmed the mistrust inspired by the Anglo-German Naval Agreement. 'The French have not had the guts either to repudiate or to act up to the League. That is the whole trouble', wrote Sir Robert Vansittart, Permanent Under-Secretary of State at the Foreign Office.[76] But 'guts' did not enter into the affair. Laval's policy was eminently defensible both on military and political grounds. Germany exploited this disarray. While Great Britain and France were distracted by the Ethiopian war Hitler delivered his first major blow against the territorial status quo.

Chapter 3

Wit's end

On 7 March 1936 Hitler, alleging a contradiction between the Franco-Soviet pact and the Treaty of Locarno, sent a force of 22,000 troops into the demilitarised Rhineland, violating the Versailles and Locarno treaties.[1] His gamble that the guarantors of Locarno, Britain and Italy, would remain passive and that France would not dare to act alone proved correct. Albert Sarraut, French Prime Minister, after bravely announcing over the radio that 'Strasbourg would not be left under German guns',[2] finally decided against forcible action.

The re-occupation of the Rhineland created a major breach in the territorial settlement of Versailles.[3] And in retrospect the crisis seemed to mark the beginning of the end for France — Anschluss, Munich, and Danzig followed in swift succession. 'If the French government had mobilised', wrote Winston Churchill, 'there is no doubt that Hitler would have been compelled by his own General Staff to withdraw, and a check would have been given to his pretensions which might well have proved fatal to his rule'.[4] Churchill's judgement reflected a widely held view that the Rhineland was France's last chance of stopping Germany without a European war.

Why, then, did the French army not expel the German columns from the demilitarised zone? France was not caught off guard—a German move had been talked about since the summer of 1935,[5] though the timing and method were a surprise. Nevertheless the French might have been expected to make some contingency plans for a German military *coup*. Moreover the balance of military strength favoured France. With her eastern allies, Poland and Czechoslovakia, she could muster a total of 160 divisions against an estimated German strength of 120. And French ministers still believed that their air force was stronger than the *Luftwaffe*.[6]

Post-1945 French reflections on the Rhineland crisis took the form of recriminations between soldiers and statesmen; soldiers stressing the hesitations of the statesmen and vice versa.[7] On one point at least there was general agreement: Britain had opposed forcible action. In the light of the French documents three considerations determined reactions to the German reoccupation: the attitude of the French General Staff, the state of public opinion, and Britain's refusal to countenance military action. The crucial factor was the standpoint of the General Staff.

In February 1936, the French government decided that no forcible action could be undertaken without the 'full agreement' of the British government.[8] On 3 March at Geneva, Flandin, Foreign Minister, assured Eden, Foreign Secretary, that France would not take any isolated action.[9] On 7 March, following the news of the German entry into the Rhineland, Eden counselled the French not to take any action without prior consultation.[10] There followed a mixture of carrot and stick. In Paris on 10 March French ministers were told that though Britain could not join in military action against Germany she was ready to consider a renewal and reinforcement of her Locarno obligations.[11] French talk of joint action against Germany, including the use of force, drew forth the comment from Baldwin, Prime Minister, that: 'at some stage it would be necessary to point out to the French that the action they proposed would not result only in letting loose another great war in Europe. They might succeed in smashing Germany, with the aid of Russia but it would probably only result in Germany going Bolshevik'.[12]

Undeniably therefore British pressure was a powerful brake on France's freedom of action. And when German troops entered the Rhineland only a handful of ministers and senior foreign ministry officials, of whom Léger, Secretary General, Massigli, Assistant Political Director, and Comert, head of the news department, were the most prominent, suggested ignoring British advice and acting on the assumption that Britain would have to follow France into war with Germany. In two meetings, on 8 and 10 March, the majority of ministers decided in favour of diplomatic negotiations.

Yet the timidity of the politicians was hardly surprising in view of the state of public opinion in France and Britain. 'I suppose Jerry can do what he likes in his own back garden, can't he?' opined Eden's taxidriver on the morning of 9 March.[13] British reactions to the Rhineland crisis cannot be separated from the Ethiopian episode. The low opinion of France, engendered by Laval's lukewarm handling of sanctions, persisted and deprived her of potential sympathy. Hitler, too, adeptly disarmed opinion in advance of the reoccupation. He carried not fire and sword but an olive branch. In the morning of 7 March *before* the entry of German troops he offered non-aggression pacts, a pact limiting air forces, and demilitarization on both sides of the Rhine frontier.

Germany's claim that the Franco-Soviet pact and the Locarno treaty were incompatible did not command wide assent in the two western democracies. Nevertheless British and French conservatives strongly deplored the ratification of the pact by the French Chamber on 27 February. The French Right wing press argued that in ratifying the pact the government had needlessly provoked Germany. An outraged and bellicose French public would doubtless have pushed the government into taking forcible action but there was no enthusiasm for chastising Germany. On 10 March the Chamber gave a very chilly reception to a suggestion of unilateral action. The Paris press, with few exceptions, refused to consider retaliatory action. Given the apathy of opinion, and with the elections only six weeks off, Ministers could be excused for accepting the advice of their military counsellors.

France's acquiescence in the repudiation of the Rhineland settlement however, was primarily the result of the General Staff's refusal to take unilateral action against Germany. The Minister of War and the Chief of the General Staff declared that it was not possible to expel the German forces without general mobilisation, involving the danger of a Franco-German war. And war with Germany could not be contemplated without the certainty of allied support.[14] Gamelin, Chief of the General Staff, told Ministers 'the idea of sending quickly into the Rhineland a French expeditionary force, even if only a token force, was a chimera' because the army was a 'static' force and 'no offensive action could be undertaken until the twelfth day of mobilisation'.[15]

Thus it was mobilisation or nothing. France was still wedded to the citizen-soldier concept of 1792. The regular army was merely a skeleton force. It lacked the men and training to deliver a swift riposte. No division could be brought up to war strength without the recall of reservists. French war plans envisaged five stages leading up to full mobilisation: the 'alert'; 'reinforced alert'; 'security'; 'general cover'; 'general mobilisation' —a steady build-up that might extend over a fortnight. Clearly, the army was too clumsy and awkward an instrument for countering the sudden thrusts of Hitlerian diplomacy.

Some writers have argued that if a mechanized, professional force on the model advocated by Reynaud and de Gaulle had existed in March 1936 France would have quickly retaliated. But it is unlikely, to say the least, that the existence of such a force would have altered the French decision. The French reasoned from fear and their inaction had little to do with the static, defensive character of the army. The simple fact, as Jean Fabry, Minister of War, admitted at a meeting of the *Haut Comité Militaire* on 18 January 1936 was that France no longer possessed a clear, decisive lead over her rival: 'from the point of view of material, Germany is on the verge of surpassing us'.[18] In fact 1934 was the last year in which the military chiefs freely acknowledged that the balance of forces favoured France.[17] At the meeting on 18 January Fabry also pointed out that the programme of French armament was no longer adequate. The Ethiopian crisis had produced a significant change in relative strengths. Fourteen divisions, about a fifth of France's total war strength, which might have been concentrated on the Rhine, had been transferred to the Alps and Tunisia.[18] France could not rely on Italian friendship.

Yet, even allowing for the transfer of the fourteen divisions as a precaution against Italy, France, with allied help, still enjoyed numerical superiority over Germany. Surprisingly, no account was taken of the potential contribution of Czechoslovakia and Poland and the numbers of German troops in the Rhineland were greatly overestimated. The French General Staff were so apprehensive of the danger of a Franco-German conflict that they failed to make a dispassionate assessment of the immediate military situation. In fact it seems clear that for some considerable time before 7 March the military leaders had tacitly written off the Rhineland on the grounds that demilitarisation could not be indefinitely enforced and the issue was not worth the risk of a major war. As early as August 1932 the war ministry had asked the foreign ministry what was to be done about German violations of the demilitarized zone. Herriot, then Foreign Minister, replied that France would have to exhaust all peaceful procedures through Locarno and the League. Military counter-measures were not mentioned. Hence in the approach to 7 March the attention of France's military and political leadership was focussed not on ways and means of preventing a German *coup* but on turning the impending remilitarization to France's advantage. On 18 February the General Staff recommended that France seek a defensive alliance with Great Britain as 'compensation' for the loss of the Rhineland 'no man's land'.[19] It would appear that both the Quai d'Orsay and the General Staff saw in a negotiated German reoccupation a means of securing a closer relationship with London. The method of German action took France by surprise—it had been expected that Germany would ask for the opening of negotiations, but the French military chiefs saw no reason to change their strategy.

France did not win the defensive alliance she wanted but her gains were far from negligible. Following the reoccupation French ministers called for sanctions by stages, including military ones. They knew what the British answer would be but there was method in their madness. In what was to become a frequent and familiar tactic over the next three years French governments by making a threat of forceful and independent action were able to extract considerable concessions. In London on 19 March the four Locarno powers—Britain, France, Belgium and Italy, renewed their obligations and agreed to open staff talks. Franco-Belgian-British staff talks followed on 15-16 April in London. It was agreed that in the event of an unprovoked German attack on France, and subject to the decision of the government of the day, two infantry divisions would be despatched on the fourteenth day of mobilisation. The practical results of the talks were, as the leader of the French delegation noted, 'very slight'.[20] Still the French had some cause for satisfaction. The offer of two divisions was the first permanent commitment accepted by Britain towards her neighbour since the collapse of the Anglo-American guarantee pact of 1919. Though the commitment was limited to western Europe only, and the staff talks were not continued the foundation of a defensive alliance had been laid.

Contrary therefore to what has often been claimed, the Rhineland crisis was not a total disaster for France. Some advantage was gained, though admittedly at the cost of tightening the harness which bound France to the British chariot. Although the strategic situation was never again as favourable to France, it is difficult to see how French leaders could have acted otherwise. The German reoccupation had been long expected but diplomatically and militarily France's hands were tied. In order to safeguard their treaty rights under Locarno, the French had to maintain consultation with their partners and scrupulously avoid any appearance of aggressive action. Army units could not be brought up to war strength without calling up reservists, and mobilisation in advance of the German *coup* would have destroyed France's diplomatic position. It might be objected that an armoured striking force would have enabled France to deliver a riposte without mobilisation. However this suggestion does not take account of the fundamental assumption that governed

French decision making, namely the belief that France, unsupported by a major ally, could not run the risk of war with Germany. If French troops had marched, German forces might well have beaten a hasty retreat but it would be rash to conclude that they would automatically have done so. Arguably they might have offered resistance.[21] The advice of the General Staff that the government in considering forcible action must reckon on the possibility of a Franco-German war was sensible and realistic in the circumstances.

The Rhineland reoccupation was a turning point for France's eastern alliances. Germany was able to fortify her western frontier, thus blocking any French offensive in support of the allies, though the fortifications were not completed until the autumn of 1938. French acquiescence in the German *coup* sowed disillusionment and dismay in eastern Europe. 'If on 7 March you could not defend yourself, how will you defend us against the aggressor', asked Titulesco, Rumanian Foreign Minister.[22] The shock of French inaction was all the greater because immediately after 7 March Czechoslovakia, Poland and Yugoslavia reaffirmed their loyalty to France. As the weeks went by alarm and despondency took hold in central and east European capitals. In Warsaw, Marshal Rydz-Smigly, Inspector General of the Polish army, confirmed his loyalty to the alliance but regretted French passivity.[23] In Prague, Krofta, Czechoslovak Foreign Minister, observed that French weakness had shaken the Little Entente. Austria felt more exposed than ever to German pressure: 'If Germany is allowed to fortify the Rhineland, we are lost', declared her foreign minister.[24] On Italian counsel, Schuschnigg, the Austrian Chancellor, resigned himself to the conclusion of a new agreement with Germany, the *modu vivendi* of 11 July 1936.

Though the Rhineland *coup* sounded the death knell of the eastern pacts it would be wrong to think that the French hastened to liquidate the pacts as tiresome liabilities. Indeed, for a while ministers seemed to suppose that Germany could be prevented from building fortifications. At a meeting of Service Ministers and Chiefs of Staff on 4 April Sarraut, Prime Minister, said:

> the essential point is that France cannot allow Germany to build fortifications in the formerly demilitarised zone. We would find it impossible to intervene effectively in order to assist our eastern allies[25]

Paradoxically, the eastern pacts were more important to France after 7 March than they had been before the *coup*. Until 7 March the military chiefs were fairly confident of holding their own against Germany in a defensive war, though it was recognised that the decisive superiority enjoyed in the early 1930s had gone for good. But the rapidity with which Germany exploited her victory and the disarray of the eastern allies made the military chiefs apprehensive lest the margin of superiority which France still possessed might be eroded before the end of the year. By May, Krupps were turning out prefabricated concrete sections twenty four hours a day and armies of workmen were constructing defences in the Rhineland.[26] Information reaching Paris pointed to the demoralization of the eastern allies and to signs of a German-Italian *rapprochement*.[27]

Consequently the General Staff placed a greater emphasis on the Czech and Polish alliances. In an appreciation of 25 June Gamelin stressed the fragility of France's position.[28] Taking into account British, Belgium and Czechoslovak forces, there was a balance between France and Germany. Yet if Germany accelerated her rearmament and Italy adopted a neutral or hostile attitude the military situation would be most precarious. Reserves of manpower were exhausted and reliance on colonial troops might prove dangerous if political unrest occurred in the colonies. Two conditions, concluded Gamelin, were necessary if France was not to be outclassed: the Franco-Italian military accord of 27 June 1935 must be retained and the Franco-Polish alliance consolidated. On 29 June the newly created Permanent Committee of National Defence (*Comité permanent de défense nationale*), which replaced the *Haut Comité Militaire*, decided at its first meeting to send aircraft to Czechoslovakia in an effort to bolster the shaky morale of the Little Entente.[29] In an appraisal of 9 July the General Staff declared that 'certain and effective help' would be given to the eastern allies by means of 'pressure' or an 'offensive' in the west. And, continued the report, if Italy remained friendly a 'central European front' might be set up which would allow French troops to be sent to central Europe.[30] This access of optimism towards central Europe was probably prompted by a letter of 10 June which Marshal Badoglio, Italian Chief of Staff, sent to Gamelin, confirming that the military accord of 27 June 1935 was still in force.[31] Badoglio warned however that unless sanctions were lifted Italy would have to reconsider the agreement. Sanctions were lifted on 15 July but events in Spain soon brought about the breakdown of Franco-Italian relations.

France's sorrows did not come singly but in battalions. On 18 July the Spanish Civil War began. On 20 July the Spanish government asked Léon Blum, leader of the Popular Front government, for arms and received a promise of help.[32] Within a month, however, the Socialist leader abandoned his promise and secured German and Italian adhesion to a Non-Intervention Agreement. Why did the French Prime Minister change his mind? Nothing would have been more natural than for the *Front Populaire* to extend a brotherly hand to the beleaguered *Frente Popular*. Two considerations seem to have been uppermost in Blum's mind. One was the danger of a general war. With Germany and Italy actively engaged in Spain, soon to be followed by the Soviet Union, there was a real danger that French aid would turn the civil war into a European war. The other consideration which motivated Blum was the possibility that France might be plunged into civil war. The Spanish war fanned the flames of class conflict in France and threatened to destroy what remained of national unity. The President of the Republic, the Presidents of the Chambers, the Foreign Minister, all impressed on the Prime Minister the danger of a general conflict. Camille Chautemps, a member of the government, and a married man who had lost three brothers in the war of 1914-18, told Yvon Delbos, Foreign Minister, and a life-long bachelor: 'they should never appoint bachelors to key positions. They should appoint fathers of

ssassination of King Alexander of Yugoslavia and M. Barthou, the French Foreign Minister,
etrus Kaleman) in Marseilles in October 1934.

h troops leaving Dortmund on October 23, 1924 in the evacuation of the Ruhr.

Above: German troops occupying the Sudetenland in October 1938.

Left: German troops marching into Cologne to re-occupy the Rhineland in defiance of the Locarno and Versailles treaties in March 1936.

families like myself, I tell you that I will not go to war under any circumstances'.[33] But the factor which probably weighed most with Blum was
the risk of civil war. In the soul-searching days that followed the original
promise of support, the paroxysms of rage and fear on the Right and Left
convinced Blum that sending arms might bring down his own government. Charity began at home.

Reinforcing these reasons, compelling enough in themselves, was
British counsel. In his postwar testimony to the parliamentary commission of enquiry Blum insisted on the pressure imposed on him by British
ministers. On 23 July the French Prime Minister and Foreign Minister
went to London. The purpose of the visit was to consider new arrangements in place of the Locarno treaties. According to the minutes of the
conference, Spain was not discussed. But Blum claimed that Eden called
on him at his hotel and asked him point-blank whether he intended to
supply arms to Spain. When he replied in the affirmative, Eden said:
'That's your affair. I simply ask one thing—please be careful'.[34] Eden's
memoirs say nothing of the alleged conversation and the French diplomatic papers are also silent. Nevertheless it is quite likely that some such
advice was given to Blum on 23 July.

The French government was certainly well aware of the temper of
ministerial and parliamentary opinion. On 30 July Blum asked his assistant, Jules Moch, Secretary General of the Prime Minister's office, to
sound out opinion in London. Moch reported that if a European war
broke out over Spain Britain would definitely stay neutral.[35] On 31 July,
Winston Churchill wrote to Corbin, French Ambassador in London, saying that if France sent aircraft to Spain 'the dominant forces here would
be pleased with Germany and Italy and estranged from France'.[36]

On 5 August Vice-Admiral Darlan, Chief of French Naval Staff, had a
meeting in London with Lord Chatfield, First Sea Lord. Blum contended
that the outcome of Darlan's talks with Chatfield 'had a considerable influence on the final decision' reached on 8 August to suspend all arms
deliveries to Spain.[37] Fortunately, both the British and French records
of the meeting are extant.[38] The French record is considerably fuller
than Chatfield's minute of the conversation, and it contains some references
to non-intervention not mentioned in the British document. The purpose
of the visit, explained Darlan, was to tell the Admiralty of certain information on the Spanish situation. Germany and Italy, said Darlan, intended to
seize the Balearic and Canary Islands. A victory of General Franco's forces
would draw Spain into the Axis camp. British and French interests would
be threatened. The Admiralty, replied Chatfield, had not received any
information as to German and Italian intentions and had 'no policy in these
matters'.[39] If the French navy really considered the situation to be so
serious the 'proper step would be for the Quai d'Orsay to inform our Ambassador in Paris'. Darlan admitted that he did not have any 'definite information' as to German plans, though there was some evidence as to Italian
designs on the Balearics.

According to Chatfield's minute, no more was said but the French record
noted a brief discussion of non-intervention. The British government,
said Chatfield, did not wish 'to meddle in any way in the Spanish Civil War'.

Darlan then asked whether while upholding non-intervention Britain and France might not try to mediate between the opposing sides in the hope of ensuring the establishment of 'a democratic government'. Chatfield was 'very sceptical of the idea' and thought mediation had little chance of success.

What influence, if any, did Darlan's mission have on decision making in Paris? In the first week of August, Delbos, Foreign Minister, was busy enlisting German, Italian and Soviet support for a non-intervention agreement but his ministerial colleagues were still divided on the issue.[40] Blum himself may have been in two minds. Ideological sympathies apart, French ministers were deeply concerned about the threat to French communications with Algeria and Morocco. It was arguable that if arms deliveries were stopped some action should be taken to safeguard French interests. However France dared not move without British co-operation. As Darlan put it: 'we do not wish to send French ships there alone. We want to follow you in what you do: if you intend to leave ships on the coast of Spain we will do so, if you intend to withdraw them, we shall also withdraw ours'.[41] Not unreasonably, the French hoped that the Admiralty would share their anxiety and be willing to consider joint naval patrols off the Spanish coast and islands. But Chatfield wanted as little to do with Spain as possible and showed no concern for the possible strategic consequences of a Nationalist victory. In effect Darlan caught the wash of the Ethiopian crisis. The deficiencies revealed by the deployment of the Royal Navy in the Mediterranean in the winter of 1935-36 and the unsatisfactory nature of Franco-British naval contacts during the crisis convinced the Admiralty of the need to steer clear of further encounters. This negative attitude to what, from the French viewpoint, seemed an overriding threat to joint strategic interests finally clinched the argument for stopping the deliveries of war material to Spain. Further deliveries would only increase the risk of a general conflict in which France would be isolated.

Almost as important as the Darlan mission in confirming the course of French policy was an interview between Sir George Clerk, British Ambassador, and Delbos on 7 August.[42] Speaking 'without instructions' and stressing that his visit was purely 'a personal one', the Ambassador complained of arms shipments to Spain and warned of the consequences of French involvement: 'I felt that in so critical a situation I must put before him the danger of any action which might definitely commit the French government to one side of the conflict and make more difficult the close co-operation between our two countries'. What Clerk did not know at the time was that immediately after the interview, Delbos attended a Cabinet meeting which, after a stormy debate, took the decision to suspend all arms deliveries.

Left wing interpretations of the origins of non-intervention have always insisted that the *Front Populaire* acted under strong pressure from London. Clearly, this interpretation cannot be accepted as it stands. The decisive considerations in Blum's adoption of non-intervention were almost certainly domestic. Moreover, there is no evidence of an official British démarche in the period from 20 July to 8 August.[43] Even if Blum's testimony is accepted, Eden on 23 July delivered only a mild admonition. Yet the Left wing view is not in fact very wide of the mark. British pressure was a factor in the situation and impinged on French decision-making. The key question to ask is did the British government really need to be high-handed in the matter? All that was necessary was that Paris should know London disapproved of intervention. The Darlan mission and Clerk interview served this purpose. Thus there was no point in making a fuss. The fact that Britain wanted nothing to do with Spain was known in Paris and this knowledge was sufficient to bridle France.

It would be difficult to exaggerate the impact of the Spanish war on French policy making. French preoccupation with the conflict helps to explain the capitulations in central and eastern Europe in 1938. The military situation created by the conflagration was a terrifying one. It was assumed in Paris that in the event of a Franco victory, France would be encircled by a triple alliance of Germany, Italy and Spain. In August, Delbos said 'he had every reason to fear that General Franco had offered the bait of the Balearic Islands to Italy and the Canaries to Germany, and if that materialised good-bye to French independence'.[44] Sea and air links with North Africa might easily be cut by air and naval forces operating from bases in the Balearics, not to mention the danger to the land frontier of the Pyrenees. Moreover, a third of the French army was stationed in North Africa and survival in war would depend on the speed and safety with which troops could be transported across the western Mediterranean.[45] For France, the Spanish war began a war of nerves which lasted until the attack on Poland in September 1939. 'Europe is on the verge of general war', declared Delbos on 28 November 1936.[46] A month later, Count Welczeck, German Ambassador, told of:

the downright hysterical nervousness that has been evident among the public here for several days and has started crack-brained rumours circulating regarding the inevitability of a war, simultaneous military attacks on France from the east and the south planned by Germany.[47]

The Spanish imbroglio had two consequences for French foreign policy. First it strengthened the dominant role of Britain in the entente. The nightmare of encirclement by Fascist dictatorships made the French cleave closer to their ally. Secondly, the strategic uncertainty created by the war practically dictated the retreat from central Europe. Presented with almost simultaneous threats to her Mediterranean position and to geographically remote allies in central Europe, France inevitably gave priority to her own security.

The strategic straitjacket which the Spanish war placed on France was strengthened by ideological hatreds. The Left believed that the Fascist dictators had to be fought and arrested, not in central Europe, but in Spain. The Right denounced Soviet intervention in Spain as a deliberate attempt to foment a European war. Ideological passions undermined national unity when it was most needed. These divisions had profound consequences for the eastern pacts. The domestic bitterness of 1936 extinguished any hope of an effective Franco-Soviet alliance. Litvinov, Soviet Commissar for Foreign Affairs, told the Ambassador at Moscow,

Robert Coulondre, that what the Soviet Union needed were good French patriots.[48] But the traditional patriotism of the Right was infected and destroyed by the conflict across the Pyrenees. Stalin, not Hitler, was the enemy.

France's difficulties were increased by Belgium's new position in international affairs.[49] In the autumn of 1936 Belgium abandoned her 1920 military agreement with France and returned to her pre-1914 policy of neutrality. The Maginot Line did not extend to the Franco-Belgian frontier and the French General Staff had made their plans on the assumption that in the event of a German attack French troops would immediately move forward into Belgium. To have extended the Maginot Line would have been ruinously expensive and would also have conflicted with war doctrine which stressed the importance of meeting a German attack on Belgian soil.

In the winter of 1936-37 Blum and his Foreign Minister, Delbos, pursued three main objectives: the enforcement of the Non-Intervention Agreement on Spain; the strengthening of the eastern alliances; and an understanding with Germany. In none of these aims were they successful and France's international position continued to deteriorate. The objectives themselves were in conflict. A revival of the eastern pacts, especially the Franco-Soviet treaty, would have queered the pitch for Franco-German *rapprochement*. Equally, an understanding with Berlin implied some disengagement from eastern Europe. The impossibility of enforcing Non-Intervention was soon apparent. On 18 November 1936, Germany and Italy formally recognised General Franco and the number of Italian troops was increased. Blum soon adopted what he called 'relaxed non-intervention'. In his own words: 'we willingly and systematically shut our eyes to arms smuggling'.[50] It was the only way Blum could ease his conscience and offer some satisfaction to followers.

The consolidation of the eastern pacts began with Poland. In July 1936, Gamelin, Chief of the General Staff, visited Warsaw and in August, Marshal Rydz-Smigly, Inspector General of the Polish army, attended French army manoeuvres. France and Poland concluded the Rambouillet agreement on 6 September which gave Poland a loan of 2,000 million francs for her armaments and railways.[51] In the view of French military chiefs, Poland was the chief ally in the east, capable of mobilising 50 divisions against 30 Czech divisions. Efforts to promote better relations between Warsaw and Prague met with no success. Gamelin, acting as a go-between, handed Rydz-Smigly a memorandum from President Benes of Czechoslovakia, renewing offers of a treaty of friendship. The Polish leader refused to commit himself, saying only that 'he did not see Poland attacking Czechoslovakia'.[52]

France had no more success with her partners of the Little Entente. On 22 October, Paris offered to enter into a pact of mutual assistance with Yugoslavia, Rumania and Czechoslovakia, on condition that the three countries changed their obligations for defence against Hungary into a general military pact of assistance against attack from any source.[53] Discussions dragged on into the spring of 1937. Finally at a meeting in Belgrade on 2 April 1937 the Little Entente states politely rejected the

French offer. Stoyadinovitch, Prime Minister of Yugoslavia, preferred to strengthen ties with Italy rather than France. On 25 March 1937 Yugoslavia signed a non-aggression pact with Italy. But the French proposal came much too late in the day. By the autumn of 1936 the uncertainties created by the Rhineland *coup* had deepened into real doubts about the value of France as an ally. On 6 November President Benes let it be known that he was not averse to the idea of a non-aggression pact with Germany. British reactions to the French plan were none too favourable. Corbin was told on 6 February 1937 that the Foreign Office had sounded out Belgrade and Bucharest and it seemed unlikely that the French offer would be accepted. The Yugoslavs, explained Eden, were alarmed at the possible effects of such a pact on Rome and Berlin. Corbin suspected, perhaps rightly, that the Foreign Secretary's concern for German and Italian susceptibilities was the principal reason for his lack of enthusiasm.

There remained the Soviet Union. The Russians had on several occasions affirmed their readiness to hold staff talks and in November 1936 the Popular Front government instructed the General Staff to open preliminary talks with the Soviet Military Attaché in Paris. It was understood that if the initial discussions proved satisfactory full staff talks would follow.

Previous contacts with Moscow had been characterised by great caution and mistrust. Save for a brief period when Barthou was at the Quai d'Orsay the Russians had made all the running. Herriot's *Cartel des Gauches* ministry restored diplomatic relations in 1924 and the first step towards an alliance came in 1927 with a Soviet offer of a non-aggression pact.[54] In May 1931, a Soviet initiative led to the opening of negotiations for a non-aggression pact. By September 1932 the pact was ready for France's signature. Four months later Moscow was still awaiting French ratification. The French did not conceal the fact that the pact was not the beginning of a 'diplomatic revolution' but had merely 'a moral or symbolic value' aimed at preserving Soviet neutrality in the event of war with Germany.[55]

Hitler's accession to power brought a sudden flurry of activity. In March 1933 Paris and Moscow exchanged military attachés. The Soviet tour became obligatory for publicists and politicians. Two leading Radicals, Herriot and Pierre Cot, travelled to Moscow in the summer of 1933. In 1934 another prominent Radical, Georges Bonnet, returned from the Soviet Union, extolling the might of the Red Army and the progress of the first Five Year Plan.[56]

These to-ings and fro-ings testified to a French desire for an entente but not for a military alliance. Paul Bargeton, Political Director of the Quai d'Orsay, said 'there was no question of an alliance, but merely, in the interests of both France and Poland, of neutralising Soviet Russia' in any conflict between France and Germany.[57] Daladier, Prime Minister, spoke of France having to secure 'the rear of her allies in the event of a war with Germany'.[58] France wanted an alliance but on her own terms. Soviet industrial and military power was to be kept on tap, for the use of France and her allies. The Socialist Paul-Boncour, Foreign Minister in the Chautemps government of November 1933, was fired by the idea of industrial agreements linking France and her eastern allies to the Soviet Union:

> Given the industrial potential which is developing in Russia, such agreements would give her neighbours and ourselves in the event of a German attack, important advantages. Granted that the USSR might not receive the same industrial and technical advantages as ourselves, the resulting co-operation would greatly help in preventing the establishment of an hegemony which she has so much reason to fear.[59]

France would not accept a Soviet suggestion that a pact should cover the Far East. Citing the precedent of the Franco-Russian pact of 1894, the French insisted on the pact being limited to Europe.[60] The Quai d'Orsay considered that in the climate of growing tension between the Soviet Union and Japan in the Far East, France had to avoid any appearance of military co-operation with Moscow.

No further progress was registered until April 1934 when Barthou began to take a keen interest in negotiations for a mutual assistance pact. The anti-German character of Barthou's approaches to the Soviet Union has been exaggerated.[61] He did not at first show any eagerness to conclude an alliance and advised the French embassy in Moscow that a projected visit to Paris by Litvinov would be inopportune.[62] Herriot, a fervent partisan of an accord, criticised the foreign minister for 'delaying tactics'.[63] It was only after the note of 17 April, closing the door to disarmament talks with Germany, that Franco-Soviet negotiations began in earnest. Nevertheless General Maurin, Minister of War, assured the Germans that Franco-Soviet *rapprochement* 'did not in any way extend to the establishment of military relations'.[64] And the pact which Laval signed in Moscow on 2 May 1935 was concluded with strong reservations on both sides. In conversations with the Germans and Italians Laval played down the importance of the pact. Litvinov at a revolutionary celebration on 7 November 1935 drank a toast to the rebirth of Soviet-German friendship and frequently abused Laval to the Germans.

In September 1936 the Soviet Union renewed earlier invitations to staff talks, and for the first time the French General Staff was authorised to hold preparatory discussions. The strict secrecy which shrouded these talks makes it very difficult to assess their course. Robert Coulondre, Ambassador in Moscow, knew very little of the exchanges and William C. Bullitt, the United States Ambassador in Paris, who received so many confidences from French leaders, was told nothing.[65] Blum seems to have handled the negotiations personally. The surprising fact was not that the talks petered out in the summer of 1937 but that they were held at all. But for Blum, the General Staff would almost certainly have refused the invitation from Moscow. The negative attitude of Daladier, Minister of National Defence and War, and of his military advisers, virtually foredoomed the talks. In a report of 24 June 1936 the General Staff gave its opinion on the desirability of staff talks.[66] Franco-Soviet military exchanges, it stated, would be seen by Germany as an attempt at encirclement. The recent ratification of the Franco-Soviet pact had served as a pretext for the reoccupation of the Rhineland: 'the mere announcement of such

talks might start a quarrel in the unstable Europe of 1936'. Another argument advanced in the report was that staff talks would upset France's
allies—Poland might be thrown 'irreparably' into the German camp.
Yugoslavia, it was pointed out, had not, as yet, given diplomatic recognition to the Soviet Union. Only Czechoslovakia would be gratified. Britain,
continued the General Staff, would certainly take a dim view of closer
contacts. The Soviet Union seemed distracted by Japanese moves in
China and the British had no wish to be entangled with Japan as a consequence of the Franco-Soviet pact. The disadvantages of military co-
operation, concluded the report, far outweighed the advantages. Without
a common frontier with Germany the Soviet Union could do little to help
France and her allies. Contact with Moscow, advised the General Staff,
should be maintained through normal diplomatic channels but an invitation to staff talks refused. On 31 July 1936 Daladier, War Minister, authorised arms deliveries to the USSR to the value of 100 million francs.[67]

This conclusion was confirmed in a report of 4 October 1936 written
by General Schweisguth, Deputy Chief of the General Staff.[68] In September Schweisguth, accompanied by General Vuillemin, of the French air
force, attended Red Army manoeuvres and talked to Marshal Voroshilov,
Soviet Commissar for Defence. During the visit, Marshal Tukhachevsky,
who was to be arrested and executed in the treason trials less than a year
later, extended the invitation to staff talks. After a guarded, though not
unfavourable, assessment of the strength of Soviet forces, Schweisguth
seasoned his military impressions with some highly speculative assertions
about Soviet political aims. Stalin, he asserted, was playing a double game,
seeking to stir up a Franco-German war while relying on the Franco-
Soviet pact as insurance in the event of Germany attacking in the east.
Here, in a nutshell, was the gospel of the French Right in the late 1930s.
Daladier, in a covering letter to the report, endorsed its conclusions and
advised against staff talks which might 'alarm certain friendly powers and
provide Germany with the excuse that she was being encircled'.[69] In
particular, recommended Daladier, no talks should be held without a
prior Franco-Czech military accord.

French Ministers were in no doubt about the antipathy of some sections
of British opinion towards the Soviet Union. In May 1936 Corbin had
reported on the strength of feeling in the Conservative party.[70] The
British attitude, as the Ambassador wryly observed, was rather a dog in
the manger one. Not only were the British unwilling to conclude a military alliance but they also contested France's right to sign military conventions with other countries. In a long discussion on 16 April 1937 Sir Robert
Vansittart, Permanent Under-Secretary at the Foreign Office, warned
Corbin that a Franco-Soviet military agreement would alienate influential
groups of British and American opinion.[71] On 15 May Eden repeated
the warning to Delbos.[72] Such plain speaking was well-timed. By April
1937 Franco-Soviet discussions appeared at last to be making some progress. Predictably General Staff appraisals of April-May 1937 stressed
much more strongly than hitherto the necessity for prior agreement with
London before concluding a military accord: 'French security rested
above all on a close entente with Great Britain'.[73]

The attitude of France's other allies in the east though important was not the determining factor in the breakdown of the military exchanges in 1936-37. The truth of the matter was that the General Staff did not want alliance with Moscow. On 17 February 1937 Potemkin, Soviet Ambassador, informed Blum that his country would support France by all available means.[74] If Poland and Rumania opened their frontier, Soviet forces could be fully deployed against Germany. In the event of refusal some Soviet forces could be sent by sea to France. Aircraft would be sent to Czechoslovakia and France. In addition France would receive raw materials and munitions. On the face of it, this was an extremely generous and comprehensive proposal but the offer to send Soviet troops to France must have seemed to the conservative-minded French generals more like a threat than a pledge. Moscow's efforts to translate the alliance into practical terms only served to frighten the French military leadership.

Negotiations moved at a snail's pace. Delbos, Foreign Minister, did not receive a record of the 17 February interview with Potemkin until 26 March, and Gamelin did not see the document until 9 April.[75] Gamelin's reply to the communication of 17 February must have dashed any hopes in Moscow of reaching agreement. His reply was a long-winded negative: 'France, if she was not attacked by the mass of German forces' was ready 'to act offensively' and 'all French forces' would be concentrated on an 'offensive action' to the extent that they were not required on other fronts or overseas.[76] As for Poland and Rumania, 'the state of discussions' with these two countries did not allow a solution to the problem of transit facilities for Soviet forces. Moreover, added Gamelin, in wartime both Poland and Rumania would need all their railway capacity for the movement of their own forces. France was not in a position to send armaments to the Soviet Union but the offer of Soviet supplies was acknowledged.

Despite Gamelin's damper, discussions continued and a preliminary agreement dated 15 April 1937 authorised the General Staff to proceed with full staff talks.[77] The military chiefs were still unwilling to accept defeat and in two memoranda of May-June they voiced their disapproval of staff talks. An undated note of May stipulated two prerequisites for military co-operation: prior agreement with London and mutual assistance pacts between the Soviet Union, Poland and Rumania.[78] On 9 June, the generals expressed themselves even more firmly: 'the risk of a German-Polish combination was particularly serious' and such a coalition would create a formidable military bloc of 100 million in central Europe.[79] In view of the political trials being held in Moscow, staff talks should be postponed. But Blum's days were numbered. On 21 June the Senate, citadel of the 'two hundred families', refused the government's request for full powers to stop the export of capital and Blum resigned. No more was heard of staff talks until the British and French military missions went to Moscow in August 1939.

Mussolini's announcement on 1 November 1936 of the formation of the Rome-Berlin axis imposed further limits on France's freedom. Over the following months exchanges of Nazi and Fascist notables multiplied. Amid these signs of Italo-German collaboration what action did the western democracies take to strengthen their own entente? France's hesitations in the face of German rearmament helped to bring about a change of leadership from Paris to London. By 1936 Great Britain was the leading rider in the Anglo-French tandem. In Paris on 24 June 1936 Duff Cooper, Secretary of State for War, described Franco-British friendship as 'a matter of life and death'. Attempts to translate interdependence into diplomatic and military terms were little more than perfunctory. In the fifteen months from August 1936 to October 1937 Eden had brief meetings with French ministers in Paris and Geneva but no formal meetings of Ministers took place until the Franco-British conference in London on 29-30 November 1937. Military collaboration was non-existent. Both countries started to rearm in 1936-37 but no effort was made to concert defence arrangements. The British Defence White Paper of February 1937 announced a five year programme of rearmament costing £1,500 million, with the emphasis on the creation of a powerful air force. In the course of the year the idea of equipping a land force for continental intervention was quietly abandoned. British defence policy was a doctrine of limited liability according to which Britain's main contribution in war would be largely confined to the exercise of sea and air power. And the French seemed satisfied by this scheme of things, not until the winter of 1936-37 did they ask for the preparation of a British striking force of two armoured divisions.[80]

Reasons for the failure to forge a closer Franco-British connection are not hard to discover. The chief obstacle was British opinion. The arguments that had prevented a military alliance in the 1920s still commanded assent. 'This country will not support an exclusive Anglo-French military alliance—we may take that for granted', Hugh Dalton, the Labour leader, declared on 26 March 1936.[81] The rejection of a military pact sprang from a detestation in principle of military agreements because they were seen as a prime cause of the war of 1914. Also, there was the conviction that while the two neighbours had much in common, Britain should maintain her separateness and work for a European settlement. Intimacy with France might alarm Germany and Italy and so hinder rather than help appeasement. The creation of a Franco-British military pact would have been interpreted as a confession of failure in foreign policy, a tacit admission that the ideological barriers were insuperable. Moreover, given the confidence which the British government still had in the French army and Maginot Line the doctrine of limited liability made some sense. British air and sea power would complement French land armaments.

Another consideration in British policy towards France was the fear of being enmeshed in central Europe. In a letter of 28 March 1936 Sir Austen Chamberlain analysed for a French friend the post-Rhineland mood:

> there is a great fear of France's entanglements in the East...Some of our Right wing politicians feel very much as yours do about the Franco-Soviet pact. They regard it almost as a betrayal of our Western Civilisation.[82]

The Left and a large section of moderate opinion, continued the letter, while not condemning France for the Franco-Soviet pact yet 'reproaches her with slackness in applying sanctions to Italy'. In June 1936 Philip Kerr, Marquis of Lothian, advised Eden that France should be offered a British guarantee only 'on condition that she abandons the fatal policy of encircle-ment and preponderance which has destroyed all chances of European appeasement for eighteen years'.[83] French domestic divisions did not help matters. Thomas Jones, formerly deputy secretary to the Cabinet, told an American correspondent that Britain's attachment to France was being sapped by 'a growing recognition . . . of the divisions of French opinion, the growth of Fascism especially, the corruption of the Paris press and of the Deputies'.[84] And, for many conservatives, the Popular Front was more of a stumbling block than the rise of fascism. Bullitt, American Ambassador in Moscow until the summer of 1936, found a sympathetic audience at the Astors for his story that Stalin had engineer-ed the appointment of Delbos as Foreign Minister.[85]

France's dependence on her ally fostered resentments. René Massigli, Assistant Political Director of the Quai d'Orsay, was 'very bitter' about reactions to the Rhineland crisis and spoke of the British 'as traitors'.[86] The Americans were treated as confidants. In 1937 Blum told Bullitt, who had been appointed to Paris in October 1936:

> America alone of the great powers was genuinely interested in the same policies that he was trying to put through. The British Government was working with him wholeheartedly and sincerely in certain fields but because it was a Conser-vative Government it disapproved highly of his domestic policy and the sym-pathy he received from London was therefore half-hearted.[87]

British rearmament was a mixed blessing: 'at the end of three years when the British were fully rearmed they would of course become intolerable', declared Delbos.[88] On the surface, however, Franco-British relations flowed smoothly and amicably. Eden claimed that Delbos 'showed many acts of friendship . . . not least in using his influence, during the Abdica-tion crisis, to restrain his country's press'.[89]

The British and French governments pursued separate, and to some extent, divergent approaches to Germany and Italy. Blum believed that the Ethiopian affair had wedded the two dictators for better, for worse. He interpreted the German-Austrian agreement of 11 July 1936 as evidence that Mussolini did not intend to oppose Hitler in central Europe. Italy, argued Blum, would have to seek satisfaction in the Mediterranean and a clash of Franco-Italian interests was therefore inevitable. Italian interven-tion in Spain confirmed this reasoning. Consequently, French Ministers took no official initiative towards improving relations, though according to Blum's secretary, André Blumel, three unofficial approaches were made in 1936-37.[90] Mussolini's state of mind, if his words to the Germans are to be believed, was hardly encouraging. France, said the *Duce* on 23 September 1936, was 'sick and old' and 'of no interest until such time as the internal crisis is over'.[91] On 29 October 1936, the French Ambassador Count Charles de Chambrun, left the Rome embassy and the Italian government insisted that his successor should be accredited to the 'King of Italy, Emperor of Ethiopia'. Since the Popular Front Ministry refused to recognise the Italian conquest, deadlock resulted. For nearly two years France had no ambassador in Rome. In January 1937 Mussolini may have made a tentative effort to break the deadlock. According to Blum's testimony, the Italian Ambassador, Cerruti, told him that the *Duce*

detested Hitler and wanted an alliance with France.[92] If France withdrew support from the Spanish Republic, Italy would obtain some assurance of General Franco's goodwill towards France. Blum replied that if
Italy wanted better relations she could start by respecting the Non-Intervention Agreement.

While the Latin sisters scowled at each other the British government
negotiated the Gentleman's Agreement of 2 January 1937, according
Italy equality of rights in the Mediterranean. At the start of negotiations
in the early autumn of 1936 Count Ciano, Italian Foreign Minister, made
it plain that he did not want French participation. Eden, in his own words,
'did not wish to insist'.[93] Paris was kept informed of the progress of
talks. Delbos was worried by the effect on German and Italian opinion
of a separate Anglo-Italian accord. On 12 December 1936 he told Sir
George Clerk, British Ambassador, that France also wanted an understanding with Rome.[94] This, replied the diplomat, was a matter to be
settled between France and Italy.

If Italy could be ignored, Germany could not. The Popular Front
administration devoted much time and energy to the search for an agreement with Berlin. On taking office Blum at once declared his readiness
for an *entente,* provided Hitler accepted a new Western security pact in
place of Locarno. The Prime Minister's friends assured the German
embassy that 'in spite of all doctrinal and domestic impediments' the
Socialist leader wanted a *rapprochement.*[95] Blum's Ministers, departed
from the usual protocol and made a point of calling on the newly arrived
German Ambassador, Count Welczeck. The deep apprehensions about
the outcome of the Spanish war increased the urgency of opening conversations with Germany. The only way of avoiding a general eruption
seemed to lie in a Franco-German accord. Britain also wanted an agreement but in the winter of 1936-37 British policy tended to drift at the mercy
of various ministerial and official cross-currents. The Abdication crisis
took precedence over all other issues and in the early months of 1937
Baldwin's thoughts were focussed on retirement. By contrast, French
diplomacy was much more decided, and on the issue of colonial concessions too decided for British liking.

At the end of August 1936 Dr Schacht, German Economics Minister,
visited Paris.[96] In talks with French ministers on 26 and 28 August the
German minister spoke of his country's wish for an entente, citing as
evidence of goodwill the applause accorded to French athletes in the
recent Berlin Olympiads. Germany, said Schacht, considered the question
of Alsace-Lorraine as finally settled. Then he expatiated on Germany's
need for colonies and markets. His listeners were sympathetic. 'I am a
Marxist and a Jew', said Blum, but 'we cannot achieve anything if we treat
ideological barriers as insurmountable'. France, he said, wanted not only
a bilateral pact but also a European agreement. In return for German
co-operation he 'did not think it impossible' to examine Germany's colonial
claims, and to discuss them with the British government.

Blum and Eden met in Paris on 20 September, and two days later Eden
and Halifax conferred with Delbos and his advisers in Geneva.[97] Eden
refused to agree to separate colonial talks with Germany, suggesting

instead that if Germany accepted an invitation sent in July to attend a conference of the five Locarno powers colonies might be included in the discussions. However the guidelines of a general European settlement would have to be firmly defined before colonial concessions could be considered. The French demurred. While the wisdom of colonial concessions might be the subject of calm and leisurely deliberation in London, in Paris it was a matter of the utmost importance. France's future as a great power hinged on a Franco-German settlement. French officials pointed out that Germany's military effort was being increasingly directed towards the west. The fear in London, replied Eden, though he personally did not share it, was that in exaggerating the danger from Germany France might surrender too much.

Following the British negative, the colonial issue was not pursued in Franco-German discussions.[98] Delbos explained to Bullitt that Schacht's visit had not been followed up 'because of British opposition. The British had frowned because Schacht had mentioned colonies'. Nevertheless, added the Foreign Minister, Paris would remain independent enough to indulge in direct conversations with Germany'.[99] In a letter of 18 December to Schacht Blum stipulated that colonial concessions could only be considered as part of a wider arrangement.[100] On 23 December Delbos outlined the shape of this wider arrangement. A settlement of the Spanish war, he told the German ambassador, would provide the basis for a Franco-German pact. Germany 'should have raw materials, colonies, and loans, in return for which the only compensation required was peace'.[101] 'Being a farmer's son', said Delbos, 'he could speak for almost the entire French people in conveying the honest desire to reach—now or never—an understanding'. The Ambassador, Welczech, warned the *Wilhelmstrasse* that a turning point had been reached. If no response was forthcoming to the French overtures Germany would be dismissed as a hopeless case'.[102]

In the winter of 1936-37 British and French public statements remained extremely conciliatory. In a speech at Lyons on 24 January 1937 Blum again extended a friendly hand to Germany. France, he said, was ready to forget the Rhineland affair and let bygones be bygones. The way was still open for colonial and economic talks. Next day Goebbels, Propaganda Minister, complained to the French ambassador, André Francois-Poncet, that the speech contained nothing 'practical' or 'positive'.[103] The same criticism might, with much more justice, have been made of a speech by Hitler on 30 January in which the French overture was ignored.

Contact with Schacht had not been lost. The next move involved the British. On 2 February at Badenweiler, Schacht had talks with Sir Frederick Leith-Ross, Chief Economic Adviser to the British government. Once again the call was for colonies. In addition, the German minister suggested tripartite discussions between Germany, Britain and France. The talks at Badenweiler created some ill-feeling in France. Leith-Ross was said to have told Schacht of his regret that the Paris meetings had not gone further. 'That was of course a typical British remark,' Delbos told Bullitt, 'because the truth is that the British Government was furious with us for having those conversations with Schacht...the British would pretend to desire

Franco-German reconciliation but would continue to follow their old policy of keeping France and Germany hostile. . .'.[104]

The British outlook was not in fact as negative as Delbos claimed. The Foreign Office in principle favoured negotiations over colonies but both Eden and his senior advisers objected to the Schacht-Leith-Ross exchanges on the grounds that the Economics Minister might be disowned by Hitler, and negotiations would be more safely handled through the diplomats.[105] In this attitude there was an element of inter-departmental rivalry since Leith-Ross was a Treasury man. After 2 February meeting Leith-Ross urged that contacts should be maintained.[106] Eden's standpoint was that there was nothing to be gained by involvement in colonial and economic discussions unless the government was really prepared to make territorial offers, and such offers should be made conditional upon a wide-ranging political settlement.

But the crux of the matter was that though British and French ministers were sympathetic towards German colonial claims they did not for a moment think that their own country should be the first to offer transfers of territories. In February 1936, Sarraut, Prime Minister, thought 'the taking away from Germany. . .of the German colonies had been a mistake' and suggested that 'England, although loath to give up her African possessions, might be persuaded to return to Germany the latter's pre-war possessions'.[107] Of French colonies, not a word. A month later Neville Chamberlain, Chancellor of the Exchequer, assured Flandin, Foreign Minister, that 'if by giving up a colony lasting peace could be won he would consider it'.[108] Which colony? That was the rub. In March 1936 a sub-committee of the Committee of Imperial Defence examined the feasibility of a colonial settlement and reported that Togoland and the Cameroons might be transferred—both French territories. The French naturally had other ideas. Léger, Secretary General of the Quai d'Orsay, considered that if any colonial concessions were to be made 'France might give up one-third, but England would have to give two-thirds'.[109] Blum and Delbos entertained grandiose visions of colonial collaboration as part and parcel of world economic co-operation. They had in mind 'the creation of consortiums to develop sections of Africa . . . all the African colonies except French North Africa and British South Africa would . . . be put into a common pot . . . all would be exploited by international consortiums'.[110]

In calling for colonies Hitler was throwing dust in the eyes of his opponents but Britain and France might have wasted less time in the colonial *cul-de-sac* if they had managed to agree on a common approach. And, of this, there was little sign. Schacht arranged a return visit to Paris on 25-29 May 1937 for the opening of the German pavilion at the Paris International Exhibition. In preparation for the visit the French endeavoured to obtain British participation in any talks that might be held. Eden did not like the idea but Chamberlain was anxious to maintain some contact with Berlin and his view prevailed. Sir Eric Phipps, Ambassador at Paris, was instructed to show just enough support to keep the negotiations going. On 15 May Delbos came to London and secured Eden's agreement to the presence of a British representative at the forthcoming talks.[111] On

28 May Blum and Schacht met but the tone of their encounter lacked the warmth and sympathy of their previous conversation. Schacht had little to say and Blum insisted that a political settlement must precede a colonial arrangement.[112] The two men did not meet again until April 1945 — as fellow prisoners at Buchenwald.

The lack of firm allies outside Europe underlined France's precarious position. Blum and Delbos were hopeful of securing a greater American involvement in Europe. The French Prime Minister was a great admirer of President Roosevelt and the New Deal. The confidences which French Ministers shared with Bullitt, American ambassador, testified to the desire for closer relations. France's refusal in 1932 to repay her war debt had caused much ill-feeling in the United States. In the summer of 1936 the omens seemed favourable. American help in the negotiation of the Tripartite Financial Agreement of 25 September helped to make Blum's twenty five percent devaluation of the franc more palatable to French opinion. French Ministers talked of re-opening the debt question. On 28 November Delbos asked directly whether the United States would join with France and Britain in a démarche to bring about mediation in the Spanish civil war.[113] The Americans sensed what was afoot and did not mince their words. Bullitt spoke to Blum and cabled home:

I repeated what I had said to Delbos; to wit: that I should be a bad friend of France if I did not advise him against basing his foreign policy or any portion of it on the expectation that by debt payments or any other measure of cultivating a pleasant atmosphere France could by hook or by crook get the United States to take a position which we took in 1917.[114]

By May 1937 French Ministers were at the end of their tether. The pessimism which had pervaded French policy making in 1932-34 reappeared in stronger form. Blum and Delbos were oppressed by what seemed a Sisyphean task. On 5 May Delbos confessed that he was 'at his wit's end' to devise an effective foreign policy.[115] A fortnight later, Blum 'agreed that Hitler had the political initiative ... and he did not see any way to take the initiative out of the hands of Germany...the situation was beginning to resemble more and more the situation before 1914'.[116]

The reasons for the failure of the Popular Front's foreign policy are readily identified. The sheer physical strain of staying in office and defending the franc would have drained the energies of the ablest of leaders. In October 1936 Blum invited de Gaulle to tell him about his army proposals. While de Gaulle talked the telephone rang ten times. 'Judge', said Blum, 'if it is easy for the head of government to hold to the plan you have outlined when he cannot remain five minutes with the same idea'.[117] The deep, domestic divisions were Blum's greatest handicap. On 16 March 1937, in Clichy, the police fired for the first time on Socialist and Communist demonstrators, killing seven and wounding many others, including Blum's secretary, André Blumel. Right and Left interpreted the incident as the first round in an open class war. Abroad, the Spanish war was a source of constant anxiety. Under these enormous pressures, failure was both unavoidable and excusable. Blum's internationalist faith with its ideals of disarmament and détente was steadily eroded and by May 1937 the

Prime Minister 'could see nothing better to do than to recreate the close entente between England, France and Russia which had existed before 1914'.[118] One serious criticism that might be made of his diplomacy is the lack of any official approach to Italy. So much effort was expended on Germany, almost none on Italy. Ministers took the view that an Italo-German pact was inevitable. If this was the case then it seems difficult to justify the separate approach to Germany. Internal politics was probably the decisive consideration in the neglect of Italy. For the French Left, Mussolini was the 'assassin of Matteotti' and 'the tyrant of Italy'.[119] Given Italian intervention in Spain, Blum felt that any approach to Rome would only weaken the *Front Populaire*.

Chapter 4

Wait and See

The state of France in the summer of 1937 was mirrored in the Paris International Exhibition. The opening was to have taken place on 1 May but was postponed until 24 May. Even so, many of the pavilions were unfinished. The exhibition site had been the scene of numerous meetings, strikes and demonstrations. 'Workmen spit at you and shout "parasite" ', complained a Swiss visitor.[1] A heavy financial loss was made on the exhibition. It cost 380 million francs, takings were 160 millions. Fifty million visitors were expected, thirty million came. The dictatorships had made the greatest effort. The huge Soviet and German pavilions faced each other, sharply symbolising the ideological conflict. Some light relief from the German eagle and Soviet hammer and sickle was provided by the British pavilion:

> When you went in the first thing you saw was a cardboard Chamberlain fishing in rubber waders and beyond, an elegant pattern of golf balls, a frieze of tennis rackets, polo sets, riding equipment, natty dinner jackets and, by a pleasant transition agreeable pottery and textiles, books finely printed and photographs of the English countryside.[2]

Neville Chamberlain, however, was real enough. His advent to the premiership in May 1937 was of crucial importance for Franco-British relations. Arguably, without Chamberlain, the general course of British policy *might* have been much *different from* that actually followed until March 1939. Different leaders might well have shown a greater understanding of French difficulties. To say that the British Prime Minister and his advisers were contemptuous of French politicians and policy would be an overstatement but sympathy and respect were noticeably lacking.[3]

In the summer of 1937 France also had a change of leadership. On 22 June the Radical Socialist Camille Chautemps, who had served in the Blum government, formed a new administration. Despite defeats and bitter disappointment Blum had worked consistently for certain foreign policy goals. The policy of Chautemps, like that of Baldwin, was one of drift. Inevitably, therefore, the key decisions were made for him and France was taken in tow by her British partner.

Blum was a self-doubting intellectual, Chautemps a born politician, a wholly political animal. He was the great middleman of French politics.

'If he had not been born it would have been necessary to invent him', observed one commentator.[4] Scion of a leading Radical family he entered political life in 1919 and quickly gained a ministerial place. Like many of his fellow Radicals, Chautemps was a staunch Freemason with the rank in the Scottish rite of masons of 'Sublime Prince of the Royal Secret'. As Prime Minister in January 1934 when the Stavisky scandal burst, he obstinately refused Right wing demands for an enquiry and was hounded from office. His refusal to order an investigation was interpreted as a clumsy attempt to shield his brother-in-law, Pressard, the Paris public prosecutor, alleged to be responsible for the numerous postponements of trial granted to Stavisky. Chautemps, like Daladier, discredited by the Stavisky affair, found refuge in the Popular Front movement. Though Chautemps favourably impressed British Ministers at the Franco-British conference in London in November 1937, later impressions were less happy. Sir Eric Phipps, Ambassador at Paris, summed him up as 'a charming, quick but somewhat fluid personality . . . difficult to pin down to any definite statement or expression of opinion'.[5]

The new government was still a Popular Front ministry with Communist support. Blum served as Deputy Prime Minister and Delbos remained at the Quai d'Orsay. Portfolios were divided fairly evenly between Socialists and Radicals. None the less the administration stood to the right of its predecessor, marking the start of a gradual return to conservative policies. The appointment of Georges Bonnet as Minister of Finance, in place of the Socialist Vincent Auriol, was seen as confirmation of the government's Radical Socialist bias. Bonnet, along with Caillaux and others, had opposed Auriol's financial policy. His importance in the new government was emphasised by the postponement of the ministerial declaration to the Chambers in order to give him time to return from Washington where he had been Ambassador since January 1937.

The chief difference between British and French leaders was that French Ministers lacked the purposive, optimistic outlook which characterised Chamberlain and his collaborators. The British Prime Minister was determined to end what he regarded as the drift of Baldwin's premiership. By contrast, Chautemps described his own attitude as one of 'wait and see'.[6] Unlike the British, the French rulers had no coherent, long-range plan for the pacification of Europe. Understandably, they were realists and deeply suspicious of Germany and Italy but suspicion alone was sterile. Appeasement was pursued reluctantly and half-heartedly for lack of an alternative. Chautemps talked of going to Germany, of visits to France by German dignitaries, of youth exchanges, but in a despairing way without enthusiasm. His Foreign Minister, Delbos, could think of nothing better than 'making concessions to Germany piecemeal in order to stave off war'.[7]

At home and abroad France was in a worse plight than in the autumn of 1936. 'After having won a war the France of 1937 is in the same position as she was in 1887 after a lost war', the Right wing André Tardieu proclaimed in *Gringoire*.[8] The legacy of the first *Front Populaire* government was an empty treasury. The export of capital by frightened property holders and the operations of currency speculators placed the franc in desperate straits. French finance ministers struggled to stave off national bankruptcy. Since 1930, French budget deficits had increased each year, reaching over 21 milliards of francs in 1937. The economy remained stagnant.

The Spanish war caused great anxiety. General Franco's Nationalist forces were gaining control of northern Spain. The Gentleman's Agreement of 2 January 1937 had not prevented Italy from increasing her help to the Nationalists. In January 1937 it was estimated that Italy had 44,000 men in Spain, by October of the same year the figure was said to be 60,000. Attacks by Italian submarines on British and French ships trading with Republican held ports had reached alarming proportions. The consolidation of the Rome-Berlin Axis was carried a stage further with Mussolini's visit to Germany in September 1937. On 28 September the *Führer* and *Duce* boasted of an alliance of '115 million men united in an unshakeable resolution'. Events outside Europe brought no comfort. Japanese intervention in China in July 1937 posed a threat to France's Asian empire, especially Indo-China. But Léger, Secretary General of the Foreign Ministry, explained to Bullitt in October that:

> as long as the present tension existed in Europe it would be impossible for France . . . to take part in any common action in the Far East which might involve or imply at some later stage the furnishing of armed forces . . . it was regrettable that this situation existed which seemed to facilitate aggression in the Far East but the situation was a fact and had to be faced.[9]

The immediate threat to French interests was in central Europe. Czechoslovakia, the linchpin of French influence, was under siege. With her army of 34 divisions and alliances with France and the Soviet Union, Czechoslovakia was a pillar of the peace settlement in the east. Before dismantling the settlement Germany would have to eliminate Czechoslovakia. In the event of a Franco-German war the French General Staff counted on Czechoslovakia and Poland to provide a second front. Czech sympathy for France was strong. At the Paris Peace Conference Czechoslovakia had been France's protégé and French influence had helped to shape the new state. The constitution was inspired by that of the Third Republic, and the Czechs even had a mini-Maginot Line, constructed by French engineers. In 1934 Jean Paul Sartre and Simone de Beauvoir were in Prague:

> We went into an almost empty dance hall; and as soon as the manager found out that we were French, the band struck up the Marseillaise. The few scattered couples . . . let out a cheer for France, Barthou and the Little Entente. It was a most depressing moment.[10]

Depressing was the word, for in 1934 and later, the French public showed little interest in Czechoslovakia. The weakness of Czechoslovakia was her ethnic composition. The most militant and numerous of the ethnic groups was the Sudeten German minority of over three millions, inhabiting the area of the Sudetenland along the frontier with Germany. By September 1937 the rumbling of Sudeten German grievances was too loud to be ignored. Sudeten claims provided Hitler with a convenient lever for his ambitions in central Europe and the German speaking minor-

ity received subsidies and encouragement from the Reich.[11] The first reactions of Czechoslovak leaders had been to pooh-pooh the danger of a
German attack and to do what they could to eliminate sources of friction
in the Sudetenland. In the winter of 1936-37, President Benes made 'inces-
sant trips' to frontier districts 'apparently making every effort to placate'
the German speaking minority, reported the United States Minister in
Prague.[12] For a while it looked as if Czechoslovakia might come to
some bilateral understanding with Germany. In December 1936 Benes
discussed with two German emissaries the possibility of a German-Czech
settlement. France let it be known that she had no objection to such a
course.[13]

By the summer of 1937 both London and Paris were counselling Benes
to reach agreement with Henlein, leader of the Sudeten German party.
The French Minister at Prague, Victor de Lacroix, was under no illusions
about the nature of the problem. Commenting on 13 July on a démarche
made by his British colleague, Newton, the French envoy remarked that
though the British diplomat was certainly sincere in his efforts and tried
to inform himself objectively he was 'soaked' in German influences: 'the
Austrian graces of the ancient Habsburg aristocracy are not without
charms for him'.[14] It was essential, warned Lacroix, that Britain's bene-
volent interest in the minority problem should not be allowed to exceed
certain limits:

> we must not lose sight of the fact that the Henlein party is in the pay of the Reich
> and receives its directives from Berlin . . . It will never declare itself satisfied
> with the fate of the Germans of Czechoslovakia unless Berlin authorises it to do
> so.[15]

As Sudeten German demands grew louder, French doubts and hesitations increased. Professions of determination to defend Czechoslovakia
were combined with reservations about France's ability to maintain herself in central and eastern Europe. This was not a development that can
be dated precisely because it was much more a matter of attitudes than of
specific decisions. On 22 April 1937 Bullitt reported 'general agreement'
in government circles that 'recent developments' were closing the door
to 'French influence' in the east.[16] 'Night and day' said Delbos in May,
'he was occupied in thinking . . . how he could keep Central Europe from
falling into the hands of Germany . . . it was clear that France was no longer
strong enough to maintain the status quo in Central Europe'.[17] The old
theme of demographic inferiority was stressed. France with only 40 million
inhabitants, stated Herriot, President of the Chamber of Deputies since
1936, 'could no longer regard herself as a great power of sufficient military
strength or human resources to maintain her position in central and eastern Europe and bring effective support to her allies'.[18] Of the ministers
and officials with whom Bullitt talked, only Léger, Secretary General of
the Quai d'Orsay, made a brave but lonely attempt to keep the flag flying,
insisting, though 'with some diffidence', that Belgium's return to neutrality
would not diminish French influence.[19]

In September 1937 the Czechoslovak government began to show serious
concern for its country's security. On 21 September Blum led a French

delegation to Prague for the funeral of the former President, Thomas Masaryk. He was asked whether France would consider an indirect attack as a *casus foederis*. The French statesman was said to have answered in the affirmative while making it clear that he could not speak officially for the French government.[20] Prague's fear was that Germany, acting through the Sudeten Germans, might instigate a revolt. Hodža, Czechoslovak Prime Minister, stressed the urgency of adapting the Franco-Czech alliance to cover new forms of indirect aggression. Lacroix wired:

> He repeated to me that the known determination of France and England to oppose any modification of the status quo in Central Europe would be . . . the best way of dissuading M. Hitler from an impulsive act.[21]

In Geneva at the end of the month both Benes and Hodža told French statesmen of their fears of German action. From Berlin, on 30 September, François-Poncet, French Ambassador, signalled that the Sudeten problem had pride of place in German demands: 'Czechoslovakia constitutes, by her active resistance to German plans, and through her alliances with France and Russia, the last and main obstacle to the German thrust to the south-east'.[22]

Far from strengthening French resolution, the alarm signals eroded it. Alliance obligations were reaffirmed but the tone was muted. At the Radical Socialist party congress in Lille at the end of October the reassertion of French pledges given by Delbos did not mention Czechoslovakia by name and omitted to state unequivocally what France would consider as a *casus foederis*. In the first week of November, Franz von Papen, German Ambassador in Vienna, had talks with French ministers. After conferring with the 'rather weak' Chautemps, who seemed to be 'pushed forward' by his 'aggressive' Finance Minister, Bonnet, Papen reported personally to Hitler that the French seemed willing to do their 'utmost to effect a general settlement with Germany' and would raise no objection 'to an evolutionary extension of German influence either in Austria . . . or in Czechoslovakia'.[23]

Reservations about France's eastern commitments were not limited to the politicians. The General Staff had set great store by the eastern alliances and as late as July 1936 had stressed the importance of maintaining, with Italian help, a second front in central Europe. But the Spanish war and the loss of Italian friendship closed France's options. On 4 November 1936, the Army committee of the Chamber emphasised its preference for an army which would concentrate on defending France's own frontiers. A country of 40 millions, Daladier, Minister of War, told the committee, must deny itself 'the Napoleonic luxury' of waging war beyond national frontiers.[24] The change in the outlook of the General Staff can be gauged from a report of 8 February 1938 in which Gamelin, Chief of the General Staff, set out the essential tasks of the army in war. His order of priorities read: 1. the defence of France and her empire; 2. 'offensive action' against Italy on the Alps and in Africa; 3. 'If possible' and 'at a convenient time' offensive action against Germany in order to divert part of the German forces 'for the benefit of our Central European allies'.[25]

France's presence in central and eastern Europe was underpinned by solid economic and financial interests. The end of World War I brought a redistribution of the economic interests of the great powers. Austrian and German investment in central and southeastern Europe was displaced by British, French, Belgian and American capital. With the loss of the Russian market, central and southeastern Europe became, after the British empire and South America, the third most important area for Anglo-French and American capital. Not only was Czechoslovakia the linchpin of French political influence it was also the base for further investment in the area. After 1918 French capital flowed into the successor states and French military missions spearheaded an economic penetration with which the great Parisian banks and metallurgical enterprises were associated. In Czechoslovakia mining and metallurgy, technically the most advanced and economically the most important industries, were firmly controlled by foreign capital, with Anglo-French investment in first place, followed by German. In particular the French armament firm of Schneider-Creusot, through its holding company *L'Union Européenne,* had a controlling interest in the Škoda Works. The French shareholders exerted strong influence. Arms exports to the Soviet Union were banned and in 1924 the heavy artillery shop was dismantled and transferred to the Schneider works in France.

But the 1930s witnessed significant changes. Symptomatic of the growing defensive character of French policy was the fact that in the 1930s new French investment was almost entirely directed to French colonies. After 1933 the effects of the economic crisis slowed down the export of French longterm capital. Moreover after 1933 the competition of German big business and financial interests in central and southeastern Europe grew increasingly fierce. Also, France failed to win a substantial share in the trade of eastern Europe. Agriculturally self-sufficient and highly protectionist she could offer nothing to tempt Poland and the states of the Little Entente who, with the exception of Czechoslovakia, had an agricultural surplus for export. After 1931 Germany entered the market, taking huge amounts of agricultural produce and raw materials, paying for them with manufactured goods. After the *Anschluss* in March 1938 Germany had a dominant place in the trade of the area.

However this is not to say that France readily surrendered to Germany. In the 1950s and 1960s Czechoslovak historians talked of 'an economic Munich before the political Munich'. Anglo-French capital, it was asserted, had voluntarily retreated from central Europe. In reality although there was a tendency to avoid further longterm investment, especially after Hitler's advent to power, British and French big business resisted the German challenge. Even after Munich the negotiations affecting two of Czechoslovakia's most important industrial concerns — the Vitkovice Mining and Foundry Works and the Škoda Works — do not indicate a voluntary retreat.

Thus the economic exclusion of France from central Europe was by no means inevitable. Indeed, by 1937 there was some disillusionment with Germany's inability to deliver manufactured goods and a determined French offensive might have scored some success. On 15 February 1938

King Carol of Rumania while affirming his desire to maintain and extend trade with Germany complained strongly that France was no longer buying Rumanian products.[26] Next day Hodža, Prime Minister of Czechoslovakia, called for Franco-British economic and financial help for the Danubian region, suggesting preferential tariffs between the Little Entente states, Austria, Hungary and Bulgaria.[27] Paris informed London of Hodza's ideas but nothing was done. When France sent an economic mission to central Europe in the winter of 1938-39 it was too late to be of any help.[28]

France could not even supply arms to her allies. Thanks to the Skoda works, Czechoslovakia could take care of herself but Poland and Rumania looked to France for assistance. Under the Rambouillet agreement of September 1936 France agreed to finance Polish armaments, provided the orders were placed with French industry. In January 1938, the armament firm of Schneider-Creusot told the Polish government that it could not supply the material ordered.[29] The French War Minister promised to help but then decided that owing to France's own rearmament programme the Polish orders could not be executed. The Polish General Staff were extremely annoyed and considered they had been misled. Rumania, too, complained of the slowness of French arms deliveries.[30]

It was Georges Duhamel who remarked that with the Munich Agreement of September 1938 France lost her Descartes line in central Europe.[31] Unfortunately, the Descartes line may have acted as a cultural barrier, preventing Frenchmen from putting down roots in eastern Europe. In a final report on the work of the French military mission in Prague, General Faucher, head of the mission from 1926 to 1938, lamented the fact that of two hundred officers who served at least two years in Czechoslovakia only a score ever acquired a working knowledge of the Czech language.[32]

As the storm clouds massed over Czechoslovakia, France was almost entirely preoccupied with the defence of her Mediterranean flank. France and Britain should not allow themselves to be hypnotised by Spain, Sir Orme Sargent, Assistant Under-Secretary at the Foreign Office, warned a member of the French embassy in London on 21 Oct. 1937. 'The real danger', he added, 'was elsewhere'.[33] The advice was sound but the French had reason to fear a Mediterranean conflict. In September the attacks on British and French shipping in Spanish waters produced a limited but effective demonstration of Franco-British power. A French initiative led to the calling of a conference at Nyon on 10-14 September which established joint naval patrols in the eastern and western Mediterranean. The attacks by 'unknown submarines' ceased but French leaders remained deeply apprehensive.

At a meeting of the Permanent Committee of National Defence on 3 November Daladier, Minister of National Defence and War, gave a gloomy interpretation of the international scene.[34] French planning, he said, had been based on the likelihood of a Franco-German conflict, arising out of a direct attack on France or on one of her allies. However the danger of a world conflict was now much greater than hitherto and it seemed probable that the Mediterranean would be the principal war theatre. The 50,000 Italian troops in Libya were a threat to both Tunisia and Egypt. Arab-Jewish troubles in British-administered Palestine posed a danger to the French mandate in Syria. If Germany succeeded in her colonial claims and received Togoland and the Cameroons, the Cape route, the only secure route to the Far East, would be in jeopardy, not to mention French North Africa.

Hitler, too, considered the possibility of a Mediterranean conflict between the two western democracies and Italy. On 5 November he informed his advisers of his intention to settle the Austrian and Czech questions, if necessary by force. A Mediterranean war, he thought, might come in the summer of 1938 and Germany would seize her chance to act against Czechoslovakia. Hitler was thinking aloud, not making plans for war but he saw clearly that France's concentration on the Mediterranean would greatly help his designs on central Europe.

Conceivably, French governments might have displayed greater determination in defending the peace settlement in the east if British support had been forthcoming. 'France could take a strong position only if she should have the absolute support of England', said Delbos.[35] But British policy towards eastern Europe had not changed a whit since the Peace Conference. 'We are unable to define beforehand what might be our attitude to a hypothetical complication in Central or Eastern Europe', Halifax told the House of Lords on 3 March 1937.[36] Then, as later in his career, the Foreign Secretary, Eden, was much too concerned with drawing lessons from the past. Reading G. M. Trevelyan's *Grey of Fallodon* he was much struck by the parallels between 1914 and 1937: 'What Belgium was then, Czechoslovakia is now'.[37] He told the American Ambassador that 'a declaration in advance that the British Government would go to the assistance of Czechoslovakia, if invaded, would split British opinion'.[38] Perhaps his time would have been better employed in studying the problems of central Europe. When on 8 October Corbin informed Eden of Czech fears that Germany would provoke a revolt in the Sudetenland, the Foreign Secretary 'did not seem to have deeply studied the matter' and wondered whether the 'designs attributed to Germany' were of real importance. Predictably, 'he was in no position to say what the British attitude would be' in the event of a Sudeten revolt.[39]

Of the reasons which determined France's decision not to oppose by force German expansion in central and eastern Europe the most important was the condition of France herself. The Chautemps ministry of June 1937 was granted full powers to deal with the financial crisis. The appointment as Finance Minister of such an orthodox Radical as Georges Bonnet was of some help in restoring financial confidence. His decrees solved the immediate crisis and by the end of the year he was even claiming a budget surplus. But social divisions were as deep as ever. The French Employers' association (*Confédération Générale du Patronat Français*) rejected any responsibility for social and economic unrest. The Left complained of the rise in the cost of living and accused the government of half-heartedness in applying the social reforms of the Popular Front. The Right countered by calling for longer working hours and the restoration of authority. After a lull during the August holidays industrial unrest affected much of the economy. Troubles culminated in a strike at the

Goodrich tyre factory on 23 December 1937. Workers occupied the factory and received reinforcements from all over Paris. At one point of the strike 30,000 workers were mobilised in defence of 'Fort Goodrich', forcing police to withdraw. Despite the possession of full powers, the government was singularly ill-equipped to restore domestic peace. Temperamentally, Chautemps tended to wait on events. The government was no longer sure of its parliamentary majority. The Popular Front alliance was wearing thin and Socialists and Radicals showed more interest in resuming old battles than in maintaining their partnership. The value of the franc and the gold reserves continued to decline. The gold stocks of the Bank of France valued at 160 milliards of francs in 1934, had fallen to 81 milliards by December 1937.[40] In November a sharp fall in world prices was seen on the *Bourse* as the beginning of a new recession.

The diplomatic initiatives came thick and fast from London: an exchange of letters with Mussolini in August, conversations with Count Dino Grandi, Italian Ambassador in London, an invitation to the German Foreign Minister, von Neurath, to visit London, and then Halifax's visit to Germany in mid-November. A renewal of the entente came low on Chamberlain's list of priorities and British and French Ministers did not meet until the end of November. France was not in favour in Downing Street. In a private letter, Sir Orme Sargent of the Foreign Office instructed Phipps that reports of what Frenchmen thought of their government should not be sent in telegrams but by private letter or despatch since telegrams went 'automatically to Cabinet ministers, certain of whom are only too glad to quote and exploit any criticism of that terribly pseudo-Communist government in France, to the coat-tails of which our Foreign Office is as usual tied, when it would be so much nicer to have it tied to the good Conservative and anti-Communist coat-tails of Hitler and Goering'.[41]

From the press, French ministers learnt that Lord Halifax, Lord President of the Council, had accepted an invitation to visit Germany on 17 November. Eden, who was in Brussels for a conference on the Far East, 'lamely explained' to Delbos that 'though the visit was purely private and unofficial we had of course intended to inform the French Government well in advance of any final decision'.[42] According to Eden, Delbos was anxious that no encouragement should be given to German moves against Czechoslovakia. Not that the French Minister was opposed to a settlement with Germany, on the contrary, he explained to the American Ambassador that although 'France and England could not offer Germany "concessions" in Austria and Czechoslovakia . . . in the colonial sphere France and England had something to give and could therefore demand something in exchange'.[43] This idea of barter was in tune with Halifax's reflections after talking to the German Chancellor on 19 November. There was something to be said, thought Halifax, for the 'bargain of a colonial settlement at the price of being a good European'.[44] Nor were the French inflexible on central Europe. In conversation with Sieburg, Paris correspondent of the *Frankfurter Zeitung*, who acted as an unofficial intermediary between Paris and Berlin, Delbos and Léger pointed out that France 'had no essential objection to a further assimilation of certain of Austria's domestic institutions with Germany's. The Czech question

was more difficult . . . but discussion of . . . protection for the Sudeten
Germans within the framework of the Czech state was quite feasible'.[45]
On 28 November 1937, Chautemps and Delbos arrived in London for
the first full conference with British ministers since July 1936. They were
accompanied by Léger and Massigli. Chautemps had first asked Chamberlain to visit Paris but then accepted an invitation to London. The
Foreign Office welcomed the visit 'as a timely antidote' after the recent
Halifax-Hitler meeting.[46] Chamberlain and Eden were both impressed
by Chautemps, finding him 'quite candid and straightforward' and they
were particularly relieved that the French Ministers did not 'appear to be
in any way under Russian influence'.[47]

The fortnight following the *Anschluss* in March 1938 has been seen as
the point at which Chamberlain, in Coulondre's words, 'took over the
reins of the Franco-British team and guided it until the outbreak of war'.[48]
In fact the British take-over finally came with the Franco-British conference of 29-30 November 1937. Reading the record of the conversations
it is difficult to escape the conclusion that if France had a last chance to
retain the initiative in central Europe it was during this conference. Unfortunately, before coming to London, Chautemps and Delbos had virtually decided that France could not maintain her influence intact in
central Europe.

In the two days of talks that opened in the morning of 29 November,
Germany and central Europe figured prominently in discussions but
French ministers showed far more interest in Italy and Mediterranean
problems. French ministers were flanked by their advisers: Léger, Massigli, Corbin and his Counsellor, Roland de Margerie completed the
team. Chamberlain was assisted by Eden and Halifax. In the morning
session, proceedings were opened by Halifax with an account of his visit
to Germany.[49] Hitler's views, as relayed by Halifax, seemed relatively
moderate but remarks made by Field Marshal von Blomberg, War Minister,
were noted with alarm by French Ministers. Blomberg had declared that
'just as France had her position in western Europe and the Mediterranean,
so Germany was entitled to a similar position in central Europe'. Chautemps
was anxious to clarify the connection between 'the colonial problem and
that of European appeasement'. According to Halifax, Hitler had talked
of colonies as 'the only direct issue between Germany and Great Britain'.
French Ministers were clearly afraid that Hitler might try to buy off Britain
with a separate colonial settlement, leaving France in the lurch in central
Europe. Chamberlain assured the French that the British government
would insist on the colonial question forming part of a general European
settlement.

Later in the afternoon session, colonies were again discussed. Chamberlain broached the subject of what colonies might be given to Germany
as part of some general settlement. Tanganyika, which had been mentioned in Germany, was, he said, too important strategically to be ceded to
Germany but Belgium and Portugal might be approached to see if they
would contribute to a settlement. Anticipating French anxieties that France
would be asked to disgorge more than her fair share, Chamberlain quickly
added that Britain 'would not consider for a moment' asking France to

sacrifice more than she was prepared to sacrifice herself. Delbos was quick to voice his dislike of the idea of approaching Belgium and Portugal. It would give a bad impression, he remarked, if the great powers appeared to rely on the smaller powers to pay the expenses of European understanding.

The co-ordination of policy towards Germany and central Europe dominated discussions. Delbos had no illusions about German intentions. In Austria, Germany was working towards the inclusion of National Socialist Ministers in the Austrian government and the eventual aim was a plebiscite. As for Czechoslovakia, Delbos envisaged demands from the Sudeten German minority for a 'federal constitution' leading to '*de facto* autonomy' and finally union with Germany. What were the implications for France's treaty with Czechoslovakia? asked Chamberlain. At this point Delbos showed his cards:

> . . .this treaty engaged France in the event of Czechoslovakia being a victim of an aggression. If uprisings among the German population occurred and were supported by armed intervention from Germany, the treaty committed France in a manner to be determined according to the gravity of the facts.

In brief, the French government had not yet decided what to do about the treaty, or rather they had already decided not to guarantee the existing territorial and political settlement in Czechoslovakia.

With sharp logic Chamberlain exploited the gap in French defences. Since French Ministers seemed to have made up their minds not to use force to defend the *status quo* in central Europe how in fact did they propose to prevent German action? Delbos replied:

> that depends to a large measure on the respect which a united Great Britain and France are able to impose, the agreement of the two powers could make Germany more reasonable.

> There were two possible methods: to leave well alone, and the results of that were clear, or to take an interest in Central Europe in a firm and conciliatory spirit. In this later hypothesis the situation did not seem really desperate.

The word 'conciliatory' was the cue Chamberlain needed and he observed that there was 'much of value' in what Delbos said. Germany, he believed, would hesitate to use force and if peaceful methods were employed in central Europe there was some chance of rendering German actions less dangerous and of retaining Italian sympathy for Austria. Britain was unwilling to be involved in war on account of Czechoslovakia—'a distant country with whom England had little in common'.

But Delbos did not surrender without a fight. France, he said, 'had repeatedly advised Czechoslovakia not to give the Germans any cause for complaint' and the same advice must be given to the Germans and an equal effort made in both countries:

> If French opinion had the impression that because of France's loyalty to her obligations English opinion was turning in upon itself, there would be deep disappointment. . .

Eden intervened to reassure Delbos that France was not being asked 'to reconsider her obligations or not to honour them'. It was simply that British opinion considered that certain Sudeten German grievances were justified and attention should be given to them before the international crisis grew worse. Chamberlain added a timely reminder of the general principle on which they had agreed; 'each question represented only a part of a general arrangement'.

The harsh reality of their alliance obligations was too much for the French ministers and Chautemps beat a retreat, taking his tune from Chamberlain:

... in effect each problem, considered in isolation, had a precise and brutal aspect, and there was a tendency therefore to see the questions in terms of force and violent solutions. The abandonment of a weak nation naturally aroused feelings of indignation. But it was not necessary to see the matter in such a direct and crude way. The Czeck question was perhaps rather more delicate for France because of the treaty uniting the two countries. But if the problem was considered in general terms ...

For Chautemps, the 'important point was to maintain peace' and there was nothing to be gained by seeking to anticipate the forms which German aggression might assume against Czechoslovakia. Frightened by what they glimpsed, the French ministers closed their eyes to the Czech problem.

Opening the afternoon session on 29 November Chamberlain summed up the morning's discussions:

It seemed desirable to try to achieve some agreement with Germany on Central Europe, whatever might be Germany's aims, even if she wished to absorb some of her neighbours; one could in effect hope to delay the execution of German plans, and even to restrain the Reich for such a time that its plans might become impractical in the long run. M. Delbos will ask M. Benes during his stay in Prague, without exercising any pressure on him, how far he is able to go in making concessions to the Sudeten Germans ...

The French Ministers made one belated effort to extract a British commitment on central Europe. Delbos, suggested Chautemps, would be in a much stronger position in Prague if he could speak in the name of both countries and say that once the Czechs had made all possible concessions to the Sudeten German minority they would be entitled to count on British and French sympathy in the event of aggression. Chamberlain and Eden at once rejected the idea.

Discussion of Italy revealed serious divisions of opinion. The conference confirmed that the French government was primarily preoccupied with the Mediterranean, not central Europe. Eden noted that the French ministers showed 'more irritation' over Italy than on any other subject.[50] While Chamberlain doubted whether Mussolini really wanted to cause trouble in the Mediterranean, Chautemps and Delbos saw evidence of Italian mischief everywhere: troops concentrations in Libya, anti-French propaganda in Syria and North Africa, designs on the Balearics. Italy, they submitted, was determined to divide Britain and France. Yet Chamberlain was not to be deflected from his approaches to Italy. French Ministers took what precautions they could, requesting that France be kept informed of negotiations and insisting that Italy be told of France's interest in participating in an Anglo-Italian agreement.

Consideration of the Far East brought general agreement that Britain and France could not act alone against Japan. Eden summed up the situation: 'it did not seem possible to do anything other than await events from day to day, and to try to obtain the help of the United States'.

Thus French Ministers accepted that the initiatives in approaches to Berlin and Rome should rest with London. Only in Prague did the French retain the initiative, though the guidelines of their action were defined in London. Reporting to the Cabinet on the results of the conference, Chamberlain said that 'at one time it looked as though the French were going to press for some more forthcoming attitude on central Europe' but 'no encouragement had been given them . . . finally they had agreed that appropriate concessions might be made by Czechoslovakia and that an attempt should be made to reach a general settlement with Germany'.[51]

The French Ministers returned home like new men. Delbos was 'for the first time in the past year extremely satisfied with himself and full of confidence'.[52] So depressing had been the record of French policy since March 1936 that Chautemps and Delbos made the most of what, on the surface at least, seemed a cheering manifestation of Franco-British collaboration. Some of the ghosts that had haunted the French had been laid. Before going to London Delbos had been told 'that there was real disagreement between Chamberlain and Eden' and that 'Chamberlain desired to give Germany a free hand in Central Europe in return for a promise by Germany not to ask for British colonies'.[53]

In reality Franco-British harmony was more apparent than real. Both governments agreed that a settlement with Germany had priority and this meant a conciliatory approach to the Sudeten German problem. But how far should conciliation be carried? What would Britain do if France fulfilled her treaty obligations to Czechoslovakia? These key questions were not explored. On Italy, there was a marked divergence of views. No attempt was made to discuss and co-ordinate defence arrangements. In practical terms, therefore, the results of the conference were slim indeed and in the lull before the storm a last opportunity was missed to forge a real Franco-British alliance.

Staff talks were not discussed in London. Effective diplomatic co-operation between London and Paris presupposed at the very least some on-going military contacts. Yet, apart from the Anglo-Franco-Belgian staff conversations on 15-16 April 1936 and naval co-operation in the Mediterranean in September 1937, there were no continuing staff talks. What high level contacts there were verged on the farcical. In the summer of 1936 Gamelin had a secret meeting with Field Marshal Sir Claude Deverell, Chief of the Imperial General Staff. It was arranged that both men should meet on the train to Vimy where they were to attend the opening of a war memorial to the Canadian army. Deverell entered Gamelin's compartment, asked for news of the Davis Cup and after some desultory attempts at conversation fell asleep.[54]

A major re-shaping of British defence policy took place in the autumn of 1937. On 22 December, defence proposals were submitted to the Cabinet calling for the abandonment of the idea of sending an army to the Continent. This change of policy was justified largely on financial grounds—after provision for the navy and air force almost nothing was left for the army. Optimistic reports on the French army helped to make the proposal more acceptable. The British even told themselves that they were doing the French a good turn. In September 1937 the Secretary of State for War, Hore-Belisha, had attended French army manoeuvres in Normandy and then visited the Maginot Line in the Strasbourg area. He was the first British Secretary of State for War to inspect the fortifications. He returned with glowing reports of French army morale and praise for the Maginot Line; although the fact that he received Daladier in his bath did not help his reputation in the British army.[55] In the Cabinet discussion of the new defence proposals on 22 December Hore-Belisha argued that when the French realised Britain could not send a continental force they would be more inclined to extend the Maginot Line to the sea.[56]

Of this review of defence which had been in progress for several months, French Ministers were given no inkling on 29-30 November. There was one ray of light in an otherwise gloomy picture. On 29 November Sir Thomas Inskip, Minister for the Co-ordination of Defence, gave the French ministers figures for British aircraft production. They were astonished to learn that monthly production was 300 aircraft and Chautemps admitted that French output was only 60 a month, one fifth of the British.[57] Next day Chamberlain assured the French that if they wanted to have further information through the air attachés, the government would be glad to reply to questions and show installations. A German air mission had recently toured British airfields and it went without saying that the government would be happy to do as much for the French.

Chamberlain's statement was much less generous than it may have sounded. It was simply an offer to reply to questions, not an invitation to staff talks. On 17 December Corbin asked Eden for naval staff talks arguing that since in wartime both governments would wish to concert their fleet movements in the Mediterranean and Far East it made little sense to refrain from making plans in peacetime. France, said the Ambassador, had reason to believe that Germany and Italy were collaborating in the Mediterranean.[58] But the British could not be budged. A Foreign Office suggestion in early 1938 that exploratory meetings might be held with the French elicited the reply from the Chiefs of Staff that 'the very term "staff conversations" has a sinister purport'. It was pointed out that the army had nothing to offer the French; naval talks were undesirable since 'If France were in alliance with us against Italy, Germany would be almost certain to come in against us'; air contacts, it was conceded, might be helpful but it would be unwise to hold them because the French might deliberately leak information and so bring about 'the very situation which we wish to avoid, namely the irreconcilable suspicion and hostility of Germany'.[59] Not until 24 March 1938 were the French offered for the first time air staff talks and the conversations which followed were carefully limited in scope.

The astonishment of French Ministers on hearing the figures of British aircraft production was genuine since they had been given to understand that the French air force was as strong as the British. In early November Pierre Cot, Air Minister, circulated to colleagues an extremely over-optimistic comparison of British and French air strengths.[60] The report concluded that in October 1937 France had more modern aircraft than

Britain. It was argued also that the French air force was better organised for war than the Royal Air Force; France had 500 bombers against 170 British. France's monthly production was 50 aircraft and Britain's output about the same. Moreover, France's military and industrial structure was better prepared for war than that of Britain. In commenting on this piece of special pleading the French Foreign Ministry did not dispute Cot's statistics but drew attention to the great gap in monthly production between France and potential enemies. France, urged the Quai d'Orsay, should aim at the same level of production as the Axis powers since inaction might be taken 'as proof that the French government is henceforth ready to acquiesce in Italian initiatives'.[61]

Italy remained in the forefront of French thinking. On 8 December Daladier, Minister of National Defence and War, told the Permament Committee of National Defence that though Germany remained the principal adversary, France might be attacked first by Italy in the Mediterranean.[62] Plans were to be prepared on the assumption that Germany and Italy would be hostile and might be aided by Franco's Spain. Britain would probably assist France. In the event of war the 'most urgent task' would be to defeat Italy. When Gamelin suggested asking for British air support for Belgium and Luxembourg, Daladier 'insisted again on the fact that the principal preoccupation of the English at this time was not there, but in the Mediterranean'. The conclusion of the meeting was that Spanish neutrality must be assured and France's alliances strengthened through military conventions.

Daladier's reference to British preoccupation with the Mediterranean suggests a lack of liaison between senior French Ministers. Chautemps and Delbos could hardly have derived the impression from the London conference that the British government was apprehensive of Italy. On the contrary, Chamberlain wished to reach agreement with Rome. Quai d'Orsay information suggested that the Far East, not the Mediterranean, was a source of anxiety. On 10 December Corbin wired: 'for an increasing number of Englishmen, Japan is tending to become public enemy number one, and this is a fact of general importance since it could have repercussions on the attitude of Great Britain towards Europe'.[63]

After the London conference on 29-30 November, Delbos packed his bags for a tour of east European capitals: Warsaw, Bucharest, Belgrade and Prague, though the visits did not include Moscow to the great resentment of the Soviet leadership.[64] The journey was the last official visit of a French Foreign Minister before the outbreak of the Second World War. Everywhere great crowds gathered to welcome Delbos. Perhaps they sensed that it was a farewell visit, a last inspection of the outposts of French influence.

Significantly, the first stop in the foreign minister's travels was Berlin on 3 December. It was not an official visit. The Minister's train stopped for half an hour at the Silesia station *en route* to Warsaw and von Neurath, German Foreign Minister, boarded the train for a brief conversation. Neurath was assured that in the recent conference there had been 'no talk of any intention to block Germany's development' and the journey to Warsaw and the capitals of the Little Entente 'was not aimed at this in any way'.[65] Tactfully, Delbos did not define what he meant by 'development'. He expressed satisfaction at the progress made in Franco-German understanding through youth exchanges, and contacts between ex-servicemen.

In Warsaw, on 4 December, Delbos was given a warm welcome but received no satisfaction on the issue of Polish-Czech relations.[66] Colonel Beck, Polish Foreign Minister, complained of the treatment of the Polish minority in Teschen and condemned Prague's links with Moscow, alleging that Czechoslovakia was the centre of Comintern propaganda against Poland.

The triumphant reception accorded to Delbos in Prague on 16-17 December at the end of his progress of central Europe offered a timely testimony of Czech friendship for her ally. Over 200,000 people greeted Delbos on his arrival. During the visit President Benes explained the standpoint of his government.[67] Autonomy for the Sudeten German minority was geographically impossible. The Sudetens represented 21% of the population and he was doing his best to give them adequate rights and representation. There were three Sudeten ministers in the Cabinet. His policy, he said, was 'essentially Western', insisting on the word 'Western'. Germany had twice approached him with proposals for a bilateral agreement but he would do nothing without the consent of Paris and London. The country's pacts with the Little Entente and the Soviet Union had been inspired by French diplomacy and they were strictly subordinate to the French alliance. Should the Soviet Union draw closer to Germany against France, Czechoslovakia would be 'immediately at France's side'. But Benes did not believe a conflict was likely in the near future because Germany was not yet prepared. The interview closed with Benes's promise that everything possible would be done for the Sudeten Germans 'within the framework of the constitution'.

The omission of Moscow from the French Foreign Minister's itinerary was an indicator of how far relations had deteriorated since the honeymoon period of 1933-34. By 1937-38, France and the Soviet Union were engaged in constant bickering. French politicians and the press accused Moscow of interfering in internal affairs. The Soviet government attacked French foreign policy, claiming that in the London conference of 29-30 November Chautemps had said that a strengthening of the entente would allow French disengagement from the east. For all practical purposes France had put the pact into cold storage. A Soviet request to be allowed to send a mission to French army manoeuvres in September 1937 was refused. While Franco-Soviet relations were not on the agenda of the London conference, there were informal hints of French feelings. Jacques Kayser, a Vice-President of the Radicals and a close adviser of Chautemps, stressed the purely 'negative value' of the pact in preventing a German-Soviet *rapprochement*.[68] But the Russians did not delude themselves about the pact. Ivan Maisky, Soviet Ambassador in London, dismissed it as 'not worth two pence'.[69]

Yet the Soviet alliance was too valuable a piece of insurance to be jettisoned. Chautemps told the Americans he was 'quite ready to give the Germans all the assurances possible that France would never make a military alliance with the Soviet Union directed against Germany or indulge in military conversations . . . and he would tell them frankly his own highly unfavourable opinion of the Soviet Union and Bolshevism but he could not formally abandon the treaty . . .'.[70] When the League Council met in Geneva at the end of January 1938 Delbos and Litvinov continued the old arguments. The French Communist Party, said Delbos, seemed to take its orders from Moscow.[71] Litvinov insisted that there were no connections whatsoever between the Soviet government and foreign communist parties. In Paris Chautemps was reproached by the Soviet Ambassador for treating the Russians 'like poor relations'. Recounting the interview to Phipps the French minister claimed to have replied that the Russians were 'not poor but dangerous' and the French government 'could never show the Soviet government the same implicit confidence' that they showed London.[72] Doubtless Phipps purred with approval.

On 15 January 1938 the Chautemps ministry fell, defeated not by a hostile vote in the Chamber but by dissensions between its Socialist and Radical Socialist members. For three days France was without a government. After Georges Bonnet and Léon Blum failed to muster sufficient support, Chautemps agreed to return and announced on 18 January his second administration in less than eight months. It was little more than a caretaker ministry or, as Chautemps euphemistically described it, 'a government of transition'.[73] Delbos continued as Foreign Minister, though the Soviet government, angered by his refusal to visit Moscow, was said to have made attempts to bring about his removal.[74] Daladier replaced Blum as Deputy Prime Minister but retained the Ministry of National Defence and War. Paul Marchandeau became Minister of Finance, though Bonnet stayed in the government as a minister without portfolio.

Against the backcloth of European events, the myopic manoeuvres of the politicians suggested a lemming-like urge for self-destruction. On 17 January Corbin sent a cry of distress from London: 'the persistence of our internal quarrels' was discouraging British opinion.[75] 'France's weakness', Chamberlain told an American correspondent on 16 January, was 'a public danger'.[76] Though lip service was paid to the idea of a government of 'National Union' from 'Thorez to Reynaud', in practice fear and prejudice decided the issue. The comments of Chautemps on the crisis reveal the narrowness of his political vision. Admitting that his government of 18 January was based on too small a group to have the necessary authority to govern, he said he would like to form 'a national government' but would not include the Communists 'because they would report every conversation to Stalin'.[77] Yet, in the absence of the Communists, Blum and the Socialists would probably refuse to join a government and so his ministry would have to be based on the Radical Socialists and parties of the Right and would not be 'an effective national government because it would leave out the chief representatives of the working classes'. If Blum tried his hand, Chautemps continued, he would try to include the Communists but in that case the Radical Socialists would refuse their support. Herriot might be able to form a national government since his prestige was such that he could retain Communist support in the Chamber without actually including them in the government. But the great danger was that the Communists would demand immediate staff talks with Moscow and

ral (*Marie-Gustave*) Gamelin, Chief of the French General Staff (*and newly appointed* *of the French Armies*), at Aldershot on a four-day visit to Britain in June 1939.

rench Prime Minister arriving at Croydon Airport for talks at Downing Street about the
crisis on September 18, 1938. From left: Lord Halifax, Mr. Chamberlain, M. Daladier,
ger and M. Corbin.

Right: the French Premier,
M. Daladier (left) and his Foreign
Minister M. Bonnet, leaving
10 Downing Street after conferring
with Neville Chamberlain on
September 26, 1938.

Far right: Paul Reynaud, the
new French Premier, entering
10 Downing Street March 28, 1940.

Below left: M. Leon Blum
Centre: M. Camille Chautemps
Right: M. Yvon Delbos

help for Spain and such a policy, Chautemps feared, 'would produce a declaration of war by Germany'.

By mid-February Chautemps and Delbos seemed resigned to the erosion of French influence in central and eastern Europe. A sense of fatalism dominated them. The Prime Minister thought it 'probable' that 'central and eastern Europe would slip into the hands of Germany without war'.[78] Not that Chautemps was blind to the consequences of German expansion:

> Every Frenchman with whom he had talked during the past ten days had recall-ed to him the example of Sadowa and . . . suggested . . . that if France should permit Austria and Czechoslovakia to fall into German hands . . . the power of the Reich would be so enormous that France would inevitably be overthrown within a few years. He felt nevertheless that Hitler would be clever enough to give France no opportunity to intervene to protect Czechoslovakia.[79]

On 21 February Delbos remarked to Bullitt that since 'England had embarked on a policy of turning over central and eastern Europe to Germany. . . It would be possible for France to retire behind the Maginot Line'.[80] Though careful to add that 'he himself would continue to oppose such a policy', the Foreign Minister admitted that 'it was a policy which . . . was likely to be adopted'. That same day Daladier said that if the threat to France's communications with North Africa were removed then 'France would be able to live safely behind the Maginot Line no matter what might happen in central and eastern Europe'.[81]

While the trend of French policy was becoming increasingly clear, it is a myth to suppose that French leaders wished to wash their hands completely of eastern Europe. This was the thesis of Flandin but it was never more than a minority viewpoint. The mass of parliamentary opinion, though accepting some loss of power as inevitable, nevertheless wished to retain a say in the area. Jean Mistler, chairman of the Chamber Foreign Affairs Committee, spent two weeks in central Europe in January 1938. Reporting to his committee on the visit he described German pressures and concluded: 'We must, ourselves too, work in the east and strengthen . . . the influence of France. Our foreign policy in that part of Europe can only benefit and it needs to do so'.[82]

On 22 February a meeting of the Chamber foreign affairs committee set the scene for the major parliamentary debate on foreign affairs which opened three days later.[83] Delbos spoke at length, rejecting the opposing schools of thought in French policy. He laid great emphasis on the interdependence of internal and external policies. A policy of firmness, as advocated by Reynaud and the Communist, Gabriel Péri, would be dangerous because France would be tempted to take initiatives beyond her strength. Instead, the government proposed 'a policy of prudence . . . we must hold on to all that can be held'. A note of ambiguity in his rejection of the Flandin thesis was noticeable: 'I do not believe that it is necessary to accept a pessimism which calls for France to retreat behind the Rhine and wait for better times. Even if this was the case, it would be better not to say so'.

The parliamentary debate which followed on 25-26 February aired the views of the opposing schools of thought.[84] On the one side, Flandin, former Prime Minister and Foreign Minister, argued for a withdrawal from the East and an understanding with Germany and Italy. France, he stated, should fall back on her own resources and empire. On the other side, the Right wing Paul Reynaud, supported by the Radical Socialist Ernest Pezet and the Communist Gabriel Péri, pleaded for a traditional and forceful diplomacy. 'The overthrow of our policy would not only imperil the peace, it would be the abandonment of our reason for living', declared Reynaud. Between the Scylla of withdrawal and the Charybdis of total commitment Delbos steered an uneasy and unconvincing middle course. The debate drew from him a general reaffirmation of French pledges—so faint-hearted as to be virtually valueless. According to one observer, the Foreign Minister before making his speech had wanted 'to run away' but had been 'propped up' by his officials. Thanks to their efforts, Dalbos had finally devised a declaration which, though uninspiring, was yet firmer than his own 'colourless' drafts.[85] A French Foreign Ministry official told the Prague correspondent of *Le Temps:* 'I have seen the statement, the Czechs will be happy, but between ourselves it is only words—naturally one must not say so'.[86] The government received a strong vote of confidence but the vote, reported the German Ambassador, was 'more an expression of helplessness than of strength'.[87]

Chapter 5

Retreat

On 12 March 1938 German troops marched into Vienna and on the following day a cowed Austrian cabinet announced the incorporation of their country into Germany. Hitler, by two bloodless victories, in two years had almost reversed the verdict of 1918. French leaders were in no doubt about the possible consequences of such an exhibition of force. 'A general conflict may break out at any moment', warned Gamelin on 14 March.[1] Some days later the French Military Attaché in Vienna signalled:

> ...the prestige of France in Central Europe, already gravely damaged by the events of 7 March 1936, has emerged from the Austrian affair, however expected and inevitable it may have been, almost completely annihilated, even among those who claim to be the most loyal.
> For everyone here, Germany is the great victor of the war.[2]

After the first reactions of shock the French press raised a hue and cry for scapegoats. For the Right, the *Front Populaire* was the main culprit. Blum's rule, it was asserted, had weakened and divided the country. Friendly approaches to Italy, it was argued, would have resulted in Mussolini opposing an *Anschluss* as he had done in 1934. The Left replied in kind. The *Anschluss* was the culmination of a series of surrenders beginning with Ethiopia and followed by the Rhineland and Spain.

The main sequence of events is well-known: on 12 February 1938 the Austrian Chancellor was summoned to Berchtesgaden and bullied into appointing the Austrian National Socialist, Seyss-Inquart, as Minister of the Interior with control over the police; on 16 February Seyss-Inquart entered the Austrian government; on 20 February in a speech to the Reichstag, Hitler declared that the Germans of Austria had the right to invoke the Wilsonian principle of self-determination. Germany's intention was clearly to provoke a 'voluntary' *Anschluss,* by encouraging the Austrian National Socialists to take their own action. On 24 February Schuschnigg, the Austrian Chancellor, declared that he would not give way to German pressure; on 9 March he asked the Austrians to show, by a plebiscite, whether or not they wished to remain independent. Hitler replied on 11 March with a two point ultimatum, demanding the postponement of the plebiscite and the resignation of Schuschnigg; next day German forces entered Austria.

The build-up of tension over Austria lasted a month and gave the British and French governments ample opportunity to devise a common line of action. Rumours of a German move against Vienna had circulated since the spring of 1937, and at the end of the year 1937 French military intelligence considered that German action would not be long delayed. Then, at the beginning of March, the Deuxiéme Bureau reported that a *coup* was imminent: 'the operation will be sudden and all will be settled within a few hours.'[3] Although neither France not Britain had treaty commitments to Austria, both powers were pledged as a result of the Stresa declaration of April 1935 to consult with Italy in the event of any action which affected Austrian independence.

On 15 February London and Paris received details of the conditions imposed by Hitler on Schuschnigg in the Berchtesgaden agreements. The Austrian Chancellor sent an urgent appeal for Britain and France to speak firmly in Berlin. Léger telephoned the French embassy at Vienna to say that before asking the government to support the Chancellor he wished to be sure of Austria's will to resist German pressure.[4] Delbos was prepared to act in Berlin but Eden was 'extremely doubtful of the wisdom of any separate or joint communication'.[5] Sir Alexander Cadogan, Permanent Under-Secretary of State, commented: 'French want to make a joint protest in Berlin. What folly We are riding them off'.[6] François-Poncet was instructed to tell the German Foreign Minister, von Ribbentrop, that France 'in no way intended to disinterest herself in the situation of Austria'. When the envoy carried out his démarche on 17 February he was firmly told to mind his own business: 'the German-Austrian relationship', said Ribbentrop, 'was a German family matter...that concerned Germany and Austria alone'.[7]

France had called on 15 February for joint action in Berlin as a confirmation of interest in central Europe; on 17 February Delbos suggested a minatory démarche: 'the French government considers...that a very clear warning should be given to the German government'.[8] Germany, he proposed, should be questioned about the 'meaning' of the Berchtesgaden talks. Furthermore, Britain and France should declare that the maintenance of Austrian independence was essential for European peace and any act of force against the status quo would be resolutely resisted. Both governments, continued Delbos, should consider ways and means of giving financial and economic aid to Austria and Czechoslovakia. On 24 February Delbos asked for a reply to his proposals; on 25 February came the British reply: French proposals for a joint approach were rejected since a démarche would only encourage in Schuschnigg 'dangerous illusions'. Words without deeds were useless. Economic aid to the Danubian area would be useful provided Germany co-operated. But the best course of action, concluded the British memorandum, was to seek some agreement with Germany and proposals were being prepared for submission to Germany.[9]

On 2 March the French returned to the attack. Paris pointed out that the destinies of Austria and Czechoslovakia were linked and though France had no treaty obligations towards Austria she had an alliance with Czechoslovakia. Germany's programme of expansion had to be arrested, failure to do so would only confirm the violent methods pursued since

1935. It would be 'regrettable' if London was not willing to help.[10] The same day Corbin was told that threats were of no avail unless Britain and France were prepared to execute them. The solution to the problem of central Europe lay in a 'general accommodation' with Germany which would include safeguards for 'the independence of the small states'.[11]

After receiving the German demand for his resignation on 11 March, Schuschnigg at once requested the advice of the British government. He was quickly told that no responsibility could be taken for 'advising him to take any course of action which might expose his country to dangers against which His Majesty's Government are unable to guarantee protection'.[12] Paris was informed of this message. Delbos immediately asked for British intervention in Rome and consideration of possible action in Berlin.[13] The two western democracies would not protect Austria and Schuschnigg drew the inevitable conclusion. In the evening over the radio he announced acceptance of the German ultimatum and took farewell of his hearers with the words: 'God protect Austria'. London and Paris delivered protests in Berlin. François-Poncet 'protested most emphatically against the coercion supported by violence of an independent state'.[14]

Judging only from the diplomatic exchanges between Paris and London, it seems that Austria might have been saved if Britain had co-operated with France in joint action in Berlin. Appearances in fact were deceptive. French requests for British support in defence of Austrian independence were no more than diplomatic flourishes, designed firstly to satisfy parliamentary opinion and secondly to reassure Czechoslovakia. A major foreign affairs debate was fixed for 25-26 February. 'He could see no way to prevent Hitler from swallowing Austria', Chautemps explained to Bullitt on 21 February, but he had allowed Delbos to suggest a joint démarche 'for purely domestic reasons in order that Delbos might go before the partners of the *Front Populaire*...and show them that France had attempted to do something. He had not been under the illusion that England might join France in such a démarche'.[15] A meeting of the Chamber foreign affairs committee on 16 February had sharply criticised the government's foreign policy. 'If France and England had said in advance that they would not accept a Nazi minister in Austria', affirmed Gaston Bergery, 'there would not be one today'.[16]

Pressure for French diplomatic action came from Prague. On 18 and 22 February Benes insisted that if Britain and France 'did not wish to be driven out of central Europe' they should affirm their determination to defend the territorial settlement.[17] In an interview with Lacroix on 22 February Benes declared that Britain was in a worse plight than in 1914. Czechoslovakia was resisting Hitler but she could not do so alone. Lacroix remarked that Britain and France still enjoyed a preponderance of force over Germany and Italy. Benes answered:

> ...if France and England do not display this force...their superiority will disappear through disuse and in two years it will hardly count any longer. Twice or three times, M. Benes asked me: "do you believe that the political, social and moral state of the democracies will allow them to take this indispensable stand?"[18]

The French government did not for a moment consider going to war for Austria. When word of the German ultimatum reached Paris in the afternoon of 11 March France was without a government. The previous day Chautemps had resigned, pleading personal exhaustion and lack of parliamentary support. Daladier, not unjustly, accused him of 'running away from office'.[19] Four Ministers—Chautemps, Delbos, Daladier and Bonnet—met at 4 p.m. on the 11th at the Hotel Matignon and decided that certain military measures might be taken, provided British support was forthcoming.[20] The measures proposed were only 'alert precautions' involving no more than the recall of some reservists and the closing of the frontier with Germany. Nothing in fact was done. Even if British co-operation had been given, all that was envisaged was an expression of displeasure, not an attempt to intimidate Germany.

Nor was there ever any question of British resistance to German designs on Austria. Indeed, as the Austrian crisis gathered momentum after the Hitler-Schuschnigg meeting of 12 February, the mood was almost one of 'If it were done when 'tis done, then 'twere well It were done quickly'. As Cadogan put it on 15 February: 'Personally, I almost wish Germany would swallow Austria and get it over...I shouldn't mind if Austria were gleichgeschaltet'.[21] It was widely felt that the Versailles prohibition on the Anschluss had been wrong from the start and a vassal Austria was inevitable. It was of little use for Delbos or Benes to pontificate on the importance of Austria as a pillar of the peace settlement when that settlement had long ceased to carry conviction. More important was the fact that France's call for a common stand over central Europe ran counter to Chamberlain's strategy of friendly negotiations with Germany. Commenting on the SOS from Schuschnigg, Sir Orme Sargent remarked on 16 February: 'neither Herr von Schuschnigg nor M Delbos...know that we are about to make proposals to Herr Hitler for an Anglo-German settlement, which includes a vague and tentative reference to Austria as an instance where Germany could collaborate'.[22] French pressure for action on Austria threatened to disrupt British appeasement plans and Cadogan minuted: 'I want to stop the French butting in'.[23] Henderson met Hitler on 3 March and submitted general proposals for collaboration, including a colonial settlement. 'Mention should be made of Czechoslovakia and Austria as illustrative of the general principle of collaboration', noted his instructions.[24]

The Austrian Chancellor was convinced that the only salvation for his country lay in a revival of the Stresa front. It was a forlorn hope. In the winter of 1937-38 France and Italy waged a cold war in which official contacts were kept to the bare minimum. In early December 1937 Chautemps had 'looked with considerable equanimity on the possibility that Germany might annex Austria because he believed that this would produce an immediate reaction of Italy against Germany'.[25] He 'could see no basis...for any rapprochement with Italy'. 'It was virtually impossible to do anything with Italy', he told Bullitt in January 1938, diplomatic relations 'had practically been severed...neither the Italian Chargé d'Affaires in Paris nor the French Chargé...in Rome had any conversations of...importance'.[26]

Yet not all French diplomats were of the same mind towards Italy. For senior officials such as Léger and Massigli, Italy was beyond the pale but Jules Blondel, Chargé d'Affaires in Rome, and Gabriel Puaux, Minister in Vienna, believed there was a chance of enlisting Italian help for Austria. Blondel, acting without instructions, told the Italian Foreign Minister, Count Ciano, on 24 February that an accord between France, Italy and Britain could save Austria. Ciano's reply was not encouraging: Italy had 'gone to the Brenner once: she will not go twice'.[27] Austria had to be saved by the Austrians. But Blondel was not too depressed, considering that the Italians were in the throes of 'a crisis of conscience' and might yet adopt a more sympathetic attitude. His report received no reply from the Quai d'Orsay.

From Vienna, Puaux wired on 7 March that if the Gamelin-Badoglio convention of 27 June 1935 could be resurrected the 'independence of Austria might yet be saved'.[28] If no military action was taken, the French government would shortly be faced, as on 7 March 1936, with a *fait accompli*. In a personal letter of 8 March to Massigli, Political Director, he drove home his point: 'the government must consider the consequences of its refusal to talk to Mussolini. Why has a semi-official emissary such as Monzie not been sent?'[29] All he received for his pains was a scolding. Delbos replied: 'I acknowledge receipt of your telegram and of your personal letter. You attempt to compare the present situation with that which preceded 7 March 1936. I cannot share this viewpoint, of which the impropriety as well as the inconsequence will not have escaped you....'.[30]

Despite the appeals of Schuschnigg, the French government refused to open discussions in Rome. Italy's acceptance of the Berchtesgaden agreements of 12 February was seen as a sign that she had tacitly abandoned Austria. The French memorandum of 18 February calling for joint Franco-British action in Berlin stated: 'However desirable Italian co-operation may still be, this is of a very uncertain character in view of the circumstances in which Signor Mussolini has just abandoned Dr. Schuschnigg to his fate'.[31] It was only after hearing of the German ultimatum on 11 March that Delbos asked London to seek Italian help. Blondel was told to see Ciano. When the French diplomat rang up the Palazzo Chigi and applied for an interview he was curtly told that if the object of the interview was Austria the 'Italian Government had no reason to concert with France or Great Britain'.[32]

While France and Italy glowered at each other, Britain opened formal negotiations in mid-February. Although the record of Chamberlain's conversation with the Italian Ambassador, Count Grandi, on 18 February reveals the prime minister's concern for Austria and interest in enlisting Italian support, it is clear that such support was not an essential part of the negotiations but merely a desirable adjunct. In the discussions with Italy Eden was preoccupied with the Spanish issue and the need to secure withdrawals of Italian troops as a preliminary to agreement. Replying to the French memorandum of 18 February, the British government agreed 'that, however desirable Italian co-operation as regards the affairs of central Europe may be, such co-operation cannot be counted upon in present circumstances'.[33] A Cabinet paper of 28 February defined the place of Austria in the framework of Anglo-Italian talks:

> It had been originally intended to seek from Italy a reaffirmation of the Stresa Resolution regarding Austria. Recent events have shown that Italy is not prepared to move where Austrian independence and integrity are concerned.[34]

The paper favoured a suggestion of Lord Perth, Ambassador in Rome, that before the final conclusion of talks, Mussolini 'might be informed that we trust that he will . . . do his utmost to restrain Berlin from any further encroachments on Austrian independence'.[35]

The prospects of recreating the Stresa front of 1935 were, to say the least, very slight, although until the Italian archives are opened it would be unwise to be dogmatic on this point. Still, on the evidence available, it seems unlikely that earlier and more intensive efforts from London and Paris on behalf of Austria would have had much effect on Mussolini. As Ciano put it: 'What in fact could we do? Start a war with Germany? At the first shot we fired every Austrian without a single exception, would fall in behind the Germans against us'.[36]

The *Anschluss* did not lead to closer links between London and Paris. Instead, relations sharply deteriorated and French requests for consultations on Czechoslovakia were refused. Relations had deteriorated in the early months of 1938. French monitoring of telephone calls between the two capitals brought distressing revelations. French Ministers were shocked by conversations 'between distinguished British representatives in Paris' and Sir Robert Kindersley, London partner of Lazard Brothers, predicting 'that a tremendous financial crash in France was inevitable in March'.[37] Phipps picked up anti-British whisperings. Both the Communists and the Right were recounting stories of British interference in French internal affairs. It was particularly alarming, said Phipps, that these tales were being given credence in Radical Socialist and moderate political circles.[38]

February brought distressing news of British defence policy. On 17 February General Lelong, Military Attaché in London, was told by the Secretary of State for War, Hore-Belisha, that the army's tasks, in order of importance were: the defence of British soil, the protection of vulnerable points of the Empire, the maintenance of British interests in the Near East, help for allies. This order of priorities was formally confirmed on 7 March when Chamberlain spoke in the House of Commons in support of the government's White Paper on Defence. After home defence, defence of trade routes, imperial defence, the 'fourth and last objective' was the support of 'any allies we might have in case of war'.[39]

The changes of leadership at the Foreign Office in January and February were a further source of anxiety in Paris. At the end of January Sir Robert Vansittart, Permanent Under-Secretary of State, brother-in-law of Phipps, and close friend of Léger, Secretary General of the Quai d'Orsay, was replaced by Sir Alexander Cadogan. His new post of Chief Diplomatic Adviser was, in his own words, 'largely humbug'.[40] On 20 February, Eden and Cranborne, Parliamentary Under-Secretary, resigned. That evening Phipps was summoned to the Quai d'Orsay where he found assembled Chautemps, Delbos, Léger and Corbin, all gravely perturbed.[41]

They recalled that at the London conference of November 1937 both governments had promised to consult together before embarking on major policy changes. At 10.20 p.m. the same evening Chamberlain telephoned Chautemps saying that there would be no change in British policy and promising to keep in close touch. Chautemps was not reassured. With the elimination of Vansittart, Eden and Cranborne 'the three Englishmen closest to the Quai d'Orsay', the French Prime Minister thought it 'certain that England would be inclined to make ever-increasing concessions to Germany'.[42] Delbos dismissed Chamberlain's assurances as 'valueless' and one of his assistants added that in practice the promise of close contact would 'probably consist of a few crumbs of routine information about once every two weeks'.[43]

Such was the shock occasioned by Eden's departure that Chautemps even talked of the Foreign Secretary's resignation leading to a change of government in France. On 25 February, Phipps suggested that as a mark of confidence the French government might be given more information about British approaches to Germany and Italy. A senior Foreign Office official minuted that no reply was necessary: 'it is a familiar gambit of French Foreign Ministers to tell us that unless we agree to do something or other the French government will fall'. In any event, concluded the official, a change of government might not be a disaster since Chautemps might then replace Delbos at the Quai d'Orsay.[44]

The French certainly felt that they were being treated in cavalier fashion. The Chamberlain-Grandi conversation of 18 February was seen as a breach of confidence. On 22 February, Corbin complained that contrary to the assurances of close co-operation given in November 1937, France had not been kept informed of Anglo-Italian developments.[45] Halifax (Eden's successor as Foreign Secretary) replied that London saw no need to inform the French in detail of every stage of the negotiations since the contacts were within the framework of talks as originally conceived in the November conference and discussed between Eden and Delbos on 28 January. This attitude brought a swift rejoinder from Delbos:

> I am touched by the message that Lord Halifax asked you to give me and I ask you to thank him for it, assuring him that I, too, have retained happy memories of our meeting in the London talks.
> But, all personal considerations aside, it is necessary for London to understand that the French government has the right to insist on having the fullest information concerning the objectives of British policy, at a time when it seems to be undergoing, in certain respects a change of direction.[46]

Corbin saw Halifax on 25 February and strongly criticised the methods of the British government which, without prior agreement with France, had approached Germany and defined its attitude towards German colonial claims. France and Britain, said the Ambassador, were in danger of returning to the position of 1935 'when there was no sincere co-operation'.[47] The Ambassador continued, not without a touch of irony, 'a policy of trust . . . cannot rest exclusively on declarations of goodwill, it must be reflected in deeds'. By his own account, Halifax seems to have reassured Corbin, promising a statement of 'our general thought'.[48] However when Henderson presented Hitler on 3 March with proposals for a settlement he stressed that 'no information would be given the French, much less the Belgians, Portuguese, or Italians concerning the subject of the discussion'.[49]

On 10 March Chautemps had resigned, and three days later Blum took office for a second time as leader of a predominantly Socialist Ministry. The Socialist leader's call for a Cabinet of 'national union' with Communist participation was rejected by the Right which demanded a government of public safety. Laval at the time was trying to form a Pétain government.[50] Leading Radicals—Chautemps, Delbos, Bonnet and Marchandeau—were out of office. Blum appointed the Socialist Joseph Paul-Boncour as Foreign Minister and personally took charge of the Treasury. Daladier continued as Minister of National Defence and War and Deputy Prime Minister, telling confirmation of his political ascendancy.

Blum's return to power was a red rag to the British prime minister and kindred spirits. Chamberlain did not have the 'slightest confidence' in the new government, suspecting it of being 'in closish touch with our Opposition'.[51] On one point at least Downing Street and the Foreign Office saw eye to eye—the Blum government was a disaster. 'France had no government and Paul-Boncour was not a foreign minister who at so serious a moment could be a worthy partner in a discussion of the European crisis', declared Cadogan.[52] French requests for a meeting of ministers were refused. Herriot who pressed for an early meeting was told: 'such meetings' were 'quite useless until the days of transitory French governments were over'.[53] Not content with expressions of displeasure, the Foreign Office hinted at action to unseat Blum. On 17 March Sir Orme Sargent, Deputy Under-Secretary, minuted: 'we should definitely not allow French ministers to come to London...to discuss Spain and Czechoslovakia...I should go so far as to say that anything we can do to weaken the present French government and precipitate its fall would be in the British interest'.[54]

Given such antipathy, the odds were heavily weighted against a successful reassertion of French interests. None the less Blum and Paul-Boncour tried to tighten the ties between the two governments and sought to reaffirm their conception of French security. The French public shed few tears over the Austrian débâcle. The annexation was regarded as unfortunate but unavoidable. Only two newspapers—the Right wing L'Epoque and the Left wing L'Humanité expressed regret that France had not intervened to save Austria. What mattered next, said André Tardieu, was the future and the future was the defence of Czechoslovakia.

The first step taken by the new ministers was the confirmation of the treaty with Czechoslovakia. On 14 March, Blum and Paul-Boncour reaffirmed France's obligations to the Czechoslovak Minister in Paris, Ossuky. The promise was reiterated in sessions of the parliamentary foreign affairs committees and in a semi-official announcement on 6 April.

While Ministers reasserted diplomatic commitments, the military chiefs assessed the consequences of recent events. Czechoslovakia, reported Gamelin, was completely encircled. Only Poland could intervene quickly and effectively. But the Chief of the General Staff rejected the Flandin thesis that France should abdicate her European role, though the argument did not carry much conviction. In the event of war, he said, Czechoslovakia would be restored in the final peace settlement. Yet France could not fight without allies: 'more than ever, it is . . . necessary to have with us England and Poland'.[55]

Thanking the French government for its friendly and categorical declarations of support, Benes pointed out that the best guarantee of peace would be a Franco-British declaration.[56] Everything hinged, therefore, on the British attitude. In the afternoon of 12 March, Corbin reminded Halifax of French obligations towards Czechoslovakia. The Foreign Secretary agreed on the urgency of joint discussions and promised to take the matter up with the Prime Minister. At the same time, he could not resist probing French defences and asked what action would be taken if Germany attacked Czechoslovakia. French intervention, replied Corbin, would divert large German forces to the Rhine. By 17 March, the French Ambassador detected a hardening of policy towards central Europe. In recent briefings to journalists the Foreign Office News Department had been quite negative about the prospects of British help, drawing attention to a despatch from the British Minister at Prague, Newton, stating that the country was militarily indefensible.

On 21 March, Paul-Boncour instructed Corbin to make a final assault before Chamberlain made an announcement to the Commons on 24 March: 'no effort should be neglected to divert the British Cabinet from decisions which will have serious consequences':

> Since the *fait accompli* of the *Anschluss* it is no longer a question of the treatment of the Sudeten minority of Czechoslovakia, and the fate of the Czechoslovak state: it is the destiny of Europe itself which is now being decided . . . Does London think it expedient, fair and clever to abandon to Germany central Europe and the Danubian area . . .[57]

France, said Paul-Boncour, did not seek a guarantee for Czechoslovakia but a declaration of British support for herself in the event of a Franco-German war arising out of the Czech treaty. Corbin acted on his instructions in the evening of 22 March. Tactfully he eschewed the uncompromising phraseology of the instructions. Halifax gave a short answer: no guarantee or undertakings could be given 'by reason of public opinion here and in the Dominions'. This negative was softened by the addition of a note of uncertainty: 'whatever might be the formal pronouncements made . . . the inexorable drive of facts, once a war started, might be expected to be so strong that it was . . . probable that this country might be drawn in. . .'.[58]

Halifax's gentlemanly way of saying no, left Corbin with charitable thoughts: 'it is impossible not to note the firm desire for co-operation with France which appears in Halifax's comments'.[59] Yet the Ambassador was too experienced a diplomat to swallow Halifax, hook, line and sinker. In their talk of 22 March, the Foreign Secretary made much of the constraints of Dominion opinion. Corbin reported to Paris that while frequent allusions to the Dominions were appearing in the press and in speeches, the references were vague and imprecise. A brief enquiry among Commonwealth diplomatic representatives had revealed that whatever official consultations had taken place had not been conducted through the heads of missions. The Ambassador concluded that although Commonwealth governments did not wish to be embroiled in European quarrels, they were still sensitive to the attraction of international ideals such as collective security, international law and justice. Given a different outlook in Downing Street: 'It would not perhaps be impossible for British Ministers to unite these different viewpoints into a common policy'.[60]

British decision making was not affected by diplomatic pressures from Paris. In meetings of the Cabinet Foreign Policy Committee, Halifax showed a different side of himself, complaining that the 'the French were never ready to face up to realities, they delighted in vain words and protestations'.[61] Without consulting Paris and without full benefit of military advice, the Cabinet decided that Czechoslovakia was indefensible and that no guarantee should be given to France for the defence of her ally. It was agreed that France should be asked to join with Britain in bringing pressure to bear on Prague to reach a speedy settlement of the Sudeten problem. As one analyst of British policy writes: 'the government intended to freeze France's hopes of British military help, not merely in the case of war fought on behalf of Czechoslovakia but in the case of any German aggression on the Western Frontier; and they wished to induce her to betray the alliances freely made in 1925 and 1935'.[62]

A formal statement of the British position was communicated to the French on 24 March, and on the same day Chamberlain made an announcement in the Commons. In the British memorandum transmitted to Paris it was recognised that France had commitments to Czechoslovakia and would fulfil them if the need arose. After this tactful assertion of French responsibility for her ally, the extent of Britain's commitment to France was then carefully de-limited. Britain would 'come to the assistance of France in the event of an unprovoked act of aggression on her by Germany' but 'could certainly not go so far as to state' what her action 'might be in the event of an attack upon Czechoslovakia by Germany'.[63] In short, if France fulfilled her obligations to Czechoslovakia she could not count on British help. At this point the note of uncertainty, already sounded by Halifax, was repeated: 'Where peace and war' were concerned 'legal obligations' were not alone involved and 'the inexorable pressure of facts' might well prove 'more powerful than formal pronouncements'. Various practical arguments were adduced. A guarantee for Czechoslovakia would have no value because as a result of the *Anschluss* the heart of the country lay open to attack. Even if Britain went to war she could offer in the early stages no more than the 'economic pressure' of blockade, 'slow in operation and tardy in its effects'. Britain was militarily unprepared: 'Quite frankly, the moment is unfavourable, and our plans are not sufficiently advanced'. Finally, the pill was sweetened with an offer of air staff talks.

It might be argued that the French, as in the month before the *Anschluss,* were simply going through the motions, perhaps intent already on thrusting the responsibility for Czechoslovakia on to Britain. French ministers, thought Chamberlain, would be glad 'to find some method to relieve them of their engagements'.[64] This argument is certainly a plausible one in respect of the Daladier government which took office on 10 April. Yet the evidence suggests that in the week or so following the occupation of Austria, the Blum government genuinely strove to help Czechoslovakia. In Paris in mid-March, as in London, the formulation of policy still possessed some fluidity and no hard and fast decisions had been reached.

The *Anschluss* had caused much greater alarm in Paris than in London. National pride had been wounded and the solemn assertions of diplomatic pledges were designed in part to restore self-confidence. Policy-making was complicated by the fact that the annexation of Austria was seen not only as a threat to Czechoslovakia but as a challenge to France's whole position as a great power, especially her Mediterranean interests. On 14 March, the Deuxième Bureau interpreted events in Austria as confirmation of previous suspicions that the two dictators had come to an agreement on the basis of central and eastern Europe for Germany, and the Mediterranean for Italy.[65] The General Staff had for some months regarded North Africa and the Mediterranean as the most likely theatre of war, reported the British Air Attaché in Paris.[66] The Air Attaché quoted Massigli as saying that 'Italy was now bound hand and foot to the German chariot', though he 'begged that this should not be passed on to London'. Léger, too, was 'absolutely convinced' that 'there was a definite understanding between Germany and Italy' for division of spoils.[67] Cadogan commented: 'The French are inclined to be hysterical where Italy is concerned'.[68] French fears were not entirely unfounded. The Italians, as the Foreign Office knew, had been concentrating troops in Libya, and the rapid advance of Franco's forces on the Aragon front towards Barcelona in the second half of March endangered France's Mediterranean flank.

On 15 March the Permanent Committee of National Defence met to consider two questions: firstly what help could be given to Prague in the event of a German attack? Secondly, could help be given to the Spanish Republic?[69] Meeting under Daladier's chairmanship, the committee brought together Blum, Paul-Boncour, Gamelin, Marshal Pétain, Léger, the Navy and Air Ministers and their chiefs of staff. Paul-Boncour explained that the British had countered French requests for support for Czechoslovakia with the question: what in effect can you do to help? Daladier replied that France could not help her ally directly: 'the only aid' that could be offered was 'indirect...by mobilising, so as to pin down on our frontiers German forces'. Gamelin added that mobilisation could be followed by an attack but since such attacks would be against fortified areas, lengthy operations would be involved. Under this barrage of pessimism Blum clutched at one last hope: 'Russia would intervene'. Coldly Gamelin disposed of the Soviet alliance. The transport of troops through Poland and Rumania presented serious difficulties and Soviet mobilisation might alienate Warsaw and Bucharest. Bleakly Blum summed up the discussion: French mobilisation and an offensive would tie down German forces in the west but Germany could not be prevented from attacking Czechoslovakia.

However the major part of the meeting was devoted to a study of the possibilities of French intervention in Spain. The idealism of Blum and his foreign minister elicited a biting comment from Daladier: 'one would have to be blind not to see that intervention in Spain would unleash a general war'. Léger confirmed that Germany and Italy would consider French intervention as a *casus belli*. Desperately Blum cast about for some way of helping his Spanish brethren. Perhaps France, he suggested, might intensify her supplies of arms without directly intervening? Gamelin immediately killed the idea. Such action, he said, would only weaken France's own military readiness without offering decisive help to the Spanish government.

The meeting of 15 March confirmed the impotence of France. As Léger put it: 'France could only react to events, she could not take the initiative'.[70] Nothing, it seemed, could be done to save either Prague or Madrid without the danger of a lengthy war. Moreover, intervention in Spain would antagonise British opinion and France could not risk a major war without the certainty of British assistance. The 15 March meeting leaves no doubt that the General Staff had not prepared any plans for the defence of the eastern allies. The weakness of the air force, a source of growing anxiety during the previous six months, was openly avowed on 15 March by General Vuillemin, Chief of Air Staff. He admitted that in a Franco-German war the air force would be wiped out in fifteen days. At the same meeting the Air Minister, Guy la Chambre, conceded that the rate of aircraft production was only 40 a month.

From the record of the 15th March conference it is clear that Blum and Paul-Boncour were sincerely anxious to help Czechoslovakia. And no final decision was taken on the 15th. 'If the government has decided to commit itself fully to the support of Czechoslovakia,' wrote Gamelin on 16 March, the British could be told that Franco-British intervention on behalf of Czechoslovakia would also bring in Poland and the Little Entente. The strategic outlook, he said, would not be unfavourable since Germany was not yet ready for a European war. Should Italy enter the fray, Britain and France together could soon defeat her. Even if Czechoslovakia was in difficulties at the outset of hostilities 'all would be settled at the peace treaty'. Then, almost as an afterthought, Gamelin added: 'as regards the present weakness of our air force, I consider that there is no need to acknowledge it to England'.[71] This was cold comfort indeed to the government and far from strengthening the French case Gamelin's draft reply would have been grist to the British mill. The reference to the restoration of Czechoslovakia at a peace conference would have been seized on as a tacit admission that Prague was a lost cause from the start. Newton, Minister in Prague, had already reminded London that 'should war come...all that we could hope to achieve would be to restore after a lengthy struggle a status quo which had already proved unacceptable and which, even if restored, would probably prove unworkable'.[72] As for the deficiencies of the air force, this was an open secret in London.

In the circumstances, the decision lay with London and every day that passed without a final statement of British policy diminished the credibility of French policy. Blum's political opponents were intriguing all the time. The French prime minister soon realised the hopelessness of his position. The confirmation of alliance pledges in his ministerial declaration to the Chamber on 17 March omitted to mention Czechoslovakia by name, though in a draft shown to Phipps, Czechoslovakia had been included.[73] The Commons statement of 24 March and the memorandum communicated to Paul-Boncour on the same day effectively extinguished any hopes of enlisting British help.

In eastern Europe the outlook was equally gloomy. The disintegration of the eastern alliances was all too painfully apparent. On 5 April, Paul-Boncour summoned to the Quai d'Orsay France's representatives in Moscow, Warsaw, Prague and Bucharest.[74] They were asked to say what help France could expect from eastern Europe. Léon Noel, Ambassador in Warsaw, stressed that Poland would only support France in the event of a direct German attack in the west. Beck considered Czechoslovakia to be unstable and the Polish press had just started a campaign against Prague. The Warsaw press was filled with extracts from French newspapers saying that France would not fight for the Czechs. What, then, asked Paul-Boncour, could France do to win over Poland? The wisest course, replied the Ambassador, was to convey an impression of military and political firmness. Rumanian friendship for France was still strong, reported Adrien Thierry, Minister in Bucharest, but Rumania would not march if Germany attacked Czechoslovakia. As for relations with the Soviet Union, 'for a Rumanian peasant, German domination' was 'preferable to Russian control'.

Robert Coulondre, Ambassador in Moscow, pointed out that Soviet military power was considerable and sizable forces were 'massed on the Soviet frontier' but the problem was one of transit facilities across Poland and Rumania. Paul-Boncour suggested that Moscow might pay for her passage across Rumania by recognition of Bessarabia, formerly part of the Tsarist empire. But the Czechoslovak government, he thought, would be better placed to put this question to Moscow. Prague could also ask for details of Soviet military help. At this point, Victor de Lacroix, Minister in Prague, intervened to say that he 'believed' the question of Soviet military aid had been examined by the Soviet and Czechoslovak General Staffs. Evidently nothing was known for certain. It was agreed that Prague should be advised to ascertain from Moscow the nature and extent of Soviet assistance. Poland should be asked for a statement of her intentions in the event of a German attack on Czechoslovakia. Lastly, it was agreed that Franco-Rumanian relations would be re-animated by accelerating deliveries of war material.

Nothing was done to revive relations with the Soviet Union. Litvinov stated frankly on 23 March: 'France has no confidence in the Soviet Union and the Soviet Union has no confidence in France'.[75] Though Blum had courageously opened preliminary staff talks in the autumn of 1936, the attempt was not repeated in March 1938. Of course, time was lacking but in any case the government's precarious position in the Chambers excluded any contacts. The Soviet proposal of 18 March for a conference of Britain, France, the United States and the Soviet Union to discuss measures to prevent further aggression was sympathetically received in Paris but rebuffed in London. Significantly, at the Quai d'Orsay conference of 5 April the subject of direct Franco-Soviet military contacts was not raised. France was not even willing to act as a middleman. The Czechs were advised to make their own enquiries in Moscow.

The first week in April brought a major change in Franco-Italian relations. On 6 April, Paul-Boncour told an Italian emissary, Puricelli, President of the Milan Fair, that France wanted a settlement and would send a negotiator to Rome to discuss the question of recognition of the Italian conquest of Ethiopia.[76] Such a *volte-face* seems surprising given the declared hostility of Blum and senior Quai d'Orsay officials to Italy. Yet the initiative came from Blum. According to Bonnet, the prime minister telephoned him, saying he wished to re-establish good relations and offering him the Rome embassy.[77] It is unlikely that French ministers had undergone a change of heart towards Italy but they were under increasing pressure to open negotiations. The Right clamoured for a *rapprochement* and on 16 March Laval called in the Senate foreign affairs committee for the restoration of relations. But the main factor was the fact that Anglo-Italian negotiations were nearing completion and a continued refusal to talk to the *Duce* would adversely affect French interests in the Mediterranean and Middle East.

British ministers would neither receive French colleagues nor go to Paris but two distinguished statesmen crossed the Channel to bolster French morale. Lloyd George went to Paris on 21-22 March, followed by Winston Churchill on 26-28 March. Lloyd George's visits to the tomb of Napoleon at the Invalides and to the unknown warrior were received with amused irony by the French Right which found the belated display of affection for France a little unconvincing. Phipps endeavoured to destroy any good that might come of the visits. Léger was told to let everyone know that Lloyd George 'represents very little more than himself in the England of today'.[78] Over dinner Corbin reassured Chamberlain that there was no possibility of the French government having been misled by anything Lloyd George might have said since 'he did not count for anything in France at present'.[79] Churchill met a host of personalities, including Blum, Herriot, Flandin, Gamelin, and impressed on them the need for immediate staff talks and a solid alliance. Again, Phipps warned that Churchill spoke only for himself.

No prescience was required to predict the direction of events. In a secret note of 29 March Gamelin submitted to Daladier his prognosis for the coming months.[80] Short of an internal crisis in Germany or a sudden *volte-face* by Italy, Hitler, said Gamelin, would settle the Czech question and consolidate his control over eastern Europe by winning over Poland. He would then turn against France, attacking through Switzerland and probably Belgium. As for France's obligations to Czechoslovakia, the German Ambassador wired Berlin on 8 April: 'a diminution, either open or concealed, of French obligations . . . will take place, and thus give rise to the gradual isolation of that country'.[81] In a memorandum dated 9 April Paul-Boncour replied to the British communication of 24 March. Without attempting to overturn the political and military arguments marshalled against Czechoslovakia, the French minister agreed that 'nothing should be left undone to eliminate occasions of friction or conflict' and France was 'ready unreservedly' to co-operate to this end.[82]

Thus France surrendered to her British partner. Would a strong stand by French ministers in the week following the *Anschluss* have modified British policy? Perhaps, but the French government would have had to be a stable one, backed by a large parliamentary majority. French policy was not made in a vacuum. Given the domestic constraints Blum and Paul-Boncour could offer no more than a flicker of resistance. Blum had too many troubles. He was terribly broken by the death of his second wife and in no state to ride out the political storm. The strike movement which had been renewed in the autumn of 1937 presented a grave threat. In March there were sit-in strikes in Citroën and Panhard factories. Industrial action was unashamedly aimed at influencing the government's foreign policy. The Left wanted to save Czechoslovakia in Spain. 30,000 workers of the Paris 'Red Belt' suburb of Boulogne-Billancourt passed a unanimous resolution calling for intervention in Spain 'in order to finally defeat Hitler and Mussolini and assure world peace'. Speculation about the duration of the Blum ministry started almost from its inception. Laval claimed to be working in the Senate to 'demolish' the government and begged the British not to do anything to bolster up Blum.[83] The temptation to make literary capital out of the crisis was too much for Phipps. He wrote on 22 March:

> We are all praying for its fall, but the franc remains annoyingly steady. As Caillaux put it yesterday 'the franc remains steady because the government is expected to fall, and the government does not fall because the franc remains steady'.[84]

French diplomats were acutely aware of the damage caused by the ministerial crises. On 12 March Corbin wrote: 'I have no need to say that the establishment in France of a solid and lasting government would greatly help to dispel the indecision and hesitation of the British Cabinet'; on the 13th: 'I cannot conceal. . .the unfortunate impression produced in British political circles by the impossibility of forming in France a Cabinet of national union, despite the lesson which Germany's *coup* has given us'.[85] In a personal letter of 17 March to Paul-Boncour Roger Cambon, Chargé d'Affaires in London, wrote:

> . . . Our political credit sinks each day. . .
> The declarations of Neville Chamberlain to parliament would be in fact quite different if our country held its place. Yesterday morning, in the Cabinet, our opponents asserted that to go into Europe with a firm policy at the side of France would be pure folly. . .[86]

Judging from the tone of the press, Blum and Benes had few friends.

The *Anschluss* marked the start of a vicious press campaign against the government and the Czech alliance. The mood of the campaign was exemplified in an article which appeared in the *Marseilles-Matin,* quoted without criticism in the Paris press:

> The French nation is not cannon fodder. No, M. Blum and M. Boncour, France will fight only for her own independence, and you shall never have the French Army at your disposal to sacrifice it to interests which are not French, interests of eastern peoples . . .

One of the instigators of this offensive was believed to be Sir Charles Mendl, the British Press Attaché.[88] It would be wrong to conclude that such opinions were representative of the mass of the public. Given a longer life and using the traditional levers of influence over the press, the government might have created a strong pro-Czech lobby.

On 8 April, the Senate drove Blum from office for a second time. Matters came to a head over the Prime Minister's request for full powers to carry out financial reforms, inspired in part by the ideas of Keynes. The government proposed a mild system of exchange control, also revaluation of the gold reserves of the Bank of France, tighter controls on stocks and shares in order to prevent tax evasion, surveillance of industrial cartels and monopolies. All this was too much for the senators to stomach and the proposals were thrown out by a majority of 214 to 47. Tired and dejected by the struggle of the previous weeks Blum may have deliberately provided the Senate with the opportunity to overthrow him. On 14 April Winston Churchill, writing 'as an old minister now in retirement' sent Blum a friendly word:

> My dear Monsieur Blum,
>   I have thought much about you in these anxious and trying days, and I feel bound to express to you the gratitude which so many English people cherish towards you for the great and real advance in the understanding between our two countries which marked your memorable Premierships. It is not for a foreigner, however friendly, to meddle in French politics. But I have never seen the good feeling between Britain and France so strong as during your tenure of power . . .[89]

For Churchill the wish was father to the thought. Whatever the feelings of 'English people', official relations between the two governments were frosty indeed.

PART TWO
Personnel and Machinery
of
Policy Making

Chapter 6

Enter Daladier and Bonnet

On 10 April 1938, the Radical, Edouard Daladier, formed a new cabinet composed largely of fellow Radicals, with a sprinkling of independent Socialists and some rightwingers. His administration, with only minor changes, lasted until March 1940. He appointed a fellow Radical, Georges Bonnet, as Foreign Minister. These two men were to lead France first to Munich and then into the Second World War. The physiognomy of each man complemented the other. The stockily built, bull-necked, shortish Daladier looked so much like a bundled-up Teddy Bear, with a disposition which often bordered upon the bearish, the dominant impression was one of stolid, purposeful strength; Bonnet had a taller build with a prominent nose and a mobile foxy countenance, giving a general impression of restlessness and subtle manoeuvrability.

Daladier, born at Carpentras, near Avignon, in 1884, was a few years older than Bonnet. As a baker's son, his was a more plebian origin than that of the foreign minister. He progressed by scholarships from the local *lycée* to Lyons—where one of his teachers was Edouard Herriot—thence to the *Ecole Normale* and the Sorbonne. He prided himself on being a man of the people, saying: *'Je suis sorti du peuple'*, meaning, as an unkind critic said, he was proud to be no longer there. Unlike Bonnet, his early career was academic. When war came in 1914 he was lecturer in history at the *Lycée Condorcet* in Paris. During the First World War he fought at Verdun, rising from the ranks to become a captain by 1918. After the armistice, he joined the Radical Socialists as a protégé of Herriot and was elected deputy for Vaucluse in 1919, a constituency which he represented until 1940.

Daladier, in company with Georges Bonnet, Camille Chautemps, Henri Queuille and Albert Sarraut, was one of the 'Big Five' members of French Radicalism between the wars. Each of the twenty three administrations formed between 1930 and 1939 numbered at least one of these politicians The *Cartel des Gauches* victory of 1924 brought Daladier and Bonnet into the public eye, however Daladier's ascent in the Radical hierarchy was much swifter than that of his running mate. He challenged Herriot for the presidency of the party and the *guerre des deux Edouards* became a byword in the politics of the time. In 1927 he won the Radical throne and retained it until 1932. In that year he became War Minister and in January 1933 Prime Minister.

The Stavisky scandal of January-February 1934 almost ruined his career. On 29 January 1934 he succeeded Chautemps and tried to form a ministry of all the talents capable of riding the storm of anti-parliamentary agitation. The key issue was the position of Jean Chiappe, the Paris Prefect of Police. The Left demanded his head, alleging his involvement in the scandal. The Right insisted on his retention in office. The immediate measures taken by Daladier savoured more of comic opera than of statesmanship. Over the telephone he offered the Prefect the post of Resident General in Morocco. Refusing to be kicked upstairs in this way. Chiappe remonstrated with the Prime Minister. According to Daladier, the Prefect threatened to start a riot. Chiappe's own version of the conversation was that he had merely said he would be out on the street. The comic element was heightened when the Prime Minister transferred the head of the *Sûreté Générale* to the *Comédie Francaise*, whose director had been dismissed because a production of Coriolanus was thought to have provoked Royalist demonstrations. Though Daladier had second thoughts and cancelled these changes, the public was far from pacified. Street demonstrations culminated in the 6 February riots which threatened to engulf the Chamber of Deputies. Daladier ordered the police to open fire and some seventeen people were killed. Within hours, popular indignation had driven him from office and he was branded 'the executioner'.

The way back to office started on the Left. Though Daladier led his party into the *Front Populaire*, there was little conviction in his alliance with Socialists and Communists. He was photographed raising a clenched fist and embracing the Communist leader Maurice Thorez but for him the people's flag was palest pink. He advised against staff talks with the Soviet Union in September 1936 and claimed to be a most determined enemy of Communism.[1] Léon Blum appointed him Deputy Prime Minister in the first Popular Front ministry of June 1936. He survived Blum's fall in June 1937 and continued in office under Chautemps with whom he was politically much more in sympathy. In March 1940, Paul Reynaud supplanted him as Prime Minister but he continued as Minister of National Defence and War and was Foreign Minister for a few weeks from May-June 1940. After the defeat, Laval claimed that Daladier had taken the initiative in suggesting the overthrow of Reynaud's government and its replacement by a Daladier-Laval ministry. The story cannot be corroborated and seems unlikely, to say the least.[2]

The Vichy government of Marshal Pétain first imprisoned Daladier and then put him on trial at Riom in February 1942 charging him with responsibility for the defeat of 1940. His able and well-documented defence proved such an embarrassment to the regime that the trial was suspended and never concluded. Daladier was deported to Germany for the duration of the war. Freed in 1945, the *taureau* of Vaucluse, as he was popularly known, returned to the political arena. Re-elected in 1946 for his old constituency, he became a year later president of a new Radical group, the *Rassemblement des Gauches Républicains.* In 1957-58 he was again president of the Radical party.

Despite these honours he held no significant place in postwar France. Some old familiar faces of the Third Republic — Auriol, Blum, Herriot,

Reynaud, Ramadier — returned to play a part in the early years of the Fourth Republic but Daladier was handicapped by his political record. In 1946, the Communists, whom Daladier had hounded and locked up in September 1939, contested the validity of his election as deputy for Vaucluse.[3] The former leader still retained his old fire. 'This old sergeant-major of a politician', observed one of those who listened to the persuasive defence of his Munich policy, 'practises eloquence with greater aplomb than our present raw recruits'.[4] But eloquence was not enough. Communists and younger Radicals continued to vilify him. Radicalism, too, was in decline, and slowly faded from the postwar political map, reviving only for a brief period in the mid-1950s under the inspiration of Pierre Mendès-France. Having pronounced against the constitution of the Fifth Republic in 1958, Daladier resigned the presidency of his party. Defeated in the elections of November 1958, he retired from politics and devoted his last years to writing his memoirs. He died in 1970 the last of the four heads of government who signed the Munich agreement of 30 September 1938.

Daladier cut a rather tragic figure. Until the Stavisky scandal, he was thought to have had the makings of a strong man who would reinvigorate an etiolated Republic. In the early 1930s the Young Turks of Radicalism — Gaston Bergery, Pierre Cot, Guy la Chambre, Pierre Dominique, Eugène Frot — looked to him for dynamic leadership. Bertrand de Jouvenel confessed in March 1934:

> There were many of us in the party and outside who considered that once in power Daladier would be capable of taking vigorous action to restore the prestige of the state.[5]

His mismanagement of the 6 February riots disfigured the image, which he had sedulously cultivated, of the strong, silent man. A severity of manner remained with him. 'In newsreels', it was said, 'he always looked like the chief mourner of his own country's funeral'.[6] Memories were short, however, and by the spring of 1938 he was again seen as a strong man who would restore order and authority.

Unlike the men of his native Midi, Daladier was a man of few words and silence lent him an air of wisdom. Unfriendly observers were quick to point out that he was silent because he had nothing to say. A widower, he lived modestly with his two sons and a sister. His friend, the Marquise de Crussol, provided a link with Parisian social life. In contrast to the Comtesse Hélène de Portes, mistress of Paul Reynaud, she does not seem to have interfered much in Daladier's political life, though her friends had access to the Prime Minister.[7] Parisians could not resist a play of wit at the expense of the two ladies. The Comtesse de Portes was nicknamed 'La Porte à Côté'— the side door, while the other, the Marquise de Crussol, better known by her maiden name of Bézier, because of her family's sardine canning business, was described as 'La Sardine qui s'est Crue Sole' — the sardine which took itself for a sole.

Gossip had it that Daladier drank too much and André Geraud, who under the pen name of Pertinax was one of the best known and most well-informed journalists of the period, spread stories of the Prime Minister being worse for drink at the conference in Munich in September 1938. The stories may well have had some substance for when British and French ministers met in Paris in November 1938 the British delegation noted that Daladier certainly looked as if he was 'drinking heavily' and much the worse for wear.[8]

In Paris a taciturn nature and a Napoleonic cast of feature were distinct assets; in London the French leader was not judged over-impressive. 'Compared to our own Ministers who were resplendent in stars and ribbons', recorded Harold Nicolson in April 1937, 'he looked like some Iberian merchant visiting the Roman Senate'.[9] An earlier visit to London in 1935 had left an unfortunate impression. The Prime Minister, Ramsay MacDonald and the Foreign Secretary Sir John Simon, solemn and dignified, were waiting to meet Daladier in one of the French embassy drawing rooms. Daladier and one of his colleagues were late. 'In the hall downstairs they argued noisily and at length, then they came up to meet the British without even throwing away the butts of their cigarettes'.[10]

The French Prime Minister was not in fact the man of destiny so many had believed him to be, on the contrary those who knew him well considered him to have an irresolute personality with an inherent self-distrust: Daladier 'ce n'est pas le taureau de Vaucluse c'est la vache hésitation' was one verdict.[11] After meeting the French minister at the Franco-British conference in April 1938, Neville Chamberlain did not think him 'so strong as his reputation'.[12] Moods of self-doubt fettered his powers of initiative and decision; after being talked into making up his mind he would go back upon it or he would make himself inaccessible to advisers like Gamelin, Chief of the General Staff, who demanded a ruling from him.

Bonnet was born in 1889 into a well-to-do legal family of the Dordogne, the country of Montaigne and La Boétie. After studying at the *Ecole libre des sciences politiques,* the nursery of the Republic's governing elite, he went as an *auditeur* to the *Conseil d'état.* His marriage in 1911 to Odette Pelletan, grand-daughter of Eugene Pelletan, one of the founding fathers of the Republic, gave him a place in a leading political family. Active war service in 1914 interrupted his civil career. In 1918 Clemenceau appointed him director of demobilization services. A spell followed as one of the secretaries to the French delegation at the Paris Peace Conference. In the Left wing triumph of 1924 Bonnet won a parliamentary seat, having failed to secure election in 1919. His constituency was the Dordogne, virtually the rural heart of France and solidly Radical voting since the 1880s.

In the Chamber he soon distinguished himself as a financial specialist. In contrast to some of his more famous contemporaries such as Blum, Reynaud and Tardieu who campaigned for major reforms. Bonnet was no visionary. The end of the war witnessed a spate of social and economic criticism and in *Lettres à un Bourgeois de 1914* (1919) Bonnet called for the renewal and modernisation of French society but in the 1920s no more was heard of reform. Paul Painlevé took him under his wing and he first cut his political teeth as a junior minister in Painlevé's government of 1925. Though out of office in 1926, he was believed 'to have considerable influence' with the government of the day.[13] He again held office as Minister of Commerce and Trade in Chautemps's ministry of 1930.

For Daladier, the 1930s were a political golden age; save for the years 1934-36 he was in office continuously from 1932 to 1940. Bonnet was less fortunate. Having climbed the middle slopes, the summit eluded him. He was Minister of Finance in the Daladier government of January-November 1933 and played a leading part in London defending the gold standard at the London Economic Conference. His main achievement was the creation of a National Lottery. The Stavisky affair cut short his advance. He was accused of having lunched with Stavisky at the Lausanne Conference in July 1932 and of having employed one of the swindler's lawyers. The attack failed. It was proved that the Minister had not employed the lawyer nor had he met Stavisky at Lausanne. Yet enough mud had been thrown for some of it to stick. Bonnet's reputation, like that of Chautemps, was tarnished. While Bonnet was innocent of any complicity in the affair, his characteristic evasiveness encouraged critics to think the worst. During Doumergue's government of February 1934, Bonnet became president of the Chamber commission on constitutional reform, and opposed major changes.

The *Front Populaire* swept the Radicals back to power as partners in Blum's government of June 1936. But not all Radicals welcomed the new alliance. Bonnet's political standpoint, more to the right of centre than that of Daladier, made him chary of the combination of Communists, Radicals and Socialists. In the Chamber he led a group of about eighteen like-minded Radicals in opposition to Blum's financial policy. He was too clever an opponent to be disregarded and Blum decided to muzzle him with the offer of France's Washington embassy. Although he did not speak English, Bonnet accepted the offer in December 1936 and took up his duties on 16 January 1937. It was not his first excursion in diplomacy; in the 1920s he served with the League of Nations secretariat in Geneva, and in 1927 Briand entrusted him with a mission to the German Foreign Minister, Stresemann. In 1932 he represented France at the Lausanne Conference. Though Bonnet accepted the offer of the Washington embassy with some reluctance since his main interest was in domestic politics, he quickly, by his own account, proved himself *persona grata*. Other accounts suggest that as Ambassador he did not leave a good impression.[14]

With the fall of Blum's ministry in June 1937 Bonnet's star took a sharp upward turn. Though he had been in Washington only a few months, Chautemps offered him the post of Finance Minister and the Ambassador returned home post-haste. In January 1938 the premiership came tantalisingly close. On 14 January Chautemps resigned and President Lebrun asked Bonnet to form a new government.[15] He provisionally accepted the invitation, promising a definite reply the next day. Friends advised him to form a ministry at once and to have the list of ministers published before the parliamentary committees convened and intrigues were set on foot. Bonnet drew up a list which included old friends such as

Joseph Caillaux, Henry Berenger, Lucien Lamoureux, Paul Marchandeau, Emile Roche and Pierre Etienne Flandin—all predominantly conservative in outlook. The Socialists refused to support an adversary of the *Front Populaire,* even Bonnet's fellow Radicals were doubtful and divided. 'During voting', noted a colleague, Bonnet 'could not prevent himself getting up from his chair to count the raised hands'.[16] Sceptical of his chances, he asked Lebrun to promise a dissolution of the Chambers, if the vote in the Chamber of Deputies should go against him. The attempt of the monarchist President MacMahon to replace a republican Chamber in 1877 had ended in his resignation. Lebrun did not want to disturb the last year of his septennate. Bonnet was hardly popular. The *Populaire* talked of the 'impossible Bonnet Cabinet' and, under the heading 'The failure of M. Bonnet', the Paris correspondent of *The Times* wrote on 16 January:

> An ambitious politician, personally extremely unpopular, and with little follow-ing even in his own Radical party. With his contacts with the banks and big business he symbolised in the most blatant manner the political reaction against the *Front Populaire.* . .[17]

Bonnet failed, though he had the satisfaction throughout his life of signing himself 'former prime minister'.

Bonnet was Minister of State in the fourth Chautemps government formed on 18 January 1938. A measure of his growing influence can be gauged from the fact that following Chautemps's resignation on 10 March he was one of four ministers, including Daladier, who met in the afternoon of 11 March to decide on possible counter measures against German action in Austria.[18] When Blum succeeded in forming a new administration on 13 March he again tried to eliminate a dangerous opponent by offer-ing Bonnet the Rome embassy.[19] After asking Laval's advice, Bonnet accepted the offer but the ministry was too short lived to bring about an improvement in relations with Rome. Bonnet did nothing to smooth the path of the Popular Front cabinet. While Blum and Paul-Boncour reaffirmed France's loyalty to her treaty commitments, Bonnet confided to Bullitt 'his personal and confidential opinion' that without 'a promise of support from Great Britain it would be impossible for France to go to Czechoslovakia's aid. Publicly he would have to state the opposite just as others now in office stated the opposite'.[20] On 25 March the Foreign Office learnt that Bonnet was anxious to go to London to meet one or two 'influential people', including the Foreign Secretary.[21] Halifax was advised not to see the former minister because he was known to be intriguing against Blum.

The summit of Bonnet's career came on 10 April 1938 when Daladier appointed him Foreign Minister. The move to the Quai d'Orsay was a welcome change from the Ministry of Finance in the *Rue de Rivoli,* where he had spent so much of his career. His tenure of the foreign ministry lasted almost eighteen months, a reasonable record by the standards of the time. On 13 September 1939 Daladier remodelled his Cabinet and Bonnet was shunted to the Ministry of Justice, *place Vendôme.* When in

March 1940 Paul Reynaud replaced Daladier as Prime Minister Bonnet lost his post in the ministerial reshuffle.[22]

With the French collapse in June 1940 Bonnet seems for a while to have followed Laval. Laval's political following at this time included a number of the former foreign minister's allies — Gaston Bergery, Anatole de Monzie and Jean Montigny. And the former minister may well have been a member of the delegation led by Laval which on 21 June stormed Lebrun's office and helped to bully the weak-kneed president into revoking his decision to leave for Algeria.[23] As deputies gathered in Vichy for the decisive parliamentary session on 10 July which ended the Third Republic, Bonnet was counted as 'a supporter of Laval'.[24] Hitler was now master of France and on 31 July, Bonnet journeyed to Paris in order to assure the German occupation authorities of 'his personal readiness for future collaboration'.[25] Four months later, accompanied by his former private secretary, Jules Henry, the ex-minister visited the American Chargé d'Affaires 'to, plead the cause of peace and appeasement'.[26]

The Vichy regime did not provide any pasture for the politicians of the Third Republic. Bonnet held no political office, save membership of the 'National Council' created by Flandin in December 1940, but the council never met. Bonnet's own account of his semi-retirement at Perigueux, in the Dordogne, stressed his support for the resistance. He claimed to have intervened with Laval to secure the release of Herriot from house arrest in 1942, and to have successfully defended a Frenchman accused of shooting a German officer.[27] German records tell a different story. In February 1941 he appears to have confided to the Gestapo his hopes of joining Laval in a new Vichy cabinet to replace the one recently formed by Admiral Darlan.[28] Early in June 1943, the Germans received word that Bonnet was thinking of leaving France to join opposition groups abroad. As if to scotch such rumours, the former minister appeared in Vichy, fulminating against dissident generals and politicians. Later, he assured the Germans that he had never contemplated leaving France. In the autumn of 1943, Bonnet and Albert Chichery, a former president of the Radicals, were alleged to be involved in a plan to prevent General de Gaulle assuming power in the event of a successful allied invasion.[29] Whatever the truth of these stories, it would seem that Bonnet's retirement was much more active than might appear from his memoirs.

Intrigues and manoeuvres of one kind or another enforced a hasty exit. The ex-minister believed his life was threatened from all sides — Vichy *Milice*, Communist *Maquis* and the Gestapo. The collaborator of 1940 had become a *Résistant*. Indeed, if his own testimony is to be believed Bonnet was virtually running an intelligence and resistance network of his own. On 5 April 1944, under cover of accompanying his wife for urgent medical attention, he left for Switzerland. From the safety of neutral Switzerland he claimed to have sent regular reports to Robert Murphy in Algiers, who was political adviser to General Eisenhower.[30] Asylum in Swizerland turned into a lengthy exile, for legal proceedings were opened against him in France and the Provisional Government refused him a passport. Only in March 1950 was he able to return. The enforced leisure was put to good use in writing two volumes of memoirs.[31] Friends who had played a more active part in Vichy were less fortunate and had to suffer the full force of the *Epuration*. Paul Baudouin and Pierre Etienne Flandin, who had been members of Vichy governments, were tried by the High Court.

After returning to France in 1950, Bonnet slowly rebuilt his political base in the Dordogne, proving himself, in the words of a friend, 'an electoral machine'.[32] The obstacle to his return to national politics was the Constitution of the Fourth Republic which declared persons sentenced to 'national disgrace' for their wartime activities ineligible for election. This provision excluded Bonnet until an amnesty in 1953 allowed him to stand for election. By 1956 he had recovered his fief and was again deputy for the Dordogne. If his aim was to stage a political comeback as Blum, Herriot and Reynaud had done, he was deluded. Memories of Munich were too strong. The Fifth Republic had nothing to offer a veteran of the Third, though seemingly Bonnet did not despair of recognition, if only through a fleeting handshake. One observer of the scene in the National Assembly after the investiture of General de Gaulle as President of the Fifth Republic in June 1958 wrote:

> And during an interval . . . countless deputies trying to get sufficiently close to the government bench to be able to shake the great man's hand. In particular, Georges Bonnet was seen manoeuvring his way to where de Gaulle sat and managing to extract from him a handshake; one observer said it was 'a very short and dry one', another that 'it looked as though de Gaulle had touched a slug, so quick was he in withdrawing his hand'.[33]

But the author of this description, Alexander Werth, Paris correspondent of the *Manchester Guardian* in the 1930s, was no fan of Bonnet. In truth, the former minister was better received than might have been expected. In May 1961 he dedicated to de Gaulle his book *Le Quai d'Orsay Sous Trois Républiques* and received an appreciative letter of thanks in the General's own hand which said that as Foreign Minister in 1938-39 Bonnet 'eminently contributed to the preservation of the prestige and future of France'.[34]

Some politicians, like old soldiers, never die, they only fade away. Re-elected in 1962 and again in 1967 Bonnet continued a political career, which, in successfully spanning four regimes, rivalled the Vicar of Bray and Talleyrand for sheer doggedness. Daladier lost his seat in 1958, Reynaud in 1962. Of those who had held senior office in the interwar governments, only Bonnet remained in active politics. The end came in the elections of June 1968 when he lost his seat by a narrow margin to a Gaullist candidate. Ironically, his defeat was due primarily to the Communists who did not vote for him as strongly as they had done in 1967.[35] He outlived Daladier and Reynaud and died in 1973.

Many politicians attract more than their fair share of enemies and critics, but Bonnet has been singularly unfortunate. 'Clever, but ambitious and an intriguer', considered Neville Chamberlain who had known him since 1932. 'The quintessence of defeatism' Churchill called him. Pertinax who knew the leaders of the 1930s as well as anyone considered him incapable of following any line save that 'of least resistance'. He was 'without morality', wrote Gamelin, Chief of the General Staff. 'His long nose', declared Georges Mandel, 'sniffs danger and responsibility from afar. He will hide under any flat stone to avoid it'.[36]

The Foreign Office was united almost to a man in condemnation of the French foreign minister. Surprisingly, however, Halifax was prepared to give Bonnet the benefit of the doubt. In December 1938 Oliver Harvey, the Foreign Secretary's private secretary, dismissed the French minister as 'a public danger to his own country and to ours'. But Halifax commented on reports in April 1939 that Bonnet was about to lose his post: 'we have got on well together, although I know that he is not everybody's cup of tea'. In December 1939 the Paris embassy reported Bonnet as saying that he would have preferred the war to have been postponed until 1940 or 1941, though he did not doubt the ultimate victory of the western powers. This despatch elicited a chorus of criticism from senior officials. Vansittart was particularly venomous: 'As to M. Bonnet he had better trust to time and oblivion rather than to coloured self-defence. He did a lot of really dirty work in 1938 . . . if I ever had to play cards with M. Bonnet again I would always run through the pack first, just to make sure that the joker had been duly removed'. Halifax remarked: 'I am disposed to think but I know it is a minority view that M. Bonnet is not so black (or so yellow) as he is often painted'.[37]

Villain or no villain, Bonnet had a better side to his character. That modesty was not his forte goes almost without saying, witness the five volumes devoted to his own career—a career which in terms of high ministerial office covered only sixteen years from 1924 to 1940.[38] And though his memoirs contain plenty of malicious anecdotes about the failings of others, he himself did no wrong. Nevertheless, he was not without friends. Alexander Werth, Paris correspondent of the *Manchester Guardian* in 1938-39, and a stern critic of the foreign minister's policies, described how during the 1914-1918 war Bonnet acted as counsel for the defence in the courtmartial of a German officer. Bonnet considered the man to be innocent. He was sentenced to death. Before the execution, Bonnet stayed the whole night with the officer in his cell and after the German had been shot he smuggled his belongings to his family in Germany.[39] In *Les Hommes de Bonne Volonté* Jules Romains supplies a not unsympathetic sketch of the minister. The character Jerphanion says:

> I like him (*Bonnet*) a lot. I like very much to talk to him. He listens . . . They say he has an overbearing taste for power, that he is ill when an administration is formed without him. This does not prove that he is a bad person. There are children who are ill when one excludes them from a game; actors who are ill when they are not given parts in a play. . .[40]

Bonnet, it seems, had an ease of manner and approachability which went deeper than the professional charm of his calling. Geneviève Tabouis, foreign editor of *L'Oeuvre*, though no admirer of the minister's diplomacy, paid tribute to his rare charm and intelligence. If Madame Tabouis is to be believed, Bonnet's young, ambitious and attractive wife, Odette Bonnet, popularly known as Madame *Soutien-Georges*, shared responsibility for the bad impression which her husband left in some quarters. Her salon was a fashionable gathering place for Parisian society. She was said to be 'so wildly ambitious for her husband that when a new ministry was being formed he was afraid to go home at night unless he had captured a post for himself'.[41] But her devotion to her husband was not in doubt. Shortly after Munich she wrote to an English friend:

> ...Georges has been admirable, so calm, so resolute. He never despaired. On the two final days, all the newspapers, ministers and even his assistants abandoned him...You see what a cool mind and willpower can do for the destinies of peoples.[42]

His intelligence and abilities were considerable. Elie J. Bois, editor of *Le Petit Parisien*, considered him to have 'the makings of a good, perhaps a great foreign minister'. Paul-Boncour, a strong critic of Munich, acknowledged the 'kindness and help' of Bonnet when the latter served under him in 1932. Even the Church put in a good word for him. The Nuncio at Paris thought him 'a decent fellow'. Impressed by Bonnet's mastery of his brief as French delegate to the Lausanne Conference in June 1932 Ramsay MacDonald asked 'Why isn't he in the Cabinet?'[43]

Bonnet the man and statesman has generally been condemned without any attempt to understand his personality and motives. His colleague Anatole de Monzie, Minister of Public Works in the Daladier Cabinet of 1938, provided a more discriminating appraisal than most observers. Though the two men were friends, Monzie was no sycophant. He wrote:

> Whilst very courageous in the long run, he is much less so in the heat of the moment...Because he is reticent, he is accused of lying or of deceit. False accusation...Bonnet is discreet so that his policy may be successful...There is in him an obvious ability, an excessive flexibility. He jumps too quickly on to the bandwagon, on to all bandwagons. What does it matter to me? . . . If he aims for the goal and means to reach it by devious means, I care only for the goal. Now I note that having adopted the peace party, he is sticking to it with the foresight of a statesman.[44]

Deviousness was also a personality defect. It was noted that his 'blue eyes' seemed 'to be veiled, bathed in mist, as though he wanted to conceal thoughts he dared not show even when he had nothing to hide'.[45] A former political ally who worked closely with the foreign minister recounted that when Bonnet was under attack or in a tight corner he would lie automatically to extricate himself.[46] According to René Massigli, Political Director of the foreign ministry in 1937-38, the Minister's secretive nature was the cause of many misunderstandings.[47]

The deviousness of which he was so often accused by friend and foe was partly an occupational deformation. Engulfed in the whirlpool of domestic politics he ventured further than most into the darker corners of the political workshop and paid a heavy penalty for his ambition. And yet, as a leading Radical, Bonnet was a typical product of the great centre party which made the Republic its own, because lacking a clear-cut ideology and organisation, it was many things to many Frenchmen. The inevitable compromises of a political career accentuated character traits, transforming an innate reticence into secretiveness and even mendacity.

Not surprisingly, Bonnet's defects worked to the discredit of his diplomacy and yet his policy contained much that was sincere and sensible. Though his aim in the Munich crisis of 1938 was to avoid fighting for Czechosolvakia and to put the blame for a retreat on to others, his long-term goals were Franco-German reconciliation and a European settlement. The strategy may well be questioned yet it should be recognised that he pursued an ideal, albeit misguidedly. The quandary was real and agonising: how could France avoid an unwanted collision with Germany in central and eastern Europe without losing face and honour? Bonnet's answer was to bring into play two policies, namely, a public and traditional policy which stressed the maintenance of France's alliances, and a semi-secret one of extreme concessions, based on disengagement from eastern Europe.

While Bonnet had to share with Chamberlain much of the opprobrium over Munich, Daladier was given the benefit of the doubt and treated as an appeaser in spite of himself. He was 'convinced that a firm policy could alone stop Hitler. But he was at a loss how to do it'.[48] Daladier, however, had much more faith in conciliation than has been realised. His choice of Bonnet as Foreign Minister was a clear pointer to his outlook. Paul-Boncour's story of how on 10 April after hearing his defence of French pledges in eastern Europe Daladier decided not to keep him on at the Quai d'Orsay is well-known.[49] Less well-known, though rumoured at the time, was the intervention of the British Ambassador, Sir Eric Phipps, who reported:

> We were nearly cursed by having Paul-Boncour again at the Quai d'Orsay. I therefore had Daladier and Reynaud informed indirectly that it would be most unfortunate if Paul-Boncour were to remain . . . Daladier himself was in full agreement . . . Finally after an interview of over an hour with Paul-Boncour he did the right thing . . . I felt it was my duty to take a certain risk, though it was a very small one as my messages were quite indirect and I can always disavow them.[50]

But the choice of Bonnet was Daladier's own—London would have preferred Chautemps. The significance of Bonnet's appointment was not missed. It was predicted that the new minister would 'put French relations with Italy on a sensible basis as soon as possible' and would 'welcome any opportunity' of coming to 'a reasonable understanding with Germany'.[51]

Critics of French policy have tended to treat Bonnet as a scapegoat for the capitulations of 1938-39. In March 1939, eighteen eminent French intellectuals, including several Nobel prize winners, addressed an open letters to President Lebrun, Daladier and the Presidents of the Chambers in which Bonnet was accused of bringing about the collapse of the country's security and prestige.[52] In particular, the foreign minister was charged with the pursuit of a double line, officially paying lip service to French commitments while secretly undermining them. This pre-war indictment which received wide publicity was revived by the postwar parliamentary commission of enquiry.

The impeachment was well-founded. Bonnet's journalistic following were surprisingly frank concerning the adoption of a semi-secret diplomacy. Alfred Fabre Luce wrote: Bonnet 'could not free himself in a day from the Popular Front majority which supported him... He could not even pose the Czechoslovak problem openly before public opinion'. Another supporter, Louis Thomas, was even more candid: 'No hope of direct communion with Frenchmen... it was a time for secret debate... So much the worse if... the public understood little or nothing: secrecy was indispensable'.[53] Thus the guidelines of French policy in the crisis over Czechoslovakia were never clearly defined. After a somewhat cryptic ministerial declaration to the Chambers on 12 April, only two further affirmations of French pledges were issued.[54]

But the mistake of Bonnet's accusers was to see in the foreign minister a spider-like, Machiavellian figure, spinning a web of secrecy to hide his betrayal of French interests. Undoubtedly the first consideration for the Daladier government—indeed for any French government—was national honour. France had legal obligations to defend Czechoslovakia, not to mention moral ties, but a Franco-German war was too frightful to contemplate. It seemed imperative therefore to devise some compromise arrangement which would satisfy Germany and yet leave France's reputation untarnished. The government opted for a graceful retreat, *force majeure* being the plea. Yet if national honour was to be saved, ministers had to maintain a common front and eschew public discussion of the problem. As Léger put it on 4 September: 'No French politician would be willing to leave on record that he had consented to discuss so delicate a matter'.[55] Another factor in determining secrecy was the divided state of opinion. The Czech alliance was a subject of bitter controversy. Intensive debate on the issue, it was feared, would only divide opinion still further and so prejudice diplomatic negotiations. Lastly, some secrecy was dictated by the government's dependence on Communist and Socialist votes in the Chamber. Many on the Left called for the defence of the eastern allies.

Daladier's outlook in 1938 was largely inspired by earlier essays in conciliation. As Prime Minister in 1933 he had not only agreed to join in Mussolini's Four Power Pact—as had Paul-Boncour, his Foreign Minister—but he had also made unofficial contact with Hitler through the journalist Count Fernand de Brinon, president of the *Comité France-Allemagne,* and later Vichy ambassador to the German occupation authorities. Plans for a secret Daladier-Hitler meeting and a subsequent Franco-German declaration seem to have been mooted.[56] Nothing came of it all because of the fall of the government in October 1933. Even before that event, however, he was characteristically beginning to have misgivings, fearing the reactions of Paul-Boncour and of the Chamber. The attempts of 1933 were not forgotten. On his return from Munich he defended the agreement with the words: ·'It's my policy, it's the Four Power Pact'.[57]

What credence, if any, therefore, should be given to Daladier's denunciations of German aims in the conferences with British ministers in 1938? Were they only windy rhetoric, part of the verbal demonstrations of French honour? The answer is that the French leader was naturally irresolute about most matters and was certainly in two minds about Germany and attempts to appease her. His apprehensions — genuine enough — that Hitler was bent on destroying Czechoslovakia and subjugating Europe set him apart both from his foreign minister and from British ministers. Bonnet was the more extreme in his opinions and said to be 'even keener than Daladier in steering clear of France's obligations'.[58] In the consistency and persistency of their pursuit of conciliation Chamberlain and Bonnet had much in common. At the height of the Czech crisis in September 1938 Bonnet was all for a settlement at almost any price, while Daladier seemed resigned to war. In London Halifax acted as a brake. Chamberlain was prepared to accept Hitler's Godesberg terms but Halifax, after losing a night's sleep, plumped for refusal.

Daladier did not share Chamberlain's faith in Hitler as a man of his word. His first and last encounter with Hitler was at Munich. On his return he told the American Ambassador that Chamberlain 'had been taken in a bit by Hitler'. He 'was an admirable old gentleman, like a high-minded Quaker who had fallen among bandits' and his 'last conversations with Hitler had not been helpful'.[59] Sour grapes maybe. Daladier was annoyed that without consultation Chamberlain had stolen a march on him by concluding with Hitler the Anglo-German agreement on 30 September. Daladier also deluded himself that some settlement could be reached with Germany, if only a *modus vivendi*. Jean Zay, his Minister of Education, records him telling the Cabinet on 30 September that contacts with Hitler and Goering might be fruitful.[60] The essential difference between the two Prime Ministers was one of temperament and training. Imbued with a strong sense of mission Chamberlain pursued appeasement ruthlessly and fanatically. By contrast, with his knowledge of history, Daladier was deeply suspicious of Germany but could think of no sane and viable alternative to appeasement. Distrusting himself, he constantly had second thoughts about the wisdom of French policy.

The strongest motive which impelled French ministers was fear. Daladier and Bonnet were frightened men. As Daladier told British ministers in April 1938:

> ...We should be blind if we did not see the realities of the present situation. We were confronted by German policy...designed to tear up treaties and destroy the equilibrium of Europe. In his view, the ambitions of Napoleon were far inferior to the present aims of the German Reich...it was clear that, if and when Germany had secured the petrol and wheat resources of Rumania, she would then turn against the Western Powers.[61]

There was a general awareness that France's survival as a great power was threatened not only by Germany but also by her internal convulsions. 'All problems, economic, financial, social and political', the government stated in a parliamentary declaration on 12 April, 'are part of the single problem of security'. France, Daladier told a gathering of ex-servicemen on 12 November 1938, had to choose 'between a slow decline or a renaissance through effort'. 'There could be no greater tragedy', he continued, 'than to see one's country, through a falling birth rate, the slowing down of production, disordered finances and the undermining of its currency, running the risk of sinking to a second class power'. The government's policy was aimed at 'saving both the Peace and the grandeur of France'.[62]

Although apprehensions of Germany and of national decline were uppermost in the minds of French statesmen, other motives were also at work. French ministers, like their British counterparts, detested war. The war of 1914-18 in which both the prime minister and foreign minister had seen active service left them with an enduring horror of bloodshed. They shrank from a holocaust which might destroy not only France but Europe. In a broadcast of 21 August Daladier declared his resolve 'to do everything to spare Europe the annihilation of its civilisation'.[63]

But the 'civilisation' of the French statesmen was that of the sixteenth *arrondissement*. War was dreaded not for its own sake alone but as a harbinger of social revolution. France might survive another conflagration but not the 'wisely-built' Republic, endowed with liberal institutions, affording security, dignity and independence to its citizens. Thus spoke the Republic of property, panicking at the prospect of losing its privileged position. Geneviève Tabouis recorded the following conversation with Bonnet in September 1938:

> For a time he stared at the ceiling, then going over to window, he peered down at the Seine.
> 'If war comes', he said, 'that is where I shall end up'.

Tabouis asked why he would want to commit suicide:

> 'I won't throw myself into the Seine. . .if war comes, there will be a revolution. and the people will throw me into the river'[64]

In September Joseph Caillaux, the man of Agadir, chairman of the Senate finance committee in 1938, voiced his fears that 'heavy air bombardments of factories round Paris' might 'well cause another Commune'.[65]

Almost as strong as the detestation of war was the hatred of Communism, indeed the governing elite dreaded Communism more than National Socialism. In a private talk with the German Ambassador on 22 May, Daladier described his vision of Armageddon: 'the catastrophic frightfulness of modern war would surpass all that humanity had ever seen. . .Into the battle zones. . .Cossack and Mongol hordes would pour'. In September in conversation with Bullitt the prime minister was even more explicit:

> Germany would be defeated in the war. . .but the only gainers would be the Bolsheviks as there would be social revolution in every country of Europe. . . Cossacks will rule Europe.[66]

The conclusion of the German-Soviet pact on 23 August 1939 and the coming of war only hardened Bonnet's deep conservatism. 'He warmly approves of the dissolution of the Communist Party', reported Phipps

on 28 September 1939 and 'spoke bitterly of the harm done to France'
by the Popular Front. Bonnet, continued the Ambassador, was:

absolutely convinced that Stalin's aim is still to bring about world revolution. . .
Germany, as Russia's nearest neighbour, will be the first victim. . .he wonders
whether it will be possible to prevent the disease from spreading: one important
barrier in our two countries is constituted by our large middle classes, whose
interests should be jealously guarded by both Governments.[67]

Someone in the Foreign Office minuted sardonically: 'M. Bonnet should
meet Colonel Blimp'.

The French ministers were animated by a deep-seated dislike of Versailles. 'Both are convinced', wired the American Ambassador, on 15 September 1938, 'that the treaty must be revised and at bottom regard an alteration in the Czechoslovak state as a necessary revision—the necessity for
which they pointed out nearly twenty years ago'.[68] These views were no
secret. Daladier, as Benes noted, was 'a man who for many years had
never forgotten to point out whenever occasion offered that he had not
been at Versailles. . .that France could not make herself responsible for
the disordered central European states'.[69]

Was there then an alternative to a Franco-German duel? Though the
primary, motivating instinct of French diplomacy was fear, Daladier and
Bonnet hoped against hope that a *détente*, if not an *entente*, might still
be realised. With the Czech dispute settled, French ministers looked
forward 'to negotiations. . .to bring together Germany and France in
genuine friendship'.[70] Daladier's desire for *rapprochement* was no panic
reaction to the Czech crisis but sprang directly from the agony of the
trenches. At Marseilles in October 1938 he told the Radical party congress:

When at Munich I heard the heart of the German people beating, I could not
prevent myself thinking, as I had done at Verdun, . . . that between the French
and German peoples . . . there are strong ties of mutual respect which should
lead to loyal collaboration.[71]

While Chamberlain and Halifax were on the whole close and loyal
partners, Daladier and Bonnet waged a war of succession.[72] Early on in
their careers the two politicians seem to have been good friends, with
Daladier, as Bonnet tells the story, helping to give his car a push when
the engine was slow to start after a long night's discussion. Bonnet's
ambitions probably drove the two of them apart. He had only narrowly
failed to form a government in January 1938 and kept his eye on the premiership. Also, whispers reached Daladier of Bonnet's criticisms of
France's military strength and the prime minister scented a move to out-
flank him by impugning his record as minister of national defence and war.

Of the two men, Daladier commanded a greater popular appeal. By
the summer of 1939 many referred to him affectionately as 'Dala'. His
simple and direct manner was reassuring. Moreover, as war minister since
June 1936 he had won the army's confidence—no mean feat. His oratory
carried an attractive ring of Jacobin militancy, though his more important
speeches were ghosted by a young secretary who afterwards became a
well-known novelist. Unhappily, Bonnet had none of the qualities which

might have endeared him to a wider public. He lacked Daladier's prowess in debate. His main asset was his financial expertise and banking background. Through his wife he was connected with one of the major French banks and one of his former secretaries was a director of Lazards. In short he was, as the German ambassador signalled, 'an avowed agent of authoritative economic circles'.

Chapter 7

The Cabinet

The role of the Cabinet in the formulation of French foreign policy raises special problems. In contrast to the British Cabinet which decided in 1919 to continue the War Cabinet methods of record keeping and secretarial organisation, the Cabinets of the Third Republic did not keep an official record of their deliberations. The establishment of a Cabinet secretariat and an effective Prime Minister's office were administrative innovations of the Fourth Republic. In the absence of an official record, the historian has to glean what he can from memoirs and private papers. The task is a difficult one because for certain crises there are almost as many versions of a discussion as there were ministers present. There was no voting, or counting of noses. Ministers usually made notes after the Cabinet had met. When in 1940 Paul Reynaud detected one of his colleagues taking notes during a meeting he was quick to register disapproval.[1] And ministers often came away from their confabulations none the wiser. Jean Zay, Daladier's Minister of Education in 1938-39, testified that after a Cabinet one of his colleagues would often ask: 'But what exactly has been decided?'[2]

The lack of official minutes and of a Cabinet secretariat illustrates an essential difference between the British and French Cabinets of the period. The British Cabinet was the supreme policy-making body, the pinnacle of the British system of government. Yet much of its strength resided in the fact that it was the Prime Minister's own team of ministers who accepted his authority. By contrast, the governments of the Third Republic tended to be anarchical affairs in which Ministers were almost autonomous authorities, directing their departments with little or no reference to the head of government.[3] Indeed the office of Prime Minister was unknown to the law until 1934. The Prime Minister was no more than first among equals, without special authority. Constitutionally, this was also the British position but in practice, thanks to the Cabinet Office, British Prime Ministers beginning with Lloyd George were able to ignore the parity and achieve the primacy.

To fortify themselves, it was customary for French Prime Ministers to hold one or more major departments.[4] In 1934, Daladier coupled the premiership and the Foreign Ministry; in 1938 he held the portfolio of national defence and war. The burden of running a major ministry combined with the daily struggle to hold together a parliamentary majority imposed a great physical and mental strain. After six to eight months of office, many leaders were glad to give way to their rivals. Any pretensions of co-ordinating government action and translating large views into large policies were quickly sacrificed to day-to-day requirements. There was no Prime Minister's office properly speaking. An organisation of sorts had been set up in the early 1920s and Bonnet—as Under-Secretary of State in the Painlevé government of 1925—had recommended the use of the Hôtel Matignon as a permanent base but it was not until 1934 that Flandin established a Prime Minister's office at the Hôtel Matignon. In practice the body which mattered was the prime minister's private office or *Cabinet* and this would usually concern itself with his particular departmental responsibilities—foreign affairs, war or finance. As early as 1918, Blum had advocated the creation of a secretariat which would be able to co-ordinate and supervise the different branches of government. In particular, he urged that the prime minister should not overtax himself by holding a senior department. On coming to power in June 1936 Blum entrusted Jules Moch with the task of organising a secretariat which would work closely with the traditional *Cabinet.* Unfortunately, Blum's ideas foundered on the resistance of individual ministers who jealously defended their independence.

Under the Third Republic, the presidency was a very different institution from that of the Fifth Republic.[5] In the Fifth Republic General de Gaulle was always a ruling influence—and in defence and foreign affairs, ministers were often mere executants of a policy initiated and directed by the General. The makers of the Third Republic saw the president as both the formal head of state and the nominal head of the executive. Consequently the presidency quickly became the focus of the suspicions which had previously been concentrated on the monarchy and empire. After the experience of two independent-minded presidents, Thiers and MacMahon, checks and balances were built up. Parliament excluded any candidate who was likely to assert himself. Raymond Poincaré, who was at the Elysée from 1913 to 1920, was the only outstandingly able incumbent of an office which had become a sinecure for mediocrities.

Albert Lebrun, the last President of the Third Republic, was not entirely a nonentity. He was born in Lorraine and trained as an engineer. Shortly before his election to the presidency in 1932, Madame Lebrun, daughter of a Director of the School of Mines, is said to have exclaimed nostalgically: 'When I think that if Albert had not gone into politics he could now have been Inspector General of Mines'.[6] The solid, bourgeois respectability of the Lebruns made them attractive targets for malicious anecdote. The president's heavy-going personality was a source of amusement abroad. King Boris of Bulgaria who was an excellent mimic entertained a royal gathering at Balmoral with a first rate imitation of Lebrun. From a parliamentary viewpoint, Lebrun was a safe candidate for the Elysée, safe enough to be re-elected for a second septennate in April 1939. He seems to have aged quickly. Though he was only 69 years in 1940, a year younger than Neville Chamberlain, a visitor reported that his memory was 'evidently failing rapidly. It was difficult for him to remember with any accuracy names or dates, or even facts'.[7]

Still, this picture may be exaggerated and in the 1930s Lebrun was not without a mind of his own on a number of issues. The victory of the *Front Populaire* made him think of resigning and he tried to dissuade Léon Blum from taking office. According to André Blumel, Blum's private secretary, Lebrun told the Socialist leader: 'I must summon you, and I will summon you, but don't you think it would be better to give up the idea of forming a government? There have never been Socialists in the government, don't you think it will lead to strikes?'.[8] Upon the outbreak of the Spanish civil war he insisted that no arms should be sent to Spain until the Cabinet had discussed the matter.[9] When the major decisions were made in 1938, Lebrun was not of central importance. Hearing in August 1938 that two Socialist ministers, Frossard and Ramadier, had resigned, Lebrun, who was in the country, telephoned Daladier offering to return to Paris. Daladier replied that there was no need to do so; the two ministers had been replaced and in the next day's post the President would receive the papers which required his signature.[10] Again, when the French ultimatum was sent to Prague on the night of 20-21 September Lebrun was out of Paris. But he could be obstinate. After Munich, a majority of ministers was said to favour a dissolution of the Chambers but the chief obstacle was the President 'whose one wish was to finish his term of office next April quietly'.[11]

Under the Third Republic, ministerial meetings were of two kinds: informal meetings of the Cabinet under the chairmanship of the Prime Minister, usually held at the Hôtel Matignon; formal meetings of the Cabinet, presided over by Lebrun at the Elyseé. Ministers smoked at informal sessions but not at formal meetings. Copies of foreign ministry papers went automatically to the President, Prime Minister and Foreign Minister and discussion of foreign affairs was usually reserved for full and formal meetings.

Depending on the personalities and preoccupations of the President and Prime Minister, the Foreign Minister might enjoy virtually a free hand. Théophile Delcassé, Foreign Minister from 1898 to 1905, was very much his own master. The Prime Minister, Emile Combes, was so absorbed by the Church question that he would remark: 'Don't let us concern ourselves with that, gentlemen, it is the business of the Foreign Minister and the President of the Republic'.[12] But the combination of a Prime Minister or a President interested in foreign policy and a Foreign Minister with ideas of his own could prove explosive. Briand explained his foreign policy to the Cabinet as if he were giving a lesson in a primary school, usually repeating what was in all the newspapers. As Prime Minister from 1926 to 1929, Poincaré suspected Briand of withholding information from the Cabinet, complaining that 'after a council of ministers Briand appears to accept the majority of his colleagues, and then goes off to the Quai to take a line in some respects different'.[13] The British Ambassador at Paris, Lord Crewe, observed:

If it were not for the very remarkable tact and skill with which Doumergue (*President*) presides over the Council of Ministers, the machine might scarcely remain in working order. Important questions of foreign policy must hardly ever be examined by the Cabinet Councils, held at the Ministry of Foreign Affairs, under Poincaré's chairmanship.[14]

Another major difference between the British and French Cabinets of the period was the absence on the French side of established Cabinet committees. The permanent Foreign Policy Committee and the transient Committee on Czechoslovakia in 1938 had no French counterparts. Informal, *ad hoc* consultation was the rule. Senior ministers would have a quiet word together without anybody knowing. In 1936-37 Blum is said to have arranged meetings between certain ministers 'for the purpose of discussing questions of foreign policy involving military commitments— questions that could not be aired in general meetings of the Cabinet'.[15] For detailed discussion of defence policy the prime minister and service ministers met with the Chiefs of Staff in the Permanent Committee of National Defence but meetings were relatively infrequent. Chamberlain had an Inner Cabinet of four, including himself, which met regularly in September 1938. There was no equivalent in Paris. On 10 April 1938 it was announced that the French Prime Minister had formed an inner cabinet which would meet daily to discuss all important questions, including finance and foreign affairs, but there is no evidence that regular meetings were in fact held.

Bonnet testifies that he and Daladier talked over foreign policy and constituted an inner cabinet so far as foreign affairs were concerned.[16] Until Munich, Bonnet had virtually a free hand. There was little reason for Daladier to interfere since he was in broad agreement with his Foreign Minister. However in the last week of September 1938 Daladier seemed to assert himself much more. After the Prague *coup* in March 1939 the Prime Minister tightened his hold on decision-making and Bonnet's influence waned. Although President Lebrun followed international affairs closely and was not without opinions of his own, decision-making rested largely with Daladier and Bonnet, with Léger, Secretary General of the Quai d'Orsay, playing an increasingly influential role in the summer of 1939.

Daladier, in the opinion of one of his ministers, was competent and authoritative at Cabinets 'where pencil in hand he imagined himself back in his old school teaching days, explaining a complicated problem to attentive pupils'.[17] But his personality and methods of working attracted considerable criticism. He was said to have 'a way of signing papers which he had not himself prepared and to the content of which he had not necessarily given careful consideration'.[18] His main fault was indecision. According to Jean Jeanneney, President of the Senate, he was 'inclined to listen to the advice of the last person' who entered his room. Blum considered him unsociable and anxious to avoid meeting anyone outside his own small circle.[19]

As compensation for a taciturn and irresolute nature, Daladier was gifted with considerable guile. He tried hard to be a dictator, borrowing more than one idea from Jacques Doriot's *Parti Populaire Francais*. In 1938-39 he emasculated his party, systematically eliminating all traces of independent authority.[20] His personal following of little known deputies served as a power base within the Chamber and in the party at large. The premiership was transformed into a much stronger office than hitherto. By skilfully playing on external threats, the French prime minister gave himself a much longer innings than many of his predecessors. 'No French Minister in recent times', wrote Neville Chamberlain on 13 July 1939, 'has had his people so solidly behind him'.[21] The compliment was not undeserved. Nevertheless, French society in 1939 was still deeply divided. It would be more accurate to say that no French leader of the decade had been so solidly entrenched in power as Daladier.

This consolidation of power was largely the prime minister's own work and owed but little to popular esteem. At times, he seemed to envy the dictators and sought to emulate them: 'Ah', he would say, 'if only I was served like Hitler'.[22] In October 1938 one of his colleagues observed that he 'had evidently been impressed by Hitler's method of working because since returning from Munich he had shut himself up' and 'had not consult-ed members of the cabinet regarding the preparation of decree laws'.[23] Shaken by the hurricanes, domestic and foreign, the Chambers granted Daladier full powers to govern by decree laws. From the Munich crisis the government drew a renewal of the full powers granted in April 1938. Thanks to these powers Daladier survived in office but he was slow to exploit the opportunity of thoroughgoing reform. On 16 November 1938 the British embassy in Paris reported that Daladier was considerably discredited by his failure to use effectively the powers given to him for two months in April and renewed in October.[24] After the German occupation of Prague in March 1939 he obtained further powers.[25] There followed a whole crop of authoritarian measures. On 21 March 1939 the government promulgated a list of 13 decrees aimed at strengthening security. Another batch followed in July, giving the Cabinet extensive control of radio and information services.

Arguably, the decree laws sapped France's main source of strength, her liberal parliamentary tradition. In theory decree laws required parlia-mentary ratification but they could operate without it. The bill renewing Daladier's plenary powers in March 1939 stipulated that the decrees 'will be submitted for ratification to the Chambers before 31 December 1939'. In practice though deputies were reluctant to approve decrees and so saddle themselves with responsibility for unpopular measures. A 'Law for the Organization of the Nation in War-time' passed on 11 July 1938 empowered the government to govern by decree from the opening of hostilities. Thus when war came on 3 September 1939 many felt, like Simone Weil, that the country was under 'a mild dictatorship'. The twilight war in the winter of 1939-40 strengthened still further Daladier's ascen-dancy. Paul Baudouin even claimed that 'all the powers for directing the war had from the beginning been concentrated in the hands of the Minister of National Defence. All intelligence was centralised by Daladier, who objected to passing it on to his colleagues'.[26]

Personalities outside the government and civil service often exercised greater influence as informal advisers than individual ministers or the Cabinet as such. If Pertinax is to be believed, Daladier's official advisers did not carry much weight with him and he was particularly influenced by two men introduced to him by the Marquise de Crussol: Daniel Serruys, appointed High Commissioner for the Economy in September 1939, and Emmanuel Arago, grandson of Pierre Dupuy, founder of *Le Petit Parisien*.[27] But there is no strong reason why Pertinax's opinion should be accepted. One man on whom Daladier leaned heavily for counsel was his *Directeur du Cabinet,* Marcel Clapier. Clapier started his career as a local official in Daladier's constitutency of Vaucluse and became *Directeur du Cabinet* in 1932 and remained with the minister throughout his political life. He accompanied Daladier to the Munich conference. Another member of the Prime Minister's inner circle was Jacques Kayser, a journalist and vice-president of the Radical party. He had been one of the 'Young Turks' of the party in the early 1930s.

On foreign affairs Daladier sometimes consulted the journalist, Count Fernand de Brinon, president of the *France-Allemagne* committee.[28] The two men were in close touch during Daladier's 1933 premiership and were still in contact in 1938. De Brinon accompanied the French delegation to the London conference on 29-30 April 1938 and was said to be 'closely connected' with the French prime minister. In the last week of September 1938 Brinon's conduct was little short of treasonable. He passed on to the German embassy particulars of cabinet discussions which gave Berlin a fairly accurate picture of cabinet opinion. In forwarding the information to Germany the embassy added that a personal meeting with Brinon had not been possible 'owing to the observation' under which he was being kept—presumably by French intelligence.

It is tempting to speculate on the identity of Brinon's informants—perhaps Monzie or Pomaret, Minister of Labour, though Daladier himself may not have been innocent. The Prime Minister may have wanted to keep open a private line to Berlin. It is not clear whether Brinon and Daladier remained in touch after Munich. In December 1938, reports reached the Foreign Office that Brinon was in German pay and received regular information on cabinet discussions from two ministers. The British embassy in Paris was unable to verify either of these allegations but confirmed that no one had any confidence in the journalist who was widely suspected of being on Berlin's payroll.

Surprisingly, the man on whom Daladier relied greatly for counsel was not a Frenchman but the United States Ambassador, William C. Bullitt. Bullitt, formerly Ambassador to the Soviet Union, took up his Paris post in the autumn of 1936. By the summer of 1939 he had formed a very close relationship with the French leader and his advice was listened to and often heeded. He cabled home on 29 August 1939:

> I have seen Daladier constantly and intimately throughout this crisis. I do not telegraph half of what he says to me for the simple reason that there is nothing he doesn't say . . . he asks my judgement about nearly everything of great importance not only in the field of foreign policy but also in the field of domestic policy, and what's more, he is apt to do what I advise. . .[29]

Daladier felt he could turn to Bullitt for disinterested advice and such was his confidence in the diplomat that he even tried to get the house next door to Bullitt at Chantilly.

The Foreign Minister was much more gregarious and accessible than the Prime Minister and consequently his circle of counsellors and associates was fairly wide. Indeed, in later life, the two statesmen changed little. After his political retirement in 1958 Daladier lived a secluded life, shunning publicity and spending much of his time on a house-boat at Avignon, whereas Bonnet welcomed visitors and tried to continue an active political life.

The leading members of Bonnet's circle was Joseph Caillaux, the former prime minister and minister of finance, the banker Paul Baudouin, the independent deputy Gaston Bergery, the publicist Alfred Fabre Luce, the former prime minister, Pierre Etienne Flandin, the Radical deputy and former minister, Lucien Lamoureux, and the former navy minister, François Piétri. Among ministerial colleagues Bonnet had three major allies: Paul Marchandeau, Minister of Finance until November 1938, Anatole de Monzie, Minister of Public Works, and Charles Pomaret, Minister of Labour.

As an elder statesman and chairman of the Senate Finance Committee, Caillaux had more influence over the Senate than anyone else. He had twice turned Blum out of office. As Prime Minister in 1911 he had been an advocate of conciliation in the Agadir crisis. In 1938 through the newspaper *La République* he urged the conciliation of Germany and canvassed the idea of imperial self-sufficiency. He complimented Bonnet upon his 'sensible and realist attitude' in the Munich crisis.

Paul Baudouin was managing director of the Banque de l'Indochine. After the First World War he had entered the Inspectorate of Finance, the elite corps of the French civil service. Before leaving government service for banking he served as secretary to several ministers of finance. In 1937 he was said to be closely connected with Jacques Doriot, leader of the *Parti Populaire Francais*.[30] In the early months of 1938 while Flandin was preaching the doctrine of imperial self-sufficiency and withdrawal from the east, Baudouin was propounding similar notions. In a widely read article of February 1938, he proposed that the 'traditional policy' of eastern pacts should be abandoned, leaving France free to concentrate her energies on the development of empire. 'Important concessions' might be 'necessary to avoid a conflict' but 'to gain time' was 'to live'. The nature and extent of the concessions was not specified. 'It is a crime against our country', said Baudouin, 'to maintain that war with Germany is inevitable'.[31] In February 1939 he was sent as a semi-official envoy to Mussolini, whom he had met in 1935 and 1937. In June 1940 he became Foreign Minister in the first of Marshal Pétain's governments at Vichy.

Gaston Bergery, one of the stormy petrels of French politics, had been elected Radical deputy for Nantes in 1928 but left the party in 1932 and showed great interest in Communism. His first marriage was to a daughter of Krassin, first Soviet Ambassador to France after the restoration of diplomatic relations in 1924. Having lost his seat in 1934, he formed an extra-parliamentary *Front commun,* a prototype of the *Front Populaire.* Re-elected as an independent in 1936 he was disappointed at not being included in Blum's government. He never again achieved the influence he had wielded in 1924 when as Herriot's private secretary he had been called the *'Père Joseph'* of the *Cartel des Gauches*. In 1938-39 his newspaper *La Flèche de Paris* gave consistent support to Bonnet's diplomacy. His pacifism led him to sympathise with Sudeten German claims and he continued to advocate appeasement after 15 March 1939.

The publicist Alfred Fabre Luce was a member until Munich of Doriot's *Parti Populaire Français*.[32] He argued that Germany and Italy did not necessarily want war with the western democracies. Given British and French rearmament, Germany and Italy would be ready to negotiate and make concessions. Britain and France could only increase their strength by limiting their interests to western Europe and the Mediterranean. France must withdraw from the east or become a German vassal. During the Czech crisis Fabre Luce kept in close touch with Bonnet.

Flandin, Foreign Minister during the Rhineland crisis of March 1936, was president of the Right wing *Alliance démocratique*. After the Rhineland, he did not hold Cabinet office again until December 1940 when he became Marshal Pétain's Foreign Minister at Vichy. A tall, flamboyant figure, he was noted for his English ways and taste for Savile Row suits: 'to the average run of deputies', said Pertinax, 'Flandin was a fellow "who had his personal laundry done in London" '.[33] At his trial in 1946 and in his memoirs he argued that had France shaken off the British collar in 1936 and taken swift action against Germany she would have averted further decline in her fortunes, whereas by the time of Munich France had no choice but to placate an over-mighty Germany and play for time.[34] So he claimed the credit for a policy of resistance to Germany in 1935-36 and for one of appeasement in 1938-39. The claim to have resisted Germany in 1935-36 may largely be discounted but his advocacy of conciliation in 1938 is not in doubt. In the major foreign affairs debate on 25-26 February 1938 he fiercely attacked traditional policies and called for withdrawal from the east and *rapprochement* with Germany and Italy. In March 1938 Phipps signalled that the ex-minister had returned from Berlin 'firmly convinced that we must all lie down and lick the Nazi boot'.[35]

Flandin worked well with Bonnet whom he considered 'the most conscious and steadfast pacifist in the Cabinet'.[36] In the Munich crisis, Flandin, in a poster which was promptly torn down by the Communists, challenged the right of the government to declare general mobilisation without consulting parliament. He also won notoriety for sending a congratulatory telegram to Hitler after the Munich conference. Communists caricatured him as 'Flandin, the French Seyss-Inquart'. His views were too well known for Germany's liking. It was felt that his zeal might do the German cause more harm than good. After the occupation of Prague in March 1939 little was heard of him, a withdrawal dictated by amatory exploits, not by political considerations.[37] The coming of war did not alter his outlook. In October 1939 Phipps found him 'even more defeatist than I had supposed . . . he fears Communism in France'.[38]

In comparison with Caillaux and Flandin, Lucien Lamoureux and François Piétri were lightweights. Lamoureux was a friend of Laval, though never a member of any of Laval's administrations. In February 1939 on a visit to Germany he acted as a semi-official emissary for Daladier and

Bonnet.[39] He was Finance Minister in Paul Reynaud's government of 21 March 1940. Piétri was a leading member of Colonel de la Rocque's *Parti social français*, formerly the *Croix de Feu*. He was Navy Minister in 1934 and came close to being appointed to the Quai d'Orsay. In October 1934, following Barthou's assassination, the Prime Minister, Doumergue, considered him as a possible successor, finally selecting Laval. Both the British and Germans noted that Piétri was one of the few honest and reliable French politicians, free from any allegations of shady dealings.[40]

Perhaps the most influential figure outside the Cabinet was Edouard Herriot, President of the Chamber of Deputies from 1936.[41] He was a richly Rabelesian man, of great appetites—for women, scholarship and the table. Anecdotes abounded of his gastronomic accomplishments, in restaurants he would often order almost the entire menu. At the same time he possessed wide interests in literature, the arts and politics. His geniality and zest for life made him a popular leader and by the mid-1930s he was well-established as the philosopher and mentor of the Radicals, although he was not without his failings. According to Bonnet, he was particularly vain. When annoyed with someone he would receive them coldly, extending a single finger to them, and then, with his glasses pushed to the back of his head, he would stare fixedly at the ceiling, his interest clearly elsewhere. In June 1936 Blum offered him the post of foreign minister but Herriot preferred the presidency of the Chamber.

Herriot's firm and decided views on foreign affairs did not make him popular in London. In a conversation with Phipps on 26 March 1938 he said it was absurd to ignore the Soviet Union. As for Italy, she was bound 'hand and foot' to Germany. Germany was the greatest threat: 'France and Great Britain should be welded into one great defensive machine . . . intimate staff talks should begin at once'. Non-intervention in Spain, continued Herriot, was a 'snare and a delusion'. Still, the Radical statesman did not exclude the 'possibility of fruitful talks' with Germany. 'Quite deplorable', minuted Sir Orme Sargent, 'one can only hope that Herriot will not be called upon to "save" France'. Cadogan was less inclined to take Herriot at his word: 'With M. Herriot in control, an Anglo-French policy will be difficult to conduct—or even to define. But M. Herriot is an awful wind-bag, if he were in power his views might moderate'.[42]

The French Cabinet in 1938 was not as deeply divided on foreign policy as some commentators have supposed. That divisions existed over Czechoslovakia is undeniable but they were not as deep as sometimes described. Despite certain rumblings, there were no rebellions. The accepted picture of a Cabinet split between appeasers and resisters is misleading. The so-called *mous*, the ministers who supported Bonnet's line of extreme concessions, even at the cost of abandoning Czechoslovakia, were in a minority; likewise the *durs* who wanted to resist some of Germany's demands.

Around Bonnet were grouped Paul Marchandeau, Finance Minister, Anatole de Monzie, Minister of Public Works, and Charles Pomaret, Labour Minister. Paul Marchandeau, Finance Minister until November 1938 when Daladier made him change places with Paul Reynaud at the ministry of justice, was a loyal ally of Bonnet.[43] He was a quiet, unassuming personality and his major achievement was in local affairs. As Mayor of Rheims he had presided over the postwar reconstruction of the city. On foreign affairs Bonnet and Marchandeau were in agreement, although in financial matters they differed. In financial questions Bonnet was rigidly orthodox while Marchandeau showed greater flexibility. As Finance Minister in 1938, he had Socialist support. Within a few days of the declaration of war in September 1939 Marchandeau resigned, pleading the weight of local responsibilities. Understandably he had not forgiven Daladier for having forced him to change places with Reynaud. Monzie felt a twinge of conscience because he and Bonnet had not spoken up for their colleague.

The man who was most closely in league with the foreign minister was Anatole de Monzie. With his Basque beret and taste for colourful velvet waistcoats he was a picturesque character who combined a successful legal practice with politics and writing. He had a reputation for being an adventurer. It was rumoured that he had been implicated in the Stavisky affair as a former friend and legal adviser of Madame Stavisky. He was also alleged to have connections with several shady companies. His political views were difficult to fathom. Phipps, the British Ambassador, detected an 'apparent absence' of moral fibre.[44] Unlike Marchandeau who was a staunch Radical, Monzie switched from Right to Left more out of caprice than conviction. Yet on foreign affairs he held firm views. His great ambition, having held a number of Cabinet posts, was the Quai d'Orsay. On international affairs his outlook was conditioned by deep dislike of the peace treaties. He opposed the League of Nations because it owed so much to Anglo-Saxon inspiration. But dislike of the peace settlement did not mean automatic support for Germany's revisionist ambitions. In February 1938 he urged the Chautemps government to oppose any move towards an *Anschluss*. The Franco-British entente was of little interest to Monzie. He preferred to ignore Britain, stressing France's roots in the Latin Mediterranean world. Hence his unswerving advocacy of Franco-Italian *rapprochement*. But his horizon was not completely bounded by the Mediterranean. Unlike other associates of the foreign minister who could see no further than across the Rhine or the Alps, Monzie was one of the first French politicians to visit the Soviet Union and played a prominent part in promoting Franco-Soviet understanding in the 1920s.

Pomaret and Monzie were close friends.[45] They both joined Daladier's government on 23 August 1938 following the resignation of two Socialist ministers, L. O. Frossard and Paul Ramadier. The new ministers called themselves 'Independent Socialists' but this was no more than a flag of convenience. Pomaret kept his post as Labour Minister until 16 June 1940 when for a few days he was Minister of the Interior. In his own words he was 'a convinced partisan of Munich', though in August 1939 Monzie found him lacking in pacifist zeal.

The opposing trinity of *durs* were not in fact as hard as they might appear. The arch-resisters were Georges Mandel, Minister of Colonies, Paul Reynaud, Minister of Justice until his exchange of portfolios with Marchandeau in November 1938, and Auguste Champetier de Ribes, Minister for Ex-Servicemen and Pensions. All three were men of the Right. Champetier de Ribes, leader of the small group of Christian Democrats, followed the lead of Mandel and Reynaud.

According to Litvinov, Mandel and Reynaud were the only two French ministers trusted by the Soviet government. Mandel (his real name was Louis Rothschild) was popularly known as the Tiger's cub because he had been Clemenceau's henchman in the First World War. Some critics have dismissed him as a paper tiger. In May 1940 Reynaud appointed him Minister of the Interior. As a faithful follower of Clemenceau, he was expected to pounce on the defeatists, but never did. Under Vichy he was first imprisoned and finally shot by French fascists in 1944. Nevertheless it would be unfair to condemn Mandel for his relative inaction in May-June 1940. Militarily, the issue was almost decided and time was short. And Mandel laboured under a major disability—his Jewish origin. The Right wing press attacked him mercilessly. In May 1938 *Je Suis Partout* even demanded that Blum, Mandel and Reynaud be shot for warmongering. Not that Blum offered any comfort. In his opinion a Jew could not lead French resistance to Germany.

Mandel consistently defended what he believed to be France's real interests. He opposed Laval's Italian policy in 1935 and called for strong action against Germany after the reoccupation of the Rhineland. His opposition to Bonnet's diplomacy covered almost the entire field of foreign policy—Czechoslovakia, Spain, Italy, the Far East. On 15 September 1938 Bullitt called Washington that a few days previously Daladier had been involved 'in a considerable argument with Mandel who had wished him to mobilise the French army'.[46] As Minister of Colonies in 1938-39, he organised and expanded a formidable intelligence network. By April 1938 he favoured helping the Republican forces in Spain, though Bonnet was intent on closing the frontier to arms shipments. He also opposed any concessions to Italy. Bonnet and Mandel also differed on the Far East. Following Japanese protests the French government had stopped sending military supplies to General Chiang Kai-shek's forces. Bonnet believed it was best not to risk offending the Japanese armies in China since France would have great difficulty in defending her Far Eastern possessions. But Mandel thought the best defence of French interests was to prolong and strengthen Chinese resistance and a military mission was sent to Chiang Kai-shek.

But one Mandel did not make an opposition and Reynaud was much less forceful than his colleague. Like Mandel in 1940, Reynaud was to disappoint those who saw him as a saviour. A small, dapper man of a farming family in the French Alps, he had a passion for physical fitness and was often to be seen cycling in the Bois de Boulogne. This was supplemented by daily exercise in a gymnasium in his apartment in the Place du Palais Bourbon, just behind the Chamber of Deputies. Such pursuits did not distract him from the advancement of his career. He rapidly built up a lucrative law practice, enabling him to travel and indulge a variety of interests. Success at the bar led to the acquisition of property in the Basses-Alpes, and commercial interests in Central and South America. However this business background put him at a disadvantage in competition with Daladier since the public tended to prefer the latter's more humble origins. Nor did Reynaud's independent and consistent stand on a number of domestic and foreign issues endear him to the electorate. A brilliant mind and first-class oratory made him almost too clever for many Frenchmen. Since 1934 he had been a consistent advocate of devaluation, though enemies linked his devotion to devaluation with business concerns in South America. In the Ethiopian conflict he had called for the effective application of sanctions. Also, he supported de Gaulle's proposals for a professional, mechanised army. In the early part of 1938 he won wide publicity with his call for the inclusion of the Communists in a government of national union. 'From Thorez to Reynaud' was the cry.

Yet a close look at Reynaud's conduct in the spring and summer of 1938 suggests that he was not as firm an advocate of resistance to Germany as his memoirs claimed. Bonnet told Phipps that though Mandel was bellicose, Reynaud was not.[47] Although generally regarded as a partisan of a Franco-Soviet military alliance, it is significant that he was ready to deny reports that he wanted a military pact with Moscow. On a visit to London in May he agreed with Halifax on the need to put 'all the pressure possible' on Benes to enter into direct contact with the Sudeten German leaders. Speaking to the German ambassador on 10 May as 'an old acquaintance and not as a member of the Cabinet', he affirmed that 'everything must be done to avert the destruction of the civilised old world'. A 'radical solution' of the Czech problem was needed.

Although Mandel, Reynaud and Ribes may have wanted France to stand firm in defence of Czechoslovakia, they did not carry their dissent from official policy to the point of resignation.[48] Hearing on 22 September that an ultimatum had been sent to Prague on the night of 20-21 September, the trio went to see Daladier. According to Reynaud, the prime minister was told that if an ultimatum had in fact been sent they would resign. Daladier replied that the Czechs had asked for an ultimatum and proof of their request would be given by Bonnet at the next Cabinet. Other sources reveal that before seeing Daladier the three ministers had been dissuaded by Herriot from resigning. Winston Churchill, who was then in Paris, also counselled against resignation. One gesture of dissent was made. When on 30 September ministers gathered at Le Bourget to welcome Daladier on his return from the conference in Munich, Mandel and Reynaud stayed away. An opportunity of registering a more forceful protest came on 1 October when Duff Cooper, First Lord of the Admiralty, telephoned Mandel to say he was resigning. The three ministers conferred but did not follow the example.

Why did Reynaud not react more forcefully against the treatment of Czechoslovakia in 1938? One reason, as already suggested, may have been that privately he favoured conciliating rather than antagonizing Germany. Another consideration was that a rebel against foreign policy was in a much more difficult situation than a rebel against domestic policy. On social and economic issues France was profoundly divided but the division was between Left and Right and politicians had no hesitation in voicing their views. Unlike Spain, Czechoslovakia cut across class and party interests and an uncompromising attitude might have completely isolated a politician. After the feelings of relief which followed Munich, it was understandable that Mandel, Reynaud and Ribes should have preferred to remain in office rather than risk political suicide. The opportunity of resignation, for what it was worth, was missed on 22 September. Moreover, since national honour was at stake, the three dissident ministers were under great pressure not to rock the boat. Seeing the country in such dire economic and political straits, political leaders eschewed outright opposition in the summer of 1938.

Still, the main reason why Reynaud did not lead a rebellion over Czechoslovakia may well have been personal ambition. He was a highflyer aiming at the premiership. Daladier knew this and the two men were deadly rivals. In part this may also have been an *affaire des femmes*. The jealousies between the two Dulcineas were widely believed to explain the rivalry between the two men. After Munich, Hélène de Portes, Reynaud's mistress, asked Bonnet to intervene with Daladier in order to secure her lover's appointment as Minister of Finance.[49] Consequently, Reynaud moved cautiously and the reward came in November when Daladier offered him the portfolio of finance. Lastly, Reynaud's character should not be overlooked. Roland de Margerie who served as his private secretary in 1940 testifies that he was too prone to reflection and indecision. As a good lawyer, he was much to conscious of the pros and cons of a particular issue. Despite flashes of statesmanship he was, like Bonnet, primarily a *parlementaire*, absorbed in the political mêlée.[50]

The most striking feature of the Cabinet was not the conflict between the Bonnet and Reynaud groups but the balancing role of the majority led by Daladier. Chautemps, Deputy Prime Minister, César Campinchi, Navy Minister, Guy La Chambre, Air Minister, Raymond Patenôtre, Minister of National Economy, Albert Sarraut, Minister of the Interior, Jean Zay, Education Minister,—all Radicals—were content to follow a conciliatory course without going to the extremes of concession recommended by Bonnet. In September Cabinets, Guy La Chambre gave valuable support to Bonnet but he was not a permanent member of the Foreign Minister's clan. He believed the weakness of the air force imposed a conciliatory diplomacy.[51] Patenôtre and Zay had serious misgivings about official policy but could suggest no alternative.[52] The eel-like Chautemps, though sometimes supporting Bonnet, usually wriggled towards the majority.

On the basic issue of conciliation the Cabinet was united. Benes, it was agreed, would have to make substantial concessions to the Sudeten German minority. No one, not even Mandel, questioned this assumption. On 19 September the Cabinet accepted the Anglo-French plan for the cession of the Sudetenland to Germany. What provoked disagreement was the question of how much pressure was to be applied on Prague. In the last week of September, Bonnet, Monzie and Pomaret stood out sharply as the peace at almost at any price group but the issue was not one of surrender or resistance. Most ministers, including Daladier, objected not to the substance of Hitler's demands, but to the form of their presentation and strove to reach an acceptable compromise.

The Cabinet in 1938-39 did not play a critical role in the making of policy. The prime movers were the Prime Minister and Foreign Minister. The decision to present Prague with an ultimatum on the night of 20-21 September was made by Daladier and Bonnet alone, though President Lebrun was consulted by telephone. Ministers were often kept in the dark about important developments. Monzie complained that as the international situation deteriorated in September 1938 and again in August 1939 the Cabinet met less frequently.[53] Patenôtre also felt that ministers were inadequately informed on foreign affairs. For example, it was only on 23 November 1938 after several weeks of negotiations that Bonnet informed the Cabinet of the plans for a Franco-German declaration and a visit by Ribbentrop. In the Czech crisis, Daladier and Bonnet deliberately chose to play their cards close to their chest. In a speech on 4 September at the Pointe de Grave, Bonnet reaffirmed French alliance obligations. Between 4 September and the Munich conference, neither the prime minister nor the foreign minister made a single public speech. The government imposed its silence on the public. On 13 September public meetings on international affairs were banned.[54] Bonnet's balancing of the double line was so well done that colleagues were puzzled. A strong press campaign against helping Czechoslovakia prompted Jean Zay to ask on 22 September:

> Have the British given up or have we been irresolute? Bonnet's *Pointe de Grave* speech reiterating our engagements is only days old. Have we had two diplomacies?[55]

Reynaud did not submit completely to Daladier and Bonnet's leadership. On 8 July the Cabinet was informed of a despatch from François-Poncet, warning of German mobilisation measures against Czechoslovakia and suggesting that war might come within six weeks. Afterwards Reynaud wrote to Daladier, calling for an acceleration of armaments and government talks with the unions:

> . . . If you think that too frequent Cabinets might alarm opinion, the inner cabinet could meet regularly. . .
> It will be said that it is dangerous to alert opinion. The greater danger, however, is its present passivity. It is this passivity which encourages the dictators. . .
> It is necessary, in my opinion, to impress on our opinion and abroad that France is strong and will not allow herself to be taken by surprise. Let us beware of weakening opinion by giving it the impression that something is being withheld. To hide the truth from the country would also deprive national defence of an upsurge of energy of which it stands in urgent need.[56]

The appeal went unheeded. The summer holidays in August were a timely tranquillizer. There were no meetings of the Cabinet from 31 July to 31 August. Even Léger was a partner in this attempt to anaesthetize opinion. At the beginning of September it was decided to implement a number of military measures. Daladier at first thought of making public these counter-measures but Léger

> persuaded him not to do this, pointing out that a small and unimportant section of French public opinion might criticise the French measures and thereby convey a completely false impression to the German Government with dangerous results . . . the smaller friends of France, including Czechoslovakia, will not be informed, for fear of leakage and of undue encouragement to the latter to be unyielding in the present negotiations.[57]

Chapter 8

Parliament

The Third Republic has been seen as the type of a 'parliamentary, rather than cabinet, sovereignty', its governments—the creatures of a fickle legislature.[1] However in the making of foreign policy, governments enjoyed a substantial measure of independence. The constitution of 1875 gave the executive considerable freedom of action in foreign affairs. The executive could negotiate treaties without the obligation of keeping parliament informed, and the president was obliged to make treaties known to parliament only when 'the interest and security' of the state allowed.

Until 1914 the role of parliament in the shaping of foreign policy was hardly more than that of a rubber stamp upon policies predetermined by the administration of the day.[2] The changes wrought by the First World War; the establishment of the League of Nations; the pursuit of general disarmament; the Wilsonian ideal of open covenants openly arrived at; all generated greater interest in international affairs, but opinion still showed much indifference to foreign issues and this indifference was a powerful stabilising factor. In 1849, Guizot had written to the British Foreign Secretary, Lord Aberdeen; 'You may count on the fact that foreign policy does not concern the French at all and will not be the cause of any important event'. This insight had not lost its force and there is much to be said for the view that from 1815 to 1940 French opinion gave priority to 'introversive goals': wealth, peace, social cohesion in preference to power and glory. Wages, prices, the forty-hour week, holidays with pay, these were the immediate preoccupations in the mid-1930s. One observer of the general elections of May 1936 noted an 'almost unbelievable indifference to international affairs'. 'On the whole, our country hardly follows foreign affairs', wrote Senator Charles Reibel, a member of the Senate foreign affairs committee in 1939. Spain, of course, was an exception but much of the passion aroused by the Spanish war was ignited by France's internal tensions.

Between 1918 and 1939 parliamentary influence on the making of foreign policy increased, although the amount of direct influence exercised was small. Normally upon taking office, a government would issue a ministerial declaration, defining its foreign policy in broad terms. The only way for deputies to obtain further information was through parliamentary questions, written or oral, and through the foreign affairs committees of the Chamber of Deputies and of the Senate. The amount of debating time reserved for foreign affairs was strictly limited and written questions upon international affairs were rare. Thus the growth in parliamentary influence during the interwar years was reflected not so much in direct parliamentary interventions—which were few, as in the importance of the foreign affairs committees.

The absence of an established parliamentary tradition of control meant that the Daladier administration of 1938, was free to pursue its foreign policy in a manner which, at times, savoured of discredited secret diplomacy. The government was buttressed by two additional sources of strength: special powers and a firm parliamentary majority. On 12 April 1938 Daladier presented the customary ministerial declaration to the Chamber. The passage dealing with foreign policy read:

> The government is determined to defend everywhere the interests of France and the integrity of her Empire. In all cases—in the case of strengthening our bonds with our friends or in the case of proving our loyalty to all pacts and treaties we have signed or in the case of entering into equitable negotiations, it is indispensable that all the national energies be united. We want peace with all peoples whatever their political regime, but a just peace not an abdication of France.[3]

This vague declaration, which made no reference to any specific country, supplied the first indication of the new government's diplomacy. 'Never', commented a foreign correspondent, 'had a ministerial declaration been so uncategorical in its statement on foreign policy'.[4]   Some deputies protested that it was impossible to give the new cabinet a vote of confidence on such a woolly and laconic statement. But the Chamber was told nothing more, and Daladier received a grant of full powers, enabling him to govern by decree laws. Theoretically decree laws needed parliamentary ratification but in practice deputies were reluctant to approve decrees and so saddle themselves with responsibility for unpopular measures. Employing his powers Daladier sent the Chambers away on holiday in June and foreign policy was not discussed again until 4 October and then only cursorily. The Munich crisis came and went without parliament being consulted.

Daladier's treatment of parliament showed plainly that an administration enjoying the confidence of the parliamentary majority could 'not only survive criticism' but actually avoid 'all discussion of its foreign policy'.[5] As a self-styled ministry of national defence preserving a semblance of the Popular Front the government commanded votes from the Left and the Right. The confidence of the majority extended to foreign policy. The ministry could rely upon a fair measure of agreement with its declared aims, namely, a peaceful settlement of the Sudeten German dispute, paving the way for a European détente. Léon Blum, speaking at the Socialist party congress at Royan in June, pledged his support for the government and congratulated Daladier upon his handling of the Czech problem. A ministerial crisis, declared Blum, was not in the interest of the Popular Front, though he reminded his audience that France must maintain all her pacts, including the treaty with the Soviet Union. Curiously, the Franco-Czech treaty was not mentioned.

In their hurry to settle the Czech question and reach an understanding with the dictators, Daladier and Bonnet were prepared to exert extreme pressure on Prague, pressure, which it was anticipated, would not meet with the approval of the Popular Front majority. Ministers feared the danger of a parliamentary backlash bringing about the fall of the government. As a precaution, therefore, the Chambers were curbed and muzzled. The government's approach to parliament was also determined by another consideration. It was feared that full discussion of foreign policy would only create a Tower of Babel. Existing divisions would be deepened and the government's negotiating position *vis-a-vis* Germany would be destroyed.

In 1938 and 1939, key decisions in foreign policy were taken when the Chambers were in recess. Of course, this was not deliberate policy but simply a reflection of the fact that the Chambers were on holiday for most of the time. In 1938, parliament was adjourned from 13 April to 31 May and on 17 June Daladier read a decree closing the session. From mid-June to October, deputies and senators were on holiday. Even when they were sitting discussion of foreign affairs was minimal. Only two foreign affairs debates were held in 1938—a major review of international affairs on 25-26 February 1938, and a brief discussion of the Munich Agreement in a special session on 4 October. Appeals from Caillaux and Flandin for the recall of the Chambers in September 1938 fell on stony ground. Daladier would not 'contemplate summoning parliament before its normal session, even in case of war' and was resolved to take 'all the necessary measures . . . and stand the consequences', reported Phipps on 8 September.[6] Fearful of the Right gaining influence, the Socialists accepted this situation: 'parliamentary debates might weaken rather than strengthen the will of the government . . . Flandin, Caillaux . . . might thus gain influence . . . a cabinet crisis now might be most serious', Blum informed the British Labour leader, Hugh Dalton.[7]

After Munich, parliament was recalled from its summer recess and met on 4 October for a special twenty four hour session.[8] Thanks to a smart piece of political sleight of hand, the Chambers were deprived of a vote and debate on Munich. The government requested a vote not directly upon the Munich Agreement but upon a procedural point, the adjournment of an *interpellation*. The voting upon this technicality was naturally interpreted as a vote approving the government's foreign policy, although some deputies, notably the Right wing Louis Marin, voiced their anger at being deprived of a debate. However, with only Communists and some Right wingers voting against, the motion of adjournment was passed by a large majority, 535 votes for, 75 against. The leaders of the main political groups were given only a quarter of an hour to speak on the motion of adjournment, perhaps a *mauvais quart d'heure* for some. Given the limited time allowed, no meaningful debate was possible.

For the Communists, Gabriel Péri condemned the Munich Agreement. On the extreme Right, Henri de Kérillis, conducted a post-mortem of

French diplomacy. Munich, he stressed, was the end of French influence in central Europe. But neither Péri nor de Kérillis were representative of the Chamber. Blum was much more attuned to the parliamentary mood and speaking for the Socialists emphasised the general feeling of joy and relief that peace had been saved. His well-known phrase—'cowardly shame and relief' is often cited as exemplifying his reaction to the Munich Agreement. This was not the case. The phrase appeared in *Le Populaire* on 20 September when the danger of war appeared to be receding and Blum envisaged its avoidance with a mixture 'of cowardly shame and relief'.[9] And though Blum's private feelings probably were the same on 4 October he did not voice them in the debate.

In the Senate the Deputy Prime Minister, Chautemps, gave a brief recital of the Munich crisis and then asked at once for full powers to be granted.[10] Next day the voting of full powers was an overwhelming vote of confidence in the government's handling of the international situation. In the division on 5 October, 21 senators abstained, including two former foreign ministers, Laval and Paul-Boncour. Though politically poles apart, they both realised, in Laval's words, that the Agreement was 'the greatest diplomatic humiliation to which France has ever had to submit'.[11] Needless to say, they could not bring themselves to vote with the Communists against the government.

It is often assumed that the interplay of internal conflict and external threats automatically debilitated French governments in the 1930s. This was not true of the Daladier ministry. Munich, though disastrous abroad, was a source of strength at home. The Prime Minister astutely exploited foreign and domestic tensions. The secret of his survival was simple: he appealed persuasively for national unity against the external danger, and pleased the conservatives by burying the Popular Front.

Early efforts to get on better terms with the Rome-Berlin Axis had only partly restored the confidence of French investors. In the eyes of Daladier and Bonnet, the recovery of the economy depended on the restoration of business confidence and this meant the sacrifice of the Popular Front. The first portent of change was Daladier's attack on the social legislation of the Popular Front, particularly the forty-hour week which conservatives denounced as an obstacle to increased industrial production. In a broadcast of 21.7.1938, the prime minister announced that workers would be allowed to exceed the forty-hour week maximum. On 30 August the Cabinet approved two decrees modifying the application of the forty-hour law. With many Frenchmen away on holiday until September, the timing of the broadcast was a minor masterpiece of political skill. The Left was taken by surprise and before it could recover from the shock the international crisis came to a head in September. The threat of war silenced the prime minister's critics. The majority of deputies and senators accepted their exclusion from policy-making. As late as 27 September the Presidents of the two Chambers assured the British Ambassador that there was 'no actual demand' for the recall of parliament 'even in parliamentary circles'.[12]

The peaceful outcome of events was a tremendous boon to Daladier. The enormous relief with which the public greeted the Munich Agreement gave him a huge, though momentary, popularity. He toyed with the idea of dissolving parliament and going to the country.[13] A Radical landslide in the elections would free him from dependence on Socialists and Communist votes. It was decided to ask for a renewal of full powers and in the event of a refusal to dissolve parliament. The Socialists jibbed at giving the government a second grant of plenary powers. Herriot's personal intervention, fortified with a promise from Daladier not to tamper with the forty-hour week, persuaded the Socialists to abstain, instead of voting against the government. The voting was 331 for, 78 against, with 203 abstentions, of which 156 were Socialists. The Popular Front majority of June 1936 was finally shattered. 'We are voting for you, you will govern for us', the Right wing told Daladier.[14]

In October Daladier moved further to the Right. At the Radical party congress at Marseilles on 27-29 October he roundly condemned the Communists. On 1 November the Radical Finance Minister, Paul Marchandeau, exchanged portfolios with the Right wing Reynaud. Reynaud's deflationary programme angered the unions who called a general strike at the end of the month. The strike was a failure. In the Cabinet, only the Radical Jean Zay, Education Minister, warned against the danger of trying to govern France without the participation of the working classes. However Reynaud's reforms restored the confidence of the moneyed classes. The *Times* talked of the 'French miracle' and 'from the spring of 1939 the problem of the franc practically ceased to exist'.[15]

Hitler's annexation of Bohemia and Moravia on 15 March 1939 marked the only occasion between the *Anschluss* and the outbreak of war when parliamentary pressure decisively shaped the conduct of French policy. In March, parliament was sitting and fierce denunciations of Germany's aggression helped to stiffen official reactions.[16] But for the parliamentary explosion, backed by wider public alarm, Daladier would probably have contented himself with a mild protest in Berlin. The flare-up was all too brief. Following the example of Munich, Daladier utilised the Prague *coup* to consolidate his position. On 17 March a bill was introduced to give the government full powers up to 30 November 1939 to take all necessary measures for national defence. Daladier emphasised the necessity of countering with similar weapons the totalitarian states, whose successes were achieved by speed and surprise. Despite strong Left wing opposition, the bill was passed by the Chamber of Deputies on 18 March by 321 votes, with 264 against. The Senate passed the bill the next day.

According to one highly-placed official of the period, the request in March for full powers was a piece of bluff designed to extricate the government from an awkward position in international affairs.[17] Reynaud was said to have persuaded Daladier to ask for the powers. A flurry of activity followed in government departments with officials trying to find projects for decree laws. For lack of new ideas, old plans were rehashed.

After 12 May 1939 there was no further discussion of foreign affairs. Daladier had the stage to himself. He was anxious to get parliament out of the way as soon as possible. On 14 June he asked Chamberlain not to announce the date of the British general election until after August so as to avoid providing ammunition for political opponents who wished to have a French election in the spring of 1940. The four year term of parliament would end in May 1940. Daladier had in mind the proroguing of parliament 'for a couple of years' since it was 'of the highest importance' that given the international situation discussion of foreign affairs should be 'avoided' in France. 'Your account of Daladier's intentions concerning prorogation of parliament makes my mouth water', Chamberlain replied to Phipps.[18] The British prime minister believed he had a lever with which to persuade Daladier to restore relations with Italy. On 27 June Daladier closed the parliamentary session.

On 25 July the French heard rumours that the date of the British general election had been fixed for 25 October. Chamberlain was asked not to announce the date before the end of August. The British leader renewed the undertaking given in June but did not take the French into his confidence as to the date of the election, although the Germans were told that the date was 14 November.[19] In the event, the French parliament was prolonged not prorogued. On 30 July the Cabinet approved an emergency decree which prolonged by two years the legislative life of the 1936 parliament. Despite the imminence of war, the recall of parliament was again delayed for as long as possible, perhaps in the hope of a last minute diplomatic solution to the Danzig dispute. The Chambers were recalled for a special session on 2 September and were immediately asked to vote supplies for war.

As well as trying to keep the Chambers out of the way and stifling discussion of foreign policy, the executive starved parliamentarians of information upon international affairs. Pre-1914 governments published Yellow Books upon the Moroccan crises of 1905 and 1911, and in the 1920s diplomatic documents had been made available upon the international conferences of the period, but for the Rhineland crisis of 1936, the *Anschluss* and Munich there was nothing. On 4 October Daladier promised the Chamber that all the diplomatic papers on the Czech crisis would be published in a Yellow Book, however, such a publication, he affirmed, would contain little that was new because 'perhaps for the first time in the history of the world everything was done and said in public'.[20] It was a ridiculous claim and the Right wing deputy, Louis Marin, demonstrated its absurdity by pointing out that parliament in fact knew very little indeed of the diplomatic exchanges. The deputies, said Marin, had neither maps nor documents. What scanty information they possessed came from the British White Papers and Commons debates. In response to requests from the Chamber foreign affairs committee, Bonnet promised a Yellow Book but the government were in no hurry and the diplomatic collection was not published until December 1939. The French parliamentary record did not compare favourably with the British. Though Chamberlain was not anxious to recall parliament sooner than necessary in September 1938, the House of Commons did at least meet before the conference in Munich. On 28 September the House was given a lengthy account of the crisis. Parliament reassembled on 3 October and debated the Munich Agreement until 6 October.

The Chambers were not entirely defenceless. Through the foreign affairs committees of the Chamber of Deputies and of the Senate, deputies and senators were able to exert some influence on the formulation of policy. The fact that the meetings of the committees were not restricted to parliamentary sessions gave them some importance as watchdogs. The membership of the committees was the key to their influence. Members were elected annually by a system of proportional representation of political groups so that the committees formed a parliament in miniature. Frequent re-election of members, who were often former prime ministers and foreign ministers, gave a marked continuity of personnel and technical expertise to the committees. The Senate committee in 1938-39 included Laval, Millerand and Paul-Boncour. The Chamber committee had two former foreign ministers, Delbos and Flandin.

The committees' primary function was the collection of information upon foreign affairs. This information was supplied in two ways: firstly the foreign minister would attend committee meetings and answer questions, secondly committee chairmen had access to official files. The usual procedure was for the chairman to request the foreign minister or prime minister to attend their meetings and report upon official policy. But the procedure lacked constitutional force, and Briand when foreign minister allowed eight months to go by without putting in an appearance before the committees; normally, however, a minister would have courted disaster had he refused to attend without giving satisfactory excuses.

Although the ministerial report did not usually divulge secret information, reference would be made to diplomatic despatches and the minister might even read extracts from certain documents. Committee members received a much fuller picture of events than they would otherwise have had. The tradition was that proceedings were secret and, in theory, the public knew no more than the brief reports published in the *Bulletin des Commissions*. In practice several committee members were journalists and a good deal of information might find its way into the press. As for access to official papers, committee members did not have a general right of access but chairmen were allowed to see foreign ministry documents, though it is not clear whether they were allowed to see outgoing as well as incoming telegrams.[21] In 1935, for example, Bérenger, chairman of the Senate committee, received copies of secret agreements which Laval concluded with Mussolini in Rome on 7 January. The privilege of seeing foreign ministry papers was withdrawn in July 1940.

Bonnet claimed that he had the support of Jean Mistler, chairman of the Chamber committee since 1936, and Henry Bérenger, chairman of the Senate committee. Jean Mistler was a man of many parts—author, academic, diplomat, politician.[22] In the 1920s he lectured at the University of Budapest and also worked at the Quai d'Orsay. In 1934 he held cabinet office in two governments. He worked with Chautemps in 1937 for Franco-German *rapprochement* and prided himself on being the only French deputy who had not yet set foot in the Soviet embassy. On 14 June 1938 he was said to share Caillaux's opinion that France would never willingly fight for Czechoslovakia. Alexander Werth, Paris correspondent of the *Manchester Guardian*, saw him as 'one of the most active pacifists' in Paris. Until March 1939 Mistler seemed confident that Germany had no hostile intentions towards France and was only interested in the Ukraine.

By July 1939 he had changed his tune and believed that Germany now imperilled France's security, though regretting that Munich had not proved a success since a 'friendly arrangement' over Danzig might have been possible. Berlin had considered inviting him to the Chancellor's fiftieth birthday party on 20 April 1939 but the message of sympathy for Czechoslovakia issued by the Chamber foreign affairs committee made its chairman *persona non grata*.

Henry Bérenger, chairman of the Senate committee since 1931, strongly seconded Bonnet's diplomacy.[23] Bérenger was senator for Guadeloupe and before 1914 had been a well-known journalist. His fixation was Italy. He had always been passionately Italophile and in his *Resurrections Italiennes,* published in 1911, praised Italy as a future ally of France against Germany. Under Clemenceau he was High Commissioner for Fuels from 1918-20 and acquired a reputation for profiteering and shady dealing. Though he never again achieved high office, he was very much a denizen of the *couloirs*. Briand sent him as ambassador to Washington in 1925 and he negotiated the Mellon-Bérenger agreement of 29 April 1926 regulating French war debts but the Chambers refused to ratify it. On 7 October 1938 on behalf of his committee he thanked Bonnet for his 'courageous and tenacious action for peace'.

In addition to the chairmen, Bonnet had other allies in the committees. In the Chamber committee, Flandin and Bergery sympathised with the foreign minister's policy. But there were also staunch opponents such as the Socialist Solomon Grumbach, the Communist Gabriel Péri, and the Right wing Henri de Kérillis. Feelings ran high after the Prague *coup*. When the Ambassador at Berlin, Coulondre, who had been recalled to Paris on 19 March as a gesture of disapproval, told Mistler that he would have to return to Berlin with a solid Anglo-Franco-Soviet alliance the chairman replied: 'do not speak in front of my colleagues of your return to Berlin, you will be disgraced'.[24] As a counterweight to his critics in the Chamber committee, Bonnet could muster support from a pacifist and Italophile group in the Senate committee, led by Laval and his friend, Gaston Henry Haye, Mayor of Versailles, later Vichy ambassador to Washington.[25]

In the main, however, the government encountered little trouble from the committees because their direction was firmly in the hands of the chairmen who had access to ministers and could control the information given to members. Press communiques often mentioned that the chairmen were keeping in semi-permanent contact with the minister. Bérenger in August 1939 ignored the appeals of senator Jacques Bardoux for a meeting of the committee.[26] Moreover, the chairmen tended to conduct a semi-official diplomacy of their own. Bérenger had talks with Mussolini and with Goebbels in 1932 and 1933. On the eve of war, both Bérenger and Mistler made frantic efforts to secure Mussolini's mediation in order to avert a Franco-German war over Poland.[27]

None the less the committees were not mere ciphers. Following the Berchtesgaden agreements between Germany and Austria on 12.2.1938, the Chamber foreign affairs committee met on the 16th and examined France's position in central and eastern Europe.[28] Mistler, who had

toured central Europe in January, reported on his impressions. The
Foreign Minister, Delbos, was not present but members called for his appearance. Bergery, who later in the year was an ardent appeaser, spoke
strongly in favour of an active diplomacy in the east. The end of Austria,
he told colleagues, would also mean the extinction of Czechoslovakia.
'Do you think', he asked, 'that we can imitate Belgium, falling back in the
west and arming ourselves so that no one can attack us'? 'If France and
England', he continued, 'had said in advance that they would not accept
a Nazi minister in Austria, there would not be one today'. Gabriel Péri
and Florimond Bonte, both Communists, called for the strengthening of
ties with Czechoslovakia and condemned what they termed 'the policy of
renunciation and surrender followed since 1933 and 1934'. Only Flandin
argued for a withdrawal from the east. Mistler's conclusion drew general
approval: 'the committee must make known its viewpoint. It must, as is
customary, play its role of surveillance and criticism'. Later in the month,
on the 22nd, Delbos appeared before the committee and defended government policy, advocating a diplomacy of 'prudence'.[29]

The Chamber committee was not afraid to express strong criticism of
the Quai d'Orsay. On 8 June 1938 the committee met to consider the
ratification of the Montreux Convention of 8 May 1937 by which France
had agreed to surrender capitulatory rights in Egypt, thus ending for
French residents their exemption from Egyptian laws. Committee members felt that the changes which they had proposed in the Convention had
not received serious attention in the foreign ministry.[30] Strong distrust of
the Quai d'Orsay was voiced. 'The Quai d'Orsay does what it likes and
practises a policy of surrender', complained the deputy Felix Grat. Louis
Marin spoke of the need to teach the functionaries a lesson and asked
Mistler to see Bonnet. 'He will tell me: "It was one of my predecessors who
was responsible" ', replied Mistler. Though the chairman advised against
an adjournment, a vote of adjournment was passed. The vote of displeasure produced results. Bonnet appeared next day to answer questions
on the Convention which was finally ratified by parliament on 16 June.

On 6 October the Chamber committee met for the first time since
17 June. The meeting opened with a long narrative by Bonnet of the
Munich crisis.[31] His report was liberally larded with extracts from official
papers, though his offer to read the text of the Agreement was brushed
aside with cries of 'No, no, quite unnecessary'. The gist of the minister's
statement was that Munich had saved peace and spared Europe a war
which might have destroyed its civilisation. The Agreement, he said, was
a distinct improvement on the Godesberg terms. France must now work
for national unity.

Bonnet got small thanks for his pains. The Socialist Grumbach preferred to talk of the débâcle suffered by France and proposed the creation
of a sub-committee to examine in detail the provisions of the Munich
Agreement. Marin, supported by Mistler, demanded the publication of an
official collection of documents similar to the British White Paper. The
Christian Democrat Ernest Pezet, Vice-Chairman of the committee,
asked why the government had not confessed a year ago its inability to
aid Czechoslovakia. Another member, Bonte, was angry because the

committee had not met for over three months and asked Bonnet for his opinion. 'I have none', was the reply. Mistler then came to Bonnet's rescue, explaining that he had called a meeting as soon as possible after Munich. In fact, he added, one deputy had requested an earlier meeting but the individual in question had forgotten that his membership of the committee had expired three months ago. Mistler reminded members of the committee's function: 'the role of the committee was not to make policy but to appraise it. We do not negotiate treaties but assess them'. The chairman closed the meeting with a vote of thanks to Bonnet for his 'patient and courageous action . . . for the defence and maintenance of peace'.

In the winter of 1938-39 the growing criticism of Munich, and more particularly of the foreign minister, was echoed in the Chamber committee. At a meeting on 14 December 1938, Bonnet was given a very rough passage.[32] The session lasted four hours. Bonnet's calm optimism contrasted sharply with the disquiet of the deputies. The minister delivered a lengthy account of Franco-British and Franco-German relations since October. The questions and discussion which followed brought a devastating attack by the Right wing de Kérillis:

> If we have had little opportunity to hear you, our Radical colleagues at Marseilles have had the chance to hear from you an important speech, in the course of which you did not mention at any point our eastern alliances and in which you replaced the word 'alliances' by the term 'friendships' . . . there are some men, Minister, who pass for your friends, there are organs which are considered to have your inspiration . . . which announce that France must hand over the Ukraine . . . there must be in the interest of the government, and in the interest of the country and in the interest of parliamentary institutions, a closer contact between government and assemblies, . . . for months we have not managed to see you. . .

Pressed for a reply, Bonnet said there was nothing he would like more than a foreign affairs debate. A major foreign policy debate took place from 13-26 January 1939 and it seems reasonable to conclude that the discontent expressed in December ensured an early debate.[33]

The Chamber committee did not see the minister again until 1 March 1939 when he reported on recent developments and answered questions. 'No negotiations, neither official nor semi-official, had been undertaken with Italy', the committee was told, though Baudouin had in fact been sent as a semi-official emissary in the first week of February.[34] Hitler's Prague *coup* brought another outburst of criticism from the committee. Bonnet attended a meeting on 15 March and outlined the international crisis.[35] There was a general demand for a foreign policy debate on Czechoslovakia and Bonnet promised to consult Daladier. The Communist Péri delivered a vehement denunciation of government policy but the most remarkable philippic came from de Kérillis:

> We are a country dishonoured . . . a country which destroys its alliances. . . . France was the guardian of great principles, that was all that remained to us . . . You have destroyed that at Munich and you have just reaped what you sowed . . . You said: 'We must be strong'. Have you made an effort since Munich? No. Because of the spirit of Munich we have done nothing . . .

Doubtless the reactions of the Chamber committee after 15 March helped to stiffen the government's diplomacy but on specific issues the committee was helpless in the face of official stonewalling. In response to many requests, the government promised a Yellow Book dealing with the Czechoslovak crisis. But after its second meeting the sub-committee on the Munich Agreement was not convened again. On 14 December Marin asked what had happened to the Yellow Book promised in October. Bonnet said he was having difficulty securing the agreement of other governments for the publication of documents but 'hoped to overcome them' and promised the documents 'in a few days'. When the committee met on 15 February 1939 Marin requested an explanation of the delay in publishing the collection. Mistler promised to look into the matter. His colleagues felt the government should also publish documents for the Rhineland and *Anschluss*. On 8 March Mistler announced that he had been given the draft of a Yellow Book, containing 33 documents, but no date of publication had been fixed because of the need to secure the approval of other governments. The draft collection, he continued, would be deposited in the archives of the committee so that members might consult it.

Parliament and its committees scrutinised the Daladier ministry's foreign policy but showed little interest in trying to control it. The committees have been described as 'channels of information about foreign policy, rather than agencies in making it'.[36] This description requires some qualification. Admittedly, as watchdogs of the legislature, the foreign affairs committees were not as sharp-toothed as the finance committees, which at certain periods in the interwar years ranked almost as a second cabinet.[37] Under Caillaux's chairmanship the Senate finance committee was largely responsible for the overthrow of Blum's two Popular Front governments. However, as well as being 'channels of information' the foreign affairs committees could on occasion act as influential pressure groups in the making of policy. They could shake a weak administration such as Blum's second ministry in March 1938 or buttress a strong one such as Daladier's government of April 1938.[38] At times they exercised what seemed to be a decisive pressure on the government. In 1922 Poincaré, chairman of the Senate foreign affairs committee, sent a telegram to the foreign minister, Briand, who was then attending an international conference, making it clear that he was not to conclude any agreement without the approval of the committees and parliament.[39] Some measure of the importance which the government attached to the committees can be gauged from the frequency of the foreign minister's attendance at meetings. From April 1938 to September 1939 the Chamber committee had 22 meetings, including purely business meetings for the election of officers, of which Bonnet attended eight.

What was the explanation for the relative passivity of parliament and its committees? Certainly the nature of the parliamentary tradition counted for much. For the majority of senators and deputies the purpose of the Chambers and committees was to conduct an audit of policy, not to act as agencies in its making. Another consideration was the consensus which existed on foreign policy. Until Munich, few could quarrel with the government's declared aim of international *détente*. Even after the crisis, the growing body of criticism was not strong enough to deflect the government from its course. A major factor, too, was the strength of the parliamentary majority. Despite the dissolution of the Popular Front majority in October 1938 parliamentary support remained firm. Daladier profited from an evolution to the Right which had been evident since the autumn of 1937. The propertied classes had had more than their fill of the Popular Front and were prepared to support any government which sought peace abroad and order at home.

Some of Daladier's strength derived from opposition weakness. Munich cut across party lines. Unlike Ethiopia in 1935 and Spain in 1936, there was no clear division between Left and Right. Traditionally the goal of Franco-German understanding had attracted men of the Left (Gambetta, Rouvier, Ferry, Caillaux); in 1938-39 many on the Right (Flandin, Piétri, Baudouin) were drawn to it. Potentially the Socialists were a strong opposition since many of them were disillusioned with the government's social and economic record but Munich divided their ranks. The secretary of the party, Paul Faure, and his supporters, like the British Clydesiders, were passionately for peace and rejoiced over Munich. On foreign affairs, therefore, parliamentary opposition was weak and divided. Sniping from the Communist Péri and the Right wing de Kérillis had only nuisance value. Nearly all the political groups contained dissident voices but there was no concerted resistance to the government. Marin and Tardieu on the Right had reservations about Franco-German understanding but, unlike de Kérillis and Reynaud, they were not prepared to do business with Moscow. The traditionally ultra-nationalist, Germanophobe Right had lost its identity. The Christian Democrats were few and undecided. Only Georges Bidault, at that time a relatively unknown figure, advocated in his newspaper *L'Aube* a firm line towards Germany and called for Bonnet's resignation.[40]

Chapter 9

Quai D'Orsay

In post-Liberation France, national recovery seemed conditional upon establishing the responsibilities for recent disasters. In 1946 the National Assembly created a parliamentary commission to investigate the 'political, economic, diplomatic and military events' which contributed to the collapse of 1940. The commission drew up an indictment of the French foreign service: 'the diplomats negotiated', ran the report, and created 'juridical constructions which reflected rigid adherence to a system rather than political views grounded in realities'.[1] Thus old prejudices died hard. After 1914, secret diplomacy was blamed for the outbreak of the First World War. Similarly, after 1940, diplomats, as well as politicians, were blamed for the fall of France. But there was a world of difference between 1914 and 1939. In the years immediately preceding the Second World War the diplomats exercised comparatively little influence on events. The disregard which the dictators displayed for their professional advisers was strikingly paralleled in the two western democracies. The British Foreign Office and the French Foreign Ministry were frequently bypassed by the statesmen.

In London the inability or unwillingness of French leaders to keep secrets was almost proverbial. But while British secrets might not be safe in Paris, French officials were remarkably tight-lipped about their own. Though several ambassadors published memoirs, the central administrators of the Quai d'Orsay have said little about themselves. Philippe Berthelot, Secretary General of the Foreign Ministry from 1925 to 1933, destroyed his personal papers and published no memoirs. Alexis Léger, his successor, did not write about his diplomatic career. If he kept a diary for the 1930s it would be an invaluable source since the official archives shed little light on the policy making process within the Foreign Ministry.[2]

Alexis Léger, permanent head of the Foreign Ministry from 1933 to May 1940, was an enigmatic individual, as complex as his poetry.[3] Indeed, he is better known in works of fiction than in the histories of the period. Under the name of 'Léger' he figures in a number of novels: Marcel Proust's *A la Recherche du Temps Perdu*; Louis Chadourne's *Le Maître du Navire*; Jules Romains's *Les Hommes du Bonne Volonté*; Louis Aragon's *Les Communistes* and Jean Paul Sartre's *Les Chemins de la Liberté*. Diplomacy was not his first choice of career. He studied medicine for a while and then entered the diplomatic service in 1914, serving at Peking from 1916 to 1921. Like Berthelot, he owed much to the friendship of the foreign minister, Aristide Briand, whom he accompanied to the Washington Naval Conference in 1921. In April 1925 Briand returned as foreign minister in the Painlevé government and Léger's career began in earnest. It was rumoured that he had gained Briand's friendship through a certain Madame de Vilmorin who at one time had a political salon. As well as favouring Léger, Briand restored his protégé, Berthelot, to the post of secretary general. Poincaré had disgraced him in 1922 for using his position to help his brother who was in the Bank of Indo-China. Upon Berthelot's retirement in 1933, Léger was the natural successor.

While Paul Claudel, Jean Giraudoux and Paul Morand openly combined literary and diplomatic careers, Léger gave precedence to diplomacy and wrote little in the 1930s. The decision can hardly have been an easy one and Léger had much in common with the Leader of his poem, Anabase, who in the midst of all the parleyings with ambassadors and princes, is continually distracted by the fascination he finds in the contemplation of his own soul. 'The highly wrought verbal texture' of Léger's verse, with its 'ceremonial aloofness' and 'sustained elevated tone' hints at the complex personality of the diplomat.[4]

On 18 May 1940, Paul Reynaud remodelled his government, taking the ministry of war for himself and giving Daladier the Quai d'Orsay. The chief casualty of the changes was Léger. He was brusquely and ungraciously sacked — a victim, it seems, of the intrigues of Reynaud's mistress, Hélène de Portes. He refused to accept the sop of the Washington embassy. After the armistice of 1940, he moved to the United States and resumed his literary career under the name of Saint-John Perse. In revenge, the Vichy government deprived him of his French nationality. After the Liberation of France he refused an invitation to return to diplomacy and did not return to give evidence before the postwar parliamentary commission of enquiry. In 1960 his literary achievement was crowned with the award of the Nobel prize.

Léger, like Berthelot, was depicted as the power behind the throne. Foreign ministers reigned but did not rule. In point of fact, his role as the 'permanent master of French foreign policy' has been exaggerated.[5] Several factors helped to foster the illusion that the secretary general was more powerful than was actually the case. The office itself, which corresponded to the post of Permanent Under-Secretary of State in the British Foreign Office, was relatively new. It was first created in 1915 but not permanently established until 1920. Its purpose was to supply an element of continuity and stability in the face of frequent ministerial changes. As first incumbent, Berthelot undoubtedly wielded great influence, although there were limits to his power. He was never, for instance able to discover from Briand precisely what the minister had said to the German foreign minister, Stresemann, at Thoiry in 1926. Briand requested his leading advisers not to discuss major policy questions with the German ambassador, reserving them for his personal attention alone.[6] Needless to say, the very newness of the post encouraged suspicions that Berthelot was a deputy foreign minister. Moreover, the diplomacy by conference which followed the First World War imposed new and heavy demands on the Ministry's central services. The increasing amount of business handled by the central officials reinforced the impression that the secretary general was the real master of policy. Personality, too, lent support to this belief. Both Berthelot and Léger were born to the roles of grey eminences, priding themselves on being models of discretion. The public knew a little of them and suspected much more.

The critics of the central administration were numerous and vociferous. A parliamentary report of 1933 indicted the Quai d'Orsay on several counts: inadequate intelligence services, insufficient consultation between the ministry and agents in the field, lack of administrative coherence. Many conversations took place, it was alleged, of which records were never kept.[7] In January 1933 a commission under Henry Bérenger, chairman of the Senate foreign affairs committee, was set up to study the the working of the foreign ministry. There were calls for the streamlining of the administration. Five years later the criticisms of 1933 were still being repeated. And the 1946 parliamentary commission of enquiry into the disasters of the 1930s alleged that the permanent officials had acted as a barrier between the minister and representatives overseas. Some of the harshest criticism came from former ambassadors. Léon Noel, Ambassador in Warsaw from 1935 to 1940, claimed that 'the mistakes made during this period by our diplomacy' were 'due essentially to the lack of realism of the leading officials...especially Alexis Léger' who 'did not take account of the opinion of our heads of mission'.

To what extent were these criticisms justified? The postwar commission of enquiry relied heavily on the testimony of Jean Dobler, Consul General at Cologne from 1931 to 1937. Dobler claimed that from the autumn of 1935 he repeatedly warned Paris of the danger of a German move against the Rhineland. Certainly his warnings do not seem to have been acknowledged but Paris was aware of the danger and Dobler may well have been piqued by the lack of attention paid to him. Like many diplomats stationed in one place for any length of time, he may have thought himself forgotten.

It is difficult to substantiate the charge that permanent officials tended to screen the minister from agents in the field.[8] Conferences between the minister, leading advisers and groups of ambassadors may, as François-Poncet claimed, have been rare. In nine years as Ambassador at Berlin, François-Poncet recalled having attended only one such conference— on 3 April 1936. Paul-Boncour called a conference of French representatives in central and eastern Europe on 5 April 1938. Still, it is arguable that such gatherings, organised perhaps on a regional basis, should have been the norm rather than the exception. But there was frequent consultation between the Minister and individual ambassadors. Also, it would seem that agents in the field themselves enhanced the importance of the central staff. Roland de Margerie, Secretary at the London embassy in 1938-39, recalls that since the Minister had little or no time to read reports these were often written with a view to winning the attention of a particular official. Much more well-founded is the charge that senior officials had spent too much time in Paris. Alexis Léger, Secretary General, René Massigli, Political Director in 1937-38, Emile Charvériat, Political Director in 1938-39, Charles Rochat, Assistant Political Director, had served in Paris almost continuously throughout the 1930s. Some lengthy tours of duty abroad might have made for a more balanced and experienced leadership.

Much more serious was the criticism contained in the parliamentary report of 1933 to the effect that the foreign ministry's services were inadequate and lacked cohesion. The administrative structure was cumbersome and antiquated.[9] An old-fashioned distrust of telephones and typewriters persisted into the 1920s. The establishment of the post of secretary general did not lead to any thoroughgoing modernisation. Though the number of missions increased between 1914 and 1939, the personnel of the foreign ministry fell from 526 to 404 in the same period. The reduction in manpower was not the result of any mechanisation. A small cipher staff had to encipher and decipher by hand. Cipher machines were only in experimental use. These shortcomings had practical consequences for the conduct of diplomacy. As Ambassador at Ankara in 1939-40 Massigli found his negotiations for a Franco-Turkish alliance hampered by the delay which instructions took to reach him from Paris. He noted that instructions for his British colleague always arrived before his own. The leisurely, amateurish ways of the Quai d'Orsay placed France at a serious disadvantage.

Nor was Léger a model of efficiency. According to Jean Chauvel, Assistant Director of the Asiatic and Oceanic department in 1938-40, the secretary general would arrive at the ministry about 11 a.m. in the morning, leave at midday for lunch and return about 4 p.m. in the afternoon, though often working late into the evening.[10] Much of his day was spent closeted with a small group of regular visitors. His frequent absences for one reason or another did not help subordinates. The best moment to catch him was at the end of the afternoon, even then his door might be locked or the caller would be imperiously waved away. Léger's last barricade was a thick pile of papers on his desk. If the matter was urgent, Chauvel returned the next day. Another manoeuvre was to wait until the end of the week and then Chauvel, with the aid of Léger's secretary, would place his file on top of the pile. Chauvel also suggests that Léger was not as well-informed as might have been expected. He had spent some years in China and had been assistant director of the Asian and Oceanic department. Traditionally the Asian section came under the personal supervision of the secretary general. Yet when Chauvel consulted him, Léger had little to offer but general advice.

Complaints about the dominance of the central staff and lack of consultation were an understandable reaction against the steady erosion of the established role of the ambassador. The telephone completed a devaluation which had begun with the invention of the telegraph. The central services could keep a much tighter rein on their agents overseas. Instructions sent by wire or bag could be cancelled or modified up to the last minute. Also the huge increase in the amount of paperwork, especially in the last year or so of peace, left the diplomat with scant time for reflection and personal initiative. Before 1914, private correspondence between diplomats and permanent officials had greatly helped in the formulation of policy but in the interwar years private letters were few and far between.

The decline in the position of the ambassador was part and parcel of a general decline in the influence of professional diplomats. Long-term trends were undermining the authority of the central officials as well as of the ambassador. The chief factor at work was the post-1918 emphasis on personal diplomacy, conducted by heads of government and their foreign ministers. The new approach was summed up by the British Prime Minister, Ramsay MacDonald, in a letter to Herriot in October 1932:

> you will never get the mind of any country from its dispatches and its interviews with the press. If you assume that any country in Europe is playing an evil game, surely the best thing to do is to ask it to come and talk matters over...I would not write...long letters; and that I think is how our international business must be done more and more.[11]

Pressure of work also weighed heavily on central staffs. The enormous increase of incoming correspondence in all foreign ministries in the 1930s 'forced overworked departmental staffs to give priority to cables that required action and to defer the analysis of situation reports to a later time which sometimes never came'.[12]

In 1938 the Right wing periodical *Je suis partout* and the like portrayed the foreign minister as the prisoner of his permanent officials. In truth, Bonnet was far from defenceless. Through his private office he could bypass the central staff and follow a personal diplomacy. The minister's private office, or *cabinet* as it was known, was staffed by personal assistants, drawn from family, party or home town and usually allotted liaison tasks with the press, parliament and constituency.[13] In contrast to the British practice of selecting ministerial assistants from the permanent staff, the French *cabinets* of the interwar years tended to be an independent team, recruited directly by the minister and responsible only to him, though paid by the government as civil servants. Ministers came and went in relatively quick succession but while in office their personal advisers were capable of harassing and thwarting leading officials. As Briand's principal private secretary in 1915, Berthelot is said to have 'dealt with the most important matters, summoning editors to give them instructions, presenting telegrams for the minister's signature — the contents of which had not been seen by the permanent officials.'[14]

Bonnet's chief assistant in 1938, Jules Henry, was a devoted aide who worked closely with Francois Piétri, former Navy Minister and one of the minister's major political allies.[15] Frequently Bonnet managed affairs through his office, keeping senior functionaries in the dark. In February 1939 Daladier and Bonnet were seeking an agreement with General Franco's Nationalist forces. The Foreign Minister informed Phipps of the terms of a proposed Franco-Spanish agreement, requesting him to tell Halifax 'in a private letter only' because he had 'not told any of his officials at the Quai d'Orsay'.[16] In May 1939 Bonnet conducted negotiations with Poland 'personally' and did not inform 'Léger or any of the regular services' of the progress of the talks; all documents were handled by his *cabinet*.[17]

Allegations have been made, notably by M. Massigli, Political Director in 1938, about Bonnet's methods of working.[18] It is said that he would withhold for several days the notes of his interviews with foreign envoys. And when these notes were communicated to senior staff they might be at complete variance with the version given by the envoys themselves to officials. Also, it is claimed, that Bonnet, unknown to Léger, might by telephone significantly modify instructions cabled to French missions. Pertinax states that when Bonnet did not want officials to know of his calls to Berlin he would ring François Poncet from the Chamber of Deputies. It has also been suggested that since the cipher service came under the control of the Minister's *cabinet* Bonnet had the opportunity to restrict the normal distribution of telegrams. Normally, telegrams would be decoded in longhand and copies made for distribution. However on occasion the minister asked for the longhand notes to be brought immediately to him before copies had been made.[19]

Some of these charges can be corroborated. In 1938 and 1939 the Minister kept negotiations with Poland very much in his own hands. On 1 June 1938, Massigli sent Léon Noel, the Ambassador in Warsaw a copy of a Polish memorandum which had been handed to Bonnet on 26 May and retained for three days.[20] On 29 June 1938 Massigli wrote to Noel:

> Since the minister has initiated with Lukasiewicz (*Polish ambassador*) negotiations of which we are only very inadequately informed it is impossible for me to send you the instructions which you were expecting. . .[21]

Regarding the alleged discrepancies between Bonnet's memoranda of talks and the notes of his interlocutors, the verdict must be *not proven*. What can be said, however, is that the Foreign Minister's notes of conversations often give only the briefest summary of an interview and look very thin in comparison with the records made by the diplomats themselves. Generally, Léger and Massigli drafted written instructions which the Minister signed. Often a telephone call from the Minister's private office would precede and follow written instructions. This was normal procedure. Yet certain diplomats, notably Massigli and de Margerie in London, testify that although the Minister's telephone calls did not explicitly conflict with written instructions, their tenor and emphasis was often contrary to the spirit of the instructions. But again proof is wanting. M de Margerie, Secretary at the London embassy in 1938-39, writes:

> I cannot give . . . an example of the differences between the written instructions of M Georges Bonnet and his words on the telephone . . . M Corbin and I studied the matter in 1946, and concluded that we did not possess any documentary proof in this matter.[22]

Again, there is no documentary evidence for the other allegations against Bonnet. In a letter of 2 October 1938, Pierre Comert, head of the press and news services of the Quai d'Orsay, accused the minister of having tried to suppress in France a British Foreign Office communiqué of 26 September 1938.[23] Victor de Lacroix, French Minister in Prague in 1938, was convinced that one of his key telegrams to Paris at the height of the Munich crisis had been edited in the Quai d'Orsay. Bonnet was not accused by name but the inference was plain — someone acting on the minister's authority had tampered with the text of the original telegram.

In an anguished letter of 30 April 1948, Lacroix begged Massigli, who was then Ambassador in London, to search the embassy archives for evidence that might confirm his recollections.[24] Massigli was unsuccessful but pointed out that it was clear not everything of importance had been transmitted to London at the time.

What remains, then, of the charges against Bonnet? Although the most serious accusations lack documentary proof, it is not insignificant that a number of experienced and normally reticent civil servants should have chosen to make such allegations. Bonnet's personality tended of itself to create mistrust. Bonnet's methods of working differed little from those of his predecessors. Theophile Delcassé, for example, conducted a highly personal policy, employing unofficial contacts and bypassing often both central officials and representatives overseas. Similarly, Briand and Delbos did not see fit to report all their conversations with foreign statesmen and envoys. What the diplomats really disliked were not the methods — which might have been followed by any other minister — but the personality and policy of Bonnet. As his friend and colleague de Monzie put it:

> What can you expect...with Bonnet. He is a decent and honest man, but he suffers from an almost physical inability to tell the whole truth. There are always things held back and not made clear, so that finally no one knows how much truth there is in what he says...This holds true for his talks with diplomats, as well as his reports to the Council of Ministers...[25]

In fairness to Bonnet it must be said that his methods of working simply reflected the lack of established procedures in the day-to-day running of the Foreign Ministry. In the British Foreign Office it was understood that the Secretary of State would keep a full record of conversations with foreign envoys and that this record would be quickly made available to the appropriate officials. At the Quai d'Orsay much depended on the whim of the Minister of the day. He might retain notes and memoranda for his own personal use or they might immediately be passed on to senior advisers. Barthou was systematic and methodical in circulating memoranda of talks but there was no long-standing arrangement in the matter. However the full truth is likely to remain the *secret* of Bonnet. He took great care to keep his record clean. Massigli recalled that none of the memoranda which he submitted to the minister in September 1938 were ever returned to him with any written comment.

As Foreign Minister, Bonnet could also wield considerable influence outside the Foreign Ministry. The press and news department of the Foreign Ministry, like the cipher section, was controlled by the minister's *cabinet*. Through the press department and by means of secret subsidies the minister could exert powerful pressures on the press.

In 1935 the Prime Minister, Laval, had warned the British Foreign Secretary, Eden, that France was not to be judged by its press.[26] Despite the absence of official censorship the government had always exercised a strong influence on the press. Foreign influences vied with official ones. Before 1914, Russian roubles had gone in large amounts to French newspapers. In the 1920s the Americans were said to have spent 'enormous sums in the French press to influence public opinion'. From 1935 onwards

Italian lire were poured into the coffers of certain papers. It is even alleged that British Intelligence and the Trade Union Congress distributed subsidies to some newspapers. Only the Germans seem to have abstained from exploiting the venality of the French press, possibly because they had no need to buy sympathy. On the whole, however, foreign subsidies were limited to the small circulation papers and periodicals in the 1930s. The major influence was that of the French government, encompassing the whole of the press.

The foreign ministry press department was established in 1920, and from 1925-30 each major ministry had a press office with a group of journalists on its payroll.[27] Encouraged by Laval and Tardieu, the senior government departments adopted the practice of distributing monthly 'envelopes', as the payments were discreetly called. Following official example, the Bank of France and business interests adopted the practice.

The pivot of official influence was the Havas news agency, counterpart of Reuters and United Press.[28] Havas combined news and advertising services and had built up a virtual monopoly of press advertising. It also controlled the majority of shares in Radio Luxembourg and other radio stations. The agency was linked to powerful financial interests such as the Banque de Paris et des Pays Bas. Since the Second Empire the agency had been generally regarded as a semi-official organ, its overseas representatives were counted as unofficial diplomatic agents, working in close liaison with resident French envoys. Léon Renier, a Havas director, said: 'without betraying any secrets I can say that Havas could not exist for an hour if it quarrelled with a government'.

The Daladier government established formal ties with the agency. Negotiations initiated by Blum in 1936 were reopened by Bonnet and in an agreement of 11 July 1938 the government assumed responsibility for ten years for the deficit on news services in the Havas budget. In addition, there were informal contacts; the Political Director of Havas, Léon Bassée, was a friend of the foreign minister.[29]

As well as links with Havas, the minister possessed other levers of influence: secret government subsidies — the notorious *fonds secrets*, also private monies made available by sympathetic business concerns, and perhaps most important of all, informal day-to-day contacts with proprietors, editors and journalists. The journalist Jean Luchaire, later a prominent Vichy supporter, was paid 20,000 francs a month by Bonnet for the expenses of his weekly review *Notre Temps*, which backed the minister's diplomacy.[30] Pertinax, editor of *L'Europe Nouvelle*, alleged that Bonnet on several occasions tried to bribe him into abandoning his criticism of official policy. Bonnet's own mouthpiece was *L'Homme Libre*, a small circulation daily, founded by Clemenceau in 1913. In December 1938 the Foreign Minister acquired a controlling interest in the paper. From that time onwards the newspaper consistently sang the praises of Bonnet.

Informal contact with the press counted for a great deal. During the interwar years it was quite normal for the Foreign Minister to receive twice a day the diplomatic correspondents of the major dailies.[31] In September 1938 Bonnet saw the foreign press corps every day. Some journalists, to their credit, did not take kindly to official guidance. There was a long-standing feud between Pertinax and the Quai d'Orsay. According to Léger, the journalist had been forbidden access to the Foreign Ministry since the days of Briand. Certainly Bonnet and Pertinax seem to have waged a private war. In June 1939, one of Pertinax's overseas despatches was intercepted by Bonnet and communicated to London. Among the foreign press correspondents, Thomas Cadett of *The Times,* and Alexander Werth of the *Manchester Guardian,* roused the wrath of the Foreign Minister. Leading foreign journalists were often nominated by the Quai for the award of the Légion d'Honneur. Werth's nomination was blocked by Bonnet.

The quarrel between Cadett and Bonnet is instructive because it reveals the extent to which the Foreign Minister had the support of the British Ambassador, Phipps, and of his Press Attaché, Sir Charles Mendl.[32] Cadett had got into the embassy's bad books as a result of his attitude to the Munich crisis. He and the correspondent of the *News Chronicle*, formerly frequent visitors to the embassy, stayed away and Phipps reported that they were 'not in sympathy with the Munich and subsequent policy of His Majesty's Government'. Mendl, Press Attaché, was particularly annoyed by Cadett's comment on hearing the news of Chamberlain's visit to Hitler at Godesberg on 22 September: 'This time, he will, I suppose, go in livery'. Gossips passed on remarks in this vein to the embassy. At the beginning of January 1939 Cadett was telephoned by Mendl who told him on the instructions of Phipps that 'it was the policy of HMG to minimise Franco-Italian differences. The Ambassador greatly hoped that the . . . correspondent . . . would eschew all sensationalism . . . and generally conform himself to the British Government line'. Cadett was incensed by these instructions and complained to his editor, Geoffrey Dawson, who felt that the message 'had not been very happily conceived'. The Foreign Office was much less concerned than Phipps about Cadett and considered there was nothing objectionable in his writing but felt the embassy 'must accept some responsibility for letting Mr Cadett get out of hand'.

Worse was yet to come. On 30 January 1939 the *Times* carried a report about a declaration which Bonnet had made to the press after a Cabinet meeting on 29 January. The minister was reported as saying that Italy had not been given a square deal in the Rome Agreements of January 1935. He was said to have spoken without consulting colleagues and Daladier was extremely annoyed. The same day the Quai d'Orsay denied that Bonnet had made any statement to the press. Bonnet protested to Phipps, claiming that Cadett was 'running a campaign against him'. Roger Cambon, Counsellor in London, told the Foreign Office that Bonnet wanted to expel Cadett. A Foreign Office enquiry followed and confirmed the truth of Cadett's report—other journalists had reported the same story. Indeed, Roland de Margerie, Secretary of the French embassy, in informing the Foreign Office of the Quai d'Orsay's *démenti* 'conveyed the impression that he himself believed the story to be perfectly true'. Phipps was censured for not checking the accuracy of the press report before forwarding Bonnet's official protest. He was also told to impress on Bonnet the danger of expelling the journalist. The outcome of the affair was a compromise. Bressy, Bonnet's chief assistant, sent for Cadett and told him no action would be taken. But the *Times* warned Cadett 'to mind his P's and Q's in the future and if possible to cultivate friendlier relations with the Quai'.

But the French Foreign Minister was not without friends in the foreign press corps. On 29 April 1939, Percy Philip, correspondent of the *New York Times*, broadcast for the BBC from Paris.[33] The Polish Ambassador in London, Count Raczynski, complained to the Foreign Office that in his talk Philip had suggested 'that a settlement of the Danzig question in Germany's favour should have been reached long ago and that this was an issue on which Frenchmen could not be expected to fight'. But, before receiving this complaint, the Foreign Office news department had initiated their own enquiries. It was learnt that the BBC had been given to understand that Philip was expressing in his broadcast the views of Bonnet.

Although the foreign ministry had ample means of influencing the press, it did not need to deploy its resources to the full. By reason of its ownership the Paris press was cautious and conservative. The large circulation Parisian papers: *Paris-Soir*, *Petit Parisien*, *Le Journal*, *Le Jour-Echo de Paris*, *Le Matin*, *Le Figaro*, were all controlled by Right wing political and business interests. *Paris-Soir*, owned by the former textile magnate, Jean Prouvost, professed itself non-political but usually came down in favour of the government of the day.[34] The semi-official *Petit Parisien* belonged to the Italophile Pierre Dupuy. Its editor, Jules Elie-Bois was said to be in the pay of the Quai d'Orsay. *Le Journal* was avowedly Right wing and against fighting for Czechoslovakia in 1938. The *Matin*'s proprietor, Maurice Bunau-Varilla, was an admirer of Hitler. *Le Jour-Echo de Paris* of Léon Bailby spoke for the ultra Right, opposed to the Popular Front and against any contact with Moscow. In September 1938, Bailby impressed on Phipps his repugnance and indignation 'at the really criminal and Bolshevik attempts to render a general conflagration inevitable'. The *Figaro*, which had on its editorial board the historian Lucien Romier and the former diplomat Count Wladimir d'Ormesson, was not without sympathy for Czechoslovakia but gave priority to the need for a realistic diplomacy and internal recovery. Prominent among the editors and journalists who gave firm and consistent support to Bonnet's diplomacy were Jules Sauerwein of *Paris-Soir*, Stephane Lauzanne of *Le Matin*, Pierre Guimier of *Le Petit Parisien*, Emile Roche and Pierre Dominique of the Radical daily *La République*. Only a handful of writers in the small circulation journals took issue with Bonnet: the Communists Gabriel Péri and Paul Nizan of *L'Humanité* and *Ce Soir* respectively, Henri de Kérillis in *L'Epoque*, Georges Bidault in *L'Aube*, Emile Buré and Pertinax in *L'Ordre*, Geneviéve Tabouis in *L'Oeuvre*.

The leading evening paper *Le Temps* was, on foreign affairs at least, a semi-official organ.[35] The newspaper was owned by coal, iron, steel and insurance interests. The two managing directors were Jacques Chastenet, representing the coal owners association (*comité des houillères*), and Emile Mireaux, for the steel industry (*comité des forges*). Chastenet had visited Hitler in 1933 and returned much impressed. He had little time for Czechoslovakia and was sympathetic towards German claims. 'M Hitler has often, both publicly and privately, posed as a champion of peace', announced *Le Temps* on 1 September 1938, 'there is no reason to doubt his sincerity'. After Munich, there was much talk of France renouncing or remodelling her eastern pacts, especially the Polish alliance. Chastenet shared Bonnet's view that the alliance should be radically revised and offered to do some kite flying on the subject. When an article appeared in *Le Temps* the Poles protested and Bonnet duly issued the customary *démenti*. But not all the staff of *Le Temps* toed the editorial line on foreign policy. The paper's Prague correspondent, Hubert Beuve Méry, later director of the postwar *Le Monde*, sharply disagreed with his editor. In October 1938 he resigned in protest against Munich.

The *Anschluss* was followed by a violent press campaign against the Czech alliance.[36] The campaign ranged from the sheer vituperation of the *Eclaireur de Nice* insisting that 'the bones of a little French soldier are worth more to us than all the Czechoslovaks in the world', to the sophisticated casuistry of *Le Temps*, denying that France had any legal obligations to actually defend Czechoslovakia. In the early summer the campaign died down and government influence seems to have been directed towards restricting or discouraging discussion of the international scene. By its nature, such influence did not advertise itself but different observers detected signs of official pressures. At the end of August the German Ambassador reported that the press was showing 'the greatest reserve' towards Germany, avoiding all signs of aggressiveness, an attitude which could 'doubtless be traced to instructions from official quarters'. In September, Bonnet complained frequently that the British press was more bellicose than the French and the British embassy noted that the Paris press 'soft-pedals quite remarkably'. But there were limits to the power of the foreign minister. The German Ambassador recounted the following conversation with Bonnet on 10 August 1938:

> If I had any complaints regarding the newspapers here which he was in a position to influence, he was always at my disposal; but he did not wish to conceal that he could undertake no action against Left wing newspapers of the calibre of *Humanité* and *Populaire*.

In the winter of 1938-39 the government concentrated its efforts on maintaining a favourable climate for Franco-German relations.[37] Negotiations for a Franco-German declaration were shrouded in secrecy. On 9 November Bonnet suppressed a Reuters report on the progress of negotiations. Amid growing press criticism of the Axis powers, Bonnet sought wider powers. On 12 November 1938 he submitted to the Cabinet a draft decree empowering the Foreign Minister to take immediate action against newspapers and individuals who published any matter judged offensive to foreign heads of state. Under existing law, action could only be taken upon the written complaint of the ambassador of the country in question. Jean Zay, Education Minister, suggested that Bonnet's proposal should also provide for the suppression of German propaganda in France. In the face of further objections from colleagues Bonnet withdrew his draft decree. However, the minister did not hesitate to use the means at his disposal. On the occasion of the signing of the Franco-German declaration on 6 December, the Foreign Minister asked *Paris-Soir* to publish a laudatory article by Jules Romains. In January 1939 Franco-German economic talks were in progress and the Ambassador at Berlin, Robert Coulondre, asked Bonnet to make 'a major effort' on the press so as to ensure Germany was given no grounds for complaint. Later, the Ambassador boasted to the German State Secretary, von Weizsäcker, of his success 'in keeping the French press and the Strasbourg radio station in order'.

The reshaping of French foreign policy after 15 March 1939 did not produce any relaxation of official influence, on the contrary, Daladier tried to tackle the dictators with their own weapons. A much stricter control of the press was established. Among a batch of 13 decrees issued on 21 March was one which made the unauthorised publication of military information in any form a punishable offence. This decree gave the government wide powers to censor and, if necessary, confiscate newspapers, letters and telegrams. On 30 July, further decrees were promulgated which provided for the creation of a Commissariat General for Information, under the control of the Prime Minister's office. The first Commissioner General was the playwright, Jean Giraudoux. French radio services were amalgamated and placed under a Director General, responsible to Daladier.

In comparison with the formidable Nazi propaganda machine, the Daladier government's influence on the mass media was relatively slight.[38] Yet the extension and consolidation of official direction in 1939 was hardly a healthy symptom. The government's treatment of the press was of a piece with its handling of parliament. On 18 August 1939, Daladier sent for newspaper directors and asked them not to publish anything 'that might offend the susceptibilities of Germany and Italy'. Analysing in 1940 the causes of France's fall, the historian Marc Bloch singled out the failure of successive governments to inform and educate opinion. The public became increasingly distrustful of the written and spoken word, thus widening the chasm between rulers and ruled. However, it would be wrong to see the government as exclusively concerned with disseminating official attitudes. The creation of the Commissariat General for Information was a belated bid to restore a sense of national purpose and identity. To counter Goebbels, France would broadcast her *mission civilisatrice*. Ironically, the first task of the new Commissioner General was to suppress the Communist press following the news of the German-Soviet pact of 23 August 1939.

If Bonnet was not in fact in thrall to his senior advisers how effective were those officials in defending the traditions of French diplomacy?[39] The Right wing *Gringoire* baptised Léger, Massigli and Comert the 'sinister trio', intent on sabotaging the appeasement of Germany and Italy in 1938. For critics of Munich they were 'three brave men opposed to the Minister'. After Munich the self-styled 'peace party' called on Bonnet to settle scores with these leading officials. For various reasons Léger was not moved but Bonnet struck at his deputy, René Massigli, Political Director, and Pierre Comert, head of the press and news department. Massigli was shipped off as ambassador to Ankara and Comert shunted to the American section of the Quai d'Orsay. Caillaux was delighted at what he described as the 'cleaning out of the Augean stables at the Quai d'Orsay', though disappointed that Léger would live to fight another day.

Incontestably, there was little love lost between the Minister and his senior advisers. His personality and policy of appeasement *à outrance* were not calculated to endear him to the permanent staff.[40] In his memoirs Bonnet did not conceal his antipathy for Massigli while Comert was passed over in silence. But he maintained that all was well between himself and Léger. The contention is hard to accept. The friction between the two men was so well known that when in 1938 the Foreign Minister assured Phipps that, notwithstanding reports to the contrary, he and Léger saw eye to eye the Ambassador commented in his report: 'in that case the eyes must be astigmatic'. Two of Bonnet's friends, Chastenet, editor of *Le Temps*, and Bressy, his private secretary, even spread stories that Léger gave instructions for certain incoming telegrams to be shown first to him before going to the Minister.

Although Léger, Massigli and Comert were lumped together as opponents of the Minister, there was no common action between them.[41] Relations between Léger and Massigli were no more than formal and correct and Léger does not seem to have supported Comert. It would be quite wrong to assume that the permanent officials were opposed in principle to conciliation on the Czech issue. The Secretary General's opinions on the Czech crisis are difficult to determine. He was away on holiday in August and the French documents for September contain little trace of his thinking. In conversations with foreign envoys the Secretary General was firm, telling Bullitt in May 1938 that 'if Germany should attack Czechoslovakia, France would automatically go to war at once and England would follow'. Still, this was no more than a reassertion of France's obligations. In practice, however, Léger did not oppose concessions over Czechoslovakia. In July he joined forces with Bonnet in advising the Czechs to accept the Runciman mission. During the night of 20-21 September he helped Bonnet to draft the terms of the French ultimatum to Prague, urging acceptance of the Anglo-French Plan for the cession of the Sudetenland. It was the Secretary General who on 11 September suggested to London the summoning of a four power conference, and he saluted Chamberlain's Berchtesgaden visit as a 'noble and courageous gesture'. Finally the head of the Quai d'Orsay boarded the plane for Munich, convinced that it would be folly for France to fight.

Why did Léger manage to retain his post? One obvious reason was that his opposition to Bonnet had been muted and he was prepared to go much of the way with ministerial opinion. Another factor, stressed by Roger Cambon, Counsellor in London, was that Léger had Daladier's confidence and was kept on 'to keep watch over M. Bonnet'. Lastly, there may well have been some truth in Pertinax's allegation that:

> Bonnet had made a very large sum of money on the Stock Exchange at the time of the Munich Agreement and this was known to Léger who had thus been able to retain his place during the recent purge at the Quai.[42]

Only Massigli and Comert could claim some title to independence of thought and action in the crisis over Czechoslovakia and both officials paid dearly for their dissent.[43] Massigli had been a leading figure at the Quai for over a decade and was recognised in London as 'in season and out of season a good friend of Anglo-French relations'. In 1944 General de Gaulle appointed him Ambassador in London. The bad feeling between Bonnet and the Political Director was common knowledge. In October 1938 Massigli was said to have been given the choice of two embassies — Warsaw or Ankara. His reply was: 'The post I want is the one which is as far away as possible from Paris. I have had enough of the present regime at the Quai d'Orsay'. The Bonnet-Massigli feud became a permanent one, with Bonnet claiming in his memoirs that the Political Director was a 'difficult character' who had quarrelled with most of his colleagues, including François-Poncet.

That Massigli was sympathetic towards Czechoslovakia and condemned the Munich Agreement is not in question. Returning from the delirious welcome given to Daladier at Le Bourget on 30 September, he wrote: 'Poor people, I am overwhelmed with shame'. And he had been under no illusions about the probable course of German policy. Deputising for Léger in August, he stressed to Campbell, British Chargé d'Affaires, the importance of Czechoslovakia as a barrier to German penetration in southeastern Europe. Germany, however, he believed, would not be satisfied in the east but would turn west rather than become embroiled with the Soviet Union. But bold words were not followed by bold deeds. Massigli had nothing to offer in place of appeasement. In September he considered that, lacking a promise of British support, the wiser course for France would have been to explain the situation 'frankly' to her Czech ally and urge the negotiation of a settlement. In the event of a German attack on Czechoslovakia the Political Director did not favour an immediate declaration of war. In mid-September he argued that France should submit her case to the League Council and await a finding upon aggression. In a note of 17 September he wrote:

> If the British Government pushes us along the path of surrender it must consider the resulting weakening of French security, which, on numerous occasions, has been declared inseparable from British security. To what extent might a reinforcement of the ties of Franco-British collaboration compensate for this weakening in the common interests of the two countries? This is a matter to which the attention of the British leaders should now be drawn.[44]

In short, Czechoslovakia, like the Rhineland in 1936, was seen not as a redoubt to be defended but as a bargaining counter in the pursuit of a Franco-British military alliance. That had been the policy of Daladier and Bonnet from the outset, though Massigli only seems to have suggested it when events had left France with no choice.

Comert would seem to have been the lone opponent of surrender to Germany. He was an extremely able and gifted official. As director of the information services of the French mission in London in the First World War, he had won the confidence and trust of many British and allied journalists and leaders. Visiting Paris in October 1938 the American journalist, William L. Shirer, noted: 'outside of Pierre Comert no one at

the Quai d'Orsay with any idea at all of the real Germany'.[45] Sir Basil
Liddell Hart, defence correspondent for the *Times* in the 1930s, thought
Comert was 'one of the most progressive and internationally minded
Frenchmen' he had ever known.[46] On a trip to France in 1935 Liddell
Hart found that French military planners were not interested in British ideas
of armoured warfare. Comert explained that he had not been able to arrange
visits to the War Ministry because no one wanted to see Liddell Hart. However, the Quai d'Orsay official arranged meetings with a number of younger
officers, including Captain Beauffre who was to become one of France's
leading strategists.

As director of the League of Nations information service from 1919 to 1933
Comert had been one of the principal pillars of the League. At the Quai
d'Orsay his left wing opinions and independent, critical attitude did not
make him a pliant subordinate. During Laval's tenure of the Foreign
Ministry in 1934-35 he had incurred the minister's displeasure by quoting
from *Mein Kampf* in press conferences. But Comert was not anti-German
but anti-Nazi. In fact he had nearly been sacked for Germanophile views.

Comert's general opinions on foreign affairs in the 1930s are difficult to
discover. Despite his career as head of press and news services he always
shunned personal publicity. Nevertheless he soon crossed swords with
Bonnet, though the two had been friends in the early 1920s. The main
battle between the minister and the official concerned the British Foreign
Office communiqué of 26 September 1938. In the afternoon of 26 September
Halifax authorised a communiqué stating, *inter alia*, that if Germany
attacked Czechoslovakia France would assist her ally and would be supported by Britain and the Soviet Union.[47] The statement came, in
Monzie's words, as a 'stab in the back' to Bonnet and his associates who
at that time were working frantically to keep France out of a war for
Czechoslovakia. Their counter-offensive took two forms: circulation
of the communiqué within France was restricted as much as possible,
and it was rumoured that the statement had not been officially authorised
and need not be taken seriously. Geneviève Tabouis, diplomatic correspondent of *L'Oeuvre*, was favoured with a personal telephone call from
the Foreign Minister, warning her 'to be careful about the communiqué
as it had not been officially confirmed'. Bonnet dismissed the statement
as another manoeuvre of Churchill and Vansittart. The French morning
press of the 27th barely mentioned the communiqué. Alerted by a friendly
colleague of the rumour emanating from the minister's office, Comert
informed the ambassador in London, Corbin. The ambassador wired
Paris underscoring the official character of the communiqué. According
to Comert's testimony, the wire never reached the press and news section
because Bonnet restricted its distribution. When in the afternoon of the
28th *Le Temps* finally published the text of the communiqué the invitations to a conference in Munich had been received and accepted.

In October 1938 Comert was offered the post of Assistant Director of
the American section — in effect this was a demotion since American affairs
were largely handled by the minister's *cabinet*. Still, the press chief won
one small victory. Before accepting the new appointment he asked Bonnet
to issue an official denial that, contrary to what certain critics were saying,

the press section had been in any way responsible for the spreading of false news'. The Minister complied. In his memoirs he contended that the removal of Massigli and Comert was part of a routine reshuffle, but on 26 October 1938 Phipps reported: 'Bonnet told me in confidence the other day how glad he was to have shunted Comert; but he has typically issued a communiqué white-washing the latter'.[48]

There were no rebels among the ambassadors. The doyen of France's diplomats was André François-Poncet, Ambassador at Berlin since 1931 and a firm believer in Franco-German *rapprochement*. He had been a brilliant student at the *Ecole Normale Supérieure* and his early career was academic. In the 1920s he entered politics and served as a junior minister in two cabinets. Through marriage he acquired substantial holdings in the steel industry and soon became known as a *Comité des Forges* man, a champion of big business. He knew his own abilities and was not without a strong streak of vanity. He once remarked to British diplomats that the British Foreign Office was wonderfully organized, whereas the Quai d'Orsay was chaotic. And for this reason 'it was possible for a member of the British service of moderate attainments to become a successful ambassador, while to be a successful French ambassador a superb intelligence was required'.[49]

Outwardly his Berlin mission was successful. He spoke fluent German and entertained on a lavish scale. Though not a career diplomat, he was industrious and zealous, holding daily conferences for embassy staff. His reporting was regular and full, almost to a fault. Hard-worked foreign ministry officials in Paris found the distinction of his literary style poor compensation for the prolixity of the Berlin despatches. François-Poncet was said to be the only foreign diplomat who enjoyed Hitler's liking and respect.[50] Personal charm played a part in this success but the main reason for his being *persona grata* was that he eschewed plain speaking and evinced considerable sympathy for German policy.

His memoirs contrived to minimise both his own personal role and French responsibility in the abandonment of Czechoslovakia. Chamberlain was made the villain of the piece. In reality the ambassador probably exercised a not inconsiderable influence on French policy making.[51] He was very much a Foreign Minister *manqué*—in fact when the Daladier government was being formed in April 1938 the ambassador was rung up by Reynaud and asked if he would accept the Quai d'Orsay. He replied in the affirmative but heard no more of the offer. The Ambassador sympathised openly with the German thesis that Czechoslovakia 'allied to Russia' constituted 'a perpetual menace' to Germany. He had no trust whatsoever in the goodwill of President Benes and told Henderson, his British colleague, who could hardly believe him, that the 'French government would go so far as to jettison Benes'. Czechoslovakia, he told the German Foreign Minister, Ribbentrop, on 23 June, should be regarded not as an 'apple of discord' but as an opportunity for 'mutual consultation and exchange of views'. His personal solution, broached in early June, was for informal French, British and German discussions led by himself, Henderson and Ribbentrop to draw up plans for the neutralisation of Czechoslovakia under a three power guarantee. The Czechs would be told to accept the settlement. Transferred to Rome in October 1938 Francois-Poncet worked enthusiastically for a Franco-Italian reconciliation.

Robert Coulondre, Ambassador to the Soviet Union from 1936 until October 1938, has been hailed as one of the few far-sighted diplomats of the 1930s. Of the post-1945 flood of memoirs only his met with unqualified approval: 'No European diplomatist', Sir Lewis Namier averred, 'comes out better from the ordeal of those years than M Coulondre'.[52] Historians, relying upon Coulondre's *apologia* have commended him as a realist who, hostile to appeasement, sought in vain to construct a Franco-Soviet military alliance. Such an interpretation does not tally with the evidence which shows the ambassador to have been much more conciliatory towards Germany than he later cared to admit.

In Moscow in 1938, as the documents confirm, he was a firm advocate of Franco-Soviet staff talks; yet later in the year in Berlin he worked studiously for Franco-German understanding. What was the explanation of his attitude? Von Weizsäcker, State Secretary of the Wilhelmstrasse, dismissed him as a cautious bureaucrat who wrote and talked for the Yellow Book. The judgement was unduly severe and reflected the fact that after the panache of François-Poncet, Coulondre was a rather reserved, unprepossessing personality. Still, Weizsäcker's verdict offers part of the key to the Ambassador's record. At one level, Coulondre was no more than a solid, conscientious civil servant, dedicated to the job in hand. In Moscow it made sense to work for a genuine Franco-Soviet alliance, as ambassador in Berlin from October 1938 Coulondre obediently toed the official line which aimed at a *détente* with Germany. Coulondre could compartmentalise his thinking and adopt a narrow focus. Thus he was convinced of the necessity of defending Czechoslovakia but was not prepared to make a nuisance of himself in Paris by broadcasting his views:

> Of course, it was only upon the Russian aspect of the (*Czech*) problem that it behoved me to give an opinion. The French Government alone was in a position to formulate an overall policy.

At a deeper level, however, the explanation of Coulondre's conduct lay in his appreciation of French interests. The documents confirm that in the summer of 1938 he pleaded for staff talks with Moscow but in his mind there was no stark choice between Moscow and Berlin. At no stage was a real Franco-Soviet alliance seen as an alternative to a Franco-German understanding. The original purpose of the Soviet pact had been to insure France against the danger of a German-Soviet *rapprochement*. In 1938 this purpose was still valid but the insurance had to be much stronger since Germany was much more formidable than in 1935. Staff talks with Moscow would provide the extra leverage France needed in negotiation with Germany.

Of French diplomats, Coulondre alone seems to have had the distinction of exercising a direct influence on decision making in Paris. His relations with Daladier in the summer of 1939 were close. Common backgrounds helped—both were men of the Midi and it was said that on the telephone they spoke to each other in Provençal. On 30 August 1939 he wrote personally to Daladier, pointing out that Hitler was hesitating and that the only way to deal with him was to stand firm. Whether by accident or design, the letter was brought to Daladier during a Cabinet meeting on 31 August, called to consider Mussolini's proposal for a conference on Danzig and the Polish Corridor. The letter was read out and hardened opinion against the Italian proposal.

Coulondre's confrère in London was Charles Corbin, 'the steely, grey, Frog ambassador', as Chips Channon called him.[53] Appointed in 1933 Corbin spoke English fluently and came to London already possessing many British friends. Socially his mission was a success. Austen Chamberlain noted that the ambassador had turned the embassy in Albert Gate 'into a fashionable place where one met the right people'. He had the advantage, too, of having as Counsellor, Roger Cambon, a distinguished diplomat, who had been at the embassy since 1924.

Sir John Wheeler-Bennett singled out Corbin for praise. In 1938 the ambassador 'could not have been a stronger opponent of his country's policy of surrender'. Though the record shows traces of disagreement with Bonnet's diplomacy, it would be an overstatement to call the diplomat a strong opponent of surrender. On holiday in August Corbin conferred with Gamelin and both were agreed on an 'energetic attitude'. Back at his post the Ambassador seems to have presented to Paris a more favourable impression of British readiness to support France over Czechoslovakia than Halifax's declarations warranted. Perhaps that was his discreet way of putting a spoke in Bonnet's wheel. Through Léger the Foreign Office heard that Corbin had informed Paris:

> Several political men in Great Britain, and among them members of the Government, seemed to think that the French Government were not reacting with sufficient vigour to the German military preparations.

Léon Noel, Ambassador to Poland since 1935, was convinced in March 1938 that France could not help Czechoslovakia. When on 5 April 1938 Paul-Boncour called a conference of representatives in central and eastern Europe, Noel gave his opinion that the military and diplomatic situation precluded French assistance to her ally. Whilst he was explaining his standpoint a top-ranking official interjected: 'This is defeatism'.[54] But it was a voice in the wilderness, for Noel claimed that : 'when the conference was over all my colleagues who had been present thanked me for having expressed their personal views'. The only point of disagreement between Noel and Bonnet concerned how much the Czechs should be told. After a mission to Prague in mid-April, Noel recommended that from the end of June the Czechs should be told fairly and squarely that France could no longer help them. Daladier and Bonnet, chose otherwise: 'The plan was clear. To avoid any parliamentary difficulty it was a question of allowing the British government to take the responsibility for the abandonment of Czechoslovakia'.

Though Bonnet's counsels prevailed in the crisis over Czechoslovakia the tensions and conflicts left their mark on the Quai d'Orsay.[55] The removal of Massigli and Comert only added to the atmosphere of distrust and unease which pervaded the ministry. Munich, recorded one official, 'profoundly affected and divided a generally rather sceptical personnel'.

When Jean Chauvel took up the post of Assistant Director of the Asian and Oceanic department in January 1939 he found a group of leading officials determined to oppose the minister. Prominent in this cluster which drew its inspiration from Léger were Henri Hoppenot, Assistant Director for European Affairs, and Charles Rochat, Assistant Political Director. But Bonnet's influence was short-lived. In the early months of 1939 Daladier grew increasingly mistrustful of his foreign minister and by April there was open talk of his replacement. In June, Phipps lamented that Léger's influence over Daladier was 'unfortunately increasing daily'. The chief beneficiaries of Bonnet's eclipse were the permanent officials. With his fall on 13 September 1939, Daladier took over foreign affairs but in wartime his existing responsibilities as Prime Minister and Minister of national defence and of war were onerous enough and he could not possibly maintain a close oversight of the Quai. To ease the burden, Champetier de Ribes, Minister for Ex-Servicemen and Pensions since April 1938, was appointed Under-Secretary of State for Foreign Affairs, and Coulondre became Daladier's *Chef de Cabinet* for foreign affairs. Daladier kept his office in the war ministry. Every morning Champetier, Léger and Coulondre would go to the ministry in the *Rue Saint Dominique* for a conference with the prime minister.

The final picture is necessarily a complex one. The polemics of the period distinguished sharply between *bellicistes* and *pacifistes* or *durs* v. *mous;* and this terminology of resisters and appeasers has influenced much of the writing on French policy. Yet the old labels convey little of the reality. In practice there was no simple, sharp division between resisters and appeasers. Faced with the disparity between France's resources and commitments, the diplomats all turned in some measure towards conciliation and concessions. This is not to deny that critical differences existed between the politicians and their advisers. Léger and Massigli fought a rearguard action against what they considered excessive pressure on Prague, though the Secretary General was much more circumspect than his second-in-command. On 27-28 September the Secretary General claimed to have spent 'a long night of argument with Bonnet over the issue of his instructions' for the conference in Munich on the 28th.[56] And during the conference he tried to stiffen Daladier's attitude, prompting him to raise objections. Also, he distrusted Italy and did not work *con amore* for Bonnet's goal of a détente. But such skirmishing did not deflect ministerial policy from its objectives.

Not only officials in Paris but representatives overseas felt grave misgivings about their country's foreign policy. Roger Cambon, Counsellor in London, was quite 'sick' at the terms of the Anglo-French plan of 18 September, providing for the cession of the Sudetenland to Germany.[57] The Ambassador in Washington, Count René Doynel de St. Quentin. 'could not reconcile himself to the idea that four statesmen representing four of the great powers of Europe should take it upon themselves to dismember a smaller power, . . . such a procedure was a step backward'. That the diplomats stayed at their desks in 1938, as many were to do in 1940, is hardly surprising. Their political masters gave no lead. No French minister resigned over Munich in 1938. The tradition of loyal service to the state, irrespective of the policies of particular governments, overrode reservations about national policy.

Though Berthelot and Léger were ultra-secretive about their personal contribution to policy-making, the general standards of secrecy in the Quai d'Orsay have been much criticised. The most famous leakage of the 1930s was the premature disclosure of the Hoare-Laval plan on Ethiopia in December 1935. The French secured such a bad name for themselves that in February 1938 the British Chiefs of Staff gave as one of their reasons against the holding of staff talks with France the danger that information might be deliberately leaked to Germany.

There is no doubt that the Foreign Ministry was careless in its handling of information. As early as November 1937 the Germans were reading reports from the French embassy in Berlin, though it is not clear whether they had broken the main diplomatic codes, or only a non-confidential code.[58] On 18 February 1937 Noel, Ambassador in Warsaw, obtained a full report of a talk between Reich Marshal Goering and Marshal Smigly Rydz of the Polish army. He forwarded it to Paris, stressing its secrecy. The same day, to the great embarrassment of Noel and his Polish informant, the gist of the telegram was published in the French press.[59] The Quai d'Orsay was distrusted by other ministries. In October 1938 Daladier asked for papers from the French embassy in London to be sent direct to him, instead of through the Foreign Ministry.

But seen in the general context of French politics, the indiscretions of the Quai were not exceptional. State secrets had always been bandied about. In May 1915, Delcassé complained bitterly of 'Cabinets in which everything is said and which meet in public'.[60] Eavesdropping was the norm and much of what went on was close to comedy. An official of the ministry of the Interior wrote:

> The Sûreté Nationale listened in on the Prefecture of Police which paid it back in kind. The *Action Française* and *Humanité* had our lines tapped, but we had theirs too. As everybody was quite aware of this, what always astonished me was that so many people went on confiding so many secrets to the telephone.[61]

At the end of their working day Bonnet and Léger would come together and listen to the digests of monitored telephone calls between embassies. Doubtless the stories of 'who's in, who's out' provided enough material for the two men to dine out on. Ministers, however, had access to a direct line —the 'interministerial' which was free from interference. Of course, the tapping of telephones, official and private, continues and the affair of *Le Canard Enchaîné* in 1973 helped to publicise an extremely unpleasant and long-standing practice.

Three elements seem to have been involved in the leakages from the Quai: sheer carelessness on the part of some diplomats; an element of manipulation of information for political purposes; and lastly, the deliberate betrayal of secrets to foreign powers. Of carelessness, there was plenty. Coulondre, Ambassador in Moscow, coming from the world of security which surrounded the Soviet leadership, was shocked to find in Paris that highly confidential conversations were carried on in front of servants. And yet as Ambassador in Berlin from October 1938 Coulondre was quite indiscreet on the telephone. In February 1938 a dispatch from Lacroix, Minister in Prague, was deciphered by the Italians and published in the *Giornale d'Italia*.[62] Lacroix suspected a leakage from the Quai but the fault was his own since he had used a non-confidential cipher, known to the Italians. Massigli, Political Director, censured him and confessed himself 'shocked' by the information which Lacroix confided to telegrams. No cipher, advised Massigli, however confidential was absolutely secure and it was safer to put certain information in a personal letter rather than in a telegram which usually received wide distribution.

The premature publication of the Hoare-Laval plan best exemplifies the leakage of information for political purposes. The journalist Geneviève Tabouis has told how she obtained the essentials of the plan and published it in order 'to ruin its chances' by exciting opinion against it.[63] But Laval's opinion that it was Sir Charles Mendl, Press Attaché at the British embassy, who leaked the details, should not be overlooked. Mendl was a rather shadowy personality who may well have had much to answer for—Laval believed him to be working for British Intelligence.[64] Still, whatever the source of the leak, the premature disclosure helped to wreck the plan. Well-timed leaks were the stock-in-trade of negotiations. After the meeting of British and French ministers in London in April 1938, the French press waxed strong on the success and importance of the talks. Questioned about the attitude of his country's press, Bonnet took the offensive, pointing out that when he and Daladier got back to the French embassy after the first day of talks, British journalists already knew the gist of the day's business. But the Foreign Office had information that it was Bonnet who had talked to the press and divulged details of discussions.[65]

There is, however, some evidence of deliberate transmission of information to Germany.[66] In March 1936, François-Poncet expressed alarm because the Germans were so well-informed about the details of French Cabinet discussions on 7 and 8 March. In September 1938 the journalist de Brinon passed on to the German embassy in Paris particulars of Cabinet deliberations which he had almost certainly received from certain ministers. In April 1939 information about the activities of British intelligence in Germany was communicated to the German embassy in Paris from a source close to the Deuxième Bureau.

The French Foreign Minister distrusted his own department and sent a letter to Halifax in July 1939 by special messenger 'since he did not want the matter to pass through . . . the Departments for fear of leakages'.[67] He also expressed great distrust of the ambassador in London, Corbin. But Bonnet himself was hardly the soul of the discretion. On 22 March 1939 British ministers gave him in confidence the current British air production figures. Within a fortnight this secret information was dinner table gossip in Paris. In July 1939 Bonnet's name was linked with two journalists, Aubin and Poirier, arrested for spying.

Consideration of the Quai d'Orsay leakages raises the wider question of the effectiveness of French intelligence services. Here there were certainly shortcomings.[68] There was nothing to equal the scoop of pre-1914 days when the Deuxième Bureau deciphered telegrams from the German embassy in Paris to the *Wilhelmstrasse—les verts,* as the intercepts were called. Unfortunately, French intelligence seems to have had no inkling of the secret German-Soviet contacts in July-August 1939. However in August 1939 the French had broken the Italian diplomatic cypher and were reading communications between the Italian embassy in Paris and Rome.[69] And the Deuxième Bureau had one notable success: documents were obtained which enabled it to reconstruct the cypher machine used by the German army.

How successful was French counter-intelligence in combating Axis activity in France in the late 1930s? Without access to French intelligence files no precise answer can be given. The few indicators available convey only a blurred and vague picture. A report on the activity of German intelligence in France in 1937 offered the government alarming prognostications but no hard facts:

> Since 1934 German intelligence has been officially re-organised. Extending unceasingly its goals, adding to its resources and improving its methods, it could anticipate obtaining in France in 1937—where it has implanted itself with un-believable ease—the most satisfying results, if strong and systematic counter-measures are not energetically taken.[70]

After the Rome agreements of January 1935 Italian intelligence promised to cease all activity in France. There was even a measure of co-operation with French counter-espionage. By 1937 this understanding had broken down. Italian agents were again active in France and co-operating with German intelligence. However the number of arrests was small. By November 1937 only four arrests had been made since June 1936.[71]

In fairness to the French the question of leakages must be judged in the context of the behaviour of British, Italian, Belgian and other diplomats. Coulondre and his colleagues were not alone in their indiscreet use of the telephone. German intelligence considered that the 'Italians, French, Belgians, Dutch and Balkan diplomats observed no discipline whatever in their use of the telephone'.[72] Also, the most notorious case of lack of security was the British embassy in Rome, where from 1935 to 1940 the safe was regularly burgled. British ministers did not always follow the strict rules of Cabinet secrecy. Walter Elliot, Minister of Health in 1938-39, consistently leaked Cabinet secrets.

Chapter 10

The Armed Forces

On 14 July 1939, the 150th anniversary of the fall of the Bastille, the French army held its annual parade along the Champs-Elysées. Some 30,000 troops, drawn from every part of the French empire, took part. As a mark of Franco-British solidarity, the Chief of the Imperial General Staff, Lord Gort, took the salute jointly with General Gamelin, Chief of the French General Staff. Royal Air Force squadrons of Wellesley and Blenheim bombers thundered overhead. Intimations of impending war made the display more memorable than any previous review since the victory march after the armistice of 1918. Ten months later the army which had been praised by Chamberlain and Churchill alike as the finest in Europe was in full retreat from the victorious *Wehrmacht*. By 15 May 1940 France's military hegemony was gone for good.

At the time it was widely assumed that Germany had possessed an overwhelming superiority of men and material in the battles of May-June 1940. We now know that the German and French armies were well-matched in land armaments. On the French side the crucial failure was one of generalship, a failure to envisage alternative strategies. However although quantitatively the opposing armies were well-matched, qualitatively Germany had the advantage, especially in the air. The 1930s witnessed a gradual decline in France's military might. In 1925 with a peacetime army of 640,000 men France was supreme on land; a decade later, with the exception of the Soviet Union, she remained the strongest military power in Europe. Even in 1935 the French air force ranked second in Europe, though by then much of its equipment was obsolescent. But by 1938 Germany had outstripped France in the air and almost overtaken her on land.

In 1939 in land armaments France occupied third place among the powers, in naval and air armaments fourth place. From Table I it is evident that the turning point for the French army came in 1938. In January 1938 France could still mobilise more divisions than Germany. Discounting British help on land, France, supported by Czechoslovakia and Poland, had a numerical superiority over Germany and Italy combined. Yet within sixteen months the whole situation changed for the worse. The 34 Czechoslovak divisions were lost after Munich and Germany achieved a marked lead over France. The 16 British divisions listed offered no more

Table 1

Contemporary Estimates of Land Forces of the European Powers, 1938-1939
(strengths, expressed in divisions, are war strengths)

	January 1938	*April 1939*
Germany	81	120-130
Italy	73	85
France	100	100
Gt. Britain*	2	16
USSR	125	125
Czechoslovakia	34	
Poland	40	40

*British forces available for the Continent
Sources: Committee of Imperial Defence: 'A Comparison of the strength of Great Britain
   with that of certain other nations as at January 1938' (Cabinet Paper, 24/273);
   Documents on British Foreign Policy, 1919-1939, Third Series, VI, Appendix V;
   General M. G. Gamelin, *Servir,* II (Paris, 1946), p. 351; 'Etude du problème
   stratégique à la date du 10 April 1939', *French foreign ministry archives.*

than paper support since the British programme of military expansion
from 2 to a projected 32 divisions had made but little progress on the
outbreak of war in September 1939. Only a military alliance with the
Soviet Union could have redressed the balance for France.

As regards the peacetime strength of the French army, a major caveat
must be made. The numerical strength of the French army was not fixed
and unchanging during the inter-war years. Fourteen divisions, a fifth
of the army's peacetime strength, were posted overseas. Even in the mid-
1920s at the height of French power it is claimed that 'the army at home
was desperately struggling to maintain itself as a fighting force'.[1] Risings
in Morocco and Syria required the transfer of large forces from Europe,
completely upsetting the order of French mobilisation. In fact there was
an appreciable fall in the size of the French army between 1921 and 1933.
One reason for this decline was the reduction in the length of military
service, fixed at three years in 1913, reduced to eighteen months in 1923,
and then cut again to twelve months in 1928. Another factor was the
unpopularity of the army as a career. The pacifist temper of opinion,
coupled with low pay and poor conditions of service, acted as a brake
on long-term enlistment. Following Hitler's reintroduction of conscription in Germany in March 1935 the length of service was fixed at two
years. Though the measure brought little benefit because the years 1935
to 1940 were the 'lean years' when the number of conscripts available
was much reduced as a result of the fall in the birth rate between
1914 and 1918.

It is in the context of declining manpower and pacifist ideals that the
decision to build fortifications in 1929 has to be understood. The Maginot
Line is often taken as a symbol of the defensive mentality of the French
General Staff. However the French cannot be blamed for thinking de-
fensively. The attrition of 1914-18 seemed to have justified the nation
in arms concept. France had survived only by the complete mobilisation
of her resources, together with those of her allies. After 1918 manpower

Table 2
Contemporary Estimates of First-Line Air Strengths of the European Powers, 1935-1939
(in numbers of military aircraft of all types)

Year	France	Germany	Gt. Britain	Italy	USSR
1935	1,696	728	1,020	1,300	1,700
1936	1,010	650	1,200	—	—
1937	1,380	1,233	1,550	1,350	—
1938	1,454	3,104	1,606	1,810	3,280
1939	1,792	3,699	2,075	1,531	3,361

Notes
1. There were no agreed definitions as to what constituted first-line aircraft, consequently estimates differed considerably.
2. Totals for France and Gt. Britain are for metropolitan and overseas strengths. Reserves are not included for any of the powers.

Sources: 'Note sur les possibilités comparées des Aviations françaises et étrangères, 20 Juin 1935', *Service historique de l'Armée de l'Air;* 'La production aéronautique militaire française' in *Revue d'Histoire de la Deuxième Guerre Mondiale,* January 1969, pp. 111-16; the low estimate for German strength in 1936 comes from *Documents diplomatiques francais, 1932-1939,* 2 Série, II, no. 23; *Documents on British Foreign Policy,* Third Series, VI, Appendix V; Basil Collier, *The Defence of the United Kingdom* (London, 1957), p. 66 and p. 78; *League of Nations Armament Year Books.*

Table 3
Present Day (1973) Estimates of actual total production for the Luftwaffe

Year	
1935	1,823
1936	2,530
1937	2,651
1938	3,356
1939	4,783

Source: Stephen Roskill, *Hankey: Man of Secrets,* III, (London, 1974), Appendix B, pp. 664-5.

was the primary problem — 60 million Germans against 40 million Frenchmen. With the passing of the one-year service law of 1928 fortifications of some kind became indispensable as a means of enabling fewer men to fight more effectively. Fortifications, it was judged, would provide the necessary cover for general mobilisation, and also act as insurance against an *attaque brusque*. As the veterans of 1914-18 became too old for service in the reserves the army was more and more dependent on young, untried, short-service soldiers without battle experience. The Maginot Line, it was believed, would offset complete reliance on a field army. The fact that the Maginot Line was not continued to cover the Franco-Belgian border proved the fatal flaw in France's defences in 1940. Yet in the early 1930s the French military leadership still assumed that in the event of war with Germany French armies would be free to sweep forward into Belgium. Gradually Belgium disengaged herself from the military links with France and in 1937 she adopted a policy of full neutrality. By then, however, given the state of the French economy, it was clearly too expensive to extend the Maginot Line to the Channel ports.

On the eve of the Second World War, it was the state of the French air force that gave most cause for concern in London and Paris. Though in December 1937 Neville Chamberlain conceded that France possessed 'a powerful army' the condition of her air force was another matter.[2] In November 1937 the Chiefs of Staff noted: 'present reports indicate that lack of equipment, inefficiently executed reorganisation and political interference in the Service, has very seriously affected the fighting value of the French Air Force'.[3] Should the historian look for 'guilty men'? 'When in France they are looking out for "guilty men" ', wrote Winston Churchill, 'it would seem that here is a field which might well be searchingly explored'.[4]

Of the sorry state of the air force, there is no doubt. The most telling testimony came from General Joseph Vuillemin, Chief of French Air Staff, who admitted in March 1938 that in a war with Germany the air force would be wiped out within fifteen days.[5] The decline was all the more to be regretted since in 1918 France had been the leading air power with an estimated 34,000 military aircraft. In the three years from 1935 to 1938 French production never exceeded a monthly figure of 100 aircraft, and was often as low as 30-40.[6] In 1937-38 Germany was turning out about 450-500 aircraft a month, rising to 700 in 1939.

The chief cause of French deficiencies was the delay in air rearmament. Rearmament did not begin until 15 March 1938, fifteen months after the start of land rearmament. Until the spring of 1938 relatively little was spent on the air force. The French air estimates for 1937 accounted for 19% of the total defence budget, in Great Britain the corresponding figure was 54%.[7] So the air force remained the Cinderella of the services. The pleas of the Air Minister, Pierre Cot, for more money were refused. 'We will end up by having the weakest air force because we have spent so little', Cot told the Permanent Committee of National Defence on 8 December 1937.[8] Germany, warned the air minister, was producing 500 planes a month, Great Britain 175-200, France a mere 50. Daladier, Minister of National Defence and War, explained that the credits voted were not sufficient to meet the cost of the existing programme of land armaments, let alone increased expenditure on the air force. The parsimony practised towards the air force was based in part on a failure to appreciate the full importance of air power. The General Staff treated air power very much as an adjunct to land forces. Overshadowed by the army and navy the air force had fought a long battle for independent recognition. An independent air ministry was not created until June 1933. In September 1938 Gamelin, Chief of the General Staff, considered that the 'role of aviation is apt to be exaggerated, and that after the early days of a war the wastage will be such that it will be more and more confined to acting as an accessory to the army'.[9] Another brake on French aircraft production in 1937-38 was the Popular Front government's reorganisation and partial nationalization of the aircraft industry.

On 15 March 1938 Guy la Chambre, who had succeeded Pierre Cot as air minister in January 1938, announced a new expansion programme called Plan V which aimed at creating a first line strength of 2,600 aircraft by 1940, with 2,120 aircraft in reserve, giving a total strength of 4,720 planes.[10] The plan was approved and remained the basis of air rearmament until the outbreak of war. What must be stressed is that the record of French air power was not one of complete decline. A simple comparison of the numerical strengths of the major European air forces does not do full justice to France's efforts to make up for lost time. In effect there was a remarkable upsurge of production in the years 1938-1940. In these two years French aircraft production achieved the same results as Germany had done in four years.[11] In 1939 France produced a total of 1,261 aircraft in the first eight months of the year, a monthly production rate of 157, compared to a total of 432 aircraft in the previous twelve months. Against the background of previous delays and deficiencies it was an astonishing recovery. By September 1939 British and French air strength combined was only slightly inferior to that of Germany. And, in fairness to the French, it must be stressed that they were not aiming at air parity or supremacy over Germany. It was taken for granted that considerable support would be forthcoming from the Royal Air Force and that the two air forces together would be in a strong defensive position.

French deficiencies in the air might have been offset by large purchases of American aircraft. In 1938-39 the French government was involved in protracted negotiations for the purchase of American aircraft.[12] But for various reasons, some of which are not entirely clear, the opportunity of filling the gaps in French strength was missed. One major obstacle was the Neutrality Act of 1935, confirmed in 1937, which forbade the export of war materials to all belligerents. The American Ambassador, Bullitt, warned Bonnet in June 1938 that if war came in Europe the Neutrality Act would be applied in all its rigour and the delivery of aircraft already ordered would be very difficult. Though tentative enquiries about purchases of American aircraft were initiated in the early months of 1938, large orders were not placed until after Munich. Even then the results were meagre. In the autumn of 1938 it was proposed that France should buy 1,000 aircraft from the United States, giving her a total air strength by mid-1939 of 2,617 planes. But Reynaud's watchword 'to defend the franc is to defend France' carried the day and for reasons of financial stringency the order was reduced to 600 aircraft in January 1939. The puzzling fact is that although France's gold reserves rose in January and February 1939 enabling Reynaud to make the United States an offer of ten billion francs in gold in part settlement of First World War debts, no attempt was made to spend the money on orders for more aircraft. No further orders were placed until September 1939 and by then only 200 of the 600 aircraft ordered in January had been delivered. Some blame must be attached to the French government. In May 1938, Roosevelt wrote to Bullitt: 'all along we have done everything we properly could to facilitate French purchases of planes in this country. The delays which have ensued have been due to their own dilatory methods of doing business'.

British assistance was regarded as indispensable at sea. In 1939 France occupied fourth place among the leading naval powers but her place was far from secure. Given a hostile Italo-German alliance, the French

Table 4

Contemporary Estimates of Naval Strength of the leading powers 1939

	Capital Ships	Aircraft Carriers	Heavy Cruisers	Submarines
Gt. Britain	15	6	15	57
United States	15	5	18	87
Japan	9	5	12	59
France	7	1	7	78
Italy	4	—	7	104
Germany	5	—	2	65
USSR	3	—	—	150

Source: *Jane's Fighting Ships 1939*

Table 5

Military expenditure in France, Germany and Great Britain, 1930-1939, as a percentage of GNP and national income

(in thousand millions of local currency)

Year	France Nat. Inc.	Mil. Exp.	Francs Per Cent	Germany GNP	Mil. Exp.	Rm. Per Cent.	Gt. Britain Nat. Inc.	Mil. Exp.	£ Per Cent.
1930-1	332	15.1	4.3	—	—	—	—	—	—
1931-2	312	12.9	4.1	58	.8	1	—	.1	—
1933	259	11.7	4.5	59	1.9	3	3.7	.1	3
1934	237	10.2	4.3	67	4.1	6	3.9	.1	3
1935	221	10.4	4.7	74	6.0	8	4.1	.1	2
1936	239	14.4	6	83	10.8	13	4.4	.2	5
1937	304	20.8	6.8	93	11.7	13	4.6	.3	7
1938	347	28.4	8.2	105	17.2	17	4.8	.4	8
1939	407	92.7	22.8	130	30.	23	5	1.1	22

Sources: for France: Alfred Sauvy, *Histoire Economique de la France entre les deux guerres*, I, p. 277, pp. 370-1, II, p. 319, pp. 576-7. Different data for French expenditure and national income are given in H.C. Hillman, *The World in March 1939, Survey of International Affairs, 1939-1946* (London, 1952), p. 454 and p. 456; and also in Charles P. Kindleberger, *Economic Growth in France and Britain, 1851-1950* (London, 1964), p. 338. I have followed Sauvy's statistics. For Britain and Germany; the table is based on Berenice A. Carroll, *Design for Total War: Arms and Economics in the Third Reich* (Hague, 1968) p. 184.

fleet would be unable to control the Mediterranean. In 1937 France's naval primacy in the Mediterranean was threatened by Italian naval expansion. The French government seemed unaware of the danger and the naval estimates in the 1938 budget were actually reduced. The navy replied with a broadside from its Chief of Staff, Vice-Admiral Darlan. On 29 July 1937 Darlan warned ministers that unless the estimates were increased the country's survival in war would be gravely imperilled. France, he pointed out, depended on naval supremacy in the Mediterranean for the safety of her trade, troop transports and communications with North Africa. Thus a war at sea could not be envisaged without the certainty of British participation: 'we must align our foreign policy completely with that of Great Britain'.[13] Particularly alarming was the strength of Italy's submarine fleet. The outcry from the admirals, backed by public protests, secured the voting of supplementary estimates in January 1938, though the slowness of naval building and industrial strife prevented any appreciable improvement in French sea power.

Sooner or later, France had to relinquish her military leadership but the transfer of power to Germany came sooner than it might have done because defence expenditure was drastically curtailed in the years 1932 to 1935—just at the time when German rearmament was getting into its stride.

Between 1930 and 1933 French defence spending was cut by 25% and the defence estimates for 1930 were not exceeded until 1937. This curtailment of expenditure had little or nothing to do with the onset of the Depression which did not affect France until 1933-34. Spending was reduced as a contribution to the Disarmament negotiations then in progress at Geneva. The heaviest expenditure occurred in the years 1936 to 1939 when the economy was badly hit by the Depression. On 7 September 1936 the *Front Populaire* government of Léon Blum approved a four year programme of land armaments, costing 14 milliards of francs. But by that date, it was too late. In military equipment, though not as yet in manpower, Germany was overtaking France.[14]

Yet French governments deserve more credit than they have been allowed for their financial exertions between the two wars. In 1930, after the greatest war in her history, France set aside 4.3% of her national income for defence—in 1913 at the peak of the pre-war arms race the figure was 4.2%. Even allowing for the depreciation of the franc, more was being spent in real terms than in 1913 and the evidence would seem to confirm Gamelin's claim that 'a formidable military effort' was accomplished after 1936.[15] Bearing in mind too that British and German rearmament was fuelled by an expanding national income, the French record is all the more impressive and in 1939 France made a proportionately greater effort than her neighbours. One important reservation must be made. The statistics do not show what proportion of the sums voted were actually spent on armaments, as distinct from the construction of the Maginot Line, pay, rations and so forth.

The social and economic cost of the struggle to retain military primacy was ruinous. Given the belief in the necessity to balance the budget, defence spending left next to nothing for social welfare and industrial investment. In 1930-31 over half of government expenditure went to cover debt charges and a further quarter went to defence, leaving less than 25% for all the normal expenses of administration, including the civil service, education, and war pensions. On 27 June 1939, the Chamber was told that there was no money for the provision of old âge pensions which the deputies had voted three months earlier. Here was a real dilemma for the Ministers of the 1930s. External security could only be assured at an ever increasing cost but the consequent neglect of outstanding social needs created internal conflict and destroyed national unity. Arguably the generals may have been obsessed by the internal enemy. Their call for more spending on arms has been seen as an attempt to torpedo the Popular Front's social reforms.[16]

Despite weaknesses in the air and, to a lesser extent, at sea, France's fate in 1940 was decided on land and the French army therefore merits close attention. Like all the great organisations which emerged from the Consulate and Empire, the army was a centralised, bureaucratic body. This was at once its strength and its weakness. 'No one could change anything in our army', avowed the Deputy Chief of the General Staff, General Schweisguth, in 1935, 'but it is because of this very fact that we survived at all'.[17] The spirit of *fonctionarisme* which enabled the regime to weather the storms of Boulanger and Dreyfus, in the long term weakened the army. It is even said that between the two world wars the General Staff was 'deprived of all constructive thought'—the consequence of years of exhausting struggle against internal foes: parliament, the government of the day, and the treasury. Nor did the army stand high in public esteem. Pacifist sentiment and the hopes of general disarmament made the military virtues seem outdated. Only in 1938-39 did the army begin to recover a little of the prestige it had enjoyed in 1914.

New ideas and initiatives might have revitalised the army if younger men had been given their head. But the army was dying from the top, crushed by the inertia of its old men. Clemenceau's plans for a young army in which divisional generals should be retired at 62 and brigade generals at 58, were discarded. The military gerontocracy remained firmly entrenched in power. Touring the Maginot Line in the autumn of 1939 General Ironside, Chief of the Imperial General Staff, observed that many divisional commanders were 60 or over.[18] Gamelin, Chief of the French General Staff from 1931 to 1940, was 67 in 1939; his deputy, General Georges, 65. In May 1940 Gamelin was replaced by the 72 year old General Weygand. Marshal Pétain, whose influence profoundly shaped military policy-making throughout the 1930s, was 84 when he formed the Vichy government in July 1940. And the generals all lived to a great age: Gamelin died at 86, Pétain was 95 and Weygand 98.

The mistake of the military leadership lay not in the adoption of a defensive strategy—no other course was practicable in the 1920s—but in the failure to review and redefine strategy and tactics in the light of changing ideas and technology. The lessons of the First World War were codified in an official manual issued by the War Ministry called the *Instruction sur l'emploi tactique des grandes unités* which as late as 1936 insisted that despite the technical advances in warfare since 1918 the guiding concepts of the Great War remained valid. The shapers of military doctrine ignored the prophets of modern warfare—General Estienne in France. Captain Liddell Hart in Britain. After the publication of de Gaulle's *Vers l'Armée de Métier* in 1934, Gamelin issued a circular reminding the army that the sole authority for war doctrine was the General Staff. French military intelligence translated General Guderian's *Achtung Panzer* and sent a copy to every garrison library in France. A provincial tour in the winter of 1937-38 revealed that the pages of not a single copy had been cut.[19] The lack of curiosity about German military thinking was in part the result of a language barrier. English and German were obligatory studies but in practice priority was given to English and the majority of officers were only interested in achieving a pass standard in German in examinations. Consequently they were ill-equipped to keep abreast of recent military developments in Germany.[20]

Much obviously hinged on the quality of the military chiefs and General Maurice Gamelin, Chief of the General Staff, was not an outstanding leader. Neither his own staff, nor the British in 1939-40, had much confidence in him. When General Beauffre joined the General Staff in the early 1930s a colleague warned him there was one thing he must know: 'Gamelin is a drip'.[21] The Chief of the General Staff was a fussy, pedantic person. A high-ranking British officer who saw him after the outbreak of war commented: 'a nice old man, not remotely equal to his enormous job'.[22] Not that Gamelin was ignorant of the opinions of some of his subordinates. In 1937 it was brought to his notice that General Bourret, a member of Daladier's staff at the War Ministry, had said of some matter: 'all that is Gamelinesque nonsense'.[23] This indiscretion cost the officer his post.

Coming from an old military family of Alsace-Lorraine, Gamelin was a disciple of Marshal Joffre and served under him in the war of 1914-18. Educated by the Jesuits at the College Stanislas, he remained 'a convinced Catholic' all his life but, and this was one of his main recommendations, he was no bigot in an army which was still divided by quarrels between Catholics and Freemasons.[24] His liberal-minded stance in politics was an even stronger qualification for office. Three of his closest friends were men of widely different political persuasions: the Right wing André Tardieu, the Radical Socialist journalist and politician Maurice Sarraut, and the Socialist Albert Thomas. After the Great War, Gamelin headed a military mission to Brazil and from 1925 to 1928 was commander-in-chief in the Lebanon, then under French mandate. At this point his ambitions were largely satisfied. Even after becoming Chief of the General Staff in 1931 he had no wish to cling to office and in 1937 he and Madame Gamelin had already bought an apartment for their retirement. Indeed, when war came he seemed to go into semi-retirement, living a life of monastic calm at his headquarters at the Château de Vincennes. Frugal and abstemious, he took a siesta and retired to his room punctually at 8 p.m., each evening, not appearing next day until 8 a.m., during which time he was not to be disturbed.

Why, then, did Gamelin preside over the army's fortunes for almost a decade? The explanation lay in his mediocrity. His self-effacing manner and modesty of ambition made him indispensable at a time when the army was under great stress. It was no longer the assured, self-confident force of 1914. Moreover, the unease felt by the military chiefs at the political and social convulsions of the Republic was compounded by the disarmament policy pursued by the Left wing governments which followed the electoral victory of 1932. The impulsive and abrasive personality of General Maxime Weygand, Chief of the General Staff until 1931 and then Inspector General of the Army until 1935, stretched civil-military relations almost to breaking point.[25] In January 1934, Daladier, Prime Minister and War Minister, quarrelled openly with Weygand.

After the intransigent Weygand with his Right wing associations, Gamelin was a godsend. He could be relied on to follow the government's lead and keep the army out of politics. Nevertheless, civil-military relations remained extremely fragile. The continuing tensions were manifested in the Gerodias affair in January 1937.[26] General Gerodias, of the Deuxième Bureau of the General Staff, circulated to all army commands a document of Spanish origin which purported to give Soviet instructions on the methods of carrying out a military *putsch*. Gerodias acted without the authorisation of Gamelin. The document soon found its way into the press. The Popular Front Chamber was in an uproar, scenting some Fascist plot. Daladier, without consulting Gamelin, relieved Gerodias of his post and exiled him to a provincial command. Gamelin was furious. He acknowledged that Gerodias had acted wrongly but considered the punishment excessive and claimed that he himself had been slighted by Daladier's high-handed action. His threat of resignation elicited the comment from Daladier: 'You are even more difficult than Weygand'.[27]

That ultra-Right wing groups were strongly entrenched in the officer corps seems certain, though it is difficult to say whether they posed a serious threat to the state. Gerodias alleged that the Spanish document had been handed to him by Commandant Loustaunau-Lacau, an officer attached to Marshal Pétain's staff. Loustaunau-Lacau was also implicated in the Right wing terrorist organisation, the *Cagoule*. In February 1938 a network of cells in the officer corps was discovered. The organisation was known as *Corvignolles* and dedicated itself to the denunciation of Communists and anti-militarists in the ranks. It seems that there were connections between the *Corvignolles* and the *Cagoule*.

Not only was the General Staff at odds with the political leadership, it also had its own internal dissensions. Gamelin heartily disliked General Georges, his deputy. General Bourret, Daladier's assistant, referred to the General Staff as 'a band of Jesuits', declaring that 'he would have Georges and Colson'.[28] The Duke of Windsor, who was attached to Gamelin's headquarters in 1939-40, was amazed to find that the army was still divided by conflicts between Catholics and Freemasons.[29] The consequence of this malaise in the army and in its relations with the government was that Gamelin's activity was essentially political. His role was a peacekeeping one. In fact he was much easier to get on with than Weygand and he was the one man who seemed capable of holding the army together. The price paid for this achievement was a high one. Given a similar span of office, a different leader might have realised much in the way of rethinking and modernisation. In the circumstances, however, Gamelin had no choice but to concentrate on preserving unity and avoiding a head on collision with the government.

What Liddell Hart called the 'haziness and contradictoriness of mind' prevalent in the top-levels of the army was mirrored in the confused and ill-defined policy-making machinery. There were numerous committees, dignified with high flown titles but no unified chain of command or supreme commander.[30] A law for the organisation of the nation in wartime of 11 July 1938 affirmed the primacy of civilian control and confirmed existing legislation. It was laid down that the 'general direction' of the war would be exercised by the Cabinet and a *Conseil Supérieur de la Défense Nationale* would be formed to this end, with a membership of Cabinet ministers, Marshal Pétain, the Chief of Staff. 'The military direction of the war', it was said, would be in the hands of a *Comité de Guerre,* composed of the President of the Republic, the Prime Minister, Service Ministers, Chief of Staff of National Defence, Chiefs of Staff, Foreign Minister.

Below these Cabinet committees, each of the three services had its own 'superior council', headed by the minister and chief of staff. Such was the machinery laid down for wartime policy-making. Peacetime arrangements were much less precise. After the 1914-18 war, the *Conseil Supérieur de la Défense Nationale* soon proved too large and unwieldy and was transformed into a secretariat and study body, with specialist sub-committees on various aspects of defence policy and planning. In 1923, Poincaré was considering the setting up of a much smaller defence policy committee, though parliament did not like the idea. In 1932 the *Haut Comité Militaire* was established. The *Conseil Supérieur de la Défense Nationale* continued to exist but rarely met and decision making passed effectively to the *Haut Comité Militaire,* which had as its members the Prime Minister, Service Ministers, Chiefs of Staff, and Marshal Pétain. No official minutes of meetings were kept. On 6 June 1936, the *Haut Comité Militaire* was replaced by the *Comité Permanent de la Défense Nationale,* with the same membership but administratively a much more effective organ because it was linked to the secretariat and specialist services of the *Conseil Supérieur de la Défense Nationale.*

Although the need for a defence ministry was recognised in the 1920s, the ministry created in 1932 was no more than a piece of window dressing, or as one official report put it, only a change of heading on official stationery. After three months, nothing more was heard of the new ministry. In June 1936, Blum revived the Ministry but subordinated it to the war Ministry. Daladier, War Minister, became Minister of National Defence and War. He held both portfolios continuously until 1940 and blocked moves to endow the National Defence Ministry with independent authority and direction over the three service ministries. Equally serious was the failure to create before September 1939 a Ministry of Armaments.

The alliance of Daladier and Gamelin, fortified by inter-service rivalries, was strong enough to prevent the creation of a supreme commander in peacetime. By a decree of 21 January 1938, Gamelin was appointed Chief of Staff of National Defence while retaining his existing designation as Chief of the Army General Staff. But he was not given a separate National Defence Staff and his authority rested entirely on his position as Chief of the Army General Staff. In truth he did not aspire to be generalissimo, complaining that the burden of the two posts was too onerous, though his functions as Chief of National Defence Staff were largely nominal. Perhaps he wisely knew his own limitations. Both he and the government opposed parliamentary pressure for the appointment of a supreme commander in peacetime. Gamelin countered calls for a generalissimo with the argument that the supreme command was 'above all a question of personal prestige' which would easily resolve itself on the outbreak of hostilities.[31]

Gamelin's mission was to keep the peace not only between the army and nation but also between the three fighting services.[32] Pierre Cot, Air Minister in 1936-37, found the air force jealous of its new-found independence and eager to assert itself against the army. And Vice-Admiral Darlan, Chief of Staff of the Navy, was even more jealous of the independence of the fleet. Consultation and co-ordination between the service chiefs was minimal. Ambassador Bullitt complained to Daladier that in September 1938 the army 'seemed to be entirely unaware of what they could count on from the air force . . . and seemed to be making their plans without regard to the air force'. Indeed, Gamelin admitted that it was only on 28 September that he learnt indirectly of the advice tendered a few days earlier to the government by the Chief of Air Staff, General Vuillemin, to the effect that the air force was not ready for war.

Until the creation of the Permanent Committee of National Defence (Comité Permanent de la Défense Nationale) on 6 June 1936, policymaking machinery was cumbersome and confused. Gamelin claimed that important decisions had been taken either in full Cabinet without consulting the Chiefs of staff, or in small ad hoc meetings without official minutes.[33] With the setting up of the Permanent Committee of National Defence there was no excuse for lack of consultation. And yet the improved machinery was little used. In 1938, for example, the Permanent Committee met only twice, on 15 March and 5 December. Surprisingly, Gamelin on 12 September 1938 rejected a suggestion of Daladier that the army council—Conseil Supérieur de la Guerre might be convened. Probably the main reason for the relative neglect of the central policy-making machinery was the fear that more frequent consultation would lead to an erosion of the independence of the three services.

If there was little consultation between the services, there was even less between the Chief of the General Staff and the Prime Minister. 'To serve', the title of Gamelin's memoirs, was an apt choice—the army served its civilian masters but service was not supplemented by trust and confidence. Weeks went by without any contact between Gamelin and Daladier. Daladier explained that liaison was difficult because Gamelin and he did not share the same building—the Chief of the General Staff had his office at the Invalides, not at the war ministry.[34] According to Gamelin, Daladier had too many responsibilities and was consequently immersed in administrative and parliamentary matters. His account of relations with the prime minister has a note of unconscious humour. After weeks of trying to see Daladier, he would eventually be received, but no sooner had the conversation got under way than a secretary would enter to announce another visitor. The real reason for the infrequent contact between the two men was that they did not like each other. Gamelin claims that all would have been well if Daladier, like his predecessors at the war ministry, General Maurin and Colonel Fabry, had been a personal friend whom he could telephone or call on at any time. However the war provided ample opportunity for contact. From 1943-45 Gamelin and Daladier were fellow prisoners at the castle of Itter in the Tyrol.

Between the General Staff and the Quai d'Orsay the lines of communication were even more defective.[35] Each of the Service Ministries had a liaison officer attached to the Quai but until 1938 there was no committee for the co-ordination of liaison work. Neither the *Haut Comité Militaire,* nor its successor the Permanent Committee of National Defence, required the attendance of the Foreign Minister or his assistants. The Foreign Minister, Paul-Boncour, and Léger were present at a meeting of the Permanent Committee on 15 March 1938 but Bonnet did not attend the meeting on 5 December. Liaison between the Quai and War Ministry was inadequate. On 12 March 1938 Léger complained to Gamelin that the War Ministry had not kept him sufficiently informed of German moves against Austria. Gamelin replied that the liaison officer, Lieutenant-Colonel de Villelume, had been told to keep the Quai fully informed. But de Villelume may have been careless since Gamelin had his own doubts about the officer.

In his testimony to the postwar commission of enquiry, de Villelume argued that the War Ministry was always mistrustful of the Quai and very sparing in the information released. There were other instances of friction or lack of understanding between the generals and diplomats. In February 1936, the Quai tried to ascertain what measures, other than precautionary ones, the army was prepared to take in the event of a German threat to the Rhineland. The replies received were, as Massigli noted, evasive. The Quai d'Orsay's questioning obviously annoyed the war ministry. On 23 April 1936 Gamelin told Bargeton, Political Director:

> The Quai d'Orsay must understand that the present organisation of our army is such that, without mobilisation, we can occupy our defensive lines, stop an attack, but any offensive action in enemy country is out of the question.[36]

After the *Anschluss* liaison improved. In 1938-39, fortnightly meetings of the Deputy Chiefs of Staff were held at the Quai d'Orsay under the chairmanship of the Political Director and full minutes were kept.

Clearly, the General Staff exerted a considerable influence on the conduct of diplomacy. Diplomatic moves had to conform to a fundamentally defensive strategy. And no other strategy was practicable in the conditions of the time. However the generals can be criticised for being ultra-defensive, cautious to a fault, overestimating German strength in March 1936 when France still had a military lead over her adversary. Their defensive mentality excluded not only a preventive strike against Germany but also a riposte to German violations of the peace treaties. Following the Rhineland *coup,* diplomats like Léger and Massigli who wanted firm action found themselves cabined and confined by the government's military counsellors. And the advice of the generals carried the day. Again, in 1938, the General Staff, though fully conscious of the strategic value of Czechoslovakia, did not in any way encourage the government to fulfill France's pledges. The weight of advice was against fighting for Czechoslovakia. Thus the appreciations of the generals were a powerful constraint on policy-making.

Yet the generals seemed incapable of exercising a positive initiative. In 1936, the Blum government opened preliminary staff talks with the Soviet Union—much to the dismay of the generals. That the talks fizzled out in May 1937 was not surprising. What is surprising though is that Gamelin who was fully alive to the military value of an Italian alliance does not seem to have made any efforts to persuade Blum to open talks with Rome. The most serious failure of the 1930s lay in the lack of a close understanding between statesmen, diplomats and generals. Common sense required that diplomatic and strategic preparations should go hand in hand but no reappraisal of foreign and defence policies took place.

PART THREE
Undeclared War

Chapter 11

Czechoslovakia 1938

By far and away the most important problem which faced the new Daladier government was the threat to France's central European ally, Czechoslovakia. When the new ministers took office on 10 April 1938, the Czech alliance was already the focus of attention. The *Anschluss* had been followed by what the Czechoslovak Minister at Paris called a 'hellish' press campaign against Czechoslovakia.[1] On 12 April the semi-official *Le Temps* published an able and mischievous attack on the alliance. The jurist Joseph Barthélemy argued that since the Franco-Czech treaties of 1924 and 1925 had been linked to the Locarno treaties, now denounced by Germany, France was no longer under any legal obligation to go to war 'to maintain the Sudetens in the allegiance of Prague'. The article received wide publicity. Thousands of copies were translated into German or bad Czech and distributed throughout Czechoslovakia under the title: 'Czechs. France says: "Nothing doing"'. From Prague, de Lacroix, the French Minister, reported that the article had 'had the worst possible effect' and suggested the Quai d'Orsay published a refutation. A Hungarian newspaper carried the headline: 'the Foreign Ministry's newspaper abandons Czechoslovakia'. Not until 17 April did an editorial in *La Temps* attempt to refute the Barthélemy thesis.

Despite the press onslaught, the first act of the new government was reassuring. On 11 April, Bonnet assured the Czechoslovak Minister, Osusky, that French policy would remain unchanged.[2] On the same day in Prague, President Benes asked Lacroix if he was certain that the government would confirm France's engagements. France, replied the envoy, 'would always be faithful to her word'.

The British government wasted no time in seeking to influence the new ministry. Bonnet, who had spent a 'great part of the night in the Chamber', paid his first official call on Phipps, the British Ambassador, in the afternoon of 13 April.[3] The military and political arguments against fighting for Czechoslovakia which had been marshalled for Paul-Boncour were paraded for his successor. But Phipps did not content himself with generalities. He made a specific request. Instructions, he suggested, should be sent to Lacroix to act jointly with Newton, the British Minister in urging the Czechs to make substantial concessions to the Sudeten German minority. 'Disposed to agree' Bonnet asked for a little time for reflection, explaining that 'his greatest desire was to work in close collaboration' and his 'chief object was . . . to work for peace and to avoid being stampeded by the warmongers' but 'he must be given a little time to undo the work of his predecessors'. Following this meeting, Phipps sent a note to the Quai d'Orsay, stressing that both governments must 'exercise all their influence in Prague, preferably conjointly'. He proposed that a note should be sent to Prague in this sense, asking to be kept informed of the progress of talks with the Sudeten German leaders. Bonnet's cautious reaction was a wise one. With a meeting of British and French ministers in the offing, it made no sense to give away France's bargaining position. No action, therefore, was taken on Phipps's proposal. In a conversation with Newton on 25 April Lacroix denied any knowledge of a plan for joint Franco-British representations. What he had told Benes, on the instructions of Paul-Boncour, was that the French government had every confidence that Prague would go to the limit of concessions 'compatible with the maintenance of sovereignty'.

A word must be said about the diplomats whom Bonnet saw most. They were: William C. Bullitt, the American Ambassador, Sir Eric Phipps, his British colleague, and Count von Welczeck, the German Ambassador. Bullitt had been an adviser of President Woodrow Wilson and was a member of the American delegation to the Paris Peace Conference. In 1933 he was appointed first United States ambassador to the Soviet Union. The Moscow mission turned him from being an ardent admirer of the Soviet Union into a bitter enemy. After the disillusionment, dreariness and isolation of Moscow the Paris embassy seemed like the promised land. Bullitt took up his duties in October 1936. France was his spiritual home. With fluent French and family connections he settled down easily into a round of dinners and junketings. He leased a château at Chantilly and stocked the cellars with 18,000 bottles of wine.

After his arrival in October 1936 he quickly developed close ties with French leaders.[4] His personality and sympathy for France were obvious assets but his chief recommendation was his relationship with Roosevelt. Like his London colleague, Joseph P. Kennedy, he was a personal choice of the President and enjoyed direct access to the White House. He came to be regarded as the President's personal spokesman and felt 'he had a tacit mandate' to act as Roosevelt's eyes and ears in Europe. He had almost daily telephone contact with the White House. No other envoy enjoyed such intimate relations with French statesmen. With Blum and Daladier, Bullitt developed a close personal friendship, sitting with Blum at the bedside of Madame Blum the night she died. Daladier asked him to act as guardian for one of his sons in the event of his own death. Relations with French diplomats were much less close. Bullitt had no time for the traditions of the Quai d'Orsay. Writing of the new French ambassador to Washington, Count René Doynel de Saint-Quentin, he told Roosevelt on 10 January 1938:

> When Saint-Quentin comes to see you, you will face the quintessence of the Quai d'Orsay. . . He is upright and honourable, and his point of view and that of Léger and rest of the permanent officials of the Quai d'Orsay seems to me fatal. . .

Phipps dismissed his American colleague as a 'lightweight' who was not liked by his staff. Though the estimation was not free of professional malice, it is true that Bullitt was not sufficiently discriminating in his reporting. He tended to ply Washington with ill-digested dinner table gossip and attached too much weight to the impressions of the last person with whom he had talked. 'On the whole', writes his biographer, his 'dispatches from Russia were more contemplative and interpretative... the greater part of the Paris dispatches tend to report, with little comment, casual conversations in the Quai d'Orsay, and dinner-time gossip'.[5] Daladier, not Bonnet, was Bullitt's hero and by September 1938 the ambassador's reports revealed considerable distrust of the foreign minister. Later in the year, Bonnet regained some of Bullitt's confidence by showing him the texts of British notes received during the Czech crisis.

The British Ambassador, Sir Eric Phipps, was an almost daily caller at the Quai d'Orsay.[6] He came to Paris from Berlin in April 1937. As Ambassador in Berlin from 1933-37, he had quickly perceived the ruthless character of the Third Reich, though it is said that 'on the ultimate issue of Nazi intentions' his reports were 'perhaps indecisive'. He was criticised for being pro-French. Sir Nevile Henderson, his successor, claimed 'it was common talk that there was no British embassy there at all, only a branch of the Quai d'Orsay'. Paris suited him well. It was the plum of the foreign service and Phipps knew the capital, having been educated there. He had also served three times as Secretary at the Embassy.

Phipps and Bonnet worked well together. Immediately after Munich the French minister wrote to Halifax, paying tribute to the ambassador:

> I have always been able to speak to him in complete confidence. . . I know that he has always accurately reported my thinking.

But Bonnet would not have written such a glowing testimonial if he had known all that Phipps said of him. While Bullitt was somewhat naïve in his judgement, Phipps had a strong streak of cynicism. On 17 September 1938, the eve of a Franco-British conference in London, he proposed to Halifax that French ministers should be interrogated individually regarding the state of the French air force:

> it would be well for the Prime Minister, for instance, to put the same questions to Daladier that you are putting to Bonnet in another room . . . Veracity is not . . . the strongest point of the average French politician, but there is a rather better chance of extracting the truth from him when he is not in the presence of another Frenchman. . .

The mistake of Phipps was to identify himself too closely with one section of the French governing class—the trinity of Bonnet, Flandin, Caillaux and their acolytes. Consequently, he lost a sense of balance and perspective in his assessment of the French scene. Bonnet, as Gamelin said, discouraged everybody and much of the Minister's pessimism rubbed off onto the Ambassador. The prime example of this myopia was his report of 24 September 1938 on the theme 'all that is best in France is against war, *almost* at any price' with its reference to a 'small, but noisy and corrupt, war group'.[7] The Foreign Office was stung to censure and asked the Ambassador to obtain samples of a broader spectrum of opinion. Phipps stuck to his story, explaining that by 'small, but noisy and corrupt, war group' he meant 'the Communists who are paid by Moscow and have been working for war for months'. These September reports permanently damaged his standing in the Foreign Office. British consuls in France were told to send their reports of opinion direct to London, so as to prevent the Embassy 'doctoring them'. A move followed to get the date of his retirement settled as quickly as possible. Oliver Harvey, private secretary to Halifax, wrote:

> I must record my view that Phipps in Paris has done his utmost to discourage the French from anything resembling positive action in fulfilment of their treaty with Czechoslovakia. He has skilfully worked on Bonnet's fears and weaknesses and he has consistently reported his views without seeking or encouraging the views of other more important Frenchmen such as Blum, Herriot, Reynaud or Mandel,...In all this he has faithfully interpreted the views of the present Cabinet. But I do not think it wise to blanket other opinion to the extent he has...

Another, though less frequent, visitor to the Quai d'Orsay was the German Ambassador, Count Johannes von Welczeck. He was a career diplomat of the old school, having begun his career as Consul-General in India before the First World War. This was followed by a period at the legation in Chile, where he met and married a wealthy Chilean lady. Later, he served in Hungary, and then as Ambassador to Spain from 1926 to 1936. In April 1936 he was appointed to Paris. He was connected with the French aristocracy through his step-aunt, the Countess Jean de Castellane and he was the only German ambassador since 1914 to be admitted to the exclusive diplomatic club, the 'Union'. Paris was his last post. He did not serve Germany in the Second World War, being placed on the semi-retired list from January 1940 until his final retirement in 1944.

Welczeck was never as close to French ministers as his British and American colleagues. Moreover, he was away from Paris for quite lengthy periods — for much of September 1938, March-April 1939 and August 1939. 'In times of crisis', as Weizsäcker noted, 'Hitler sent the heads of missions away on compulsory leave'.[8] Nevertheless, Welczeck's dispatches contain statements attributed to Daladier and Bonnet which, if known at the time, would certainly have wrecked their political careers. On 9 August 1938, Bonnet was reported as saying: 'we would have to go to the extreme limits of compromise in the Sudeten German question, even though this did not suit the Czechs'. On 2 September 1938 Welczeck wired the following account of the foreign minister's views:

> ...After a repetition of the general peace talk which I have often heard from him, he added that...he himself, Daladier, and other members of the Cabinet were sincere admirers of the Führer...he, Bonnet, wished for nothing more ardently than to see the Führer in Paris as the guest of the French Government ...In the present situation he wanted to leave no room for doubt that France, and Britain at her side, were firmly resolved to hasten to the assistance of the Czechs if they were attacked by German troops...In France and Britain, however,...nothing was so ardently desired as peace...We could depend upon it that Czechoslovak Government would be forced to accept Runciman's verdict,

which, in all probability, would mean the fulfilment of 70, 80, or 90 percent of the Sudeten German demands.

Should the historian dismiss all such evidence out of hand as hopelessly biassed and untrustworthy? Not at all. Naturally, like all sources, Welczeck's reports need to be handled with some caution but there is no reason to discount the general sense of his reporting. Welczeck, it must be remembered, was a trained diplomatic reporter and Bonnet was not. Also, the German Ambassador had no ideological axe to grind. On Bonnet's own testimony, the Ambassador was barely tolerated by Berlin. Phipps acknowledged that he had 'no sympathy with some of the tenets of the present German regime'. Moreover, taking Welczeck's dispatches over the eighteen months of Bonnet's tenure of the Quai there is a remarkable consistency about the views attributed to the foreign Minister, and some confirmation of their tenor can be found in the assessments made by Bullitt and Phipps. Lastly, Bonnet's attitude to the German documents has been inconsistent and, at times, contradictory. When in 1951 the Parliamentary Commission of Enquiry confronted him with extracts from Welczeck's reports of 9 August and 2 September 1938 the former Minister denied their authenticity and flatly asserted that the Ambassador had lied. His denials would have carried more conviction had he produced, as requested, his own memoranda of the interviews. Yet, in later editions of the memoirs, he quoted freely from the German documents, citing them almost with the same respect as the French diplomatic papers.[9]

On 27 April, Daladier and Bonnet flew to London for a two-day conference with British Ministers.[10] The guidelines of their policy were already well-defined, and London knew in advance the general stance of the French government. In Paris, on 24-25 April, Hore-Belisha, Secretary of State for War, had talked to Daladier and Gamelin. Daladier, noted the British minister, 'seems to be ready to fall into line with us'. Gamelin considered 'it was impossible for France to give military assistance to Czechoslovakia'. Other reports from Paris, notably from Mendl. Press Attaché, indicated that there was no question of France defending her ally. Further evidence of the state of mind in which the French delegation approached the negotiations comes from the German record. The German Embassy in London received two reports from an informant who claimed to have had a private talk with Daladier on 28 April and also to have spoken to the French Prime Minister's adviser, Fernand de Brinon.[11] The pith of these reports was 'Daladier's hope that Chamberlain and Halifax would themselves suggest that pressure should be put on Prague' so that the French 'could acquiesce without seeming to have taken the initiative'. In forwarding the reports to Berlin, the embassy added that it had confirmation of their conclusions 'from another quarter'. Not that the British were unprepared for their guest. Cadogan impressed on Halifax that the French had come over for '2 reasons — (1) to boost themselves (2) to tighten our leading string. We must look out for (2)'.

The first day's meeting passed off fairly amicably, covering, in Cadogan's summary, 'non-contentious stuff, such as Anglo-Italian agreement, procedure at Geneva, Spain and — less contentious — Staff conversations'.[12]

In the evening the French ministers spent the night at Windsor Castle as guests of King George VI and Queen Elizabeth. Their stay added a touch of comedy to the official courtesies. In their rooms they discovered cards requesting the wearing of Court dress—knee breeches. Hastily, Corbin was summoned and advised that the cards should be ignored. Another trial was yet to come. The palatial accommodation lacked one amenity—central heating, and the weather was cold for the time of year. The bedclothes were too light and Bonnet rummaged for extra clothing. Still, Bonnet, as his memoirs testify, was flattered at having stayed 'with the King and Queen' — so much so in fact that, according to the journalists, he could talk of nothing else.

The second day's talks on 29 April concerned Czechoslovakia and the French ministers, by asking for a firm promise of support for their ally, almost brought proceedings to breaking point. In the previous day's discussion on staff conversations the French had already shown their teeth a little by asking for naval talks. Over Czechoslovakia Daladier spoke as an opponent of German expansionism:

> We should be blind if we did not see the realities of the present situation. We were confronted by German policy readily translated into action, designed to tear up treaties...In his view the ambitions of Napoleon were far inferior to the present aims of the German Reich...if and when Germany had secured the petrol and wheat resources of Roumania, she would then turn against the Western Powers...
> ...war could only be avoided if Great Britain and France made their determination quite clear to maintain the peace of Europe...

Chamberlain disagreed with Daladier's diagnosis and 'doubted very much' whether Hitler 'really desired to destroy' Czechoslovakia. Cadogan was less polite and dismissed Daladier's discourse as 'very beautiful but awful rubbish'. But the French prime minister soon hauled down his flag. After a luncheon adjournment during which the two prime ministers had a private talk, the two delegations agreed that Britain and France would jointly urge concessions in Prague.

French behaviour at the April talks set the pattern for future meetings.[13] The French Ministers at first resisted and then gave way, conveying the impression of bowing to British pressure. They acted in this manner for a variety of reasons. Uppermost was Daladier's desire to preserve French honour, a show of resistance was for the record. It was essential that France should speak up for her ally. Yet this is not to say that Daladier was two-faced and therefore the denunciations of German aims can be discounted. The French minister was a victim of his own temperament. He favoured conciliation but knew Germany was not to be trusted. However doubts and misgivings were no substitute for a policy. Finally, the demeanour of the French ministers was based on much hard calculation. Bonnet's 'whole policy', as he confided to Bullitt, 'was based on allowing the British full latitude to work out the dispute'. In making great play of their suspicions of Germany and their solicitude for Czechoslovakia, the French sought to bluff the British into thinking that France would fight for her ally. 'Are the French bluffing to try to get more out of us?', asked Halifax's secretary. The British government might well believe that if the worst came to the worst France would do no more than man the Maginot Line but there was no certainty in the matter. Both sides strove to keep each other guessing about their real intentions. At Windsor Castle, Daladier and Bonnet told Halifax that 'bad though the situation was, France would have to honour her obligations if Czechoslovakia were attacked but she would welcome and press on Benes any solution, even a Federal one...'. The French government rightly assumed that in order to guard against the danger of being dragged into war by France, British Ministers would readily take the initiative in Berlin and Prague. Inevitably, the leading strings would be tightened but France's diplomatic defences might be the stronger. British support, it was reasoned, might yet deter Germany from attacking Czechoslovakia and, if the worst happened, Britain would be committed to France.

Although Daladier's demand for a Franco-British declaration to the effect that while every effort would be made to reach a settlement the destruction of Czechoslovakia would not be permitted was rejected, French Ministers did not leave empty handed. By asking a high price for their co-operation, they secured important gains. Though Chamberlain won their agreement to joint pressure on Prague, in return he had to promise a British démarche in Berlin. Germany would be told that London and Paris were doing their utmost to produce a settlement in Czecho-slovakia. Chamberlain also promised further action in Berlin, if the need arose. Should concessions in Czechoslovakia fail to produce a settlement, Germany would be given a warning on the lines of Chamber-lain's 24 March statement to the Commons. Lastly, British resistance to naval staff talks with France was overcome and it was agreed that con-versations would be opened after Hitler's visit to Rome in May.

The success of the London conference strengthened Daladier's hand at home against a number of mischief makers in and outside the govern-ment. The troublemakers in the Cabinet were Reynaud, Minister of Justice, who wanted more Socialists in the government, and Camille Chautemps, Deputy Prime Minister, who disliked Daladier and was said to covet the Quai d'Orsay. The arch-intriguer was alleged to be Herriot, who disliked both Daladier and Chautemps, and wanted a broad-based Ministry, embracing the Communist Maurice Thorez and the Right wing Louis Marin.

In accordance with the strategy elaborated in London the French made no move in Berlin, leaving the running to their British partner. No opportunity was missed, however, of reminding Germany of France's desire for a peaceful settlement. Conciliation seemed all the more necessary after the Sudeten German leader, Conrad Henlein, in a speech at Carlsbad on 24 April, demanded the reshaping of Czechoslovak foreign policy and self-government for the German-speaking minority. On 30 April, Bonnet assured Welczeck of his 'admiration for the rise and achieve-ments of the new Germany'. Czechoslovakia, said the minister, offered 'an opportunity of reaching an understanding with Germany' and 'any arrangement' was better than 'world war'.[14] But Germany did not relax the war of nerves. When François-Poncet assured the German Foreign Minister, Ribbentrop, on 17 May that 'the French government ... would do everything to contribute to a settlement of the Sudeten German problem' he received a testy answer. If Germany had to intervene in Czechoslovakia and France attacked her, threatened Ribbentrop, the whole of Germany would be swept by a wave of nationalism. Reluctantly perhaps the Ambassador restated his country's obligations: France would 'honour her promise, whatever Germany's military strength'.

In May, France probed the intentions of two of her eastern allies, Poland and the Soviet Union. The approaches were characterised by considerable ambivalence. In his memoirs Bonnet claimed that he made strenuous efforts to enlist the support of Poland, Rumania and the Soviet Union; alas, all to no avail. Only France was 'faithful found among the faithless'. On closer scrutiny, Bonnet's diplomacy was much less straight-forward than it might appear. Coulondre, Ambassador at Moscow, wrote: 'there was no clear speaking in Warsaw and no talking at all in Moscow because that would not have pleased either London or Berlin . . . I could not prevent myself from wondering what Maxim Litvinov thought of the attitude of his French colleague. One sensed so much in all that M Bonnet said the desire to shelter France from the approaching storm'.[15] The Polish Ambassador, Lukasiewicz, reached a similar conclusion. After a meeting with Bonnet in August 1938 he recorded: 'with this we ended yet another talk, confirming my opinion once again that M Bonnet's intentions to establish any real co-operation with Poland . . . were only formal and without practical meaning'. 'Was it really the help of Rumania that was sought in 1938 or rather her refusal?' declared the former Rumanian foreign minister. The central purpose of Bonnet's diplomacy in fact was not to fashion an alliance for Czechoslovakia but to furnish France with excuses for not fighting for her ally. Coulondre in Moscow, and Noel in Warsaw, campaigned in vain for the strengthening of the Soviet and Polish pacts.

Since the breakdown of preliminary staff talks in June 1937 the Franco-Soviet pact had been in a state of limbo. In March 1938, Paul-Boncour instructed Coulondre to ascertain the progress of Czech-Soviet military relations. On 18 April, Coulondre reported his findings and asked if Bonnet wished him to continue enquiries. A few days later hints came from London that the Franco-Soviet pact was regarded as undesirable. On 22 April Corbin cabled a report of a conversation between one of the embassy's informants and a member of 'the small group which surrounds the Prime Minister and busies itself with foreign affairs . . . with more zeal than competence'.[16] According to the Downing Street adviser, Barthou had told London that one of the principal reasons for a Franco-Soviet alliance was Soviet military strength. However, given the decline in Soviet strength, should not the French consider a 'revision' of their relations with Moscow? On 24 April Coulondre signalled that Czechoslovakia had received from Moscow a formal offer of staff talks. On the same day an internal Quai d'Orsay memorandum reached a sober and realistic assessment. Given the domestic crisis in the Soviet Union and the danger that war represented for the stability of the regime 'everything suggests that rather than isolation the Soviets would prefer an entente with Germany even at the cost of very substantial sacrifices. . . We must not forget that if the U.S.S.R. is not with us, she will be against us'.[17] The memorandum noted some signs of the Soviet Union and Germany drawing closer together.

Coulondre was not slow in offering counsel. The firm conviction of the inevitability of a European war, stressed the Ambassador on 28 April, was one of the chief determinants of Soviet policy: 'What for other governments appears as a menace is a certitude here. It is as if they had some material proof of the imminence of war'.[18] The Soviet leaders, he continued, really wished to co-operate with the western powers over Czechoslovakia but their outlooks differed from those of western leaders: 'contrary to the Soviets, we consider that peace can yet be saved through a European détente. If we achieve it, it will be by dint both of concilia-tion and firmness'. Coulondre was not an advocate of enlisting Soviet participation in a stop-Hitler alliance. In his opinion, consideration of Soviet proposals would add the necessary touch of firmness to French policy: 'it is more a matter of anticipating an initiative by Germany than of preparing a riposte . . . more a matter of maintaining peace than of preparing for the war which the Soviets consider inevitable'.

Staff talks were again in sight. In the second week of May, Bonnet met Litvinov in Geneva and the Soviet minister proposed Franco-Soviet military conversations. Not that Bonnet was in a fighting mood. Report-ing to the Cabinet on a meeting with the French minister at Geneva, Halifax said Bonnet had made it clear he wanted the British government 'to put as much pressure as possible on Dr Benes . . . in order to save France from the cruel dilemma of dishonouring her agreements or becom-ing involved in war'.[19] Nevertheless, the Soviet proposal could not be ignored. Accordingly, Coulondre was recalled to Paris to discuss pro-posals. On 20 May, it was agreed that the talks should be initiated through the Moscow embassy. Chastened by previous failures, Coulondre made a point of securing the approval of Gamelin and Léger. The plans were modest indeed: secret talks on a two-power basis only—Franco-Czech, Franco-Soviet, Czech-Soviet. The sudden threat of war over the weekend of 19-21 May killed the proposals. On 23 May Coulondre revisited Bonnet and found him 'hesitant', apprehensive lest 'the prospect of Soviet military help would incite certain French elements to be bellicose'.[20] Daladier agreed that the talks should proceed but enjoined the 'greatest prudence'. But Coulondre heard no more.

Poland's conduct towards Czechoslovakia in 1938 caused much indigna-tion in France. According to Bonnet, the bid to enlist Polish help reached its climax towards the end of May 1938. On 22 May, Bonnet received from the Polish Foreign Minister, Colonel Beck, a note saying that it was impossible for Poland to make a *démarche* in Berlin similar to the one made by Britain on 21 May. Bonnet's narrative of these transac-tions was brilliantly dissected by Sir Lewis Namier. As well as destroying Bonnet's reliability as a historian, his analysis threw strong doubt on the latter's statesmanship. For some months the correspondence columns of the *Times Literary Supplement* witnessed a vitriolic polemic between the two men.[21] The contest was an unequal one and Namier's main contentions emerged strengthened by Bonnet's clumsy defence. Namier made short work of Bonnet's history, showing that it was not until 22 May that the minister asked Beck to take action in Berlin. The Polish reply did not reach Paris until 26 May (not 22 May as stated by Bonnet). The gravamen, however, of Namier's indictment was that the Polish note of 26 May, far from being an absolute refusal to take action, offered the possibility of friendly Franco-Polish discussions. In effect, Poland suggested for the first time a discussion of the Czech problem. Namier alleged that Bonnet the historian, by suppressing the opening and concluding paragraphs and doctoring the remainder of the text had transformed what was a veiled Polish 'offer' to negotiate into a completely negative document. He concluded: 'The Polish offer, for what it was worth, was first torpedoed by Bonnet the statesman, and next obliterated by Bonnet the historian'. There the matter rested. While having had the best of the fight, Namier did not show conclusively that Bonnet 'torpedoed' the Polish offer.

With the publication of Lukasiewicz's papers and the opening of the French archives, some reassessment can be made of Franco-Polish relations in 1938. On 15 April Lukasiewicz wired Warsaw that since the Daladier government seemed likely to last for some time, first contacts would be of great importance. It would be wise, he counselled, if Poland abandoned her 'present tactics' of rejecting French advances and manifested a readiness to enter into discussions of central European affairs.[22] Beck replied:

> ...I do not think that Franco-Polish discussions on central Europe, however far they are carried . . . will reach a satisfactory conclusion. I do not believe the present government has decided to change its foreign policy... I instruct you to maintain for the future great reserve on the question of central Europe.

But Beck's attitude soon changed. On 30 April Bonnet had given Lukasiewicz an account of the London conference. 'Both the French and British Governments', said the minister, 'wanted to be assured of the assistance of the Polish Government' in the settlement of the Czech question.[23] The conversation was friendly and Bonnet 'stressed repeatedly that France would always remain true to its alliance with Poland, which is much closer to it than Czechoslovakia'. Impressed perhaps by the demonstration of Franco-British solidarity in London and by Bonnet's friendly words, Beck went out of his way to be conciliatory. In a talk with Noel on 4 May he affirmed Poland's willingness to co-operate with France and Britain in damping down the conflict in central Europe. As for Czechoslovakia, 'one cannot ask us to give her our guarantee but we have no hostile intentions towards her'.[24] Noel noted that for the first time since his arrival in Warsaw in 1935 Beck was 'relatively' objective and moderate in his references to Czechoslovakia.

The scene seemed set for a Franco-Polish *rapprochement*. On 19-20 May a crisis blew up over Czechoslovakia. London and Paris received reports of German troop movements and Halifax instructed Henderson to deliver the warning which had been agreed on in the London conference. On the morning of 22 May, Lukasiewicz asked to see Bonnet in order to present the formal Polish reply to the request for assistance which the French Minister had made on 30 April. The reply, like Beck's utterances of 4 May, was extremely conciliatory—judged in the context of the asperities that had hitherto marked Franco-Polish relations. Having heard the Polish reply, Bonnet did not reply directly but proceeded to describe Henderson's *démarche* in Berlin on 21 May. 'Would the Polish Government', he asked, 'be willing to make a *démarche* in Berlin similar in tone and contents to the one made by the British Government?'.[25]

Beck's reply to Bonnet's question was the note of 26 May which was remarkably conciliatory in tone. The request for a *démarche* in Berlin was rejected because '*ipso facto*' it would 'mean Poland's acceptance of a unilateral commitment, not provided for in Polish-French agreements'.[26] But the final paragraph of the note left the door open for further talks:

> In conclusion, I would affirm, as I did on March 7, 1936, that we are ready to fulfil our treaty obligations within the limits of the present agreements and that we are prepared to enter friendly discussions on any new factors based on a mutual comprehension of the interests of the two countries.

Again, as on 22 May, Bonnet did not reply directly to the Polish declaration but opened with general remarks. When he did turn his attention to the text of the reply he did not seem to understand it fully and 'paid no particular attention to the statement that our declaration in Berlin similar to that of the British would amount to undertaking a new unilateral commitment'.

To describe Beck's note of 26 May as an 'offer' is misleading. No more was involved than a restatement of Polish goodwill, though this reassertion was in itself significant. Bonnet's declarations on the importance of the Polish alliance to France, noted Lukasiewicz, 'could . . . be taken as a starting point for broader political discussion'. Yet the ambassador 'doubted whether this is advisable, especially as regards the . . . Franco-Soviet pact'. But to avoid any discussions 'would unnecessarily excite the suspicions of the French':[27]

> We could, for instance, share with the French government our opinion regarding Germany's mood, and we should not hesitate to make remarks on the policy of Czechoslovakia . . .

But Beck had lost interest in the matter. On 9 June Lukasiewicz was told:

> Please refrain from further discussions of this matter. The situation is not ripe for the negotiation of a Franco-Polish agreement on policy in eastern Europe. It is not worth initiating conversations, especially in view of Bonnet's naive attitude towards these problems.

While the Poles backpedalled, the French made a belated effort to follow up the 26 May note. On 30 May Massigli advised Bonnet:

> For the first time M Beck informs us officially of his grievances towards Czechoslovakia . . . The Polish Government declares itself ready for a discussion . . . Under these two headings the Polish communication offers us possibilities that it would be mistaken to neglect.[28]

If France did nothing, continued Massigli, Beck would say that none of his initiatives had been taken up. Next day Bonnet forwarded the text of the 26 May note to Noel, requesting his advice. In a letter of 1 June, the Political Director explained to Noel that Bonnet had retained the note for three days before passing it on to his officials. Noel was an advocate of closer relations with Warsaw. On 31 May, before receiving the text of the 26 May note, he had reviewed the whole field of Franco-Polish relations and urged the holding of staff talks—'often projected, always postponed'. He was not enthusiastic about Beck's note, considering that in refusing to act at Berlin the Polish Foreign Minister had taken 'a step backward' since his interview with the ambassador on 4 May. Nevertheless, concluded Noel:

> I think . . . there would be more disadvantages than advantages in not replying to the initiative taken by M Beck . . .
> It would, in my opinion, be good policy to tell M Beck that the French Government is always ready for "friendly discussions" and . . . will consider with interest the views of the Polish Government.

This in fact was the line Bonnet took when he saw Lukasiewicz on 11 June. France, he said, 'had noted with pleasure the last paragraph of the memorandum . . . opening the way to a better understanding of Franco-Polish relations'. Moreover, the French government fully sympathised with the position of the Polish minority in Czechoslovakia and had urged that the minority receive the same treatment as the Sudeten Germans. Then came a specific request. On 4 May Beck had been reported as saying that Poland had no hostile intentions towards Czechoslovakia. Would Poland, asked Bonnet, be prepared to make a declaration in this sense? Lukasiewicz denied any knowledge of the 4 May interview between Noel and Beck. Thereupon, Bonnet formulated a new demand: did Poland consider as binding the Covenant of the League of Nations which excluded aggression?

Franco-Polish discussions dragged on throughout June and into July, although senior foreign ministry officials and the ambassador at Warsaw seem to have been kept on the fringes of the negotiations.[29] Bonnet persisted in seeking from Poland a written promise not to attack Czechoslovakia. On 17 June, on Beck's instructions, Lukasiewicz gave Bonnet an undertaking that Poland would not attack Czechoslovakia and remained faithful to the League Covenant. This was not enough for the French foreign minister. On 7 July Noel asked Beck for written confirmation of the declaration of 17 June. Beck refused, considering 'the French démarche to be rather a search for pretexts than real action'.[30]

Namier's charge against Bonnet was that the Minister had 'torpedoed' the Polish 'offer'. It has also been argued that the Minister's real fault was one of omission: a 'failure to comprehend the veiled offer contained in the last paragraph of the Polish note'.[31] Massigli told a member of the Polish embassy that Bonnet 'apparently had not grasped the essential points' of the note. But in a letter to Noel of 1 June the Political Director stated that Bonnet had not yet made up his mind what to do about the note. And this would seem to be the most likely explanation of the Foreign Minister's conduct. He was much too shrewd to have missed the import of the document. According to Lukasiewicz, he was given a word for word translation of the note. He 'wrote down' the text and read it over twice. Bonnet was simply slow in making up his mind until prodded into action by his permanent officials. No sinister significance need be attached to the fact that he kept back for a few days his notes of the interview with Lukasiewicz on 26 May. Bonnet did not 'torpedo' the note because discussions continued in June and July, resulting in a considerable measure of agreement. Poland was promised support for her minority in Czechoslovakia and offered in return a declaration not to attack Czechoslovakia. Bonnet's fault lay in seeking a written statement from Beck in July, thus jeopardising the limited understanding achieved after 26 May.

One of the Daladier government's first tasks was to try to make friends with Italy. The decision to appoint an Ambassador to Rome had been taken by the Blum government and on 6 April Paul-Boncour had expressed his readiness to send a negotiator. The Daladier ministry, like the outgoing government, had mixed feelings about Italy. The Duff Coopers who visited Paris in mid-April 1938 found French Ministers 'very sceptical' about the value of the Anglo-Italian Agreement of 16 April.

> Daladier went so far as to say that it had saved Mussolini from disaster. They all take the view that Italy's word is not worth having, and that she will always betray her allies . . .[32]

However the signature of the Anglo-Italian Agreement left France with no choice but to negotiate a parallel accord in order to protect her Mediterranean interests.

Following the retirement of the French Ambassador, de Chambrun, in October 1936, France had been represented by the Chargé d'Affaires, Jules Blondel. The Italian Ambassador to Paris, Cerruti, had been withdrawn in October 1937. Bonnet immediately gave some thought to the appointment of an Ambassador: Flandin, Piétri, Mistler, Monzie were short-listed, though Flandin was the favourite, reported Phipps, since 'it would suit the government to get rid of him'.[33] Finally, it was decided to await the conclusion of an agreement before appointing an envoy. The French request for talks coincided with the signing on 16 April of the Anglo-Italian Agreement. Mussolini decided that talks would have to proceed slowly until after Hitler's visit to Rome in May. Ciano, his Foreign Minister and son-in-law, arranged 'a little obstructionism'. On 14 May the *Duce* made a 'very strong, anti-French speech' at Genoa. This calculated insult aroused anger and disappointment in all but the most dedicated Italophiles. Bonnet tried to salvage what he could of the negotiations. 'A soothing, special report was given out' by the Havas news agency, saying that 'influential French circles did not draw any pessimistic conclusions from the speech'.

On 22 May, Bonnet sent for the Italian Chargé d'Affaires, Prunas, and reaffirmed his desire for an understanding.[34] The interview took place at Bonnet's house, away from the disapproving eyes of the permanent officials. The Italian diplomat was reminded of France's efforts at Geneva to achieve a settlement of the Ethiopian affair. As for Spain, France primarily wanted an end to the war and the nature of the régime was secondary. Moreover, France was making great efforts to prevent a conflict over Czechoslovakia. But Mussolini regarded the talks as 'broken off' and Daladier spoke bitterly of the *Duce*. Bonnet would not take no for an answer. In June he sent Ciano a message of goodwill through the film star, Madeleine Carroll. Ciano, who was not unmindful of feminine charms, proved resistant to these blandishments. The film star was told that so long as French supplies continued to reach Republican forces in Spain there was no hope of a Franco-Italian accord.

Spain had been a bone of contention between Paris and Rome since the outbreak of the civil war in July 1936. The Blum government of March 1938 had allowed considerable quantities of munitions to cross the Pyrenees frontier. In the London talks of 28-29 April French ministers had been asked to close the land frontier with Spain. When in May Corbin presented 'lame excuses about material going over the French frontier' Cadogan renewed the pressure, speaking to him like 'a Dutch uncle'.[35] But Cadogan lacked a sense of proportion, being ready to equate French and Italian intervention: France could not expect Italy to give the 'same assurances as they have given us while they "intervene" as much as Musso does'. The Pyrenees frontier was closed to arms deliveries on 13 June, although Daladier had strong misgivings. Bonnet, however, was ready to join forces with the British against his colleague. 'Speaking very privately and confidentially' to Phipps, 'he urged' Halifax to lay 'great stress with Daladier on the importance' Britain attached 'to the Pyrenees frontier remaining closed'. Daladier, said Phipps, was inclined to listen to the voices of Mandel, Reynaud and Herriot 'who sing pro-Soviet and anti-dictator, particularly anti-Mussolini, songs to him'.[36]

Given their dependence on a Popular Front majority, Daladier and Bonnet had to walk warily in their approaches to Italy. Ideologies apart, Daladier was genuinely concerned about the threat to France's Mediterranean interests. Bonnet was less preoccupied with the strategic threat, telling the German Ambassador on 16 June that he would 'welcome any régime d'ordre in Spain'. The French foreign minister's main concern was the class war in France. The ambassador reported him as saying:

> that the Communists living in the so-called Red Zone around Paris, of whom the great majority are foreigners, had provided a large contingent of volunteers for the Spanish Civil War. According to reports he had received, almost 80 percent of these volunteers had been killed or had died, so that this zone had luckily become much more thinly populated.[37]

By early July the French were becoming increasingly restive. The frontier had been closed but Mussolini refused to open negotiations. Yet the Portuguese frontier remained open and supplies were reaching Franco's forces. In a letter of 5 July to Chamberlain Daladier complained that despite all that France had done to assist Britain in her relations with Italy she was placed in a humiliating position by Italy's refusal to talk. Chamberlain's reply of 8 July was conciliatory:

> We have our own difficulties with Italy but we hope and believe that with a little patience and tact we shall overcome them and in the meantime you can rely upon it that we shall do all we can to influence Italy to change her attitude to France.

British influence achieved nothing and there was no change in Franco-Italian relations until after Munich.

In Prague the French marked time. Bonnet did not apply the extreme pressure on Czechoslovakia which he encouraged London and Berlin to believe he was exercising. Until July France trod lightly in her official representations, though a number of semi-official agents were employed to corrode Czech confidence in the alliance. Such was the confidence of President Benes in the French government that he thanked Daladier and Bonnet for the 'firmness' and 'generosity' they had displayed in the London talks.[38]

Some time elapsed before the British government realised that the French foreign minister, though profuse in promises, was apt to be remiss in their fulfilment. As agreed in London, the British and French envoys carried out a *démarche* in Prague on 7 May. Paris was informed of the instructions sent to Newton who was told to concert with his French colleague. The British representations stressed the unfavourable military situation of Czechoslovakia and counselled the Czechs to make 'a supreme effort' to reach a settlement.[39] Britain, Prague was told, could not undertake any further commitments. The French Minister, Lacroix, found the Czech Foreign Minister, Krofta, 'deeply distressed' by the British approach and apprehensive lest the Germans should come to hear of it via the British embassy in Berlin. Lacroix saw Krofta separately and his language was comparatively mild. The motif of his instructions was sympathy for Czechoslovakia's plight, punctuated by reminders of the importance of retaining British support. The French minister was told that in his interview with Krofta:

> all references to the conditions of a settlement of the Sudeten problem should be formulated in the most generous terms so as to leave the greatest freedom of action in this matter to the Czech government . . .
> You will inform your interlocutors in confidence that the French government appreciates the value of the effort of conciliation represented by the proposed Nationalities Statute . . .

Nevertheless, continued the instructions, a further Czech effort at conciliation would encourage and reinforce British action in Berlin. British intervention in Berlin was a significant manifestation of British interest in central Europe, 'Nothing must be neglected to ensure its success' concluded Bonnet, and he had 'full confidence in this matter in the wisdom of the Czechoslovak statesmen'.

On 19 May, persistent reports of German troop movements in the direction of Czechoslovakia led to an international crisis. Local elections were taking place in Czechoslovakia and tensions were increased by the shooting of two Sudeten German farmers by a Czech major at Eger on 20 May. The Czechs were said to have mobilised two classes of reservists—in fact only one class was recalled. Nor was the tension limited to Prague. Women and children were reported to be leaving the British embassy in Berlin and by the evening of 21 May it seemed certain to one observer that Germany intended 'either to confront Benes with an ultimatum or to march in'.[40] Though the origins of the weekend crisis remain obscure and disputed, the sudden flare up highlighted the deep reluctance of France to defend her ally.

As tensions mounted, the opportunity of involving the British was too good to miss. On 21 May Bonnet urged Halifax to deliver the warning agreed upon in the London conference. Henderson in fact had already been told to see Ribbentrop. If Germany attacked Czechoslovakia, France would have to fight and 'in such circumstances His Majesty's Government could not guarantee that they would not be forced by circumstances to become involved also'. In conversation with Phipps, Bonnet berated the Czechs for having mobilised without consulting Paris and said he would warn Prague of the serious consequences of such 'hasty action'.41 Emboldened by this statement and believing the minister to be 'only too ready to follow any lead that we may give at Prague' Phipps suggested that the Czechs be told that 'by mobilising two classes they 'had in effect broken their treaty with the French'.

But Bonnet was too wily to be netted so easily. More evidence was required of British reluctance to support France in a conflict. Halifax soon obliged. 'We can't go to war' affirmed Cadogan and on 22 May a telegram was sent to Paris warning the French 'not to be under any illusion' that because Germany had been admonished Britain 'would at once take joint military action' in defence of Czechoslovakia. Bonnet took down 'copious notes', promising that 'if Czechoslovakia were really unreasonable, the French Government might well declare that France considered herself released from her bond'. Contrary to what Phipps had been given to understand, the Czechs were not scolded for their military precautions. When Bonnet saw the Czechoslovak Minister, Osusky, in the late evening of 21 May he uttered no word of censure. His questions were largely concerned with eliciting more information about the Czech measures. Osusky was told of the 'surprise of the British Government' on hearing of the mobilisation. The envoy explained that 'this was not a mobilisation but an accelerated call-up of one class of reservists' . . . intended as 'a simple police measure for the election period'. Bonnet urged that this fact should be announced publicly as quickly as possible.

By 23 May the crisis had blown over. François-Poncet reported that neither his own attachés nor the British military attachés had detected any abnormal troop movements.42 None the less the crisis left its mark on the policies of the powers. Hitler's hatred of Czechoslovakia took shape and form. In a military directive of 30 May he declared: 'it is my unalterable decision to smash Czechoslovakia by military action in the near future'. Execution of the directive was to be assured by 1 October 1938 'at the latest'. The British government regretted its intervention in Berlin almost as soon as the alarm was over. 'To avoid at any price being involved in a conflict created by the situation in Czechoslovakia remains the dominant preoccupation of a great number of Members of Parliament', signalled Corbin on 26 May.

Halifax urged Bonnet to persuade the Czechs to countermand their military measures. On 23 May the French foreign minister acted but in his own way. Compliments came first. The Czechs were congratulated on their calmness and mastery of the situation. The request for total or partial demobilisation was then supported by reference to British intervention in Paris:

This is the advice tendered by the British Ambassador on behalf of his government. Moreover, the British Military Attaché in Berlin has noted that at present there is no concentration of German troops on the Czech frontier. . .[43]

Finally came a touch of flattery:

The wisdom of M Benes and his assistants has had too happy an influence on the attitude of the British government over the past days for the Czech leaders not to be encouraged to persevere on the same course, whatever obstacles might be encountered.

The main result of the May crisis in Paris was to intensify the determination of the French ministers to avoid war at almost any cost. The trend of French sentiment had been apparent for some time. On 28 April François-Poncet informed Paris that the 'hesitation of French opinion' towards Czechoslovakia, as reflected 'in a certain number of regrettable articles' had been 'carefully noted' by Berlin.[44] And though in the evening of 21 May Bonnet issued a press statement reasserting French obligations its wording was not such as to inspire confidence in French determination to fulfill the pledges. More telling than the tepid press communiqué was the fact that during the crisis France made no official *démarche* either through François-Poncet in Berlin or Welczeck in Paris. On 25 May Bonnet told Welczeck that the French government 'recognised the effort' made by Germany towards preserving peace in the recent crisis:

I pointed out to Count Welczeck that if I had not asked him officially to come earlier it was because I feared that in this period of tension it might have been considered that I was making a comminatory *démarche*. . . .[45]

A reminder of French engagements to Czechoslovakia was followed by an explicit statement of the goal of French policy: 'if the problem of the minorities in Czechoslovakia was settled peacefully, economic and disarmament problems might be considered. . .'. Welczeck was reminded not only of French alliance obligations but also of the pressure France had brought to bear on Prague during the May crisis. In reality, of course, Bonnet had done little, though Welczeck did not know the true situation. Bonnet then mentioned the 'secret and quite private meeting' which Daladier had had with Welczeck in the evening of 22 May. The Prime Minister and Ambassador had talked 'in a frank and friendly manner as one ex-Serviceman to another'. Daladier's interview with Welczeck had also been exploratory, not comminatory. The Prime Minister's statement of the dilemma in which France found herself *vis-à-vis* Czechoslovakia and his allusions to 'Cossack and Mongol hordes' could have left Berlin in no doubt that the alliance was seen as an embarrassing liability.[46]

The chief effect of the May crisis on British policy was the decision, in Cadogan's words, 'to use the big stick on Benes'[47] The Czechs were to be told that they must negotiate with the Sudeten Germans on the basis of Henlein's demands of 24 April. In order to humour Henlein it was felt that the Czechs should meet at least in part his demand for total demobilisation. The Czechs maintained that they could not demobilise the class of reservists called up over the weekend of 20-21 May until after 12 June when the period of local elections ended. Newton was directed to ask for demobilisation and Paris was asked to second his efforts. Bonnet agreed to instruct Lacroix in a similar sense but the instructions sent on 31 May presented France in the guise of friendly counsellor, herself under pressure from unsympathetic allies:

> Since Sir Eric Phipps has requested with great insistence our intervention . . . I think it is necessary that the extent of English preoccupations should be known to the Czechoslovak Government. Please take up again with M Hodza (*Czech prime minister*) the discussion on this subject, invoking the interest that Prague attaches to the maintenance of British goodwill. . .[48]

On 31 May Halifax gave another turn of the screw. He suggested to the French government a joint *démarche* to put the 'greatest possible pressure' on Benes.[49] The moment had come for the Czechs to be told that if they were really unreasonable France would consider herself released from her bond. Bonnet played for time. On 1 June he promised to instruct Lacroix accordingly, requesting only that British and French representations should be made separately since Lacroix would have to go 'somewhat further' than his British colleague. London accepted this *modus procendi*. Newton acted promptly on 3 June, Lacroix saw the Czech Prime Minister, Hodza, on 5 June, and Benes three days later. However Lacroix's visits were exploratory, not minatory. Bonnet instructed him as follows:

> The information that you have transmitted to me on the state of the negotiations between the, prime minister and the representatives of the Sudetens does not allow me to pronounce as fully as the British Government believes itself able to do on the character and substance of M Henlein's proposals . . . I ask you, therefore, to obtain urgently the necessary details on the proposals submitted to M Hodza. . .

Lacroix was critical of the British pressure and wired Paris on 5 June: 'In my view, before asking us for *démarches,* the British Cabinet should inform us of the arguments which it believes can be used to support its own'.

Bonnet's doubleline might have gone unnoticed but for the indiscretion of Lacroix who disclosed to Newton on 8 June the tenor of his instructions. On 11 June Halifax requested Phipps to seek, without giving away Lacroix, an explanation for French inaction. Cornered on 13 June, Bonnet put on a bold front, pleading that 'after careful reflection and consultation with M Léger' he had decided to act through Osusky, who had been given a memorandum 'couched in very strong terms'.[50] Osusky had taken the document to Prague and reported 'very favourably on the effect of his mission upon M Benes'. The interview ended with Bonnet promising 'to continue to support us at Prague whenever we feel that it is necessary'. Phipps was not offered a copy of the memorandum, nor did he seek to embarrass the minister by asking if the specific warning about the Franco-Czech treaty had been given.

The account of 13 June interview with Phipps which Bonnet forwarded to Corbin and Lacroix differed considerably from Phipps's own record.[51]

No mention was made of the Osusky memorandum. Bonnet is recorded as holding forth firmly and unequivocally. Phipps had been told that it was impossible for France to exercise at present a new initiative in Prague. Representations had been multiplied at the request of the British government but whilst undeniable proofs of goodwill came from Prague, Germany maintained an enigmatic attitude. France had her treaty with Czechoslovakia and intended to uphold it. The digest concluded:

> It goes without saying, of course, that if on a specific point an intervention in Prague would be helpful the French government is ready at any time to exercise its influence, but in the present state of affairs it is in Berlin, and not at Prague, that action appears to be most necessary.

Corbin was asked to ensure that Phipps had reported faithfully to Halifax in the above sense.

By the end of June, Halifax finally managed to extract from Bonnet a copy of the Osusky memorandum dated 9 June. The document spelt out clearly the line of French argument in Prague. The French excused their representations by pleading the importance of winning over British public opinion to the Czech cause. The Czechs were gently reproved in terms of studied vagueness: delay in granting concessions would have 'serious consequences by strengthening the hands of those elements which in the various countries concerned were in favour of a policy of reserve and abstention'.[52] In conclusion, the Czechs were again complimented on their mastery of a difficult situation. As for the Franco-Czech alliance, not a word of warning.

That was not the end of the affair. At the close of an interview on 7 July Halifax handed a note to Corbin 'excusing himself for not commenting on it for lack of time'.[53] The note upbraided Bonnet for his sins of omission and commission. Corbin, who did not have an opportunity to read the note until he returned to the embassy, advised Paris that the document 'calls manifestly for a reply from us which will gain for being expressed with a frankness equal to that of the Foreign Office'. Bonnet's reply dated 16 July was received in London on the 18th. The Foreign Minister argued that French representations in Prague had been frequent and firm. He had 'never ceased' to urge 'a policy of conciliation'. Lacroix, for example, had seen Benes on three occasions between 8 and 25 June. Bonnet had twice asked Osusky to return to Prague in order to make representations in person. The memorandum handed to Osusky on 9 June had been given to Benes on 10 June. On 11 June a meeting of the Czech Cabinet had decided to open negotiations with the Slovak, Hungarian and Polish minorities and to accept Henlein's Carlsbad proposals as a basis for negotiation. This decision, implied Bonnet, had been the consequence of French pressure. As for a warning of the possible revision of the Czech alliance, no mention had been made of it since:

> Such a threat . . . without justification, would have appeared incompatible with the very spirit of the existing agreements between France and Czechoslovakia, for it would have implied doubt towards the goodwill or even the good faith of the Czech leaders.

Bonnet concluded with a review of recent moves in Prague. Lacroix had visited Hodza on 18, 21, 27 June. New instructions had been sent on 29 June and on 1 July Lacroix had seen both Benes and Hodza.

The weight of French pressure on her ally in the spring and early summer of 1938 was largely of an indirect nature, though all the more insidious for being so. It was a secret diplomacy which left few traces. The public record of French diplomacy had to be kept clean. Hence the muted, muffled tone of official representations in May and June. But the activities of private or semi-official emissaries could, if necessary, be disavowed. Moreover, France's official agents in Prague—de Lacroix, and General Faucher, head of the French military mission—were judged in Paris to be over-sympathetic towards Czechoslovakia.

British complaints that Faucher was encouraging the Czechs to be 'unduly obstinate' were tacitly conceded by Bonnet.[54] He remarked that the general was 'disposed to regard himself as a Czech general' and promised 'to talk' to him. Lacroix, an austere Protestant, and an extremely conscientious diplomat, gave Bonnet cause for anxiety. On 31 May he had made his own viewpoint crystal clear, telling Paris:

> I do not know if it is possible to save this country, but in any case we must neglect nothing in order to try to do so, in spite of and, if necessary, against certain Czech elements.

Recalled to Paris for consultations on 15 July, he was, in Bonnet's words, 'surprisingly optimistic' believing that Benes would go a long way in making concessions. The Foreign Minister gained his confidence by showing him the evidence of British pressure on the French government. On his return to Prague his dispatches were much more sympathetic to Bonnet and at the same time critical of British policy.

Prague attracted a constant stream of French visitors, mostly politicians and journalists.[55] Some of the visitors were well-intentioned. In mid-July Marc Rucart, Minister of Health, returned with the conviction that Benes was doing his utmost to work out a reconciliation with the Sudeten Germans. Others were less charitably disposed. At the end of April, Noel, Ambassador in Warsaw, was asked to go to Prague. His first reaction was to decline the invitation in view of the delicacy of the mission. He accepted when told by Bonnet that if he did not go a journalist would be sent. Since the journalist in question had a reputation for venality the Ambassador decided to go himself. Lacroix knew of the visit and entertained Noel at the Legation. Benes was told of the shortcomings of the French air force and of the hostility of the French Right for his country. 'After our conversation', wrote Noel, 'the President could not doubt that on the French side everything would be done to prevent France from fulfilling her obligations'. In June, Jules Romains was commissioned to tell Benes 'certain things'— presumably not protestations of French loyalty. Another visitor was Georges Monnet, Minister of Agriculture in Blum's first Popular Front government, who was despatched in early July to sound out Czech opinion on the idea of neutralisation, though Lacroix had been told nothing of neutralisation proposals. Of the journalists, two of the most frequent visitors were Fernand de Brinon, foreign editor of

L'Information, who was close to Daladier, and Jules Sauerwein of *Paris-Soir*. Both were noted for their pro-German propensities.

Benes's task in defending Czechoslovakia from her friends and foes was one of overwhelming difficulty. The enemies within were almost as dangerous as those without. Signs of divided counsels in Prague had been observed by Lacroix since early February. Many Agrarian party leaders called for an understanding with Germany. Benes was not helped by the activity of his prime minister, Hodza, an Agrarian leader in the government coalition. Insisting on the 'confidential character' of the information, Hodza told Lacroix on 24 May that he had been in 'semi-official' contact for several weeks with Sudeten leaders.[56] He claimed that this contact had eased relations between the police and Sudeten party organisations during the May crisis. Probably, more was involved than Hodza cared to admit. On 26 June the prime minister made an approach to Newton which he himself admitted might be described as 'treasonable'. His proposal was for 'private messages and conversations between representatives and leaders of public opinion' in Czechoslovakia and Britain. The appeal was not repeated to Lacroix. The French were already active enough.

At the end of June the French for the first time showed their teeth in Prague. The increasing tempo of German military preparations could no longer be ignored. The Czechs themselves seemed to be inviting greater pressure. News of Hodza's approach to Newton was passed on to Paris and Bonnet was asked to back up British efforts. The tone of French representations was unmistakably peremptory. On 30 June Lacroix was instructed 'to renew without any delay' his previous counsels to Benes and Hodza; this time stressing 'the anxiety' with which France had noted 'the slowness of the present negotiations'.[57] Czech leaders were to be told that 'any delay would seriously compromise the situation'. Much worse was soon to follow.

In the first week of July Daladier took a hand in events. On 5 July he wrote to Chamberlain, arguing that Germany might misinterpret Franco-British pressure on Prague as 'a sign of weakness': 'a complementary effort' was needed in Berlin.[58] In short the French Prime Minister was asking for another British warning on the lines of the message sent to Berlin during the May crisis.

Daladier's appeal was prompted by the storm signals across the Rhine. François-Poncet's reporting was remarkably prescient. The ambassador described increasing evidence of German mobilisation and work on the western fortifications. On 6 July he wired:

> thus from the 15 August onwards Europe will again face a particularly critical period...
> ...According to the plan which the Führer has decided on, the first useful pretext offered by the Prague government will be seized. An unexpected and lightning attack will be launched against Czechoslovakia, whose fate will be militarily settled before any of the allies of this state have had time to move. Germany will then propose to France and to England....a conference...[59]

However one event in particular had impressed French Ministers. On 27 June Hitler received a French visitor, General Le Rond. Le Rond was treated with a mixture of flattery and intimidation. A Franco-German understanding, said the German Chancellor, was necessary 'to save European civilisation'.[60] He wished to visit Paris, especially the *Louvre*. Colonial claims were not urgent and autonomy for the Sudeten German minority within the present frontiers of Czechoslovakia would be acceptable. Then after this show of sweet reasonableness Hitler cracked his whip. If the oppression of the Sudetens continued he would 'impose order'. Le Rond returned to Paris and reported that Hitler certainly meant business. It seemed vital therefore to mobilise British assistance in Berlin while simultaneously counselling caution in Prague. Daladier's letter was well-timed. With a state visit to France by King George VI and Queen Elizabeth only a fortnight away the French premier doubtless expected that Chamberlain would feel obliged to make some gesture of friendship.

Chamberlain's reply of 8 July was negative but the negative was well-wrapped in reassuring general statements. 'Franco-British solidarity', wrote Chamberlain soothingly, was 'the kernel of our foreign policy'. But 'the general attitude of this country on the Czechoslovakian question has been more than once defined both to your Government and in public statements'.[61] All that the British Prime Minister would concede was action, if necessary, in Prague and in Berlin to dispel any misunderstanding about British intentions. But the British government was not willing to make a special *démarche* in Berlin.

Since Chamberlain would not oblige, Daladier acted in his own way. On 12 July in a speech at a banquet given by the Paris Provence and Languedoc association he reaffirmed French obligations to Czechoslovakia. However the tone of his speech was hardly reassuring to the Czechs and probably did more harm than good. Hitler was given a pat on the back for his pacific resolution in the weekend crisis of 21 May. France's obligations to Czechoslovakia, Daladier reminded his audience, were 'ineluctable and sacred'. Equally ineluctable was the French dilemma:

> The French government, like the French people . . . was in fact animated by two emotions, equally strong, . . . the desire not to have to execute these engagements and the determination never to repudiate our word if, by misfortune, this desire could not be fulfilled.[62]

Such mental and verbal contortions could only have confirmed Hitler's conviction that France would not fight for Czechoslovakia.

By the middle of July, Czech-Sudeten negotiations were at their most critical stage. Though the long-awaited draft Nationalities Statute was about to be published, London and Paris believed that Benes would soon reach what he considered the limit of concession. Sudeten German behaviour gave small hope of a settlement. Deadlock was in sight. Britain and France reacted in two ways: pressure on Benes was stepped up, and secondly London considered the sending of a mediator.

On 16 July Bonnet promised London 'to impress' on Lacroix the 'vital necessity' of keeping Benes 'up to the mark'.[63] The promise was kept. French ministers were deeply anxious about the situation. The Quai d'Orsay was flooded with reports of German military preparations. Bonnet, in his own words, was extremely impressed by the fact that 'numerous personalities' returning from Prague, in particular 'one of my government colleagues', reported that Benes 'did not at all appreciate the situation and might still have illusions about the attitude that England and France would take in the event of German aggression'. Lacroix was told to see Benes 'so as to dispel any illusions, and to affirm what would be the attitude of France'. The Foreign Minister handed Lacroix 'for his personal use' a note of guidance dated 17 July. This note was a major onslaught on Benes and marked the beginning of the end of the French alliance. Its importance can be gauged from the fact that in the French 'ultimatum' sent to Prague on the night of 20-21 September Bonnet referred specifically to only two previous warnings—the instructions of 17 July and an interview with Osusky on 19 September.

In the note of instructions handed to Lacroix on 17 July Bonnet began by pointing out the strength of the Sudeten position. In recent elections Henlein's party had gained 90 percent of Sudeten German votes. Next Bonnet turned to the military defence of Czechoslovakia. Here 'certain illusions must be dispelled'. The Rumanians had said plainly that they would not only stay neutral in the event of a German attack on Czechoslovakia but would also 'oppose the overflight of their territory by Russian aircraft and the passage of Russian troops'. The Poles had said the same. Yugoslavia would remain neutral. Having disposed of the eastern allies, Bonnet moved on to Britain. The British attitude in the London talks of November 1937 had been 'completely negative' towards central Europe. Some progress had been made in the April talks but the British government had not taken any commitment and had restated its views 'in a series of notes of which the most important are known to M de Lacroix'. Bonnet then tackled the argument that if France acted alone Britain would follow: 'Nothing could be more false than such a conception'. Indeed, he continued, if France were not directly attacked and did not have the certainty of British help it would be difficult to persuade French opinion of the need to defend Czechoslovakia. Moreover, continued the minister, 'the English Government has declared in the clearest possible manner to France that in no case will it allow itself to be presented with a *fait accompli*. Sir Eric Phipps stated this to me again categorically today'. The note concluded with a forecast of the probable course of events. If Benes did not reach an understanding with Henlein, Britain would probably propose arbitration and France would support such a move. France had shown over the past months its solidarity with Czechoslovakia. The advice now offered was given 'in the spirit of a perfectly disinterested friendship and with the conviction that a world war would have the worst consequences for the independence of Czechoslovakia'.

Lacroix returned to Prague on 18 July. It had been agreed that he would wait two or three days before speaking to Benes in the sense of the new instructions. However a Cabinet meeting in Prague was called for 19 July and the French envoy asked for an interview before the meeting. Now Benes was assailed from all sides. On 16 July Newton had delivered a plain warning that if the Czechs 'appeared' to be dilatory in reaching a settlement and Henlein asked for a plebiscite, British opinion would not think him 'unreasonable'.[64] Benes countered Lacroix by 'claiming to know that at present Berlin was encouraging' the Sudeten Germans to be intransigent and 'did not want an accord'. Once again, reported the French Minister, the Czech President 'asked bitterly whether the French government now considered Czechoslovakia as a burden'.[65]

As the hopes of a direct Czech-Sudeten settlement dwindled various alternative solutions were canvassed. In early May Halifax considered the possibilities of a plebiscite or neutralisation under a guarantee. A month later, François-Poncet proposed that the fate of the Czechs should be decided by direct negotiations between France, Britain and Germany. Halifax had dismissed the idea as 'inopportune'.[66] On 18 June British proposals for neutralisation were put to the French. Czechoslovakia's treaty relations with France and the Soviet Union would be revised, leaving the obligations to Czechoslovakia intact but eliminating Czechoslovakia's undertaking to come to the help of France and the Soviet Union against Germany. François-Poncet favoured the proposals but Massigli was critical. In a note of 8 July he pointed out that Britain's plan would deprive France of the Czech alliance without any compensation. If German ambitions were seen as limited to central Europe, neutralisation might give some stability, but if there was a real danger of Germany expanding in the east or west it would be disastrous to throw away Czechoslovakia.

Halifax, however, had another idea in reserve — mediation. On 1 July Paris was told that London had in mind the sending of a mediator. On 20 July Benes was informed that Britain proposed to send Lord Runciman as an independent mediator. On the same day, in Paris, Halifax told the French Ministers of the offer and secured their approval. Much upset by the proposal Benes asked for French advice. On 23 July Bonnet told Osusky that after 'mature consideration' he advised full acceptance.[67] It would be useful, he argued, to involve the British government as directly as possible in the Sudeten affair. Osusky then asked whether he should consider the Minister's reply 'as that of a Minister of a country having alliance obligations towards Czechoslovakia and anxious to free itself of them in part, or else as the reply of a leader assuming responsibility for the political and military interests of France in Czechoslovakia'.[68] Greatly taken aback and plainly embarrassed Bonnet twice asked the envoy to repeat the question. Needless to say, he had no short answer. But the Foreign Minister's advice was seconded by the Secretary General, Léger. On 25 July both Bonnet and Léger advised immediate and unconditional acceptance of the offer of a mediator. To Bullitt, Bonnet spoke frankly: 'if the Czechs should refuse British mediation the British then would make it clear that they were not prepared to go to war in order to maintain the dominance of 7 million Czechs over 3½ million Germans. It would then be possible for France to take a similar attitude'.[69]

Runciman accepted his mission with the words: 'I am being cut off like a small boat from a great liner'.[70] Few spared a thought for the anguish of the Czech statesmen. Bonnet had seen Osusky on 20 July and spoken sharply. The time for deception and ambiguity was over and the French Foreign Minister came into the open and delivered what was tantamount to an ultimatum:

I have had a conversation with M Osusky. It was a question once again of indicating clearly to M Osusky the French position . . .

The Czechoslovak government must know fully our position: France would not go to war for the Sudeten affair. Certainly, publicly we will affirm our solidarity as the Czechoslovak government wishes—but this assertion of solidarity should allow the Czechoslovak government to obtain a peaceful and honourable solution. In no case should the Czechoslovak government believe that if war breaks out we will be at its side . . .

I replied that, of course, if I had to speak publicly I would recall the ties which unite us to Czechoslovakia. But the Czechoslovak government must be convinced that neither France nor England will go to war . . .[71]

Visiting Benes the next day Lacroix found the Czech President deeply disturbed by Osusky's report of the conversation with Bonnet. The President read out to the French envoy several pages of the report, as if seeking some disavowal of its contents. Benes had the impression that Bonnet 'believed allegations representing him as opposing an entente between the Czechoslovak government and the Sudetens'.[72] It seemed, said Benes, 'that the interpretation to be placed on the memorandum (*memorandum given to Osusky on 9 June 1938*) given to Osusky last month was that if this entente was not realised the French government would be obliged to reconsider the extent of its agreement with Czecho-slovakia'. The realisation that France might reconsider her alliance, continued the Czech president, was 'a terrible blow'. Lacroix summed up his impression of the audience: 'I see M Benes besieged by difficulties of all kinds which he has had to face since the absorption of Austria . . . I could say since 7 March 1936. For the first time this afternoon I think I observed in him a kind of collapse . , .'. The idea that France might not honour her obligations was too much to bear and Benes, reported Lacroix, had kept returning to the subject asking him: 'Do you think this is true?'

Chapter 12

'Better Late Than Never'

On 19 July King George VI and Queen Elizabeth landed at Boulogne, beginning the first royal visit to France since 1914. From Boulogne to Paris the British party were impressed 'by the number of people who had gathered in the fields and villages to wave as the train went by'.[1] Paris was bedecked and glittering for the occasion. A railway station át the Bois de Boulogne had been specially built for the visit. No public criticism was made of the fact that twelve million francs had been spent on the decoration of the apartments of the Quai d'Orsay palace at a time of financial stringency when social reforms such as old age pensions had been postponed on the grounds of expense.

The brilliant reception and dinner at the Quai d'Orsay on 21 July was a moment of triumph for the Foreign Minister's wife, Odette Bonnet. Press and public acclaimed the five day visit as a timely and magnificent celebration of the entente. 'It would be impossible to recall a period in which the relations between the two countries were more intimate', declared the King at an Elysée banquet. The German embassy in Paris interpreted the visit as marking the foundation of a new ideological front of the democracies. But the after dinner mood of self-sacrifice and *camaraderie* quickly evaporated.

Since April international tensions had helped to intensify the long-term pressures on the French franc. On 4 May the franc was devalued for the third time in three years. The conciliatory approaches to Berlin and Rome in the early summer had somewhat restored the confidence of the bankers but in early August the drain on the franc was resumed. Heavy buying on the Bourse of gold and dollars in preference to French francs and sterling caused panic in Paris. The Daladier government was too conservative-minded to impose the obvious remedy—exchange controls. On 12 August Daladier wrote to Chamberlain expressing his alarm at the outflow of gold from France and asking for a meeting.[2] In his reply of 17 August Chamberlain offered sympathy but nothing else. The request for a meeting was declined: 'If the difficulty could be averted by any support from us, you may be sure that I should be eager to offer it, but material assistance is not possible'. Daladier's appeal was dismissed as a move to prepare French opinion for another devaluation. Sir John Simon, Chancellor of the Exchequer, was particularly cynical. The French, he

200

said, were looking for another fillip after the Royal visit and Daladier's London lionising in April.

The storm was weathered. Daladier, by attacking the social legislation of the Popular Front, regained the confidence of French capitalists. In a radio broadcast of 21 August he announced that the forty hour week would have to be modified. Two Socialist members of his Cabinet, Frossard and Ramadier, resigned in protest but the majority of their brethren, prompted by concern for the international situation, did not oppose Daladier. Their positions were filled by Monzie and Pomaret, a change which was 'generally considered a further weakening of French policy'.[3]

Despite the toasts and speeches, Franco-British relations were strained in July and August. The Halifax-Bonnet exchange of notes over French pressure on Czechoslovakia had been frank but far from friendly. Spain and Italy were also contentious matters. On 6 July, Léger complained to the Paris correspondent of *The Times* that France had only agreed to close the Pyrenees frontier as a result of British pressure and reluctance to delay the application of the Anglo-Italian Agreement.[4] Léger considered that a grave crisis in Franco-British relations would arise if Britain did not press Italy to negotiate with France. Halifax was sympathetic: 'This is the precursor of the storm that I have dreaded, unless we measure what we are doing—which is to imperil our friendship with France for the sake of what is still a will o' the wisp', he minuted on 11 July. The malaise persisted into August. In a secret and private letter of 11 August Campbell, Chargé d'Affaires in Paris, wrote: 'the atmosphere of Anglo-French relations has lost something in mutual confidence'. A number of instances were cited in which London seemed reluctant to give Paris early information of British moves. Captain Wiedemann, Hitler's adjutant, met Halifax and Cadogan on 18 July and discussed the possibility of a visit to London by Goering. Paris learnt of the Wiedemann visit through the *Daily Herald*. Chamberlain and the German Ambassador in London, Dirksen, had met on 22 July but again the French had been told nothing. Moreover, continued Campbell, the Foreign Office had tended to pooh-pooh French reports of increased German military activity. Finally, concluded the Chargé d'Affaires, on 10 August the Paris embassy had been instructed not to tell the French about British representations in Rome concerning recent Italian reinforcement for Spain; on 11 August the news of the *démarche* appeared in *The Times*. 'I realise the fear of leakages by the Quai d'Orsay', wrote Campbell, 'but these seem to take place even when the Quai are not told things'.

On 20 August Sir Orme Sargent, Deputy Under-Secretary, replied, disclaiming any wish to be 'cagey' about Anglo-German relations.[5] Each case, the embassy was told, had to be decided as it arose and no general rule of telling the French everything was practicable. In Paris, on 20 July, Halifax had given French ministers a full account of the Wiedemann interview. As regards the Chamberlain-Dirksen meeting, nothing new had been discussed and it was felt that there was no need to say anything to Paris. However, on one charge the Foreign Office pleaded guilty. Concerning German military preparations, Sargent wrote: 'I must confess that we have been somewhat uneasy about the manner in which we have treated the French'. An appeal to Hitler against building up tension had been sent on 11 August but it was essential for its success that it be kept secret. In fact, although Sargent did not say so, Henderson had asked particularly that the French should not be informed. So much for the plans of the Foreign Office. The secret was not kept and Radio Luxembourg broadcast a report of the British move.

While Daladier wrestled with the financial crisis which, as François-Poncet warned, could only encourage 'the partisans of war' in Germany,[6] Czechoslovakia was left to the ministrations of Lord Runciman. However, the French government did not leave the field entirely to Runciman. Daladier and Bonnet had their own man in Prague. In July they had considered the sending of a French mediator to work alongside Runciman. Their candidate was René Brunet, a Socialist deputy and professor of international law. He was well-known to Bonnet, having served under him as an under-secretary of state at the ministry of finance in 1937. On 23 July Osusky rejected the idea of a French mediator and Bonnet promised that no one would be sent. But in August Brunet was sent as a private observer. He cultivated close relations with the Sudeten leaders and kept Paris posted. In fact he knew more about the Sudeten leaders than the Czech government. On 21 September, for example, Bonnet and his associates were closeted together at the Quai d'Orsay: Monzie, Pomaret, Mistler, Bergery, and René Brunet who had returned from Prague. Bonnet was telephoning Lacroix in Prague. President Benes, explained Lacroix, was trying to get in touch with the Sudeten deputy, Kundt, but could get no reply to his telephone calls. At that moment, Brunet pulled out of his pocket a notebook and said: 'I have a special number for Kundt, here it is'.

The Runciman mission gave London and Paris a much-needed respite, but the breathing space was short-lived. On 17 August Daladier received a disturbing report from the French Military Attaché in Berlin, General Renondeau.[7] Renondeau's assistant had talked to his British colleague, Major Strong, who had recently returned from London. Strong was said to be convinced that neither Britain nor France would intervene militarily in the event of a German attack on Czechoslovakia. Colonel Mason-MacFarlane, the British Military Attaché, was 'personally quite opposed' to armed intervention in defence of Czechoslovakia. Confirmation of Germany's readiness to fight and France's own weakness came on 21 August when General Vuillemin, Chief of French Air Staff, returned from a five-day visit to Germany. Interviews with Hitler and Goering convinced him that Germany would risk war with France. The carefully stage-managed display of German air power strengthened Vuillemin's highly pessimistic appreciation of his own air force.[8]

Although Germany continued to mobilise, no word of warning came from London. On 22 August Bonnet instructed the London embassy to ask for a new British warning on the lines of the 21 May démarche. Cambon, Chargé d'Affaires, was told by Halifax on 25 August: 'I have no doubt that the French government would feel that we had done everything that was possible in the sense of a discreet repetition of warning'.[9] Cambon was told of the appeal of 11 August but not of its brusque rejection. Halifax seized the opportunity to tighten the leash, reminding Cambon of the assurances given by Bonnet on 22 May and 16 July that 'the French Government would not dream of taking any action which might have the result of exposing them to German attack without ample consultation with His Majesty's Government'.

Bonnet looked next to Moscow. On 26 August Litvinov was informed through the Soviet Ambassador at Paris, Souritz, that German military measures made it likely that force would be used against Czechoslovakia in September. The French and Czech General Staffs, said Bonnet, were in contact. France wished to know what assistance the Soviet Union could give to Czechoslovakia. At their May meeting in Geneva, Litvinov had stated that in view of her alliances with Poland and Rumania it was for France to secure from these powers rights of passage for Soviet troops and aircraft. Despite great efforts, said Bonnet, the result was negative: 'the Polish Government has informed me categorically that it will prevent the transit of troops or aircraft over its territory and the Rumanian Government, in more moderate terms, has given me an identical reply'.[10] Coulondre was directed to see Litvinov as a matter of urgency 'to ask him under what conditions Prague could count on Soviet help, given the practical difficulties which I (*Bonnet*) have encountered up to the present'.

Replying on 2 September to Bonnet's questions, Litvinov confirmed previous declarations that the Soviet Union was determined to fulfil 'by all possible means' its obligations to Czechoslovakia, provided France fulfilled her own.[11] According to the French Chargé d'Affaires, Payart, the Soviet Commissar for Foreign Affairs first tried to return the ball to France's court by asking what practical steps France intended to take. Payart replied that his country had 'clearly defined' its position and was now asking the Soviet Union to do likewise. Litvinov then proposed three courses of action: an appeal to the League of Nations, secondly a conference of Britain, France and the Soviet Union and a common declaration against aggression, thirdly Franco-Czech-Soviet staff talks. Litvinov 'excluded *a priori*' any possibility of Soviet troops forcing a passage across Poland or Rumania.

The Soviet stress on the League was grist to Bonnet's mill, but the suggestion of staff talks was sufficiently practical to be embarrassing in Paris. When on 6 September the Foreign Minister informed Phipps of the terms of the Soviet reply, the staff talks proposal was suppressed. And to complete the picture of an uncooperative eastern Europe, Bonnet insisted that, contrary to what Léger had said only two days earlier, Rumania would not allow Soviet aircraft to overfly her territory: 'Russia's one wish', concluded Bonnet, was 'to stir up general war'.[12]

However Bonnet's own officials and the Ambassador, Coulondre, were much less pessimistic about Soviet policy. An internal Quai d'Orsay memorandum of 6 September did not mince words.[13] Litvinov's reply, it stated, might be described as 'evasive' but due regard should be paid to the frame of mind of the Soviet leadership. Information 'gathered from certain Parisian circles' might have given Moscow the impression that France would not fight for Czechoslovakia. Bonnet was reminded of Litvinov's words to Coulondre: 'France will perhaps mobilise, but will she go to war? And if the present government is resolved to do so, will it

not be overthrown?' It must not be forgotten, continued the memorandum, that the Soviets have on several occasions proposed a military
convention 'which we have always refused'. The Soviet Union, therefore,
had grounds for mistrusting France. The next step, recommended the
note, was to seek a further interview with Litvinov and ask him whether
the Soviet Union would give armed assistance in the following circumstances: if Poland was neutral, if she supported France, if she attacked
Czechoslovakia.

In Moscow Coulondre maintained an optimistic front, telling Potemkin,
Litvinov's deputy, on 11 September that though the Soviet reply might
not have been 'sufficiently explicit' any difficulties would be resolved
personally by the two foreign ministers in Geneva.[14] That same day Bonnet
and Litvinov discussed the situation. According to Bonnet's notes, and
these are the only source available, Litvinov insisted that Soviet troops
would only cross Poland and Rumania with the prior authorisation of the
governments concerned.[15] Bonnet then asked what kind of help would be
forthcoming, especially in the air. Litvinov replied that this was a matter
for specialist discussions—in other words, staff talks. In conclusion, the
Soviet minister emphasised the importance of a common Anglo-Franco-
Soviet declaration against aggression.

Though Warsaw would have no truck with Moscow, Bucharest was
willing to turn a blind eye to the overflight of Soviet aircraft. The Rumanians really had no choice in the matter since their anti-aircraft defences
were too weak to stop Soviet aircraft. After a talk with the Rumanian
foreign minister, Bonnet had a second interview with Litvinov in which
he suggested that the Soviet Union might take advantage of 'this offer
of overflight'. Bonnet testifies that Litvinov declined the offer, insisting
again on the need for prior formal consent.[16]

At that point Franco-Soviet exchanges ended. Apart from some minor
contacts between Gamelin and the Soviet Air Attaché in Paris in the last
week of September, the Soviet Union was excluded from the meetings and
conferences that followed. 'For London and Paris', wrote Coulondre,
'Moscow was no longer in Europe'.[17] Coulondre though did his best
to keep the lines open. On 17 September he informed Bonnet of Soviet
fears of a four-power pact. It was being said in Moscow that if such a pact
took place: 'the necessary conclusions would immediately be drawn from
it: positions would be examined, and the pacts with France would be
denounced'. The Soviet Union, continued the ambassador, had two
choices: to go into isolation and hope Germany turned west, or to seek a
pact with her:

> In any case, in order to avoid here untimely reactions and above all a *volte-face*,
> it is necessary to do all we can to avoid giving Moscow the impression of being
> set aside, and to ensure that she receives all possible reassurances.

Coulondre could not have spoken more plainly.

Germany was now poised to strike Czechoslovakia. The Deuxième
Bureau had a clear picture of German preparations: On 30 August Colonel
Gauché, head of the Deuxième Bureau, told the British Military
Attaché:

> Germany is ready for immediate war against Czechoslovakia with a *couverture* on the western front and it rests entirely with the politicians if war is to be averted. The German Government is still under the impression that neither Britain nor France will fight to save Czechoslovakia.[18]

Hitler was known to be inspecting units and defences in the west. The Runciman mission had served as a useful stop-gap but a settlement seemed as remote as ever. Benes now offered the Sudeten leaders a 'Third Plan', promising a measure of autonomy and economic help for the Sudetenland. On 1 September Henlein went to Germany for consultations with Hitler.

Predictably, the German military threat was countered by renewed Franco-British pressure in Prague. On 2 September Bonnet boasted to Welczeck of his direct line to Prague: 'hardly a day went by without his telephoning Prague . . . even though he allowed Britain to take the lead . . . French influence was no less energetic and lasting'.[19] Though not as hot as Bonnet wanted Welczeck to believe, the line to Prague was much busier than in June-July. On 1 September Lacroix was instructed to speak to Hodza 'in the firmest possible language':

> The Czechoslovak Government must never lose sight of the fact that the first condition of our assistance is the certitude that on the Czech side there exists at all times the considered determination to neglect nothing in the search for an accord. . . With all the firmness that our friendship for Czechoslovakia and our determination to keep the obligations undertaken towards her commands you will tell M Hodza . . . . that the time for sterile arguments and procedural expedients has gone.[20]

Two days later, Newton delivered a stiffly-worded warning. Benes was told that if it came to a choice between Henlein's Carlsbad demands and war, he should have no doubts about the attitude of British opinion. Bonnet, however, held his full fire for the time being and refused to instruct Lacroix in the same sense as Newton.

On 2 September the Sudeten Germans rejected the 'Third Plan'. Benes then asked them to write down in full their demands. On this basis the Czech government drafted a 'Fourth Plan'. It was submitted to the Sudeten leaders on 6 September. Henlein's deputy, Kundt, admitted that the plan fulfilled 'in its essential content' the eight-point Carlsbad programme of 24 April.[21] Benes pointed out to Lacroix the 'far-reaching nature of the concessions', demanding 'with great emphasis that France should now fully and uncompromisingly back the Czech standpoint'.[22] But Bonnet was like Bunyan's Mr Facing-both-ways. In Prague on 8 September Lacroix assured Benes that France wished to maintain her traditional friendship with Czechoslovakia; in Paris the French Foreign Minister told Osusky that this assurance in no way absolved Czechoslovakia from her duty to solve the Sudeten problem and above all to ensure that war did not result from the dispute. Henlein's motto since the spring had been: 'we must always demand so much that we can never be satisfied'.[23] He was now in danger of being satisfied. An excellent pretext for the rupture of negotiations came on 7 September when Sudeten deputies claimed that Czech police had brutally dispersed a peaceful gathering at Moravska Ostrava.

Benes urged French ministers to defend Czechoslovakia's cause in London—not for Czechoslovakia's sake but in their own interests: 'if France does not at once realise the gravity of the situation, the consequences for the political evolution of Europe will be incalculable.'[24]

The French were active in London but not in the sense desired by Benes. In September Franco-British relations turned largely on procedure not principle. Both partners desperately wanted to avoid a war for Czechoslovakia, neither wanted the responsibility for the abandonment of Prague. Bonnet's desire to shelter under Chamberlain's umbrella is well-documented, less well-known is Léger's readiness to follow the Minister. On 4 September Phipps made it 'quite clear' to the Secretary General 'how impossible it was to say before the event what action Great Britain would take and how absolutely vital it was that no important action should be taken by the French government without previous consultation with Great Britain'. Léger 'fully' understood the position and promised 'faithfully' to adhere to the British ruling.[25] Halifax had told the French on 25 August that 'the right policy for both our Governments was to do everything in our power to keep the Germans guessing'. In practice, both allies did everything they could to keep each other guessing about their ultimate intentions.

In vain French ministers sought a plain statement of British policy. On 7 September Corbin was told to insist on some British pressure being exercised in Berlin. 'I have good reasons to think', wrote Bonnet, 'that M Ribbentrop continues to believe that in the event of a conflict over Czechoslovakia England will not be at the side of France'.[26] Corbin asked Halifax to remove 'any ambiguity' by uttering a warning in Berlin. Janus-like, Halifax merely restated the ambiguity. On 9 September Bonnet returned to the attack. France had information from an extremely reliable source that Hitler was resolved to attack Czechoslovakia because he was convinced Britain would not intervene. This time Halifax gave Corbin an unqualified negative. British opinion would not be prepared to defend Czechoslovakia against German aggression.

With the suspension of Czech-Sudeten negotiations on 7 September the Nuremberg Rally was the focus of attention. It was expected that Hitler's closing speech to the Rally on 12 September would bring an announcement of German intervention in Czechoslovakia. In France, reservists rejoined their regiments and the French government put on a final brave show. On 2 September Bonnet had treated Welczeck to another dose of his 'general peace talk' but laced on this occasion with a very unBonnet-like bravado. Daladier and he were 'sincere admirers' of the Führer but if Czechoslovakia were attacked then France would 'hasten' to the defence of her ally—'America would not stand aside, neither would Russia'.[27] On 8 September Daladier told Phipps that if Germany attacked Czechoslovakia France would march 'to a man'.

Yet British stonewalling was unnerving. On 10 September 'desperately anxious' for a way out of the *impasse,* Bonnet made a new assault on London. Having had no success through official channels, the Minister addressed 'as a friend' a private question to Halifax with the request that it should not be officially recorded.[28] The question was: 'We are going to march, will you march with us?' Halifax's reply, though retaining the ambiguity of previous pronouncements, was negative enough to please Bonnet. He now had ample ammunition to silence Cabinet colleagues, like Mandel and Reynaud, who were critical of his lack of firmness towards Germany. In addition, Bonnet requested a copy of the warning of 22 May which Phipps had delivered orally, stating that Britain was not automatically obliged to go to war if France resisted German aggression against Czechoslovakia. Halifax complied while making it clear that the warning was not being renewed but the French Minister was wily enough to extract from Phipps confirmation that the *démarche* 'still applied'.

Although Halifax seemed unresponsive to French pleas, the pressure from Paris was not without effect. In the first ten days of September British ministers and their advisers met on numerous occasions to discuss the advisability of sending Hitler another warning. Following Bonnet's request for action on 7 September, a message was drafted. At length, on 9 September a message of warning was sent to Henderson at Nuremberg but the ambassador secured its cancellation. While the Foreign Office drafted and redrafted messages of warning, Chamberlain had his own plan for a personal meeting with Hitler and by 8 September his mind was made up. The only sop for the French was a statement which Chamberlain made to the press on 11 September, declaring 'that we contemplated the possibility that this country could not stand aside if a general conflict were to take place in which the security of France might be menaced'.[29] This was too much for Bonnet's peace of mind. On 13 September he complained to Phipps that the press statement might give public opinion the wrong impression:

It was to be feared that public opinion in our two countries, wrongly convinced of the superiority of our armaments, might push blindly the Governments into a war which could be a disaster.[30]

In a quiet, unassuming way Corbin, Ambassador at London, tried to stiffen his country's diplomacy. In a letter of 2 September to Bonnet he discreetly attempted to counter both Halifax's desire to keep France in tow and any publicity the Foreign Minister might be giving to such pressure:

You will have noted in the account that I have sent you of my interview with Lord Halifax that the Secretary of State referred to the *démarche* made by the English ambassador in Paris on 22 May. He has already mentioned it to M Roger Cambon. This insistence could create misunderstandings. Doubtless the English Government wishes to be kept informed of the military measures that we might judge it necessary to take—because of the effect that they could have on the political situation—this in no way means that they disapprove or advise against them. . .[31]

Corbin reported that some members of the Foreign Office wished to see more vigorous French counter-measures. On 10 September the ambassador sent a strong hint that some plain speaking in Paris would help in London: 'several political personalities' had told him that 'one of the reasons why the British Government experienced such difficulty in reaching a decision was because it was not yet quite sure of the likely attitude of the French Government in the event of war'.[32]

Wittingly or unwittingly, however, Corbin weakened his own position by slightly misrepresenting Halifax's statements. On 9 September, on Bonnet's instructions, he complained that the uncertainty of British policy was encouraging Hitler in his designs. In reply Halifax gave a sharp and incisive definition of policy: he did not think that 'British public opinion would be prepared . . . to enter upon hostilities with Germany on account of aggression by Germany on Czechoslovakia'.[33]

When on 11 September Phipps read to Léger a French translation of the British record of the conversation, the Secretary General at once detected 'a distinct change for the worse'. At Phipps's suggestion, Corbin's record was compared with the British. The discrepancy between the two records was plain. Corbin had reported Halifax as saying on 9 September that 'in the event of France discharging her obligation to help Czechoslovakia one would be faced with a new situation, as a result of which England would without doubt be drawn into the conflict after a delay which obviously could not be fixed in advance'.

Halifax insisted on his own account being taken as the authoritative record while conceding somewhat testily that though his remarks of 9 September had not been qualified, previous qualifications still held: 'it was also probable that if France was obliged to act in discharge of her obligations, British public opinion would realise that we could not allow France to be in trouble, without wishing to do our best to help her'. Corbin did not improve his standing in Paris by then overstating the significance of Halifax's qualifications: 'they affirm unequivocally that England will come to our aid . . . this engagement, given spontaneously, exceeds by far the agreement of 19 March 1936. . .'

While the Russians were relegated to the sidelines, the Americans were wooed and flattered. London and Paris made a great show of taking Washington into their confidence. President Roosevelt of the United States was anxious to deploy American prestige and influence. In January 1938 he had proposed an international conference of small and neutral states to discuss with the United States the fundamental principles of international relations. The desire to act was strong but Roosevelt lacked a coherent, defined policy and was prone to pressures, not only from advisers, but also from European governments. The French did their utmost to resolve in their favour what one State Department official termed 'the eternal question mark of American foreign policy'.[34]

From May onwards Bonnet angled for American pressure on Prague, and occasionally, on Berlin. His strategy was simple: if France knocked loud and long enough she would be answered and any answer, affirmative or negative, would help her diplomacy. During the May crisis Washington was asked to tell Prague that the 'Czech government would not have the sympathy of the American government if it should not attempt seriously to produce a peaceful solution . . . by making concessions to the Sudeten Germans which would satisfy Hitler and Henlein'.[35] Bonnet's readiness to sacrifice Czechoslovakia did not help the task of his Ambassador in Washington, Count de St. Quentin. On 16 May Bonnet told Bullitt that war with Germany 'on a point of honour' would be more terrible than the war of 1870: 'he would fight to the limit against the involvement of France in war'. Next day the American Under-Secretary of State, Sumner Welles, read to St. Quentin Bullitt's telegram. The same day St. Quentin wrote to Massigli, informing him of the statements attributed to Bonnet. Up to the present, commented the Ambassador, he had tried in his mission to present Czechoslovakia as the basis of 'our policy as a great power'. He would continue to do so in order 'not to accentuate the impression, which could be dangerous in this country, of our *effacement*'. St. Quentin feared that Sumner Welles would probably inform the British ambassador of Bullitt's report.[36]

On 4 July Bonnet broadcast direct to the United States, stressing 'common ideals' and the interdependence of nations. Patience and pressure were rewarded in mid-August when Roosevelt and his Secretary of State, Cordell Hull, both warned the world of the possibility of American involvement in a future conflict. In the first week of September Bonnet again badgered Washington for its moral support. The occasion was the unveiling on 4 September of a memorial at the Pointe de Grave, near Bordeaux, erected to commemorate the embarkation of Lafayette in 1777 and the landing in 1917 of the first American troops in France. In his speech the French Foreign Minister dwelt on Franco-American spiritual solidarity, emphasising that France did not want American help for war but for safeguarding and organising peace. For the first time since Daladier's speech of 12 July French commitments were reaffirmed, although curiously Czechoslovakia was not mentioned by name. Bonnet's declaration read: 'France, in any case, will remain faithful to the pacts and treaties she has concluded. She will be faithful to the agreements she has undertaken'. This mild statement surprised Bonnet's ministerial allies and de Monzie afterwards claimed that the alliance reference was not part of the original text and had been inserted *en route* to Bordeaux.[37] Whatever its genesis the reminder of 4 September was the last public expression of France's pledges.

However the impact of the Pointe de Grave ceremony came not from Bonnet's speech but from incidental remarks attributed to the American ambassador, Bullitt, who accompanied the Foreign Minister. Speaking at a banquet in Bordeaux he was reported as saying that the United States and France were 'united in war and peace'. Press reports of the speech created an immediate furore in the United States with isolationists breathing fire and thunder against the administration.[38] On 9 September Roosevelt dismissed stories that the United States was aligning itself with Britain and France in a 'stop-Hitler bloc' as '100 per cent wrong'. In the memoirs Bonnet described Roosevelt's remarks as a turning point for French diplomacy. American isolationism had triumphed and France could expect neither men nor money from the United States. All the more reason, therefore, it was argued, for not rushing to arms in defence of Czechoslovakia. In fact there was no turning point. In the Pointe de Grave address Bonnet explicitly disclaimed any desire for American material assistance. He never deluded himself that such help would be forthcoming. What he did want, though, and continued to press for, was an American moral endorsement of appeasement. Despite Roosevelt's press statement of 9 September, French diplomatic pressure was maintained in Washington. Bonnet, too, was responding to domestic pressure. A strong body of French opinion, especially on the Left, believed that if Roosevelt spoke out against the dictators they would retire in confusion. Bonnet harnessed this sentiment for his own ends. But high-sounding talk of 'common ideals' did not hoodwink American diplomats. 'Both the British and the French', wrote Moffat, chief of the Staff Department's European division, on 17 September, 'are trying their hardest to bring us into the picture now so that we can share responsibility for the "sell-out" '.[39]

At Nuremberg on 12 September Hitler violently abused Benes and demanded self-determination for the Sudeten Germans. The speech was the signal for riots in the Sudetenland and Henlein crossed into Germany. The Czech government proclaimed martial law and sent in some 40,000 troops. Order was soon restored. Nevertheless the short-lived Sudeten revolt pricked the French bubble. At a meeting of the French Cabinet in the afternoon of 13 September mobilisation was discussed. Daladier, it was said, wanted to mobilise; Bonnet was against. 'Seven Ministers sided with Bonnet . . . Bonnet threatened to resign if mobilisation was decided on . . . Daladier and Bonnet were sent for . . . by Lebrun and urged to stand together', so ran one report of the meeting.[40] On the previous day Gamelin had told Daladier that a French offensive against German fortifications in the west would be a 'modernised battle of the Somme'.[41]

Bonnet's nerve had snapped. The American aviator, Colonel Charles A. Lindbergh, had just returned from a visit to Germany, deeply impressed by the overwhelming superiority of the *Luftwaffe*. His alarmist appreciation, followed by the Sudeten revolt, completely shattered the French minister. The danger of being suddenly pitchforked into war was too frightening to contemplate. All Bonnet could say was that peace must be saved at any price:

> I repeated all this with emotion to Sir Eric Phipps telling him that at no price should we allow ourselves to be involved in war without having weighed all the consequences and without having measured in particular the state of our military forces.[42]

Of calmer calibre, Daladier kept his nerve but he was not the man of 8 September when he had declared 'most positively' that France would march. Asked 'point-blank' on 13 September whether he adhered to the opinions expressed on 8 September, he replied 'with evident lack of enthusiasm' that if Germany used force France would have to follow suit.[43] Later in the day at a second interview with Phipps he was quoted as saying: 'at all costs Germany must be prevented from invading Czechoslovakia because in that case France would be faced with her obligations'. These words were hardly a call to battle and the language, Chamberlain told his Cabinet next day, was 'significant'.

Phipps concluded that the French had been bluffing and by way of confirmation they produced their proposals for conciliation. On 12 September Léger suggested the summoning of a four power conference. Next day Bonnet repeated the suggestion and on the same day Daladier proposed a three power meeting. When the French Prime Minister asked to speak to Chamberlain on the telephone, he was told to give the message through Phipps. Without consulting French Ministers or the full Cabinet Chamberlain wired Hitler at 11 p.m. in the evening of the 13th a proposal for a personal meeting. Shortly after midnight on the 14th Daladier was sent a curt message to the effect that 'before deciding on Daladier's proposals' Chamberlain was 'exploring . . . another possibility of direct action on Berlin'.[44] In the early evening of 14 September Halifax asked Phipps to inform Daladier immediately of the Prime Minister's plan to fly to Germany the next day. At 8 p.m. before the ambassador had seen Daladier, Chamberlain sent instructions that the French prime minister was not to be told until 9 p.m., at which time a press release would be issued in London. Daladier, wrote Phipps, was none too pleased that his own *conversation à trois* idea had been passed over.

Bonnet's collapse was confirmed on 14 September when all the pent-up tensions of the past months exploded in an outburst of anger against the Czechs. 'We cannot sacrifice ten million men in order to prevent three and half million Sudetens joining the Reich', Phipps was told.[45] France, continued Bonnet, preferred a neutralised Czechoslovakia with autonomy for the Sudetens but 'in the last resort' a plebiscite would be acceptable. Runciman, urged the minister, should still produce a plan. The French minister's wrath was reserved for the Czechs, not the Germans. He 'expressed great indignation with the Czechs who, it seems, mean to mobilise without consulting the French . . . he has therefore given a broad hint to Benes that France may have to reconsider her obligations'. Bonnet's one thought was concessions: 'we are not ready for war and we must therefore make the most far-reaching concessions to the Sudetens and to Germany'.

The 'broad hint' to Benes was not in fact given but the Czechs were reprimanded for daring to take military precautions in the Sudetenland without consulting Paris. Bonnet's mood was reflected in press comment. Bullitt noted that 'during the past few days the French newspapers have published many maps showing the racial divisions in Czechoslovakia and . . . public opinion has begun to develop the attitude: "Why should we annihilate all the youth of France . . . in order to maintain the dominance of seven million Czechs over three million Germans'.[46] In the *Populaire* Blum preached conciliation: 'everything must be attempted, every method must be tried out to the full'.

The meeting between Chamberlain and Hitler at Berchtesgaden on 15 September was warmly welcomed in France. Bonnet was 'gleeful'. The Chamberlain-Hitler encounter, cabled the American Ambassador, was a 'personal triumph' for the French Foreign Minister since 'the chief aim' of his diplomacy had been to engage British intervention.[47] Blum gave whole-hearted approval to the meeting. Herriot and Reynaud, though apprehensive for the future, praised Chamberlain and were both, as Phipps was at pains to point out, 'unable to suggest any alternative course of action'. The official mood was exemplified in *Le Temps* which hailed the British Prime Minister's visit as marking perhaps 'a whole new policy of co-operation'.

From Prague came a final appeal from Benes. On 15 September the Czech President wrote:

> We have always been faithful friends of France and will remain so. . . I address this urgent appeal to the French government in the hope that it will support us in our struggle and that it will remain faithful to us, whatever happens, in conformity with the spirit of our treaty of alliance.[48]

Bonnet replied, assuring Benes of France's 'profound sympathy in the national ordeal which he was facing with so much courage and sacrifice'. But then came the sting in the tail. Lacroix was told:

> You can assure him (*Benes*) that nothing has changed in the attitude of the French government such as it has always been represented to him, nor in the recommendations that you have had to make to him in the execution of my instructions, notably those of 17 July.[49]

While Hitler and Chamberlain discussed the fate of their country, the Czech leaders prepared for the worst. The Runciman mission had turned into a Trojan horse. Runciman had concluded that any settlement would have to be based on self-determination and the idea of a plebiscite had been canvassed in the British and French press since early September. In a note of 12 September Prague informed Paris of its total opposition to the idea of a plebiscite.

In an interview with Osusky on 16 September Bonnet asked Prague to consider the cession of the Sudetenland in return for a guarantee for the remainder of the Czech state. The advice was followed by a warning:

> I repeated to him that there was no question of France marching in this affair if she did not have complete agreement on all points with Great Britain . . . I earnestly requested M Osusky to warn M Benes in Prague not to continue in the illusions in which he had lived for so many months.[50]

In Prague the same day Lacroix saw Benes and asked whether cession might solve the problem. Then 'not without great hesitation' Benes recounted how in 1919 during the Paris Peace Conference he had considered 'the cession of three regions of an area of 8,000 square kilometres and a population of over 900,000 Germans'. Lacroix wired:

> M Benes did not forbid me to inform your Excellency of the confidences which he gave me, but he adjured me that no one should be told that the idea came from him, so great was his fear of the claims of the other minorities. . .
> Conscious that your Excellency will take into consideration the recommendation of M Benes as to secrecy if the scheme outlined in the telegram appears to offer a possible solution to the Czechoslovak problem, I suppose that it might be suggested to the Prague government as coming from its friends: I could study it with M Benes.[51]

In his testimony to the parliamentary commission of enquiry in 1948 Lacroix alleged that his telegram had been tampered with in Paris so as to turn what had been an incidental recollection by Benes into a tentative proposal for cession. The former envoy offered no proof of his allegation.

When he left Prague in April 1939 he did not take any papers with him and the Legation's archives were all burnt. It seems unlikely, to say the least, that Lacroix's telegram was doctored in any way. Benes related that at Lacroix's request he had explained the historical background to the Sudeten problem, alluding to his ideas of 1919. Lacroix was asked not to inform Bonnet but to send a private letter to President Lebrun. But if Benes was not making a tentative proposal what was the point in suggesting a letter to Lebrun? In fact what really distressed Lacroix and angered Benes at the time was the fact that Bonnet not only failed to respect the request for secrecy but defended the Anglo-French plan of 18 September for the cession of the Sudetenland in terms of Benes's remarks of 16 September. On 19 September Osusky was told by the French minister:

> They decided in favour of this solution especially as de Lacroix had reported in his despatch of 17 September that President Benes had explained to him that he himself was considering the cession of the Sudeten territory to Germany. . .

After reading Osusky's report Benes telephoned Lacroix asking him to protest to Paris. Under the pressure of events, the Czech leaders, as Hodza put it, were 'thinking aloud' about cession and on 15 September Benes had reminisced in similar vein to Newton. Then on 17 September Benes sent Necas, Minister of Public Health, to Paris with proposals for cession.

After years of sporadic contacts Anglo-French ministerial conferences came fast and thick. Daladier and Bonnet were invited to London on 18 September for the third Anglo-French summit within less than a year. Their mood towards British Ministers was none too friendly since they had been given no indication of the outcome of Chamberlain's colloquy with Hitler at Berchtesgaden. Daladier's proposal of 13 September for a three power meeting had been spurned. Yet, on the larger issue of conciliating Germany, French Ministers before travelling to London had resigned themselves to the cession of the Sudetenland to the *Reich*. On his own testimony, Daladier, before leaving for London in the morning of Sunday 18 September was visited by André Blumel, a former *chef de cabinet* to Blum. Blumel gave him particulars of the cession proposals which Benes's minister, Necaš, had brought to Paris.[52] While Chamberlain and Hitler conversed French Ministers had waited. No meetings of the French Cabinet were held between 13th and 19 September. Until the results of Berchtesgaden were known there was nothing to discuss. Of the general temper of French leaders, one document in Daladier's personal papers speaks volumes. A memorandum dated 17 September concluded:

> It is better to resolve the Sudeten affair by a general peace than by a general war, for it seems there is only this alternative: a general peace or a general war.[53]

In London British Ministers closed ranks against the French visitors. On 17 September Halifax stressed to colleagues how 'very important' it was 'that we should avoid allowing the French to say that they came to London and found that we had decided to give the show away'.[54] The darkest hour of the Anglo-French conference was before lunch on 18 September. Chamberlain had opened proceedings with what his Home

Secretary later called 'the sedative of a, long narrative' in which the Berchtesgaden expedition was presented as purely and simply exploratory.[55] The British Prime Minister had gone to discover what Hitler wanted and now wished to know the views of his French friends 'on the decision which had now to be taken'. In reality the honest broker role was no more than a convenient pose intended to throw the onus of reaching a decision onto the French ministers. Personally, Chamberlain accepted Hitler's demand for self-determination for the Sudeten German minority.

As lunchtime drew near Daladier made a last flourish of the rhetoric of resistance: 'Germany's real aim was the disintegration of Czechoslovakia . . . in a very short time Germany would be master of Europe'. But he was soon deflated and his concluding note was conciliatory: 'the problem, therefore, was to discover some means of preventing France from being forced into war as a result of her obligation'. During the luncheon adjournment the two prime ministers had a private talk and it was almost certainly then that the French leader referred to the Czech proposals for the cession of the Sudetenland. When the conference resumed at 3.30 p.m. the French delegation readily accepted a British suggestion that some arrangement for the cession of the Sudetenland might be acceptable to Germany.

But there was a price to pay for French agreement. The French ministers asked for and received a British promise of a guarantee for Czechoslovakia. Daladier, it is said, had 'built better than he knew. He had committed Great Britain to opposing Hitler's advance in the east'.[56] This is to read too much into a guarantee which never in fact materialised. What Daladier won was a British promise of participation in a general, international guarantee, conditional upon Czechoslovakia's acceptance of an Anglo-French plan of cession and upon the neutralisation of her foreign policy. It cost Chamberlain little to promise participation in a guarantee which could only come into force with the agreement of all the guarantors. 'A British guarantee for Czechoslovakia', explained Daladier, 'would therefore help France . . . to stop the German march to the East'. More candid, however, was Bonnet's reasoning that France 'would be making a very big concession in agreeing to the cession of Sudeten territory . . . French public opinion would only be prepared to accept such sacrifices if in return . . . Britain would guarantee the neutrality of Czechoslovakia'. In other words, French ministers wanted a guarantee in order to tranquilise domestic opinion, not eastern Europe.

At the end of the conference Chamberlain asked 'one last question': what would be the position if Benes said 'No' to the Anglo-French plan? Daladier hummed and hawed; he did not think a refusal 'would be possible'. Chamberlain narrowed the question. Should the decision to involve France in war be left to Benes? Daladier conceded that it 'seemed difficult' to leave such a matter to Benes and 'the strongest possible pressure would have to be brought to bear' on Prague. When the British Cabinet met next day the Home Secretary, Sir Samuel Hoare, complimented Chamberlain on his success in ensuring that the decisions taken were joint ones 'for which we could not be saddled with the major share of responsibility'.[57]

On 19 September the French Cabinet approved the Anglo-French plan while reserving the question of what should be done if Benes refused the proposals. Shortly after the Cabinet Bullitt put to Bonnet the same question as Chamberlain had asked Daladier. What would France do if Benes refused? Without hesitation Bonnet answered: 'France positively would not march in support of Czechoslovakia'.[58] Thinking he knew France better Bullitt repeated the question. This time Bonnet did not mince his words: 'we will not let Benes drive 40 million French people to their deaths in order to maintain the domination of 7 million Czechs over 3½ million Germans'.

After the meeting of the Cabinet Bonnet had at once summoned the Czechoslovak Minister, Stefan Osusky.[59] The envoy was informed of the details of the Anglo-French plan: a guarantee of the great powers would replace Czechoslovakia's treaties with France and the Soviet Union; the Sudetenland would be transferred to Germany, the operation would be supervised by an international body; France offered financial and economic help. Bonnet's own note of the conversation reads:

> . . . I reminded him of our previous talks, in June and in July. Although I had continued, as the Czechoslovak government desired, to proclaim publicly our solidarity with Prague, Prague knew very well that it was not with a view to war — which England and ourselves did not want to wage — but so as to allow the Prague government to reach a peaceful compromise. . .

Bonnet, according to his own record, 'begged' Osusky 'to transmit immediately' the Anglo-French plan to his government, advising its acceptance. However on Osusky's testimony the French Foreign Minister used much stronger language: 'in the event of the Anglo-French proposals not being accepted by the Czechoslovak Republic, the British Government . . . would deny France its solidarity in the event of a conflict between the Czechoslovak Republic and Germany'. Osusky protested vehemently that a decision was being imposed since if Czechoslovakia did not accept the plan the French alliance would be of no value. Bonnet conceded that this was the position. 'On leaving me', recorded Bonnet, the Czechoslovak Minister 'did not hide an emotion which I well understood'. Osusky in fact was in tears when he left the Quai d'Orsay. 'Here you see the condemned man. He has been sentenced without even being heard', he said.[60] Foreign Minister and envoy did not meet again until after Munich.

In Prague at 2 p.m. in the afternoon of 19 September Lacroix and Newton presented jointly French and British texts of the Anglo-French plan. Benes was given two days in which to reply. 'Our audience', wired Lacroix, 'has been extremely painful'.[61] Few words were exchanged because Benes, in his own words, was 'literally stupefied'. Decisions had been taken affecting Czechoslovakia's vital interests without his government being consulted. Hitler, said the President, would not be satisfied for long: 'I am not telling you what I think of the proposal that you have brought me. You know it very well yourselves'. Benes was distressed by the thought of 'his poor people who had with goodwill made so many efforts for peace and who had now been suddenly stripped of the guarantees on which they had counted'.

Czech opinion was in a state of shock. René Brunet, Bonnet's private observer in Prague since August, reported that until 19 September most Czechs had believed that whatever happened France and Britain would be at their side. The emissary had done his best to explain and defend the French viewpoint: France could not separate from Britain and the maintenance of peace came first. More French propaganda was required:

> as all that appears in the French press concerning Czechoslovakia always arouses the most lively interest here and is more or less reproduced in the Czech newspapers. I cannot insist too much, though I am sure that you have already given the necessary instructions, that your press department ensures the publication of the greatest possible number of articles explaining and justifying the attitude of France.[62]

Paris and London had been told that the Czech reply to the Anglo-French plan would be ready in the afternoon of 20 September. But more pressure was required before the Czechs surrendered. And all the documents, including Bonnet's personal papers in the French archives, make nonsense of Bonnet's assertion in the memoirs that between the afternoon of the 19th and 8 p.m. on the 20th 'no pressure . . . was exercised by the French and British envoys'.[63] At midday on the 20th Lacroix telephoned Bonnet that the Czechs were hesitating between two courses: acceptance or appeal to arbitration. The Foreign Minister gave instructions and Lacroix delivered the following message:

> According to the information reaching the French Government, the Czech Government is hesitating between acceptance of the proposals and an appeal to arbitration. M Bonnet has just telephoned and instructed M de Lacroix to say that the appeal to arbitration would be a very dangerous thing; that it would be an irreparable mistake which would allow England to disengage itself, compromise the negotiations and open the way to the arbitration of M Hitler.

Newton also acted in the same sense. Shortly after 7 p.m., Lacroix informed Paris that although the Czech reply might be evasive the Czechs would surrender in response to an immediate and formal warning. A personal appeal from Gamelin to General Krejci, Chief of the Czech General Staff, would be best.

The many weeks of Franco-British pressure were now bearing fruit. The Czechs were actually inviting an ultimatum. Phipps renewed his initiative of 22 May: 'the moment seemed to have come', he told Bonnet, 'when we should inform M Benes that, unless his reply was an acceptance pure and simple, France and Great Britain would wash their hands of Czechoslovakia'.[64] Bonnet 'did not demur'. He telephoned Daladier the information from Lacroix and presumably spoke of the British Ambassador's ultimatum proposal. Within a short while the Foreign Minister was urging Phipps 'most insistently' that Benes should be given the proposed warning.

At 9.15 p.m., Bonnet had on his desk the official Czech reply, calling for arbitration under the German-Czech arbitration treaty of 1926. Shortly after, Lacroix wired that the intervention of the French General Staff with the Czech General Staff would change the terms of the Czech reply. Within minutes of the receipt of this telegram Lacroix telephoned to say that the Czech reply was not to be regarded as final. The Czech Prime Minister, Hodza, had just put to him a decisive question. Hodza declared that if his country could be told that France would not defend her the Anglo-French plan would be accepted. 'I admit *a priori* that France will not march', said the minister, adding that he spoke with Benes's agreement and intended to make a similar approach to Newton.[65]

Hodza requested a reply before midnight or at the latest during the early hours of 21 September. At the Quai d'Orsay, Daladier, Bonnet, Léger, and Jules Henry, Bonnet's chief assistant, went into conclave. Daladier decided that there was no time to consult the Cabinet. Several Ministers were out of Paris and time was of the essence. By midnight the French reply was ready and received the approval of Lebrun, whom Bonnet telephoned at Rambouillet. At 2 a.m., Lacroix and Newton warned Benes of the consequences of a negative reply to the Anglo-French plan. 'The pressure was of such a nature', wrote Benes on 23 September, 'that it had the character of an ultimatum'.[66] By 8.30 a.m., on the 21st Benes had ready a draft reply, accepting in principle the Anglo-French plan. Paris was then asked for written confirmation of the ultimatum which Lacroix had presented orally during the night. At noon, in a letter to the President, Lacroix confirmed in writing what he had said during the 2 a.m. audience. Benes was told that refusal of the Anglo-French plan would break 'Franco-British solidarity' and so 'deprive French assistance of any practical value'. Czechoslovakia would then be responsible for determining a resort to force by Germany and France would draw her own 'conclusions'.[67]

At Godesberg on 22-23 September Hitler rejected the Anglo-French plan and Chamberlain was given a memorandum, demanding occupation of the Sudetenland by 1 October. Hitler's imposition of a deadline, coupled with a demand for more territory than the Anglo-French plan offered, touched the raw nerve of French policy — the dread of having to choose between war and humiliation. Though deeply disappointed by the rejection of the Anglo-French plan, Chamberlain was prepared to accept the Godesberg terms, justifying them as 'a wonderful opportunity to put an end to the horrible nightmare of the present armament race'.[68] But for Daladier, Godesberg was unacceptable. France would be inflicting on herself a humiliation almost as grievous as war. When the French Cabinet met in the afternoon of 25 September Ministers followed Daladier's lead in rejecting the German memorandum. But it was not a total rejection. Although Daladier and a majority of Ministers would not give Germany more than the areas already conceded under the Anglo-French plan, they were willing to make some concessions in the search for a face-saving formula. It was agreed that an international commission might 'authorise . . . symbolic and progressive occupations' of the Sudetenland.[69]

After the Cabinet meeting Daladier and Bonnet flew to London for another conference with British ministers. As on previous occasions French ministers met only the inner circle of British Ministers — Chamberlain, Halifax, Hoare and Simon, though at least one British minister queried this procedure. However the procedure worked to Chamberlain's advantage since despite several ministerial meetings on the 24-25 September the Prime Minister had not succeeded in persuading the majority of his colleagues to accept the Godesberg demands. When the French and British delegations assembled at 9.15 p.m. on the 25th Daladier opened proceedings with a complaint. He claimed that he had not received a copy of the Godesberg memorandum until 10.30 a.m., that morning. Maybe in this instance the British were not to blame for keeping their ally ill-informed since Phipps said he had handed Bonnet's secretary a copy of the memorandum at 10.20 p.m., in the evening of the 24th.[70]

The French Ministers were then subjected to a rigorous cross-examination on their military plans in the event of a German attack on Czechoslovakia. Daladier's shadow boxing convinced no one. Hoare thought the French 'weak and secretive', Chamberlain considered them 'very evasive'.[71] Nothing that was said served to dispel the disbelief in France's will to fight. Then Daladier dropped his guard and made the first move towards compromise, proposing that 'an international commission should be set up with a definite time-limit . . . so that within a week the German districts might be evacuated'.[72] Though Hoare seized hopefully on the proposal, Chamberlain damned it with faint praise and continued browbeating the French minister. At this point Hoare pushed a note across to Chamberlain 'suggesting that he and Daladier should meet alone after the meeting and try to clear up any differences'.[73]

At midnight the conference was adjourned while the British Cabinet met for the third time that day. The British Prime Minister secured approval for a last effort at conciliation. He proposed to send his chief adviser, Sir Horace Wilson, as the bearer of a personal message to Hitler. If the appeal failed Wilson was to warn Hitler that France would fight and would be supported by Britain. About 10 a.m., in the morning of the 26th Chamberlain and Daladier met privately, with only Corbin present as interpreter since Chamberlain's command of French and Daladier's English were far from perfect. The French statesman was told of the Wilson mission and handed copies of the written message and the oral warning. Wilson was authorised to say that: 'The French Government have informed us that, if the Czechs reject the memorandum and Germany attacks Czechoslovakia, they will fulfil their obligations to Czechoslovakia. Should the forces of France in consequence become engaged in active hostilities against Germany we shall feel obliged to support them'.[74] Daladier was 'absolutely in accord with the proposed statement' and now affirmed resolutely that France 'intended to go to war'. The private colloquy between the two leaders was followed by an interview with Gamelin who had been summoned to report on French war plans. When the conference resumed at 11.20 a.m., it was merely to note the decisions already reached.

When Chamberlain told his Cabinet of the pledge to the French Duff Cooper registered his amazement at what seemed a 'complete reversal' of policy.[75] The French themselves were less impressed. By a cruel irony the commitment that France had sought since 1919 for her eastern alliances had been given when the alliances were in full dissolution. Not only had the British undertaking come too late in the day, it had also been given in a casual, almost offhand manner. The private discussion between the two statesmen was not minuted, nor did the terms of the guarantee form part of the record of the conference. And if Bullitt is to be believed, Daladier misunderstood the pledge given.[76] Contrary to what Sir Samuel Hoare later claimed, the French were not given the 'specific pledge of a British expeditionary force'.[77] The wording of the guarantee was imprecise. As for the oral warning entrusted to Wilson, it was not delivered at the first meeting with Hitler and Wilson was instructed that it should be given 'more in sorrow than in anger'.[78]

On their return to Paris on 26 September the French quickly put the new pledge to the test. Bonnet asked Halifax for 'very early replies' to the following questions: if France became involved in war with Germany, would Britain mobilise at the same time as France; introduce conscription, pool the economic and financial resources of the two countries?[79] Before replying, Halifax tightened the leading string. He secured confirmation from Bonnet that no offensive measures, including a declaration of war, would be taken without full consultation and agreement with London. In the evening of 28 September he replied to Bonnet's questions. Assistance to France, he stated, would mainly consist of the exercise of sea and air power, and the most that could be sent to France, if it were decided to send a land force, would be two divisions—perhaps not fully equipped. Conscription and the pooling of resources raised constitutional issues on which parliament would have to decide. By the time the replies were sent Czechoslovakia's fate had been settled. On the afternoon of the 28th Chamberlain and Daladier had accepted Hitler's invitation to attend a conference in Munich the following day. Nevertheless Bonnet's exercise was not wasted. Halifax's answers were doubtless put to good use in parliamentary lobbies and Parisian salons.

The Right wing *Je Suis Partout* announced on 16 September that the French people were faced by a massive 'campaign for war'. Nothing was further from the truth, on the contrary the final stages of the crisis witnessed a massive campaign to prevent France honouring her treaty obligations. As early as 10 September observers noted the appearance of 'numerous apparently inspired articles' suggesting that France was looking for a way out of her obligations.[80] The opening salvo in the peace offensive was fired by the Radical deputy for the Sarthe, Jean Montigny, a friend of Bonnet and Caillaux. On 19 September he addressed an open letter to the government, asking 'Shall France go to war for Czechoslovakia?'[81] The letter was published in *Le Temps* on 21 September. War, Montigny argued, would mean a long struggle in which France would be practically alone. France should think very carefully before embarking on a war outside her frontiers. His prescription for France's troubles was simple: French workers should work harder, the state must restore its authority, Britain should introduce conscription. Communism, not Nazism, was the real enemy. France, concluded the deputy, should not 'sacrifice herself' for the 'triumph of communism'. Forwarding a report of the letter to Berlin, the German embassy commented: 'the statements of deputy Montigny sum up excellently all the arguments which are daily used by us here'.[82]

Counter-moves to stiffen French opinion were feeble in the extreme. Winston Churchill and his friend, General Spears, formerly Military Attaché in Paris, telephoned Bonnet on 15 September breathing fire and thunder but only succeeded in raising the minister's hackles. In the afternoon of 22 September the *bellicistes* Mandel, Reynaud, de Ribes talked of resigning but were dissuaded by Herriot and Churchill. Mandel's most energetic action was to tell the Czechs: 'Do not accept the Anglo-French plan. Resist. It only needs a few Germans to be killed for Georges Bonnet himself to be obliged to declare war'.[83]

The action of Bonnet and his coterie was sustained and determined. Hearing that the Reynaud group had threatened to resign, Monzie, accompanied by Pomaret, asked to see Daladier. Bluntly, Monzie declared that if Daladier gave way to Reynaud then he and Pomaret would resign. Neither faction was sure of Daladier's position. On 23 September the Prime Minister told a delegation of 50 Radical deputies that if Germany attacked Czechoslovakia France would fulfill her engagements. He was said to have spoken without consulting Bonnet who was reported in a state of collapse.

Hitler's Godesberg demands had produced 'a complete swing over of public opinion,' reported Phipps on 26 September. 'The population is growing accustomed to the idea of war, despite an inherent strong aversion and is becoming reconciled to it', wired the German Chargé d'Affaires.[84] This shift in opinion was not encouraged in any way. Indeed, the *Bonnetistes* worked unremittingly to nip it in the bud. Emile Roche, director of the Radical *La République*, introduced Caillaux to Monzie. Although in his seventies Caillaux, as president of the Senate Finance Committee, was still an influential figure. Monzie presented the man of Agadir to the numerous trade unionists—postal workers, miners and teachers—who thronged his ministry of Public Works. Such was Caillaux's pessimism about the outcome of a conflict that all he could talk of were possible peace terms. On 25 September he insisted to Phipps that the 'possible losses of a war' would have to be evenly shared by Britain and France 'that is to say, if colonies have to be surrendered, both countries will contribute equally'.[85]

Flandin, too, was doing his bit. He had seen Daladier on 13 September and wrote confirming his counsel on 24 September. The government, he stated, could not go to war without recalling parliament. Daladier was urged to insist on Britain mobilising at the same time as France and also introducing conscription. Flandin, like Caillaux, was preoccupied with the thought of defeat and its consequences. Britain, he advised Daladier, would have to cede an amount of territory 'strictly equal to that of France'.[86] The same day he assured Phipps that 'all peasant class were against war' and raised the Communist bogey:

> Communist leaders who are the most active in egging on war are already telling their men that if there were . . . heavy air bombardments they would rise up, declare that France had been betrayed by her Government and set up a Communist regime.

Flandin's most well-known intervention came on 28 September when he had Paris covered with posters declaring: 'You are being deceived . . . a plot has been organised by secret forces to make war inevitable . . .' Sarraut, Minister of the Interior, had the posters removed next day but the damage was done.

Bonnet himself was far from idle. In a letter to Daladier of 24 September he recapitulated all the military and political arguments against France going to war for her ally:

.... If France declared war against Germany her position would be weaker than at any time since 1919. In fact, France in this case would have to withstand alone on land the force of the combined German and Italian armies, without counting Japan which, in the Far East, will doubtless attack Indo-China . . .
For five months, night and day, in the course of our confident collaboration, we have struggled for peace. I beg you to continue in this course. It is the only one which can save the country . . .[87]

According to Gamelin, the letter was backed up by a threat of resignation.

Monday 26 September was a field day for the Bonnet brigade. Daladier had already prepared an order for general mobilisation and also the text of a radio broadcast, explaining the necessity of French intervention in defence of Czechoslovakia. The Foreign Minister urged his acolytes to lobby Daladier and Lebrun. When the British Foreign Office issued a communiqué in the afternoon, stating that France would defend Czechoslovakia and would be supported by Britain and the Soviet Union, the French Foreign Minister did his utmost to suppress it.[88] One of Bonnet's allies, François Piétri, a former navy minister, transmitted to the Belgian government details of France's military unpreparedness, requesting that the information be relayed to London because the British did not know enough about French deficiencies.[89]

On the morning of the 26th another friend of Bonnet, Marcel Boussac, textile industrialist and founder of the fashion house of Christian Dior, had telephoned Lucien Lamoureux, Radical deputy for Allier.[90] Lamoureux was in his constituency. Boussac asked if he would go to Paris to help counter *belliciste* propaganda in the Chambers. Lamoureux hesitated, and Boussac tried again, saying that Bonnet urgently needed his help. The deputy hastened to Paris. Briefed by Bonnet from official files, he sallied forth into the parliamentary lobbies. Although the Chambers had not been recalled, many deputies were returning to Paris. At the Chamber of Deputies, Lamoureux found 'a very strong current of opinion in favour of France standing firm'. Next day he worked tirelessly among clusters of deputies, seeking to convince them that the differences between the Anglo-French plan and the Godesberg memorandum were not great enough to justify a war. By the evening of the 27th Lamoureux reported to Bonnet that parliamentary opinion seemed to be swinging back in favour of conciliation. Monzie was busy. His Ministry had become the headquarters of a powerful pressure group. The minister encouraged the leaders of the teachers and postal workers unions to publish a peace petition. Monzie himself wrote to Daladier, saying that France's first obligation under the Franco-Czechoslovak treaty was not to declare war on Germany but to take her case to the League of Nations.[91]

While the artillery of words thundered, statesmen and diplomats frantically drafted and redrafted compromise timetables, promising Germany the substance of her demands but preserving the appearance of peaceful and orderly negotiation. War seemed imminent; trenches were being dug, gas masks distributed. On the evening of 26 September Hitler delivered a frenzied speech at the Berlin Sportpalast repeating his

Godesberg deadline of 1 October. Czechoslovakia had mobilised on the 23rd; by the 27th France had recalled nearly a million men; on the morning of the 28th Britain mobilised the Fleet.

After Hitler's speech of 26 September Bonnet and his advisers drafted a compromise timetable. According to this scheme, certain areas promised in the Anglo-French plan were to be evacuated before I October and occupied by German troops on that date. An international commission would then be responsible for the delimitation of a new Czech-German frontier. Corbin presented the French timetable to Halifax on the morning of the 27th but, independently, Chamberlain and his Foreign Secretary had drafted their own timetable which, though similar to the French one, was more detailed in its provisions, giving precise dates both for German occupation of the Sudetenland and the work of the international commission. France had not reached the limit of concession. When during the late evening of 27th, Phipps informed Bonnet of the British arrangement, the Foreign Minister did not believe the concessions were far-reaching enough. If the British initiative was unsuccessful, François-Poncet was authorised to offer Hitler 'immediate occupation of a more important area'.[92]

On the morning of 27 September the French Cabinet held a confused and stormy meeting.[93] Bonnet spoke out strongly for peace at any price. The Czechs, he told colleagues, had been warned on two occasions since June that France could not go to war and could only offer diplomatic support. The most France could do was to mobilise a few classes of reservists. There was no air force worth speaking of, and the diplomatic situation was gloomy. He was against general mobilisation: 'at all cost a compromise must be found'. Bonnet, by his own account, was in a small minority: 'I met very strong opposition from most of my colleagues. The question of my resignation was undoubtedly in the air. The statement issued at the end of the meeting did not even mention my name, only that of Daladier'. The Cabinet broke up in confusion. It was decided that more reservists would be recalled but there would be no general mobilisation. In the meantime France should continue her effort of conciliation. But Bonnet's own future seemed in jeopardy. According to Jean Zay, Daladier was anxious to call another ministerial meeting to settle 'the Bonnet business' but later abandoned the idea. Later in the day Bonnet had a long talk with his chief assistant, Jules Henry, saying that in two days he would no longer be Foreign Minister. At 4 p.m. he saw Daladier and reminded him of his letter of the 24th. The Prime Minister, recorded Bonnet, 'seemed overcome. He no longer spoke of my resignation. He let me leave, telling me to act for the best'.

The advocates of conciliation received strong encouragement from the intervention of the United States. For some months Bonnet had been bent on securing an American initiative; on 26 September Washington acted. Roosevelt sent a message to European capitals urging the statesmen not to break off negotiations. Daladier expressed his pleasure and gratitude at the presidential initiative and encouraged Roosevelt: 'he still hoped a moment might come when it might be possible to call a conference . . . such a call must come from President Roosevelt'.[94] In the small hours of 28 September the French government received a second message from Washington, calling for a conference of the interested powers. Before making this second appeal Roosevelt had sounded Chamberlain and Daladier. 'Delighted' by the suggestion, Daladier had listed the powers he wished to see at a conference: France, Britain, Germany, Poland and Czechoslovakia.[95] Despite Daladier's blackballing of Italy, Roosevelt sent a special message to the *Duce*. On the night of 27-28 September Bonnet hastened to utilise the American initiative. After conferring with two of his Italophile supporters, Piétri and Frossard, the minister asked Mussolini to back the American appeal. But Halifax had already solicited the Duce's mediation and the French approach was at once rebuffed: 'Not a hope', said Ciano, 'it is not our intention that France shall interfere'.[96]

Though French diplomacy had no success in Rome, its contribution to decision-making in Berlin was far from negligible. France's readiness to go to the extreme limit of concession must have greatly influenced Hitler's decision to call a conference in Munich. At 8.20 a.m., on the morning of the 28th, François-Poncet telephoned the German State Secretary, von Weizsäcker, requesting an interview with the German Chancellor:

> I explained to him the main lines of the French proposal, emphasising that it went much further than anything so far put forward. He promised to arrange matters. He did not conceal from me that the English proposal concerning the occupation of the Egerland was of no use.[97]

At 9.15 a.m., fearing that Hitler would not inform the army chiefs of the French offer the Ambassador sent his Military Attaché, General Renondeau, to speak to the Chief of Army Staff. After communicating a memorandum and maps of the French proposal Renondeau was told to leave no doubt in the mind of the army chief that France, Britain and Russia would fight for Czechoslovakia. 'You are winning the day', the Ambassador told Hitler at 11.15 a.m.:

> It is only a matter of being patient for a few days. What we ask of you is to allow the civilians to march in front, the members of the international commission who will declare: 'this district is incontestably German. Germany can take possession of it; . . . in sending the army and its guns first . . . you will become the aggressor . . .

Britain and France had now reached the limit of conciliation. Chamberlain sent a final appeal for a conference which would give Hitler 'all essentials without war and without delay'.[98a] This message was seconded by Mussolini. At 2.40 p.m. Hitler agreed to a conference, provided Mussolini attended.

At 3.25 p.m., Ribbentrop telephoned the French embassy to say that Hitler had issued invitations to Chamberlain, Daladier and Mussolini to attend a conference in Munich the following day. The invitations were immediately accepted. The fact that there was no time to prepare for the conference or to concert with London mattered little since the essentials had already been conceded. Bonnet and Gamelin met and produced some plans 'for occupation of certain Sudeten areas by German troops and . . . suggested occupation of others by French, British and possibly Italian troops'.[99] At Léger's request, Bonnet drew up a note of instructions for the French delegation. Germany was only to be given territory in which the German population was in a clear majority. An effort had to be made, said Bonnet, to preserve certain industrial centres of Czechoslovakia. An international guarantee must be obtained for the new frontiers. Finally, Bonnet suggested that the conference should transform itself into a general conference of all the powers and consider 'all European problems.[100] But the success of the conference was everything for the Foreign Minister. He urged Phipps to tell London 'how absolutely vital . . . it was that an arrangement should be reached . . . at almost any price'.[101] Bonnet, like Halifax, stayed at home. Daladier was accompanied by Léger and Rochat, head of the European section of the Quai.

When the conference opened on 29 September Daladier thanked Hitler for his initiative: 'the plan for such a meeting had . . . already existed before, but circumstances had unfortunately prevented its realisation . . . However, there was a French proverb: "Better late than never" '.[102] Mussolini produced a working draft which was accepted by Chamberlain and Daladier as 'a basis for discussion'. The text of the agreement which finally emerged differed little from the Italian draft which was itself based largely on a British timetable, proposed by Chamberlain on the 27th and seconded by Daladier. Benes had sent a personal message to Daladier begging him not to forget the 20 years of alliance and to ensure that Czechoslovakia was given a hearing in decisions affecting her interests. Though the Czechs were excluded from the conference, Daladier made some effort to speak for them but achieved nothing of substance.

The French delegation received two luncheon invitations, one from the British delegation and one from Goering. Moody and morose, Daladier refused the Field Marshal and failed to turn up for the British. Goering then arranged to have lunch near the French party. In the evening the atmosphere became more relaxed. The French Prime Minister settled on a sofa and ordered Munich beer. At 2.15 a.m., on the 30th the agreement was signed, providing for the evacuation and occupation of the Sudetenland in successive stages between 1 and 10 October. The whole operation was to be supervised by an international commission, composed of representatives of the four powers and of Czechoslovakia. Britain and France renewed their offer of a guarantee and Germany and Italy agreed that after the settlement of Polish and Hungarian claims they would join in an international guarantee of the new Czech frontiers. Mastny, the Czech delegate, was in tears. Daladier had little taste for English humour and 'declined' Chamberlain's suggestion that 'he should take the Agreement to Prague'. When at 2.30 a.m., François-Poncet telephoned Bonnet the terms of the Agreement, the minister cut short his explanations: 'Peace is saved . . . that's the main thing'. At midday Goering called to say goodbye to Daladier. The Field Marshal expressed the hope that their meeting might be the starting point for Franco-German understanding. Daladier concurred. He 'had already thought about it' and 'had a certain number of ideas' but time was needed before they could 'take shape'.

As Daladier stepped out of his aircraft at Le Bourget the sight of the waiting crowds filled him momentarily with apprehension. In reality he was the hero of the hour. Never again would he be so popular. The drive from the airport to Paris was a triumphal progress. Seated next to him in the open car was Bonnet. Waiting to welcome him at the war ministry, Rue Saint-Dominique, were Gamelin and colleagues. The crowd sang the *Marseillaise*. Monzie embraced the Prime Minister. Bullitt rushed up with a bouquet. Ministers then assembled at the Elysée for a brief meeting of the Cabinet at which Lebrun formally conveyed to Daladier the nation's gratitude. The euphoria persisted for several days. A Paris city councillor proposed that an avenue be renamed 'September 30'. Bonnet 'wisely' declined an offer from Perigueux, his constituency, to name one of the streets in his honour.[103]

Chapter 13

Strategy and Diplomacy

For France, Munich was a bloodless Sedan, completing the decline which the Rhineland coup had begun in March 1936. Much more was involved than the destruction of a loyal ally. In less than three years without a shot fired France had been deprived of her European primacy. Yet even in September 1938 the decay of French power might still have been arrested. By 30 September there were no more than 10 German divisions in the west, some of which were reserve units, facing 23 French divisions, with 10 in reserve. Since the concrete in the Siegfried Line was not yet dry there would have been nothing to stop a determined French offensive. The failure to oppose Germany swung the strategic balance decisively in her favour. With Germany nearing the peak of her rearmament and accumulating more trained reserves, France's position could only deteriorate. In addition, the French army had lost the support of 34 Czech divisions.

Why then did France acquiesce in the emasculation of her ally? Gamelin saw clearly what was at stake. On 27 September he warned Daladier that if France did not try to stop a German attack then within a decade she would be 'a second class power'.[1] In a report of 12 October Gamelin catalogued the strategic consequences of Munich. 'German occupation of the Sudetenland', he wrote, had brought 'a reversal of the general situation in central Europe'. Czechoslovakia 'amputated of more than a quarter of its population, cut in two . . . is almost incapable of fulfilling its role as an obstacle to German expansion in the east'. The Danubian area was now open to Germany.[2]

As the *Te Deums* for Munich died away, defenders of the settlement pleaded military necessity and after 1945 the military factor was considered decisive. 'I thought that France could only go to war as the leader of a democratic coalition. . . . France could not make war alone against Germany', Daladier told the French National Assembly in 1946.[3] Supporters of Munich insisted at the time and afterwards on three arguments drawn from the military situation: a French offensive directed at German fortifications between the Rhine and Moselle would, it was said, have been a long and difficult operation. German forces might have been diverted but nothing could have been done to prevent the invasion of Czechoslovakia. Secondly, it was argued, French forces would have had to march through Belgium and Soviet help would have been required but Belgium refused to allow troops to cross her frontier. Nor would Poland and Rumania allow Soviet troops to cross their territory. Thirdly, the Chief of Staff of the French air force believed that his aircraft would be destroyed within the first week or so of hostilities.

While these arguments call for closer consideration, it is now clear that France could and should have fought in 1938. From a purely military viewpoint, 1938 offered a last chance of fighting Germany on better or at least even terms. Yet the issue of war or peace was not decided primarily on military grounds. Chamberlain's Home Secretary, Sir Samuel Hoare, conceded that 'military weakness' was not 'the principal cause of the Munich agreement'.[4] Until March 1939 British and French ministers clung desperately to the hope of a European détente. In September 1938 the fate of Czechoslovakia was predetermined by the political assumptions which had inspired Franco-British diplomacy since the previous autumn.

The outlook which animated British and French statesmen in 1938-39 is too well-known to require analysis. Pacifist sentiment was a powerful propellant. It was felt that war would be utterly disastrous for victors and vanquished alike. A European détente based on an agreement with the dictators was seen as the best way of avoiding war. Sympathy for Czechoslovakia's predicament was noticeably absent. It was widely assumed that Czechoslovakia was not a viable entity and must succumb sooner or later to a combination of internal tensions and German pressures. This attitude towards Czechoslovakia reflected a fairly general dislike of the Versailles settlement. Daladier and Bonnet had no liking for the peace treaties. British ministers had no time for France's eastern pacts, believing that France occupied 'an unreal position' in central and eastern Europe and that once Germany regained her 'normal strength' her predominance was inevitable.[5] Another important determinant of policy was detestation of Bolshevism.

Reinforcing these political considerations were certain strategic preoccupations. Since the outbreak of the Spanish civil war, French governments had placed increasing emphasis on France's Mediterranean and imperial interests. Though the Mediterranean region had always been of central concern, it was given absolute priority in the years 1936-39. The Mediterranean came first, central and eastern Europe second. It was argued that France did not have the resources to maintain her interests in both areas. The policy pursued after 1936 was one of seeking a settlement with Germany while aiming at a containment of Italy's Mediterranean ambitions. French war plans were based on the belief that Czechoslovakia would help France by opening a second front in the east. Wedded to an essentially defensive strategy the French General Staff had no plans to help its eastern allies. As the German noose on Czechoslovakia tightened after the *Anschluss* the French military leadership conducted a preliminary study of the feasibility of helping Prague. A report submitted shortly after the seizure of Austria concluded that 'there could be no question of France helping Czechoslovakia directly by an offensive across Germany'.[6] Two possibilities of action were outlined: firstly France by massing her forces on the Rhine frontier might hope to divert substantial German divisions and so deprive the German army of sufficient strength to crush Czechoslovakia outright; secondly France might try to occupy German territory as security for a settlement of the conflict. On the prospects of successful action the report was pessimistic:

> If our organisation is ill-adapted to the kind of battle which we will have to fight in the Rhineland, one can also say the same for the instruction of our army in this respect.
> Speaking only of the infantry one could very probably count on one's fingers the units which have been trained to fight over ground strewn with shell holes, and criss-crossed with trenches and obstacles...

In a paper of 8 February 1938 Gamelin examined France's military situation.[7] France and Britain, he stated, were inseparably linked by a community of interests which could only be defended by joint action. Chief of these interests was the preservation of the axis of their colonial empires, stretching from the Mediterranean to the Indian ocean. The principal antagonists were Germany and Italy and of the two, Italy, implied Gamelin, was the more immediately dangerous because she straddled the Mediterranean, 'the vital artery' of the Franco-British empires. Scouting for possible allies Gamelin found little comfort. Belgium, the Netherlands and Scandinavian states would probably remain neutral; Nationalist Spain would side with the Axis powers, Republican Spain with the western democracies; the Little Entente 'was all ready to disintegrate . . . leaving Czechoslovakia to resist alone German pressure'; Poland's attitude depended on a number of factors and she could not be counted on 'in all circumstances'; the Soviet Union was 'shaken by her internal political crisis and to a great extent distracted by Japan in the Far East'; in the Balkans Greece and Rumania would at the outset of a war adopt a wait and see policy; Turkey's eventual alignment was uncertain. Outside Europe, the United States would only intervene if her interests were directly threatened; in Asia Japan seemed for the present fully absorbed in the conquest of China. In conclusion Gamelin defined the tasks of the French armed forces. First priority was given to the defence of metropolitan France and her empire, next came an offensive against Italy in the Alps and in Africa. An offensive against Germany in order to divert German forces for the relief of eastern allies was relegated to third place.

In their impatience to dispose of the *Duce* the French seemed to be closing their eyes to German designs in central Europe. The *Anschluss* confirmed the political and military leadership in their conviction that Mussolini was completely in Hitler's pocket. 'But when one asks how the French are going to fight for Czechoslovakia', minuted a Foreign Office official on 24 March, 'the only answer one gets is that they will march in Libya'.[8] After his Paris visit in March, Winston Churchill reported to Chamberlain that in the event of a German attack on Czechoslovakia French plans were to hold the Maginot Line and mount an offensive in Africa. Although in London the preoccupation with Italy seemed obsessive, it was natural enough in the circumstances. The success of Franco's forces, aided by Italian troops, presented a much more serious and immediate threat than German pressure on Czechoslovakia. Moreover, the Popular Front Ministries of the period responded to the anxieties of their parliamentary majority. Powerless to save Republican Spain, Communists and Socialists vented their spleen on fascist Italy. Another consideration was the extent of Britain's own Mediterranean interests. Mindful of Franco-British naval co-operation in September 1937, Daladier argued that there was a much better chance of enlisting British help in the Mediterranean theatre than in central Europe.

The main difference between British and French appreciations of the international situation was that the British Chiefs of Staff were much more conscious of the Japanese factor and of the danger of simultaneous action by Germany, Italy and Japan. In December 1937 the Chiefs of Staff had warned:

> Without overlooking the assistance which we would hope to obtain from France . . . we cannot foresee the time when our defence forces will be strong enough to safeguard our trade, territory and vital interests against Germany, Italy and Japan at the same time.[9]

Asked for their views on the military implications of a possible German attack on Czechoslovakia, the Chiefs of Staff reported in March 1938: 'if such a struggle were to take place it is more than probable that both Italy and Japan would seize the opportunity to further their own ends . . . the problem we have to envisage is not that of limited European war only but of world war'.[10] By contrast in his report of 8 February Gamelin said comparatively little of Japan and assumed she would be fully engaged in China for some time. Another difference in defence thinking lay in the premises of planning. French leaders recognised they were dependent on British help at sea and in the air whereas British Ministers tended to assume that home and imperial defence could be separated from the defence of France and the maintenance of a European balance of power. The Cabinet and its military advisers raised the spectre of world-wide action by Germany, Italy and Japan but were unwilling to take practical steps to exorcise the danger.

In addition to the specific arguments against a French offensive in September 1938, Gamelin always insisted that a strong Franco-British alliance was a prerequisite for French intervention. Yet apart from some routine technical exchanges, there was an almost complete lack of co-operation between French and British staffs. No attempt was made to prepare for joint action against Germany and Italy. The French would gladly have accepted full staff talks but the British Chiefs of Staff obdurately resisted the idea. In the Franco-British discussions from April to September 1938 the military factor was the shuttlecock in the game of diplomacy. Instead of seeking means to help Czechoslovakia, both London and Paris manoeuvred for position. In February 1938 the British Chiefs of Staff counselled against giving any impression 'of mutually assumed military collaboration' with the French.[11] Chamberlain and Halifax, however, were in favour of some limited contacts and the British memorandum of 24 March informing Paris that no British commitment for Czechoslovakia was possible also carried an offer of air staff talks. But there was agreement in London that conversations should be kept to a bare minimum. On 11 April the Chiefs of Staff advised that the political assumptions of talks should be 'a strict interpretation of our treaty obligations to France and Belgium; that is to say Germany alone should be assumed the aggressor, and the conversations should not be permitted to comprehend the extension of a conflict to other nations'.[12] In brief, no discussion of common action in defence of Czechoslovakia or against Italy in the Mediterranean.

When British and French ministers conferred in London on 28-29 April, Chamberlain astutely spiked French guns by suggesting a change in the agenda order: item 7 (staff talks) was brought forward before item 4 (Czechoslovakia). The French were informed that 'two divisions would be the maximum military force which could be sent to France on the outbreak of war'.[13] And Chamberlain carefully entered a caveat: 'if the government of the day decided in favour of sending such a force'. An offer of air and army staff talks was made, and after some pressure from the French Ministers, naval talks were also conceded 'though these should only be taken up as soon as opportunity offered'. Chamberlain made it plain that staff talks must not jeopardise efforts to improve relations with Rome and Berlin. The results of British approaches to the Axis powers made 'it necessary to be very careful not to undo any good which had been achieved . . . by exciting Italian and German suspicions that we were now devising fresh combinations to injure those two Powers'. The conversations that followed were low-level contacts, conducted through normal attaché channels. 'We were precluded by Cabinet instructions', wrote a member of the British Air Staff, 'from any discussion of strategic plans with the French staffs'.[14]

All this was much less than the French Chiefs of Staff wanted. In a note of 24 April on 'Franco-British military co-operation' the secretariat of the Permanent Committee of National Defence proposed the establishment of an inter-allied body which would be responsible for the co-ordination of military and economic policies.[15] The argument advanced in the memorandum was the familiar one of French demographic inferiority. Forty million Frenchmen were faced by seventy five million Germans and forty million Italians: 'France cannot for long withstand effectives three times as numerous'. Britain should be asked to send a force to the Continent commensurate with her population, even if this meant conscription. This note of 24 April seems to have been the first occasion on which the French General Staff advised the government to ask for a substantial British expeditionary force. As regards Air Forces, the French Air Staff suggested that fighter and bomber squadrons of the Royal Air Force should be stationed on French territory—in north-eastern France and in North Africa.

In the discussions on Czechoslovakia on 28-29 April British ministers listed all the gloomiest facts which they had been able to collect. Following the *Anschluss,* the government 'had instructed their Chiefs of Staff to make a full examination of the Czechoslovak problem from the military point of view. The result of that examination . . . was to reveal what an exceedingly difficult military problem . . . the defence of Czechoslovakia presented'.[16] No papers were communicated to the French delegation and none were requested. Halifax next reviewed Polish and Soviet strengths, adroitly sidestepping any judgement on Czech military power. It was 'extremely doubtful', expounded the Foreign Secretary, 'whether Russia could be counted upon to make any great contribution, if indeed she could make any contribution at all'. Daladier countered by putting in a good word both for Czechoslovakia and the Soviet Union. 'The Czechoslovak army was by no means to be despised', he declared, and 'Russia still possessed the strongest air force in Europe, comprising 5,000 aeroplanes!' Halifax had not mentioned Soviet air power. The British approach was skilful: the general military picture was roughed out in broad strokes, leaving no time for adequate analysis of individual aspects.

But the relative optimism displayed by French Ministers was as much a game of bluff as British pessimism. In defence, as in diplomacy, both governments endeavoured to keep each other guessing. Daladier, as he later confided to Bullitt, knew full well that the British were 'consistently describing their state of preparedness as worse than it really was'.[17] In the same conversation with Bullitt, however, the French Prime Minister admitted that 'with the present disparity between the French Air Force and the German Air Force it was impossible for France to go to war to protect Czechoslovakia....he had considered the position of Czechoslovakia entirely hopeless since the annexation of Austria'.

At the Franco-British conference on 25 September Chamberlain again harped on the impossibility of defending Czechoslovakia. The two governments, he said, had no alternative but to accept Hitler's Godesberg terms. British Ministers did their best to extinguish any sparks of French resistance. Assisted by the Chancellor of the Exchequer, Sir John Simon, Chamberlain cross-examined Daladier on the state of French armaments. Under heavy fire from Simon, Daladier made a diversionary move, suggesting that Gamelin could be asked 'to give to another conference' a full technical exposition of French war plans.[18] Not so lightly warded off Simon pursued his quarry, Chamberlain, however seized on the proposal. 'Would it be possible', he asked, for Gamelin 'to come across to England to-morrow?' Thus Daladier was neatly hoisted with his own petard and contact between French and British Chiefs of Staff, hitherto evaded, came about almost by accident.

Upon arrival in London in the early morning of 26 September Gamelin went immediately to Downing Street and reported to Chamberlain and Daladier. At 11.15 a.m., accompanied by General Lelong, Military Attaché in London, he went to the Cabinet offices in Richmond Place for a meeting with the Chiefs of Staff and Service Ministers. Gamelin stressed the need for a 'real co-ordination of the efforts of the two nations'.[19] At midday the three Service Ministers left for a meeting of the Cabinet and the conference continued with the Chiefs of Staff only. No British record of the Chamberlain-Gamelin meeting has been traced but in a verbal report to the Cabinet the Prime Minister said that in Gamelin's opinion 'the Czechoslovak army would give a good account of itself . . . if it were forced to retire to the eastern part of the country it would continue to exist as a fighting force'. The Chiefs of Staff were told that the Czechs 'could hold out certainly for a few weeks, but perhaps not for a few months'.[20]

Gamelin in fact was almost warlike. France, he informed Chamberlain, could mobilise a 100 divisions, in addition there were at least 30 Czech divisions. The Czech army was ready to withdraw to Moravia in order to save its forces from a German pincer attack. Gamelin even listed German weaknesses: unfinished fortifications, shortage of trained reserves, lack of raw materials. Ultimate allied victory was assured. Gamelin sounded martial and managed momentarily to put 'heart' into Chamberlain but in Cadogan's words: 'Cross-examination of Gamelin showed that "active hostilities" probably meant a squib offensive (to bring us in) and then retirement on Maginot Line to wait (6 months) for our "Kitchener armies".'[21] From the Military Attaché in Paris, London already had good reason to suspect that Gamelin was bluffing. Colonel Gauché, head of the Deuxième Bureau had said on 20 September: 'Of course, there will be no European war, since we are not going to fight'.[22] Since no offensive plans had been prepared to help the eastern allies Gamelin could only talk in generalities. After seeing Gamelin off on his way back to Paris General Lelong, Military Attaché, told Liddell Hart: 'perhaps by next Spring or Summer they would be ready for a major offensive' in the west.[23]

Gamelin's brave talk in London was essentially an improvisation for the record and the General Staff had no plans for helping Prague or any of the eastern allies. The alliance with Czechoslovakia was never cemented by a military understanding. Despite the fact that France was given several months notice of the probability of a German attack on Czechoslovakia, no preparations were put in hand. The feasibility of helping Prague was touched on in cursory fashion at the meeting of the Permanent Committee of National Defence on 15 March 1938. 'France might be able to attack' in the west, said Gamelin, but 'since the attacks would be against a forti-fied zone, lengthy operations would be required'.[24] From March to September Gamelin's drill hardly varied; while admitting in principle the possibility of a French offensive he carefully qualified his pronouncements so as to make an attack seem quite impractical. On 27 April Daladier asked Gamelin to let him know what action France could take against Germany. The army, replied the Chief of the General Staff, could launch an offen-sive but its effectiveness would depend on the attitude of Britain, the Soviet Union and Poland. And this was a diplomatic question which concerned the government, not the General Staff. So the ball was returned to Daladier. On 22 May the French Prime Minister again requested the advice of his military counsellors. 'I will attack', replied Gamelin, 'but in front of me I have fortifications'.[25] 'But me no buts' might have been Daladier's rejoinder. On 12 September Daladier put to him for the third time the question of what could be done to help Prague. An early French offensive, said the general, would resemble 'a modernised battle of the Somme'.[26] That was enough for a veteran of 1914-18 and Daladier did not trouble Gamelin again.

Gamelin's London visit on 26 September had an interesting sequel. In a telegram of 27 September which Sir John Simon drafted, the French government were told:

> General Gamelin made it plain to us on Monday that, in his view, if German forces now invaded Czechoslovakia, Czech resistance is likely to be of extremely brief duration. This disturbing estimate is confirmed by our Military Attaché in Berlin who has just returned from Czechoslovakia...[27]

The conclusion of these 'actual facts' was that nothing could be done to prevent a German *fait accompli*, and the French were asked to give an undertaking that they would not carry out any offensive action without previous consultation and agreement with London.

Next day Colonel Fraser, Military Attaché in Paris, challenged the telegram. What he had heard in talks with Colonel Petitbon, Gamelin's 'most confidential staff officer', and other French officers, did 'not at all agree with the appreciation of the capacity of Czechoslovakia for resistance reported by the Foreign Office as having been given by General Gamelin to the Prime Minister in London'.[28] Petitbon's opinions, emphasised the Attaché, were 'certainly those of his chief'. Gauché, head of the Deuxième Bureau, had stated 'most categorically that the morale of the Czech army . . . was high'.

But London's trump card was the opinion of the Military Attaché in Berlin, Colonel Mason-MacFarlane. On 27 September the Attaché had reported personally to Halifax and his 'gloomy picture of Czech morale' was cited in the Cabinet meeting that evening. 'What does he know about it?' was Cadogan's reaction and the French might well have said the same.[29] The man who did know at first hand the state of Czech morale was Colonel Stronge, Military Attaché in Prague, and he sharply disagreed with his Berlin colleague. He wrote later:

> At the height of the Munich crisis he (*Mason-MacFarlane*) came to Prague to form his own impressions of things . . . Somehow or other, he got entangled in the wire on the Czech side of the frontier, emerging therefrom bleeding and displeased in the very early morning, to be confronted almost at once by, apparently, a nervous young soldier who, instead of issuing the customary challenge, regarded this unexpected apparition with a look of some consternation and then let him pass. . .
> When we got down to discussing the military situation in the Legation he stoutly maintained that the morale of the Czech army was poor and would not listen to any denial. . .[30]

On 27 September, in fact, Newton, Minister at Prague, wired Halifax that his Attaché dissented and considered the Czechs had 'confidence in their cause, their leadership and may render a good account of themselves'.[31] On 1 November 1938 Newton himself censured the Foreign Office. He forwarded to London a note of a talk between Stronge and his German colleague, Colonel Toussaint. Toussaint agreed that in September the morale of the Czech army had been excellent. 'This view', wrote Newton, 'is in striking contrast with the opinion which was formed by Colonel Mason-MacFarlane and impressed with such force upon the French government at the height of the crisis'.[32]

Gamelin blamed Bonnet for the views attributed to him in the telegram of the 27th and when British ministers visited Paris on 23 November the general attempted to set the record straight. Rumour had it that while Gamelin talked to Chamberlain and Daladier on the morning of

26 September, in another room Bonnet gave Halifax his own version of Gamelin's views. Yet Bonnet was not to blame. The Paris telegram of 27 September was drafted by Sir John Simon and where Czechoslovakia was concerned the minister's motto would seem to have been *nil nisi malum*.

On paper, the position of the French government was impregnable. France could not envisage a European war without the certainty of allied support, especially from Britain. But did the generals and politicians really wish to fight for Czechoslovakia? In the discussions about the Czech alliance, it was, as the German Ambassador at Paris shrewdly saw, 'not so much a question of seeking possibilities of really giving help to Czechoslovakia as of seeking difficulties which would make help appear hopeless'.[33] If the government had been determined to save Czechoslovakia, London might have been persuaded to agree to full staff talks. But the French knew that British help on land would be no more than a moral gesture in the first months of war. Much hinged, therefore, on the strength of Germany's western fortifications. If the fortifications could have been pierced between the Rhine and Moselle, Belgian neutrality would not have mattered.

Estimates of the strength of the Siegfried Line in the summer of 1938 exemplify the way in which the French General Staff painted the military situation blacker than it really was. On three occasions — 15 March, 22 May, 12 September — Gamelin asserted that the fortifications were a major obstacle to an offensive. In point of fact, though much of the concrete was in position, it was not yet dry and the works could not be occupied. This fact was known to the French at the time. On 8 September Daladier quoted Gamelin as saying that 'another year or even more would be necessary, to make the Siegfried Line 'really formidable'.[34]

A real desire to save Czechoslovakia implied at the very least staff talks between Paris and Prague. No such talks were ever held. Indeed, not only were the French reluctant to honour the alliance but they also sought to dissuade the Czechs from measures of self-defence. In June 1938 General Faucher, head of the French military mission in Prague, let it be known that he approved of Czech defensive measures. Halifax then asked Paris whether Faucher's help 'could not be enlisted in keeping the Czechs alive to the realities of their situation'.[35] Bonnet promised that pressure would be put on the general 'to urge moderation in Czech military circles'. Alarmed by reports of Czech mobilisation on 13 September Daladier berated the Czechs for not consulting him before taking action. In fact the Czechs had not mobilised. In a personal letter of 15 September Faucher reminded Gamelin that the Czechs had not yet received a reply to a request for staff talks which they had made in June. Faucher concluded his letter with two questions:

> Do the indispensable precautionary measures taken in Prague increase the risks of conflict or may one not consider on the contrary that it is the lack of precautions which will increase these risks? Is it thought that French public opinion will be more unanimous if, at the moment of the announcement of mobilisation in France, it is announced that German troops are at the gates of Prague?[36]

By 21 September it was known that Hitler was ready to attack any day but London and Paris still maintained their exhortations not to mobilise. On 18 September Faucher, on Benes's insistence, sent a personal appeal to Gamelin. It was curtly acknowledged on the 20th. Not until the afternoon of 23 September was the advice not to mobilise withdrawn. 'It was now a matter for the Czech government to decide for itself on the measures that might be thought necessary by the worsening of the situation', declared Lacroix.[37]

As for the Soviet Union, conjecture and surmise were the order of the day. No serious attempt was made to reach a balanced appraisal of Soviet military power. The Franco-Soviet pact of 1935, like the Franco-Czech treaty, had not been followed by a military accord. Estimates in Paris of Soviet intentions and military preparedness were almost wholly pessimistic. According to Bullitt, in May 1937 Gamelin 'did not believe the Russians would wish to march'.[38] At the London conference in November 1937 Gamelin was said to consider 'even Rumania a better asset than the Russian army'.[39] On 15 March 1938 the Chief of the General Staff said the Soviet Union could give no practical help in a war for Czechoslovakia. French politicians were equally gloomy. In a conversation with Bullitt on 16 May Bonnet referred to 'the latest reports' from Coulondre which showed that 'neither he nor the French General Staff believed that the Russian army could take any offensive action in Europe'.[40] Daladier, too, said that although 'the Russians had 6,000 planes . . . there was some doubt as to their quality and it seemed exceedingly unlikely that the Soviet Union would take any offensive action in Europe to help Czechoslovakia'.[41] The Quai d'Orsay was resolved to put a good face on the situation: 'our interest at the present time is to allow it to be thought, without deluding ourselves, that the Soviet army is strong . . . It seems, in any case, that one can accept the fact that the U.S.S.R. is a reservoir of manpower and that her troops are well-armed and equipped'.[42]

This pessimism in official quarters contrasted with the glowing reports of Soviet might and achievement which had circulated in 1933-34. In part the Soviet internal crisis was responsible for the change in attitude. Stalin's purges took a heavy toll of the country's military and political leadership. More important however in shaping French opinion was France's own internal convulsion. After the Popular Front French conservatives fought shy of any contacts with Moscow. Soviet intervention in Spain and stories of Comintern interference in French politics strengthened the suspicions of Soviet intentions. The French Ambassador in Moscow, Robert Coulondre, wrote:

> When I went to France in May 1938 hardly anyone spoke to me of Russia, and when I spoke of Russia in political circles, I was barely listened to. I could count on one hand those who with the cool lucidity of Paul Reynaud were able to free themselves from all ideological considerations.[43]

More typical of the champions of a Soviet military alliance was Pierre Cot, Air Minister from June 1936 to January 1938. Monzie wrote in

September 1938: 'he, at least, does not deny the ideological *parti pris* to which his strategic reasoning is subordinated'.[44]

Coulondre tried to break down the barriers of mistrust and ignorance. All his initiatives were met by resistance or indecision in Paris. His mission in Moscow was difficult enough in the circumstances. In Stalin's Moscow, the diplomatic colony was cut off from the usual sources of information. According to one resident in the 1930s, there was 'a continual exchange, in bad French, of inaccurate political information, mostly picked up from servants'.[45] Despite this setting of rumour and gossip the French embassy supplied Paris with information which, if not entirely accurate, was reasonably balanced. The authorities turned a deaf ear. The Military Attaché, Colonel Palasse, was acknowledged as 'one of the few who rated the Red Army at its true worth'.[46] On 26 July 1938 Palasse reported to Daladier: 'It seems that the government, the country, and the officers have confidence in the value of their army. Doubtless this is the explanation of the very firm attitude of the Soviet government towards Japan'.[47]

The belief in Paris that nothing good could come out of the Soviet Union frustrated Coulondre's efforts. When the Air Attaché, Commandant Donzeau, showed interest in buying Soviet fighter aircraft, Coulondre backed him and opened negotiations directly with the Commissar for Aviation — in itself no mean achievement at that time. On 17 March 1938 the Attaché was given details of a new Soviet aircraft. It was understood that France would provide technical assistance and plans of her proto-types in exchange for Soviet designs. In June the Attaché was told that the negotiations must be limited to exchanges of prototypes only and Paris was not interested in buying Soviet aircraft already in production. In effect this amounted to a breaking off of negotiations since the Soviet Union bought its prototypes abroad and did not design its own. In a letter of 13 June 1938 Coulondre recorded his dismay: 'In truth, the Air Ministry does not want technical co-operation with Moscow. I am greatly surprised. The Air Ministry is abandoning Soviet co-operation just when, after years of efforts, we were at last about to realise it'.[48] The Russians, he added, were not yet capable of designing their own aircraft but their mass pro-duction methods had surprised even American observers. The Ambassador continued: 'They are very mistrustful here and reactions . . . are often lively: is this the right time to provoke them? Moreover, technical co-operation was the only concrete result of the Franco-Soviet pact'. Such questions, he insisted, were too important to be left to an individual mini-stry. It was a matter for a 'government decision'. Some months later, Coulondre asked Gamelin for an explanation of the Air Ministry's attitude. Claiming to have supported the proposal, Gamelin said he had been told by the Air Ministry: we will never accept 'such a humiliation'.[49]

Ideological mistrust, the Soviet purges, the fear of alienating Poland and Rumania, all combined to prevent the holding of staff talks in 1938. In a memorandum of 7 March 1938 Daladier, then War Minister, had con-cluded that given the lack of a common frontier with Germany and the hostility of Rumania and Poland 'it would be inopportune to discuss military arrangements with the Soviet Union'.[50] Moreover, the 'present state' of the Soviet army would render any negotiations 'hazardous'. The role assigned to the Soviet Union was purely secondary, supplying Poland and Rumania, containing Japan. In mid-May Coulondre was recalled to Paris to discuss Litvinov's offer of staff talks. But the May crisis intervened and French leaders were too frightened to pursue the Soviet proposal.

On 2 September 1938 Litvinov renewed the offer of staff talks. Coulondre did what he could to support the proposal. On 15 September he wired home: 'I consider moreover that it is necessary to open without further delay the military conversations, if for no other purpose than to exhaust the means of dispelling all ambiguity'.[51] On 24 September, following Chamberlain's meeting with Hitler at Godesberg, Coulondre tried again: 'I consider that we should immediately begin the staff talks suggested by M. Litvinov . . . it is equally important to take the necessary dispositions for the co-ordination without delay of the action of the two countries in defence of Czechoslovakia . . . I would be grateful if your Excellency would send me the necessary instructions'.[52]

That same day Gamelin at last took action. He summoned the Soviet Air Attaché and informed him of French and probable German dispositions. Would the Soviet Union support France? he asked. At 11 a.m. on 26 September the Soviet Attache returned to the French War Ministry with the reply of the Soviet High Command. Gamelin, however, had flown to London in the early hours of the morning and the Soviet reply was telephoned through to him. The Soviet High Command, it was stated, had concentrated on the western frontiers 30 divisions of infantry, supported by cavalry and armoured units. The air force was 'in full readiness'.[53] But Gamelin was nothing if not cautious. He did not mention the Soviet dispositions to his British hosts since he did not wish to raise the subject without prior agreement with Daladier. One small consolation awaited Coulondre. On 28 September the War Ministry asked him to find out if Soviet factories could supply gas masks in large quantities.

France could have encouraged and facilitated Czech-Soviet military co-operation but very little was done. In the first week of April 1938 Paul-Boncour had instructed Coulondre to ascertain the state of Czech-Soviet military relations. On 18 April the Ambassador reported: 'everything or almost everything remains to be done to prepare for effective Soviet military help to Czechoslovakia'.[54] Military missions had been exchanged but no formal staff talks had been held. Some informal discussions, conducted by Fierlinger, Czech Minister in Moscow, had taken place in 1936 and these were resumed on an informal basis in the spring of 1938. Czech and Soviet intelligence services had an agreement for the exchange of information. On 23 April Moscow made an offer of formal military assistance.[55] There the matter seems to have rested until July. Benes, no doubt, was glad to have the Soviet offer but preferred not to offend British and French susceptibilities by opening negotiations. In early July, however, Benes asked Bonnet 'to sound Russia' as to the help she would give. Bonnet agreed with Phipps that this request indicated 'what a dangerous frame of mind Dr Benes was in'.[56] On 22 August, under pressure from Faucher, Daladier at last agreed that the subject of Soviet aid should be seriously studied but insisted that the discussions should be secret and take place between Czechoslovakia and France only. Prague was asked to send a representative to Paris.[57] Impatient of the French, the Czechs tried to initiate staff talks directly with the Soviet Union. A Soviet mission toured Czech airfields. In August the Chief of the Czech Air Force visited Moscow. Though given a warm welcome, he was told by Litvinov that staff talks had to be tripartite, not bilateral.[58]

Certainly in September 1938 there was no question of Soviet ground forces directly helping Czechoslovakia. Poland and Rumania would not have allowed Soviet forces to cross their frontiers. Even given Rumanian permission, the poor railways through the Carpathian Mountains were not capable of carrying sizeable numbers of troops: 'As regards Rumania, the opinion of our technical advisers is definite: the passage of Soviet troops across her territory is without practical interest', recorded a Quai d'Orsay memorandum of 6 September.[59] But this is not to say that the Soviet Union could have given no practical help. Apart from the question of Soviet aircraft overflying Poland and Rumania, the substantial Soviet ground forces concentrated in the western Ukraine might have served to neutralise Poland, enabling Czechoslovakia to deal with her main enemy. In fact Moscow sent a formal warning to Warsaw that the Polish-Soviet non-aggression treaty would be denounced if Polish forces crossed the Czech frontier. More importantly, there is the factor of French behaviour in the six to eight months before Munich. By the summer of 1938 it was too late to start organising practical help for Czechoslovakia and Hitler and Stalin already had good reason to think that France did not want to defend her ally. However the early initiation of Czech-Soviet-French staff talks might have influenced Hitler's assessment of the situation.

Although the French General Staff stressed the strength of Germany's western fortifications as an obstacle to an offensive, it was British and French weakness in the air which many observers considered decisive. On 22 September General Ismay, Secretary of the Committee of Imperial Defence, judged the air situation was the 'crux of the matter'.[60] Two days before, Colonel Gauché, head of the Deuxième Bureau, had said there would be no European war since France could not face the risk of the German air threat.[61] The danger of massive air attacks was taken seriously. Guy la Chambre, Air Minister, took no chances, and sent his wife and child to Brittany in the last week of September. Undeniably, the British and French air forces were inferior in quantity and quality to the German air force. But this inferiority was not as significant as it seemed at the time and afterwards. British and French appreciations tended to discount Czech and Soviet air strength. Combined, the air forces of Britain, France, Czechoslovakia and the Soviet Union were more than a match numerically for Germany and Italy together. Moreover, comparisons of British, French and German air strengths were based on the unlikely assumption that Germany would begin a war for Czechoslovakia by an aerial knock-out blow against the western democracies. Finally, evaluations of the air situation were considerably distorted by the ready credence accorded to the impressions of two individuals; General Joseph Vuillemin, Chief of French Air Staff, and Colonel Charles A. Lindbergh.

General Vuillemin, Chief of French Air Staff, went to Germany in mid-August 1938 to return a visit which General Milch, Inspector-General of the *Luftwaffe*, had paid to France in 1937. The Vuillemin visit was ill-timed. According to the Assistant Air Attaché in Berlin, the visit took place on Bonnet's insistence, against the advice of the Ambassador and Air Attaché.[62] Treated to carefully staged displays of German air power, Vuillemin returned to Paris oppressed by the conviction of its overwhelming superiority. The air chief had never had much faith in his own air force. On 15 January 1938 and again on 15 March he had declared that in a war with Germany the air force would be wiped out in a few days.[63] Daladier testified that Vuillemin was a pessimist by temperament, and he certainly had no great gifts of leadership.[64] His chief recommendation was his first world war career as a flying ace and his pioneering of night flying. Growing public and parliamentary unease over the condition of the air force had led to the replacement of Pierre Cot, Air Minister since June 1936, by Guy la Chambre in January 1938. La Chambre then appointed Vuillemin, thinking perhaps that the latter's first world war reputation would help to restore public confidence.

The political and military significance of the Vuillemin visit was summed up by François-Poncet on 18 August: 'It seems that they (*Germans*) are concerned to give foreign visitors the impression of the formidable force of . . . German aerial equipment and that at the same time they wish to suggest to our compatriots that Germany's friendship is not difficult to conquer and that it is within their reach'.[65] Goering asked Vuillemin what France would do if Germany attacked Czechoslovakia. The air force chief replied that his country was in honour bound to defend her ally. The Quai d'Orsay made a special effort to broadcast this soldierly reply. But Goering also declared that, if necessary, Germany would fight and this statement, according to François-Poncet, 'deeply affected' Vuillemin. And on the subject of the air force general's audience with the German Chancellor the French foreign ministry preserved a discreet silence. Hitler, had turned on his pro-French *camaraderie*: 'He loved France . . . Germany would never attack France . . . he would very much like to visit the areas in France in which he had fought as a soldier'.[66]

The pessimism purveyed by Vuillemin deeply influenced French policy in September. After Munich, Monzie told the German Chargé d'Affaires that 'the most bitter experience of the last weeks' had been the recognition that Germany possessed a 'terrifying' air superiority. Vuillemin 'after his Berlin visit had laid the foundation for this opinion'.[67] On 18 September, just before Daladier's departure for London, the air chief sent the Prime Minister a letter containing 'fresh, pessimistic information'.[68] Vuillemin's opinions were invoked by the Bonnet cohort to justify the abandonment of Czechoslovakia. When in the Cabinet on 19 September some Ministers expressed misgivings about the Anglo-French plan, Monzie and Bonnet turned to Guy la Chambre. The Air Minister then read one of Vuillemin's recent reports. Monzie noted later: 'Whatever happens, it would be folly to go to war'.[69]

Vuillemin's final sortie came on 26 September when in a letter to Guy la Chambre he dispensed a number of gloomy prognostications.[70] No more than 700 aircraft of all types were available for use in metropolitan France, wrote the Air Chief. Such was the weakness of the air force that it could not provide adequate cover for the army's mobilisation or for the evacuation of civilians. Bombing raids on Germany would have to take place at night and would have only a very limited effect on German industry. However, certain features of Vuillemin's letter deserve attention. Curiously, he did not reiterate his statement of 15 March that the air force would be destroyed within 15 days. The estimate given in the letter was that at the end of the first month of war the air force would lose 40% of its strength. Doubtless, an extremely serious situation but not quite as black as previous statements suggested. Also, the assumption of Vuillemin was that Germany would at once launch an all-out air offensive against France. And, of course, no account was taken of Czech or Soviet air strength.

Reinforcing the reports of Vuillemin were the impressions of the American aviator, Colonel Charles A. Lindbergh, whose solo flight from the United States to France in 1927 made him a household name. In 1929 he married the daughter of an influential Senator, Dwight D. Morrow. In 1932 the kidnapping and murder of the Lindbergh's son brought the family a great deal of public sympathy and attention. In the summer of 1938 he paid flying visits to several European capitals. Air Marshal Sir John Slessor, a member of Air Staff in 1938, found him 'a striking example of the effect of German propaganda'.[71] Nonetheless, his impressions of the relative air strengths of the major powers exercised considerable influence in government circles in Paris and London.

After visiting the Soviet Union and Czechoslovakia at the end of August, Lindbergh arrived in Paris on 8 September. At Daladier's request, Bullitt invited the aviator to dine with him at his country house at Chantilly. The French Air Minister, Guy la Chambre, was also present at the dinner. Lindbergh retailed his assessments of German, Czech and Soviet air power and Guy la Chambre discussed the French air force. In his diary Lindbergh wrote: 'the French situation is desperate . . . France is producing about 45 or 50 warplanes per month. Germany is building from 500 to 800 per month . . . One is forced to the conclusion that the German air fleet is stronger than that of all other European countries combined'.[72] On 21 September the United States Ambassador in London, Joseph C. Kennedy, invited Lindbergh to London. Over the next few days the aviator had a busy round of meetings with officials and politicians.[73]

Lindbergh, however, as he admitted to Slessor, was 'not a military expert'.[74] As the Labour leader, Hugh Dalton, put it: 'he had flown the Atlantic, but knew no more about military aircraft than our own Amy Johnson'.[75] His impressions of the air strengths of the European powers were a hotchpotch of fact and fiction. German air strength, he said, was greater than that of all other European powers combined. The best he could say of the Soviet Union was that she 'probably' had 'sufficient planes to make her weight felt in any war she entered.[76] In reality the Soviet air force was numerically as strong as the German air force. And Lindbergh had his own axe to grind. 'The present situation', he told Slessor, 'was largely the fault of the unwise attitude of France, Great Britain and the

United States . . . at Versailles'.[77] Later, he crusaded for isolationism in the America First movement.

The effect of Lindbergh's opinions on the French Foreign Minister was devastating. On 13 September Phipps wired:

> Bonnet was very upset and said peace must preserved at any price . . . Colonel Lindbergh had returned from his tour horrified at the overwhelming strength of Germany in the air and terrible weakness of all other powers. He declares that Germany has 8,000 military aeroplanes and can turn out 1,500 a month . . . French and British towns would be wiped out.[78]

Bonnet, it seems, invented his own statistics and, figuratively speaking, the sky was the limit. Lindbergh in fact had not given any estimate for total German air strength. The impact of Lindbergh's views was all the greater coming so soon after Vuillemin's mission. The British Military Attaché at Paris summed up the situation:

> The Führer found a most convenient ambassador in Colonel Lindbergh, who appears to have given the French an impression of its (*German air force*) might and preparedness which they did not have before, and who at the same time confirmed the view that the Russian air force was worth almost exactly nothing.[79]

Although Lindbergh's instant assessments, fortified by Phipp's alarmist reporting, impressed ministers in London, some officials kept their heads amid the general stampede. Towards the middle of the month Phipps sent in a series of alarmist dispatches. On 13 September he relayed Bonnet's reactions to Lindbergh; on the 16th he reported that Guy la Chambre had said France only had 500 aircraft; on the 24th he reached a crescendo:

> To embark upon what will presumably be the biggest conflict in history with our ally, who will fight, if fight she must, without eyes (Air Force) and without real heart must surely give us furiously to think.[80]

The Air Ministry drafted a sharp reply. If by the phrase 'without eyes' was meant a lack of reconnaissance aircraft, this was not true. France was understood to have 210 modern reconnaissance planes. However, if the words in question, continued the Air Ministry note, were intended to mean that France had no defence or striking force, then:

> in the considered judgement of the air ministry, based on information from all sources and compared with the proportion of German aircraft which might reasonably be expected to be employed against France in the event of a European war, the quoted statement appears to the air staff to be a misrepresentation of the situation.[81]

The sting came in the final paragraph of the note:

> It is not within the province of the air staff to comment on the significance of the defeatist attitude of certain sections of the French public. But it does appear that the attitude is influenced to an excessive degree by misinformation . . . and that this misinformation has been propagated by individuals associated with the air ministry and air force.

On the 27th Phipps was told that too much importance should not be attached to Lindbergh's figures and other reports on German and French strengths. Lindbergh had told the Air Ministry that 'during his recent visit to Germany he saw nothing of the German air force and very little of the industry; his impressions were almost entirely based on what he saw or heard during a visit two years ago, even then he saw only one air force unit'.[82] On the 30th Phipps explained his earlier reports. The figure of 500 aircraft, attributed to the Air Minister, had been given by a journalist. The estimate of 8,000 aircraft attributed by Bonnet to Lindbergh, had not been confirmed. According to Bullitt, Lindbergh had 'not felt justified in giving any figures'.[83]

Appreciations of the air situation in 1938 tended to neglect or underrate Soviet air power. A French Air Staff study of 10 March 1938 concluded that with a total strength of 4,130 aircraft and a monthly production of 450 the Soviet air force was 'incontestably' a force to be reckoned with both quantitatively and qualitatively.[84] But the same study considered that the effective deployment of Soviet air power in central Europe called for 'excessively long, complex and costly preparations'. Soviet aircraft would have to be based in Czechoslovakia since their operational range would be stretched to the limit if they flew from the Ukraine. On 15 March Vuillemin told the Permanent Committee of National Defence that Soviet air support would be 'very difficult' since there were only 40 or so suitable airfields in Czechoslovakia and the Germans could soon put these out of action.[85] Another Air Staff study of September reached similar conclusions. Czech bases were too few and too small for Soviet heavy bombers but, with adequate preparation, Soviet medium bombers and fighters might operate from Czechoslovakia.

Yet, where there's a will, there's a way. Given several months of technical preparation, suitable bases for Soviet aircraft might have been prepared. Rumania was willing to turn a blind eye to the overflight of Soviet aircraft. Daladier estimated that as many as 200 Soviet aircraft had been flown to Czechoslovakia in the spring and summer of 1938.[86] The Czech air force of 500-600 first line aircraft was in good shape and, with substantial Soviet support, Czechoslovakia might have prevented Hitler from winning the air mastery on which the success of his offensive planning depended.

In the 1936 Rhineland crisis, a handful of ministers and senior foreign ministry officials had advocated a *riposte* to Germany. The General Staff had strongly counselled against military intervention. In September 1938 there were no such divisions. Though there was agreement that if Germany invaded Czechoslovakia general mobilisation would be necessary, no member of the government or General Staff urged intervention in defence of Czechoslovakia's territorial integrity. It was agreed, even if reluctantly, that Czechoslovakia would have to submit to the Anglo-French plan for the cession of the Sudetenland. In the end the abandonment of Czechoslovakia was determined by political presuppositions, not by military necessities. Sympathy for the claims of the Sudeten Germans, exasperation with the Czechs, pacifist sentiment, a sense of diminishing power, all combined to render the idea of fighting a European war for Czechoslovakia seem absurd. Indeed, 'the military situation', as Daladier told British ministers in April 1938, 'was really determined by the political situation'.[87] As early as 9 May Bullitt had derived:

> The definite impression . . . that French and British action with regard to Czechoslovakia will be based on the assumption that the ultimate dissolution of Czechoslovakia is inevitable and that the best that can be hoped for is that such dissolution will take place without bloodshed in such a way as to save the face of France and England.[88]

By mid-September the Ambassador was reporting that 'the number of persons who believe that France should fight to maintain her traditional power and prestige in central and eastern Europe has diminished steadily'.[89]

All this is not to deny the importance of military considerations in the making of policy. The military arguments were not simply pretexts for inaction and surrender. No doubt Bonnet was sincere when he told Bullitt on 16 May that a war for Czechoslovakia 'would mean the defeat and dismemberment of France'.[90] Yet the Foreign Minister gave no consideration to the implications for France of the loss of her central European ally. Obviously, too, the military factors were important in defining the long-range frame work of British and French policies. But, having said this, one major qualification must be made. The implication of the military arguments against fighting for Czechoslovakia was that if France had been stronger on land and in the air, and if only her allies had supported her, Czechoslovakia would have been saved. In fact this is extremely doubtful. Rearmament and appeasement were not alternative strategies but different facets of the same policy. Armaments were intended to facilitate a European détente, not a 'Grand Alliance' to stop Germany. The aim of Franco-British diplomacy was the negotiation from strength of a European settlement and additional armaments were seen as levers to successful negotiations with the dictators. Lunching with Bullitt on 3 October 1938 Daladier said that 'if France could do something to strengthen her position in . . . aviation the discussions which inevitably would come during the next twelve months might be carried on in an atmosphere of give and take'.[91] 'If I had had a thousand bombers behind me . . . I would have been in a much stronger position at Munich to resist Hitler's demands, and perhaps we would not have been forced to sign what we did sign', the French Prime Minister told his advisers.[92] Significantly, Daladier assumed that a conference in Munich would still have met. In short, Czechoslovakia might have been spared some of her humiliations under the Munich agreement but a loss of territory was probably inevitable.

Why did the French General Staff accept the loss of such a valuable ally? Firstly, given the constraints of a defensive strategy and the priority given to Italy and the Mediterranean, there was almost nothing France could do for Czechoslovakia. Secondly, the General Staff deluded itself that although Czechoslovakia might have to cede some territory she could still remain a military power. A General Staff note of 9 September argued that even with satisfaction of Sudeten German claims Czechoslovakia could remain a strong ally, blocking further German expansion: 'The main thing is that Czechoslovakia must not be neutralised as a state'.[93] This idea was soon overtaken by events. The international guarantee offered to Czechoslovakia under the Anglo-French plan of 18 September was conditional upon neutralisation. By 22 September the General Staff had abandoned any hope of saving Czechoslovakia as an independent military power. General Dentz, Gamelin's deputy, regarded the annexation of Czechoslovakia as a *fait accompli*.[94]

Chapter 14

'L'Effort Du Sang'

The euphoria which greeted the Munich agreement was quickly replaced by heartsearchings and confusion. Twenty years of diplomacy were in ruins: Czechoslovakia abandoned, the eastern pacts in dissolution, the League in its last agony. Domestic divisions were as deep as ever. Daladier talked of dissolving parliament and holding fresh elections for a Munich majority. Leaders of ex-servicemen's organisations called for a non-party government of national safety. While the Right and much moderate opinion clamoured for longer hours in the factories, the Left felt betrayed and broken. The Popular Front was dead. In the *mêlée* one note of unity was sounded. All political leaders were united in calling for the closest possible co-operation with Britain.

The aftermath of Munich witnessed a new phase in Franco-British relations. In the crisis over Czechoslovakia, France had generally toed the British line. The Czech alliance had been seen as an embarrassing liability which could not be liquidated without British help. With the burden gone, French policy took on a much more self-assertive and independent character. French and British Ministers clashed on two crucial issues: the extent of Britain's continental military commitment, and the attitude to be adopted towards Italy. Italy had been a sore subject since 1936-37 but defence arrangements were a new source of contention. The French, who had hitherto expressed themselves satisfied with the offer of two divisions, began to press in the autumn of 1938 for the sending of a sizeable expeditionary force. And from January 1939 onwards, they demanded the introduction of conscription. London, in turn, sought to pressurise Paris into conciliating Rome — all to no avail. Apart from the Baudouin mission in February 1939, Daladier steadfastly refused to woo the *Duce*.

Chamberlain, it is said, tightened his links with Paris in the last stages of the Czech crisis.[1] Diplomatically, both partners had perforce to work in close harness but of wider political and military co-operation there was none. Although the British pledge of 26 September brought a superficial strengthening of relations between the two countries, it was a decidedly hollow victory for France. The territorial settlement in the east was on the verge of collapse and nothing had been done to prepare for co-operation in war. Gamelin's visit to London on 26 September merely underlined the lack of common defence arrangements.

Nothing was more illustrative of Chamberlain's lack of sympathy for France than the signing of the Anglo-German declaration at Munich on 30 September. Urged to consult Daladier who was still in Munich, Chamberlain replied that 'he saw no reason whatever for saying anything to the French'.[2] That same evening Corbin informed the Foreign Office of the French Prime Minister's surprise on reading of the declaration in the French press. Lamely, Cadogan could only say that the declaration was a 'total surprise' for the Foreign Office and appeared to have been improvised.[3] Next day, Chamberlain sent an analeptic letter to Daladier: 'Closely united . . . I look forward to renewed and continuous co-operation with you in further efforts for the consolidation of European peace through an extension of the goodwill and confidence which so happily inspires the relations between our two countries'.[4]

In fact such was the 'goodwill' and 'confidence' between the two countries that on 28 September a Foreign Office paper proposed a 'self-denying ordinance' with the French on the grounds that:

> The French Government probably possesses a certain amount of evidence of what will be described as a defeatist attitude on the part of certain important sections of British public opinion, and we certainly here in the Foreign Office have sufficient evidence to make the position of certain members of the French Government extremely unpleasant. Any washing of dirty Anglo-French linen in public . . . would of course be very gratifying to the German Government and might do us a very great deal of harm in the United States of America . . . It might perhaps be best if a member of HMG spoke to a member of the French Government on the subject.[5]

The proposal was not followed up because it was judged that the 'widespread support' won by Daladier had removed the temptation for Bonnet and associates to indulge in recrimination.

In a letter of 1 November to Phipps, Halifax defined the object of Britain and France as being 'to uphold their preponderant position in Western Europe . . . They should also firmly maintain their hold on the Mediterranean and the Near East . . . also keep a tight hold on their Colonial Empires and maintain the closest possible ties with the United States of America'.[6] Not only did French leaders endorse this lay-out but they also perceived that the loss of 34 well-equipped Czech divisions had transformed the strategic outlook. Predominance in the west could only be maintained by a greatly increased British contribution to continental defence. Within only days of Munich, General Dentz, Gamelin's deputy, told the British Military Attaché: 'Take care of French public opinion: France does not intend to allow England to fight her battles with French soldiers'. What the French were expecting, reported the Attaché on 18 October, was summed up in the phrase of Gamelin's staff officer, Colonel Petitbon: 'l'effort du sang'.[7] In short, conscription. But it was to take the British government several months to realise that the loss of Czechoslovakia would have to be compensated by a larger British commitment.

'The greatest lesson of the crisis', wrote Halifax on 1 November, 'has been the *unwisdom* of basing a foreign policy on insufficient armed strength'.[8] No special insight was needed to appreciate this fact. Gamelin had made the same point on 12 October: 'we will never be able to negotiate with Germany except from a position of strength'.[9] Yet the British were painfully slow to draw the obvious conclusion, namely, that the two democracies could only defend their European and overseas interests by a close military alliance. The French military were quick to see what was needed. On 23 November Gamelin advised the government that full staff talks with London should be held immediately. He proposed the creation of an interallied military committee to co-ordinate staff talks.[10] Though both governments were determined to defend their colonial empires, no steps had been taken to concert defence arrangements overseas. Again, the French were quick off the mark. On 27 September Mandel, Minister for Colonies, had called for Franco-British planning for joint action in Africa and the Far East. On 13 October General Dentz stressed that overseas military co-operation was just as important as in the European theatre. The sooner preparations were started the better. The Quai d'Orsay, he suggested, should be asked to advise on the timing of an approach to London.[11]

No invitations to staff talks were forthcoming but the British were generous with advice. 'Every opportunity of encouraging her by precept and example to rearm as soon as possible', had to be taken, wrote Halifax, otherwise 'we might have to face alone the full weight of German military power in the West'.[12] In other words, defence was on a self-help basis. The British government remained obdurately insular and selfish. France had to be pushed and prodded into exerting herself lest Britain's security should be endangered. Still, some Frenchmen asked for British pressure. On 3 October Sir Maurice Hankey, Secretary to the Cabinet, reported a plea from General Weygand that the only hope for France was for 'the British Government to exercise early and continuous pressure on M Daladier to set the French defences in order'.

Nor was defence the only area in which pressure was exercised. Phipps reported that his French friends had 'begged' him to point out to French ministers 'how vital it is for French finances to be put on a sound basis, for French workers to work for longer and more reasonable hours than they are allowed to by the forty-hour week, and for a strong line to be adopted in the matter of strikes'.[13] The Ambassador admitted that he was already speaking 'in this sense' to Ministers but a personal message from Chamberlain to Daladier 'would be more effective'. Halifax preferred another of Phipps's ideas—a visit by Chamberlain and himself to Paris before Christmas. Such a visitation 'would obviously afford the best opportunity for speaking on these subjects, both informally and effectively'. In the meantime, the Ambassador was to lose no opportunity in private conversations for 'rubbing in the lessons of the recent crisis'.[14].

The Embassy's intervention in domestic broils alarmed Halifax's private secretary, Oliver Harvey. His disquiet came to a head at the end of October. On 26 October Phipps reported Caillaux's delight at 'the cleaning out of the Augean stables at the Quai d'Orsay'. The 'departure of Massigli and the shunting of Comert to the American department' had given the elder statesman great satisfaction. Phipps was asked for his impressions of 'Léger's activities' in September. By his own account, he refrained from expressing an opinion and reported: 'Caillaux would evidently like Léger to be shunted as well'.[15] Harvey commented:

I cannot help feeling that Sir Eric Phipps is getting into dangerous waters if he lends himself in any way to the encouragement of the removal of high officials of the Quai d'Orsay. Reports are already too current in Paris that the Embassy has been intervening overmuch in French internal politics. . .If now Léger is to be removed, we may find ourselves badly short of friends in the Quai. . .[16]

The danger, in Harvey's opinion, was that the school of Caillaux and Flandin would gain the upper hand and seek 'direct agreement with Germany behind our backs and at our expense'. Halifax did not 'see any evidence of Phipps acting unwisely'. As for the general direction of French policy, he thought it 'inevitable that recent events and German strength' would make it 'more restricted and more defensive on narrower lines'.[17] However Harvey remained suspicious of Phipps and sought his retirement.

Much more serious than the lack of staff talks was the insufficiency of British and French rearmament in 1938-39. Increases in the Territorial Army and in the Air Force announced in October marked an acceleration of the tempo of rearmament but not a change in its scale. 'Acceleration of existing programmes was one thing but increases in the scope of our programme. . .was a different proposition'[18], Chamberlain told his Cabinet on 31 October. The introduction of conscription and the creation of a ministry of supply did not come until April 1939 and then only in limited forms. The most serious shortcoming was the failure to prepare an adequate expeditionary force. Only in February 1939 was a force of 6 divisions authorised.

France's land armaments were still formidable. Vast sums had been expended on fortifications and the army had always had the lion's share of defence spending. Nevertheless, the Maginot Line was not extended to cover the Belgian frontier. Though the cost of extending the Line to the sea would have been prohibitive, a much more determined effort to fortify the frontier might have been made in the winter of 1938-39. The basic weakness, however, was the defensive character of French war plans. A radical revision of strategy and tactics was needed. More effective use might have been made of existing resources. Gamelin urged the creation of a Ministry of Armaments but nothing was done until September 1939. The weak link in French defences was the air force. Since serious air rearmament only began in March 1938 it is difficult to see how more could have been done to accelerate production in the autumn of 1938. Industrial resources were probably fully stretched in air rearmament. But gaps and delays in production might have been filled by large purchases of American aircraft.[19]

British and French ministers met in Paris on 24 November. The main lines of the British position were decided well in advance of the conference. As regards defence arrangements, Chamberlain proposed to take 'a firm line' and stick to existing plans for land forces. France would have to be content with the maximum of two divisions already promised. The Cabinet was told that it would also be 'necessary to make it clear . . . that our Air Force was being built for our own defence'.[20] Halifax 'was inclined to discourage any extension of the scope of Staff Conversations. . .although he might be willing that Staff Conversations should be extended to cover

French assistance to this country'.[21] The chief concern of British ministers was the state of the French air force. Sir Samuel Hoare thought it 'very important' that 'we should make some specific statement to the French Government in regard to their Air Force and that we should not allow ourselves to be put off by generalities'.[22]

Chamberlain did not attach much importance to the visit, regarding it 'as more in the light of a gesture to the French people and the French Government and not likely to result in any great advance in diplomatic relations'.[23] The French, he noted in his diary, would be given 'an opportunity of pouring out their pent-up feelings of gratitude and affection'.[24] The primarily social character of the visit was underlined by the presence of Mrs Chamberlain and Lady Halifax. The 'pent-up feelings' of the French included some boos as well as cheers at the *Gare du Nord,* and Chamberlain was only with difficulty dissuaded from driving round Paris in an open car. In reality, little remained of the enormous popularity he had enjoyed in France in the first week of October when *Paris-Soir* opened a fund for a country house to be presented to him. After a month the fund closed at £ 1,500. The supply of 'lucky umbrellas' in the shops soon exceeded demand, although some Frenchmen continued long afterwards to call their umbrellas 'mon Chamberlain'.

During the official talks between British and French ministers, Halifax's secretary, Harvey, hobnobbed with Reynaud's *chef de cabinet,* Gaston Palewski. What he heard was 'distinctly disquieting'. Strikes were spreading and mistrust of Daladier and Bonnet growing. Daladier was said to be 'drinking heavily and much deteriorated'. A 'defeatist' and 'pacifist' minority favoured contracting out of world politics. France, concluded Harvey, was 'in a bad way'.[25] Doubtless Harvey paid too much attention to Palewski. As Reynaud's henchman, Palewski was hardly the man to hold a brief for Daladier and Bonnet. After another visit to France in February 1939 Harvey reached much less pessimistic conclusions.

The Franco-British conference opened with Bonnet's reading of the text of the proposed Franco-German declaration. The French Ministers were congratulated on an agreement which 'constituted another step towards appeasement in Europe'.[26] The core of the conference was concerned with a discussion of armaments and defence measures, especially in the air. Daladier reaffirmed the guiding principle of appeasement — negotiation from strength. The Franco-German declaration could only have 'real value' if France continued to rearm: 'Co-operation with Great Britain was necessary in all possible ways'. The importance of the Mediterranean theatre was emphasised and Daladier talked of moving the French army against Italy in the event of war. An Axis attack, said Daladier, would fall on France first. Chamberlain disagreed: 'the first blow might well...be struck against Great Britain'. Daladier was ready to allay British anxieties. The pledge of immediate assistance to Britain which Delbos had given in December 1936 still applied.

After this preliminary sparring, the Ministers got into their stride. Wiser after the interrogations inflicted on him in September, Daladier decided that attack was the best form of defence. That there were weaknesses in the French air force, he readily admitted, but the situation had greatly improved: 'France now had 2,600 aeroplanes and was hoping by the end of next spring to have a production of 400 a month with 4,000 planes by the end of the year'. French industry, he added, 'was capable of an output of 80 modern aeroplanes . . . a month'. This attempt to impress was too clumsy to carry conviction. An Air Ministry breakdown of French air strength, prepared for ministers, gave France a total metropolitan strength of 1,596 aircraft. The figure of 80 a month was a patent falsehood. French production figures for November and December 1938 were 37 and 39 respectively. However, what caught Chamberlain's attention was Daladier's forecast of future strength. He expressed his astonishment that within six months France would have quintupled her present production. Daladier retreated: 'he hoped that the figures which he had given would be reached by next spring. . .he hoped to have an important number of aeroplanes by the spring. . .' Chamberlain pressed home the attack, expressing 'a little doubt as to the accuracy of the French figures'. Daladier 'admitted that he himself was always inclined to be sceptical when presented with figures purporting to show the increase of aircraft production. . .In any event France was determined to obtain as many aeroplanes as possible'.

Driven back on the defensive in the air, Daladier switched to land forces: 'he wished to emphasise the need for greater support from Great Britain . . . It was not enough to send two divisions after three weeks. More divisions were needed and. . .they should be motorised'.[27] Conscription was not mentioned. But Chamberlain would not budge. It was two divisions or nothing. The only concession made was an offer of further staff talks within the framework of the exchanges since April 1938.

Although French pressure for a larger British contribution to continental defence made no headway in November and December, a change was taking place in Foreign Office opinion. Halifax, who on 7 November counselled against widening the scope of military contacts, cautiously suggested at a meeting of the Committee of Imperial Defence on 15 December that 'a time might come when the French would cease to be enthusiastic about their relations with Great Britain if they were left with the impression that it was they who must bear the brunt of the fighting and slaughter on land'.[28] The main factor in changing the British attitude was the growing recognition that France could no longer be relied on to act as a shield. Anxiety about the direction of French policy was strengthened by reports of Bonnet's desire to revise the eastern pacts. First reactions to the news that the eastern pacts might be drastically revised were complacent. In early October, Sargent wrote: 'It is curious that it should have taken two and half years for a realistic and logical people like the French to appreciate such an obvious fact'.[29] By 1 November Halifax admitted to Phipps that there was a risk 'that France may in certain political circumstances turn so defeatist as to give up the struggle of maintaining adequate defences even for the safety of metropolitan France'.[30] In mid-November Sargent was sunk in gloom, and urged that France be asked to confirm the pledge of immediate assistance given by Delbos on 4 December 1936. Pacifism was strong in France and there was no prospect of a resolute government: 'for the present we have to deal with a Prime Minister incapable of taking a decision, and with a foreign minister who is completely untrustworthy'. Bonnet, opined Sargent, might be 'sorely tempted to achieve an easy and spectacular success' in a Franco-German agreement which would enable Hitler to drive the thin end of a wedge into the entente.[31]

French pressure also made some contribution to the change of climate. It was known that Corbin was urging his government to press for a larger British expeditionary force. Corbin's Counsellor, Roger Cambon, deepened Foreign Office depression about France. Germany, he told Strang, head of the Central Department, on 17 November: 'desired to separate Great Britain and France and he was afraid that . . . Daladier and Bonnet, who were both weak men, might be tempted further along the path of *rapprochement* with Germany than was desirable. . .M Bonnet was a man to whom it was necessary to speak plainly'.[32]

The subject of British aid to France was given a public airing in late November when the *Times* published several letters over influential signatures, arguing that Britain should never again send a large army to the continent. After such a correspondence both Strang and Sargent considered that there was a real danger of France losing heart and making the best terms she could with Germany. Britain, it was felt, would have to make a major gesture such as the announcement of conscription. Vansittart spoke plainly: 'If we are not going to provide the French with bigger assistance on land than we now contemplate, we are going to lose France and the next war'.[33]

After November France was increasingly at loggerheads with Italy and pressures for a greater British commitment were intensified. On 7 December Bérenger, chairman of the Senate foreign affairs committee, insisted on the need for a large British force, hinting that without further help France would be demoralised.[34] At a meeting of the Chamber foreign affairs committee on 14 December Bonnet stressed the inadequacy of British help, quoting from a report 'by a particularly well-qualified expert':

> It is considered, on the English side, that the French army constitutes a covering force which allows the British empire to gain the necessary time to go from a peacetime state to a war footing, without having to modify too drastically the social and economic organisation of the country. . .[35]

The government, said Bonnet, was determined to oppose this British conception: 'it would be dreadful for the morale of the French army for Frenchmen to feel that they would be alone for so long before having the support of their allies'. A larger British field force was an 'engagement that must be obtained in the course of the next months'.

In a report of 22 December the Military Attaché at Paris analysed the French mood. It was unlikely, he concluded, that France would go to war to preserve the Polish Corridor or to save Poland from paying her contribution to an independent Ukraine. 'In the opinion of the French it is Great Britain who provides the only source from which 34 Czech divisions lost in central Europe can be replaced'.[36] The Secretary of State for War, Hore-Belisha, saw Gamelin in Paris on 1 January 1939 and found him 'far less optimistic' than on previous occasions. Gamelin and a colleague 'both expressed the view that German troops would be on the Alps, and that Italian troops would be in the

Siegfried Line. Hitherto they had regarded the Italian front as a simple proposition because of the weakness of Italian soldiers'.[37]

In the event, however, it was not French pressure but increasing uncertainty about Hitler's intentions which forced the British government to make the first major concession to Paris—full staff talks. From mid-January onwards a large number of secret reports poured into London. The upshot of these reports was that Hitler was planning a surprise attack in the west. Various possibilities were mentioned—an attack through Holland or Switzerland, or a sudden air strike against Britain. Previous reports had all stressed Hitler's preoccupation with eastern Europe. The new threat to the west provoked an immediate extension of British commitments in Europe. On 1 February the Cabinet agreed that a German attack on Switzerland or Holland would constitute a *casus belli* because it would offer clear evidence of an attempt to dominate Europe by force. Full staff talks with France were now unavoidable. 'Hitherto we had avoided very close contacts between our Staffs and the Staffs of potential allies . . . for fear of finding ourselves involved in specific commitments . . .' Chamberlain told his colleagues on the 1st:

> The Foreign Policy Committee was satisfied that the right course was that conversations should now proceed for the formulation of joint plans notwithstanding that these plans would constitute more binding obligations than had hitherto been contemplated.[38]

The British volte-face took the French by surprise. It is clear from the French archives that the government had not received the same secret information as London. On 10 January the Military Attaché at Berlin informed Daladier that the most likely area for German expansion in 1939 was still eastern Europe—Rumania was a probable target—and Hitler would stand on the defensive in the West.[39] A week later the conclusion was confirmed, though less emphatically. When British estimates of German plans were passed on to Paris at the end of the month they were received with polite scepticism. Corbin told Halifax: 'Such information as was at the disposal of the French Government, which he had given instructions should be placed at the disposal of the Foreign Office, led them to feel that the more probable point of danger was Rumania'.[40]

On the morning of 29 January, Phipps handed Charvériat, Political Director of the Quai, a memorandum confirming the information given to Corbin the previous day. In a note of the interview Charvériat wrote:

> Up to now information from German sources has not confirmed any unusual preparations or special troop movements. . . In any case the occasion would be favourable to indicate clearly, from this evening, to the British Government that a recourse to conscription is the essential element for the effective participation of England in the common defence. . .
>
> Our Ambassador at London confirms today that such a demand would meet the wishes of numerous British circles and might, in present conditions, decide the attitude of the British Government. . .[41]

Hoppenot, Assistant Director of European affairs, was critical of the British memorandum. It showed signs, he wrote, of hurried drafting and a certain emotionalism. The memorandum stated that Germany was supporting Italian claims but the French impression was that Berlin was exercising a moderating influence on Rome. Hoppenot pointed out that the memorandum cited only one single fact in support of its conclusion—the formation of a reserve regiment in Bavaria.[42]

On the evening of the 29th, Phipps had interviews with Daladier and Bonnet who had been out of Paris during the day. If Hitler attacked in the West Daladier believed that the 'most likely plan would seem to be a very comprehensive one through Holland, Switzerland and Tunis at the same time'.[43] But Daladier, like his diplomats, was more concerned with conscription that a discussion of Germany's next move. He asked 'anxiously' whether Britain 'would not soon introduce compulsory military service'. Phipps replied that 'this seemed to be impossible'. 'He then expressed the fear', reported the Ambassador, 'that the arming of our small army was out of date ... if any French plan ... could eventually be of use to us he would gladly place them at our disposal'. The official French reply to the British memorandum was delivered on 1 February. It repeated Daladier's request for conscription, although Corbin 'made little concealment of the fact that in his personal view this reference had been mistaken'.[44]

The decision to regard a German attack on Holland or Switzerland as a *casus belli* meant a vast expansion of the projected continental force of two divisions. The British Chiefs of Staff carried out a smart about-turn. Until the end of January, assistance to continental allies had been last in the order of priorities. Now the Chiefs of Staff recognised that 'France might give up the unequal struggle unless supported with the assurance that we should assist them to the utmost. If France were forced to her knees, the further prosecution of the war would be compromised'.[45] Introducing the Army Estimates on 8 March, Hore-Belisha told the House of Commons that the War Office proposed a potential expeditionary force of 19 divisions.

As for the much belated staff talks, various factors contrived to delay their opening still further. Detailed proposals were sent to Paris on 3 February but the talks did not begin until 29 March. The first delays occurred on the French side. By 22 February no reply had been received from Paris and Halifax sent a testy letter to Phipps:

> I find it rather difficult to understand why the French Government who are usually so anxious to push ahead with conversations between our two Staffs should have so long delayed an answer... I trust that they are not proposing to use this occasion to suggest in their reply the conclusion of more binding political agreements... the scope we propose for the conversations ought to be wide enough to satisfy even the French General Staff.[46]

On 24 February Paris accepted the proposals and said that Gamelin was ready to meet British representatives in Paris or London. This reply caused embarrassment in London since the Cabinet had decided on 8 February that the talks would be conducted in London below Chiefs of

Staff level, although it was agreed that 'such conversations should take place at a later date'.[47] Phipps had been told to await the French reply to the offer of staff talks before communicating British views on procedure. The French government were informed of these views on 25 February but no reply was received until 11 March when Paris suggested that talks should begin in London on the 15th. On 13 March Halifax informed Phipps that talks could not start on the 15th since the British Chiefs of Staff were:

> working on a memorandum in which we set forth our conception of the broad strategic problem ... we think the French representatives will find that they will require some little time to study it. What we have in mind is that the French representatives should, before the conversations open, send to London a paper commenting on our own paper.[48]

The reason for this procedure, as Lord Chatfield, Minister for the Co-ordination of Defence since 2 January, explained to the Cabinet was that it 'enabled us to take the initiative, and might avoid our being faced with a series of French proposals with which we were not in agreement'.[49]

Yet the main delays were on the French side. The reason given by Charvériat, Political Director, was the need for secrecy. Interested departments had been consulted orally and not in writing. However oral consultation should surely have expedited rather than retarded decision-making. One factor involved in the delay was France's pre-occupation with the Mediterranean. The British note of 3 February proposed that staff talks should proceed on the assumption of a war against Germany and Italy combined. But what the French feared most in February was a separate Franco-Italian conflict in North Africa. On 6 February, therefore, Corbin was instructed to ask for a statement of Britain's attitude towards an attack on France initiated by Italy alone. Before Corbin had time to act, Chamberlain announced on 6 February that 'any threat to the vital interests of France from whatever quarter it came' would evoke 'the immediate co-operation of this country'.[50] Thus both London and Paris exchanged all-round guarantees. Bonnet had already reaffirmed on 19 December, and again on 26 January 1939, Delbos's December 1936 pledge of immediate French assistance to Britain. Britain's limited Locarno obligation of assistance against unprovoked aggression by Germany was transformed into a general guarantee.

Why, then, did the French delay their reply until 24 February? The answer was that behind the scenes Gamelin and the foreign ministry were engaged in a tug-of-war for control of the staff talks.[51] Gamelin believed that as Chief of National Defence Staff he should have complete control of the talks. Charvériat called a meeting on 20 February of representatives of the Chiefs of Staff to consider the terms of the French reply but the matter was not finally settled until the Permanent Committee of National Defence met on the morning of 24 February. After a discussion between Bonnet, Léger and Gamelin, it was agreed that Gamelin should co-ordinate and centralise all staff talks.[52] In March, the actual quantity of documentation sent to Paris caused further delay.

The document sent to Paris as a discussion paper was 90 pages long, with 430 paragraphs 'covering every aspect of allied strategy'.[53]

However, the main bone of contention between London and Paris was Italy, and the issue was not resolved before the outbreak of war. In October 1938 it was widely assumed that Mussolini's appeal had been decisive in persuading Hitler to call the conference in Munich. The *Duce*, in François-Poncet's words, was the 'key to Hitler'.[54] Talks at Munich with the Italian Foreign Minister, Ciano, and the Italian Ambassador to Berlin, Attolico, seem to have convinced Daladier that Italy wanted to restore good relations. For almost two years France had been without an ambassador in Rome. On 3 October Daladier told Bullitt that 'diplomatic relations with Italy should be resumed at once'.[55] Next day, France recognised the Italian conquest of Ethiopia, thereby removing the obstacle to the appointment of an envoy. The transfer to Rome of François-Poncet, one of France's most distinguished diplomats, emphasised the importance which the government attached to the restoration of relations.[56] It was hoped that François-Poncet would secure Italian ratification for the Rome agreements of January 1935.

The renewed endeavour to reach agreement was bedevilled by a number of tensions and obstacles. One factor was British diplomacy. On 26 October the British government decided to implement the Anglo-Italian agreement of 16 April 1938. Mussolini's announcement of the withdrawal of 10,000 'volunteers' from Spain was accepted as proof of goodwill. But the approaches to Italy followed the established pattern of telling France as little as possible. Paris was not consulted in advance and by the time Phipps was asked to inform the Quai d'Orsay French ministers had read the news in *Le Temps*. Fuel was added to the fire by the fact that it was again from the press that French Ministers learnt of Chamberlain's plan for a Rome visit in January 1939.

Anglo-Italian confabulations aroused fears that Italy was driving a wedge between Britain and France. On 3 October Ciano held out the hope to London that 'once the Agreement came into force negotiations between France and Italy could be resumed . . . general European détente would follow'.[57] But François-Poncet was not optimistic. On 3 November he 'fully' expected Italy 'to continue for some time to come to drive a wedge' between Britain and France 'by blowing cold on France and hot on England', though he hoped 'later on to warm the Italian breath'.[58] Léger, as always, was deeply suspicious of Italy. According to Phipps, when Italy was mentioned he looked like 'a cross between a mule and a viper'.[59]

The main French anxieties were Italy's involvement in Spain and the attitude of a future Spanish government. Italy's presence in Spain was regarded as a continuing threat to France's interests. Even if Italy withdrew completely at the end of the civil war, it was feared that a Nationalist regime under Franco would support the Rome-Berlin Axis. In October 1938, France had an ambassador accredited to the Republican government but no representative with the Franco forces. Britain had sent an agent to represent her interests in December 1937. France had tried to reach some agreement with Franco. When Franco-

Italian talks began in April 1938, Bonnet also opened semi-official negotiations with the Franco government at Burgos. His intermediaries were Quinones de Leon, a former Spanish ambassador to France, and Lasmartres, French Consul-General at San Sebastian. Franco refused to receive a French representative at Burgos until two questions were settled: the ownership of the gold of the Bank of Spain which had been entrusted to the French government for safe custody, and the closing of the Pyrenees frontier to arms deliveries.

On 26 May the French government decided to close the Pyrenees frontier but Franco's Foreign Minister, General Jordana, still insisted that the question of the gold had to be settled before an agent could be appointed.[60] At the end of July Bonnet secured through the French Court of Appeal an initially favourable decision on the gold, although it was to be only the first stage in a long legal battle. In August, contacts were resumed and Bonnet laid down certain conditions for a settlement. Franco was to be asked to accept the following terms. In the event of a European war, Spain would remain neutral. Secondly, Italian and German troops would leave Spain at the end of the war. Thirdly, Spain would make iron ore deliveries to France. As a negotiator, Bonnet proposed to send the deputy Jean-Louis Malvy, Minister of the Interior in 1914-17. In 1917, along with Caillaux, he had been arrested for intelligence with the enemy. Malvy's advantage was that he had met Jordana in 1925. All was arranged when *Humanité* got hold of the news and unleashed a violent attack on the government. Daladier decided that Malvy would have to go as an unofficial emissary. Malvy refused.

After Munich, Spain was still at the centre of French preoccupations. The corollary of disengagement from central and eastern Europe was a new emphasis on the empire, especially the North African territories. The sense of humiliation which replaced the immediate euphoria of Munich rendered opinion highly sensitive to the security of the Pyrenees frontier and Mediterranean communications. Complicating the issue was the fact that the whole of the Left and much moderate opinion still wanted a Republican victory and bitterly resented Italian intervention. The much publicised withdrawal of 10,000 Italian troops in October left Italy with over 40,000 men in Spain, including air force units. On 31 October Bonnet hankered after 'some arrangement' whereby Majorca could be controlled by an international force of the four Munich powers until the end of the civil war.[61] At the Anglo-French talks in Paris on 24 November, Daladier suggested an armistice which might be followed by a 'monarchist restoration of some kind'.[62] He suspected Mussolini of wanting a free port in the Balearics. Chamberlain said an armistice would not work 'without a prior understanding with Italy', and showed more interest in learning whether the French had considered following the British example in appointing an agent at Burgos.

Franco-Italian relations which had thawed somewhat in October were quickly frozen again in November. When François-Poncet arrived at the Rome embassy on 7 November Mussolini had already decided that he did not want a *rapprochement* with France. The *Duce* was even annoyed to hear that some Italians had applauded the Ambassador on his arrival at the station. The Italian leader had drawn up a series of demands: a condominium with France in Djibouti, French Somaliland and also in Tunisia; Corsica to be ruled directly by Italy.[63] At a first meeting on 9 November Ciano made it clear to François-Poncet that Spain was a major obstacle to agreement. On the French side, Jacques Kayser, a vice-president of the Radical party and a close associate of Daladier, stated that no agreement with Italy would be acceptable without assurances of Italian withdrawal from the Spanish mainland and islands.

France was regularly pilloried in the Italian press. This baiting came to a head on 30 November in an organised outburst of anti-French feeling in the Italian Chamber. A speech by Ciano was interrupted by black-shirted deputies with cries of 'Nice, Corsica, Tunis'. The effect on French opinion was immediate and lasting. It was assumed in Paris that the demonstration had been deliberately timed to coincide with the expected paralysis threatened by the French trade unions' call for a general strike on the same day. On 17 December Italy denounced the Rome agreements of January 1935. Affirmations of loyalty flooded in from Corsica and North Africa. In the first week of January Daladier set sail in the battleship *Foch,* escorted by destroyers, for a tour of Corsica and French North Africa. The visit was a huge success. Daladier regained much of the popularity which he had enjoyed on his return from Munich. The quarrel with Italy supplied a much-needed rallying point for wounded national pride. The Italian demonstration of 30 November and the manifestations of bad temper which followed it were particularly embarrassing for the Bonnet brigade. Italian demands struck at the heart of their post-Munich strategy, according to which France had to hold fast to her Mediterranean position, leaving Germany to her eastward drive. In October and November the Quai d'Orsay inspired press had heavily backed the Italian horse, painting a rosy picture of France, Italy and Germany working in harmony.

Bonnet got over the difficulty by speaking with two voices. On 14 and 16 December he made formal declarations to the Chamber and Senate foreign affairs committees that France would not yield an inch of her territory. However, 'in strict confidence' the Minister dropped hints to Phipps that 'after a decent interval' France might consider non-territorial concessions such as representation for Italy on the Suez Canal Board, lowering of Canal dues, a free port at Djibouti.[64] After a Cabinet meeting on 28 January he told journalists that Italy had not been given a square deal and France should not forget that she was indebted to Italy. These remarks were seized on by the French and foreign press. Predictably, the Quai d'Orsay denied that Bonnet had spoken to the press.[65] Daladier took a tougher line than his Foreign Minister. It was noted that while in public speeches Bonnet said that not an inch of territory would be given away, Daladier added 'and not a single one of our rights'.[66]

France looked to Britain and Germany for diplomatic support. In Paris on 6 December Ribbentrop was not forthcoming and reaffirmed Axis solidarity. Bonnet put a good face on this negative reaction, telling Phipps that his 'distinct impression' was that Italian claims would not be 'backed up by Germany'.[67] Needless to say, Goebbels's propaganda machine loudly supported Italy. London was much more co-operative than Berlin. The

Foreign Office agreed that the 'ice-creamers', in Cadogan's words, should be given 'a crack on the head'.[68] Instructions were sent to Perth, Ambassador in Rome. Perth was reluctant to act and suggested that the French were 'inclined to over-dramatise the whole affair and that it would be much wiser on their part and on ours now to let it sleep'.[69] On 12 December Cadogan, on Chamberlain's authority, asked Perth to let the Italians know that their behaviour was causing the Prime Minister 'considerable difficulty about his projected visit to Rome'.[70]

As the date of the Rome visit drew near, French anxieties increased. The French press described the visit as 'regrettable'. Replying to questions in the Commons on 12 December, Chamberlain stated that no treaty or pact with France contained any specific requirement that Britain should render military assistance in the event of a Franco-Italian war. Two days later, Bonnet summoned Phipps to tell him how disappointed French opinion was by the 12 December statement.[71] The French were further alarmed by a leading article in the *Times* of 17 December which, in commenting on Italian claims, referred to 'one or two legitimate grievances'. Indeed, the French government could think of little else but Italy. Asked to advise on French and Italian air strength, Vuillemin reported on 19 December that although the Italian first line strength of 950 aircraft almost equalled that of France (1000 aircraft), the French air force had 106 fast fighters compared to 10 Italian and was confident of holding Italy in the air.[72]

On 26 December Bonnet expressed the fear that Mussolini might 'decide to provoke a general conflagration'. It was essential, he impressed on Phipps, that British Ministers 'should not encourage Mussolini to hope for any concessions from France even of a non-territorial nature'.[73] Though the injunction was immediately weakened by a confidential hint that in time some such concessions might be made. Mussolini should be told, said Bonnet, that any alteration in the status quo in the Mediterranean would be a violation of the Anglo-Italian agreement. In a letter of 27 December to Lord Winterton, Chancellor of the Duchy of Lancaster, Waldimir d'Ormesson, foreign editor of *Figaro,* summarised French opinion. The proposed visit to Rome was 'extraordinarily perilous'. France could not surrender any territory because the logic of the Munich policy meant keeping a firm hold on the Mediterranean and overseas possessions. He had not opposed Munich but supported Chamberlain loyally in the French press:

I may add that at the time. . .I would have judged it insane to oppose Germany's expansion in the east. I even believe that this expansion was rather desirable. . .

Still, continued d'Ormesson, the policy of allowing Germany to expand in the east had overturned the European balance of power:

It makes us no more than a strictly western and colonial power. This evolution can certainly be justified. On one clear condition, however: it is that in this area, at least, we are absolutely firm and unyielding. . .What is certain is that we French cannot retreat any more, we have reached the extreme limit at which the slightest hesitation, the weakness would bring disaster.[74]

That same day Bonnet instructed Cambon to see Chamberlain and point out that the Italian aim was obviously to divide the two countries. Italian policy revealed clearly the 'dangers which threaten England and France when their policies are not in perfect harmony'.[75] In the absence of Chamberlain and Halifax, Cambon left an *aide-memoire* at the Foreign Office on 29 December. British ministers, said the French note, would have to avoid 'the temptation of playing the part of honest broker between France and Italy'.[76] Another possible pitfall was that in refusing to act as honest broker they might give Italy the impression that they were disinterested in the dispute.

In January 1939 while London pondered the reports of an impending German attack in the West, Paris was almost wholly absorbed by the Spanish problem. The great Franco offensive against Catalonia, which had begun on 23 December, rolled forward relentlessly. All was over but the shouting. It was feared in Paris that Italy would try to keep her troops in Spain. On 6 January Reynaud felt obliged to intervene. He telephoned the Quai d'Orsay, stressing the desperate plight of the Spanish Republican forces in Catalonia and suggested that 150 machine guns might be sent in order to avert an immediate collapse. Léger was asked to pass the message on to Bonnet.[77] Gamelin was extremely worried about the whole Mediterranean situation. He warned Hore-Belisha on 1 January of the danger of a sudden Italian air attack on the British fleet at Alexandria. A week later, he told Daladier that the question of Franco-British co-operation in the defence of Africa, especially Somalia and the Red Sea and Persian Gulf areas, was urgent.[78]

On their way to Rome on 10 January British Ministers stopped in Paris for an informal meeting with the French leaders. It was an impromptu affair — without secretaries or interpreters. Chamberlain and Halifax sipped tea in Bonnet's office and tried to talk French. Daladier, who had just returned from his triumphal tour to North Africa and Corsica, was in fine fettle. He could not, he stressed, make any concessions to Italy: 'any French Government attempting in these conditions to make concessions would be swept away'.[79] The French Ministers suggested that Mussolini be asked to confirm the assurances given in the Anglo-Italian agreement regarding the territorial inviolability of Spain and her islands. Chamberlain preferred 'to wait and see'. Then Bonnet urged that the *Duce* be asked to withdraw all his troops from Spain.

Neither Daladier nor Bonnet had any objection in principle to the victory of Franco. Their sole concern was the safeguarding of French interests. Bonnet had told Ribbentrop in December:

> The French Government had no liking for Bolshevism and was opposed to all seeds of disorder...It remained faithful to the principle of Spain for the Spaniards and would have no objection to the victory of General Franco or of any one else, provided this victory was not achieved by foreign aid.[80]

Nevertheless, the Popular Front conscience was stirred by the moving appeals for help from the Spanish Republic. And in the second week of January the Daladier government was under heavy pressure to save beleaguered Barcelona. A foreign affairs debate in the Chamber began on 13 January and it was expected that at some point Bonnet would have to defend government policy. The Foreign Minister's political future was at risk. He had become, as Harvey noted, 'the most vulnerable member of the Cabinet'.[81] On 15 January the executive committee of the Radical party passed a resolution calling on the government to examine the situation created by Italian involvement in Spain.

Bonnet had no joy in London or Rome. At Geneva on 16 January Halifax dined with the French minister and reassured him about the Rome visit. Mussolini and Ciano had repeated that Italy had no territorial designs on Spain. Later, in the train from Geneva to Paris, Bonnet asked Halifax to urge Italy to withdraw another 5,000 men as a gesture of goodwill. Halifax was alarmed by what he heard of French opinion and told the Cabinet on 18 January that France was toying with the idea of seizing Minorca so as to have a bargaining counter with which to induce Italy to leave Majorca.[82] In Rome, Mussolini was determined that his moment of glory should not be delayed by any last minute French aid to Barcelona. The dictator informed London that any intervention by France would be countered by Italian reinforcements. Instead of giving Mussolini the reply which his insolence deserved, London passed on the threat to Paris, with appropriate admonitions. The consequences of French intervention, counselled Halifax, would be 'terrible':

> In these conditions, the British Government requests the French Government not to do anything in this matter without first having alerted and consulted it.[83]

With the fall of Barcelona on 26 January, the question of reaching some settlement with Italy and Nationalist Spain became a matter of extreme urgency. The first approach was to Italy. At the end of the month amid great secrecy Paul Baudouin, director of the Bank of Indo-China, was sent to Rome, empowered to listen to Italian claims and to offer certain non-territorial concessions.[84] Baudouin testified that Daladier approved of the mission but was sceptical of its chances, whereas Bonnet was confident and optimistic. At his first meeting with Ciano on 2 February Baudouin insisted that the talks must be subject to two conditions: only a general settlement of France-Italian questions could be envisaged, and secondly France could not cede any territory or make any surrender of sovereignty. Ciano accepted these terms and in further discussions the same day and on 3 February Italian claims were examined: a free zone in the port of Djibouti, French Somaliland; Italian representation on the Suez Canal Board; the status of Italians in Tunisia; and finally Spain.

Nothing came of the Baudouin mission. By 9 February much of the press, led by *Humanité, Populaire* and *L'Ordre,* was in full hue and cry against the French Foreign Minister, denouncing his secret diplomacy and accusing him of acting without the knowledge of the Prime Minister. The secret of Baudouin's mission had not lasted long. On 3 February Mussolini informed Berlin of the visit and Ribbentrop mischievously released the information.[85] However the banker's visit would not have remained secret. On the day of Baudouin's arrival, François-Poncet was at the station to meet a member of his staff. The Ambassador recognised

Baudouin and was intrigued when the banker did not call at the embassy. The savage press attacks alarmed Daladier. On 9 February, in Bonnet's presence, the Prime Minister told Baudouin that for fear of dividing French opinion the feeler would not be followed up. Bonnet added: 'such is our present position. It remains to be seen whether we maintain it'.

Accusations against Bonnet of conducting a secret diplomacy were strengthened by the news that Count Fernand de Brinon, President of the Franco-German friendship committee, had met Ribbentrop on 6 February. Cross-examined by the postwar parliamentary commission of enquiry, Bonnet claimed that the timing of the Brinon visit to Berlin was 'a pure coincidence' of which he had known nothing.[86] Brinon ostensibly had gone to attend an equestrian event in Germany. Yet Coulondre, Ambassador at Berlin, did not accept Brinon's story that the visit was a purely private one. According to the German record, Brinon 'indirectly and in a discreet manner' suggested to Ribbentrop 'mediation between France and Italy'. In the circumstances, Bonnet's claim that the government was in no way associated with the affair seems highly improbable. Bonnet in fact protested too much his innocence, telling the Chamber foreign affairs committee on 1 March: 'I have not sent on a mission either M Brinon to Berlin or M Baudouin to Rome'. Coulondre complained to the Quai d'Orsay — not because semi-official emissaries were being used — but because he had not been informed and had been placed in a false position.

The collapse of Republican resistance in Catalonia at the end of January brought a host of problems. The immediate problem was the flood of refugees. It was estimated that nearly 500,000 refugees entered France in February 1939. The vast majority were fed and sheltered and then repatriated, although some died for lack of care. Not everyone welcomed them. *Gringoire* published a picture of a burglar and murderer, with a large bag of stolen art and religious treasures, entering France and saying: 'I'll find plenty of work here'. Next there was the vexed question of diplomatic recognition and associated tangles — the fate of the gold of the Bank of Spain, the Republican fleet interned at Bizerta, and the future course of Spanish foreign policy. On 2 February the Senator, Léon Bérard, a friend of Laval, and later Vichy ambassador to the Vatican, was despatched to Burgos as an official 'observer'. His long nose was a ready-made subject for the cartoonists and one cartoon showed Bérard and Bonnet touching noses — an arc de triomphe through which General Franco walked.

On 3 and 6 February Bérard met General Jordana, Franco's Foreign Minister.[87] On 18 February he returned to Burgos as France's official envoy. Further meetings followed with Jordana and agreement was reached on 25 February. By the Bérard-Jordana agreement of 25 February France accorded *de jure* recognition to the Franco regime, undertaking to restore all Spanish property and securities in France, including gold, art treasures, ships and arms. The agreement supplied another instance of the way in which the Prime Minister and Foreign Minister bypassed the Cabinet. In the memoirs Bonnet stressed that the sending of Bérard and subsequent agreement had Cabinet approval. In truth, the negotiations were discussed in the Cabinet on only two occasions; on 14 February when it was decided that Bérard should return as official envoy and on the 27th when the agreement was approved.[88]

On 24 February the Popular Front Chamber of 1936 voted for recognition of Franco by 323 votes to 261. Daladier's hurried recognition shocked Herriot, father-confessor of Radicalism. 'One might almost be dreaming', he told Jean Zay, 'when one remembers who led the processions of 1935'.[89] But the Popular Front was dead in 1939. In May 1939 even Blum agreed with Halifax that France should give no cause to Franco for saying that she was not implementing the Bérard agreement. Recognition was not the end of the Spanish problem. On 2 March Marshal Pétain was appointed first French Ambassador to Nationalist Spain. The Marshal expected to be received by Franco immediately on arrival. The Generalissimo however left him to cool his heels for a week at San Sebastian before condescending to grant an audience at Burgos. The delay in receiving Pétain was designed to bring pressure on Paris to return the Republican fleet interned at Bizerta. The refugees and the contentious points of the Bérard agreement ensured that for several months to come, Franco-Spanish relations were far from smooth. The influx of refugees posed a military problem. Of the 500,000 who entered France, 250,000 were soldiers. The Franco government would only take back 300 a day and Bonnet claimed that it 'required two army corps to guard these refugees, and ... this situation would make it impossible for France to mobilise in that area in case of trouble'.[90]

'All the information I get seems to point in the direction of peace', Chamberlain confided in his diary on 19 February.[91] The French government had other ideas. In mid-January London had been alarmed by the possibility of a sudden German descent in the West. A month later, it was France's turn to sound the alarm. The enemy, of course, was Italy. After the Baudouin mission, relations between Paris and Rome swiftly deteriorated. Insults were freely exchanged. 'France must be spat upon', announced one of the Duce's mouthpieces. 'The French are only thinking about Mussolini, and against him they are absolutely raging', noted Harvey after a short visit to Paris.[92] Such was the obsession with Italy that the Japanese occupation of the French island of Hainan on 10 February was interpreted at the Quai d'Orsay 'as one of the first steps preparatory to the precipitation of events by Mussolini'.[93] Germany was no problem. Economic negotiations were in full swing and Coulondre's impressions were encouraging.

From 14 February onwards reports reached Gamelin of a steady concentration of troops in North Africa.[94] Italy had not honoured her undertaking in the Anglo-Italian agreement to reduce her troops in Libya. By 24 February the Italian garrison was estimated at 88,000 men and the figure, it was thought, would soon reach 100,000. Counter-measures followed, including the recall of reservists. On 17 February Gamelin summoned a meeting of the chiefs of staff. A week later, the Permanent Committee of National Defence considered the African situation. The main fear was of a lightning descent on the port of Djibouti between 15 March and 1 April. Little could be done to withstand a determined onslaught on the port but France could take the offensive against Libya and preparations were put in hand. The military balance was over-whelmingly in France's favour. Italy, the French General Staff believed, could not maintain more than 150,000 men in Libya, whereas France could at once mobilise in her North African territories 441,000 men. The gravity with which the French government saw the situation was conveyed in a cable from Bullitt to Roosevelt. The government and army chiefs, wired Bullitt, 'believe unacceptable demands will be made by Mussolini between tenth and end of March...France may expect Mus-solini to make war at any time after the middle of March'.[95]

The British government could not have chosen a worse moment to intervene in the Franco-Italian quarrel. In a speech of 23 February Halifax explicitly disclaimed any intention of 'mediating' between France and Italy.[96] Yet only five days later London proposed British 'good offices' to induce both sides to refrain from further troop concentrations in Africa. The lever for British intervention was Chamberlain's pledge of 6 February that 'any threat to the vital interests of France...must evoke the immediate co-operation of this country'. Halifax argued that 'anything which affects vital French interests cannot but be of concern to His Majesty's Government'. Phipps was told to suggest to Bonnet 'as tactfully as possible' that 'no reasonable opportunity should be neglected' of improving Franco-Italian relations. Halifax hoped that no reply on Italian claims would be made 'without prior consultation with London'. The driving force behind this pressure was Chamberlain's determination to get 'Franco-Italian conversations going'. Léger chided Phipps: this was not a case of the Czechs and the Sudetens—care was being taken to keep the British *démarche* secret because of the effect it might have on French opinion. And Bonnet's formal reply of 8 March firmly declined the offer of 'good offices'. Characteristically, however, on 4 March Bonnet verbally authorised Halifax to tell Rome that if Italy abstained from sending further reinforcements to Libya, France would not reinforce her garrison in Tunisia.

There is no evidence that Italy planned an attack on Tunisia or Djibouti. Indeed, the Italians would have been very ill-advised to challenge the French since France was in an extremely strong defensive position. Eastern Tunisia was protected by the fortifications of the Mareth Line. And French forces heavily outnumbered the Italian garrison in Libya. By 2 March Leger seemed inclined to play down the danger: 'Italy could not face a war, and knew it...It was, however, highly probable,... that she might risk a raid either at Djibouti or in Tunisia...and then say... "Now let's talk"'.[97] In reality the French were deeply perturbed by the challenge to their political primacy. Arab nationalism was stirring, egged on by Italian propaganda. As Corbin put it: 'the native population of Tunis, and indeed of all North Africa, were watching the struggle between France and Italy; they understood only concrete facts and, if the French were seen to be making too great practical concessions, the result...on the whole future of French North Africa would be very serious'.[98]

Chapter 15

A Free Hand in the East?

On 30 September Coulondre went to offer his sympathy to Fierlinger, the Czechoslovak Minister in Moscow. 'When I entered his study' wrote Coulondre, 'I felt that coldness which penetrates one in a house where there is a dead person. Fierlinger was dressed in black'.[1] Amid the general rejoicings in France Czechoslovakia was almost forgotten. In a personal letter of 1 October to Léger, Lacroix apologised for striking a melancholy note and asked for some consideration for Czechoslovakia to be shown in the French press.[2] In Prague, General Faucher, chief of the French military mission, resigned his post. His officers chose to wear mufti rather than be seen in uniform. Czechs who had served with the French army in the Great War returned their decorations.

Reports from East European capitals told an all too familiar story. On 4 October Coulondre had the 'disagreeable' task of explaining to the Kremlin France's Munich diplomacy. In two sentences Potemkin, Deputy Commissar for Foreign Affairs, summed up the situation: 'My poor friend, what have you done? For us, I see no other outcome than a fourth partition of Poland'.[3] 'Our international prestige', cabled Coulondre, 'has been seriously injured by this crisis and our morale, already shaken, will suffer from it'.[4] From Bucharest on 3 October the Military Attaché wired Daladier:

> Certainly all sympathy for France is not dead in Rumania . . . but French power now seems very distant . . . central and eastern Europe is no more than a ramshackle structure at the mercy of the first German blow. The situation has to be recognised and the consequences accepted or efforts made . . . to try to set up, if there is still time and if the game is worth the trouble, a barrier capable of stopping German expansion.[5]

What was France's reaction to the collapse of her influence in the East? Memorialists and analysts of French policy have greatly over-simplified what was in effect a complex and confused response to the post-Munich situation. Bonnet claimed that while seeking to strengthen relations with the dictators he had at no time relaxed France's grip on her eastern interests. His critics, however, alleged that when the German Foreign Minister, Ribbentrop, visited Paris for the signing of the Franco-German declaration in December 1938 he was given assurances of a free hand in the East. Bonnet, it was said, had bartered away his country's eastern pacts in exchange for a worthless promise of German good behaviour in the West. Not only Bonnet's political opponents but also the British Foreign Office were suspicious of the Minister's diplomacy. The Deputy Under-Secretary, Sir Orme Sargent, wrote on 22 December: 'we are inclined to suspect that Ribbentrop may have left Paris with the impression that Bonnet has given him a free hand to do what he likes in eastern Europe'.[6]

After Munich, the aims of French policy were unchanged: firstly the preservation and consolidation of the entente, secondly the defence of the Mediterranean and empire, thirdly the search for an understanding with Berlin and Rome as a prelude to a European *détente*. These objectives met with wide support among Ministers and officials. Even those, like Gamelin, Mandel and Reynaud, who were, to say the least, sceptical of the chances of agreement with Germany conceded that the effort should be made, if only by way of securing additional proof of German bad faith.

Disagreement centred on the means to be used in reaching an understanding with the dictators. At one extreme, Flandin and his followers demanded a complete withdrawal from the East:

we will settle our affairs with neighbouring totalitarian states by direct negotiation, we will renounce all our traditional ideologies, even the ideology of Geneva...we must have a policy for the empire.[7]

Of course, such opinions had been held for some time but they were now voiced vociferously. One of Bonnet's journalist friends, Alfred Fabre Luce, wrote:

After Munich, there was open talk in Paris of denouncing our eastern alliances...
the *Paris-Soir* surveys of our colonial conquests were, for an informed observer, evidence enough of our retreat from central Europe. Germany possessed in fact "a free hand in the east"[8].

At the other extreme, were the advocates of a reassertion of traditional ties, notably Mandel and Reynaud. The need for an understanding with Germany was not questioned but, it was argued, no attempt should be made to bribe Germany by recognising eastern Europe as her sphere of influence.

Yet what counted in the end was the broad mass of official opinion. By and large foreign ministry officials refused to be dogmatic about eastern Europe. There was no suggestion of abandoning the east, nor of reasserting French interests. It was a wait and see policy, marking time until German intentions became clearer. A Quai memorandum of 16 November 1938 pronounced: 'a waiting policy, very much on the alert...we will not denounce any of our existing accords with Poland and with Russia. In order to revise them we will wait until our friends come to us as suitors'.[9]

Bonnet was much closer to Flandin's standpoint than to his own officials. He contemplated 'some revision of France's engagements towards Russia and Poland', reported Phipps on 12 October. In early

December he wished 'to loosen the ties that bind France to Russia and Poland'.[10] On 31 December Phipps took further soundings. Bonnet declared that the Rhineland *coup* had completely altered the situation between France and Czechoslovakia. Asked if this also applied to Poland and Russia, Bonnet 'replied in a decided affirmative' and 'again repeated' that he would like to slacken the treaties. Though *sotto voce* sympathetic to the Flandin school, Bonnet steered a middle course. In October the deputy Jean Montigny, a friend of Caillaux, led a delegation of fellow Radicals to ask Bonnet to denounce the pacts with Poland and the Soviet Union. The minister listened 'approvingly' and then remarked 'sadly':

> If I was free, I would carry out your policy; but I am not: I would have against me the majority of the Cabinet, led by Reynaud and Mandel, and I cannot count on Daladier, for Gamelin believes that in the event of war Polish military assistance would be indispensable.[11]

One consideration which Bonnet did not mention to Montigny, though it may well have been the most important, was his ambition to succeed Daladier. The septennate of President Lebrun expired on 10 May 1939. It was known that Lebrun did not wish to be considered for a second term. Daladier, it was thought, might wish to succeed him at the Elysée and Bonnet would then be in the running for the premiership which he had narrowly missed in January 1938.[12] It was imperative, therefore, not to do anything which might damage his chances.

Much less easy to define was Daladier's stance. True to his reputation of '*le Taciturn*', he said little and evaded contact when Léon Noel, Ambassador at Warsaw, was in Paris for discussions about the Polish treaty in November 1938.[13] Probably his attention was almost entirely concentrated on domestic affairs. The government had been given further plenary powers and new decree laws had to be drafted to deal with the financial and economic crisis. Moreover, industrial troubles came to a head at the end of November. While endorsing the main outline of French diplomacy the Prime Minister left considerable initiative to his Foreign Minister. Still, an element of calculation may have been present in Daladier's reserve—the more Bonnet did in foreign affairs, the safer his own reputation.

As for the military chiefs, Gamelin in a note of 12 October examined future strategy.[14] Faced with Axis solidarity and *de facto* German pre-dominance in central and eastern Europe, France should maintain close partnership with Britain and defend the Mediterranean theatre. If Hitler re-opened colonial claims, they must be refused. However, Gamelin did not advocate withdrawal from the east. Further German pressure in the east had to be resisted, otherwise France's position in western Europe would be undermined. For Gamelin, the way to renewed influence was through the Mediterranean. The first objective was a favourable settlement of the Spanish question. Once secure in the West, France could then consolidate her position in the eastern Mediterranean and Levant. Relations with Turkey might be improved: 'the maintenance of the Balkan entente' was 'essential'. The Chief of the General Staff had little to say of Poland and the Soviet Union. 'Russia remains an enigma', he wrote; Poland's duplicity was clear and she might already have joined the German camp. The design which had informed French policy since 1937 was still valid. France, advised Gamelin, must be ready to resist the combined strength of Germany and Italy. The lesson of recent events was plain: Germany could only be approached from a position of strength. Consequently, armaments and industrial production had to be greatly increased.

But the French Chiefs of Staff were not in complete accord. On 14 October Gamelin asked for the views of navy and air staff. In a reply of 25 October Vuillemin took issue with the note of 12 October.[15] Gamelin had expressed confidence in France's ability to stand on the defensive in the early stages of a conflict until allied help was available. Vuillemin stated that although a defensive stance against Germany and Italy combined might be possible for the army, it would be disastrous for the air force. There was nothing to oppose 5,000 German and Italian aircraft. By 1 April 1939 France would have less than 500 modern fighters. 'We must decide on the policy that the state of our military forces imposes on us', he concluded. While Gamelin had merely hinted at the need to secure Italian neutrality, Vuillemin insisted that it must be the first priority of policy. The air chief even suggested ways and means of winning Italian favour: 'Perhaps this result might be obtained by the observation of a strict neutrality towards Republican Spain and by a radical break with the Soviets'. Poland would then support France. Germany, continued the air chief, seeing the defection of Italy and aware that France, Britain and Poland 'closely united and determined to resist her' would be less tempted to expand in the East.

The French government endeavoured to find some crumbs of comfort in the Munich settlement. Writing to French missions on 3 October Bonnet stated that the Munich agreement, unlike the Godesberg demands of 23 September, had the 'character of a settlement, concluded under the guarantee of the four powers, the execution of which was essentially under the control of ... an international commission'.[16] In the event the Czechs never received the promised guarantee and German manipulation of the commission ensured that Hitler received almost as much territory as he had demanded at Godesberg.

The German members of the commission were instructed that the areas to be ceded to Germany should 'in principle coincide' with the Godesberg demands.[17] In meetings in the first week of October the British and French representatives allowed themselves to be browbeaten. 'The intervention of the representatives of the German General Staff . . . has made work very difficult. The latter, in effect, assert, in a peremptory tone, . . . that the German Command formulates such and such a demand', wired Francois-Poncet on 3 October.[18] The French Ambassador complained to the German State Secretary, von Weizsäcker. Bonnet instructed the French delegation to secure a frontier line 'which takes account as fully as possible of vital Czech interests'.[19]

In practice, however, the French government was not prepared to put up a fight. Matters came to a head on 4 October when the German team led by Weizsäcker demanded that for the purpose of determining territory of predominantly German character a figure of 51% based on the 1910 statistics should be taken. Mastny, the Czech representative, suggested a figure of 75% based on the census of 1930 and threatened to break off negotiations. As a compromise François-Poncet proposed 66% of the 1918 census. In the small hours of 5 October Ribbentrop summoned the Ambassador and delivered an ultimatum: if the Czechs did not accept the German figure 'before midday' Hitler would 'order the army to occupy the Godesberg line'.[20] Bonnet telephoned fresh instructions: rather than nullify the Munich agreement François-Poncet was to accept the German demand.[21] The Czechs acquiesced with bitterness and reproach. François-Poncet feebly excused himself, pleading *force majeure:* 'the problem was presented in such a way and the circumstances were such that it was hardly possible to do otherwise and . . . sick at heart I had to adapt myself to the necessities of the situation'.[22]

The trend towards disengagement from central and eastern Europe was confirmed by the French government's approach to the international guarantee for Czechoslovakia. Under the Munich agreement, Czechoslovakia was promised an international guarantee. It was agreed that Germany and Italy would join Britain and France in a guarantee after the settlement of Polish and Hungarian minority claims. The Czechs intimated that they wanted the guarantee as soon as possible. The Vienna Award of 2 November settled the Hungarian claim and by mid-November the guarantee was well overdue.

In Paris on 24 November British Ministers explained that only a general guarantee, as distinct from an individual guarantee, could be envisaged. This meant, said Halifax, that each signatory of the guarantee would judge for himself when the obligations should come into force and 'the guarantee would only come into force as a result of a decision by three of the four powers'.[23] Such a guarantee was not 'out of conformity with the letter' of the Anglo-French plan of 18 September. 'It was hardly in conformity with the spirit', quipped Bonnet. France, said Daladier:

> was in a very difficult position. She had guaranteed Czechoslovakia individually against unprovoked aggression . . . He feared that it would have a very adverse effect upon France's position if she were now to say that the new guarantee was subordinated to certain conditions. In any case, he did not see how in practice the situation could arise in which the guarantee would be brought into operation. Czechoslovakia was already in the wake of Germany.

The spark of French resistance was soon extinguished. 'It was essential remarked Halifax, that 'a repetition' of the September crisis 'should be avoided for, in the future, France and Great Britain would be in a far worse position'. Meekly, Daladier agreed that 'practical considerations should be borne in mind'. And, without more ado, French Ministers accepted Chamberlain's suggestion that the Czechs should be asked whether they wanted the joint guarantee as proposed by Britain rather than 'a sham guarantee which could not work'.

When Ribbentrop came to Paris for the signing of the Franco-German declaration on 6 December Bonnet raised the matter of the guarantee and received, in the words of the French record, a 'very ambiguous' reply.[24] Ribbentrop promised to examine the question on his return to Berlin. No attempt was made to jog his memory until 21 December when Coulondre 'of his own initiative' asked whether Ribbentrop had given the matter any further thought.[25] 'Could not this business be forgotten?', asked the German State Secretary, von Weizsäcker. Czechoslovakia, the French Ambassador was told, was in Germany's sphere of influence and a German guarantee should suffice. No vigorous assertion of French interests was forthcoming from Coulondre and in a report to Paris he cautiously describ- ed the interview as no more than 'an exchange of personal views in the course of a courtesy visit', adding that 'it would not be appropriate to take official cognisance of it'.

Obviously the French government was playing for time and a casual observer might have been excused for thinking that Czechoslovakia had been allied to Britain, not France. It had been agreed in the Franco- British meeting on 24 November that both governments would ascertain the views of the Czech government on the proposed joint guarantee. On 8 December Newton was instructed to consult Prague. Next day Corbin told Cadogan that his government had already been in touch with the Czech government but it had 'proved impossible to elicit . . . any definite views on the subject'.[26] Lacroix, however, confided to Newton that he had not made any specific enquiries. Told to make 'discreet enquiries' Phipps learnt that approaches had been made through Osusky, the Czecho- slovak Minister at Paris. On 22 December Halifax informed Paris of British enquiries at Prague and requested a report on French findings. The Quai d'Orsay did not reply until 18 January. In the meantime, on 10 January, Chamberlain and Halifax met French Ministers in Paris. The mood of Daladier and Bonnet had changed since November. They now definite- ly preferred a joint guarantee as envisaged by Britain. It was agreed that there was no choice but to raise the matter officially in Berlin.

But the British and French governments were past masters at prevarica- tion. It was not until 26 January that Halifax instructed the British Chargé d'Affaires to concert with Coulondre in making an exploratory démarche. Coulondre did not receive instructions until 4 February when he was told to join his British colleague in an approach. On 8 February the British and French missions sent notes to the Wilhelmstrasse, stating that the time had come to implement the guarantee promised in the Munich agreement. The German reply, dated 28 February, was delivered on 2 March. 'Tran- slated into clear language', commented Coulondre, it said that the western powers had 'no longer any right to interest themselves in central European affairs'.[27] On 15 March German troops entered Prague. The German coup, Halifax told Corbin, had one 'consolation'. It had brought to an end the problem of the Czech guarantee 'which troubled his conscience and which was manifestly insoluble'.[28]

In his memoirs Bonnet strove to refute the charge that he had given Ribbentrop carte blanche in the East. He wrote: 'so little had France disinterested herself in eastern Europe that on 10 December . . . I directed M Coulondre to inform Ribbentrop . . . of our anxieties concerning Memel . . . it is obvious that if on 6 December I had given Ribbentrop a free hand in the East I would not, four days later, have instructed our Ambassador to make a *démarche*.'[29] In reality, the record was not as straightforward as Bonnet implied. As signatories of the Memel Convention of 1924, Britain and France were under a treaty obligation to interest themselves in the fate of the Baltic port. Alarmed about the possibility of a German move, the Lithuanian government asked Paris to raise the matter with Ribbentrop during his visit. According to the Lithuanians, the French agreed to do so provided the British concurred. In the afternoon of 7 December Phipps was told to ask Bonnet to raise the matter with Ribbentrop. Unable to see the French Minister who was closeted with Ribbentrop, the Ambassador gave the message to Jules Henry, Bonnet's private secretary. Henry confirmed that the Lithuanian government had made representations in Paris but denied that France had promised to discuss the matter with Ribbentrop. It had been decided to make enquiries through Coulondre in Berlin. Unsure of Henry, Phipps urged that Bonnet be told of Halifax's message. He then saw Léger and obtained a promise that the latter would speak to Bonnet in the evening.

Phipps's efforts were in vain. Next day, the Foreign Minister told Phipps that he had no confirmation of an impending *coup* in Memel and had not mentioned the matter to Ribbentrop. But reports of a possible *coup* were still reaching London and on 10 December Halifax authorised the British Chargé d'Affaires in Berlin to join with Coulondre in making representations. The British envoy was authorised to refer to the clause in the Anglo-German declaration of 30 September providing for consultation and discussion of international problems. Bonnet agreed to act and promised to instruct Coulondre in similar terms. However, the following day the British diplomat discovered that his French colleague's instructions explicitly precluded him from reference to the recently signed Franco-German declaration. Coulondre defended his government: 'it was undesirable to expose both the Paris and Munich declarations to the certainty of a rebuff'.[30] The British Chargé d'Affaires prepared a note but Coulondre 'was reluctant to leave anything in writing and wanted to mention Memel quite casually amongst other subjects'.[31] On 12 December Coulondre was told that the Wilhelmstrasse was not even prepared to discuss the matter. Next day, Bonnet explained to Phipps that the French government had 'thought it better to base their representations . . . on Statute of Memel rather than on Franco-German declaration, which might have to be invoked before long on other subjects such as the Ukraine'.[32] On 23 March Hitler annexed Memel. A few days before the *coup*, Halifax had told Corbin that he did not think any 'useful purpose' would be served by repeating the December warning. Corbin was of the same mind. Even Léger, who was thought to be a custodian of France's traditional influence, considered the return of Memel and Danzig to Germany as a 'foregone conclusion'.[33]

With the dismemberment of Czechoslovakia, France's remaining major allies in the east were Poland and the Soviet Union. Of the two, Poland ranked first. She was the only country with whom France had a full military alliance. The historical links between Paris and Warsaw were long-standing. Léon Noel wrote on 25 October:

One has only to recall the services that Poland rendered to France at the time of the Revolution by drawing on herself the blows of the coalition armies to measure the price of her co-operation in wartime.[34]

Nevertheless, Poland's 'duplicity', as Gamelin termed it, in September 1938 caused much resentment in France. Poland, like Hungary, concentrated troops on the Czech frontier and delivered an ultimatum on 28 September demanding cession of the district of Teschen. Daladier even went so far as to say to Bullitt that 'he hoped to live long enough to pay Poland for her cormorant attitude . . . by proposing a new partition of Poland to Czechoslovakia'.[35] Though the Flandin group with their call for the abandonment of the alliance were in a minority, there was broad agreement that the alliance should be reconsidered.

The first move towards revision of the Polish alliance came from Léon Noel in Warsaw. On 25 October he urged a reappraisal of the pact, arguing that French commitments under the 1921 treaty were 'too vague and too wide'.[36] The alliance should not be dissolved lest Poland joined Germany but a new treaty was needed which would change the rigid military alliance into a pact of 'friendship and consultation'. A suitable peg for negotiations, suggested the Ambassador, might be Colonel Beck's 26 May declaration expressing Poland's desire for friendly discussions. Noel had an ally in Gamelin who was thinking along similar lines. The ambassador followed up his letter of 25 October with a visit to Paris in November. Bonnet told him that there was no need to revise the 1921 treaty since the agreements 'contained enough loopholes' to keep France out of war.[37] However, the Ambassador was persuasive and after hearing his arguments Bonnet declared himself ready to denounce both the Polish and Soviet treaties. This was much more than Noel wanted and he counselled Bonnet against such a drastic solution. He returned to Warsaw with assurances that he would shortly receive instructions for the opening of negotiations.

The Ambassador's views clearly met with approval in the Quai d'Orsay. A memorandum of 19 November argued, in phrases taken verbatim from the letter of 25 October, that Poland 'with its numerous and well-trained army', its geographical position and population of 34 millions, was too important for France to neglect. In war Poland would provide 'an extremely precious support'.[38] Abandonment of the alliance would simply drive Poland into Germany's arms. A revision of agreements, concluded the Quai d'Orsay paper, was desirable but some links had to be retained.

Relations between Paris and Warsaw were cool and correct. The General Staffs exchanged routine intelligence information but nothing more. Gamelin and Marshal Smigly-Rydz who had exchanged New Year greetings in 1937 and 1938 omitted to do so in January 1939. On 22 November Bonnet gave the Polish Ambassador, Lukasiewicz, details of the proposed Franco-German declaration, pointing out that the declaration was purely bilateral and would not affect the Franco-Polish treaty. It was said that Mandel had persuaded Bonnet to see Lukasiewicz.[39] In Warsaw, Noel had not received instructions to open negotiations for the revision of the alliance. Under the four year Rambouillet agreement of 1936, Poland was given a further payment of 95 million francs for her armaments. But

Lukasiewicz, the Ambassador in Paris, was under no illusions about French feelings. On 17 December he wrote:

> there is no lack of indications that should France be required . . . to fulfil obligations resulting from its alliance with us, the effort to evade these obligations would be undoubtedly greater than the action towards fulfilling them.[40]

Uncertainty prevailed in the Cabinet. At a meeting on 24 December Marchandeau complained that although Poland was supporting Italian claims against France, she was still receiving financial help. Daladier replied that this raised the question of French engagements. 'But what engagements. . .Is there an alliance?', asked Zay. Several Ministers discussed the issue.[41]

As for the Franco-Soviet pact, the matter of revision hardly arose since most observers pronounced it defunct. Although neither Paris nor Moscow attached much value to the pact, both were content to leave it in cold storage until German intentions became clearer. Lunching with Litvinov at the Soviet embassy in Paris on 1 October, Bonnet tried to brave it out, stressing that France had kept constantly in touch with Moscow. The French government, he said, had wanted a general conference of all the powers.[42] On 4 October Coulondre informed Paris of Soviet anger. The press talked of a British and French capitulation. The Soviet government, he considered, would keep the pact for the time being simply as an insurance against isolation, however worthless it might now seem: 'in these conditions what other course remains for her but to return to the policy of entente with Germany that she abandoned in 1931?'[43]

The break between Paris and Moscow was not necessarily an inevitable one. Whatever French leaders thought of Soviet intentions, they might at least have tested them in staff talks. In a dispatch of 4 October Coulondre submitted a lengthy review of Soviet policy. He maintained that the integrity of Czechoslovakia had been seen as a matter of Soviet security: 'the sincerity of Moscow's intentions, in this respect, can only be doubted with difficulty'.[44] According to Coulondre, the reactions of the Soviet leaders had changed from initial timidity to a surprising firmness at the height of the crisis. On 2 September Litvinov had concentrated on action through the League of Nations, exlcuding *a priori* the possibility of Soviet troops forcing their way across Rumania and Poland. By 23 September the situation had changed and Poland had mobilised troops on the Czech frontier. Poland was sent an ultimatum in which no mention was made of the League. Thus Soviet policy became more assertive and independent. Litvinov's attendance at League deliberations in mid-September, argued Coulondre, finally convinced him of the inadequacy of the League.

Perhaps after Munich all was not yet lost. But a renewal of close Franco-Soviet relations required a diplomatic revolution which French leaders were not prepared to consider. On 18 October, shortly before leaving Moscow for Berlin, Coulondre went to the heart of the matter. The question of alliances was paramount since a situation might arise any day in which they would work against each other. Poland, supported by Germany, might attack the Baltic states, and the Soviet Union, wishing to assist them, might request French aid. Clarification of relations with

Moscow and Warsaw was absolutely necessary. France had to keep one or the other treaty and make up her mind to maintain her alliance come what may. As matters stood, the Soviet treaty was on its last legs: 'I have the painful duty to note that, in present conditions, it has become pointless and hardly offers us more than disadvantages'.[45] Moscow, too, he added, considered the pact worthless and would only conserve it 'to mask its isolation'. France must expect from the Kremlin 'imminent action, without doubt semi-official and indirect' to sound out German plans.

A dispassionate appraisal of the Soviet alliance was beyond France's rulers. Domestic preoccupations dictated that the Soviet Union be kept at arm's length. Rightly or wrongly, French Ministers believed that through the agency of the Comintern the Kremlin was busily subverting the social and political order in France. After Munich, the Popular Front was, in Bonnet's words, 'definitely dead'. He and Daladier, Phipps was told, were determined 'to cut adrift from the Communists'.[46] At the Marseilles congress of the Radical party on 26-29 October Daladier pilloried the Communists. His speech was acclaimed by the German press as if he had been a fellow Nazi. As industrial unrest grew in November, Communists were blamed for trying to sabotage the government's foreign and domestic policies. On the eve of the general strike called for 30 November Litvinov was quoted as saying: 'And now Daladier is finished'.[47] The last thing the Daladier government wanted was a *rapprochement* with Moscow. On 16 December French newspapers published an appeal for the dissolution of the French Communist party on the grounds that it was directed by a foreign power. Daladier was said to have seen the appeal before publication. On 6 December the German Embassy in London forwarded to Berlin an agent's report of Bonnet's opinions:

> A French friend of mine...who is a close friend of Bonnet, had a long talk with the latter in Paris last week. Bonnet showed him reports from the French Secret Service, proving that Moscow had been at the back of the recent strikes... Moscow was not really concerned about French workers but was using the discontent aroused by the Decree laws in order to foment revolution...or at least to sabotage the Franco-German negotiations and the Munich policy... Bonnet further told my friend that...the Soviet Government had only one purpose, which was to provoke war between Germany and the Western Powers ...In conclusion, my friend asked Bonnet about the Franco-Soviet Pact. Bonnet replied that nowadays one allowed such pacts to die a natural death without denouncing them. In his opinion it was already dead.[48]

Estimates of Soviet military power which had been uniformly pessimistic in 1937 reached a nadir in the autumn of 1938. Coulondre instructed his Military Attaché, Colonel Palasse, to draw up a report on Soviet military strength. Without concealing Soviet deficiencies — bad transport and communications, a purged High Command, Palasse indicated the strong points: a well-equipped army, supported by at least 4,500 tanks and 3,500 aircraft. Coulondre sent the report to Paris. A few weeks later, Palasse received a note signed by General Dentz, on Daladier's behalf, rejecting his conclusions and inviting him to be 'more moderate in his appreciation of Soviet military power'.[49] The Deuxième Bureau believed that 'militarily' the Soviet Union was 'entirely impotent'.[50]

The belief in London and Paris that Hitler's next move would probably be against the Ukraine dictated extreme caution towards Moscow. On 20 October Bonnet even claimed that the Russians 'far from seeking to denounce their Pact with France' were 'showing an almost feverish desire to maintain it' since they dreaded 'a German attack on the Ukraine'.[51] Although in 1936-37 London had advised Paris against concluding a military agreement with Moscow, no action was taken to induce France to denounce the pact. On 22 October Sargent wondered whether the French should be told that:

> we consider that in the altered circumstances of today they ought not to continue to be tied by their Russian treaty inasmuch as it can in future only constitute a dangerous liability for France, all the more dangerous because if they did get involved in a war with Germany in defence of Russia they clearly could not count upon the collaboration of Great Britain.[52]

But Cadogan was very doubtful about such a course: 'we are not in a very good position to advise the French to relax their hold on anything that may, in their eyes, give them added security'.[53] Halifax hesitated 'to advise' denunciation 'as the future' was 'far too uncertain'.[54] On 24 November Bonnet assured British ministers that if Germany encouraged a separatist movement in the Ukraine, then it would be an 'internal Russian question'.[55]

The Franco-German declaration of 6 December widened the breach between Paris and Moscow. On 22 November Bonnet assured Souritz, Soviet Ambassador in Paris, that the declaration in no way affected the Franco-Soviet pact. Next day, Souritz telephoned with a request for a full text of the declaration. Bonnet declined the request but supplied further particulars. On 26 November the Ambassador said he had not heard from Moscow. Bonnet took the opportunity to complain about the Comintern's activity in France, stressing that the 'campaign against the government, by newspapers and organisations incontestably supported by Moscow' might 'profoundly alienate French public opinion'.[56] Although Litvinov suspected that Bonnet had concluded a secret deal with Ribbentrop, he had not abandoned all hope in the western powers. On 20 November the French Chargé d'Affaires in Moscow, Payart, acting 'in a purely personal capacity' visited Litvinov. Speaking as 'an advocate of collective security', he asked if the Soviet Commissar 'thought such a policy feasible at the present time' and received the reply: 'we shall probably. . .have to return to the old way of collective security'.[57]

In France the Soviet Union was not entirely bereft of friends. Pertinax in L'Ordre, Tabouis in L'Oeuvre, and of course Humanité and Populaire, continued to defend the pact. Mandel admitted to Souritz that he felt 'slightly guilty' about his support of official policy but said the system of collective security was not easy to maintain.[58] Another minister, Raymond Patenôtre, Minister of National Economy, visited Souritz on 21 December. Describing himself as 'an advocate of close co-operation with the Soviet Union', he had heard that Moscow was on the point of denouncing the pact 'which would be nothing short of a catastrophe for France'.[59] The Soviet envoy denied that his government had any such intention. Another member of the government, César Campinchi, Minister of Marine, kept

in touch with Souritz. Like Patenôtre, he believed the pact should be strengthened.

Such sympathy appeared to have little influence on official opinion.
In a leading article of 27 December 1938, believed to have been inspired
by Bonnet, *Le Temps* reviewed France's treaties with Poland and the
Soviet Union, stressing that both treaties were based on the League Covenant and drawing attention to the difficulties of interpreting the Covenant.
The articles asked whether 'France can at the same time defend the integrity of her colonial empire and risk being involved on the continent in
dangerous ventures'.[60] A memorandum of 29 December, emanating from
the legal department of the Quai d'Orsay, analysed the terms of the Franco-
Soviet pact and concluded that the treaty was virtually defunct.[61]

Despite the trend towards some measure of political disengagement
from the east, there were belated efforts to maintain an economic presence
in the area. On 16 February 1938 the Czechoslovak Prime Minister,
Hodza, had appealed for Franco-British economic and financial help for
the Little Entente and other Danubian states. Lacroix had seconded the
suggestion, reminding the Quai d'Orsay that on several occasions since
1936 he had warned of German economic pressure in the region.[62] At
the London talks on 28-29 April Daladier proposed that economic aid
should be given to Czechoslovakia, Rumania and Yugoslavia. It was agreed,
though with evident lack of enthusiasm on both sides, that such assistance
should be given 'as might be possible'.[63] The idea was filed and forgotten.
After Munich, the idea of economic aid was revived. A despairing telegram
from Belgrade on 21 October may have helped to alert the Quai d'Orsay:

> It becomes more and more evident that if we do not wish to make the necessary
> effort to put our relations with the countries of this region of Europe on a com-
> pletely different footing, notably by directing towards them certain of our pur-
> chases made up to now in America or elsewhere, there will be nothing more to
> do than to leave the Führer to colonise completely this part of Europe.[64]

On 12 November 1938 an economic mission led by Hervé Alphand,
Director of the Trade Agreement division in the Ministry of Commerce,
departed for Rumania, Bulgaria and Yugoslavia. Alphand's brief was to
study the possibilities of French investment and trade. The mission was
composed of two groups: officials drawn from the Quai d'Orsay and the
Ministries of Commerce, Finance and Agriculture; bankers and industrialists. Certain agreements were concluded on the spot and in a report of
19 December 1938 the mission presented a balance sheet of French interests in eastern Europe. An inter-ministerial committee met on 30 January
1939 to decide on further measures, notably grain purchases.

But the lethargy which seemed endemic in French government and
administration prevailed. By the end of February 1939 despite several
approaches by the Rumanian Ambassador in Paris nothing had been done
to follow up the measures proposed by the Alphand mission:

> In Paris . . . although the Rumanian Ambassador has made several *démarches*,
> private and public, industrialists and bankers have been in a state of uncertainty,
> because of the lack of precise and co-ordinated guidance from the interested
> ministerial departments.[65]

Similarly, as early as June 1938 the Polish government had asked the French government to finance through the *Banque de Paris et des Pays Bas* the electrification of a new Polish industrial complex. With government approval representatives of the French electricity industry had talks with the Polish government. However at the end of February 1939 negotiations were still in progress.[66]

Astonishingly, the French government which had shown so little interest in military contacts with its Czech ally in the recent crisis became very interested in the winter of 1938-39 in buying munitions from the Skoda works. Following initiatives from the French Minister at Prague, Lacroix, and the President of the Skoda works, a mission was sent to Czechoslovakia in early November 1938.[67] In mid-December it was decided to spend up to 355 million francs on Czech war material. But the French were too dilatory to win even this booby prize. While Paris haggled over the small change of the agreement, time was running out. In December the Czechoslovak government and the Skoda company, in which the French group of Schneider-Creusot and Union Européenne had a controlling interest, received an ultimatum from Berlin. Germany wanted arms deliveries urgently from Skoda and in the case of refusal threatened reprisals. Schneider said they could not accept such terms but the Czechoslovak government decided to acquiesce and suggested that Schneider sold its shares to a group of Czech banks. The arrangement was to be completed by 31 January 1939. On 17 January 1939 Paris was told that its arms orders could not be fulfilled. Germany had already staked a claim to the material ordered by France.

On 26 January 1939 in a speech to the Chamber, Bonnet affirmed for the first time since his *Pointe de Grave* statement of 2 September 1938 France's eastern pacts:

> So, gentlemen, let us dispose of the legend that our policy has destroyed the engagements that we have contracted in eastern Europe with the USSR and with Poland. These engagements remain in force and they must be applied in the same spirit in which they were conceived.[68]

Poland was singled out for a special word of friendship. This declaration did not signify a fundamental change of course. Relations with Warsaw and Moscow remained cool and distant. The phrase 'these engagements remain in force and they must be applied in the same spirit in which they were conceived' was much less reassuring than it sounded. The opinion of Bonnet's advisers was that the Franco-Soviet pact depended entirely upon the League of Nations Covenant. Since the League had virtually collapsed it could be argued that the pact was also finished.[69] Hence for Bonnet to say that the pact had to be 'applied' in the 'spirit' in which it was conceived was really saying very little.

Nevertheless, Ribbentrop took umbrage and scolded France for forgetting her place in Europe. In defence, Bonnet explained that the speech had been mainly intended for domestic consumption. The domestic situation was in fact the key to the parliamentary declaration. The Foreign Minister was faced with growing criticism. In January, Bullitt, who had just returned to Paris after three months in the United States, cabled:

> Both the British and Polish Ambassadors and several French friends with whom
> I have talked have spoken to me with regard to the growing hostility to Bonnet...
> it appears that after Munich Daladier reaped all the thankfulness while Bonnet
> reaped all the rage.[70]

On 14 December, in the Chamber foreign affairs committee, Bonnet had
faced a barrage of criticism and calls for an early debate on foreign policy.
Bonnet himself testifies to the movement of opinion. Two former friends,
E J Bois, editor of *Le Petit Parisien,* and George Boris, also a journalist,
quarrelled with him over his post-Munich policy.[71] Given his ambitions
for the premiership, it was inevitable he should trim his sails somewhat.
Another factor was a revival of interest in Poland. In December, Colonel
Beck, Polish Foreign Minister, went on holiday to Monte Carlo. Returning
to Warsaw he broke his journey not in Paris but at Berchtesgaden for a
meeting with Hitler on 5 January. Lukasiewicz informed Beck: 'a large
section of the press reproached Minister Bonnet for not having taken the
opportunity of meeting you'.[72]

Bonnet's personal views about the Polish alliance remained unchanged.
On 20 January Noel returned to Paris to ask why no steps had been taken
to revise the alliance. Bonnet assured the ambassador that his views were
the same as in November but it was necessary to wait a while because
Ribbentrop's December visit was too recent. If he acted immediately he
would be accused of playing Germany's game. In the meantime Bonnet
took care to give Berlin advance notice of his impending parliamentary
declaration. On 24 January he read out to Welczeck excerpts from the
draft of his speech, emphasising that the reaffirmation of interest in eastern
Europe 'had been framed for domestic consumption'.[73] To guard against
any possible misunderstanding in Berlin, Bonnet instructed Noel to see
Ribbentrop during the latter's Warsaw visit of 26-27 January. Noel was to
stress the importance which France attached to the Franco-German
declaration of 6 December.[74]

Ribbentrop, however, was not mollified. Welczeck was instructed to
express 'astonishment' that in the foreign affairs debate Bonnet talked of
'fostering and...extending French friendships in eastern and central
Europe'.[75] Welczeck raised the matter in an interview with Bonnet on
11 February. The German and French records of this conversation are
completely at variance.[76] The subjects covered in the conversation are
the same in both records but Bonnet, according to his own notes, defended
the stand he had taken in the Chamber on 26 January, whereas Welczeck
records the minister apologising for the public statement. So Bonnet, by
his own account, refused to accept Ribbentrop's criticism:

> France had never accepted that her friendships or alliances should be impaired
> in any way...we wished very sincerely to be at peace with Germany...but we
> would not accept any compulsion or *coup.*

But Welczeck reported the minister as saying:

> Things were often said during a foreign affairs debate...which were obviously
> designed for domestic consumption...If a French foreign Minister, against the

storm and wave of opposition, substantiated our claims to the Sudeten German territory...and then drew his own conclusions privately from the changed situation in Central Europe, he could not be expected to withdraw all along the line when facing the Chamber...

Parliamentary pressures over, Bonnet opened talks with Lukasiewicz for the revision of the 1921 alliance. On 19 February Lukasiewicz brought Beck's answer. The 1921 alliance was fundamental to Franco-Polish relations: 'there can be no question of weakening it'.[77] There was scope, added Beck, for clarifying and strengthening the military agreements and he was ready to open talks to this end. No further progress was made until Franco-Polish staff talks were held in May.

By February Franco-Soviet relations seemed permanently frozen. Litvinov dismissed Bonnet as 'a natural capitulator' and Daladier declared that he had 'no confidence in any statement or promise which might be made by the Russians'.[78] Still, Moscow made one attempt to break the ice. On 10 February Litvinov wrote to Souritz to say that the Soviet Union was ready to enter into real co-operation with the French government.[79] It is not known whether Souritz communicated the message to Bonnet. Certainly the Ambassador had no reason to trust the French Minister. 'In private circles', he wrote, 'Bonnet has not concealed the fact that without a sacrifice in the east Germany cannot be pacified and an outlet for German expansion must be created'.[80] Matters might have been helped by the presence of a French ambassador in Moscow but Coulondre's successor, Paul-Emile Naggiar, did not present his credentials until early February and then returned to France.

The distinctive trait of French diplomacy in the six months from Munich to Prague was ambiguity. Bonnet was strongly suspected of having given Germany a free hand in the east. Despite the Minister's wish *in petto* to denounce the Polish and Soviet pacts, they were maintained and even reaffirmed. None the less German predominance in central Europe was tacitly recognised. There was no fundamental objection to German expansion provided it was limited, gradual and peaceful. The drift of French policy was clear but there was no hasty withdrawal from the East. On the contrary, efforts were made to reassert economic influence. What was the reason for this apparent shilly-shallying? Some confusion and indecision was inevitable since France needed time to take stock of the post-Munich scene. The ambiguity of French policy was also a response to the uncertainty which shrouded Germany's intentions. Until Hitler's designs took shape Paris postponed major policy decisions.

Above all, however, the avoidance of firm and final decisions about eastern Europe was dictated by the need to bargain with Germany. France's anxieties were concentrated on the Mediterranean throughout the winter and spring. It was thought that as a result of the Franco-German declaration of 6 December Germany might be induced to counsel moderation in Rome. In Paris on 6-7 December Ribbentrop was not forthcoming but the French did not abandon hope. The first hint of bargaining came in a talk between Coulondre and Weizsäcker on 21 December:

You are expecting that our recent accord will induce France to show understanding for the exercise of your activity in certain European regions. At least it is necessary that our opinion should not have the impression that the sources of direct conflict have simply been diverted elsewhere. If it finds you behind the Italian claims, which you know to be unacceptable to us, it will think there has been a misdeal and the work begun will be compromised.[81]

The theme of give and take was maintained. When on 6 February Ribbentrop complained to Coulondre about Bonnet's Chamber speech of 26 January the French Ambassador replied:

France does not intend to renounce her friends and interests in any part of the continent; a great European power, she will remain present in Europe...but I had to repeat that if Berlin wished France to show proof of understanding for vital German interests, it was necessary that reciprocity should be admitted and practised; this mutual understanding would be the best safeguard for Franco-German relations.[82]

Chapter 16

Penguins and Porpoises

In the eleven months preceding the outbreak of the Second World War, the Daladier government made a final effort to come to terms with the hereditary enemy across the Rhine. The Rhineland, *Anschluss,* Munich had interrupted but not changed the long-range objective of French statesmen—the search for agreement with Germany. Relief at a hairbreadth escape from war in September 1938 brought a determination to work all the harder for a Franco-German settlement. Whatever feelings of shame Daladier may have had on his return from Munich in the afternoon of 30 September were not voiced when he met his Cabinet at 5.30 p.m. that day. 'He was convinced that contacts with Hitler and Goering would not be without influence. Both wished to come to Paris; Hitler wanted to visit the *Louvre'.*[1] That same day François-Poncet wired: 'the personal contacts between the four heads of government have been full of cordiality. This proves that ideological antagonism does not necessarily lead to war. The Munich conference suggests therefore that there is still room for a European concert'.[2]

The appeasement of Germany in 1938-39 was the culmination of eighteen years of intermittent attempts to achieve an understanding. After the war of 1870 the Germanophobe tradition dominated French thinking. On both sides of the Rhine chauvinists vied with each other in exaggerating differences of temperament and culture which were said to make any reconciliation impossible. Anatole France caricatured this mentality:

You don't like the Porpoises then?
We hate them.
For what reason do you hate them?
Need you ask? Are not the Porpoises neighbours of the Penguins?
Of course.
Well that is why the Penguins hate the Porpoises.[3]

The armistice of November 1918 seemed to augur a change of heart. It was thought that the holocaust of the trenches had destroyed many of the old hatreds. Some observers believed that the exhaustion of post-Versailles Europe made the Franco-German quarrel irrelevant. A Franco-German understanding, noted André Gide, was 'indispensable in the present situation of Europe'.[4] The internationalist school in French thinking, which the writers Henri Barbusse and Romain Rolland had kept alive, challenged the deep-seated Germanophobe sentiment. In 1919-20 Barbusse's 'League of International Solidarity for the triumph of the international cause' won support from French and foreign intellectuals, notably from Georges Duhamel, Anatole France, Jules Romains, E.D. Morel, H. G. Wells and Stefan Zweig. In the postwar decade numerous writers and academics worked for Franco-German *rapprochement.*

But Franco-German relations did not exist in a void. The peace divided the two nations almost as much as the war had done. Of the clauses of the Versailles Treaty, the most contentious was the obligation imposed on Germany to pay reparations. That Germany should pay some reparations was reasonable in the circumstances but the amount demanded—three times the country's annual income—was beyond her capacity to pay. Yet it would be wrong to see the French Prime Minister, Raymond Poincaré, as a Shylock figure, insisting on the letter of the law. French policy in the reparations issue cannot be separated from that of her allies. The United States, by insisting on the payment of allied war debts, forced the allies in turn to demand reparations. The need to survive led the governments of the Weimar Republic to propose a policy of 'fulfilment'—an effort to co-operate with the allies. The consequences of this policy were disastrous for Franco-German relations. Germany's leaders, by professing the impossible, entangled themselves in a web of contradictions. Internally, the association of fulfilment with parliamentary government harmed the newly-created Republic. Externally, the fulfilment policy fostered lies and evasions. The classic example of this deception was the clandestine rearmament of Germany in the 1920s. Weimar leaders professed their willingness to work with the allies while secretly flouting the disarmament clauses of the Versailles Treaty.

British Ministers were eager to promote a Franco-German dialogue. Britain wanted to see in France evidence 'of a sincere desire gradually to improve relations', declared Austen Chamberlain in January 1925.[5] The French Ambassador, de Fleuriau, confided that although the French government 'was compelled to move cautiously for public opinion . . . was not yet prepared for any sort of pact with Germany', 'small but influential circles' were moving towards an agreement.[6] Understandably, the strongest emotion among French statesmen, as Austen Chamberlain testified, was one of distrust. From Geneva in March 1925 he reported that Briand, Herriot, Poincaré and Paul-Boncour 'all . . . distrust Germany to the point of regarding it almost as an insult to suggest that they should make a pact with her'.[7]

The 'small but influential circles', of which de Fleuriau spoke, set up an organisation for Franco-German co-operation. In 1926, Emil Mayrisch, a Luxembourg steel magnate, established the *Comité Franco-Allemand de Documentation et d'Information.*[8] The committee was divided into French and German sections which sponsored cultural exchanges and acted as information centres. The purpose of the committee was to guide public opinion in both countries towards an *entente.* The list of founding members read like a Franco-German *Who's Who.* On the French side: Count Wladimir d'Ormesson, a well-known publicist, René Duchemin, president of the *Etablissements Kuhlmann,* one of the major French chemical concerns, Henri de Peyrimhoff, a leading member of the coal-owners association (*comité des houillères*), Lucien Romier, historian and journalist, André Siegfried, sociologist. On the German side: the novelist E R Curtius, also Franz von Papen, politician and future chancellor and von Stauss, president of the *Deutsche Bank.* The first secretary general was Pierre Viénot, a Socialist deputy. Viénot married the daughter of Emil Mayrisch and held office as Under-Secretary of State for Foreign Affairs in Blum's Popular Front government in June 1936. The *Comité Franco-Allemand* had the patronage of Marshal Lyautey, proconsul of French Morocco from 1912 to 1925. The blessing of such a distinguished Lorrainer whose family home had been burnt by the Germans in 1914 was of great assistance in launching the new body.

Two events in the mid-1920s were hailed at the time as marking the beginning of an *entente* between Berlin and Paris: the Treaty of Locarno of 1 December 1925 and the private meeting between the German Foreign Minister, Stresemann, and the French Foreign Minister, Briand, at Thoiry on 17 September 1926. But the so-called spirit of Locarno was not proof against German revisionism. For Stresemann, Locarno was the first step towards the revision of the peace treaties; for Briand, 'the first step on the road to compliance'.[9] Or as René Massigli of the Quai d'Orsay quipped: 'il y a trois choses, le Locarno spirit, l'esprit de Locarno, et le Locarnogeist'.[10] Following Germany's admission to the League, Briand and Stresemann met at Thoiry on 17 September. Over lunch they discussed a scheme for the settlement of Franco-German differences. The scheme provided for the return of the Saar to Germany without the plebiscite imposed by the Treaty of Versailles. The Rhineland was to be completely evacuated within a year and in return France would receive reparations payments in advance of the sums already agreed. Germany would raise money by the sale of German railway bonds. The scheme was a non-starter, doomed by its 'grandeur and impracticality'.[11]

Disillusionment and recriminations followed Locarno and Thoiry. Some gains there were but to list the instances of Franco-German economic co-operation — conclusion of a steel agreement between Germany, France, Belgium, Luxembourg and the Saar in 1926; the signing of a Franco-German commercial treaty in 1927 — is to chronicle small beer. Cultural and political contacts multiplied: Thomas Mann lectured in Paris; Georges Duhamel and Jules Romains spoke in Berlin. In 1927 a German delegation attended the *Semaine sociale* at the Institut Catholique in Paris, where the rector Mgr Baudrillart was a keen advocate of Franco-German amity.[12] In the same year Lucien Romier, the historian and a member of the editorial board of *Figaro,* met German bankers and industrialists in Luxembourg. He observed 'a strong desire to co-operate with Frenchmen, especially in our colonies'.[13] The Senator Henry Lémery, a former minister, was particularly interested in colonial co-operation in North Africa. He obtained Briand's permission to sound German opinion.[14] Promising though some of these exchanges were, they were essentially tactical advances and could not hide the wider strategic failure. The first postwar decade ended in disappointment.

Still, economic collaboration seemed to offer a short cut to a political settlement. In September 1931 the French Prime Minister, Pierre Laval, and his Foreign Minister, Aristide Briand, journeyed to Berlin, the first official visit of French leaders since the Congress of Berlin in 1878. Their visit resulted in the establishment of a Franco-German economic commission. In order to foster economic ties, André François-Poncet, a representative of French iron and steel interests, was appointed Ambassador in Berlin. In his first press conference, the new Ambassador spoke enthusiastically of an alliance between French and German industry. Whether the Germans were genuinely interested in French economic initiatives is very doubtful. According to one historian: 'all the talk of friendship with France was hardly more than an effort to induce the French to grant a credit'.[15] The economic commission had only a short life because political understanding was so patently lacking. The gap between French and German attitudes was revealed during the Berlin visit when Laval briefly alluded to a compromise settlement of German-Polish disputes. The German Chancellor, Brüning, 'brusquely cut him short with the observation that "in this national question, in which the whole of Germany—regardless of party—was happily of one mind, a compromise was completely out of the question" '.[16]

Once bitten, twice shy. At the Lausanne conference in June 1932 Chancellor von Papen presented the French Prime Minister, Herriot, with proposals for an understanding.[17] Germany asked for the ending of reparations and equality of rights in armaments. In exchange the French were offered a Franco-German customs union and economic co-operation in central and eastern Europe. As additional bait, von Papen offered Franco-German staff talks. Herriot gave the proposals a cool reception, considering that in return for concrete concessions France was being offered only vague and tentative compensations. Moreover, the French leader disliked the anti-Soviet emphasis which von Papen gave to the scheme.

While the statesmen deliberated, the industrialists tried to find common ground.[18] In 1932-33 industrialists from Germany, France, Belgium and Luxembourg held two conferences. Discussions ranged over the Polish Corridor, armaments, reparations, mandates and colonial co-operation. But a political settlement, as the businessmen recognised, was a prerequisite for an economic entente. And both Berlin and Paris were unwilling to conclude a political accord.

Hitler's coming to power in January 1933 did not destroy hopes of agreement; on the contrary, once Germany began to rearm, agreement became all the more necessary. Commentators on French policy have wondered how French leaders, having read *Mein Kampf,* 'could . . . seriously believe that Hitler would allow even a complacent France to exist as a first class power'.[19] Apart from a small minority who read German, the French public did not have the opportunity to read the Führer *in toto.* A full translation was published in 1934 but the German publishers *Eher Verlag* took legal action through the French courts to secure its suppression. An abridged translation was not published until the summer of 1938 and a complete version was not available until after the Second World War. Even in parliamentary circles *Mein Kampf* was at first little known. In 1934 the deputy Franklin-Bouillon 'made a great impression merely by reading out, word for word, the famous passages about Franco-German relations'.[20]

More importantly, German propaganda took great care to counteract any unfavourable impressions created by a reading of *Mein Kampf*. The *leit-motiv* of the numerous interviews which Hitler accorded to French publicists in the five years from 1933 to 1938 was his desire for friendship with France. Lest some Frenchmen might have been swayed by the enmity for France avowed in *Mein Kampf*, it was explained that the work had been written 'under the influence of defeat in war and of the Ruhr episode . . . it was occasioned by the internal political struggle. The important thing was not the words printed at the time, but the actual policy of the Führer and Chancellor'.[21] Fortunately not everyone swallowed the official gloss. In November 1933, Roger Martin du Gard received from a German professor who was a stranger to him a brochure giving texts of recent conciliatory speeches by Hitler, prefaced by Goebbels. His friend André Gide urged him to write in reply: 'whilst Hitler does not deny his *Mein Kampf* declarations, all his subsequent statements are suspect'.[22]

As the Third Reich consolidated itself, the *Comité Franco-Allemand* gradually faded into obscurity, its place being taken by a new agency— the *Comité France-Allemagne,* founded in 1933 by the journalist Count Fernand de Brinon. The new Franco-German committee focussed its action upon fostering exchanges of youth and ex-servicemen. Two leaders of ex-servicemen's associations, Jean Goy and Henri Pichot, were members of the committee. A constant theme of Nazi propaganda was the Franco-German community of arms: if only the veterans of Verdun could come together, it was suggested, then all would be well. The French Foreign Minister, Delbos, appeared to accept this line of argument. In December 1937 he declared: 'Frenchmen and Germans were the best soldiers in the world; if they agreed with one another, that would make the greatest impression on everyone else'.[23] But the *poilus* did not believe the leopard could change his spots. Leaders of a German ex-servicemen's group visiting Paris found that 'the great fear of Germany was quite obviously the determining element in the attitude of the French organisations'.[24]

In working for an agreement with Germany in 1938, Daladier and Bonnet merely followed up the initiatives of their immediate pre-decessors—Blum, Delbos and Chautemps. Chamberlain, however, had outdistanced his French partners. In the early morning of 30 September Chamberlain and Hitler signed the Anglo-German declaration, stating that Anglo-German relations were 'of the first importance for the two countries and for Europe' and promising that the 'method of consultation' should be followed in any questions concerning the two countries.[25] After reading of the declaration in the French evening press of the 30th, Daladier and Bonnet at once conferred and in all probability decided there and then that France should have a similar agreement.

What Chamberlain had achieved in a few minutes conversation in Munich was to take the French ministers over two months of negotiation.

In the first week of October there were no difficulties on the German side. The mood in Berlin was extremely favourable to France. On 4 October François-Poncet underlined the fact that at Munich, Ribbentrop, and especially Goering, had gone to great lengths to show esteem for Daladier.[26] The German press, continued the French Ambassador, had also stressed Germany's friendship for France, insisting that there was no subject which need cause disputes. Goering's phrase: 'with a man like M Daladier it is possible to do business' was being widely repeated. German commentators argued that France had only to draw the necessary conclusions from Munich. François-Poncet's own conclusion was that conciliation and armaments should go hand in hand. No possibility of an understanding with the dictators should be neglected but at the same time the democracies had to rearm and eliminate internal divisions.

Yet it was not until François-Poncet met Hitler on 18 October that a Franco-German declaration assumed shape and form. There were a number of reasons for the delay. In early October, the French had not made up their minds about the kind of agreement they wanted. On 3 October Bonnet talked in general terms about the 'initiation of immediate conversations with Germany on financial, economic and disarmament questions'.[27] A Quai d'Orsay paper of 5 October concluded that though the negotiation of a Franco-German declaration of non-aggression did not present any problems, it would be better to try to restart conversations between London, Paris and Berlin for a new western pact.[28] Before opening negotiations with France, Hitler decided to seek the approval of Mussolini. In the second week of October the Chancellor sent his special envoy, Prince Philip of Hesse, to seek the Duce's consent.[29] It seems likely, too, that there was an element of rivalry between Goering and Ribbentrop. Initial soundings for an agreement seem to have been handled by Goering without Ribbentrop's knowledge.[30]

The first indication of what France envisaged came on 13 October when François-Poncet sketched in broad outline the shape of an agreement. It comprised three points: a non-aggression pact, a consultative undertaking, and some regulation of currency matters. The French had decided to settle in the meantime for a bilateral pact. It was clear that a new western security pact in place of Locarno would require months of negotiation. The French government proposed that Ribbentrop should come to Paris for the signing of the agreement. At this stage Berlin did not commit itself. On 13 October the German State Secretary, von Weizsäcker, simply took note of the French proposals.

François-Poncet's transfer to Rome had been announced and on 18 October the Ambassador took leave of Hitler at Berchtesgaden.[31] Except where England was concerned, reported François-Poncet, Hitler was 'calm, moderate and conciliatory'. The French suggestion of a non-aggression pact was not acceptable and was replaced by a proposal for a written recognition of the Franco-German frontier. The German Chancellor was also willing to sign 'an undertaking to hold mutual consultations' but on economic and financial matters he was distinctly lukewarm. The conversation ranged widely, covering disarmament, a new western pact, and a currency settlement. Von Ribbentrop, who was present, was instructed to formulate firm proposals and future negotiations were placed completely in his hands.

What were France's motives in working for an accord? French diplomacy has been seen as mere expediency, a desire to gain time for rearmament by diverting Hitler to the east.[32] Doubtless, the agreement was in part intended to reassure Germany that her peaceful expansion in the East would not be opposed. At the same time French statesmen were not entirely opportunists. When on 7 November Bonnet told Welczeck that an agreement would mean 'the fulfilment of his life's dream' he was not altogether guilty of hyperbole.[33] The main objective of French policy remained the search for a general European settlement and a bilateral accord was seen as a way of keeping the ball rolling until a western pact could be negotiated. François-Poncet argued that to refuse Germany's desire for an accord would only give Hitler a useful alibi. His reasoning was: 'if these commitments are kept, they will greatly contribute to the improvement of the European climate; if they are not kept they will burden the culprit with a moral responsibility'.[34] Did Hitler really want friendship with France? Franco-German relations, said François-Poncet, were like a lottery in which France had to try her luck. Although Hitler was 'dissembling' and 'uncertain' France had to gamble in the hope that the Chancellor might keep his word. Hitler, believed the Ambassador, was inspired by a sincere, though 'intermittent', desire for an understanding.[35]

On the eve of his departure from Berlin and in the afterglow of Munich, François-Poncet leaned over backwards to be charitable towards Hitler. Essentially the Chancellor's attitude was one of *Realpolitik*. The Munich agreement was interpreted as proof of French disinterestedness in central and eastern Europe and any additional confirmation of French withdrawal was welcomed. The French government was anxious to secure a bilateral pact and it was only commonsense to keep Paris in a conciliatory mood. Hitler's diplomats, perhaps echoing their master's voice, did not see in the proposed declaration any harbinger of lasting reconciliation. 'No more than a friendly meeting and a platonic declaration, if anything', opined von Weizsäcker, 'will come of it in the immediate future'.[36]

By the end of October the French were in a hurry. On 31 October Bonnet told Welczeck that he hoped to receive a German draft text in the coming week. Although both parliament on 4 October and the Radical party congress on 26-29 had endorsed the Munich agreement, rumblings of discontent were to be heard from the Communists and Socialists. This criticism did not worry the government so much as the disillusionment which was taking hold of the mass of French opinion. In 1936-37 the prospects for Franco-German co-operation had seemed quite promising: youth camps, ex-servicemen's rallies, cultural exchanges had taken place. But the climate was changing. In February 1938 an anti-Hitler exhibition was held in Paris and posters appeared showing swastika covered planes bombarding the city. The first jubilation of Munich had evaporated, leaving the nasty taste that France had gained nothing for her sacrifices but humiliation. The shock was a double one: loss of prestige abroad, and economic crisis at home. In fact within days of Munich, a strong reaction revealed itself. On 3 October the Radical Socialist deputy,

Ernest Pezet, Vice-Chairman of the Chamber foreign affairs committee, wrote to a German acquaintance:

> What an illusion, alas, is yours . . . Munich induces you to return to us; and you believe that a new era of Franco-German reconciliation is opening. Everything leads me to think the contrary.
> Already our people is coming to its senses after the animal joy – understandable and excusable – of having escaped war. And now it is getting a grip on itself and feels that it has been cheated . . . some even say: betrayed . . . It is already ashamed of having betrayed an ally . . . Better perhaps that we do not meet: we have nothing pleasant to say to each other . . . [37]

An added reason for urgency was the impending visit of British ministers on 24 November. The French government wanted a Franco-German accord to be signed before the British visit so as to avoid 'the impression', Bonnet explained to Welczeck, that 'the agreement had been made under British tutelage'.[38]

On 5 November Ribbentrop forwarded to Paris a draft text. This 'rough outline', as Ribbentrop termed it, covered three matters: a general declaration of mutual goodwill, a solemn recognition of the Franco-German frontier, and an undertaking 'to remain in contact' and 'confer together'.[39] Bonnet expressed the hope that Ribbentrop would come to Paris for the signing. This was the moment for the Italians to put their oar in. When sounded out by Hesse in early October, Mussolini had been agreeable to the proposed declaration. On 7 November, however, the *Duce* asked for the signing of the declaration to be postponed until after the British visit to Paris. Obligingly, Ribbentrop promised not to rush matters. Next day, the Italians intervened again. Mussolini was alarmed lest the declaration embodied 'a joint consultation obligation'. He wanted the declaration to parallel as closely as possible the Anglo-German text of 30 September, which had referred to consultation only 'in very general terms'.[40] Although the Italians were not shown a draft text, they were assured that there was no German commitment to 'any precise formula'. 'The importance of such agreements', Weizsäcker told Attolico, 'manifestly lay not in their wording but in the intention of adhering to them and carrying them out energetically. The Anglo-German declaration was now six weeks' old but had not been 'followed . . . up so far'.[41] In German eyes, the Italians were obviously taking the declaration much too seriously. Nevertheless, they got their way. On 8 November Welczeck was informed that an agreement was not urgent and would not be signed until after the British visit on 24 November. In addition, the consultation clause would have to be watered down so as to conform with the Anglo-German declaration.

The assassination in Paris on 7 November of the German diplomat, vom Rath, at the hands of a Jewish exile, provided a pretext for the *Kristallnacht* of 9-10 November. The destruction of synagogues and thousands of Jewish homes deeply shocked international opinion. Some 10,000 refugees crossed into France. None the less the French government was not deflected from its course. The new French ambassador in Berlin, Robert Coulondre, paid his first visit to Ribbentrop on 20 November. Ribbentrop delivered a sharply-worded reminder of German policy. Germany's sphere of influence was central and eastern Europe and France should devote herself to her colonial empire. The foreign minister's thesis went unchallenged. Coulondre's tone was conciliatory. France, said the envoy, was in no way responsible for the murder of the German diplomat and the many expressions of sympathy sent to the German embassy in Paris reflected French feelings.[42]

On 19 November Bonnet renewed his invitation and on 21st Ribbentrop accepted, saying he would come during the week 28 November to 3 December. On 23 November the French Cabinet was informed for the first time of the details of the proposed declaration and Ribbentrop's visit. Until then Daladier and Bonnet had preserved strict secrecy about the negotiations. Although there was some grumbling in the Cabinet, it was directed not at the idea of a declaration but at the timing of the Ribbentrop visit. Mandel and Reynaud suggested postponement of the visit.[43] Zay asked if the agreement could be signed by the German Ambassador. Monzie suggested a ceremony in Strasbourg, instead of Paris. Undeterred by the doubts of colleagues, Bonnet on the same day told Welczeck that the French government proposed 29 November as the date for the visit and signing of the declaration.

The negotiation of the declaration was beginning to seem like an obstacle race for Bonnet. After the vom Rath murder came the threat of a general strike in France. Paul Marchandeau, Minister of Finance since April, was replaced by Paul Reynaud on 1 November. On 14 November Reynaud announced a batch of deflationary decrees. The budget was to be balanced by increases in direct and indirect taxation. The whole of the public works programme was stopped. Other economies included the dismissal of 40,000 railwaymen and restrictions on the number of new appointments in the civil service. The operation of the Popular Front 40 hour week, already modified for the armaments industry, was also modified for the railways. Reynaud's austerity programme was denounced by the Communist led Confédération Générale du Travail as a 'policy of aggression against the working class'. On 21 November strikes were called against the 40 hour week decrees and on the 25th the CGT called a 24 hour general strike for 30 November. The parliamentary groups of the Socialist and Communist parties passed resolutions demanding Daladier's resignation.

On 23 November Welczeck transmitted the French invitation for 29 November and asked for early instructions. Six days later, Ribbentrop replied. The visit could not take place until the strikes had died down. January was suggested as an alternative date. In the late evening of the 29th, Bonnet sent for Welczeck and pleaded for the visit to take place as planned: 'the longer it was postponed the more ominous might be the effect of the intrigues of all opponents of a Franco-German rapprochement'.[44] The general strike called for the next day, said Bonnet, could be regarded as a failure: 'not more than 30% would obey the call to strike'. Impressed by Bonnet's appeal, Welczeck strongly urged Ribbentrop to maintain the original timetable since postponement 'would be a most difficult test case for the Cabinet and might lead to its fall'.

Ribbentrop reverted to the original plan. The decisive consideration was the manifest failure of the general strike. Industrial unrest persisted for some days but the danger point had passed. Undoubtedly, the stern measures taken by Daladier broke the back of the strike movement. On 24 November workers occupying the Renault factory had been cleared by the police with tear gas. All mines and railways were requisitioned by decree. Civil servants were warned that if they came out on strike they would be liable to dismissal. Trade union leaders who had threatened to disrupt the railways were told that they would be in danger of criminal proceedings. Finally, some 7,000 foreign miners were notified that if they joined the strike they would be deported. By 1 December stocks and shares had revived and capital sent abroad returned home.

As in the Czech crisis, Bonnet was anxious to secure American approval for his foreign policy. On 27 November he instructed the French ambassador at Washington, René Doynel de Saint-Quentin, to inform the State Department of the terms of the proposed Franco-German agreement and to request that when the agreement was made public the United States should express its approbation in some way, even if only in a press statement. The instructions sent to Saint-Quentin also provided a lengthy apologia of French policy in the past months. Washington, said Bonnet, had told him that it could give France neither men nor money. Bullitt advised him that in the event of war Roosevelt would be obliged to apply the Neutrality Act of 1935 in all its rigour. Bonnet had been shown a letter from Roosevelt to Guy la Chambre, warning that in the event of war, delivery of aircraft already ordered by France some time previously would be most difficult. Visiting France during the summer, the Assistant Secretary of State, Sumner Welles, had told Daladier, Chautemps and Bonnet that 80% of American opinion was opposed to intervention in Europe. Bonnet concluded this review with the sentence: 'The American Government cannot at the same time deny us any support in a conflict and not approve our attempt at European understanding'.

Saint-Quentin called at the State Department on 28 November and spoke to Sumner Welles who was then Acting Secretary of State. Two days later, Welles informed him that:

> this Government did not feel itself able to make any public statement with regard to the signing of a Franco-German agreement . . . in view of the strained relationships existing between the United States and Germany it would be very difficult for this Government . . . to express approbation of an official act on the part of the German Government . . .

The American climate was hardly favourable for Bonnet's diplomacy. Following the *Kristallnacht* of Nov. 9-10, the United States recalled its Ambassador from Berlin and Hitler retaliated by recalling his Ambassador from Washington. The two countries were to be without Ambassadors to each other for the remaining three years of peacetime relations.

The German Foreign Minister arrived in Paris on the morning of 6 December, escorted by a large posse of advisers. The first official visit of a German Foreign Minister since 1933 was greeted coldly by press and public. No large crowds turned out either to cheer or protest. *Timeo Danaos et dona ferentes* epitomised the public mood. Suspicion of the secular enemy was too strong. Elaborate police precautions shielded the

German party from contact with the public. Daladier gave a luncheon for the German Minister at the Hotel Matignon but 'purposely' took no part in the talks which followed in order to mark their 'unofficial and limited character'.[45] In the afternoon, at the Quai d'Orsay, Bonnet and Ribbentrop talked together in the presence of Léger and Welczeck. The Franco-German declaration was then signed. It was a brief document under three headings.[46] The first clause affirmed 'the conviction that peaceful and good neighbourly relations between France and Germany' constituted 'one of the essential elements' for general peace. The second clause was a recognition that the existing frontier between the two countries was fixed and final. Thirdly, there was a consultation clause according to which both governments resolved, with 'due account being taken of their relations with other powers', to keep in contact and to consult on questions affecting them.

Uneasiness and suspicion clouded the official festivities. On the evening of 6 December a banquet was given at the Quai d'Orsay. Critics were quick to notice that two Cabinet ministers, Mandel and Zay, both Jews, had not been invited. In fact there was no discrimination against the two ministers. Protocol laid down that only a certain number of senior ministers were invited to a reception for a visiting Foreign Minister, and Mandel and Zay were present at a German embassy reception the next evening.[47] Another absentee, but by choice, was Gamelin. He had taken care to arrange engagements out of Paris during the two-day visit. Herriot, too, refused to attend any of the official functions.[48] In the afternoon of 7 December Bonnet had a second conversation with Ribbentrop in his room at the Hotel Crillon. The two men were alone. A dinner at the German embassy rounded off the visit. While Ribbentrop held court to Parisian society, Bonnet was observed hovering uneasily and unnoticed in the background. In the corner of an adjoining room 'Daladier was for some time left alone with Fernand Gentin, his Minister of Commerce, no one paying any attention to him'.[49] Perhaps the Prime Minister was in a morose mood after eating the *jambon de Prague* which had figured on the evening's menu.

The Bonnet-Ribbentrop conversations, like the Laval-Mussolini discussions in Rome in January 1935, were a source of much confusion and misunderstanding. In the months that followed, Bonnet's critics alleged that the Minister gave Ribbentrop a free hand in eastern Europe. In a letter of 13 July 1939 Ribbentrop himself took Bonnet to task, claiming that in the negotiations leading up to the declaration and in the talks that took place on 6-7 December it was understood that both countries would respect each other's sphere of interest. In particular, Ribbentrop cited a passage from the conversation of 6 December:

> On that occasion, I expressly pointed out that eastern Europe constituted a sphere of German interests, and, contrary to what is stated in your note, you then stressed on your part, that, in France's attitude regarding the problems of eastern Europe, a radical change had taken place since the Munich conference.[50]

On 21 July 1939 Bonnet replied:

There is one point which I am anxious to make absolutely clear. At no moment either before or after the declaration of December 6 has it been possible for the German Government to think that France had decided to disinterest herself in the East of Europe.[51]

What, then, was said on 6-7 December 1938? The most important of the talks held during the two day visit—and Bonnet obstinately maintained in his memoirs that it was the only talk he had with the German foreign minister—took place in Bonnet's office at the Quai d'Orsay in the afternoon of 6 December.[52] According to the German record, Ribbentrop stressed France's need to recognise Germany's sphere of influence in the east. Bonnet replied that 'relations since Munich had fundamentally altered in this respect' and then went on to discuss Franco-Italian relations.[53] In the French record kept by Léger there is nothing corresponding to the phrase attributed to Bonnet in the German version.[54] Does this mean that Ribbentrop's argument can be dismissed? Not at all. Though Ribbentrop in his letter of 13 July 1939 referred specifically to the remark attributed to Bonnet, his case really rested on the context of the declaration. And here the German case was a strong one. The mere fact that the declaration and visit took place at such a time signified that France was not prepared to oppose peaceful German expansion in the east. Apart from the ambiguous phrase attributed to Bonnet in the German documents, there is no evidence that the French foreign minister explicitly acknowledged the German thesis. In fact it would have been both unnecessary and impolitic for him to have done so. What mattered was that Bonnet and Léger did not deny Ribbentrop's claim and the Germans were entitled to draw their own conclusions. Plainly it was not in France's interest to adopt a clear-cut position when Germany's intentions remained unclear. Moreover France was at loggerheads with Italy and Bonnet hoped to secure some German pressure in Rome. It was essential therefore not to surrender too much too soon in eastern Europe.

'Held without any agenda, without secretaries, and not even round a table'[55] the conversation of 6 December was a case of much ado about nothing. The discussion rambled over several topics: Franco-Italian relations, Franco-German trade, political relations, Morocco, eastern Europe, Czechoslovakia, Spain, colonies. The disjointed exchange showed only too well that neither side had done much homework for the meeting. Ribbentrop in fact had little to say of importance and expatiated about German interests in the east partly as a way of rubbing in the lesson of Munich, partly to avoid being inveigled into saying too much about the Franco-Italian fracas. In December 1938 France was preoccupied with the Mediterranean, not eastern Europe.[56] Only a week before the Ribbentrop visit shouts of 'Nice, Corsica, Tunis' in the Italian Chamber had brought Franco-Italian relations to their lowest point since 1935. Talking to Ribbentrop Bonnet harped on the Italian theme in the hope that Germany might be induced to sweeten Italian bad temper. The Germans noted: 'In this and in further discussions during the Reich Minister's stay in Paris, great anxiety was expressed repeatedly about future developments in the Mediterranean. Indeed, one may say that this is really the principal matter engrossing members of the French Government these days'.[57] With the Spanish Civil War drawing to a close the French government was worried on two counts: firstly the prospect of an unfriendly Franco regime in league with Germany and Italy; secondly the likelihood of permanent Italian bases in the Balearics and on the Spanish mainland.

Ribbentrop, however, refused to be drawn on Italy and affirmed the 'perfect solidarity' of the Rome-Berlin Axis. Bonnet raised the question of the four power guarantee for Czechoslovakia. When the German Minister virtually rejected the idea of a guarantee, Bonnet 'confined himself to saying that it was actually more by force of circumstances that France had come to envisage undertaking a guarantee'.[58] Although Léger laid 'great stress' on the guarantee, neither he nor Bonnet were prepared to be troublesome in the matter. The outcome of the discussion was summed up laconically in the French record: 'M von Ribbentrop replied in a very ambiguous manner that he would examine this question on his return to Berlin'.[59] Again, when Ribbentrop instanced the Franco-Soviet pact as an obstacle to rapprochement, both Léger and Bonnet soft-pedalled its importance, stressing that it was not the work of the Daladier government. Ribbentrop was 'forgetting', explained Léger, 'the conception of the pact which was that of a collective entente to which Germany and other powers would be associated'.[60] The French record continued:

> Appearing to allude to central Europe, M von Ribbentrop noted that Berlin did not understand why certain powers wished to meddle in Germany's own interests in Europe. He had already said so in London but that had not prevented Lord Runciman from involving himself in Czechoslovakia in questions which did not concern him.

According to the French record, at no point was Ribbentrop contradicted or reminded that France had not abdicated in central and eastern Europe.

The Franco-German declaration has been described as a device 'to anaesthetize French opinion and to induce in France a mood of supine resignation towards German expansion in the east'.[61] This is to ascribe to the declaration far more importance than the Germans ever intended. There was in fact no need to induce a mood of resignation towards German expansion in the east. Such a mood had existed for the past two years. The French government had made its own decision to soft-pedal the eastern pacts. On 20 November Coulondre had not demurred when told by Ribbentrop that France must stick to her empire and leave the East to Germany. The political significance of the declaration was clearly perceived. Germany would interpret the declaration 'as implying a definitive acceptance by France of the territorial changes realised in central Europe', announced the *Revue des Deux Mondes* on 15 December. Yet the declaration did rest on a misunderstanding. Germany assumed that French recognition of her eastern interests meant a completely free hand to achieve her aims, if necessary by force. However French acceptance of German predominance in the East was based on the assumption that German expansion would be peaceful and limited.

Since the French government fought shy of defending its eastern interests it could hardly be expected to make great sacrifices for the victims of Nazi persecution. In his memoirs, Bonnet endeavoured to show that France had done her utmost for the 10,000 refugees who crossed her frontiers in November 1938: 'I expressed to Ribbentrop, at our official talk at the Quai, our indignation against the persecutions'.[62] In another version of the memoirs, the former minister claimed that Ribbentrop had refused to discuss the Jews in the 'official talk' on 6 December and he had, therefore, raised the question informally when he met the German minister at the Hotel Crillon in the afternoon of the 7th. In truth, the French government was much less sympathetic towards the Jewish refugees than Bonnet later claimed. At the time Bonnet explained to an American diplomat that he had not mentioned the matter at all on the first day's talk because the ambassadors were present and 'he was certain Ribbentrop would refuse to discuss it in their presence'.[63] When he did raise the question on the afternoon of the 7th, Ribbentrop refused to discuss it officially and insisted that in the statements to the press no mention should be made of the refugees.

In May 1938, following a request from Halifax, Bonnet had asked Mandel, Minister of Colonies, whether France could settle Jews in the empire. In a letter of 25 May Mandel opposed the idea, arguing that the settlement of Jews would require considerable capital and France could not expect her colonies to foot the bill. Also, there was a political problem. It would be foolhardly, said Mandel, to settle Jews from Germany and Poland in French colonies because at some future date they might be used as a fifth column: 'I believe it would be more than imprudent to show favour to the plans for Jewish colonisation', concluded the minister.[64] When a subcommittee of the Intergovernmental Committee on German Refugees met in London on 2 December 1938, Senator Henry Bérenger, head of the French delegation, said that France would consider the settlement in Madagascar and New Caledonia of 10,000 refugees, but 'not persons of German origin'.[65] The French government was willing to allow the 10,000 who had crossed the frontier in November to stay in France. The Americans thought the French attitude a 'negative' one since French ministers 'vigorously opposed' the suggestion of government participation in financing the settlement of refugees. Yet in fairness to the French, it must be said that the influx of refugees imposed heavy demands, socially and economically. Bonnet told the Chamber foreign affairs committee on 14 December 1938 that in proportion to her population France had done as much as Britain and the United States.[66] In 1938 France already had 3 million foreign workers—les métèques—as well as 200,000 refugees, of whom 40,000 were Jews. And in February 1939 over 300,000 Spanish refugees entered France after the collapse of Republican resistance. Of course, many of these eventually returned to Spain, but in August 1939 there were still 230,000 in France. Unhappily the refugees from central Europe were not assimilated. Whether because of their numbers or as a result of the French temperament 'the great mass...lived cut off from French contacts and led a kind of ghetto existence...immersed in their emigré universe'.[67]

Only Bonnet seems to have judged the Franco-German declaration a signal success — naturally enough since it was largely his own work. He told the German Ambassador that he had placed observers in cinemas, even in Communist districts, to monitor audience reactions when the newsreels of the signing ceremony were shown and claimed 'exceptional approval had been registered'.[68] In his memoirs he praised the declaration as a posthumous victory over Bismarck. Yet the solemn recognition of frontiers lasted less than two years. Nevertheless, during the period December to March 1939 the declaration served some purpose, providing a peg for economic negotiations and strengthening the belief that Hitler's next move would be in the east. On 15 December Coulondre wired: Germany's 'determination to expand in the east seems to me as certain as her renunciation, at least for the present, of any conquests in the west'. There was 'a general desire', he added, 'for the establishment of good relations with France'.[69]

The Munich agreement had aroused some hopes in French business circles of a new era of European economic co-operation. Before Munich in fact *Le Matin* had descanted upon the bright prospects for Franco-German economic collaboration. From October to December Bonnet had his hands full with the negotiations for the declaration. He did find time, however, to tell Otto Abetz, Ribbentrop's personal representative in Paris, on 24 October that Franco-German economic co-operation might form the first topic of an official meeting. Beyond arranging for representatives of French industry to visit Germany, Berlin gave Bonnet small encouragement. During his farewell audience with Hitler on 18 October François-Poncet had ventured to mention economics but Hitler 'having little knowledge of these matters' had referred him to the experts.[70]

Only with Ribbentrop's Paris visit did French economic appeasement begin to make some progress. Ribbentrop was accompanied by a group of economic advisers, headed by Emil Karl Josef Wiehl, director of the German Foreign Ministry's economic policy department. Without having had preliminary meetings and lacking an agenda neither side was adequately briefed for the talks. The French team, led by Count Renom de la Baume, assistant director of political and commercial affairs at the Quai d'Orsay, had yet to win for their proposals the support of Fernand Gentin, Minister of Commerce.

Despite their rough and ready nature, the December economic talks did serve to pin-point the fundamental stumbling blocks to economic co-operation. The Germans would only buy more French goods if the French government first cleared their deficit in the exchange balance between the two countries. But the French were intent on selling more of their agricultural surpluses to Germany. 'The surest foundation for a lasting political *rapprochement*', the French experts pointed out, would be for the Germans to take more French agricultural produce. 'This question', continued the French delegation, 'was of great significance . . . in domestic politics'.[71] Large German purchases of French produce would have been manna indeed for the Daladier government. In September 1938 peasant pressure groups had crusaded vigorously for peace at any price.[72] With an assured market for their produce, French farmers might have solidly backed the Daladier government's foreign policy. But the

Germans were not philanthropists: the French would have to earn their
political dividends by buying more German goods.

Although in January 1939 the two governments exchanged written
notes on economic proposals, it was not until 11 March that the French
government presented detailed suggestions. From December to March,
informal talks were held in Paris between von Campe, Commercial
Counsellor of the German embassy, and Count de la Baume of the Quai.
As well as examining the problems of Franco-German trade, projects
were discussed for collaboration in South America, the Balkans and
French colonies. French business interests, eager to maintain their
position in Spain, suggested that Spain would be 'the best field for Franco-
German co-operation'.[73] Germany, it was argued, had technical services
and Spanish goodwill and France could provide the capital. The Germans
vetoed the idea, fearing that a joint appearance, arm-in-arm with the
French, would 'discredit' them in Spanish eyes.

The relatively slow progress of economic negotiations was in part
the result of a basic German indifference, in part it was also the result
of resistance from certain ministers, notably Gentin, Minister of Commerce.[74] It was Hitler's Reichstag speech of 30 January 1939 with its
'export or die' theme which infused new life into the talks. Daladier for
one, was reported to have been 'very impressed' and at once took a
personal hand in the negotiations. A special Cabinet committee was set
up to decide on practical proposals.[75] At this period Daladier was in
unofficial contact with Goering. He confided to Bullitt on 6 February:

> Goering not only during their personal conversation at Munich but lately had
> been communicating with him in a rather surprising manner . . . Goering had . . .
> proposed that France should join Germany in finishing off England and that
> the British Empire should be divided between France and Germany . . . . [76]

Daladier 'thought he might invite Goering soon to make a visit to Paris'.
In further talks with von Campe of the German embassy, de la Baume
showed himself 'particularly eager and accommodating'.[77] By 21 February
Le Temps was calling for an end 'as soon as possible to the economic
rivalry of Germany and the West' so that 'an honest policy of rapprochement and co-operation' could get under way.[78] In a note of 20 February
prepared for the Cabinet committee on economic appeasement, the Quai
d'Orsay submitted an optimistic assessment of the prospects for agreement.
On the same date Coulondre wrote to Bonnet, complaining of the way in
which France was lagging behind Britain in economic approaches and insisting on the 'absolute necessity' to make economic proposals.[79] On 1 March
Coulondre handed Hitler a message from Daladier: France was ready 'to
pursue and to develop with the Reich the policy of collaboration affirmed
in the declaration of 6 December'.[80] Bonnet himself was far from inactive.
It was with his personal backing that his friend Baudouin-Buguet, a lawyer,
established on 28 February a *Centre Économique Franco-Allemand*. The
centre had the support of several prominent personalities, notably C. J.
Gignoux, president of *Confédération Générale du Patronat Français*,
René Duchemin, industrialist, Emile Mireaux, a director of *Le Temps*,
and Senator Aimé Berthod, an ally of Laval.

An interesting sidelight to the economic exchanges in February was a proposal that France should buy German engines for her air force. In October 1938 the Air Minister, Guy la Chambre, asked Charles Lindbergh to find out if Germany would sell aircraft engines. In January 1939 the German government said it would be willing to sell 300 Benz motors for delivery about December 1939 or January 1940. Daladier and Guy la Chambre kept their own counsel: 'Daladier especially did not wish Bonnet and the other members of the Quai d'Orsay to know about it as they were thoroughly unreliable'.[81] Technically, the proposal had serious snags. The lengthy delivery dates meant that war might well come before the French air force could take delivery. Moreover, in the event of war, it would be impossible to get parts and spares for the engines. However Daladier was willing to consider the proposal for political reasons: 'because of the improvement that might be produced by such an order in the diplomatic relations between France and Germany and because news of such a deal would tend to make the Italians less sure of German support'.[82] But the most interesting feature of the episode was the fact that Daladier deferred a decision until Roosevelt had given his advice about the possible effect on American opinion. When word came from Washington on 14 March that Roosevelt was unable to predict the effect on opinion, Guy la Chambre decided not to proceed further.

In all the talk of economic appeasement one subject was taboo— colonial concessions. The French were eager to enlist German help in schemes for colonial development and certain firm proposals were sent to Berlin but not even a whisper was heard of transfers of colonial territory. On 3 March 1938 London had submitted to Hitler a plan for a central African condominium. Hitler did not reply to the offer. As the question of central Europe loomed increasingly large, colonial appeasement slipped into the shadows. However, in anticipation perhaps of British pressure at the London conference on 28-29 April, the French General Staff on 24 April argued strongly against the idea of ceding the Cameroons to Germany.[83] A list of consequences of cession was presented: the idea of the empire would be dealt 'a moral blow'; Germany might be more tempted to attack France; the Rome-Berlin Axis would be consolidated; cession would pose a possible threat to French power in black Africa; the French and British African empires would be separated; French forces in black Africa and the south Atlantic would have to be strengthened. At the London conference, French ministers were reassured that pending a reply to the 3 March offer Henderson was under instructions not to re-open the colonial question.

The post-Munich climate was quite inimical to colonial concessions. Disengagement from central Europe was accompanied by greater interest in the colonial empire. In particular the Flandin school argued that France should redeploy her energies and resources, withdrawing from the East and consolidating her position in the Mediterranean and over- seas. This renascent self-sufficiency found expression at the Radical party congress in October. Daladier spoke of 'a vast zone of security outside Europe' which France would defend 'as she will defend her home territory'.[84] The Bonnet-Flandin group nursed the hope that the new imperial vision would in time soothe the trauma of Munich. By contrast, Mandel, Minister of Colonies, saw the colonies as a reservoir of man-power and material which would enable France to resume her traditional role in Europe. France constituted an empire of 110 millions which could furnish all the raw materials needed for national defence, he declared on 5 November.

Whatever the differences of approach between individual Ministers, popular interest in the empire was strong. Germany's revival of the colonial issue in October-November met with an indignant reaction. In a speech at Munich on 8 November Hitler proclaimed that except for colonies Germany had no more demands to make of the democracies. The mention of colonies aroused widespread resentment in France. The Right wing Marin group passed a sharply-worded resolution, calling on the government to define its position. On 15 November the Colonial committee of the Chamber declared itself opposed to any concessions. Next day, Daladier spoke: 'no cession has ever been considered, nor can it be'.[85] The Germans spared the French government further embarrassment by suddenly calling off their campaign. Ribbentrop, conciliatory for once, assured Coulondre on 20 November that 'it would be well not to broach' the colonial problem 'for a few years'.[86] In July 1939 the British again dangled before the Germans the bait of a colonial condominium. It was to include as well as British possessions, French, Belgian, Portuguese and Spanish territories. Needless to say, the French government was never informed.

By the second week in March the economic negotiations were nearing a climax. With a blare of publicity, Hervé Alphand, director of the trade agreement department in the Ministry of Commerce, was despatched to Berlin for the signing of an agreement on the Sudetenland, and for the conclusion of talks on a tourist agreement. To buttress Alphand, the French government posted off a special envoy, Lucien Lamoureux, a former minister of Commerce, to assure the German government of France's 'urgent desire' for far-reaching economic co-operation in the spirit of the December declaration.[87] On 11 March Paris made known detailed proposals, providing for an exchange of agricultural produce for German machine tools and chemicals. Certain colonial projects were also outlined. This was as far as the French government ever got, for on 15 March German troops occupied Prague and Alphand was summoned home.

The failure of French economic approaches presents no mystery: the political and economic conditions for success were so obviously lacking. Without a French economic revival and the abandonment by Germany of economic autarchy, collaboration between the two countries was bound to have a synthetic quality. Indeed, the scope for far-reaching co-operation did not exist. The Reich Federation of Industry informed the German embassy in Paris on 2 March that although enquiries had been made 'among the whole industrial organisation, no requests worth mentioning for negotiations with French industry' had yet been made.[88] German and French industrialists had already concluded the market agreements which they needed. The Germans, too, had reservations about some of the colonial schemes submitted by the French. Moreover, Germany could get all the agricultural produce she needed from central and eastern Europe. Even if Hitler had been genuinely interested in economic accords, France was hardly a tempting market. As a German minute succinctly put it: France was 'a land of crises'.[89] Not that Hitler would have wanted it otherwise, a weak France suited his book.

French thinking about the state of the German economy was confused. Bonnet, for example, argued that Germany's economic and financial tensions were such that war would be the only exit unless economic appeasement was given a trial.[90] Le Temps, in its leader of 21 February, took a similar line. Others drew different conclusions. De la Baume of the Quai d'Orsay and F.T.A. Ashton-Gwatkin of the Economic Section of the British Foreign Office maintained in February that the strains of the German economy imposed a peaceful policy.

In economic, as in political approaches, the British were the pace-makers. As early as 17-18 October 1938 a German delegation en route for Ireland, had informal talks at the Board of Trade on the possibilities of increasing German exports to British colonies. In January 1939 an Anglo-German coal agreement was concluded and in February Ashton-Gwatkin of the Foreign Office was sent to Germany to assess the chances of economic accords. Preparations were made for a visit to Germany by Oliver Stanley, President of the Board of Trade. French and British moves were separate and uncoordinated. After Ribbentrop's December visit, Bonnet merely informed London that economic questions had been 'touched upon'. Seemingly, nothing more was said until February when Ashton-Gwatkin stopped in Paris for talks with Count de la Baume. It was important, he noted, to keep 'in touch' with the French who 'clearly think there is something to be said at the present time in favour of an economic approach'.[91] On 20 February the Quai d'Orsay suggested that an exchange of views with London would be useful but no consultations took place.

Coulondre's contribution to the economic overtures calls for special mention. His memoirs were praised for their 'lucid objectivity and dispassionate frankness'.[92] Coulondre wrote:

> At the beginning of 1939 a French delegation came to Berlin and M Alphand, its leader, and myself, were agreed in asking Paris to widen the scope of the negotiations . . . I do not think that for a single moment Hitler ever thought of slowing down the production of German armaments and if he proclaimed the slogan 'export or die', it was only because he wanted at all cost to continue importing vital raw materials.[93]

In fact the French and German documents reveal the Ambassador as a leading advocate of economic understanding. His experience as assistant director of political and commercial affairs at the Quai from 1933 to 1936 was a determining factor in his appointment to the Berlin embassy. In presenting his credentials to Hitler on 22 November he had stressed the importance of 'committing the two countries to the path of reconciliation and collaboration'.[94] He soon fell under the Chancellor's spell, cabling on 24 November: 'I am inclined to think that he really desires a rapproche-

ment with France and that he thinks it possible in present circumstances'.[95] In a personal letter of 25 January to Bonnet he affirmed his confidence in the value of the 6 December declaration, saying 'it was essential that a great effort should be made in Paris on the French press in order that it does not react too unfavourably against the speech of 30 January . . . the spirit of the 6 December is still living. Let us sustain it'.[96] Optimistic to the end, he told Paris on 2 March that Germany was well-disposed and the time was ripe for an agreement.

In 1931 the German film director, G. W. Pabst, made the film *Kamerad-schaft*. With dialogue in both German and French the film was an impassioned plea for a better understanding between nations, and showed a disaster in a French coalmine just across the Franco-German frontier; German miners go to the rescue of the French workers who have been entombed and to do so they smash their way through the frontier posts. Pabst's portrayal of brotherly feeling between French and German workers was good cinema but not real life. A vast gulf separated French and German opinion. Karl Stern, a German Jew, relates how, as students, he and a friend went for a trip to Paris by motor cycle. They stopped for lunch in a French village and the innkeeper's wife who served them said: 'there is not a single French boy of your age who would have a motor cycle like you. We French are economical and careful people. You Germans come over in the most flashy cars and motor cycles, and then you claim you cannot pay us any reparations'.[97]

The well-intentioned strivings of groups and individuals did no more than scratch the surface of a tremendous problem. In the 1920s the *Comité Franco-Allemand* of Pierre Vienot embraced only an élite of intellectuals, diplomats and industrialists. It was a Franco-German club and its activity was too rarefied and academic to have any impact upon the general public. Its successor, de Brinon's *France-Allemagne* committee, was no more suited to the task of influencing opinion. Subsidised by the *Dienststelle* Ribbentrop, the committee was increasingly regarded as a German fifth column.[98] After the *Anschluss,* Paul-Boncour almost secured its dissolution. Bonnet tried hard to endow it with greater influence. Herriot was nominated chairman of the French section and contributed an article to its journal *Cahiers Franco-Allemands.* On 8 August 1938 Abetz wrote to Herriot inviting him to the Nuremberg Rally and suggesting that Hitler would receive him there. Herriot refused. Bonnet tried to persuade Daladier to write for the *Cahiers.* In March 1939 public clamour forced Bonnet to insist on the closure of the committee's Paris office. Denounced in the Chamber as a German agent, de Brinon retired to his country estate. Abetz was obliged to leave France on 2 July.

Chapter 17

A Change of Course

The German occupation of Prague on 15 March 1939 and the Italian invasion of Albania on 7 April introduced a new policy of British and French guarantees in eastern and south-eastern Europe. The guarantees were followed by protracted negotiations with the Soviet Union. The aim of this diplomatic revolution was to build a dam against further German expansion but appeasement was not dead. It used to be said that appeasement ended with Hitler's march into Prague, and, more recently, it has been suggested that the British Cabinet's decision on 1 February to regard a German attack on Holland or Switzerland as a *casus belli* 'outdated' appeasement and 'marked the real turning point'.[1] Yet appeasement had always been a mixture of conciliation and firmness. Significantly, British and French ministers now talked of the construction of a 'peace front'. In other words, the post-Prague emphasis on firmness did not cancel out the conciliatory elements in British and French policies. Germany's violent methods had enforced a change of course but the destination was unchanged: a European détente. The demonstration of firmness by the western democracies failed because it was essentially half-hearted. Only a grand alliance for war could have deterred Germany in the summer of 1939.

Germany's destruction of Czechoslovakia was not a bolt from the blue. On 11 March British intelligence forecast German action against Prague for 14 March. French intelligence was even better informed and predicted on 6 March a German move on the 15th.[2] As reports came in of the Czech-Slovak political crisis Bonnet was unperturbed. On 14 March he and Bérenger, chairman of the Senate foreign affairs committee, dined with Phipps. Their attitude, reported the Ambassador, was 'that the less we interfere in this crisis the better. . .this renewed rift between Czechs and Slovaks only shows that we nearly went to war last autumn to boost up a state that was not "viable"'.[3] Bonnet merely instructed Coulondre to ask for information about German recognition of Mgr Tiso's Slovak government. If necessary, Coulondre was to base his enquiry on the consultative clause of the 6 December declaration. However the ambassador did not act until noon on the 15th.

When in the morning of 15 March German troops marched into Prague, official reactions in London and Paris were remarkably muted. 'Question is one of saving our face', noted Cadogan.[4] 'Does it surprise you? It is after all only a consequence of the blunders made in 1919', declared Bressy, Bonnet's chef de cabinet, to journalists.[5] In the evening the French Foreign Minister received formal notification of the German protectorate over Bohemia. According to Welczeck's testimony, the Minister refrained from expressing an official opinion, giving as 'his personal view' that 'the peace and appeasement policy of the "men of Munich" had suffered a lamentable disaster...in every country warmongers who would lead Europe toward catastrophe were bound to gain the upper hand'.[6] As a mark of disapproval, Paris at once recalled Alphand, director of trade agreements in the Ministry of Commerce, who was in Germany for the conclusion of economic agreements. London cancelled the proposed visit to Berlin of Stanley, President of the Board of Trade.

Protests against the German *coup* were made but they were belated and unco-ordinated. At midday on 16 March Corbin informed Cadogan that his government were resolved to make a protest whether London did so or not. But instructions were not sent to Coulondre until 17 March and he did not act until the morning of the 18th. When he handed Weizsäcker a note of protest the State Secretary replaced it in its envelope and pushed it back across the desk. Since Coulondre refused to retrieve the note, Weizsäcker chose to regard it as transmitted through the post. The British note of protest was delivered on the same day and strengthened by Henderson's departure. While Henderson was packing his bags, the recall of Coulondre was still being debated in Paris. One practical step was taken in Paris. When on 17 March German officials arrived to take possession of the Czech legation they were stopped by police. London and Paris continued to recognise Czech diplomats.

After the initial floundering, both governments began to review their position. 'Don't know *where* we are', exclaimed Cadogan on the day following the *coup*.[7] In London and Paris ministers were propelled by parliamentary and public pressures. The pro-Bonnet press interpreted the liquidation of Czechoslovakia as proof of how artificial and unstable the state had been: Europe was still paying for the errors of Versailles.[8] But this line did not command wide support. Indignation mingled with anxiety was expressed. Many who had advocated conciliation in September 1938 had done so because of the reasonableness of Hitler's claim for self-determination for the Sudeten Germans. Annexation of non-Germans shattered the belief that Germany was only interested in the well-being of Germans outside the Reich. The Chambers were in session and the three days following the *coup* were the only occasion in the life of the Daladier government when parliamentary opinion decisively shaped foreign policy. Ministers, especially Bonnet, were made to run the gauntlet. When the Chamber foreign affairs committee assembled on 15 March members demanded a debate on Czechoslovakia.[9] Bonnet promised to speak to Daladier. Speaking to the Chamber on 17 March Daladier defended his Munich policy and asked for extended powers.[10] His speech was noisily interrupted. Attacked again the next day Daladier announced the delivery of a French note of protest. There were pressures, too, in the Cabinet. On 17 March Zay called for firm measures, in particular the recall of Coulondre. That same day Chamberlain spoke in Birmingham. Though there was no recantation on Munich, a new note of firmness was sounded.

Bonnet's political reputation was seriously compromised by the Prague *coup*. The distrust of the Foreign Minister which had been voiced since the autumn now boiled over. On 15 March 1939 the *Union des Intellectuels francais* sent an open letter to Lebrun, Daladier and the presidents of the Chambers, calling for an enquiry into Bonnet's conduct as Foreign Minister. The indictment was made up of 21 separate charges, covering the period from April 1938 to March 1939. It was alleged that the Foreign Minister had consistently pursued a secret diplomacy detrimental to France's interests.[11] The letter was signed by 17 distinguished academics, including the physicists and Nobel Prize winners Jean Perrin, Frédéric and Irène Joliot-Curie, and the historian Lucien Febvre, co-founder with Marc Bloch of *Annales d'histoire économique et sociale*.

Not that Daladier needed any prompting. Such was his lack of confidence in his colleague that on 18 March he bypassed the Quai d'Orsay and consulted Bullitt about a semi-official proposal for the resumption of negotiations with Italy. On 17 March an emissary had informed the French Prime Minister that both Mussolini and the Italian royal house were deeply disturbed by Hitler's latest adventure. It was suggested that the French government should send Laval to Rome. Bullitt advised against the sending of such an envoy since Laval 'would destroy' public confidence in Daladier's 'will to resist absolutely all demands against France which was the basis of his strength throughout the country'.[12] The advice was accepted — not that it made much difference since the Italians had decided they did not want Laval.[13]

The issue of Coulondre's recall from Berlin illustrates the tensions which beset policy-making in the immediate post-Prague period. Coulondre did not want to leave Germany.

In a personal letter of 16 March to Bonnet the Ambassador wrote: 'the events which have just occurred are going to put great difficulties in the way of the policy of détente which you have so rightly striven for since Munich...we must hold fast and gain time by all means possible until our rearmament is completed'.[14] In conclusion, however, he advised against his own recall, advancing three considerations: relations, once broken, would be difficult to mend; in his absence Italian counsels might gain the ascendancy; and the departure of the Ambassadors might only accelerate the coming of war. In Paris the Cabinet debated the issue on 17 March. Zay spoke strongly for recall but President Lebrun was against it. On the morning of 18 March while Bonnet and other Ministers were still arguing against recall, Léger urged it strongly, complaining to Daladier of the 'weak attitude and hesitancy' of Bonnet and of the 'reticence' which surrounded himself.[15] Léger won the argument and Coulondre left Berlin on 19 March. But Bonnet was not so easily defeated. Only five days later, on 23 March, he suggested to Halifax that the Ambassadors should return to their posts.

Britain and France, it seemed, had reached the cross-roads. In their

confusion British Ministers looked anxiously for signposts as to the future
direction of German policy. Rumania seemed an obvious target. When
the Rumanian Minister, Tilea, told the Foreign Office on 17 March that
Germany was demanding in the form of an ultimatum a monopoly of
his country's exports in return for a German guarantee of her frontiers,
his story was accepted. And London took the first hesitant and stumbling
steps towards the giving of guarantees. Subsequent investigation revealed
the tenuous basis of the alarm.[16] Telegrams were sent off to the Soviet
Union, Poland, Yugoslavia, Greece and Turkey asking them to define
their attitude in the event of German aggression against Rumania. Despite
the lack of any confirmation of Tilea's approach, the French government
was only too anxious to follow London's lead. Daladier considered that
'we should do all we can to encourage Poland and the Balkan entente to
guarantee each other...and to let them know that we shall support
them'.[17] Since early January in fact French sources had tipped Rumania
as Germany's next objective, although Gamelin was not too sure and
suggested on 18 March that Hungary might be first on the list.[18] Leger
was sensible and realistic about the British proposal. Such an initiative,
he told Phipps, was putting the cart before the horse: the governments
consulted would decide their attitude in accordance with British and
French intentions.

France's eastern pacts were now of little avail. Given French encouragement, Poland and Rumania might have been expected to stand shoulder
to shoulder. However, relations between Paris and Warsaw were barely
civil. On 18 March Colonel Beck asked if the French government would
help to resist a German attack on Danzig. Paris insisted that Poland
would have to sign a defensive pact with Rumania. On 19 March Bonnet
asked again if Poland would protect Rumania. Beck's reply was evasive;
the best course was not to bring in the Soviet Union but to act immediately
in Bucharest or Budapest. When on 21 March Lukasiewicz communicated
Beck's reply to Léger there followed 'hot words and almost a fist fight'.[19]
Once again, Bullitt had to act as peacemaker between the French and
their Polish allies.[20] But Léger did not change his opinion of the Polish
Foreign Minister. The Secretary General warned London that Beck was
'entirely cynical and false' and his plan was to ask Britain 'to make an
alliance with Poland'.[21]

Léger's opinion of the British initiative proved correct. In reply to
the question 'what will you do?' the threatened states answered: 'what
will you?' Chamberlain however worked out a new plan which received
Cabinet approval on 20 March. France, the Soviet Union, and Poland
were to be invited to join Britain in a four-power declaration, pledging
themselves to consult together in the event of any action which threatened
their security. What Chamberlain considered a 'pretty bold and startling
idea' was pooh-poohed by Corbin.[22] On 20 March Cadogan read out
the draft declaration, terming it 'a warning signal to Germany' but Corbin
brushed aside the draft: 'he felt convinced himself, though he could not
answer for his Government, that the publication of this bare declaration would have a much worse effect than publishing nothing at all'.[23]
Privately, Cadogan admitted: 'there is some force in his objection. We

propose to publish a Declaration that, *in the event of a further outrage, we will consult. Point: c'est tout'*.[24]

An interlude of Franco-British cordiality followed. On 21 March President and Madame Lebrun began a three-day state visit. Lebrun addressed both Houses of Parliament in Westminster Hall. His lengthy speech, faultlessly delivered, was an impressive feat:

> At 11 o'clock the bugles blew, and the North doors were opened and the Lebruns entered escorted by Lord Ancaster, as Great Chamberlain...Mme Lebrun, who looked self-possessed and amiable, indeed even chic and having considerable chien for an old bourgeoisie, smiled and conducted herself with dignity. The President (whom, I am assured, calls her Pom-Pom) was immaculately dressed, though it is absurd to look as French as he does ... by having such a success with our Royal Family Lebrun is certain to be re-elected President...[25]

Bonnet accompanied the President and talked to British ministers. At a first meeting on 21 March Halifax read the proposed four power declaration. Bonnet stressed how 'absolutely essential' it was to get Poland in, since 'Russian help would only be effective if Poland were collaborating'.[26] After telephoning Daladier, Bonnet expressed France's readiness to sign the declaration. But the declaration was a non-starter. It was already evident that Poland and Rumania did not wish to be publicly associated with Moscow. Halifax elaborated a new procedure to meet Polish and Rumanian reservations. Britain would give Poland 'a private undertaking that, if Poland came in, they would both come in also'. Here in embryo was the British guarantee to Poland.

Another meeting on 22 March, sandwiched between official festivities provided Chamberlain with an opportunity to question Bonnet about the state of the French air force. Daladier, said Chamberlain, had forecast in November 1938 that by the end of the spring French aircraft production would be 400 a month. Present information confirmed the doubts expressed by British ministers in November. Bonnet was not exactly a loyal colleague. Admitting 'that he had had his doubts about the figures given by M Daladier', he stated that in February 100 aircraft had been produced.[27] In return Chamberlain confided that the British figure for February was 600 aircraft.

Bonnet's personal views about the new course in foreign policy were voiced in a private meeting with Halifax on 23 March. The British reaction to Germany's behaviour was much too bellicose for the French Minister's liking. Halifax was told: 'we should do everything we could to avoid exposing ourselves to a charge either of encirclement or of framing a line-up on ideological prejudice'.[28] Bonnet supported his point with excerpts from recent dispatches. In a letter of 21 March the French Chargé d'Affaires at Berlin, de Montbas, treated the recent crisis as no more than a storm in a tea cup.[29] There was still a chance of economic talks with Germany, reported de Montbas. It would be unwise to refuse any overtures. The likelihood of the re-entry of the Soviet Union into European affairs aroused general misgiving in Berlin diplomatic circles. Moreover, continued the Chargé d'Affaires, it would be a mistake to leave Coulondre too long in Paris. From Rome, François-

Poncet warned of the danger of giving the dictators the impression that Britain and France were ganging up against them. Bonnet then put to Halifax two specific proposals: Coulondre and Henderson should return fairly soon to Berlin, and Britain should introduce conscription. 'If the people of France thought it was impossible to look to Great Britain for any really substantial measure of military help for, say, eighteen months the consequences might be profound and irretrievable', declared Bonnet.[30] Before the French party left London, Chamberlain and Halifax paid tribute to Lebrun and said how much they appreciated working with French Ministers.[31] This compliment was interpreted by Bonnet as a hint that London wished to see Lebrun stand for a second septennate. Lebrun had had thoughts of retirement but was persuaded to stand again on 5 April when he was re-elected by a large majority.

Within a week of the French visit the four-power declaration proposal had been scrapped and replaced by a British guarantee to Poland on 31 March. The French government played little part in the discussions leading up to the guarantee and were not consulted until all was virtually decided. The sequence of events was simple. On 24 March Beck suggested in place of the declaration a 'confidential bilateral understanding' providing for consultation between Warsaw and London. It was obvious that the Poles did not want the French to know of the proposal and when Corbin called at the Foreign Office on 25 March he was told 'as little as possible'.[32] Only on 27 March was Lukasiewicz instructed to tell Daladier of Beck's approach to London. On the previous day Chamberlain and Halifax had decided in principle to offer a guarantee to Poland and Rumania. In the late evening of the 27th Paris was asked to support the new proposals. Poland was to be offered a guarantee on condition that she went to the help of Rumania. The public announcement of a guarantee on 31 March before negotiations were completed was precipitated by another alarmist report of German troop movements on the Polish frontier. Given no time to disagree, the French could only remark that they did 'not apprehend any imminent *coup* against Poland'.[33]

Still, French statesmen had no reason to quarrel with British policy. France was at last in possession of the British commitment to eastern Europe which she had despaired of for nearly 20 years. England's frontier, Daladier told his Cabinet, was no longer on the Rhine but the Vistula. What was the explanation of the apparent *volte-face*? In a report of 4 April Corbin analysed the change. If someone had told him three weeks previously that Britain would guarantee Poland and show readiness to assist Rumania, Turkey and Greece 'I would have received the prediction with incredulity'.[34] Corbin stressed the evolutionary character of British foreign policy. The essentially conciliatory disposition of British diplomacy had remained unaltered until March 1938. The methods of the *Anschluss*, though not its nature, had for the first time alarmed opinion, and by September many people believed that Czechoslovakia was a touchstone of Hitler's intentions. After 15 March 1939 pressures from within the Cabinet, from parliament and public opinion all combined to set British policy in a much firmer mould than could have been foreseen in the immediate aftermath of the *coup*. It was Halifax, wrote Corbin, who had tightened up the draft of Chamberlain's Birmingham speech of 17 March, giving it a fairly firm character.

In the face of growing public criticism and rumours about Germany's intentions, the main impetus in British policy-making in the fortnight following Prague was a desire to make some firm stand. As Cadogan put it on 30 March: 'the great question is shall we *now*—and how— challenge Hitler and try to stop the rot? ... it's a frightful gamble'.[35] Halifax, as one of his officials recorded, was 'itching to do something'.[36] 'Your statement ... is an irresponsible game of chance', was Lloyd George's comment on Chamberlain's announcement of the Polish guarantee on 31 March.[37] Gamble was the operative word. Both British and French statesmen gambled that a guarantee would be sufficient to deter Hitler from further aggression.

In the post-Prague panic both the French and British governments were agreed that Moscow should be kept at a safe distance. A Soviet suggestion of 18 March for the calling of a conference to discuss measures against aggression was rebuffed. Over Italy, however, opinions were divided. Hearing on 17 March that Mussolini might send an ultimatum to France or occupy Albania, the Foreign Office wanted to warn him not to bully France. But the letter which Chamberlain sent to Mussolini on 20 March contained only a hint of a warning and was essentially an appeal to the *Duce* to use his influence with Hitler in favour of peace. The French government brooded over suggestions for a resumption of negotiations. François-Poncet recommended the opening of talks. Laval approached Daladier, offering his services as an intermediary.[38] On 20 March Baudouin urged Daladier to resume the February contacts. Daladier professed his 'sincere wish for an understanding' but wondered whether 'all these at first more or less secret approaches ... are not intended to weaken French morale'.[39] Nevertheless, Daladier authorised Baudouin to transmit to Rome a statement of his position. It was a reasonably conciliatory declaration. The Italian government was assured that the recent recall of a class of reservists was not directed in any way against Italy and French troops on the Italian frontiers would not be strengthened. The French government was willing to come to some arrangement over the Italian claim for a free port at Djibouti in French Somaliland. As a conciliatory gesture, Daladier proposed to forbid French press attacks on Italy and asked for similar assurances from Mussolini. Finally, as a test of goodwill, Daladier suggested that a speech which Mussolini was to make on 26 March should be conciliatory towards France.

Bonnet was not consulted about the message entrusted to Baudouin and did not learn of the affair until some days later.[40] When Mussolini spoke on 26 March it was to reassert Italian claims to Tunis, Djibouti, and representation on the Suez Canal Board. Bonnet considered that the speech did not completely close the door to negotiations and was surprised when Daladier telephoned him to say it was an intemperate outburst which left no room for compromise. From Léger Bonnet learnt that Daladier had first telephoned the secretary general for his opinion of the speech. 'This did not surprise me at all, however, since I had been warned that for some time a great deal of trouble was being taken to dissuade the Prime Minister from contact with Italy'. Apparently, Elie J. Bois, editor of *Le Petit Parisien,* had organised luncheon parties to which Daladier and Léger had been invited but not Bonnet. On these occasions Léger and Bois—so Bonnet was told—had set to work to dissuade Daladier from opening ·negotiations with Italy. But Léger and Bois were only part of the anti-Italian chorus. Jules Jeanneney, President of the Senate, was an influential figure. He believed that Franco-Italian negotiations were a waste of time and urged Daladier to get rid of his foreign minister because 'no one in France or abroad had any confidence in him'.[41]

Bonnet was not alone however in thinking that the *Duce's* 26 March speech offered a possibility of contact. From Rome on 26 March François-Poncet cabled: 'Manifestly, he (*Duce*) has been careful not to break any bridges and not to close the door to any possibility of negotiation'. Considering the *Duce's* speech a 'guarded attempt, even if clumsy' to resume contact, Halifax on 28 March was bold enough to suggest to Daladier the line he might take in reply.[42] Daladier proposed to reply in a radio broadcast on 29 March. The Italians would be told that any claims they might have should be made through the usual diplomatic channels. Phipps did what he could in an interview with the French Prime Minister and then counselled London: 'further attempts to tone down his speech would be useless'. Daladier's frame of mind can be gauged from a note drawn up by one of his entourage. The note dated 26 March and headed 'Disadvantages of negotiations with Italy' advanced a strong case against any weakening of France's position.[43]

In the Cabinet Bonnet and his allies were in a minority. At two meetings, on 27 and 29 March, the Cabinet discussed the terms of a French reply. On 27 March Bonnet supported by Monzie, Chautemps and Marchandeau pleaded for negotiations with Italy. Opposing them were Campinchi, Mandel, Reynaud, de Ribes and Zay.[44] Between the opposing clans stood Daladier. He was willing to make some non-territorial concessions but Italy would have to ask politely. When the Cabinet met again in the morning of 29 March Daladier's stance had hardened. He read the draft text of the radio broadcast which he was to deliver later in the day. In Bonnet's words, 'a very lively discussion' ensued.[45] Bonnet had not seen the draft before the meeting. It was firmly worded and the Bonnet group had no success in moderating its tone. Although Daladier was still willing to contemplate a compromise over Djibouti, some of his colleagues were unyielding. 'We'll give the Italians a pier and that's all', said Mandel.[46]

Bonnet and his sympathisers were not defeated. On 27 March Caillaux asked for British intervention in Rome.[47] In the first week of April Caillaux and Bonnet both received unofficial emissaries from the King of Italy, 'imploring' the French to compose their quarrel so that Italy would not be 'sucked definitely into the German orbit'.[48] Caillaux had requested British action in Rome but Bonnet preferred to bring British pressure to bear on Daladier. On 3 April Pierre Bressy, the Foreign

Minister's chef de cabinet, who was 'supposed to have the entire confidence of his chief', 'poured out his soul' to the British Press Attaché, Sir Charles Mendl. Bressy complained 'about the abominable campaign being waged against his chief' which 'prevented' him from making 'approaches to Mussolini through private sources'. Mendl concluded his report: 'Bressy hinted that we ought to use some pressure on M Daladier to bring about this contact'.[49]

In Rome the French Ambassador, François-Poncet, fretted and fumed. On his appointment to the Rome embassy in October 1938 he had joked that he was going to the Palazzo *far niente*. Six months later, the joke had soured. For the Italian government and for the Quai d'Orsay the French embassy at the Palazzo Farnese hardly existed. The ambassador complained to his British colleague that nothing he did seemed to have any effect. In private letters to Bonnet he urged the opening of talks and even sent one of his staff to Paris to strengthen these representations. Exasperated by failure, he confided to Lord Perth, the British Ambassador, that Daladier, instigated by Corbin, was 'extremely obstinate'.[50] He wondered if London would be prepared to influence French ministers. The British government was only too ready to oblige but hopes of immediate Franco-Italian contact were dashed by Italy's occupation of Albania on 7 April.

The Albanian episode of 7 April and the alarms and excursions which followed had far-reaching consequences for Franco-British relations. Since the middle of February, France had been keyed up to expect an Italian offensive in the Mediterranean. It was predicted that an attack would be made in late March or early April. Germany's elimination of Czechoslovakia strengthened fears of a co-ordinated Axis attack. British policy-making in the second half of March had been greatly swayed by the alarmist reports of German designs on Rumania and Poland. Now it was the turn of the French to sound the tocsin. Nerves were stretched to breaking point. On 7 April came news of General Franco's adhesion to the Anti-Comintern pact. Daladier described the Albanian *coup* as 'only the prelude to a big Italo-German offensive from the North Sea to Egypt'.[51]

Fearful of the outbreak of war, France demanded and obtained the announcement of a guarantee to Rumania and also the introduction of conscription in Britain. These were the immediate gains of a much more forceful French policy than hitherto. Over a longer period French pressure in the negotiations with Moscow helped to bring about Britain's acceptance of Soviet proposals for a tripartite pact. Why did London concede so much so fast? The British government's reading of Italian intentions was much more optimistic than the French government. It was believed in London that the *Duce* might still be prevailed upon to exercise a moderating influence on the *Führer*. But in order to make the most of the *Duce*'s influence it was necessary to settle the Franco-Italian quarrel. Concessions were made to France in the hope that French ministers would re-open negotiations with Rome. Another consideration was French firmness. France's display of firmness on important issues was a new experience for British leaders. Lastly, the British government shrank from alienating its chief continental ally. A dissatisfied France, it was feared, would soon fall prey to defeatist propaganda. And French ministers and officials soon became adept at playing on this fear.

Following the Albanian *coup,* the Quai d'Orsay was inundated with reports of impending Italian action against Corfu, Egypt and Gibraltar. The Foreign Office remained calm. After a conversation with the Italian Chargé d'Affaires on 8 April Halifax had the impression that Mussolini had shot his bolt and would not attack elsewhere. Next day this confidence was shaken by the news that Greece had information of an imminent attack on Corfu. Halifax immediately asked if France would join in promising help to Greece. When Phipps arrived at the War Ministry Daladier and Bonnet were attending a meeting of the Permanent Committee of National Defence. Daladier later promised help for Greece. 'The atmosphere here', reported one diplomat, 'is largely dominated by the thought of war, which is held to be inevitable'.[52] Even Bonnet on 9 April believed 'there might be war at any moment'. Germany and Italy were in cahoots and it was 'only a matter of where the blow would fall'.[53] French apprehensions were discounted in London. The French, Halifax told the Cabinet on 10 April, 'seemed, perhaps, to take rather a too excited view of the situation'.[54]

At its meeting on 9 April the Permanent Committee of National Defence decided on a number of important precautionary measures.[55] The Committee confirmed the strategy agreed since 1937; in the event of war France would first tackle Italy. As well as mobilising the fleet and transferring the bulk of it to the Mediterranean, the air force was placed on alert and concentrated against Italy. It was against this background of war rumours that France demanded a British guarantee for Rumania. Daladier told his ministers on 11 April that before unleashing war Hitler would try to secure Rumanian petrol. France, he declared, was at a turning point and the government must settle its policy once and for all: 'If anyone thought, like M Flandin, that peace could be obtained by allowing Germany a free hand elsewhere . . . they should speak out'.[56] From the east, Germany would turn west and 'we will be quite alone'. The Cabinet met again the following day and decided to offer a guarantee to Rumania.

In the morning of 12 April Bonnet had warned Phipps that Daladier was thinking of making a public declaration of French assistance to Rumania. London did not take kindly to the idea. Paris was told that to guarantee Rumania would 'throw away the lever which we have for bringing Poland and Turkey into a wider arrangement'.[57] The main problem, said the Foreign Office, was Turkey, and Rumania was in no immediate danger. Next morning Corbin called on Cadogan and explained Daladier's reasons for wishing to give the guarantee. The French prime minister 'still believed that Germany's main objective was Rumania'.[58] Without Rumanian oil, Germany could not wage a long war. London was reminded that Daladier had responded at once to the request to join in a guarantee of Greece, though not under any treaty obligation to do so. Similarly, the French government had supported Britain's offer of an interim guarantee to Poland. Cadogan found Corbin's case 'unanswerable'.[59] The French government, said Corbin, 'were resolved in any event to-day to announce their guarantee of Rumania'. Shortly after midday on 13 April Halifax telephoned British agreement 'in the interests of solidarity' and 'in view of the evidence French government have given us in the past of their readiness to meet our wishes'.

Paris might not have panicked after the Albanian affair had more been known of British war plans.[60] Full staff talks had only just begun. French military and political leaders were afraid that Britain intended to divert a major portion of her naval strength to the Far East, leaving France to hold the Mediterranean virtually unaided. On 11 April Daladier told Bullitt that the British Mediterranean fleet was to be transferred to the Far East. There was no truth in the statement. In fact on 10 April the British Cabinet agreed to concentrate the fleet at Malta in order to reassure France. Washington had been asked on 23 March to deploy the American fleet in the Pacific in order to allow Britain to defend the Mediterranean. American fleet movements began on 15 April but Paris was not informed about British movements until 13 April.

By far and away the most serious lack of liaison between London and Paris occurred in the opening stages of the Moscow negotiations. The story of the separate, unco-ordinated approaches to the Soviet government is well-known. On 9 April the Permanent Committee of National Defence decided to open military conversations with the Soviet Union.[61] On 11 April several French generals impressed on the British Military Attaché the need for an agreement with Moscow. 'The military, whom one did not see before, now seek my acquaintance. The other day . . . the military governor of Paris gave me breakfast. Many of the military were present. Yesterday I received an invitation from the commander of the fleet', reported the Soviet Ambassador, Souritz.[62] On 14 April Bonnet proposed a mutual assistance pact, covering Rumania and Poland; on the same day Halifax asked Moscow for a unilateral declaration of assistance to threatened states. Apprised of the British proposal, Bonnet promised his support, although after talking to Daladier he felt 'the original French suggestion . . . might have been preferable'.[63] Thus London was given the impression that the French suggestion had been dropped. Yet when on 16 April Bonnet seconded the British initiative he told Souritz: 'we will not withdraw our proposition, in which we continue to see every advantage'.[64] In Moscow, the French Chargé d'Affaires, Payart, in supporting the British move, confirmed that France still maintained her own proposal.[65]

On 17 April Moscow offered a tripartite pact and immediate staff talks. Such a pact 'would make war inevitable', Halifax told his colleagues.[66] 'Stripped of certain obvious objections', opined Léger, 'it could be the basis of an agreement'.[67] Halifax took precautions. On 20 April he extracted from Léger a promise that no reply would be sent to Moscow without prior agreement. Halifax should have known his partners better. While the British tinkered with their declaration proposal, the French forged ahead. On 29 April Bonnet handed Souritz an amended text for a mutual assistance pact, leaving his Political Director, Charvériat, to explain to Phipps on 3 May that 'in the heat of the conversation' and in order 'to dispel' Souritz's suspicions the undertaking given to Halifax had been broken.[68] On 8 May the British Ambassador in Moscow, Sir William

Seeds, presented the British reply to Molotov, who had replaced Litvinov as Commissar for Foreign Affairs on 1 May. There followed, as Seeds wrote, 'a most unpleasant ten minutes' over Bonnet's reply.[69] Molotov noted the divergences and 'kept on asking whether each government had "approved" the other's answer'. Before seeing Molotov, Seeds and Payart had concluded from what little information they had that only a draft French reply was involved. It was from Molotov that they learnt Bonnet had communicated a written text. 'Even in a private letter', Seeds considered it 'better' not 'to say' what he thought, except that he hoped 'to be better informed . . . whether I am faced by a gross and deliberate error of tactics or merely by the foolish amateurishness of a politician'.[70] Halifax's soft impeachment was reserved for 17 May when he told Corbin that if the Russians had been 'the reverse of helpful . . . their attitude might in part have been influenced by M Bonnet's action'.[71]

Why were London and Paris so much out of step? Had Bonnet, as Seeds suggested, blundered? In fact there was no gaffe on Bonnet's part. Nor had he communicated the French proposals in 'a fit of temper', as one historian suggested.[72] The submission of revised French proposals on 29 April was prompted by a cool calculation of French interests. Though Charvériat covered up for Bonnet on 3 May, the minister almost certainly had the support of his officials. In Moscow France was represented by her Chargé d'Affaires, Payart, an experienced diplomat who had served in Moscow for several years. The Ambassador, Paul-Emile Naggiar, although appointed in November 1938, did not take up full duties until the end of May. Payart made no secret of his opinion of the British proposals which 'seemed most inopportune at a time when it is necessary to attract the USSR, and to take her at her word rather than to provide her with fresh reasons for withdrawal'.[73] Soviet propaganda, he complained on 10 May, had lumped together French and British propositions and this was misleading because 'our formula gives far greater consideration to Soviet preoccupations'.[74] Not that Payart was happy with the conduct of negotiations in Paris, from mid-April onwards he made it clear that the Quai d'Orsay was not adequately briefing him. However, some difficulties were bound to arise when negotiations were handled in three different centres—London, Paris and Moscow.

Fundamentally, French moves reflected a basic difference of approach to the Soviet Union. For British Ministers, Stalin was a supernumerary. Poland, Chamberlain told his Cabinet on 5 April, was 'the key to the situation' and there was no urgency to secure an agreement. In any case, he had 'no confidence that we should obtain active and constant support' from the Soviet Union.[75] For French Ministers, a Soviet alliance was imperative. After the Albanian *coup,* the French General Staff drew up a balance sheet of forces.[76] The figures were frightening. Germany and Italy combined, it was thought, could muster 250 divisions against 120 French and British. The balance could only be redressed in eastern Europe. It was believed that Poland, Rumania, and Yugoslavia together could mobilise 110 divisions; Greece and Turkey 50. Yet many of the eastern divisions were of dubious quality and Poland and Rumania could not survive for long without Soviet help.

The sense of urgency which impelled French leaders was lacking in

London. Old habits died hard. Psychologically, British statesmen were still reassured by the Maginot Line and reputation of the French army. Even if Germany and Italy swooped on France, Britain would have a breathing space. In the first week of April, Lord Gort, Chief of the Imperial General Staff, returned from a tour of inspection in France. His favourable impressions of the French army were relayed to the Cabinet. Naturally, the French were exasperated by British complacency; hence the swelling chorus calling for conscription. British policy towards the Moscow negotiations was a bundle of negatives: 'We should not act in such a way as to forego the chance of Russian help in war: we should not jeopardise the common front with Poland, and we should not jeopardise the cause of peace',[77] Halifax declared on 26 April. On the 10 May the Foreign Secretary told the Cabinet: 'while he thought that a position might be reached in which we should have to start Staff Conversations with Russia,' he would prefer to postpone this as long as possible'.[78]

An important qualification must be made at this point. Although France forced the pace by submitting separate and fuller proposals, there was no desire for a full military alliance with the Soviet Union. Franco-Soviet relations, though slightly thawed after Prague, had remained chilly. Bonnet, noted Souritz on 15 March, had 'on two separate occasions' spoken of the 'desirability of improving our relations'.[79] Bonnet asked if France could send a delegation to discuss trade and armaments. The Soviet Ambassador suspected the Foreign Minister was under pressure from Herriot and Jeanneney. Some parliamentary pressure existed. Over 100 Radical deputies urged Daladier to improve relations with Moscow. Herriot, President of the Chamber, talked to Litvinov and was anxious to go to Moscow 'to negotiate a firm and absolute military understanding'.[80] Daladier asked for Bullitt's advice on 18 March. The American Ambassador threw cold water on the idea:

> it had been our experience that no promises made by the Soviet Union could be relied on...Nevertheless no stone should be left unturned even though one might expect to find vermin under it...Herriot...was too honest and sincere a person to be able to deal successfully with the Bolsheviks.[81]

Despite the slight thaw in relations, both countries remained intensely suspicious of each other. The Soviet proposal of 18 March for a conference of powers to discuss measures against aggression was not taken up in Paris. France supported the British suggestion of a four power declaration. 'The Russians needed watching', Bonnet told Halifax on 22 March, because 'they liked to make public declarations for propaganda purposes which did not correspond with their real intentions'.[82] Next day, Litvinov described France as 'practically done for...disaffected and disunited, at the mercy of certain...politicians whom he profoundly distrusted'.[83]

Not until the end of March was a real attempt made to secure Soviet co-operation. On 4 April Souritz was told that the Cabinet had instructed Bonnet to open negotiations. Two days later, Bonnet telephoned, asking to see the envoy on 'very urgent business'.[84] The military experts, said the Minister, were convinced that a German attack was imminent: 'it was more than likely that Germany would attempt to seize Rumania and possibly part of Poland'. Bonnet proposed immediate talks to discuss 'what measures shall be taken in the event of a German attack on Rumania or Poland'. Litvinov was not impressed. 'We suppose that Bonnet', he wrote on 11 April, 'just as much as Halifax, talks with you from time to time about the political situation mainly for the sake of being able to say to his opposition that he is in "contact and consultation with the Soviet Union". Bonnet is as little inclined to aid Poland, Rumania or anyone else in eastern Europe as he was Czechoslovakia'.[85]

France's new independent posture was manifested in two other areas: conscription and relations with Italy. Britain saw conscription as a possible bargaining counter to induce France to open talks with Italy. After 15 March the clamour for conscription grew louder every week. On 27 March Caillaux lent his weight as an elder statesman to the pressure, asking Phipps: 'why should not numbers of young Englishmen be sent to St Cyr ... to receive the necessary training to form a future British National Army'?[86] France, he added, would be glad to supply Britain with all the artillery she needed. In early April Jacques Chastenet, editor of *Le Temps*, visited London. Bonnet had charged him to impress on British contacts the necessity of conscription. R. A. Butler, Under-Secretary of State at the Foreign Office, confided that the idea of conscription was now acceptable to the government but an improvement in Franco-Italian relations would be expected in exchange for such a major concession.[87]

In Paris, Phipps was only too ready to apply pressure over Italy, but advised waiting until 'the Albanian affair' had 'blown over'.[88] But for Daladier, the Albanian *coup* was the last straw. 'M Daladier', wrote Phipps on 9 April, 'does not now believe any Italian assurances'.[89] Chamberlain voiced his vexation on 19 April: 'the French were not doing their share in smoothing out their difficulties with Italy'.[90] Halifax 'agreed to put suitable pressure on the French'. This was easier said than done. Daladier's determination not to woo Italy was fuelled by a strong suspicion of Chamberlain's motives. On 16 April President Roosevelt appealed to Germany and Italy, asking them to guarantee their neighbours against attack. Hitler was expected to reply in a speech to the Reichstag on 28 April. Daladier and Léger feared that Hitler would then propose 'another Munich conference' which would meet with Chamberlain's approval.[91] Such a conference might consider Franco-Italian differences and France would lose face. On 17 April Daladier told Bullitt he 'positively would not talk about concessions to Germany and Italy under threat of war as at Munich'.[92] Accordingly, French policy in the second fortnight of April followed a timetable, aimed at securing a maximum British commitment to the peace front before the deadline of Hitler's speech on 28 April. On 19 April Daladier and then Léger impressed on London the need for firmness: 'the immediate days before Hitler's speech will be most important, perhaps crucial. We must show more and more that we mean business'.[93] Léger was more specific: 'If before 28 April our negotiations with Rumania, Russia and Poland could be concluded, and conscription had been adopted in the United Kingdom, he would answer for it that Hitler's speech would be moderate'.[94]

The British and French governments manoeuvred for position. The military measures taken by the Permanent Committee of National Defence on 9 April were intensified; on 19 April another 150,000 reservists were recalled. The big battleships, *Dunkerque* and *Strasbourg,* were ordered to escort additional French naval forces into the Mediterranean. Daladier asked for part of the Home Fleet to be sent to the Mediterranean. Pleas for conscription reached a crescendo. Bullitt was recruited by Daladier to strengthen French representations. On 19 April Phipps was told that Roosevelt 'felt very strongly that it was absolutely essential for Britain to introduce conscription at once and before 28 April'.[95] On the same day Daladier made a 'moving appeal', saying that although conscription might 'for a long time' be only 'a gesture' it was 'a vital one for friends and foes alike'. Phipps endorsed the appeal, pointing out that the press was asking 'Are Frenchmen expected to die in the trenches whilst Englishmen provide money, ships and aeroplanes?'[96] The appeals of Daladier and Roosevelt had their effect. On 20 April the Committee of Imperial Defence decided to introduce conscription and Phipps was authorised 'in the last resort to tell Daladier'.[97] It was agreed however, that Daladier might have to be told 'to get him to get a move on with the Italians'. In the event, the news about conscription had to be used for another purpose. Obstinately, Daladier refused to send Coulondre back to Berlin. On 21 April, Phipps, recorded Cadogan, 'argued for half an hour, trying to persuade Daladier and Bonnet to send Coulondre back. . . They would not: so he had to tell them about conscription. They burst into tears and flung their arms around his neck and agreed to *anything* we liked'.[98]

Daladier's 'anything' did not include Italy. Despite the Gallic emotionalism of 21 April the French Prime Minister kept his head. The British had no more leverage, although Phipps did his best. On 21 and 22 April he tackled Daladier and Bonnet in turn. With Bonnet he was preaching to the converted but the Prime Minister was 'in a very different frame of mind' and could not be shaken even when the Ambassador 'made great play' of the forthcoming announcement of conscription.[99] Sounding out Campinchi, Reynaud and Sarraut 'without arousing their suspicions by any over-emphasis' Phipps found them 'all rabid on the subject', feeling that any moderation 'towards the Italian gangsters' would be dangerous.[100]

Desperately anxious to restart talks with Italy Bonnet bypassed his officials and sent a messenger to François-Poncet at the end of April urging the ambassador to see Ciano.[101] François-Poncet saw Ciano on 26 April and reported to Paris on the interview. Bonnet then asked Léger to help him draft an encouraging reply. Daladier kept the draft for a few days and made some minor changes in the text. On 3 May the telegram was sent off, instructing François-Poncet to open talks. Ciano was to be told that Italy must inform France officially of her claims. In a telegram of 4 May, acknowledging receipt of 3 May instructions, François-Poncet reiterated his claim that the Quai had discouraged him from opening conversations.[102] A telegram of 22 March in which he asked for authority to see Ciano had never been acknowledged. On 1 April he had informed Paris that he had to see Ciano on certain matters and suggested that the meeting might serve as a starting point for future talks. On 6 April he was told that his Counsellor could handle the matter and the meeting should be strictly confined to the business in hand. François-Poncet and Ciano met again on 10 May but nothing came of their encounter. Mussolini had no intention of starting talks until after the conclusion of the Pact of Steel with Germany.

Bonnet next encouraged Phipps to pressurise Daladier, suggesting that the Prime Minister be told 'how much importance' Britain attached to Franco-Italian *rapprochement*.[103] Halifax was getting impatient. 'His general opinion', he told the Cabinet on 17 May, 'was that we had done a great deal for France lately, indeed far more than France had done for us'.[104] On 20 May the British Foreign Secretary intervened personally. A brief meeting with French Ministers in Paris offered an opportunity for personal influence. Daladier could not be shaken. Bonnet, who was present at the meeting, preserved a discreet silence on the subject of Italy. To Halifax's arguments Daladier made a brusque and testy reply. On 26 May Halifax wondered if a personal letter from Chamberlain might do the trick. Phipps counselled patience. On 13 June Bonnet suggested that once an agreement had been signed with the Soviet Union Chamberlain might write to Daladier. Evidently, Daladier suspected that Bonnet was going behind his back. Bonnet, wired Phipps, 'feared that if I said anything to Daladier . . . the latter might think that I had been put up to do this by himself'.[105] But even Chamberlain could not charm Daladier. When on 13 July he wrote to Daladier, urging him to listen to Italian proposals the French leader refused to modify his position.

The confident and assertive character of French diplomacy after Prague reflected the influence of Daladier and Léger. Daladier, assisted by Léger, had firmly grasped the reins of power. The French Prime Minister was almost a new man. 'Tell your Ministers', he told Phipps on 18 March, 'that I am determined to go forward and that I shall not look back'.[106] Brave words were at last followed by brave deeds. In foreign policy-making the paramount influence was now exercised by Daladier and the secretary general of the Quai d'Orsay. On 15 April Léger wrote to Daladier:

Corbin wrote to me on 13 April: 'the firmness which the French Government has shown in demanding the inclusion of Rumania in the new guarantees offered by the English has had an excellent impression in London circles. . .'
I take this opportunity to put before you a brief note from our consul in Leipzig on the growing signs of German discontent towards the Hitler regime. . .[107]

Daladier was working directly through Corbin without consulting Bonnet. After a meeting with Daladier in the last week of April it was agreed that Corbin should discuss 'quite privately' with Halifax the matter of relations with Italy. In a letter of 27 April Corbin reported directly to Daladier on the results of the conversation with Halifax.[108]

The succession of international crises provided a much-needed source of strength for Daladier's domestic position. His request after Prague for further powers was accepted by the Chambers. One class of reservists was mobilised and acting under its new powers the government forbade the press to refer to the measure. Daladier wanted to throw his weight about. After dining with him on 6 April, Souritz signalled Moscow that the Prime Minister was 'assigning himself an important role in changing England's policy towards the Soviet Union'.[109] Of course, where Italy was concerned, Daladier was playing on a popular wicket. Few had wanted to stand up for Czechoslovakia in 1938 but the mood towards Italy in 1939 was quite bellicose. In opposing Italian claims, the French Prime Minister found a new popularity. 'He could not go into a cafe', he told colleagues, 'without people getting up and shouting: "March we'll follow you"'.[110] Firmness proved a valuable unifying force both in Metropolitan France and among the Moslem population of French North Africa. And Chamberlain conceded, though not without a touch of flattery, the strength of Daladier's position: 'no French Minister', he wrote on 13 July, 'has had his people so solidly behind him'.[111] But the factor which most strengthened Daladier's hand in Franco-British relations was the revival of the French economy in the spring and summer of 1939. Reynaud's austerity programme of November 1938 brought a return of financial confidence. Funds flowed back to France. There were modest signs of industrial recovery. Moreover, after the failure of the general strike of 30 November 1938 the industrial scene in 1939 was much more settled than it had been for several years.

Chapter 18

Calm Before The Storm

At dawn on 1 September 1939 German forces invaded Poland; two days later France declared war on Germany; nine months later she was defeated and occupied. Yet it would be difficult to find in Franco-German relations a more uneventful period than the four months which preceded the outbreak of war. Apart from exchanges of letters between Bonnet and Ribbentrop in July and Daladier and Hitler in August, German diplomacy towards France was concerned with relatively trivial matters such as the withdrawal of the expulsion order which the French government served on Otto Abetz, Ribbentrop's personal representative in Paris.

The absence of any Franco-German dialogue was significant. Hitler had decided that France was not worthy of his attention. When the Rumanian Foreign Minister, Gafencu, met the Chancellor in April 1939 the German leader 'raved against England, referring to France as quite secondary'.[1] In the afterglow of Munich, Hitler, uncertain of his next move, had responded to French initiatives for a *détente*. In the spring and early summer of 1939 he was increasingly preoccupied with Poland but no longer interested in keeping France in a conciliatory mood. The military and diplomatic links between Britain and France were much stronger than in the winter of 1938-39 and Hitler reasoned that France was more dependent than ever on her ally. Welczeck was given strict instructions on his return to France on 6 May not to make any overtures to Daladier. Again on 21 June he was told to avoid important political conversations.[2] Arguably, this was a misjudgement on Hitler's part. There were chinks in the French armour and by saying almost nothing to French leaders until the end of August, Hitler missed an opportunity for undermining French opinion. French Ministers, especially Bonnet, had by no means abandoned hope of an understanding. And a careful wooing of Marianne might have furthered Hitler's designs on Poland.

On the French side there was nothing to parallel the Anglo-German parleys: the meetings between the German economic adviser, Helmut Wohltat and British officials and Ministers in June-July; the talks between Sir Horace Wilson and the German Ambassador, von Dirksen; the to-ings and fro-ings of the Swedish industrialist, Dahlerus. French Ministers did not try to outbid British economic and financial offers to Germany. Nevertheless, Paris had not closed the door to negotiations. The first week of

May brought what Phipps described as a 'suspiciously simultaneous' crop of articles arguing against the idea of resisting German aggression in the east.[3] *L'Oeuvre* of 4 May carried an article entitled 'Die for Danzig?' The author was Marcel Déat, leader of the Neo-Socialists and a former Air Minister. Déat asserted that the French peasant had no wish to die for the sake of maintaining Danzig under League of Nations administration. Such extreme expressions of opinion could be dismissed and Bressy, Bonnet's chef de cabinet, admitted that they were embarrassing the Foreign Minister. Despite the significance of the statement by the semi-official *Le Temps* that negotiations on Danzig would have to be held, Daladier himself professed to attach little importance to the tone of the press and preferred to be guided by his own correspondence which while 'about equally divided' in September 1938 was now 90-100% 'in favour of resistance to further German aggression'.[4] Nevertheless doubts persisted about France's determination. And in the evening of 4 May Daladier issued a declaration, denouncing attempts 'to create abroad uncertainty as to the clarity and integrity of French policy'. French 'resolution' was 'unshakeable'.[5]

The façade of firmness did not preclude conciliatory approaches to Berlin and German diplomacy might have made more of these advances. On 9 May Coulondre paid his first visit to Weizsäcker since his departure from Berlin on 20 March. Neither official referred to the altercation during their last interview when the State Secretary refused to accept the French note of protest against the Prague *coup*. The Ambassador came with an olive branch, assuring Weizsäcker that he had returned to continue 'working for pacification in Franco-German relations'.[6]

Bonnet knew his own mind and privately was not afraid to speak it. On 19 May he received Welczeck for the first time since mid-March. Following Coulondre's recall, the German envoy had been summoned home. Predictably, there is a glaring discrepancy between the record of the interview kept by the French Foreign Minister and that drawn up by the German Ambassador. Welczeck's opening remarks were friendly. Germany, he said, was following with satisfaction the magnificent recovery of France. The assurances given in 6 December declaration were still considered valid. Then came a warning. Germany was being encircled and France would have to bear 'the main burden of the struggle conjured up by Britain and make enormous sacrifice of life'.[7] Here the records diverge. In his notes Bonnet summed up his reply to Welczeck in just two sentences: France could not accept the use of force by Germany. A great change had taken place in French opinion since 15 March.[8] Yet, in Welczeck's version, the Minister had much more to say for himself, stressing his attachment to appeasement:

> he would never deviate from the main lines of his policy and would fight for peace to the very last. In spite of everything he held fast to the idea of bringing back co-operation with Germany . . . If I met unfriendliness in the French press where he had some influence . . . he would . . . remedy matters, as far as lay in his power.[9]

But Welczeck knew that Bonnet's views carried little weight in government counsels. On 18 and 21 May the Ambassador spoke to the British Press Attaché, Sir Charles Mendl, and urged Franco-British pressure on Poland. Bonnet, he said:

> was . . . a man who would go to the utmost limits to avoid a European war up to the last moment. He regretted therefore that foreign affairs were so much more in the hands of M Daladier than M Bonnet . . .[10]

The trouble with Daladier, said Welczeck, was that 'in some respects' he was 'more like a Prussian than a Frenchman'. Publicly, Bonnet did not dissent from Daladier. In a speech to a congress of ex-servicemen at Arcachon on 21 May he disclaimed any desire to encircle Germany but stressed France's intention to resist the use of force.

Yet the proof of the pudding was in the eating. If Poland was the acid test of French resolution then the Franco-Polish alliance of 1921 had to be updated and confirmed. Poland's failure to obtain either military or financial satisfaction from France in May 1939 spoke louder than Daladier's brave declarations. The story of Franco-Polish negotiations in May 1939 is one of almost unbelievable muddle and confusion. The British guarantee of 31 March had been followed by Colonel Beck's visit to London on 4-6 April. Although no formal alliance resulted, an agreed 'summary of conclusions' was drawn up to serve as a provisional understanding. Both sides expressed their intention of converting the guarantee into an agreement of mutual assistance. However, there was much intentional vagueness. In London, Beck was discreet to the point of *suppressio veri* concerning the state of German-Polish exchanges on Danzig and showed little interest in obtaining a formal written agreement. Nor were British Ministers eager to bind themselves in a formal alliance. They were glad to postpone a formal pact, pending the conclusion of Anglo-Franco-Soviet negotiations. And in April-May it seemed that a compromise on the Danzig dispute might yet be reached. Accordingly, the 'summary of conclusions' omitted any reference to Danzig.

Colonel Beck, however, tried to secure a declaration on Danzig from the French government and very nearly succeeded. The provisional Anglo-Polish agreement had already outranged the Franco-Polish treaty of 1921 which did not provide for automatic assistance or for indirect aggression. Although France associated herself with the British guarantee, no Franco-Polish talks took place. From London, Beck travelled across France without breaking his journey in Paris. Bullitt, who was favoured with an invitation to board the Polish Foreign Minister's train at Calais, found the Minister 'most hostile towards France'. His attitude 'in alluding to all French leaders' was 'one of contemptuous superiority'.[11] Still, Beck was determined to extract the maximum commitment from France. Lukasiewicz received instructions on Beck's train to ask for the 1921 pact to be harmonised with the Anglo-Polish accord.[12]

Negotiations reached a climax in the third week of May.[13] A draft protocol was prepared and approved by the French Cabinet on 12 May. On 17 May Bonnet accepted an additional secret article whereby France would take note that Poland considered Danzig a vital national interest. It was agreed that the protocol would be signed on 19 May. At the same time separate military discussions were in train. A Polish military mission led by the War Minister, General Kasprzycki, arrived in Paris on 15 May and Gamelin signed a military protocol on 19 May.[14] However, the political protocol was not signed. On 19 May—the day fixed for the signing—Bonnet requested a postponement to the 20th; on the 20th he suggested the 24th, alleging pressure of work and an impending visit to Geneva. Lukasiewicz protested and insisted on the signing taking place as arranged. At 1 p.m. on the 20th Bonnet asked again for a postponement on the grounds that London had not accepted any commitment on Danzig. And there the matter rested. A formal protocol reinforcing the alliance of 1921 and complementing the Anglo-Polish Treaty of 25 August 1939 was not signed until 4 September 1939.

The wish to synchronise and co-ordinate the Franco-Polish protocol with the Anglo-Polish agreement was the reason finally given by Bonnet for postponing the signing of the accord. Did the French Foreign Minister have an ulterior motive? Sir Lewis Namier suggested that Bonnet's conduct of the negotiations masked more than a desire to keep in step with the British government. It may have been Bonnet's 'purpose', wrote Namier, 'to torpedo the military convention' by refusing 'at the last moment' to sign the political protocol.[15] And Bonnet himself lent some substance to Namier's charge by later claiming in the memoirs that in postponing the political accord he prevented Gamelin from concluding an ill-considered military agreement. Yet the evidence indicates that muddle not machination was at the bottom of Bonnet's handling of the affair. And if there was any double-dealing involved it probably originated in Warsaw, not Paris.

On 15 April Lukasiewicz reported on the state of negotiations.[16] Daladier and Bonnet had willingly agreed to bring the 1921 pact into line with Anglo-Polish commitments. In accordance with instructions, French Ministers had been informed that there was a secret Anglo-Polish protocol containing a precise summary of the London talks of 4-6 April. Lukasiewicz told Bonnet that Corbin would doubtless soon receive a copy of this protocol. However Corbin was given nothing and Lukasiewicz asked urgently for a copy to be sent to Paris. Warsaw was not helpful. On 25 April Lukasiewicz begged a friend in the Polish Foreign Ministry to ascertain Beck's intentions. On several occasions Bonnet had asked for a text of the protocol. 'The situation was becoming unpleasant', wrote the Ambassador.[17] No text was forwarded from Warsaw and on 20 May Bonnet asked for a postponement of the signing of the Franco-Polish accord, explaining that 'on the 19th he had telegraphed to Corbin, requesting him to ascertain whether the Danzig question was mentioned in the protocols drawn up ... in London, and had received a negative answer'.[18]

Why did Bonnet wait until the last minute before requesting a postponement of the signing? Lukasiewicz conjectured on 22 May:

I suppose that it really is a question of communicating with London. The decision ... must have been taken under the influence of Ambassador Léger, already after Minister Bonnet had committed himself...and fixed the date of signing...Since Minister Bonnet was not acquainted with the text of the London protocol, he may have hoped that the question of Danzig was treated in it in a manner analogous to the proposal in my declaration.[19]

But Beck may have deliberately given Lukasiewicz the impression that a London protocol existed in order to bluff the French into accepting a commitment on Danzig. On 20 May Halifax confirmed to Bonnet that 'no steps had yet been taken to reduce' the Anglo-Polish agreement 'to writing'.[20] Bonnet explained that he had only consented to open negotiations because he believed that London had reached agreement with Warsaw on the terms of a formal treaty. Hence Bonnet's behaviour was in part the result of Lukasiewicz's own misunderstanding as to what had been agreed in London. Even so, Bonnet could have made enquiries much sooner than he did. The Foreign Minister's methods of working proved his undoing. On 22 May Bullitt cabled home:

I have just obtained the explanation of Bonnet's extraordinary action. Bonnet had conducted the negotiations...personally and had not kept Léger or any of the regular services of the Quai d'Orsay informed of the progress of the negotiations and had all documents prepared in his private office. After Bonnet had set the hour for signature a member of his staff informed him that the British had not yet signed their political accord with Poland...As soon as he had ascertained that...the British had not yet entered into serious negotiations for a political accord...Bonnet flatly refused to sign the agreement.[21]

Later, to cover up his own mishandling of the negotiations, Bonnet spread the story that by refusing to sign the political protocol he prevented Gamelin from concluding a military agreement 'putting us completely in the hands of the Polish government'.[22]

It would be unfair, however, to blame Bonnet entirely for the confusion which marked the negotiations. Gamelin's account of the military talks shows that the Foreign Minister's private office was not the only centre of confusion.[23] Indeed, there was a horrifying lack of liaison between the Quai d'Orsay, War Ministry and Daladier's *Cabinet*. Suddenly, on 13 May, without previous warning, Gamelin was told that the Polish War Minister would arrive the next day. Taken by surprise, he arranged for a representative to meet the Polish party in order to give himself time to find out what was happening. He was 'extremely annoyed' by the arrival of the Poles since he wished to postpone negotiations until after the conclusion of a Soviet agreement.[24] Meetings between the French and Polish military staffs followed on 15, 16 and 17 May. The Poles naturally wanted the French to act against Germany as soon as Poland was attacked. Gamelin was studiously vague and reticent: 'France would do everything possible to pin down on its frontiers the maximum number of German troops...The French High Command will act for the best and according to the circumstances'.[25] But Gamelin's assistants, Georges and Vuillemin, showed an embarrassing readiness to help the Poles. Vuillemin, Chief of Air Staff, alarmed Gamelin by talking of sending French aircraft to Poland. Gamelin drew him aside and counselled caution. General Georges, Deputy Chief of the Army Staff, advised the Polish delegation that an attack on the Siegfried Line 'could not be undertaken until the seventeenth day' of mobilisation. In Gamelin's ears, this sounded dangerously like a promise of a French offensive. He explained to the Polish generals that after 17 days French troops might actually cross the German frontier but much more time would be needed for a frontal assault on German fortifications.

On 17 May the Polish War Minister showed Gamelin a military protocol relating to Danzig. It was worded as follows: 'in the event of German aggression against Poland, or in the case of a threat to her vital interests in Danzig ... the French army will automatically take action'.[26] Contrary to what Bonnet later claimed in the memoirs, Gamelin did not commit France to military action in defence of Danzig. In fact he expressly reserved the government's freedom of action by insisting on the insertion in the military protocol of the phrase: 'The French and Polish High Commands, acting within the framework of the decisions taken by the two governments'.[27] The terms finally agreed between the two staffs stipulated that from the third day of French mobilisation part of the French army would take limited offensive action. From the fifteenth day of mobilisation, the bulk of French forces would take the offensive. This timetable was much more limited than it might have seemed at first sight. Gamelin claimed to have told the Polish military chiefs that 'an offensive' did not in any way imply an attack on the Siegfried Line. Also, the phrase 'the bulk' of French forces referred, insisted Gamelin, not to the whole French army but only to the striking forces available in north-eastern France—about 35-38 divisions. All that the Poles were promised in the way of equipment was one to two battalions of tanks.

Doubts and hesitations then got the better of the French leaders. Gamelin showed the text of the military protocol to Daladier on the afternoon of 17 May. The Prime Minister asked for twenty-four hours to consider the matter. In the morning of 18 May the Prime Minister's office informed Gamelin that the protocol could be signed. In the meantime, Gamelin had cold feet. He telephoned Léger to ask for the Foreign Ministry's opinion of the business. Léger, wrote Gamelin, seemed reticent. Gamelin returned to Daladier and together they drafted a letter to the Polish War Minister, stating that the military protocol would only come into force when the political protocol was signed. On 21 May the War Minister, General Kasprzycki, left for Warsaw without waiting for the signing of the political accord. Hearing that the government 'had finally decided not to sign the political accord' Gamelin considered that 'our military protocol had no value and did not bind us at all'.[28]

So the Poles were sent away empty-handed, without a political or military accord, or the financial assistance they had also requested. The Polish government wanted to settle the matter of French credits while the military delegation was in Paris but Daladier told Lukasiewicz that financial terms would first have to be agreed with London. Negotiations trailed on through the summer and a cash credit was not granted until 7 September. As Lukasiewicz put it: 'from the political point of view, one got the impression that France and England attached no great importance to granting us financial aid in order to convince Germany of the reality and significance of their alliance obligations towards us'.[29]

The French government's handling of the Polish negotiations revealed not only an alarming absence of communication between government departments but also a serious lack of consultation with the British government. Indeed, French anxieties about British policy had not been entirely allayed by the announcement of conscription on 26 April. Daladier confided to Bullitt that he 'would not feel absolutely sure of the British will to resist until Chamberlain should have close to him someone like Winston Churchill'.[30] The British government's reception of a peace proposal from the Vatican in May revived suspicions of perfidious Albion. On 3 May the Vatican suggested calling a five power conference to be attended by Germany, Britain, France, Italy and Poland. Halifax welcomed the initiative but proposed that instead of a conference the Pope should offer to arbitrate between Germany and Poland and also between France and Italy. But on 9 May France firmly rejected the Papal proposal of a conference. Léger said that Daladier had sent for him and Bonnet in order to discuss the French reply. 'Their reasoning', explained Léger, was that at a conference 'the question of German relations with Poland and French relations with Italy . . . would be tied together and both France and Poland would be expected to make concessions to Germany and Italy with the Pope as arbitrator and Great Britain as super-arbitrator'.[31] Halifax's counter-proposal of Papal arbitration, continued the secretary general, 'showed clearly that once all questions of discussions of British colonies should be eliminated Great Britain would be very glad to arbitrate away the possessions and interests of her associates, France and Poland.'[32] Paris suspected that Mussolini was the real author of the Papal proposal and Campinchi, Minister of Marine, went to some trouble to spread this idea in conversations. Léger, reported the Papal Nuncio at Paris, was opposed to any kind of a conference and had as much as said that the Pope should mind his own business.[33]

The Franco-Polish imbroglio was a case of confusion worse confounded. At first sight it might appear strange that the French government should have involved itself in negotiations with Warsaw at such a time. Bonnet's declared objective, as he told the Chamber foreign affairs committee on 19 April, was to fix the terms of an agreement with the Soviet Union before embarking on negotiations with Poland and Rumania.[34] However, no one in London or Paris in mid-April foresaw for a moment the length and difficulties of the Moscow talks. In opening discussions with Poland in mid-April, Daladier and Bonnet assumed that an agreement with Moscow would be signed by mid-May at the latest. As the weeks slipped by the French became frantic to obtain an accord. French diplomats warned of the danger of a German-Soviet *rapprochement*. On 30 April General Bodenschatz of the *Luftwaffe* told the Assistant French Air Attaché in Berlin, Captain Stehlin, 'something is brewing in the East'.[35] Coulondre sent a full report of the conversation and the Quai d'Orsay alerted the Foreign Office. London dismissed the idea of a German-Soviet *rapprochement* as 'inherently improbable'.[36] And on 10 May Halifax told Cabinet colleagues that 'he had no information bearing on the likelihood of some secret agreement . . . between Herr Hitler and M Stalin. He found it difficult to attach much credence to these reports'.[37] The same day Payart wired that since Litvinov's departure from the Narkomindel, Soviet policy was more dependent on Stalin and liable to sudden changes: 'I am not in fact one of those who exclude *a priori* and in all cases the hypothesis either of a withdrawal of the USSR to a position of neutrality, or even of German-Soviet collusion.'[38]

On 14 May Moscow rejected a revised British proposal for a unilateral declaration. Molotov, who had replaced Litvinov as Commissar for Foreign Affairs on 1 May, imposed three conditions for effective co-operation: conclusion of a triple alliance between France, Britain and the Soviet Union, the extension of the guarantees to cover not only Poland and Rumania but also the Baltic states and Finland, thirdly the conclusion of a military convention. The Soviet reply outdistanced the French mutual assistance pact proposal which had been intended to cover only Poland, Rumania and Turkey. No sooner had the Soviet proposal been received than Paris harangued London to send an early reply. In the ten days after 14 May British policy changed considerably. Very quickly it became clear that London had to decide between a probable breakdown in the talks and the acceptance of a three power alliance. When the Cabinet met on 24 May the decision had been made. Increasing rumours of German-Soviet contacts undoubtedly played a part in changing British thinking. Halifax now conceded that 'the idea of some *rapprochement* between Germany and Russia was not one which could be altogether disregarded'.[39] Publicly, too, argued Halifax, the government was so committed to the negotiations that 'there was great force' in the view that having gone so far a breakdown would have a bad effect on opinion. Moreover, the Chiefs of Staff advanced the view that a full alliance with the Soviet Union would provide a better bargain than the original British proposal. It was pointed out that negotiations for a permanent treaty with Turkey would be helped by an early Anglo-Franco-Soviet accord.

Obviously, therefore, the pressures for acceptance of the Soviet proposal were many and they were strengthened by the knowledge that France wanted an alliance. After talking to French Ministers in Paris on 20 May, Halifax reported that they did not want the talks to break down and 'were a good deal less interested in the form that the Agreement with Russia should take'.[40] But having burnt his fingers once before, Halifax was not taking any chances:

> He had shown various alternative formulae to M Daladier and he had at one time thought of asking the French Ministers to put one of these formulae to Russia as a suggestion of their own. When, however, M Daladier had said that if he did this he would probably touch it up somewhat, he thought that it would be wiser not to authorise M Daladier to act . . .[41]

It was also plain that French Ministers were worried by the possibility of an accommodation between Berlin and Moscow. Questioned on this point by Halifax on 20 May, they replied 'that this danger could not be ignored . . . Russian policy was quite incalculable and was liable to sudden changes'.[42] On 22 May Coulondre followed up his earlier warning with a second report. He had heard that Ribbentrop's long-term goal was a partition of Poland by means of a German-Soviet *rapprochement*. Ribbentrop's idea seemed to be gaining ground and Germany would exploit to her advantage any breakdown in the Moscow talks.[43]

French eagerness to close with the Russians did not signify an uncritical acceptance of Soviet proposals. A Quai d'Orsay memorandum of the end of May was highly critical in fact of Molotov's suggestions of 14 May. Molotov's demand for a triple alliance was a manoeuvre which France should be wary of since it added nothing to the existing Franco-Soviet pact and left the question of Soviet assistance to Poland and Rumania ambiguous. 'One may wonder,' whether, in reality, 'the Polish alliance is compatible with the Russian pact'.[44] Here, then, was the heart of the matter. The Quai d'Orsay had raised the issue before but fought shy of exploring it. By May 1939 it was too late to take a dispassionate assessment of the Polish and Soviet pacts. The guarantees had been given and some means had to be devised for breathing life into them. The Quai d'Orsay sniffed danger in the Soviet insistence on the subordination of a political pact to a military understanding. Moscow, as in September 1938, it was stated, would probably ask for permission to cross Poland and Rumania knowing full well that it would be refused.

The change in British policy had not been accomplished without great misgivings and reluctance, especially on Chamberlain's part. Piqued by the necessity of a compromise, the British Cabinet decided that they were not going to play the role of suitors. Bullitt's view that an agreement with the western democracies was necessary for the Russians and 'that we should not reach it if we gave them the impression that we were running after them' was cited with approval in Cabinet discussions on 7 June.[45] Worried by the slow progress of the talks, on 5 June Halifax considered asking Moscow to send a representative to London or Paris. Unfortunately, his concern for the talks was not strong enough for him to accept a Soviet invitation to go in person. Nor was Eden allowed to go. The sending on 14 June of Mr William Strang, head of the Central Department of the Foreign Office, was an unhappy decision, confirming Soviet suspicions that the western powers were not in earnest. The French government was also worried by the situation. On 1 June Coulondre confirmed that Hitler was planning an attack on Poland and had asked his generals what would happen if Russia marched against him. Daladier drew the obvious conclusion. The Soviet Union, he told Phipps, had to be roped in as soon as possible. He had 'reason to suppose' that the Russians were 'rather offended' because a more senior person was not being sent. A British or French general, added Daladier, should go to Moscow to show 'good faith'. In confidence Phipps informed Sir Horace Wilson that Daladier's complaint was probably inspired by Léger: 'Léger . . . is on the very closest terms of friendship with Van . . . and his influence over Daladier is unfortunately increasing daily'.[46]

On 27 May the British Ambassador, Sir William Seeds, and the French Chargé d'Affaires, Payart, submitted to Molotov new Franco-British proposals for a three power mutual assistance pact linked to the League Covenant. The physical setting of the interview underlined the adverse conditions of the negotiations. Willingly or unwillingly, the western envoys were petitioners. Molotov was seated at a large desk on a raised dais, with Payart and Seeds at his feet, nursing their notes on their knees. Earlier in the month London and Paris had agreed that negotiations would in future be conducted in Moscow. Bonnet promised to tell Payart 'to take a back seat' and let Seeds 'make the running'.[47] But Bonnet in fact was determined to stay in front. On 26 May he handed Souritz the text of the Franco-British proposals.[48] On this occasion Bonnet had blundered — unless it is assumed that he was trying to sabotage the whole negotiations. When Payart and Seeds presented the proposals on the 27 May Molotov had been given ample time to study them and formulate objections.[49]

When Strang arrived in Moscow on 14 June the French Ambassador, Naggiar, also newly arrived, asked him 'point-blank whether our Government really wanted to come to an agreement with the Soviet Union or were they merely going through the motions'.[50] Strang reassured him. In truth the British were now as anxious as the French to come to an agreement. In his memoirs Bonnet staked out a large claim for the French role in the talks. France, he wrote, 'supported all the Russian demands, while striving constantly for British agreement'.[51] In reality, the French were not quite so far ahead of their ally as Bonnet the historian suggested. In June and July France allowed Britain to set the pace, and on some contentious points the French government was obstinate. The Russians insisted on the subordination of a political agreement to a military convention. Daladier and Bonnet told Souritz that France would not agree to this procedure.[52] By early July the labyrinthine negotiations had been complicated still further by Molotov's insistence on the inclusion of the Soviet definition of indirect aggression.

According to his own account, Bonnet on 10 July asked Halifax to accept Molotov's formula for indirect aggression.[53] London, he wrote, refused to give way either on the issue of indirect aggression or on the linking of the military and political agreements. This was quite untrue. In a letter of 11 July Corbin, acting on Bonnet's instructions, expressed support for the British definition of indirect aggression and said the French government would oppose the Soviet demand for simultaneous conclusion of the military and political accords. In point of fact the British position was more accommodating than the French. On 11 July Halifax, in return for acceptance of the British definition of indirect aggression, was ready to agree to the linking of the military and political conventions.

Then on 19 July Bonnet changed his mind. He sent an appeal to Halifax, urging acceptance of the Soviet definition of indirect aggression.[54] The British and French governments, said Bonnet, could always interpret Molotov's definition in such a way as to avoid having to support Soviet interference in the east European states. On this point, however, Halifax would not budge. 'A question of principle' was at stake. Britain could not become an accessory 'to interference in the internal affairs of other states'.[55] On 23 July Molotov offered the immediate initiation of military talks, explaining that once the military obligations were defined 'the outstanding political points could easily be settled'.[56] At this juncture Bonnet concluded that the political pact was 'in the bag' and telephoned the news to Herriot who congratulated him on 'having concluded this Anglo-Franco-Soviet agreement'.[57] Bonnet was guilty of wishful thinking, perhaps understandably after weeks of tortuous negotiations. However, the fundamental issue of the transit of Soviet forces across Poland and Rumania had not been broached.

The French Foreign Minister had not undergone a change of heart towards the Soviet Union. His appeal to Halifax on 19 July was probably prompted by a stiffly-worded letter of 15 July from Ribbentrop, warning France not to interfere in the Danzig dispute. Bonnet wanted to round off the political talks with Moscow in order to strengthen his country's diplomatic position but he had no enthusiasm for military discussions. On 5 May Léger claimed that Bonnet 'was opposed to bringing the Soviet Union into close co-operation with France and England'.[58] Three days later, Bonnet himself told Bullitt that 'he had no confidence whatsoever in Russian promises and doubted that, even though the Soviet Union should promise to support Poland . . . the support would be forthcoming'.[59] 'Once more', noted Bullitt, Bonnet had made it 'abundantly clear that the present French policy is Daladier's and Léger's and not his own'.[60]

Bonnet in fact had no choice but to follow the new line. In April Daladier told the Rumanian Foreign Minister, Gafencu, that 'he was going to get rid of Bonnet quite shortly'.[61] On 6 May he confided to Bullitt 'his distrust of Bonnet and said that he might replace him in the immediate future'.[62] Of course, the Foreign Minister was no doubt well aware of what was being said about him. That he did not consider resignation until mid-July was a measure not only of his political ambition but also of his determination to work for a settlement with Germany. Why, then, did Daladier delay until September before replacing him? One consideration was the need to avoid a ministerial crisis. When British Labour party leaders asked Blum in May why Bonnet was still at the Quai the Socialist leader replied that Daladier 'did not wish to sack' him 'since this would endanger his majority in the Chamber'.[63] The coming of war in September 1939 provided a justification for major Cabinet changes. Moreover, Daladier was not without a certain canniness. He had not abandoned all hope of conciliation and believed that Bonnet might yet prove useful if the international climate changed for the better.

The objective of Franco-British diplomacy in the spring and summer of 1939 was the creation of a peace front in eastern and south-eastern Europe. But French efforts to enlist Soviet aid for Rumania and Poland were not matched by exertions elsewhere. Turkey was regarded as the key to the eastern Mediterranean and Balkan area but negotiations in Ankara for a Turkish alliance were almost as protracted as those in Moscow. London quickly outpaced Paris. An Anglo-Turkish declaration of mutual assistance was announced on 12 May. The French government had wanted a tripartite pact but this was delayed until 19 October 1939.[64] London and Paris conducted separate negotiations with Ankara.

The Franco-Turkish discussions were bedevilled by a long-standing dispute over the sovereignty of the Hatay, formerly the Sanjak of Alexandretta. The issue was envenomed by the French mandates over Syria and the Lebanon. The Syrian mandate expired at the end of 1939 and France had promised independence to Syria. Arab opinion opposed Ankara's demand for the Hatay, fearing Turkish aggrandisement. In Beirut, the outlook of the French High Commission for Syria and the Lebanon tended to be anti-Turk. René Massigli, formerly Political Director of the Quai, was appointed Ambassador to Turkey in November 1938. He appreciated that any understanding with Ankara would have to be based on the cession of the Hatay. His memoirs of his Ankara mission illuminate some of the shortcomings of the French diplomatic machine. The determination which France displayed in the Moscow talks was the exception rather than the rule. Having opened negotiations in mid-February 1939, Massigli was left for several weeks without instructions.[65] A Franco-Turkish declaration of assistance, providing for the cession of the Hatay to Turkey, was not signed until 23 June 1939. The delays and tergiversations which Massigli encountered in Paris reflected in part the complexity of the interests involved but unfortunately they were also part of a general dilatoriness which infected the main branches of French government.[66]

While in April and May Paris had spurred London forward in the Moscow talks, in June the pressure was relaxed. One reason for this relaxation was Daladier's belief that there was no immediate danger of war. Since the Albanian episode in April, nerves had steadied. On 5 June Daladier told Bullitt that 'the next great moment of danger would come at the end of July after the German harvest'.[67] There was a trace of optimism in the French Prime Minister: 'Hitler was now most hesitant to begin a war. The military position of France and England was much stronger than last September . . . he felt Mussolini had aged rapidly . . . and had begun to lose his grip'.

Another factor, however, was the revival of appeasement. On 24 June the United States Chargé d'Affaires in Paris signalled that 'a second Munich' at the expense of Poland seemed to be 'in the making'.[68] Despite the government's protestations that France would honour her engagements to Poland, there were several disquieting symptoms. The diplomat detected a sense of weariness over the continuing tension in Europe, reinforced by the feeling — 'probably widespread' — that the Danzig 'set-up' was 'unsound and not worth a war'. Deputies, acting on complaints from constituents, had asked Daladier how much longer reservists would be kept on active service. Colonel Beck, too, was deeply disliked and distrusted in political circles. It was felt that if the Moscow talks broke down France would be left alone in the west. Poland, it was argued, was not worth a long war. Allied to these considerations was the 'demoralising effect of developments in the Far East'. French opinion realised that if war came in Europe the days of France's far eastern empire were numbered. Lastly, the American Chargé d'Affaires instanced the 'persistence of the feeling in influential circles that after all France should abandon central and eastern Europe to Germany, trusting that eventually Germany will come into conflict with the Soviet Union'.

In the Far East Franco-British interests were increasingly imperilled. The Tientsin dispute in the second half of June marked a major stage in the deterioration of Franco-Japanese relations. The Japanese challenged the large foreign concessions in the port of Tientsin. Britain took the view that no action would be effective 'unless we had the co-operation of the United States of America'.[69] France had a 100,000 troops in Indo-China but on 17 June Bonnet told Phipps that in the event of a European war he did not believe the territory could be defended.[70] Naval strength was crucial. The French Foreign Minister told the Chamber foreign affairs committee on 21 June: 'I was looking this morning at the state of our fleet and of the English fleet in the Far East. It is not enormous. We have one cruiser at Saigon and the other at Shanghai'.[71] Since February Daladier had argued that Britain and France had 'to concentrate their forces in Europe'.[72] In April, French Ministers maintained that it would be a grave error to send any part of the British fleet to the Far East since if the 'Mediterranean was lost, all is lost, whereas if we are victorious in Europe we can make good later on any temporary defeat . . . in the Far East'.[73] The renewal of tension over Danzig in July confirmed French thinking. On 26 July General Buhrer, Chief of Staff for the colonies, advised Gamelin: 'It seems certain to me that the European situation requires us for the time being not to disperse our military and naval efforts'.[74]

Attempts to secure common action with the United States in the Far East failed. Nor was any effort made by France to reach a settlement with Japan. French support for China in the Sino-Japanese war caused great resentment in Tokyo. War supplies were sent to General Chiang Kai-shek over the Red River railway into Yunnan province. In October 1937 following Japanese protests the line was closed to war material. Under Mandel's initiative supplies were resumed and in June 1939 a French military mission was sent to Chiang Kai-shek.[75] When in August the conclusion of the German-Soviet pact led to some improvement in Franco-Japanese relations Daladier admitted to Bullitt that 'active steps' to exploit this amelioration would have been taken but 'for the simple physical fact that no one in Paris had time to give to this problem'.[76]

One man who had strong reservations about the direction of French policy was Jacques Chastenet, editor of Le Temps. Meeting Léger at lunch on 6 June he could not resist a sally: 'And which country have you guaranteed this morning?' he asked. In a letter of 13 June to an English correspondent Chastenet claimed that a large section of French opinion was worried by the course of Franco-British diplomacy.[77] The tactic of the warmongers, he argued, was to seek to persuade French and British opinion that they were in a majority. Recent visits to France had been made by politicians such as Churchill, Duff Cooper and Eden who advocated 'a policy of adventures'. French opinion might derive the impression that such men were representative of British thinking. Why not send us, suggested Chastenet, moderate men of the Conservative party, holding different views to Churchill. Chastenet had really little cause for concern. On 15 June Eden lectured in Paris. Phipps, it seems, tried to sabotage the lecture, suggesting that 'June was a bad month for lectures and it would be better to reconsider it in the autumn'.[78] In the event, the lecture passed off quietly. Phipps was able to assure Chamberlain that Eden had said 'nothing in the least contrary to the policy of H M Government. . . Today Anthony was slightly worried because an obscure organ tried to oppose him to H M Government'.[79]

The German embassy in Paris had contacts with several French politicians, notably Flandin, Déat and Piétri but not Laval.[80] Laval was *lying low at this time and said little, although in a speech on 24 June* he called forcefully for Franco-Italian friendship. Those politicians who had sympathised with Germany's case over Czechoslovakia kept in touch with the embassy and maintained that Hitler's aims in eastern Europe could still be realised after a period of waiting. Estimates varied of how long Germany would have to wait. On 2 June Déat suggested six months to a year. On 15 June, Piétri who had just returned from London, stated that Germany could achieve her aims in Danzig within three months by diplomatic means. The use of force would lead to war. But there was a significant difference between the June utterances of the appeasement-minded politicians and their pre-Prague pronouncements. All of them, including Flandin, insisted that 'the majority of the French people were resolved to meet a fresh German *coup de force* by every means, even by means of war'.[81] Flandin was much less in evidence than in 1938. If Daladier is to be believed, the former Minister had been seriously compromised by an incident in May. Flandin apparently called on a young lady and was in bed with her 'when her *amant de coeur* broke into the apartment', beat up Flandin 'and drove him into the street, half-clothed, minus his watch, wallet and trousers'.[82]

At the end of June, official attitudes towards Germany stiffened appreciably but the change was the result not of long-term resolution but of panic. Coulondre contributed in part to the hardening of policy. On 24 June he called on Bonnet at the Quai d'Orsay and said he was convinced Germany intended to seize Danzig and the Polish Corridor.[83] In August Germany would mobilise as she had done in 1938. The Ambassador detected a certain 'hesitation' in British opinion, prompted by misgivings about the wisdom of the guarantees. France, he told Bonnet, could combat the dangers ahead in two ways: the Moscow talks should be swiftly concluded and a plain warning given to Germany that action against Danzig would lead to war. Welczeck, suggested Coulondre, should be reminded of France's determination. Bonnet replied that he had already considered seeing Welczeck and intended to give him a written statement of French policy. But Bonnet was in no hurry to summon the German Ambassador and on 29 June Coulondre reminded the Foreign Minister of his promise to give Welczeck a clear definition of France's attitude. Action should be taken as soon as possible, advised the Ambassador, and, if possible, the Foreign Office should be asked to make a similar statement to the German Ambassador in London.[84]

On Friday 30 June reports reached Daladier of an imminent *coup* against Danzig. In Paris, Ribbentrop's agent, Otto Abetz, had 'the effrontery' to telephone to various people, announcing a *coup* for the week-end.[85] Daladier at once suggested to London an 'energetic' declaration but received no support. Halifax told colleagues that the publication of a statement 'might be playing the German game' but 'newspapers had been given a certain amount of inspired direction'.[86] Daladier instructed Bonnet to make it clear to Welczeck that France would help Poland. The Foreign Minister received Welczeck on 1 July and handed him a note for Ribbentrop, stating that 'any action, whatever its form, which would modify the *status quo* in Danzig . . . would bring the Franco-Polish agreement into play'.[87] In form nothing could have been firmer or plainer. Yet Bonnet's presentation of the declaration turned what Daladier had intended as a blunt warning into a damp squib. Welczeck was told that the note 'was only to be considered as a verbal statement made in a perfectly friendly spirit'.[88] In the course of a long and friendly conversation Bonnet told how no one 'regretted . . . more than he' the failure of the Munich agreement. 'Even now', added Bonnet, 'the Eastern questions' could still be solved 'by means of negotiation'.[89] As for Abetz, Daladier issued an expulsion order against him but Bonnet proposed that he should leave of his own accord. Abetz left on 2 July but the affair simmered on for the rest of the month. Ribbentrop took the expulsion order as a personal affront and repeatedly urged Welczeck to secure its cancellation so that Abetz could return.

In a haughtily-worded letter of 13 July Ribbentrop replied to Bonnet's note of 1 July. The German Foreign Minister reiterated the German claim that in the negotiations for the Franco-German declaration of 6 December 1938 France had disinterested herself in eastern Europe and was not, therefore, entitled to meddle in the Danzig dispute. Ten days later, Bonnet answered the charge, asserting that 'at no moment either before or since the 6 December declaration has it been possible . . . to think that France had decided to disinterest herself in the east'.[90] In all probability Bonnet never bargained for such a stiff rejoinder from Ribbentrop. Having presented his note in a friendly fashion Bonnet had striven to dilute it still further. Acting presumably on instructions, Coulondre on 13 July represented the note 'as an act of consultation and loyalty' in the spirit of the 6 December declaration.[91] That same day the Ambassador advised Paris that 'polemics' on Danzig should be avoided.[92] Daladier, too, when he received Welczeck on 11 July was remarkably conciliatory. Although he complained of being deceived and ridiculed by the Prague *coup*, he asserted that he 'still held in spite of everything' to a Franco-German understanding.[93] There was even a half-apology for the expulsion of Abetz.

Despite the peremptory tone of Ribbentrop's letter, Bonnet might still have concocted a conciliatory reply but for the wide publicity which Germany gave to the correspondence. Ribbentrop gave copies of the correspondence to the Italian, Japanese and Belgian envoys. On 17 July Henderson, too, was told of the exchanges. Bonnet was aggrieved that this had been done in spite of the letter's 'entirely personal character and form'.[94] Thus Bonnet had firmness thrust upon him. Nevertheless, the ten-day delay between the receipt of Ribbentrop's letter on 15 July and the dispatch of a French reply suggests that Bonnet may have fought a strong rearguard action in favour of conciliating Ribbentrop. On 28 July he confided to Monzie that he had offered Daladier his resignation ten days earlier. Monzie does not record Bonnet's reasons for resignation but they may well have centred on the nature of the French reply to Ribbentrop.

Bonnet's offer of resignation may also have been prompted by charges that he was in touch with spies working for Germany. In July France was gripped by a spy scare. In a speech of 27 June closing the parliamentary session, Daladier alluded vaguely to 'attempts . . . being made to involve France in a network of trickery, intrigues, espionage, perhaps even worse'.[95] Following Abetz's expulsion, accusations were freely bandied about. Anyone who had met or associated with Abetz came under suspicion. On 12 July two journalists, Aubin, news editor of *Le Temps,* and Poirier, who had worked for *Figaro*, were arrested on charges of receiving money from Germany for spying. All this was meat and drink to the Foreign Minister's enemies. Word reached London that Madame Bonnet was intimate with some of the people implicated in the Aubin-Poirier case.[96] She was alleged to have written to one of the spy's friends, offering to pass on to her husband any requests. Welczeck was said to have shown Daladier proof of Madame Bonnet's involvement. Daladier, it was reported, decided to hush up the whole affair. Further speculation was caused by Poirier's death shortly after his arrest. The Patenôtres—Raymond Patenôtre was Minister of National Economy—told the British embassy that they believed evidence existed linking Madame Bonnet to the spies. So Bonnet was attacked through his wife but the gossips conceded that although Madame Bonnet might have written to someone who knew the spies she was not necessarily involved in any reprehensible way. It seems unlikely, to say the least, that the Bonnets were associated with German or Italian paid spies. After the fall of France, French exiles thundered against the machinations of a German Fifth Column and the names of Bonnet and Flandin were often linked with its activity. But no hard evidence was produced. All that the Deuxième Bureau would tell the embassy in July 1939 was that the 'ramifications of Nazi propaganda extend to every walk of life and are found in the Press, cultural associations, films, railway and tourist agencies'.[97]

Relations between London and Paris had never been as close and friendly as during recent months, observed the Quai d'Orsay in June 1939.[98] The state visits of July 1938 and March 1939 seemed to set the seal on a new found intimacy. Undeniably much had been achieved. Full staff talks had been in progress since 29 March. Visits and exchanges multiplied. A Franco-British parliamentary committee was set up on 29 June. The Royal Air Force provided morale boosting flights over France. Hore-Belisha, Secretary of State for War, was particularly active. On 4 July at a banquet in Paris he spoke of the 'closest liaison between Government Departments in London and Paris'. Gamelin went to London. On 14 July Hore-Belisha and Lord Gort, Chief of the Imperial General Staff, were present at the celebrations of the *Quatorze Juillet.* In the march past of 30,000 troops Gort took the salute jointly with Gamelin. The French crowds were especially cheered by the British participation—Royal Marines, a Guards detachment and an RAF fly past.

Yet this flurry of activity had the air of a desperate race to make up for lost time. Nor was everything sweetness and light. There were serious disagreements on two outstanding issues: relations with Italy and defence arrangements. On 13 July Chamberlain wrote to Daladier suggesting that the French leader was now 'so strongly entrenched' in power 'as to be able at least to allow Italy to formulate her proposals'.[99] Mussolini, continued Chamberlain, could still influence Hitler and the issue of peace or war might hinge on Italy. Bonnet of course held the same view. In a secret interview with the foreign minister on 10 July Henderson had impressed on him that the *Duce* could play a decisive role in the crisis. Daladier would have none of these arguments. 'Any new initiative', he told Chamberlain on 24 July, would be considered by Italy as a sign of weakness.[100] Acknowledging Daladier's letter on 3 August Chamberlain conceded that the French Minister's arguments were 'powerful ones' and agreed that the moment was no longer opportune for an initiative. However, he hoped Daladier 'would not take it amiss' if at some future date he renewed his appeal.[101]

Although French and British staffs were meeting regularly, no permanent machinery existed for the co-ordination of Franco-British war plans. On 26 July Chamberlain took the lead, asking Daladier to consider the creation in wartime of a Supreme War Council which would meet both in Paris and London. This body would be assisted by an inter-allied general staff based in Britain. Chamberlain proposed that the inter-allied staff should be set up forthwith.[102] Gamelin was not enamoured of the idea, fearing that the inter-allied staff would be an instrument of 'British imperial strategy'. The French General Staff wanted the supreme war council and inter-allied staff to be based in France, with a French Commander-in-Chief of all forces. On 3 August Daladier accepted the idea of a supreme war council in wartime but suggested that in place of the proposed inter-allied general staff a peacetime 'committee of study' should be established. On 17 August Chamberlain concurred.

The suspicions of Daladier and Léger that Chamberlain still hankered after appeasement appeared confirmed when news broke on 24 July that Robert Hudson, Secretary of the Department of Overseas Trade, had made economic offers to a German official, Wohltat, who was close to Goering. It seemed that far-reaching economic and colonial concessions had been discussed. There was 'pained surprise' in Paris.[103] Chamberlain's Commons statement of 24 July that the talks had taken place without the approval or knowledge of the government went some way towards allaying anxieties but much uneasiness remained. France would have been much more disturbed if it had been known that Sir Horace Wilson, Chamberlain's leading adviser, had also talked to Wohltat. The public outcry over Hudson's overtures helped to screen the Wilson-Wohltat contacts. Although the general reaction in France to the Hudson-Wohltat talks was severely critical, certain newspapers—the Right wing *Intransigeant,* the big business organ *Journée Industrielle,* the Radical Socialist *République*—defended the talks and said the proposals were not without merit.

No secret Franco-German discussions took place but some French politicians continued to work for an understanding with the dictators. Piétri, for example, bombarded Daladier with memoranda urging a compromise over Danzig. Monzie tried unsuccessfully to interest Delbos in enlisting Italian mediation. The former Minister replied on 29 July that it seemed to him 'more effective . . . to impress the Axis than to hope to break it at this time'.[104] Bonnet's opinions were well known. On 15 August the British Chargé d'Affaires described him as being 'only too ready to discuss a compromise on the Danzig question'.[105] In mid-July another attempt had been made to patch up the quarrel with Italy. Yves de Boisanger, Assistant Governor of the Bank of France and a friend of Bonnet, met Malvezzi, an Italian industrialist.[106] The banker stressed that if a conflict came everyone had something to lose. Britain and France could not 'for obvious reasons of prestige' retract their pledge to Poland but they had made themselves 'slaves of Poland'. Italian intervention was essential to a peaceful solution of the Danzig dispute. Boisanger emphasised the social situation in France. For several months, Communist party membership had been increasing after a loss of strength during the winter. Economic difficulties were increasing in all countries as a result of rearmament. Without a peaceful outcome of the political crisis, 'the economic crisis of 1929 would be repeated with even worse consequences'. A four power meeting, proposed the banker, could establish European peace. France was ready to send an emissary to Rome in order to open semi-official negotiations. The Italian industrialist reported the conversation to his government and Ciano saw his report on 2 August but no action was taken.

Chapter 19

Last Days

In August the months of hard bargaining in Moscow were brought to an unexpected conclusion. The Soviet insistence on a military convention as a prerequisite for a political accord had been accepted by the western negotiators in mid-July, and on 27 July Bonnet urged London that the military delegations should depart 'in the next three or four days'.[1] With a German *coup* against Danzig forecast for the end of August, and continuing reports of German-Soviet negotiations, speed was the essence of the matter. Yet nine days elapsed before the departure of the missions on 5 August, and their journey to Moscow took another week. Mandel confessed to Souritz, the Soviet Ambassador, that in London and Paris an agreement with the Soviet Union was still regarded not as the cornerstone of a military alliance against Germany but as a means of improving the position for future talks with Hitler.[2]

The head of the French mission was General Doumenc, a specialist in motorised warfare and at 60 years of age the French army's youngest general. In a letter of 27 July Gamelin sent Doumenc instructions for the mission.[3] On 29 July General Ismay, Secretary of the Committee of Imperial Defence, was in Paris for talks with Gamelin and General Jamet, Secretary General of the Conseil Supérieur de la Guerre. The main purpose of the visit was to discuss Chamberlain's proposals for a supreme war council and inter-allied general staff. Ismay also talked to Doumenc and was shown a copy of the general's instructions. The instructions struck Ismay 'as being couched in such general terms as to be almost useless as a brief', dealing 'solely with what the French wish the Russians to do' and throwing 'no light on what the French will do'.[4] When Doumenc was asked what he would say if the Russians pressed for information on French war plans he replied: 'Very little, I shall just listen'. Travel arrangements for the two missions were discussed. Doumenc wanted to go by rail from Paris to Moscow. Ismay commented: 'My proposal that air travel, if it could be arranged, would be just as quick and less embarrassing was not welcomed. I did not pursue the argument'.

On 1 August no firm decision on travel arrangements had yet been made. The French still hankered after direct rail travel from Paris. Ismay retorted that the British delegation were 'quite determined' to go by sea to Leningrad and 'if the French preferred to go through Germany, they must do so alone'.[5] Next day, Daladier and Léger agreed to sea travel, partly persuaded by the British argument that the delay involved in a sea journey was unlikely to be more than 2-3 days. The two delegations met in London on 4 August and set sail next day from Tilbury. The sea voyage lasted 6 days since the *City of Exeter,* an old merchant ship, could not steam at more than 13 knots.

Much more important than the delays in departure was the failure to co-ordinate the instructions of the two delegations. The brief given to the British mission affirmed that the two teams should 'work as one in all but name' but admitted that there had been no time to consult with the French.[6] This is difficult to understand since the British memorandum of guidance was approved on 31 July and could then have been forwarded to Paris. In fact a copy was not sent until 3 August, too late for the French delegation to study before travelling to London.[7] The meeting of the two missions in London on 4 August was no more than a formal introduction and the opportunity for a detailed comparison of instructions did not come until the *City of Exeter* was at sea. The British brief was embodied in a lengthy memorandum whereas the French directive was a document of less than three pages, laconic in the extreme.

Yet despite the leisurely sea voyage a fundamental discrepancy in the instructions of the two missions did not come to light until the first meeting with the Soviet delegation on 12 August. Marshal Voroshilov, Commissar for Defence and chairman of the Soviet delegation, flourished a document empowering him to negotiate and sign a military convention. Asked for his own instructions, Doumenc produced an order, signed by Daladier, authorising him 'to discuss all military matters'.[8] The unfortunate Admiral Drax, leader of the British mission, 'gave a slight cough' — according to Doumenc — and admitted that he had no written authority.[9] The French now discovered, as Naggiar reported to Bonnet the same day, that Drax 'was not to involve himself in precise military discussions until the terms of the political agreement had been finally fixed'.[10]

However it has been too readily assumed that Doumenc was fully empowered to sign an agreement. Mr Sidney Aster writes:

> But the French were up to their old tricks. Unknown to the British Government, Daladier had seen Doumenc privately on July 31st and warned him: 'Bring us back an agreement at all costs'.[11]

Yet there is no documentary evidence for the instruction which Daladier is alleged to have given Doumenc. Daladier's own notes for the interview with Doumenc on 31 July contain no reference to such a remark. Nor does Doumenc mention such a statement in his account of the mission.[12] Besides, it seems unfair to criticise the French for stealing a march on their allies when the British government, by accident or design, left it to the last minute to arrange a hurried joint briefing for the two missions. Even assuming that Daladier did speak to Doumenc in such a sense, it would be wrong to read too much into his words. Doumenc in fact was not empowered to sign an agreement. The written order which Daladier sent to him on 3 August was worded thus:

General Doumenc is authorised to discuss with the High Command of the Soviet armed forces all questions concerning the necessary collaboration between the armed forces of the two countries.

On 20 August Naggiar, French Ambassador at Moscow, had to cable Paris asking for Doumenc to be authorised to sign a military convention, subject to ratification by the government.[13]

On 14 August, at the third session of the military talks, Marshal Voroshilov put the key question which Britain and France had dodged since the opening of negotiations in April. Would Poland and Rumania allow Soviet troops to cross their frontiers? asked the Soviet Marshal. The French representatives, Doumenc and Naggiar, wired Paris with the suggestion that General Valin, deputy chief of the French mission, should be sent to Warsaw to brief the French Ambassador, Léon Noel.[14] News of Voroshilov's question had reached Bonnet in the small hours of 15 August. Precious time was then frittered away. Bonnet decided to act through Lukasiewicz, the Polish Ambassador in Paris. Unfortunately, the envoy was on holiday in Brittany and did not return to Paris until the afternoon of the 15th. His reaction was negative but he promised to consult Beck. Daladier and Bonnet then turned to the French Military Attaché at Warsaw, General Musse, who was in Paris on leave. Musse was told to intervene personally with the Polish General Staff. Meanwhile in Moscow Doumenc still awaited a reply to his request to send his deputy to Warsaw. At 8 p.m. on the 15th he asked urgently for a reply; on the 16th he was told that General Valin, his deputy, could not be sent 'because of the repercussions which would result'.[15]

General Musse, the Military Attaché in Warsaw, returned to his post in the evening of the 15th. Instructions to Noel to see Beck were not sent until the late evening of 16th; and the ambassador did not carry out the démarche until the 18th. Beck was warned that in refusing rights of passage to Soviet troops he would make himself responsible 'for the failure of the military talks in Moscow and for all the resulting consequences'.[16] A plain hint that without Soviet help the French and British guarantees would be of little value.

In Moscow Doumenc was anxious to restart talks with Voroshilov and decided to send one of his assistants, Captain Beauffre, to Warsaw. Beauffre was asked to give Noel and Musse a first-hand report of the Moscow talks. Naggiar manoeuvred impatiently to find a way out of the impasse. On 17 August he told Noel that it would be sufficient for the Polish General Staff to express tacitly their full confidence in Doumenc 'to work out with the Russians the programme of co-operation'.[17] On arrival in Warsaw on the 18th, Beauffre found both Noel and his attaché extremely doubtful about the chances of persuading the Poles to accept Soviet help. Musse, in particular, 'feared a priori the bad faith of the Soviets'.[18] The attaché overrated Poland's military strength. Approached on the 18th Beck reserved his reply; on the 19th he gave a firm negative: 'we have no military understanding with the USSR; we do not want to have one'.[19]

By now desperate to resolve the dilemma, Naggiar and Doumenc suggested that the best course was to interpret Beck's *'non'* as an affirmative and to say it for him. On 20 August they informed Paris that they proposed to give Voroshilov 'an affirmative answer in principle'.[20] It was essential, wired Naggiar, that Doumenc should be sent authority to sign a military convention. Daladier's reply giving Doumenc the necessary powers did not reach Moscow until 10.30 p.m. on 21 August. But by that time Berlin had announced that Germany and the Soviet Union had negotiated a non-aggression pact and Ribbentrop would fly to Moscow for its signature on 23 August.

In his memoirs Beauffre argued that if Daladier's authority had been sent 'four days sooner' then 'all might have been changed'.[21] This is doubtful to say the least. The French negotiators tried to pretend that Poland had said Yes when she had in fact said No. The Russians would have none of this equivocation. When on 22 August Doumenc told Voroshilov that the answer to the question asked on the 14th was in the affirmative the Marshal replied: 'We must have a definite reply from the Governments of these countries'.[22] Only a formal expression of Polish and Rumanian consent would have satisfied Moscow.

The reaction of the French leaders to the news of the German-Soviet pact was to blame the Poles and the Russians. The Poles, complained Daladier, had been guilty of 'criminal folly'. The Russians had 'hoodwinked' and 'deceived' French diplomats.[23] Yet the howls of betrayal and rage were hardly justified. British and French diplomacy since the *Anschluss* had made a German-Soviet alliance almost a foregone conclusion. As early as 4 October 1938 Coulondre had written to Bonnet: 'in these conditions, what other course remains for her (*USSR*) but to return to the policy of entente with Germany that she abandoned in 1931? . .'

British and French intelligence services have been criticised for not knowing what was afoot. On 22 August Daladier reminded Bullitt that 'at least six times since last January' the Ambassador 'had warned him that most serious negotiations were under way between the Germans and the Russians' but he 'had been reassured' by government agencies 'that there were no negotiations other than the commercial negotiations in progress'.[24] However, since there were no firm political negotiations between Germany and the Soviet Union until July it is less than just to criticise French intelligence for not knowing of these exchanges.

Even if the Quai d'Orsay had been as well-informed as the State Department which had an informant in the German embassy in Moscow, it is difficult to see how France could have acted otherwise in the last stages of the negotiations with the Soviet Union. Since early May French ministers had been worried by the danger of a German-Soviet *rapprochement* but they were trapped by the eastern pacts. As a Quai minute of 29 July noted: 'the principal risk is to see the Russians pose the dilemma: all or nothing— everything if the Poles are their allies— if not, a refusal to be involved in the affair'.[25] By 1939 the alliances were incompatible and the problem was insoluble. A full-blooded Franco-Soviet alliance might have driven Poland and Rumania into Germany's arms and vitiated the peace front diplomacy. Equally, to ignore the Soviet Union meant risking a German-Soviet pact and the extinction of Rumania and Poland.

Under the shock of the impending German-Soviet pact Daladier showed signs of wavering. He and Léger had assumed that a firm Anglo-Franco-
Soviet front would be enough to overawe Germany. Léger was overheard
saying on the telephone: 'We are playing a game of poker: our adversary
is bluffing'.[26] On 22 August Daladier flinched at the prospect of imminent war, telling Bullitt:

> the Poles could not hold out against the German armies for more than two
> months. Thereafter the entire brunt of the war on land . . . would fall on the
> French Army . . .
> as soon as England and France should become engaged in Europe, Japan would
> begin taking over French, British and Dutch possessions . . . Under the circum-
> stances he was faced with the alternative of sacrificing the lives of all able-
> bodied men in France in a war the outcome of which would be to say the least
> doubtful; or the worse alternative of abandoning the commitments of France to
> support Poland which would be a horrible moral blow to the French people.[27]

The United States seemed to offer a possible escape from the dilemma.
Daladier 'hoped profoundly' that Roosevelt would summon a conference
in Washington. If the President did so, he would accept 'instantly and
with deep gratitude'.[28] Next day, Bonnet seconded the appeal on the
grounds that 'no question involved in the present dispute could possibly
justify the sacrifice of 30,000,000 soldiers'.[29] In the afternoon of the 22nd
Bullitt talked to Léger at the Quai d'Orsay:

> Throughout our conversation politicians kept calling him on the telephone
> urging that it would be folly to go to war in support of Poland in view of the
> agreement between the Soviet Union and Germany . . . Léger replied that France
> must fight.[30]

But the Secretary General admitted to Bullitt that 'it was exceedingly
doubtful, to put it mildly, that France and England would be able to win
the war'.

At 5 p.m. on 22 August French ministers gathered at the War Ministry,
rue St-Dominique.[31] The Cabinet had not met since 28 July. Daladier's control of foreign policy was underlined by the fact that he spoke first and reported in detail on the events of the last few weeks. Pathetically, he refused
to believe that all was lost. Ribbentrop and Molotov had not yet signed the
non-aggression pact. A new effort, he told colleagues, would be made to
induce Warsaw to agree to the passage of Soviet troops. Predictably,
Mandel and Reynaud called for general mobilisation: 'half-measures were
of no use', said Reynaud. Daladier resisted this pressure, pointing out that
three classes of reservists had already been recalled. The army was in a
state of alert and over a million men under arms. The fleet was on a war
footing. Gamelin, said Daladier, wished to wait longer before declaring
a general mobilisation. At this point Bonnet interjected: 'From a diplomatic view point, I do not ask for mobilisation'. Silence followed. Then
Monzie pleaded for negotiations with Italy. Daladier and Campinchi
answered that France would only expose herself to another affront. Next
Guy la Chambre spoke reassuringly about the state of air defences. Urban
areas could be protected by the air force, although 'reprisal raids' on

Germany would have to be carried out by the RAF. Chautemps remarked that a declaration of war would require the recall of parliament. This was not yet necessary, said Daladier.

Following the signature of the German-Soviet pact on 23 August Bonnet made a last effort to wriggle out of the Polish pledge. At the Foreign Minister's request, Daladier agreed to summon a special meeting of Service ministers and chiefs of staff. Contrary to what Bonnet later claimed, it was an *ad hoc* gathering, not a full meeting of the Permanent Committee of National Defence.[32] The meeting marked the final campaign in the private war which Bonnet and Gamelin had waged since Munich. From a reading of his memoirs it seems that the Chief of the General Staff was more suspicious of Bonnet than of the Germans. The two men crossed swords on 11 August when Gamelin, with Daladier's approval, asked Bonnet to tell him exactly what had been said in the 'conversations held between him and Ribbentrop'.[33] Bonnet showed Gamelin the text of the letters exchanged with Ribbentrop in July. The correspondence confirmed Gamelin's belief that the foreign minister had deliberately maintained an ambiguous attitude towards eastern Europe in the winter of 1938-39. The interview was a tit-for-tat affair. Bonnet said he was worried about the state of the air force. Hitler, he stressed, was not bluffing. Was France ready to fight? Gamelin would not be tricked into any admission of military weakness. The state of the army and air force, he replied, were excellent.

On 23 August Bonnet, in his own words, was determined 'to corner' Gamelin.[34] Whatever the general said would provide the foreign minister with ammunition. If he declared France ready for war then Bonnet could not be criticised for a declaration of war. However, any confession of doubts would strengthen Bonnet's hand in working for a compromise with Germany. Service ministers and chiefs of staff met at the War Ministry at 6 p.m. on the 23rd. Daladier explained that the purpose of the meeting was to answer three questions: firstly could France remain passive while Poland and Rumania were destroyed; secondly what means were available to check Germany; thirdly what measures should be taken immediately. Bonnet put the first question to the chiefs of staff. Gamelin answered unequivocally that for France to do nothing would be disastrous. Control of Poland would greatly strengthen Germany. If France declared war in support of her ally, Polish resistance would last long enough to prevent the bulk of German forces being deployed against France until the following spring. By that date, substantial British forces would be available. In answer to the second question, Guy la Chambre reported that fighters were now being produced in large numbers and the condition of the air force 'should no longer weigh on the government decisions as it had done in 1938'. The army and navy were 'ready', declared Gamelin and Darlan, Chief of Naval Staff. At the outset of a war the army and navy could do little against Germany but they were capable of 'acting vigorously against Italy if that power entered the war'. The meeting was over by 7.30 p.m. Bonnet had received the answers he had expected but nevertheless the meeting had served its purpose and he took good care to obtain a record of proceedings.[35] It would be unfair to condemn the military chiefs for giving 'disastrously misleading advice to their political colleagues'.[36] They promised neither an offensive nor a final victory. What they did make clear was that if France did not fulfil her pledge to Poland then her military position *vis-à-vis* Germany could only deteriorate.

At 10 a.m. on 24 August the full Cabinet met at the Elysée under Lebrun's chairmanship. It seemed as if the groupings of September 1938 were being revived.[37] Daladier still clung to the hope of an agreement with Moscow: 'discussions could be resumed with the Russians,' he declared. He cited Coulondre's opinion: 'don't break with the Russians'. Poland, continued the Prime Minister, was determined to defend Danzig but it would be a mistake for her to resist a German *coup*. At this point, a letter from Gamelin was read, stating that a Polish attack on Danzig would be folly. Daladier concluded: 'they must sacrifice Danzig. They ought to have done so earlier'. Zay and his friends were amazed by the ease with which Daladier, Bonnet, Marchandeau and Guy la Chambre were ready to consider the sacrifice of Danzig. While conceding that the greatest prudence should be enjoined on Poland, Mandel, Reynaud, Campinchi and Zay insisted that a German *coup* should activate the Franco-British guarantee. Mandel repeatedly asked Bonnet whether France would still honour her pledge if Poland refused advice. Daladier summed up the government's position: the utmost diplomatic pressure on Poland to ensure that Germany had no excuse for an attack, but in the event of an attack France would fulfil her obligations.

The hope that something might be salvaged from the Moscow negotiations persisted. On 25 August Roger Genebrier, Daladier's *chef de cabinet militaire*, suggested that the Socialist Pierre Cot, former Air Minister, might succeed in arranging some agreement with Moscow.[38] Doumenc, on his return from Moscow on 28 August, still believed in Voroshilov's sincerity and declared that in three months, France and the Soviet Union would be close allies. Some comfort was drawn from the fact that the Soviet government had not denounced the Franco-Soviet pact.

In a final bid to detach Britain from Poland, Hitler on 25 August made his 'last offer' of 'an Anglo-German understanding'.[39] No offer was made to France. Instead, Hitler tried to intimidate the French, warning Coulondre on the 25th that although Germany had no intention of attacking France, yet if she helped Poland, Germany would fight to the end. Daladier promised a 'sharp reply'.[40] But there was nothing sharp, or even mildly astringent, about the letter which he sent Hitler on 26 August. It was a semi-apologetic document in which the French Prime Minister, writing as one ex-serviceman to another, affirmed his desire for a peaceful settlement of the German-Polish dispute over Danzig and the Corridor. He offered his services as a mediator. The assertion that Poland would be defended was overshadowed by professions of peace. In delivering Daladier's reply Coulondre spent 40 minutes glossing the text with 'emotional arguments'.[41] Replying on 27 August, Hitler skilfully exploited the openings provided by Daladier: France's horror of war and desire for security.

The conciliatory tone of Daladier's letter to Hitler probably owed much to Roosevelt's diplomatic intervention. On 23 and 24 August the

President sent appeals for peace to Germany, Italy and Poland. Washington forwarded the Polish reply to Berlin, re-inforcing it with a second appeal. 'Profoundly grateful' for Roosevelt's initiative, Daladier promised to 'order all French radio stations to keep pounding the President's message to Hitler into German ears'.[42] Daladier's request for American intervention on 22 August had not been taken on the spur of the moment; over the last three years successive French governments had endeavoured to bring about closer Franco-American relations. The close personal ties which Daladier maintained with Bullitt testified to the importance which was attached to the United States. However, what was not generally known at the time was the extent to which the French government was prepared to go in order to win American support. French statesmen were even prepared to offer overseas territories. In February 1939 Reynaud, Minister of Finance, firmly grasped the nettle of First World War debts to the United States, offering to hand over at once ten billion francs in gold, ten per cent of the gold reserve of the Bank of France. Bullitt did not think this was enough and suggested that the offer might be better received if France could include one or more of her colonial possessions.[43] On 4 April Daladier in a wild moment 'stated that he did not care how many islands it might be necessary to turn over to the United States' if only the debt question could be settled.[44] Wisely, Reynaud pointed out to Daladier the inconsistency of France handing over territory to the United States at a time when she refused to surrender an inch of French soil to Italy. In fact France was spared any sacrifices, financial or otherwise. In May, Roosevelt told Jean Monnet, Daladier's envoy, that he did not want anything from France at that time.[45]

The British government recalled parliament for one day on 24 August and the House was in session from the 29th onwards. As in September 1938, Daladier did not rush to recall the Chambers, though in a note of 19 August Bonnet and Léger reminded him that according to article 9 of the Constitutional law of 1875 the President of the Republic could not declare war without the prior consent of the Chambers.[46] Yet, in contrast to 1938, there was no strong demand for the recall of parliament. Nor did Daladier take his colleagues into his confidence. After meeting on 24 August the Cabinet did not meet again until 31st, though the British Cabinet met on 26, 28 and 29 August. Zay and Monzie found it strange that 'Ministers were in the most complete ignorance of events'.[47]

Bonnet was frankly more concerned about seeking a peaceful compromise than in weighing the rights and wrongs of the German-Polish quarrel. Hitler's offer of 25 August, he told Phipps, would have 'to be taken into the most serious consideration'.[48] Chautemps, deputy Prime Minister, shared the Foreign Minister's opinion. But the decision rested with the British government and the British reply was not sent until the evening of 28 August. In the meantime, the French Foreign Minister made, in his own words, 'a desperate effort to avoid war'.[49] On 27 August he suggested that King Leopold of the Belgiums might intervene in Rome and also act as a mediator in the Danzig dispute. The same day he received the Italian statesman, Count Sforza. The meeting had been arranged by Jules Romains. Sforza proposed that if Germany attacked Poland, France should send an ultimatum to Italy, asking her to support France and demanding as a guarantee of good behaviour the occupation of two or three Italian towns. This idea was not at all to Bonnet's taste. He much preferred to woo the Italians rather than bully them. On 29 August he sought Spanish help, asking General Franco to suggest a ten-day truce during which Germany and Poland would undertake not to go to war. On the same day France backed an offer of mediation made by the Belgian and Dutch governments.

The hopes of the French Foreign Minister were focussed on Rome. For several days the Minister and his acolytes had been working for Italian mediation. When the Cabinet met on 24 August, Monzie's call for the re-opening of contacts with Rome had been opposed by Campinchi, Daladier and Sarraut. After the meeting Monzie made a special effort to win over Sarraut but the Minister of the Interior would not change his mind.[50] Nevertheless, there were already some semi-official contacts with Italy. On 26 August Bonnet confided to Phipps 'in the strictest confidence' that the French government was in touch with the *Duce*.[51] So, too, was the British government, although nothing was said to French Ministers.

Bonnet was anxious to send a special envoy to Rome. After consulting Daladier, he telephoned de Monzie at noon on 26 August, saying that he would shortly be asked to go to Rome as an emissary. A few hours later the idea had been abandoned.[52] In the evening of 28 August, de Monzie, accompanied by Mistler, chairman of the Chamber Foreign Affairs Committee, visited Guariglia, Italian Ambassador. They impressed on him that the last hope of avoiding war was the *Duce's* mediation.[53]

The French government spoke with conflicting voices. Daladier was being pushed and pulled in different directions. While Bonnet and his cronies canvassed Mussolini's intervention. Léger, supported by Campinchi and Sarraut, strove to forestall any such move. On 29 August Léger told Campbell, British Chargé d'Affaires, that any last minute Italian mediation should be treated with suspicion. Claiming that Daladier 'was definitely determined to reject any proposal for a general conference of the Munich kind', he begged London 'to beware of any stories or suggestions to the contrary . . . only the view of the President of the Council was valid'.[54]

As in the Czech crisis of 1938, the French sought to delay their ally's mobilisation until the last possible moment. Representations by Noel on 29 August induced the Poles to postpone their mobilisation for several hours. These few hours were crucial since they meant that a quarter of the army never reached its units at the front.[55]

On 29 August at 7.15 p.m. Hitler offered direct German-Polish talks provided a Polish plenipotentiary arrived in Berlin before midnight on the following day. Although the French government favoured acceptance of the proposal, they did not tell 'Beck to go to Berlin at once'.[56] Indeed, Coulondre advised against Henderson's suggestion that Beck should go to Berlin.[57] Before acting in Warsaw French ministers waited for their British ally. Only at 11.30 p.m. on 30 August was Noel instructed to join with the British Ambassador, Sir Howard Kennard, in urging the Poles to accept the German demands.

In Berlin, Coulondre was growing more and more mistrustful of Henderson. On the evening of 29-30 August he asked one of his consuls, who was returning to France, to carry a message to Léger and Charvériat, Political Director of the Quai. The message was received on 31 August: 'tenir, tenir, tenir' counselled Coulondre. France must remain firm to the end. Henderson, he said, was not to be trusted. An accommodation with Japan was urgent.[58]

On the evening of 31 August Coulondre and Henderson quarrelled on the telephone — a row overheard by the German monitoring service.[59] The two men clashed over Germany's peace proposals in the form of sixteen points which had been read out to Henderson at midnight on 30-31 August but not transmitted to Warsaw. Henderson argued for their immediate acceptance, although he had not yet received an official text. Coulondre insisted that acceptance of the sixteen points would not be possible until the Polish government had officially received them.

Shortly after midday on 31 August the *deus ex machina*, for which Bonnet and his friends had been praying, arrived. Bonnet heard through François-Poncet that Mussolini proposed the calling of a conference for 5 September to consider the revision of the Treaty of Versailles. The Italian government gave London preferential treatment. At 12.50 p.m., on 31 August, the Italian Foreign Minister, Ciano, telephoned the proposal to Halifax. Chamberlain and Halifax sent for Corbin to ascertain French reactions. The Ambassador knew nothing and telephoned Bonnet who told him that Daladier and the Cabinet would have to be consulted. Chamberlain's immediate reaction was that a conference was impossible without some degree of German demobilisation.

Bonnet's telephone conversation with Corbin had been guarded because the Minister had at once run foul of Léger. The Secretary-General dismissed the Italian conference proposal as a snare and delusion intended to save Germany 'from collapse and certainly to extricate her from the *impasse* into which she has got herself and to assure her without war the territorial goals she seeks'. If a conference met to discuss Poland and the Versailles settlement 'none of our alliances, none of our friendships could survive such an ordeal'.[60] Léger dissociated himself entirely from any attempt to follow up the proposal.

The French foreign minister postponed his lunch and went to see Daladier at his flat in the rue Anatole-de-la-Forge. He urged acceptance of the proposal on two conditions: Poland should be invited and the conference should consider all European problems. According to Bonnet, Daladier concurred and promised to call a Cabinet for 6 p.m. that day.[61] However other sources suggest that the French Prime Minister disliked the conference idea as much as Léger did. At 3.30 p.m. Phipps reported Daladier as saying 'that he would rather resign than accept' the Italian proposal.[62]

Returning to the Quai d'Orsay, Bonnet went into action, summoning his supporters to his side.[63] De Monzie arrived at 3 p.m. and found the Minister finishing a late lunch. Bonnet was confident that he could win

Cabinet approval for the conference proposal and said Chautemps would support him. For the remainder of the afternoon until the Cabinet met at 6 p.m. Bonnet's *camarilla* frantically canvassed support for the Italian suggestion. Piétri, who had been in daily touch with Bonnet for the previous ten days, was asked to concert with Flandin in sounding out parliamentary opinion. Although the Chambers had not been recalled, many deputies were returning to Paris. At his own ministry of public works de Monzie received in turn three of his colleagues: Pomaret, Minister of Labour, Queuille, Minister of Agriculture, and Zay, Minister of Education. Pomaret, a stalwart advocate of appeasement in 1938 could not be won over. However, Queuille and Zay showed some interest in the conference idea. Later, de Monzie joined Bérenger and Mistler, chairmen of the Senate and Chamber foreign affairs committees respectively, in visiting Guariglia, the Italian Ambassador. All three, noted the envoy, were full of sympathy for Italy and highly critical of the lukewarm British reception of the Italian proposal.[64]

The Cabinet meeting at 6 p.m. was a confused and stormy affair.[65] Personal relations between the Prime Minister and Foreign Minister seemed to have reached their nadir. By the end of the meeting they were not on speaking terms. Bonnet's plea for consideration of the conference proposal was lifeless and unconvincing. De Monzie judged him physically intimidated by Daladier who, bristling with anger and contempt, turned his back on the Foreign Minister. Coming to the rescue of his friend, de Monzie argued forcefully for acceptance of the conference proposal. Campinchi opposed any contact with Italy. Daladier feared a second Munich at the expense of Poland and France. Chautemps, the born conciliator, suggested that news of direct German-Polish negotiations should be awaited before reaching a decision.

A fierce exchange took place between Daladier and Bonnet on the subject of British views. The Foreign Minister asserted that Chamberlain would accept a conference provided some measure of demobilisation was carried out. Daladier challenged this statement, saying that he understood from Corbin that the British Prime Minister opposed a conference. He then read out a note of a telephone call from Corbin relating a talk with Halifax earlier in the afternoon: 'They (*British ministers*) do not want a new Munich. Public opinion will not tolerate it. But we must not expose ourselves to criticism of rejecting a peaceful solution'. In Corbin's opinion, the conference proposal was 'a danger' and 'a manoeuvre'.[66]

By now Daladier had the majority of Ministers, including President Lebrun, behind him. As a final flourish, an assistant entered the meeting and handed the Prime Minister a handwritten letter from Coulondre dated 30 August. The letter had been written in the evening of 30 August and sent to Paris by special messenger. Coulondre wrote:

... the attack against Poland was fixed for the night of 25-26 August. For reasons which are not clear, at the last moment Hitler drew back. . .
We have only to continue to hold fast, hold fast, hold fast (*tenir, tenir, tenir*) . . . I have learnt from a reliable source that for the past five days Hitler has been hesitating. Irresolution has gripped the heart of the Nazi party. Reports indicate a growing discontent among the people. . .

You are a fisherman, I believe. Well, the fish is hooked. It now has to be played with the required skill so as to land it without breaking the line. . .[67]

Reading the letter out Daladier punctuated the words *tenir, tenir, tenir* by banging his fist on the table.

From the conflicting accounts of the Cabinet meeting it is difficult to know what, if anything, was decided. However, the opposing factions drew their own conclusions from the acrimonious debate. Bonnet and de Monzie assumed that colleagues had conditionally accepted the conference proposal, while the Reynaud group talked of a polite rejection of the Italian initiative.[68] Piétri urged Bonnet to send a reply to Rome at the earliest opportunity and de Monzie drafted a note thus implementing, in his own words, a Cabinet decision 'which, in reality, had not been taken.'[69] At 11.30 p.m. Piétri handed Bonnet the note drafted by de Monzie. De Monzie telephoned the Foreign Minister suggesting that if the conference proposal failed they should both resign. Bonnet disagreed. Whatever happened, he would stay in the government.

In the small hours of Friday 1 September the German army marched into Poland. But for Bonnet all was not yet lost. The Poles might be fighting for their lives but for Bonnet 'Western civilization' was 'in peril'.[70] Doggedly, therefore, he clung to the conference proposal. It was now a means not only of averting a Franco-German war but also of keeping Italy neutral. Daladier's attitude had changed overnight. When the Cabinet assembled at 10 a.m. on 1 September he raised no objection to a favourable reply being sent to Rome. General mobilisation was decreed and the Chambers were recalled for 2 September. The French and British replies to Rome, although transmitted almost simultaneously in the morning of 1 September, were quite different in character. Halifax sent a virtual rejection, Bonnet a conditional acceptance. To guard against any possible misunderstanding, Bonnet stressed to Guariglia that the French reply was 'an acceptance in principle'.[71]

Ironically, after several months of British pressure on Paris to open negotiations with Rome, it was the French government which showed most sympathy for the Italian proposal. On Daladier's behalf, Guy la Chambre informed Guariglia that the Prime Minister wished to restore Franco-Italian friendship and expressed the hope that the *Duce* could still intervene in Berlin to secure a truce 'on the basis of which a conference could be held in accordance with the Italian proposal'.[72] During the day Ciano repeated to François-Poncet what he had told the British ambassador the previous evening: Italy would never start a war against France and Britain.

At 2.15 p.m. on Saturday 2 September Bonnet received a telephone call from Ciano. Apprised of Mussolini's proposal for a conference, Hitler had made two requests: confirmation of the non-ultimatum character of British and French notes sent to the German government on 1 September, and a delay until noon on Sunday 3 September for consideration of the Italian proposal. Bonnet replied that in his personal opinion the answer would be affirmative on both points. However, he would need to consult Daladier and the British government. Somehow historians have always contrived to give Bonnet less than his due. Writing in 1972, Nicholas Bethell dismissed Bonnet's claim that he undertook to consult the British as 'a claim which is not supported by any of the official records'.[73] In fact the record of the telephone conversation published in the French Yellow Book specifically mentions the undertaking given to consult the British government.[74]

Ciano also telephoned London and received a different reception from Halifax. The British Foreign Secretary, although willing to confirm the non-ultimatum character of the notes sent to Berlin the previous day, said his government would insist on German withdrawal from Polish territory as a prior condition for a conference. Bonnet and his associates were undaunted. Piétri suggested to the Foreign Minister that a 'symbolic withdrawal' of a few kilometres might serve as a compromise arrangement.[75]

When the French Cabinet met at 6 p.m. Daladier opened proceedings with a review of the latest developments, including the telephone call from Ciano. Zay in his diary recorded:

> Bonnet insists on acceptance of the Italian proposal to wait until midday on Sunday, if necessary a shorter ultimatum could then be given and, of course, one condition must be a German withdrawal.[76]

Daladier, noted Zay, was in agreement. The Foreign Minister did not mention Piétri's proposal for a symbolic withdrawal. However, as ministers dispersed, de Monzie:

> . . . pressed Bonnet to disregard the British *non-possumus*. To demand the withdrawal of German troops from Poland was an indefensible claim . . . Could there not be a third solution . . . . A symbolic withdrawal by a few miles? . . . It was agreed that while dining that evening with Guariglia I would sound him out on this proposal . . .[77]

That evening, the leading Italophiles, Piétri, de Monzie, and Mistler met the Italian Ambassador at the home of Madame Georgette Jean-Brunhes, well-known for her literary and political salon. Guariglia welcomed the symbolic withdrawal idea. At 9 p.m. Bonnet telephoned Ciano confirming that the British and French governments would have to insist on German evacuation. Ciano did not think Hitler would accept. Then the French Foreign Minister made one last effort. At 10.40 p.m. he asked Guariglia through de Monzie to inform his government of the symbolic withdrawal suggestion. 'During the night', wrote Ciano, 'I was awakened by the Ministry because Bonnet has asked Guariglia if we could not at least obtain a symbolic withdrawal . . . I threw the proposal in the wastepaper basket without informing the *Duce*'.[78]

While the Bonnet brigade made desperate efforts to keep the conference proposal in play, Poland was fighting for its existence. Colonel Beck had informed Bonnet on 1 September: 'the question before us is not that of a conference but the common action which should be taken by the Allies to resist'.[79] Two days after the German invasion Britain and France had still not declared war on Germany in fulfilment of their pledges. London and Paris argued over the timing of their ultimata to

Germany and the attempt to synchronize them strained relations almost to breaking point. A meeting of French and British ministers during the last week of August might have prevented the delays and misunderstandings which arose on 1-2 September. Indeed, there had been some talk of such a conference. On 23 August Cambon, Counsellor in London, told Halifax that Bonnet and Daladier might visit London 'in the next day or two'.[80] Nothing more was heard of the idea. Suddenly, at 1.30 p.m. on 30 August Halifax asked if Daladier could come to London that afternoon or the next day. Bonnet was not included in the invitation. Daladier replied that he was too busy to leave Paris. It does not seem to have occurred to Halifax that he or Chamberlain might have gone to Paris.

The delays connected with the sending of the ultimata and the declaration of war have been blamed almost entirely on Bonnet. This is quite unfair to the French Foreign Minister. Not that he can be exonerated completely since he obviously procrastinated in order to gain time for the Italian conference proposal. But from the French record it is clear that Daladier and his Cabinet, and also Gamelin, were as anxious as Bonnet to delay the sending of an ultimatum to Berlin. However, with Daladier and Gamelin, military considerations were paramount. It was essential, advised the military chiefs, to gain time for mobilisation and evacuation of civilians. Nor were the French government entirely to blame for the delay which occurred on 2-3 September. Chamberlain and Halifax were in no hurry to declare war on Germany. Indeed, it is arguable that British Ministers made Bonnet a scapegoat for their own hesitation and dithering. And there is much to be said for Nicholas Bethell's judgement that Great Britain went to war in order to save the Chamberlain government from falling.[81]

On 1 September both governments were in step, although only just. The British and French notes sent to Berlin on the evening of 1 September were in the form of warnings, without time-limits. London had wanted to set a time-limit. About 5 p.m. Halifax had telephoned Bonnet suggesting that the notes carry a time-limit and that both Ambassadors should ask for their passports. Bonnet who was closeted with three of his allies, Malvy, Mistler and Michard-Pelissier, rejected the proposal, arguing that it would be tantamount to a declaration of war and constitutionally France could not declare war until the Chambers met.[82] Technically, this was correct. Daladier had confirmed to Phipps on 26 August that in order to declare war it would be necessary to call parliament. Yet the government deliberately postponed the calling of parliament until the last possible moment.

By 2 September German forces were driving deep into Poland. At 9 a.m. Lukasiewicz called on Bonnet and asked him when France would implement her alliance. The Foreign Minister countered with constitutional and military arguments. An ultimatum could not be sent until parliament met and even then, for military reasons, a delay of 48 hours would probably be necessary. Bonnet promised to speak to Daladier.

Dissatisfied with Bonnet's prevarication, Lukasiewicz saw Daladier at 12 noon. The Prime Minister said he knew nothing of the Ambassador's meeting with Bonnet at 9 a.m. Told of Foreign Office impatience with the slowness of the Quai d'Orsay he is said to have exclaimed: 'So, that joint is not yet at work, what are they waiting for?'[83] He promised to summon Bonnet at once.

When the Chambers assembled at 3 p.m. on 2 September Daladier made a statement on the situation. His statement was hardly reassuring for the Poles. The Prime Minister appealed for unity in the face of war but hinted that he had not yet given up all hope of peace: 'if renewed steps' were taken 'towards conciliation' France was 'still ready to join in'.[84] Later in the afternoon the Prime Minister is alleged to have told the Chamber finance committee that the voting of supplies did not imply that the government was being accorded the right to declare war.[85] De Monzie interpreted this alleged remark as evidence that Daladier was not fully resolved on war. Bullitt cabled Washington that he believed Daladier did not want to declare war until 'another Italian proposal' was received.[86] However, deputies and senators accepted government leadership and there was no counterpart to the angry scenes which disturbed the House of Commons later the same day. Only the Polish ambassador, Lukasiewicz, was furious and when he saw Bonnet again in the afternoon he 'lost his temper and told Bonnet exactly what he thought of him'.[87]

From late afternoon on Saturday 2 September until the early hours of Sunday 3 September messages flashed to and fro between London and Paris in an endeavour to synchronize the timing of the ultimata to Germany. But for the angry outbursts in the Commons the two governments might have reconciled their positions. Chamberlain was due to make a statement in the Commons at 6 p.m. on 2 September. Every seat was taken and all the galleries packed. At 8 p.m. Chamberlain appeared and spoke not of the sending of an ultimatum but of continuing discussions with Paris on the expiry of a time-limit. There followed, in Chamberlain's own description, 'a painful scene'.[88] 'Speak for England', someone shouted.

At 9.50 p.m. that evening Chamberlain telephoned Daladier:

> There had been an angry scene in the House of Commons after he had made his statement in which he had said that we were consulting with the French Government on the question of the time-limit to be allowed to Germany. His colleagues in the Cabinet were also disturbed . . . If the French Government were to insist on a time-limit of forty-eight hours to run from midday tomorrow, it would be impossible to hold the situation here . . .[89]

Daladier however would not budge. The French government, he told Chamberlain, had agreed to Ciano's request to wait until midday on Sunday 3 September before acting in Berlin:

> If between now and midday tomorrow the German Government gave a refusal, it would then be possible to address an ultimatum to the German Government. In that case, unless British bombers were ready to act at once, it would be better for France to delay, if possible, for some hours attacks on the French armies.[90]

It is not true to say that Bonnet 'conjured up the excuse' that the French army wanted a forty-eight hour time-limit to the ultimatum.[91] The military plea was genuine and both Gamelin and Daladier shared Bonnet's opinion. Naturally, the Foreign Minister seized on the military situation as a means of gaining time for the Italian proposal but the excuse was real enough. At its meeting at 6 p.m. on 2 September the French Cabinet had endorsed the need to gain time for military measures. 'The entire Cabinet is agreed', wrote Zay, 'except Mandel who thinks that our mobilisation was decided upon too late, and that our action in support of Poland should have been immediate'.[92] At 7.45 p.m. Daladier telephoned Bonnet to say that Gamelin favoured the delivery of the ultimatum at noon on Sunday 3 September, with a time-limit of 5 a.m. on Monday 4 September.[93] Daladier had some days previously made his own personal arrangements for the expected holocaust. On 27 August he confided to Bullitt that 'his sister today had put in two bags all the personal keepsakes and belongings that he really cared about and was prepared to leave for a secure spot at any moment'.[94]

So the two allies went their separate ways. Acting under strong pressure from his Cabinet Chamberlain decided that, whatever France did, Britain had to send an ultimatum for 9 a.m. on Sunday 3 September, with a time-limit of 11 a.m. that day. In the watches of the night of 2-3 September Bonnet had second thoughts. He appealed to Daladier to shorten the time-limit on the French ultimatum. Gamelin, says Bonnet, was now the main obstacle, strenuously seeking to delay the outbreak of hostilities. At 10.20 a.m. on Sunday 3 September Coulondre was instructed to deliver the French ultimatum at noon, with a time-limit of 5 a.m. on Monday 4 September.

As reports came in of the bad impression which the lack of synchronization was producing in London and Paris, Bonnet once more appealed to Daladier. At 11.30 a.m. on the Sunday morning Daladier agreed that the time-limit should be altered to 5 p.m. the same day. Within minutes came a telephone call from Coulondre in Berlin. In the instructions sent at 10.20 a.m. he was told that before delivering the ultimatum he should first ask for the German reply to the French note of 1 September, calling for the withdrawal of German troops from Poland. Only then, if the reply was negative, was the ultimatum to be delivered. What should he do, asked Coulondre, if the reply was 'simply dilatory'?[95] Léger spoke first to the ambassador: any German attempt at prevarication should be treated as a negative reply. Bonnet then came on the line and dictated the correction in the telegraphic instructions. The ambassador asked to have the news confirmed by one or two officials whose voices he would recognise more distinctly. Bonnet passed the telephone in turn to Léger and Bressy, his *chef de cabinet*.[96]

One final delay ensued; Ribbentrop could not receive Coulondre at noon since he was attending the reception for the new Soviet ambassador. Weizsäcker saw the ambassador but could tell him nothing about the reply to the French note of 1 September. After twenty minutes of small talk Coulondre was conducted to the Reich Chancellery and received by Ribbentrop. The German Foreign Minister confirmed that the reply to the French note of 1 September was negative. Even at this hour the French shrank from talking of a state of war with Germany. The note which Coulondre handed Ribbentrop was worded thus:

... the Government of the Republic have the honour to inform the Government of the Reich that they find themselves obliged to fulfil, as from today, September 3, at 5 p.m., the obligations which France has entered into towards Poland and which are known to the German Government.[97]

Coulondre shook hands with Weizsäcker, who was present at the interview, but not with Ribbentrop. 'France will be the aggressor', was the German Minister's only comment. 'History will be the judge of that', replied the French diplomat.[98]

As in September 1938, Bonnet's allies once more mobilised for a final effort to prevent France going to war. De Monzie gathered together an influential pacifist lobby which included such prominent personalities as Paul Baudouin, the banker, Paul Faure, the Socialist leader, Marcel Déat, leader of the Neo-Socialist group, Jean Mistler, chairman of the Chamber Foreign Affairs Committee, René Belin, a leading trade unionist, and the former minister, L-G. Frossard.[99] The schoolteachers' union circularised deputies calling for resistance to war and a general conference of all the powers. The industrialist, Marcel Boussac, acting for Bonnet, asked the Radical deputy and former minister, Lucien Lamoureux, to sound out parliamentary opinion.[100] But parliamentary opinion did not respond to these ministrations. Only a score or so of deputies, led by Laval, Faure and Adrien Marquet, addressed a letter to the government, regretting that the guarantees had been given and calling for a conference.[101] When the Chambers met on 2 September two members of this group, Bergery and Château, moved for a special secret session to debate the issue of war. Herriot, president of the Chamber, asked for a show of hands. Only 17 deputies voted for the motion. During the night of 2-3 September de Monzie repeated his 'telephone mobilisation which had succeeded in September 1938' but those 'called or awakened did not respond'.[102]

Gamelin however had the last word. He ordered his commanders not to begin hostilities until 5 a.m. on Monday 4 September.[103] From the beginning this was indeed a phoney war. Mobilisation proceeded smoothly but the patriotic *élan* of 1914 had been replaced by a mood of fatalistic resignation: *'il faut en finir'*. On 8 September the French General Staff gave orders that on no account should German troops be fired on.[104] The French government also turned a blind eye to the presence of German diplomats and mail on Italian ships. Until 8 October French air staff telephoned information *en clair* about British air missions to their anti-aircraft defences.[105]

Apart from mobilising, no effective help was given to Poland. Not until 18 August had a Franco-Polish financial agreement been signed, and only on 4 September was the political protocol, postponed in May, finally signed. Failing to secure access to Daladier, Lukasiewicz enlisted the help of Jules Jeanneney, president of the Senate. 'Too many' members of the government, complained Jeanneney, were 'hostile to the war'.[106]

Government changes were not long delayed. On 13 September Daladier announced a reconstruction of his administration. Bonnet was banished from the Quai to the ministry of Justice, *Place Vendôme*. The Prime Minister added foreign affairs to his existing duties as Minister of National

Defence and War. Four Ministers left the government: Jean Zay, Paul Marchandeau, Louis Chappedelaine, Raymond Patenôtre. Bonnet's departure from the Quai caused no surprise since a change had been predicted for several months. Too dangerous an opponent to be dropped completely, the Foreign Minister had to be found alternative employment. If Daladier had not acted on 13 September the British government might well have applied pressure to secure the Foreign Minister's removal. 'In looking back at the crisis of the last few days', noted Cadogan on 6 September, it seemed that 'Bonnet was the villain of the piece'.[107] 'Discreet measures', suggested the permanent head of the Foreign Office, were necessary to secure the removal of the French foreign Minister. Unlike his officials, Halifax was not without some sympathy for the French Minister. The only British testimonial which Bonnet received on leaving office came from Halifax. In a letter of 15 September the Foreign Secretary spoke of 'how much' he had 'appreciated' their 'collaboration' and the friendly relations which had resulted.[108]

Conclusions

The three years from 1936 to 1939 began and ended in broken promises. In July 1936 Blum promised help to the sister Spanish Republic but within a few weeks initiated the policy of non-intervention. In September 1938 notwithstanding several reassertions of alliance obligations, Daladier, on his own admission, was 'like a barbarian' ready 'to cut up' Czechoslovakia 'without even consulting her'.[1] In September 1939 although France fulfilled the letter of her Polish alliance nothing was done to honour its spirit. Poland was overrun in a matter of weeks while from the Maginot line French troops watched the Germans playing football.

The principal aim of French policy was the search for an agreement with Germany. French Prime Ministers from Blum to Daladier worked consistently for an understanding with Hitler. But the price of Franco-German amity was the liquidation of French interests in central and eastern Europe. No French government was prepared to pay such a price. Even Bonnet fought shy of denouncing France's eastern pacts. Nevertheless French Ministers were ready to go a long way towards meeting Germany's expansionist aims. Hand in hand with advances to Berlin went a gradual disengagement from the east.

After Munich, the search for agreement with the dictators went into top gear. Despite the acrimony which had soured relations between the Latin sisters since the Ethiopian crisis, the Daladier ministry strove hard to reach a settlement. Only Italian perversity prevented an agreement in the autumn of 1938. Approaches to Germany were more successful. With the Franco-German declaration of 6 December 1938, France achieved a counterpart to the Anglo-German declaration of 30 September 1938. Contrary to what was said at the time and afterwards, Germany was not given a free hand in the east. However, reading between the lines it is clear that the French government was willing to tolerate German expansion in the east, provided it was peaceful and kept within bounds.

In the winter of 1938-39 the retreat from eastern Europe continued apace. For all practical purposes, the Czech alliance was dissolved and Ministers showed little interest in securing for Prague the international guarantee promised in the Munich agreement. The Franco-Soviet pact was said to have died a natural death and the Soviet government was kept at arm's length. Bonnet and his Ambassador at Warsaw, Léon Noel, also

353

talked of revising the Franco-Polish alliance of 1921. Criticism of the government's foreign policy was not strong enough to deflect Daladier and Bonnet from their central purpose. Behind a smokescreen of soothing assurances of traditional interests the Prime Minister and Foreign Minister redoubled their efforts to reach an economic and political accord with Germany.

Hitler's annexation of Bohemia and Moravia on 15 March 1939 led to a diplomatic revolution. Britain and France gave guarantees to Poland, Greece and Rumania. Negotiations were initiated for alliances with the Soviet Union and Turkey. Under Daladier's direction, French diplomacy after 15 March was much firmer than at any time since Poincaré's premiership in the early 1920s. Unfortunately, British and French policy was not firm enough to convince Hitler that a European war would follow an attack on Poland. Neither London nor Paris was ready to construct a grand military alliance to overawe Germany. The hastily cobbled 'peace front' of March-April, for which Soviet participation was belatedly sought, was essentially a diplomatic combination designed to corral Hitler into new negotiations. Thus on the outbreak of war in September Britain and France were militarily only slightly better prepared than they had been the previous year.

With the exception of Blum, the men who held office from 1936 to 1939 were politicians, not statesmen. Chautemps, Delbos, Daladier and Bonnet were all enmeshed in the workings of the parliamentary machine. To say this is not to denigrate the individuals concerned. They simply accepted the parliamentary system as they found it. However the political institutions of the Third Republic, although well-suited to the leisurely ways of the *belle époque,* were singularly ill-equipped to adapt to the conditions of undeclared war imposed by Nazi Germany.

Yet it would be wrong to conclude from their preoccupation with political survival that France's rulers were no more than opportunists who exploited every expedient to prevent and delay war. In particular, the popular view of Bonnet as a weak-kneed, spineless individual is a gross misrepresentation. Both Daladier and Bonnet must be given credit for their sincerity of purpose. The search for peace and détente was not an ignoble enterprise, misguided though it was in the circumstances. Undeniably, France's treatment of Czechoslovakia, Poland and the Soviet Union was short-sighted and disastrous. Yet Daladier and Bonnet believed they had only a choice of evils: a European war ending in the probable destruction of France as a great power or the abandonment of Czechoslovakia and acceptance of German preponderance in eastern Europe. They chose what seemed to them the lesser — abandonment of Czechoslovakia. But while a good case can be made for Bonnet's efforts to avoid war in September 1938, there is little at all to be said for his behaviour on 31 August-2 September 1939. If his frantic activity had resulted in acceptance of the Italian conference proposal war would only have been postponed for a few months at the most.

Timidity was the dominant characteristic of the political leadership. At the critical moments—in March 1936 and September 1938—Ministers shrank from any suggestion of constraining Germany by force. This timidity had three immediate causes. Firstly there was the pusillanimity of the military chiefs. Early in 1936 *before* the Rhineland *coup* and before the construction of the Siegfried line Gamelin considered that France could not fight Germany with any certainty of victory. From 1933-34 onwards the military chiefs had tended to exaggerate German military strength, partly in order to dissuade the government against disarmament negotiations at Geneva, partly in order to induce the government to spend more on armaments. In the end the generals frightened themselves. Secondly, French public opinion was deeply divided on social and economic issues and the lack of national unity prevented a forceful riposte to German initiatives. Thirdly, from September 1935 onwards, military and political leaders were convinced that France could not contemplate war with Germany unless assured of active British help. British assistance was judged essential for the protection of French shipping and supplies in the Mediterranean.

Overshadowing these constraints was a fundamental disability, namely the continual shrinking of French power. By September 1939 France was on the verge of final eclipse as a leading power. The decline dated back at least to 1870 and some of the causes lay deep in the structure of French society and institutions. Basically, however, France lacked the inherent stamina needed to sustain a great power role. The tempo of decline was greatly accelerated by the war of 1914-18. Of course, British power was also in decline but the effects were not felt as sharply as in France. British Ministers were buttressed by a large, stable parliamentary majority and a slow but steady economic recovery.

In the face of a resurgent Germany, extreme solutions to the French dilemma found little favour. No influential politician canvassed the idea of a preventive war. Nor did the active pursuit of Franco-German collaboration attract more than a small minority of devotees. The loss of the military and diplomatic initiative after 1935 evoked two main trends in parliamentary and ministerial opinion. On one side were the advocates of a firm policy of defending the *status quo* against Germany. Their main strength was on the left, although not exclusively since Reynaud and Mandel were very much to the fore. They argued that German moves were largely bluff. But never for a moment was it suggested that France should act without Britain. Opposing them was the school of Flandin, Caillaux and Montigny, pleading for acceptance of German expansion in the East. They argued that Germany would be satiated in the East. France, it was said, could no longer play the policeman in Europe. Consequently, the eastern pacts had to be revised or denounced.

In the event, neither school gained complete control over policy-making. Blum's efforts to revive and consolidate the eastern pacts in 1936-37 were fruitless. After the fall of Blum in June 1937 the Flandin-Caillaux lobby grew more influential but did not gain the ascendancy. Chautemps and Delbos, like the good Radicals they were, sought a *juste milieu* between retreat and resistance in the East. Publicly they proclaimed their determination to defend alliance obligations, in practice they were ready to make substantial concessions to Germany. In February 1938 the French government called loudly for a Franco-British declaration in defence of

Austrian independence but had no intention of resisting Germany by force.

After the *Anschluss* a measure of consensus on foreign policy emerged. The second Blum ministry of 13 March 1938 lasted barely a month and was able to make only a few gestures of defiance. The Daladier government which succeeded it on 10 April was agreed that Czechoslovakia would have to make considerable concessions to Germany but still hoped to salvage something of the Czech alliance. Under the rush of events in September it became clear that Czechoslovakia would in fact have to be abandoned. After Munich, French Ministers struggled to retain some stake in eastern Europe. Belated efforts were made to buy arms from the Skoda works and to extend French economic interests in the area.

Given the background and upbringing of French leaders, the inevitable decline of France, the character of political institutions, and the consequent narrow margins within which governments had to operate it is tempting to argue that Daladier and Bonnet could not have acted much differently. Admittedly, French Ministers were cabined and confined by circumstance but they did retain some freedom of manoeuvre and wiser leadership might have better prepared France for the supreme contest. Eastern Europe is a case in point. France's eastern pacts, it is said, had been 'dismantled by the Rhineland *coup* . . . this left France with the choice of either coming to terms with the Soviet Union, accepting Germany's hegemony of the continent or, as eventually happened, to do neither'.[2] Against this interpretation, it might be argued that France in fact had no real choice in the matter — ideological conflicts precluded a full alliance with Moscow and national honour required the maintenance of the eastern pacts. Yet there is another way of looking at the problem. To say that France's pacts had been 'dismantled' is an overstatement. The eastern allies, although shaken and demoralised by the reactions to the Rhineland *coup,* still retained some confidence in France. Given greater determination, the Blum government of 1936-37 might have been able to re-cement the cracks in the alliances. The fact that preliminary Franco-Soviet staff talks were opened in the autumn of 1936 and continued for several months shows that distrust of Moscow was not so great as to exclude such talks altogether.

At the London conference of 29-30 November 1937 Chautemps and Delbos acquiesced all too readily in British views on central Europe. Arguably, a forceful defence of Czechoslovakia at that stage might have modified British attitudes. Another consideration is that although successive French governments recognised the necessity of British help in a war with Germany, they were strangely slow in seeking help. Thus at no time did the French actually demand full staff talks with their ally. The invitation to full military conversations came from London in February 1939. Again, French ministers were timid and over-cautious. What they sought in April and September 1938 was merely an extension of existing staff contacts.

But the greatest failure of French governments was in internal affairs. France's survival as a leading power was dependent on the healing of social wounds and recovery of national unity. An all-out effort to rebuild national unity in 1938-39 and to reshape military policy might have averted the *débacle* of 1940.

Speaking to the Chamber of Deputies on 2 September 1939 Daladier praised the reservists who were rejoining their regiments. 'In a great impulse of natural brotherliness', he declared, 'they had forgotten everything which . . . could divide them'.[3] Alas, the truth was otherwise. The most striking feature of French society in September 1939 was the distrust and hostility which one half of the nation felt for the other. The rift between left and right which had been so apparent in 1936 was as wide as ever. In the spring and summer of 1939 the Communist party picked up its strength and recovered from the setback of 30 November 1938 when its call for a general strike had gone unanswered. Observers noted, too, a growth of anti-semitism.[4] Daladier was no peacemaker. In August he suppressed the Communist press and dissolved the party on 26 September. Communist deputies were deprived of their parliamentary mandates.

Ironically, the liberal values which Daladier and Bonnet claimed to be championing in their foreign policy were eroded by domestic developments. Some contamination of the liberal ethos was only to be expected. The example of the dictators rubbed off on to western statesmen. Daladier justified his demand for full powers on 18 March 1939 with the argument that France had to counter the totalitarian states with similar weapons. Decree powers had already been given to the government in April 1938 and renewed after Munich. Consequently, over the eighteen months preceding the outbreak of war, parliament increasingly surrendered its legislative power to the executive. Well before the coming of war in fact French democracy had ceased to function effectively, and an authoritarian precedent had been set for the Vichy regime of 1940-44.

These authoritarian trends had serious consequences for foreign policy. The government used its extensive influence over parliament and the press in order to stifle and discourage discussion of international issues, notably in the Czech crisis of 1938. The tendency did not go unnoticed. A leading American State Department official wrote: 'through all this crisis what has surprised me is that the governments of the democracies have not taken their people or their parliaments into their confidence'.[5] If Blum and Paul-Boncour had been in power in the summer of 1938, instead of Daladier and Bonnet, Czechoslovakia might have fared differently. The government's influence on the press might have been deployed in defence of the Czech treaty. Commenting on the second Blum ministry's foreign policy, Welczeck wrote perceptively on 8 April 1938:

> If a new government succeeds in bridging or suppressing the internal differences, it can, with better hope of success, exert its strong influence on the press and its other means of propaganda for its foreign policy ideas—a thing which in this question the present government has done only hesitatingly, if at all. If the government knew how to inculcate in the people the conviction that sooner or later hostilities between France and Germany were inevitable, Czechoslovakia would assume an entirely different significance in the minds of the people.[6]

It is arguable that the economic and monetary crises justified the assumption of wider powers, although not necessarily as extensive as those claimed by Daladier. More's the pity, therefore, that Daladier appeared to have little idea of what to do with his plenary powers. An opportunity was missed for imaginative and constructive action on the social front. The Family Code of July 1939 came much too late in the day. There was a need, too, for the overhaul and streamlining of government. Two major shortcomings were, firstly the lack of a Prime Minister's office which might have served as a central, co-ordinating organ, and secondly the need for a body of advisers, perhaps attached to the Prime Minister's office, who could rethink and review foreign and domestic policies.

The confusion and discord which punctuated the British and French declarations of war on Germany were the inevitable sequel to twenty years of bickering and backbiting. Standing together in close array the two allies might have checked German ambitions. Their disarray was by far and away the most important single factor in Germany's recovery of the initiative. Predictably, the mistakes of 1936-39 led to much recrimination. In truth, it was six of one and half a dozen of the other or, as the French say, *c'est bonnet blanc et blanc bonnet*. Naturally, Czechoslovakia was primarily a French concern since only France had treaty obligations. Nevertheless Daladier and Bonnet were eager to shelter under Chamberlain's umbrella. And from November 1937 onwards the British government was ready to cajole and bully the French into abandoning its central European ally. As Winston Churchill wrote 'it must be recorded with regret that the British government not only acquiesced but encouraged the French government in a fatal course'.[7]

Not that French Ministers needed much encouragement. They have been dismissed as defeatists. Rather were they realists to a fault. They appreciated that France could not stand alone in Europe and their policy was pivoted on the British alliance. However, until March 1939, Britain could offer no more than two divisions for service on the continent. Moreover, British rearmament was retarded, having started only in February 1937. Even then the programme was limited in scope and did not provide for the sending of a land force to the continent. Nor were British Ministers willing to underwrite French commitments in eastern Europe. Where French ministers erred was in their supine acceptance of the conditions laid down by London. A Franco-British military alliance was an unconscionable time gestating. Almost three years passed before the renewal of the Locarno guarantee given to France on 16 April 1936 was completed by an offer of full staff talks in February 1939 and an undertaking to defend France against attack from any quarter.

The last months of peace brought a distinct change in the partnership. After 15 March 1939 Paris engaged in a tug-of-war with London and notched up a number of victories. The giving of British and French guarantees to Rumania on 13 April and the announcement of conscription on 26 April were the direct result of French pressure. The early stages of the Anglo-Franco-Soviet negotiations were much swayed by French policy. In the spring and summer Daladier refused Chamberlain's requests to open talks with Mussolini. If only Blum and Chautemps had shown the same spirit in 1936-37 the decade might have ended differently.

Abbreviations

The following abbreviations have been used: AC Papers—Papers of Sir Austen Chamberlain; CAB—Cabinet minute or memorandum in the Public Record Office; Cadogan—*The Diaries of Sir Alexander Cadogan, 1938-45*, ed., David Dilks (London, 1971); CE—*Les Evénements survenus en France de 1933 à 1945, Rapport de M Charles Serre, Député, au nom de la Commission d'Enquête parlementaire*, 2 volumes; *Témoignages et Documents Recueillis par la Commission d'Enquête Parlementaire*, 9 volumes (Paris, 1947-51); Daladier Papers—Papers of the late M Edouard Daladier; Dalton Diary—Diary and Papers of Hugh Dalton; DBFP—*Documents on British Foreign Policy*, First and Third Series; DDB—*Documents diplomatiques belges*; DDF—*Documents Diplomatiques Français* 1 Série and 2 Série; DDI—*Documenti Diplomatici Italiani*; DGFP—*Documents on German Foreign Policy 1918-45*, Series C and D; FFMA—French Foreign Ministry archives for period October 1938-September 1939; FO—Foreign Office document in Public Record Office; FPA—French parliamentary archives; FRUS—*Foreign Relations of the United States:Diplomatic Papers;* Gamelin—General Gamelin, *Servir*, 3 vols., Paris, 1946-48); GFM—unpublished German foreign ministry files, cited by serial and frame numbers; Harvey—*The Diplomatic Diaries of Oliver Harvey, 1937-40*, ed. John Harvey (London, 1970); LJ—*Le Livre Jaune Français, Documents diplomatiques, 1938-39* (Paris, 1939); Lamoureux—unpublished memoirs of M Lucien Lamoureux; Phipps Papers—Papers of Sir Eric Phipps; RDDGM—*Revue d'Histoire de la Deuxième Guerre Mondiale*; SD—*The USSR in the Struggle for Peace on the Eve of the Second World War, September 1938-August 1939, Documents and Materials* (Moscow, 1971).

French Foreign Ministry documents printed in DDF, 1st and 2nd Series are cited by their published reference numbers. In the case of volumes of the 2nd Series which have not yet been published the date and origin of documents are given.

Notes to Chapters

Introduction

1. *La Défense de la Paix* (Geneva 1946-48); *Dans la Tourmente, 1938-48* (Paris, 1971).
2. Anatole de Monzie, *Ci-devant* (Paris, 1941) p. 180.
3. General Maurice Gamelin, *Servir*, 3 vols., (Paris, 1946-47).
4. *La France a sauvé l'Europe*, 2 vols., (Paris, 1947); *Au coeur de la mêlée* (Paris, 1951); *Mémoires*, 2 vols., (Paris 1960-63).
5. *The Diplomatic Diaries of Oliver Harvey, 1937-40*, edited by John Harvey (London, 1970) p. 233.
6. Orville H. Bullitt, ed., *For the President, Personal and Secret* (London, 1973) p. 310.

Notes to Chapter 1

1. Thomas Jones, *Whitehall Diary*, edited by Keith Middlemas, I, (London, 1969), pp.116-7.
2. Colin Coote, *A Companion of Honour:The Story of Walter Elliot*, (London, 1965) p. 162.
3. *Chips:The Diaries of Sir Henry Channon*, edited by Robert Rhodes James, (London, 1967) p. 261.
4. See Judith M. Hughes, *To the Maginot Line:The Politics of French Military Preparation in the 1920s* (Cambridge, Mass., 1971), p. 12.
5. See Paul Reynaud, *Memoires*, 2, (Paris, 1963) pp. 224-65.
6. *DBFP*, First Series, XV, no. 70.
7. See Alfred Sauvy, *Histoire Economique de la France entre les deux guerres*, III, (Paris, 1972) pp. 365-93.
8. Quoted in Judith M. Hughes, *op cit.,* p. 21.
9. A. J. P. Taylor, *op cit.,* p. 64.
10. For the *présidence du conseil* under the Third Republic see Jean Giquel and Lucien Sfez, *Problèmes de la Réforme de l'Etat en France depuis 1934* (Paris, 1965), pp. 27-28.
11. See Marc Bloch, *L'Etrange Défaite* (Paris, 1957), pp. 203; Roger Leonard, 'La Haute Administration et ses Problèmes', *Revue des Deux Mondes*, April 1959, pp. 385-98.
12. See Jacques Ollé-Laprune, *La Stabilité des Ministres sous la Troisième Republique* (Paris, 1962), pp. 295-303.
13. Quoted in Daniel Halévy, *La République des Comités* (Paris, 1934) p. 52.
14. *Ibid*.
15. See Peter J. Larmour, *The French Radical Party in the 1930s*, (Stanford, 1964).
16. Anatole France, *L'Ile des Pingouins* (Paris, 1908), p. 338.
17 See Serge Bernstein, 'La vie du parti radical: la fédération de Saone et Loire de 1919 à 1939', *Revue francaise de science politique*, XX, December 1970, pp. 1136-80.
18. Memorandum by Sir Austen Chamberlain, 30 July 1935 (*A. C. Papers*)
19. *FO* 371/21612.
20. For Laval see Geoffrey Warner, *Pierre Laval and the Eclipse of France* (London, 1968); for Pétain see Richard Griffiths, *Marshal Pétain* (London, 1970).

21. For the party in the 1930s see Nathanael Greene, *Crisis and Decline: The French Socialist Party in the Popular Front Era,* (New York, 1969).

22. Quoted in Greene, *op cit.,* p. 225.

23. Quoted in David Thomson, *Democracy in France: The Third and Fourth Republics* (London, 1958) p. 40.

24. For the French economy between the wars see Sauvy, *op cit.,* volumes I-III; T. Kemp, *The French Economy, 1913-39* (London, 1972); Claude Fohlen, *La France de l'Entre-Deux-Guerres* (Paris, 1966); Pierre Sorlin, *La Société française,* II, (Paris, 1971); Martin Wolfe, 'French interwar stagnation revisited' and Joel Colton, 'Politics and Economics in the 1930s' in *From the Ancien Regime to the Popular Front: Essays in the History of Modern France in Honor of Shepherd B. Clough,* edited by Charles K. Warner (London, 1969), pp. 159-80, pp. 181-208.

25. The phrase is Henri Bordeaux's (*Histoire d'une vie,* XI, Paris, 1966, p. 54.)

26. See Edgar Morin, *Commune en France* (Paris, 1968); John Ardagh, *The New French Revolution* (London, 1968)

27. Quoted in Joel Colton, *Léon Blum: Humanist in Politics* (New York, 1966), p. 281.

28. Quoted in André Maurois, *Choses Nues: Chroniques* (Paris, 1963), p. 65.

29. *Gamelin,* II, p. 219.

30. The literature on the *Front Populaire* is immense but two important works are: Georges Lefranc, *Histoire du Front Populaire* (Paris, 1965) and *Léon Blum: Chef de Gouvernement* (Fondation Nationale des Sciences Politiques) (Paris, 1967)

31. John Morton Blum, *From the Morgenthau Diaries, Years of Crisis, 1928-38* (Boston, 1959), p. 460.

32. *Poèmes pour Tous* (Paris, 1952), pp. 51-53.

33. For the close contact between the Bank of France and the Paris press in the 1920s see Emile Moreau, *Souvenirs d'un gouverneur de la Banque de France* (Paris, 1954); for the connections between finance and politics see Dominique Desanti, *La Banquière des Années Folles: Marthe Hanau* (Paris, 1968)

34. Quoted in Colette Audry, *Léon Blum: ou la politique du juste* (Paris, 1955).

35. (New York, 1944), vi.

36. *L'Oeuvre de Léon Blum,* V, (Paris, 1963), pp. 440-1.

Notes to Chapter 2

1. Quoted in Reynaud, *Mémoires,* 2, p. 457.

2. Paul Mantoux, *Les Délibérations du Conseil des Quatre,* II (Paris, 1955), p. 271.

3. Robert Rhodes James, *Memoirs of a Conservative: J. C. C. Davidson's Memoirs and Papers,* 1910-37 (London, 1969), p. 146.

4. R. A. C. Parker, *Europe, 1919-45* (London, 1969), p. 240.

5. Secretary of State to Lord Crewe, 27 January 1927 (*AC Papers*).

6. See D. C. Watt, *Personalities and Policies* (London, 1965), p. 106.

7. Sir Arthur Salter, *Slave of the Lamp* (London, 195), p. 52.

8. See Jon Jacobsen, *Locarno Diplomacy: Germany and the West, 1925-29* (Princeton, 1972), p. 382.

9. *DBFP,* First Series, XVI, no. 747, n. 7.

10. Quoted in R. A. C. Parker, *op cit.,* p. 60.

11. *Ibid.,* p. 61.

12. A. J. P. Taylor, *op cit.,* p. 64.

13. Stephen Roskill, *Hankey: Man of Secrets,* II, 1919-31 (London, 1972), p. 209.

14. *DBFP,* 1a, I (1925-26), p. 850.

15. Secretary of State to Lord Crewe, 4 June 1926 (*AC Papers*). Paul Cambon, Ambassador at London from 1898 to 1920, gave the French view: 'It is puerile to have long-term policies with people who dislike theories, who only live for the present' (*Correspondance,* III, Paris, 1946, p. 389).

16. *Goodbye to all that* (London, 1957), p. 148.

17. *Coming up for air* (London, 1962), p. 123.

18. For Anglo-French rivalry in the Middle East see Jukka Nevakivi, *Britain, France and the Arab Middle East, 1914-20* (London, 1969).

19. *DBFP,* First Series, XVI, no. 768.

20. Quoted in Robert Rhodes James, *op cit.,* p. 143.
21. Keith Middlemas and John Barnes, *Baldwin: A Biography* (London, 1969), p. 887.
22. Roskill, *op. cit.,* pp. 149-50.
23. *DBFP,* First Series, XV, no. 70.
24. Middlemas and Barnes, *op cit.,* p. 199.
25. Secretary of State to Lord D'Abernon, 19 March 1925 (*AC Papers*).
26. Secretary of State to Lord Crewe, 20 January 1925 (*AC Papers*).
27. See J. M. Roberts, *Europe, 1880-1945* (London, 1970), p. 335.
28. The following analysis of the eastern pacts is based on *Gamelin,* II, pp. 467-69; *DDF,* 2 Série, II, no. 419.
29. See P. E. Tournoux, *Défense des Frontières: haut commandement, gouvernement, et défense des frontiéres du Nord et de l'est,* 1919-39 (Paris, 1960), pp. 332-41.
30. See Edouard Bonnefous, *Histoire politique de la troisième republique,* VI, (Paris, 1965), p. 391.
31. See Robert J. Young, 'Preparations for Defeat: French war doctrine in the interwar period', *Journal of European Studies,* June 1972, pp. 155-72.
32. This paragraph is based on Jozef Lipski, *Diplomat in Berlin, 1933-39: Papers and Memoirs of Jozef Lipski,* edited by Waclaw Jedrzejewicz (New York, 1968), p. 1-19.
33. *Nos illusions sur l'Europe centrale* (Paris, 1922), p. 20.
34. See Elizabeth R. Cameron, *Prologue to Appeasement: A Study in French Foreign Policy,* (Washington, 1942), p. 22.
35. Letter of 30 March 1935 to Sir Austen Chamberlain (*AC Papers*).
36. See Jacques Duclos, *Mémoires,* I (Paris, 1968).
37. Lord Crewe to Secretary of State, 15 February 1927 (*AC Papers*).
38. Jacques Rueff, *Combats pour l'ordre financier* (Paris, 1972), p. 52.
39. John Morton Blum, *op cit.,* p. 456.
40. Jean-Marie d'Hoop, 'La politique française du réarmement d'après les travaux de la commission d'enquête parlementaire', *RDDGM,* 1955, p. 9.
41. Rueff, *op cit.,* p. 92.
42. *FRUS,* I, 1938, p. 65.
43. The Earl of Avon, *The Eden Memoirs: Facing the Dictators,* (London, 1962), p. 49.
44. Secretary of State to Lord D'Abernon, 30 September 1925 (*AC Papers*).
45. For post-Locarno diplomacy see Jacobsen, *op cit.*
46. Survey of International Affairs 1931, quoted in Geoffrey Warner, *op cit.,* p. xv.
47. *DDF,* I Série, I, no. 286.
48. *DDB,* III, no. 127.
49. *Ibid.,* III, no. 47.
50. *Ibid.,* no. 99.
51. *DDF,* I Série, I. no. 286.
52. *Ibid.,* V, no. 75.
53. *Ibid.,* V, no. 125.
54. Volume XXVII, *Le 7 Octobre* (Paris, 1946), pp. 221-226.
55. Sir Ian Malcolm (of Suez Canal Company) to Sir Austen Chamberlain, 23 July 1926 (*AC Papers*).
56. *Dalton Diary,* 22 September 1938.
57. Hughes, *op cit.,* p. 101.
58. *DDF,* I Série, II, no. 204. For Weygand's role see Philip Charles Farewell Bankwitz, *Maxime Weygand and Civil-Military Relations in Modern France* (Cambridge, Mass.) 1967).
59. Francois Piétri, 'Souvenir de Barthou', *Revue des Deux Mondes,* 1 March 1961, pp. 65-75; Bankwitz, *op cit.,* p. 75.
60. 'Observations présentées par M. Piétri à la séance du Conseil des Ministres du 17 Avril 1934' (*Piétri Papers*).
61. *DDF,* I Série, V, no. 364.
62. *Gamelin,* II, p. 161.
63. See D. C. Watt, 'The Secret Laval-Mussolini Agreement of 1935 on Ethiopia', *The Middle East Journal,* 15, 1961, pp. 69-78 (reprinted in Esmonde M. Robertson, *The Origins of the Second World War* (London, 1971).
64. See the Laval-Mussolini correspondence in H. Lagardelle, *Mission à Rome* (Paris, 1955), pp. 275-6.

65. *DDF,* 2 Série, II, pp. 642-5.
66. The most recent account in English is Frank Hardie, *The Abyssinian Crisis* (London, 1974). For some discussion of French policy see J. Néré, *The Foreign Policy of France from 1914 to 1945,* (London, 1975).
67. See A. J. Marder, 'The Royal Navy and the Ethiopian Crisis of 1935-1936', *The American Historical Review,* 75, 1970, pp. 1327-1356 (reprinted in Arthur J. Marder, *From the Dardanelles to Oran* London, 1974).
68. For French military policy I have drawn on an unpublished study by M. A. Reussner, *Les Conversations Franco-Britanniques de l'Etat Major, 1935-39* (Service historique de la Marine Nationale, 1969).
69. Reussner, *op cit.*
70. Lagardelle, *op cit.,* p. 278.
71. *Ibid.,* p. 278.
72. See John Terraine, *The Life and Times of Lord Louis Mountbatten* (London, 1968), p. 58.
73. Letter of 16 October 1935 to Sir Austen Chamberlain (*AC Papers*).
74. Letter of 19 October 1935 to Sir Austen Chamberlain (*AC Papers*).
75. Marder, *op cit.,* P. 1350.
76. Quoted in R. A. C. Parker, 'Great Britain, France and the Ethiopian crisis, 1935-36', *English Historical Review,* April 1974, p. 302.

Notes to Chapter 3

1. Total German strength in the demilitarised zone, including police, was 36,000 (*DGFP,* Series C, V, no. 189). The French General Staff grossly overestimated the numbers of German troops, putting their strength at 6-7 divisions—90,000 men (*DDF,* 2 Série, I, no. 392).
2. The author of this phrase was René Massigli, Assistant Political Director of the Quai d'Orsay (J-B. Duroselle, 'Les incertitudes de notre politique militaire: La France et la crise de Mars 1936' in Bonnefous, *op cit.,* VI, p. 389).
3. For appraisals of the crisis see John C. Cairns, 'March 7, 1936. Again: the view from Paris' in *European Diplomacy between two wars, 1919-39* edited by H. W. Gatzke (Chicago, 1972), pp. 172-192; Maurice Baumont, 'The Rhineland Crisis: 7 March 1936' in *Troubled Neighbours,* edited by Neville Waites (London, 1971), pp. 158-169.
4. *The Gathering Storm,* pp. 170-1.
5. See *DDF,* 2 Série, I, nos. 63, 350; *Gamelin,* II, pp. 194-5.
6. *DDF,* 2 Série, II, no. 23.
7. For Flandin's testimony see *Politique Francaise, 1919-40* (Paris, 1947), pp. 193-212; *CE,* I, pp. 147-48; for Sarraut see *CE,* III, pp. 601-606; for Paul-Boncour see *CE, III.* pp. 798-801; for General Maurin (War Minister) see *CE,* IV, pp. 907-908; for Gamelin, *Gamelin,* II, pp. 205-207.
8. *DDF,* 2 Série, I, no. 196.
9. *Ibid.,* no. 283.
10. *Ibid.,* no. 301.
11. *Facing the Dictators,* p. 351.
12. Middlemas and Barnes, *op cit.,* p. 918.
13. *Facing the Dictators,* p. 346.
14. *DDF,* 2 Série, I, no. 334.
15. *Ibid.,* I, no. 525; II, no. 113.
16. *Ibid.,* I, no. 83.
17. See Robert John Young, *Strategy and Diplomacy in France: Some Aspects of the Military Factor in French foreign policy, 1934-39,* University of London unpublished, Ph.D. thesis, 1969, p. 514.
18. *DDF,* 2 Série, I, no. 82.
19. *Ibid.,* I, no. 202, 187.
20. *Ibid.,* II, no. 97.
21. See Donald Cameron Watt, 'German plans for the reoccupation of the Rhineland: A Note', *Journal of Contemporary History,* October 1966, pp. 193-99; Frank Spencer, 'Review Article: Foreign Policy Documents' *History,* October 1967, pp. 295-6.
22. I. M. Oprea, *Nicolas Titulescu's Diplomatic Activity* (Bucharest, 1968), p. 138.

23. *DDF,* 2 Série, II, no. 214.
24. *Ibid.,* II, no. 85.
25. *Ibid.,* II, no. 23.
26. *Ibid.,* II, nos. 172, 188.
27. *Ibid.,* II, nos. 182, 204, 318.
28. *Ibid.,* II, no. 357.
29. *Ibid.,* II, no. 369.
30. *Ibid.,* II, no. 419.
31. *FFMA.*
32. See Pierre Renouvin, 'La politique exterieure du premier ministere Léon Blum' in *Léon Blum: Chef de Gouvernement,* pp. 329-75; Geoffrey Warner, 'France and Non-Intervention in Spain, July-August 1936' *International Affairs,* I, 38, April 1962, pp. 203-20; David Carlton, 'Eden, Blum' and the Origins of Non-Intervention', *Journal of Contemporary History,* 6, 1971, pp. 40-55; M. D. Gallagher, 'Léon Blum and the Spanish Civil War', *Journal of Contemporary History,* 6, 1971, pp. 56-64; Jules Moch, *Rencontres Avec . . . Léon Blum* (Paris, 1970), pp. 189-217; Hans-Henning Abendroth, *Hitler in der Spanischen Arena* (Paderborn, 1973).
33. Quoted in Geoffrey Warner, 'France and Non--Intervention', p. 220.
34. *CE,* I, p. 216.
35. Jules Moch, *op cit.,* p. 195.
36. *The Gathering Storm,* p. 168. See also Thomas Jones, *A Diary with Letters* (London, 1954), p. 231.
37. *CE,* I, p. 21.
38. For the French record see *DDF,* 2 Serie, III, no. 87; for the British see David Carlton, *op cit.,* pp. 48-49. Mr. Carlton does not appear to have consulted the French record.
39. Chatfield's minute has the following note in parenthesis: 'that is, of course, not strictly true as we have certain information'.
40. Warner, *op cit.,* pp. 217-18.
41. Carlton, *op cit.,* p. 48.
42. For a French note of Clerk's visit see *DDF,* III, no. 108; for Clerk's record see Carlton, *op cit.,* pp. 50-51.
43. However Mr Carlton unduly minimises, in my view, the importance both of Clerk's account of his 7 August meeting with Delbos, and of the French note of the meeting. Clerk acted without instructions but, as Mr Carlton notes, the Foreign Office approved his action. Exercising influence in a discreet manner without involving one's government was the art of a good ambassador. And Clerk's visit, though not an official démarche, was interpreted by the French as a warning.
44. Clerk to Eden, 7 August 1936, quoted in Carlton, *op cit.,* pp. 50-51.
45. The French government took this threat very seriously. Daladier told Chamberlain in April 1938: 'Provision was being made in the French budget for important improvements to the port of Dakar, with a view to bringing troops from Dakar by the Atlantic route in time of war' (*DBFP. Third Series, I, no. 164*).
46. *FRUS,* 1936, II, p. 578.
47. *DGFP,* Series D, III, no. 164.
48. *DDF,* 2 Série, IV, no. 60.
49. See David Owen Kieft, *Belgium's Return to Neutrality* (London, 1972).
50. Quoted in Warner, *op cit.,* p. 220, n. 2.
51. See George Sakwa, ' "The Renewal" of the Franco-Polish alliance in 1936 and the Rambouillet Agreement', *Polish Review,* XVI, Spring 1971, pp. 45-66.
52. See *DDF,* 2 Serie, III, nos. 301, 308.
53. *Ibid.,* nos, 391, 448, 457; IV, nos, 9, 81, 404.
54. Stuart R. Schram, 'Christian Rakovskij et le premier rapprochement Franco-Sovietique', *Cahiers du Monde Russe et Sovietique,* January-July 1960, pp. 205-237, pp. 584-629.
55. *DDF,* I Série, II, no. 218.
56. Georges Bonnet, *Defense de la Paix,* II (Geneva, 1948), pp. 404-6; *Vingt Ans de vie politique* (Paris, 1969), pp. 205-22.
57. *GFM,* 2218H/475087-475090.
58. *Ibid.,* 2218H/475091-475094.
59. *DDF,* I Série, V, no. 139.
60. *Ibid.,* V, nos. 139, 277.

61. See, for example, William Evans Scott, *Alliance Against Hitler: The Origins of the Franco-Soviet Pact* (London, 1962), p. 257.
62. *DDF,* I Série, V, no. 458.
63. Edouard Herriot, *Jadis, d'une guerre a l'autre,* 1914-36 (Paris, 1952), p. 403.
64. *DGFP,* Series C, III, no. 365. For official attitudes at the time see also Reynaud, *Memoires,* II, pp. 155-57.
65. For Delbos's denial that any special contacts were taking place see *FRUS,* 1936, I p. 359; *ibid.,* 1937, I, p. 53; Coulondre, *de Staline a Hitler,* (Paris, 1950), pp. 48-49.
66. 'Note dur l'opportunité de conversations d'Etat-Major franco-sovietiques' 24 June 1936 (*FFMA*).
67. Daladier papers.
68. *DDF,* 2 Série, III, no. 343.
69. *Ibid.*
70. *Ibid.,* II, no. 231.
71. *Ibid.,* V, no. 299.
72. *Ibid.,* V, no. 429.
73. *Ibid.,* V, no. 480.
74. *Ibid.,* IV, no. 457.
75. *Ibid.,* IV, no. 457, n. i; *Gamelin,* II, p. 285.
76. *Gamelin,* II, pp. 286-7. This was a draft reply which may not actually have been given to the Russians but traces of its wording can be seen in the text of the preliminary military accord of 15 April (*DDF,* V, no. 285).
77. *DDF,* V, no. 285; Coulondre, *op cit.,* p. 48.
78. *Ibid.,* V, no. 480.
79. *Ibid.,* VI, no. 35.
80. *Facing the Dictators,* p. 487.
81. Middlemas and Barnes, *op cit.,* p. 951.
82. Letter of 28 March 1936 to Wladmir d'Ormesson (*AC Papers*).
83. J. R. M. Butler, *Lord Lothian (Philip Kerr)* 1882-1940 (London, 1960), pp. 354-62.
84. Thomas Jones, *op cit.,* pp. 187-188.
85. *Ibid.,* p. 210.
86. Harold Nicolson, *Diaries and Letters,* 1930-39 (London 1966), p. 250.
87. *FRUS,* 1937, I, p. 850.
88. *Ibid.,* p. 54.
89. *Facing the Dictators,* p. 430.
90. *Léon Blum; Chef de Gouvernment,* p. 360; *GFM,* 621/250374 (report from German ambassador, Rome, 12 December 1936, saying that Ciano has received an emissary from Blum).
91. *Ciano's Diplomatic Papers,* ed. Malcolm Muggeridge (London, 1948), p. 45.
92. See Geoffrey Warner, *Pierre Laval and the Eclipse of France,* pp. 143-44. There is no record of such an interview in the published French documents.
93. *Facing the Dictators,* p. 430.
94. *DDF,* 2 Série, IV, no. 139.
95. *DGFP,* Series C, V, no. 388.
96. *DDF,* 2 Série, III, no. 213. The record of the 26 August talk was found after the publication of volume III (*FFMA*).
97. *DDF,* III, no. 276, notes 1-5. No French record of the Eden-Blum meeting of 20 September has been found (*DDF,* no. 269, n. 4). But for Blum's letters to Schacht informing him of the interview see *DDF,* V, no. 420, n. 1; *DGFP* Series C, V; no. 574. Eden's chronicle is confused and he says the Blum-Schacht meeting was in October (*Facing the Dictators,* p. 502).
98. It is impossible to be certain of this point. The Franco-German contacts, like the Franco-Soviet exchanges, were conducted in considerable secrecy and much of importance may not have passed through the foreign ministry archives. In February 1937 Delbos told Bullitt: 'the entire matter was being handled with the greatest secrecy . . . Poncet had communicated with him by letter brought by personal messenger' (*FRUS,* 1937, I, p. 49).
99. *FRUS,* 1936, I, p. 383.
100. This letter has not been found in the French archives, see *DDF,* V, no. 470, n. 4; no. 442.
101. *DGFP,* Series D, III, no. 164.

102. *GFM,* 621/251358-60; *DGFP,* D, III, nos. 169, 173.
103. *DDF,* 2 Série, IV, no. 347.
104. *FRUS,* 1937, I, p. 48.
105. See Keith Middlemas, *Diplomacy of Illusion* (London, 1972), p. 112.
106. Sir Frederick Leith-Ross, *Money Talks: Fifty Years of International Finance* (London, 1968), pp. 238-239.
107. *FRUS,* 1936, I, p. 203.
108. Keith Feiling, *The Life of Neville Chamberlain* (London 1946), p. 279.
109. *FRUS,* 1936, I, p. 358.
110. *Ibid.,* 1937, I, pp. 49-50.
111. *DDF,* 2 Série, V, no. 429.
112. *Ibid.,* no. 470.
113. *FRUS,* 1936, II, pp. 578-9.
114. *Ibid.,* I, pp. 586-7.
115. *Ibid.,* 1937, I, p. 92.
116. *Ibid.,* p. 94.
117. Charles de Gaulle, *Mémoires de Guerre,* I, *L'Appel* (Paris, 1954), p. 29.
118. *FRUS,* 1937, I, p. 94.
119. Léon Blum in *Le Populaire,* 5 January 1935, quoted in Pierre Milza, *L'Italie fasciste devant l'opinion française,* 1920-40 (Paris, 1967), p. 173.

Notes to Chapter 4

1. Quoted in Thomas Jones, *op cit.,* p. 367.
2. Kingsley Martin, *Editor: A Second Volume of Autobiography,* 1931-45, (London, 1968), p. 209.
3. See Keith Middlemas, *op cit.,* p. 50 and p. 190; Interview with Sir Horace Wilson, 27 August 1963.
4. Alexander Werth, *France and Munich: Before and After the Surrender* (London, 1939), p. 135.
5. *DBFP,* Third Series, VII, no. 346.
6. *FRUS,* 1938, I, p. 1.
7. *Ibid.,* 1937, I, p. 187.
8. Quoted in Bonnefous, *op cit.,* p. 192.
9. *FRUS,* 1937, I, p. 422.
10. Simone de Beauvoir, *The Prime of Life* (London, 1965), p. 195.
11. See J. W. Bruegel, *Czechoslovakia Before Munich* (London, 1973), pp. 131-2.
12. *FRUS,* 1936, I, p. 340.
13. *DDF,* 2 Série, V, no. 228.
14. *Ibid.,* VI, no. 222.
15. *Ibid.*
16. *FRUS,* 1937, I. p. 78.
17. *Ibid.,* p. 89.
18. *Ibid.,* p. 97.
19. *Ibid.,* p. 78.
20. *DGFP,* Series D, II, no. 21.
21. *DDF,* 2 Série, VII, no. 3 (see also, VI, no. 486).
22. *Ibid.,* VII, no. 5.
23. *DGFP,* Series D, I, nos. 22, 63.
24. Quoted in P. E. Tournoux, *op cit.,* p. 283.
25. *DDF,* VIII, no. 127; *Gamelin,* I, pp. 115-21.
26. *Ibid.,* VIII, no. 164.
27. *Ibid.,* VIII, no. 176.
28. See Chapter 15.
29. *DDF,* VIII, nos. 11, 77.
30. *Ibid.,* VIII, no. 164.
31. *Mémorial de la Guerre Blanche 1938* (Paris, 1939), p. 74.
32. *Mission militaire française auprès de la République Tchécoslovaque* Cabinet du Général, no. 3369, *Rapport de fin de mission* (hereafter Faucher), 15 December 1938.

33. *DDF,* VII, no. 124.
34. *Ibid.,* no. 223.
35. *FRUS,* 1937, I, pp. 91-2.
36. *Speeches on Foreign Policy by Viscount Halifax* (London, 1940), p. 77.
37. *The Diplomatic Diaries of Oliver Harvey, 1937-40,* edited by John Harvey (London, 1970), pp. 23-24.
38. *FRUS,* 1937, I, p. 59.
39. *DDF,* VII, no. 41.
40. Quoted in Bonnefous, *op cit.,* pp. 222-3.
41. Sir Orme Sargent to Sir Eric Phipps, 29 November 1937 (Phipps Papers).
42. *Facing the Dictators,* p. 511.
43. *FRUS,* 1937, I, p. 158.
44. *Fulness of Days,* (London, 1957), p. 190.
45. *DGFP,* Series D, I, no. 46.
46. Letter of 4 December 1937 from Sir Orme Sargent to Sir Eric Phipps (Phipps Papers)
47. Feiling, *op cit.,* p. 334.
48. Coulondre, *op cit.,* p. 134.
49. For the French record see *DDF,* VII, nos, 287, 291; for the British see Chamberlain's report to the Cabinet on 1 December 1937, *CAB* 23/90 A.
50. *CAB* 23/90A.
51. *CAB* 23/90A.
52. *FRUS,* 1937, I p. 180.
53. *Ibid.,* p. 183.
54. General Beauffre, *Mémoires: 1920-40-45* (Paris, 1965), p. 71.
55. J. R. Colville, *Man of Valour: Field Marshal Lord Gort* (London, 1972), p. 77.
56. *CAB* 23/90A: R. J. Minney, *The Private Papers of Hore-Belisha,* (London, 1960), p. 59.
57. Feiling, *op. cit.,* p. 334.
    For some months the Foreign Office had shown increasing anxiety about the state of the French air force. In May 1937 Sir Orme Sargent, Assistant Under-Secretary of State, suggested that the condition of the French air force should be looked into and form the subject of Franco-British air staff talks. On several occasions the matter was raised orally with the French in the autumn of 1937. Following the Anglo-French meeting of 29-30 November detailed information was given to the French but little was forthcoming in return (*FO* 371/21593).
58. *DDF,* VII, no. 367; *Facing the Dictators,* pp. 495-96.
59. Quoted in Michael Howard *The Continental Commitment* (London, 1972), p. 118.
60. *DDF,* VII, no. 213.
61. *Ibid.,*
62. *Ibid.,* no. 325.
63. *Ibid.,* no. 333.
64. See *DGFP,* Series D, I, nos. 73, 787, the French record.
65. *DGFP,* I, no. 55; for see *DDF,* VII, no. 307; for François-Poncet's assessment of the meeting see *ibid.,* no. 330.
66. See *DDF,* VII, no. 319.
67. *Ibid.,* no. 365.
68. *Dalton Diary,* 30 November 1937.
69. Hugh Dalton, *The Fateful Years,* (London, 1957), p. 185.
70. *FRUS,* 1937, I, p. 188.
71. *DDF,* VIII, no. 60.
72. *FO,* 371/21590 (Phipps to Halifax, 21, February 1938).
73. *FRUS,* 1938, I, p. 24
74. *DGFP,* Series D, I, no. 787.
75. *DDF,* VIII, no. 1.
76. Feiling, *op cit.,* p. 323.
77. *FRUS,* 1938, I, pp. 24-25.
78. *Ibid.,* p. 27.
79. *Ibid.,* p. 26.
80. *Ibid.,* p. 28.
81. *Ibid.,* p. 29.
82. Minutes of meeting on 2 February 1938 (*FPA*)

83. Minutes of meeting of 22 February 1938 (*FPA*).
84. *JO*, Chambre de Deputes, session ordinaire de 1938, pp. 571-658.
85. *Documents and Materials relating to the Eve of the Second World*, I, (Moscow 1948), no. 4.
86. Hubert Beuve-Mery, *Réflexions politiques*, 1932-52 (Paris, 1951), p. 85. Delbos's statement ran: 'I must once again declare that our engagements towards Czechoslovakia will if necessary be faithfully fulfilled'.
87. *DGFP*, Series D, I, no. 133.

Notes to Chapter 5

1. *DDF*, VIII, no. 432.
2. *Ibid.*, Military Attaché (Vienna) to Daladier (Minister of War), 21 March 1938.
3. General Gauché, *Le Deuxième Bureau au Travail* (Paris, 1953), p. 57.
4. *DDF*, VIII, no. 156; Jean Chauvel, *Commentaire*, I, (Paris, 1971), p. 21.
5. *FO* 371/22311.
6. *The Diaries of Sir Alexander Cadogan*, 1938-45, ed. by David Dilks, (London, 1971), p. 47.
7. *DDF*, VIII, no. 189; *DGFP*, Series D, I, no. 308.
8. *Ibid.*, VIII, no. 190; *CAB* 24/275.
9. *CAB* 24/275.
10. *DDF*, VIII, no. 304.
11. *Ibid.*, no. 301.
12. *DBFP*, Third Series, I, no. 25.
13. *DDF*, VIII, no. 372.
14. *DGFP*, Series D, I, no. 356.
15. *FRUS*, 1938, I, pp. 25-26.
16. *FPA*, minutes of meeting of 16 February 1938.
17. *DDF*, VIII, no. 248.
18. *Ibid.*
19. Phipps to Halifax, 28 March 1938, (*Phipps Papers*).
20. *DDF*, VIII, no. 381; *Gamelin*, II, pp. 315-16.
21. *Cadogan*, p. 47.
22. *FO* 371/22311.
23. *FO* 371/22311.
24. *CAB* 24/275.
25. *FRUS*, 1937, I, p. 188.
26. *Ibid.*, 1938, I, p. 3.
27. *Ciano's Diary, 1937-38,* trans. Andreas Mayor, introduction by Malcolm Muggeridge (London, 1952), p. 80.
28. *DDF*, VIII, no. 330.
29. *Ibid.*, VIII, no. 341.
30. Gabriel Puaux, *Mort et Transfiguration de l'Autriche* (Paris, 1966), p. 113.
31. *CAB* 24/275.
32. *DBFP*, Third Series, I, no. 27.
33. *CAB* 24/275.
34. *Ibid.*
35. *Ibid.*
36. *Ciano's Diary*, 1937-38, p. 79.
37. *FRUS*, 1938, II, p. 256.
38. *FO* 371/21598.
39. *In Search of Peace: Speeches* 1937-38 (London, 1939), p. 112.
40. *Dalton Diary*, Vansittart to Dalton, 12 April 1938.
41. *FO* 371/21590.
42. *FRUS*, 1938, I, p. 27.
43. *Ibid.*
44. *FO* 371/21590.
45. *DDF*, VIII, no. 231.
46. *Ibid.*, VIII, no. 259.
47. *Ibid.*, VIII, no. 276.

48. *CAB* 24/275.
49. *DGFP,* Series D, I, no. 138.
50. See Warner, *Pierre Laval and the Eclipse of France,* p. 145.
51. Feiling, *op cit.,* p. 347.
52. *Documents and Materials Relating to the Eve of the Second World War,* I, p. no. 9.
53. *FO* 371/21590.
54. Sargent to Phipps, 17 March 1938, (*Phipps Papers*).
55. *DDF,* VIII, no. 432.
56. *Ibid.,* no. 475.
57. *Ibid.,* Paul-Boncour to Corbin, 21 March 1938.
58. *DBFP,* Third Series, I, no. 109.
59. *DDF,* Corbin to Paul-Boncour, 23 March 1938.
60. *Ibid.,* Corbin to Paul-Boncour, 22 March 1938.
61. Quoted in Middlemas, *op cit.,* p. 193.
62. *Ibid.,* pp. 198-99.
63. *DBFP,* Third Series, I, no. 106.
64. Quoted in Middlemas, *op cit.,* p. 195.
65. *FO* 371/21590, Air Attaché (Paris) to London, 14 March 1936.
66. *Ibid.*
67. *FRUS.,* 1938, I, p. 38.
68. *FO* 371/21590.
69. *DDF,* VIII, no. 446; *Gamelin,* II, pp. 322-28.
70. *Ibid.*
71. *Ibid.,* VIII, no. 462.
72. *DBFP,* Third Series, I, no. 86.
73. *FO* 371/21599, Phipps to Halifax, 17 March 1938.
74. *DDF,* Record of Conference on 5 April.
75. Joseph E. Davies, *Mission to Moscow* (London, 1942), p. 189.
76. *DDF,* letter of 7 April 1938 from Massigli to Blondel (Rome).
77. *Dans la Tourmente,* 1938-40 (Paris, 1971), p. II.
78. *FO,* 800/311 (Halifax Papers), Phipps to Halifax, 18 and 22 March.
79. *CAB* 23/93, Cabinet of 30 March 1938.
    Lloyd George's visit certainly made an impression on Bonnet. In July 1938 Phipps reported him as speaking with great bitterness of Lloyd George and 'the mischievous pro-war propaganda that he indulged in here last March' (Phipps to Halifax, 17 July 1938, FO 371/21612).
80. *DDF,* 'Note sur la situation actuelle dans le monde', 29 March 1938.
81. *DGFP, Series,* D, II, no. 120.
82. *DBFP,* Third Series, I, no. 136.
83. *FO* 371/21612, Phipps to Halifax, 24 March 1938.
84. *FO* 800/311, Phipps to Halifax, 22 March 1938.
85. *DDF,* VIII, no. 388.
86. *Ibid.,* VIII, no. 481.
87. *DGFP,* Series D, II, no. 120.
88. J. Paul-Boncour, *Entre Deux Guerres,* III, (Paris, 1946), pp. 90-91; *GFM,* 436/12385-88 (Czechoslovak foreign ministry documents; Osusky despatch, 26 April 1938)
89. *Blum Papers* (unpublished Léon Blum papers, Fondation Nationale des Sciences Politiques, Paris).

Notes to Chapter 6

1. For Daladier's role in the Popular Front see James Joll, 'The Making of the Popular Front' in *The Decline of the Third Republic* St. Antony's Papers, No. 5 (London, 1959); *GFM,* 621/250420-5 (this is a five page memorandum in English of a conversation which a German embassy informant claimed to have had with Daladier in London in April 1937. The informant was Professor Gerothwohl, a former diplomatic correspondent of the *Daily Telegraph.* Gerothwohl also claimed to have talked to Daladier in April 1938 during the London conference).
2. See Warner, *op cit.,* pp. 158-9.
3. For a first hand account of the police terror unleashed by Daladier see Arthur Koestler,

Scum of the Earth (London, 1941).

4. Jacques Dumaine, *Quai d'Orsay, 1945-51* (London, 1958), p. 66; *JO,* Chambre des députés, session ordinaire de 1946, 18 July 1946, pp. 2678-85; 2703-10.
5. Quoted in Daniel Halévy, *op cit.,* pp. 172-3.
6. Alexander Werth, *France, 1940-55* (London, 1957), p. 9.
7. See Pertinax, *The Gravediggers of France* (New York, 1944), p. 104.
8. *Harvey,* p. 223; *Cadogan,* p. 126; *FO,* 371/21600.
9. *Op cit.,* pp. 298-9.
10. Pertinax, *op cit.,* p. 88.
11. See Coulondre, *op cit.,* pp. 143-5; *Gamelin,* I, p. 61; Jean Zay, *Souvenirs et Solitude* (Paris, 1946), p. 249.
12. Feiling, *op cit.,* p. 353.
13. *AC Papers,* Lord Robert Cecil (Geneva) to Sir Austen Chamberlain 26 November 1926.
14. See Chauvel, *op. cit.,* p. 48.
15. See Bonnefous, *op. cit.,* pp. 415-17; Larmour, *op cit.,* pp. 234-5; Bonnet, *Vingt Ans de Vie politique,* pp. 269-73.
16. Zay, *op. cit.,* p. 429.
17. *The Times,* 16 January 1938.
18. *DDF,* VIII, no. 381.
19. Georges Bonnet, *Dans la Tourmente, 1938-48* (Paris, 1971), p. II; Paul-Boncour, *Entre Deux Guerres,* II, p. 102; Max Gallo, *La Cinquieme Colonne, 1930-40* (Paris, 1970), p. 293.
20. *FRUS,* 1938, I, p. 39.
21. *FO* 800/310, Winterton to Halifax, 25 March 1938.
22. In a testimony of 1951 to the parliamentary commission of enquiry Bonnet said he retired from public life in March 1940. In fact, in July 1940 he asked Baudouin, Pétain's Foreign Minister, for an embassy (*The Private Diaries of Paul Baudouin,* London, 1948, p. 166).
23. See Warner, *op. cit.,* p. 184.
24. Robert Aron, *The Vichy Regime, 1940-44* (London, 1958), pp. 49-50.
25. *DGFP,* Series D, X, nos. 269, 380, 411.
26. *FRUS,* 1940, II, p. 399.
27. *Dans la Tourmente,* pp. 235-45.
28. *GFM,* 4120H/E070966-67.
29. Aron, *op. cit.,* p. 456.
30. See Bonnet's testimony in *CE*, IX, p. 2612.
31. *La Défense de la Paix, 1936-40,* (Geneva, 1946-48).
32. Interview with M Gaston Bergery.
33. Alexander Werth, *De Gaulle* (London, 1965), p. 50.
34. *Dans la Tourmente,* pp. 303-07 (text of de Gaulle's letter).
35. See *Le Monde,* 2 July 1968.
36. Feiling, *op. cit.,* p. 353; Winston Churchill, *op. cit.,* p. 266; Pertinax, *op. cit.,* p. 392; *Gamelin,* II, p. 333; Major General Sir Edward Spears, *Assignment to Catastrophe,* II (London, 1954), p. 29.
37. *Harvey,* p. 233; *Phipps Papers,* Halifax to Phipps, 6 April 1939; *FO,* 371/22915, Campbell (Paris) to Halifax, 21 December 1939.
38. *La Défense de la Paix,* 2 vols (Geneva, 1946-48); *Le Quai d'Orsay Sous Trois Républiques* (Paris, 1961); *Vingt Ans de Vie Politique* (Paris, 1969); *Dans la Tourmente* (Paris, 1971).
39. Werth, *France and Munich,* p. 135.
40. Volume XXV, *Le Tapis Magique* (Paris, 1946), p. 254.
41. *They Called Me Cassandra* (New York, 1942), p. 341.
42. *Dans la Tourmente,* pp. 66-67.
43. Elie J. Bois, *Truth on the Tragedy of France* (London, 1941), p. 63; *Entre Deux Guerres,* III, p. 101; *Actes et Documents du Saint Siège relatifs à la Seconde Guerre Mondiale,* I, *Le Saint Siège et La Guerre en Europe* (Rome, 1965), no. 46; André Maurois, *op. cit.,* p. 86.
44. *Ci-devant* (Paris, 1941), pp. 54-55.
45. Elie J. Bois, *op. cit.,* p. 62.
46. M Gaston Bergery.
47. *La Turquie devant la Guerre: Mission à Ankara, 1939-40* (Paris, 1964), p. 23.

48. A. J. P. Taylor, *op cit.*, p. 197.
49. See Paul-Boncour, *Entre Deux Guerres,* III, pp. 97-101.
50. *Phipps Papers,* Phipps to Halifax, II April 1938.
51. *FRUS,* 1938, I, p. 177.
52. 'Une demande d'enquête sur les responsabilités de M Georges Bonnet', *Les Cahiers des Droits de l'Homme,* 15 March 1939, pp. 166-71.
53. Alfred Fabre Luce, *Histoire secrete de la conciliation de Munich* (Paris, 1938) pp. 13-14; Louis Thomas, *Histoire d'un jour: Munich 29 Septembre 1938* (Paris, 1939), p. 102.
54. For further discussion of this point see Chapter 7.
55. *DBFP,* Third Series, II, no. 769.
56. See de Brinon, *Mémoires* (Paris, 1949), p. 28; *Les Procès de Collaboration: Fernand de Brinon, Joseph Darnand, Jean Luchaire* (Paris, 1948), pp. 200-7; Bonnet, *Le Quai d'Orsay sous Trois Républiques,* p. 128). Published French diplomatic papers contain no references to these discussions.
57. Reynaud, *op cit.,* p. 219.
58. *DGFP,* II, no. 147.
59. *FRUS,* 1938, I, p. 712.
60. Zay, *Carnets Secrets de Jean Zay* (Paris, 1942), pp. 25-26.
61. *DBFP,* I, no. 164.
62. See Werth, *France and Munich,* p. 141; Edouard Daladier, *Defense du Pays* (Paris, 1939), p. 94, pp. 108-9.
63. *Défense du Pays,* p. 20.
64. *They Called me Cassandra,* pp. 354-5.
65. *DBFP,* II, no. 1083.
66. *DGFP,* Series, II, no. 194; *FRUS,* 1938, I, p. 687.
67. *FO* 371/22910, Phipps to Halifax, 28 September, 1939.
68. *FRUS,* 1938, I, p. 601.
69. *Memoirs of Dr. Eduard Benes* (London, 1954), p. 38.
70. *FRUS,* 1938, I, pp. 601-2.
71. Quoted in *L'Homme Libre,* 28 October 1938.
72. For this paragraph see *Dans la Tourmente,* p. 15; Interview with M Bonnet, *DGFP,* II, no. 144.

Notes to Chapter 7

1. Monzie, *Ci-Devant,* pp. 237-8.
2. Zay, *Souvenirs et Solitude,* p. 153.
3. Blum, *Chef de Gouvernement,* p. 45.
4. For this paragraph see Gicquel and Sfez, *op. cit.,* pp. 26-29; Bonnet, *Vingt Ans de Vie Politique,* pp. 69-70; Moch, *op. cit.,* pp. 138-139; Blum, *Chef de Gouvernement,* pp. 43-45.
5. For the presidency and foreign affairs see Alfred Grosser, *La IV République et sa politique extérieure* (Paris, 1961) p. 39ff.
6. Jacques Chastenet, *Déclin de la Troisième République* (Paris, 1962) p. 276.
7. Sumner Welles, *The Time for Decision* (London, 1944), p. 99.
8. Blum, *Chef de Gouvernement,* p. 46.
9. Albert Lebrun, *Témoignage* (Paris, 1945), pp. 243-44.
10. *Ibid.,* p. 246.
11. *FO* 371/21600, Phipps to Halifax, 12 October 1938.
12. Christopher Andrew, *Théophile Delcassé and the Making of the Entente Cordiale* (London 1968), p. 64.
13. *AC Papers,* Lord Crewe to Sir Austen Chamberlain, 4 January 1927.
14. *Ibid.,* 3 January 1927.
15. Pertinax, *op. cit.,* p. 2.
16. Interview with the author, 9 May 1963.
17 *Phipps Papers,* Phipps to Halifax, 23 October 1939.
18. *FRUS,* 1938, II, p. 294.
19. *Phipps Papers,* Phipps to Halifax, 23 October 1939.
20. See Larmour, *op. cit.,* pp. 241-2.

21. *DBFP.*, Third Series, VI, no. 317.
22. Coulondre, *op cit.*, p. 145.
23. *FRUS*, 1938, I, p. 94.
24. *FO* 371/21600, Phipps to Halifax, 16 November 1938; Jacques Rueff, *op cit.*, p. 113.
25. See Liddell Hart's comments *The Memoirs of Liddell Hart*, II, (London, 1965) p. 135.
26. Simone Weil, *Selected Essays*, 1934-43 (London, 1962), p. 192; Baudouin's comment quoted in Sir Lewis Namier, *Europe in Decay*, (London, 1950) p. 82.
27. Pertinax, *op cit.*, p. 104; his chief assistants were: Marcel Clapier, private secretary (general affairs); Roger Genebrier, private secretary (Political affairs); Roger Leonard, private secretary, (national defence). (Information kindly supplied by M Genebrier).
28. *Lamoureux*, VIII, p. 1297; *DBFP*, Third Series, I, no. 390; *DGFP*, Series D, II, no. 648; *FO* 371/21676, Phipps to Halifax, 15 December 1938; Monzie, *Ci-Devant*, p. 131.
29. Orville H. Bullitt (ed), *For the President: Personal and Secret* (London 1973) p. 361.
30. For Caillaux see *Phipps Papers*, Phipps to Halifax, 25 October 1938; for Baudouin see Blum, *Chef de Gouvernement*, p. 292; 'Les Données du Problème Français', *Revue de Paris*, February 1938, pp. 571-595;
31. *Revue de Paris*, February 1938, p. 585.
32. For Fabre Luce see Dieter Wolf, *Doriot* (Paris 1969), p. 286; Interview.
33. Pertinax, *op cit.*, p. 391.
34. *Le Procès Flandin Devant la Haute Cour de Justice*, 23-26 Juillet 1946, (Paris, 1947); *Politique Française*; C. E., IX, pp. 2557-2598.
35. *Phipps Papers*, Phipps to Halifax, 20 March 1938.
36. *DGFP*, VI, no. 430.
37. See Chapter 18. p. 330.
38. *Phipps Papers*, Phipps to Halifax, 23 October 1939.
39. See Chapter 14.
40. *GFM*, 2815H/D 548672-73.
41. For this paragraph see Michel Soulie, *La Vie politique d'Edouard Herriot* (Paris, 1962); Pierre Olivier Lapie, *Herriot* (Paris, 1967); Blum, *Chef de Gouvernement*, p. 164.
42. *FO* 371/21612, Phipps to Halifax, 26 March 1938.
43. Interview with M. Marchandeau; Monzie, *Ci-Devant*, p. 166.
44. *Phipps Papers*, Phipps to Halifax, 12 October 1939; Louis Plante, *Un Grand Seigneur de la Politique: Anatole de Monzie*, 1876-1947 (Paris, 1955).
45. See Charles Pomaret, 'Un Destin Hors-Serie; Anatole de Monzie', *Annales du Centre Universitaire Méditerranean*, XIV, 1961, pp. 3-18; Charles Pomaret, *Le Dernier Témoin: Fin d'une guerre, fin d'une République, juin-juillet 1940* (Paris, 1968), p. 29.
46. *FRUS*, 1938, I, p. 601; John M. Sherwood, *Georges Mandel and the Third Republic*, (Stanford, California, 1970).
47. *DBFP*, Third Series, II, no. 751; *FO* 371/21598 (*Paris-Soir* of 21 February 1938 carried a denial by Reynaud that he wanted a military pact with Moscow); *DBFP*, I, no. 243; *DGFP*, II, no. 152.
48. For this paragraph see Reynaud, *La France a sauvé l'Europe*, I, (Paris 1947) pp. 562-3; Zay, *Carnets Secrets*, p. 9; J. M. Desgranges, *Journal d'un Prêtre Député*, 1936-40 (Paris, 1960), pp. 239-240; Francisque Varenne, *Mon Patron: Georges Mandel* (Paris, 1948), pp. 175-76.
49. Bonnet, *Dans la Tourmente*, p. 70; Phipps thought Reynaud 'a first class intriguer' who would try 'to oust Daladier' (*Phipps Papers*, letter to Neville Chamberlain, 4 November 1938).
50. Interview with the author.
51. Interview with the author.
52. See Jean-Claude Broustra, *Le Combat de Raymond Patenôtre* (Paris, 1969) Marcel Ruby, *La Vie et l'Oeuvre de Jean Zay* (Paris, 1969).
53. Monzie, *Ci-devant*, p. 6. In the five days from 24 to 29 September 1938 the full Cabinet met only twice, on 25 and 27 September. In the same period there were four meetings of the British Cabinet, and at least two sessions of the inner cabinet.
54. Werth, *France and Munich*, p. 255.
55. *Carnets Secrets*, p. 8.
56. *La France a sauvé l'Europe*, I, pp. 557-8.
57. *FO* 371/21595 (Phipps to Halifax, 4 September 1938).

Notes to Chapter 8

1. David Thomson, *op cit.,* p. 110.
2. See Pierre Gerbet, 'L'influence de l'opinion publique et les partis sur la politique étrangère de la France' in *La Politique Étrangère et ses fondements,* ed., J-B. Duroselle (Paris, 1954), p. 98; J-B. Duroselle, 'Changes in French foreign policy since 1945' in Stanley Hoffmann (et al.), *France: Change and Tradition* (London, 1963), pp. 307-308; Alexander Werth, *De Gaulle: A Political Biography,* p. 84.
3. *JO,* Chambre de Deputés, session ordinaire de 1938, p. 1148.
4. Werth, *France and Munich,* p. 142.
5. John Eldred Howard, *Parliament and Foreign Policy in France* (London, 1948), pp. 64-65.
6. *DBFP,* Third Series, II, no. 807.
7. *Dalton Diary,* 22 September 1938.
8. *JO,* Chambre des Députés, session extraordinaire de 4 Octobre 1938, pp. 1526-1543.
9. Moch, *op cit.,* pp. 248-9.
10. *JO,* Sénat, session extraordinaire de 1938, 4 Octobre 1938, pp. 723-736.
11. Quoted in Warner, *op cit.,* p. 142; *Entre Deux Guerres,* III, p. 105.
12. *DBFP,* II, no. 1122.
13. Zay, *Carnets Secrets,* p. 28; *FRUS,* 1938, I, p. 84.
14. Quoted by Léon Blum *L'Oeuvre de Léon Blum,* IV, 1937-40 (Paris, 1965), pp. 203-212.
15. Paul Einzig, *World Finance, 1939-40* (London, 1940), p. 42.
16. See *JO,* Chambre des députés, session ordinaire de 1939, 17 Mars 1939, pp. 1026-1040, pp. 1050-1081; 18 Mars, pp. 1074-75.
17. See Jean Berthelot, *Sur les Rails du Pouvoir* (Paris, 1968), p. 28.
18. *DBFP,* VI, nos. 46, 449, 452; *Phipps Papers,* Chamberlain to Phipps, 14 June 1939.
19. Martin Gilbert and Richard Gott, *The Appeasers* (London, 1963), p. 221.
20. *JO,* Chambre des députés, session extraordinaire de 1938, 4 Octobre 1938, p. 1527; Jacques Kayser, 'La Diplomatie et le Parlement', *Le Monde,* 9 January 1953.
21. Howard, *op cit.,* states wrongly that committees had no access to official files but see Jacques Bardoux, *Journal d'un témoin de la Troisième* (Paris, 1957), p. 16 and p. 77; Baudouin, *The Private Diaries,* p. 195; D. C. Watt, 'The secret Laval-Mussolini Agreement of 1935 on Ethiopia', *Middle East Journal,* XV, 1961, pp. 69-77.
22. *GFM,* 621/250562-587; *DBFP,* I, no. 409; Werth, *France and Munich,* p. 51 and p. 248; Monzie, *Ci-devant,* p. 33; Mistler, 'La menace allemande et le front de la paix', *Revue de Paris,* 15 July 1939, pp. 285-294; *GFM,* 621/250757-8.
23. Bonnet, *Dans la Tourmente,* p. 58; *L'Homme Libre,* 8 October 1938.
24. Coulondre, *op cit.,* pp. 260-1.
25. Bardoux, *op cit.,* pp. 81-2; *La Vie de la France Sous L'Occupation,* 1940-44, III, (Paris, 1957), pp. 1426-1431.
26. Bardoux, *op cit.,* p. 31.
27. *DDI,* Ottava série, 1935-1939, XIII, nos. 405, 608.
28. *FPA,* minutes of meeting of 16 February 1938. In this study only the minutes of the Chamber committee have been consulted. The author was informed that Senate committee records were destroyed in the war of 1939-45.
29. *Ibid.,* minutes of meeting of 22 February.
30. *Ibid.*
31. *Ibid.,* a sub-committee 'charged with the study of the Munich Agreement' was set up on 6 October and met on 12 October under Mistler's chairmanship.
32. *Ibid.,* minutes of meeting of 14 December 1938.
33. See *JO,* Chambre des députés, session ordinaire de 1939, pp. 25-155.
34. *FPA,* minutes of meeting of 1 March 1939.
35. *Ibid.,* minutes of meeting of 15 March.
36. David Thomson, *op cit.,* p. 111.
37. For a detailed study of the finance committee see Francois Boudot, 'Sur des Problèmes du Financement de la Défense Nationale, 1936-40', *RDDGM,* January 1971, pp. 49-72.
38. Paul-Boncour, *Entre Les Deux Guerres,* III, p. 85, p. 94.
39. See Maurice Schumann, 'La Commission des Affaires Etrangères et le contrôle de la politique extérieure en régime parlementaire' in *Les Affaires Etrangères,* ed., J. Basdevant *et al.,* (Paris, 1959), p. 43.
40. Georges Bidault, *D'une Résistance à l'autre* (Paris, 1965), p. 25.

Notes to Chapter 9

1. *CE,* I, (Rapport), p. 86.
2. See *Note on the French Sources.*
3. Elizabeth R. Cameron's brief essay 'Alexis Saint-Léger Léger' in *The Diplomats, 1919-39* (Princeton, 1953), ed. Gordon A Craig and Felix Gilbert, pp. 378-405, is still the only published study of Léger the diplomat, though Jacques Charpier's *Saint John Perse* (Paris, 1962), contains interesting material based on conversations with Léger. For an invaluable guide to the diplomat and poet see *Honneur à Saint John Perse: Hommages et Témoignages littéraires: suivis d'une documentation sur Alexis Léger diplomate* (Paris, 1965).
4. Arthur Knodel, *Saint-John Perse: A Study of His Poetry* (Edinburgh, 1966), p. 176. See also Roger Little, *Saint-John Perse* (London, 1973).
5. The phrase is Feiling's, *op cit.,* p. 413.
6. *Akten zur deutschen auswärtigen politik, 1918-45,* Serie B, 1925-33 Band 1, 2, (Göttingen 1968), no. 182; also Richard D. Challener, 'The French Foreign Office: the era of Philippe Berthelot' in Craig and Gilbert, *op cit.,* pp. 49-85.
7. *JO,* Chambre des Députés, session ordinaire de 9 Mars 1933, Annexe no. 1535, pp. 493-515; Emmanuel de Lévis-Mirepoix, *Le Ministère des Affaires Etrangeres,* (Angers, 1934), pp. 140-1; Paul Allard, *Le Quai d'Orsay* (Paris, 1938).
8. Both M Massigli and M Corbin denied any conflict or friction between the central administrators and representatives in the field; for the conference of 3 April 1936 see *DDF,* 2 série, II, no. 17; interview with M de Margerie, 8 June 1972.
9. For this paragraph see Massigli, *op cit.,* pp. 133-4, p. 24, n. I; Jean Baillou and Pierre Pelletier, *Les Affaires Etrangères* (Paris, 1962), pp. 111-2. In 1939 the British Foreign Office was still using non-machine cipher systems.
10. Chauvel, *op cit.,* pp. 45-46.
11. *DDF,* I Série, I, no. 235.
12. Gordon A. Craig, *War, Politics and Diplomacy* (London, 1966), p. 216.
13. See Philip M Williams, *Crisis and Compromise: Politics in the Fourth Republic* (London, 1964), pp. 339-340; René Massigli, *Sur Quelques Maladies de l'état* (Paris, 1958), pp. 39-42.
14. Jules Laroche, *Au Quai d'Orsay avec Briand et Poincaré,* 1913-26, (Paris, 1957), p. 31.
15. Letter of Jules Henry to Piétri, 17 October 1939, recounting their co-operation in 1938 *(Pietri papers); GFM,* 2361/488281-283.
16. Phipps to Halifax, 22 February 1939 *(Phipps Papers).*
17. *FRUS,* 1939, I, p. 190.
18. Massigli, *op cit.,* pp. 24-25; interview with M Massigli, 31 May 1963; Pertinax, *op cit.,* p. 4, n. 5; (Paris, 1967).
19. Bonnet, *De Munich à la Guerre* (Paris, 1967), pp. 158-9.
20. *DDF,* 2 Série, Massigli to Noel, 1 June 1938.
21. *Ibid.,*
22. Letter of 23 June 1972 to the author.
23. 'Lettres d'il y a trente ans sur Munich', *Politique Aujourd'hui,* January 1969, pp. 109-113.
24. *FFMA.*
25. Lukasiewicz, *Diplomat in Paris,* p. 289.
26. *Facing the Dictators,* p. 274; Emile Moreau, *op cit.,* p. 104; Chastenet, *op cit.,* p. 286, n. II; for French attempts to interest the Germans see *GFM,* 8608H/E603886-7; 7659H/E547268-9.
27. *Histoire Générale de la Presse Française,* Tome III, *1871 à 1940,* Jacques Godechot, Claude Bellanger, Pierre Guiral, Fernand Terrou, eds (Paris, 1972), pp. 466-467.
28. For Havas see Raymond Manevy, *Histoire de la Presse, 1914-39,* (Paris, 1945), pp. 129-143; Moreau, *op cit.,* p. 433; *Histoire Générale de la Presse* pp. 466-67.
29. Bonnet, *Dans la Tourmente,* p. 13.
30. *Les Procés de Collaboration: Fernand de Brinon, Joseph Darnand, Jean Luchaire (Paris, 1948),* pp. 367-8; *FO* 371/22912, Cadogan to Phipps, 2 February 1939.
31. Baillou and Pelletier, *op cit.,* p. 312; Allard, *op cit.,* p. 163; *DDB,* IV, no. 206; Interview with Alexander Werth, 19 December 1962.
32. For this paragraph see *FO* 371/22912, Minute by Charles Peake for Cadogan, 9 January 1939; memorandum from Mendl to Foreign Office with covering letter from Phipps,

22 February 1939.
33. *DBFP,* Third Series, V, no. 326.
34. Raymond Barrillon, *Le Cas Paris Soir* (Paris, 1959); Geneviève Vallette and Jacques Bouillon, *Munich 1938* (Paris, 1964), pp. 287-295; *DBFP,* Third Series, II, no. 1197.
35. Vallette and Bouillon, *op cit.,* p. 109; Interview with M Chastenet, 30 April 1963.
36. For this paragraph see *DGFP,* Series D, no. 120, no. 405, no. 345; Phipps to Halifax, 14 September 1938 *(Phipps Papers).*
37. *DGFP,* IV, no. 351; Zay, *Carnets Secrets,* p. 31; Pierre Lazareff, *De Munich à Vichy* (New York, 1944), p. 143, n. I; *CE,* IX, p. 2666; *DGFP,* IV, no. 381.
38. *FO* 371/22912, Campbell (Paris) to Foreign Office, 19 August 1939; *L'Etrange Défaite* (Paris, 1946), p. 167; Agnes G Raymond, *Giraudoux devant la victoire et la défaite* (Paris, 1963), pp. 30-1.
39. John W Wheeler-Bennett, *Munich: Prologue to Tragedy* (London, 1963), p. 126, n. 2; *Phipps Papers,* Phipps to Halifax, 26 October 1938.
40. Bonnet, *Dans la Tourmente,* pp. 18-26; *Phipps Papers,* Phipps to Halifax, 26 October 1938; interview with M Chastenet, 30 April 1963; the accusation against Léger was repeated by Chastenet in 'Deux Années Dramatiques, 1938-39', *Revue des deux mondes,* March 1973, p. 558; Bonnet writes: 'On me dit qu'au moment où je devins ministre, les télégrammes étaient portés au Secrétaire Général avant de l'être à moi-même. Mais mon Cabinet apprit très vite ce fait et des instructions contraire furent données, pourque les télégrammes fussent d'abord . . . portés au Ministre' (Letter of 26 June 1963 to the author).
41. *FRUS,* 1938, I, p. 495; *DBFP,* II, no. 894; Elizabeth R. Cameron, *op cit.,* pp. 394-5.
42. *FO* 371/21600, minute of conversation with Géraud, November 1938; *FO* 371/21592, minute by Strang, 17 November 1938. Alas in this shady area of financial speculation there are no hard facts. Mr Thomas Barman, a member of the Paris office of *The Times* in the 1930s, writes: 'A friend in the Bank of France used to give me the weekly total of operations on the foreign exchange markets for French and British account, and they were most revealing. I was pledged to secrecy . . . I can, of course, remember the names of the Bankers involved in Paris and London . . . and the politicians associated with them. But to give these names might well involve me in an action for libel' (Mr Barman to the author). The financial journalist, Dr Paul Einzig, detected 'mysterious exchange 'operations' on 28 September 1938 but does not name names (*World Finance, 1938-39,* London, 1939, p. 176).
43. *Harvey,* p. 428; *FO* 371/21592, minute by Strang, 17 November 1938; Bonnet, *Dans la Tourmente,* pp. 16-18; Bonnet-Massigli correspondence, *Le Monde,* 1 June 1971.
44. *DDF;* Massigli, *op cit.,* p. 29; *DBFP,* II, no. 914.
45. *Berlin Diary* (London, 1941), p. 125.
46. *Memoirs,* I, p. 273.
47. This paragraph is based on interviews and correspondence with the late M Comert; also *CE,* VII, pp. 2175-2184; *Politique Aujourd'hui,* January 1969; Monzie, *Ci-devant,* p. 36; Geneviève Tabouis, *op cit.,* pp. 366-7; Paul Reynaud, *La France a sauvé l'Europe,* I, p. 564; Paul Nizan, *Chronique de Septembre* (Paris, 1939), pp. 120-22; P L Bret, (Havas representative in London in 1938), *Au Feu des Evénements: Mémoires d'un journaliste, Londres-Algers* (Paris, 1959), p. 14. One of the Minister's assistants, M Ripert, was said to have told assembled journalists: 'Do you really believe in this communique?' ('Une demande d'enquête sur les responsabilités de M Georges Bonnet', in *Les Cahiers des Droits de l'Homme,* 15 March 1939).
48. *Défense de la Paix,* I, p. 337, n. i; *Phipps Papers,* Phipps to Halifax, 26 October, 1938.
49. Lord Trevelyan, *Diplomatic Channels* (London, 1973), p. 20.
50. *Memoirs of Ernst Von Weizsäcker,* trans. by John Andrews, (London, 1951), p. 170.
51. *Phipps Papers,* Phipps to Halifax, 19 April 1938; *DBFP,* I, no. 459 and no. 524; *DDF,* François-Poncet to Bonnet, 23 June 1938, *DGFP,* II, no. 265.
52. *In the Nazi Era* (London, 1952), p. 168; *Memoirs of Ernst Von Weizsäcker,* p. 170; Coulondre, *op cit.,* pp. 137-8;
53. *The Diaries of Sir Henry Channon,* p. 214; *A C Papers,* letter to Hilda Chamberlain, 4 January 1937; Wheeler-Bennett, *op cit.,* p. 126, n. 2; *Gamelin,* II, p. 340; *FO* 371/21596, Phipps to Halifax, 5 September 1938.
54. Noel, *L'Agression Allemande contre la Pologne* (Paris, 1946), pp. 195-7, pp. 198-202. Official record of 5 April conference in *DDF,* does not confirm the memoirs on this

point. Noel is recorded as describing Polish policy without making any general judgement on the Czech alliance.

55. Chauvel, *op cit.,* p. 47, p. 57; *Phipps Papers,* Phipps to Sir Horace Wilson, 13 June 1939.
56. Elizabeth R Cameron, *op cit.,* p. 395.
57. *FRUS,* 1938, I, p. 618; p. 707.
58. David Irving (ed), *Breach of Security* (London, 1968), p. 16.
59. *DDF,* 2 Série, IV, no. 461, V, no. 44;
60. Alfred Grosser, *op cit.,* p. 60.
61. Pierre Tissier, *I Worked with Laval* (London, 1942), p. 61.
62. *Ciano's Diary, 1937-38,* p. 81; *FFMA,* Massigli to Lacroix, 28 February 1938.
63. Warner, *op cit.,* p. 122.
64. *Ibid.,* p. 123; Gallo, *op cit.,* pp. 293-298; for Mendl's influence see *Blum, Chef de Gouvernement,* p. 358; *Harvey,* p. 428.
65. *FO* 371/2159, Phipps to Strang, 5 May 1938.
66. *DDF,* 2 Série, I, no. 541; *DGFP,* Series D, II, no. 648; *GFM* 2805H/D548438-440.
67. *DBFP,* VI, no. 449; *ibid.,* IV, no. 553.
68. Michel Garder, *La Guerre Secrète des Services Spéciaux Français,* 1935-45 (Paris, 1967), pp. 50-72; Jacques Bardoux, *op cit.,* p. 73; F. W. Winterbotham, *Secret and Personal* (London, 1969), p. 68; David *Irving, op cit.,* p. 34.
69. *Daladier Papers,* 'La manoeuvre italienne du 22 au 31 aout pour amorcer une conférence de revision des traités', paper marked 'absolutely secret', dated 31 August 1939.
70. *Ibid.,* 'Notice sur l'activité du S. R. allemand en France pendant l'année 1937' (undated paper).
71. *Ibid.,* 'Activité du S. R. Italien en France' (memorandum marked 'very secret', dated 13 November 1937, submitted by the army's deuxième bureau).
72. See David Irving, *op cit.,* p. 33; for Walter Elliot see N. A. Rose, *The Gentle Zionists* (Frank Cass, London, 1973).

Notes to Chapter 10

1. Hughes, *op cit.,* p. 169.
2. *CAB* 23/90A, Cabinet of 8 December 1937.
3. *CAB* 24/273.
4. *The Gathering Storm,* p. 209.
5. *Gamelin,* II, p. 326.
6. See J. Truelle, 'La production aéronautique militaire française jusqu'en juin 1940', *RDGM,* January 1969, pp. 75-109.
7. *DDF,* 2 Série, VII, no. 213.
8. *Ibid.,* no. 325.
9. *Phipps Papers,* Phipps to Halifax, 4 September 1938.
10. For the minutes of the meeting of the Conseil supérieur del'Air see *DDF,* 2 Serie, VIII, no. 427.
11. Truelle, *op cit.,* p. 109.
12. For this paragraph see John McVickar Haight, *American Aid to France, 1938-1940* (New York, 1970); Orville H. Bullitt, *op cit.,* p. 260.
13. *DDF,* 2 Série, VI, no. 293.
14. See *ibid.,* 2 Série, I, no. 83.
15. *Gamelin,* II, p. 461.
16. A. J. P. Taylor, *op cit.,* p. 152.
17. For this paragraph see General Beauffre, *Mémoires, 1920-40-45* (Paris, 1965), p. 63.
18. *The Ironside Diaries, 1937-40,* ed. Col. Roderick Macleod and Dennis Kelly (London, 1962), pp. 199-200.
19. Michel Garder, *op cit.,* p. 31, n. 1.
20. This is a point made by General Faucher, head of the French military mission in Prague, (*op cit.,* pp. 32-38)
21. Beauffre, *op cit.,* p. 61.
22. Sir John Slessor, *The Central Blue: Recollections and Reflections* (London, 1956), p. 244.

23. *Gamelin,* II, pp. 259-266.
24. For this paragraph see *Gamelin,* II, xxviii and p. 264, n. I.
25. See Bankwitz, *op cit.,* pp. 103-105.
26. *Gamelin,* II, pp. 259-266.
27. *Ibid.,* p. 263.
28. *Ibid.,* p. 260.
29. J. R. Colville, *op cit.,* p. 169.
30. For this paragraph see J. Vial, 'La Défense nationale, son organisation entre les deux guerres,' *RDGM.,* April 1955, pp. 11-32; *Gamelin,* I, pp. 53-59.
31. Vial, *op cit.,* p. 22.
32. See *Blum, Chef de Gouvernement,* p. 67, pp. 92-3; *FRUS,* 1939, II, pp. 502-3; *Gamelin,* II, p. 358.
33. *Gamelin,* II, p. 216.
34. See *FRUS, 1939,* II, pp. 502-3; *Gamelin,* II, p. 222.
35. See *Gamelin,* II, p. 316 and n. 1; *CE* IX, pp. 2779-80; *DDF,* 2 Série, I, no. 223.
36. *DDF,* 2 Série, II, no. 113.

Notes to Chapter 11

1. *FRUS,* 1938, I, p. 488; *DDF,* Lacroix to Bonnet, 13 April 1938; *DDF,* Budapest to Paris, 14 April 1938.
2. *DDF,* Lacroix to Bonnet, II April 1938.
3. *DBFP,* Third Series, I, no. 142; *FO* 371/21590, Phipps to Halifax, 13 April 1938; *DDF,* Phipps to Bonnet, 13 April 1938; *DDF,* Lacroix to Bonnet, 25 April 1938.
4. Beatrice Farnsworth, *William C. Bullitt and the Soviet Union* (Bloomington, Indiana, 1967), p. 181; Robert Murphy, *Diplomat Among Warriors* (New York, 1964), p. 30; Orville H. Bullitt, *op cit.,* p. 250; *Phipps Papers,* Annual Report on the Heads of Foreign Missions at Paris for the year 1937.
5. Farnsworth, *op cit.,* p. 181.
6. *Dictionary of National Biography, 1941-1950,* pp. 670-71; *DBFP,* Second Series, XII, p. viii; Johann Ott, *Botschafter Sir Eric Phipps und die Deutsch-englischen Beziehungen* (Nürnberg, 1968); Hugh Dalton, *Memoirs, II, The Fateful Years, 1931-45* (London, 1957), p. 105; *Phipps Papers,* Bonnet to Halifax, 3 October 1938; *Phipps Papers,* Phipps to Halifax, 17 September 1938.
7. *DBFP,* Third Series, II, nos. 1076, 1099; *Harvey,* p. 188, 200.
8. Weizsäcker, *op cit.,* p. 149; *DGFP,* Series D, II, nos. 345, 422; *Phipps Papers,* Annual Report on Heads of Mission at Paris for the year 1937; *CE,* IX, pp. 2599-2613.
9. Bonnet, *De Munich à la Guerre,* p. 108.
10. R. J. Minney, *op cit.,* pp. 120-1; *Harvey,* p. 134; *DGFP,* II, nos. 143, 147; *Cadogan,* pp. 71-72.
11. The German embassy's informant was the publicist Professor Maurice Alfred Gerothwohl (1877-1941), formerly diplomatic correspondent of the *Daily Telegraph* (1919-35). Replying in 1967 to a questionnaire Daladier denied all knowledge of the interview attributed to him (*Daladier Papers*). But Daladier definitely had contacts with Gerothwohl in London. The German foreign ministry records contain a memorandum dated 24 April 1937 in which Gerothwohl related a 'fifty minute private talk' with Daladier. (*GFM* 621/250420-425).
12. *Cadogan,* p. 71; Bonnet, *Dans la Tourmente,* p. 28; *DBFP,* I, no. 164.
13. *FRUS,* 1938, I, p. 501; *Harvey,* pp. 133-4; *ibid.,* p. 133.
14. *DGFP,* I, no. 144; *ibid,* II, no. 163; *DDF,* François-Poncet to Bonnet, 17 May 1938.
15. Coulondre, *op cit.,* p. 149, p. 156; Lukasiewicz, *Diplomat in Paris,* p. 121; *Le Monde,* II, December 1947.
16. *DDF,* Corbin to Bonnet, 22 April 1938.
17. *Ibid.,* Note du Département: 'Au sujet de l'URSS: Valeur de la collaboration soviétique pour la France', 24 April 1938.
18. *Ibid.,* Coulondre to Bonnet, 28 April 1938.
19. *DBFP,* I, no. 219, n. 2; *New Documents on the History of Munich,* ed. V. F. Klochko et al., (Prague, 1958), no. 14; *DDF,* Records of Bonnet's conversations with Litvinov and Commène (Rumanian foreign minister).

20. Coulondre, *op cit.*, p. 143.
21. *Times Literary Supplement*, 24 March 1950 (letter reprinted in *In the Nazi Era*, pp. 183-186), 30 January 1953, 13 February 1953, 17 July 1953, 24 July 1953.
22. *Unpublished Polish Foreign Ministry papers*, General Sikorski Historical Institute, London (hereafter Sikorski), A. II. 49/F/13a.
23. Lukasiewicz, *Diplomat in Paris*, p. 76.
24. *DDF*, Noel to Bonnet, 5 May 1938.
25. Lukasiewicz, *Diplomat in Paris*, p. 84.
26. *Ibid.*, p. 90; p. 103.
27. *Ibid.*, p. 104; Beck to Lukasiewicz, 9 June 1938 (document published in *Sprawy Miedzynarodowe*, no. 6, June 1958, p. 69).
28. *DDF*, Massigli to Bonnet, 30 May 1938; *ibid.*, Massigli to Noel, 1 June 1938; *ibid.*, Noel to Bonnet, 8 June 1938 and 31 May 1938; *ibid.*, Bonnet's note of conversation with Lukasiewicz, 11 June.
29. *Ibid.*, Massigli to Noel, 29 June 1938.
30. Lukasiewicz, *Diplomat in Paris*, p. 115.
31. D. C. Watt, 'Sir Lewis Namier and Contemporary European History', *The Cambridge Journal*, July 1954, pp. 597-8; Lukasiewicz, *Diplomat in Paris*, p. 105, p. 91.
32. *Old Men Forget: The Autobiography of Duff Cooper* (London, 1954), pp. 218-19.
33. *FO* 371/21590, Phipps to Halifax, 13 April 1938; *Ciano's Diary, 1937-38*, p. 103; *DGFP*, I, no. 763.
34. *DDF*, 'Entretien avec M. Prunas, 23 May 1938' (Bonnet's note dated 23 May, though interview was in evening of 22nd); *Ciano's Diary, 1937-38*, pp. 120-1, p. 123; *Phipps Papers*, Phipps to Halifax, 16 June 1938.
35. *Cadogan*, p. 78; Bonnet, *De Munich à la Guerre*, p. 29.
36. *Phipps Papers*, Phipps to Halifax, 23 June 1938; also *FO* 371/21617, Phipps to Halifax, 17 July 1938.
37. *DGFP*, II, no. 256; *FO* 371/21591/C6972.
38. *DDF*, Lacroix to Bonnet, 3 May 1938.
39. *DBFP*, I, no. 171; *DDF*, Lacroix to Bonnet, 7 May 1938; *ibid.*, Bonnet to Lacroix, 5 May 1938.
40. *Harvey*, p. 143. For the May crisis see W. V. Wallace, 'The Making of the May Crisis of 1938', *Slavonic and East European Review*, June 1963, pp. 368-390; W. V. Wallace, 'A Reply to Mr. Watt', *Slavonic and East European Review*, July 1966, pp. 481-486; D. C. Watt, 'The May Crisis of 1938: A Rejoinder to Mr. Wallace', *Slavonic and East European Review*, July 1966, pp. 475-480; D. C. Watt, 'Hitler's visit to Rome and the May Weekend Crisis: a study in Hitler's response to external stimuli', *Journal of Contemporary History*, January 1974, pp. 23-32.
41. *DBFP*, I, no. 256; *Cadogan*, p. 79; *DBFP*, I, no. 271, no. 286; *DDF*, Bonnet to Lacroix, 21 May 1938; *New Documents on the History of Munich*, no. 13;
42. *DDF*, François-Poncet to Bonnet, 22 and 23 May; *DGFP*, II, nos. 175, 221; *DDF*, Corbin to Bonnet, 26 May 1938.
43. *DDF*, Bonnet to Lacroix, 23 May 1938.
44. *Ibid.*, François-Poncet to Bonnet, 28 April 1938.
45. *Ibid.*, Bonnet's record dated 27 May; *DGFP*, II, no. 210.
46. *DGFP*, II, no. 194.
47. *Cadogan*, p. 81.
48. *DDF*, Bonnet to Lacroix, 31 May 1938.
49. *DBFP*, I, no. 354; *ibid*, no. 357; *DDF*, Bonnet to Lacroix, 3 June 1938 *ibid.*, Lacroix to Bonnet, 5 June 1938.
50. *DBFP*, I, no. 406.
51. *DDF*, Bonnet to Corbin and Lacroix, 15 June 1938.
52. *DBFP*, I, Enclosure in no. 447.
53. *DDF*, Corbin to Bonnet, 7 July 1938; *ibid.*, Bonnet's reply to Halifax's note, 16 July 1938.
54. *DBFP*, I, no. 502; *DDF*, Lacroix to Bonnet, 31 May 1938; *DBFP*, I, no. 502.
55. *FRUS*, 1938, I, p. 531; Noel, *op cit.*, pp. 198-203; M Noel to the author, 19 June 1963; Jules Romains, *The Seven Mysteries of Europe*, (London, 1941), p. 23 (In a letter to the author, 31 August 1964, M Romains refused to explain what these 'certain things' were); *DBFP*, I, nos. 476-7; *DBFP*, I, nos. 241, 390; Jules Sauerwein, *30 Ans a la une*

(Paris, 1962), pp. 221-2.

56. *DDF,* Lacroix to Bonnet, 24 May 1938; *DBFP,* I, nos. 444, 448.
57. *DDF,* Bonnet to Lacroix, 30 June 1938.
58. *FO* 371/21591/C6972. (Daladier-Chamberlain correspondence, July, 1938).
59. *DDF,* François-Poncet to Bonnet, 6 July 1938.
60. *Ibid.,* Général Le Rond's report dated 1 July 1938.
61. *FO* 371/21591/C6972.
62. *Daladier Papers; DBFP,* Third Series, I, no. 481.
63. *DBFP,* I, no. 502; *DDF,* 'Note remise à M de Lacroix le 17 juillet 1938'; 'Note du Ministre' (undated).
64. *DBFP,* I, no. 495.
65. *DDF,* Lacroix to Bonnet, 20 July 1938.
66. *DBFP,* I, no. 387.
67. *DDF,* Bonnet to Lacroix, 26 July 1938.
68. *Edouard Benes, Munich,* (Paris, 1969), p. 312.
69. *FRUS,* 1938, I, p. 536.
70. Quoted in Lord Butler, *The Art of the Possible* (London, 1971), p. 66.
71. *DDF,* Bonnet's note of meeting with Ossuky, dated 20 July 1938.
72. *Ibid.,* Lacroix to Bonnet, 21 July 1938.

Notes to Chapter 12

 1. *Harvey,* p. 164; Diana Cooper, *The Light of Common Day* (London, 1963), p. 164; Bonnet, *Dans la Tourmente,* p. 29; *Bulletin of International News,* XV, 1938, p. 18; *DGFP,* I, no. 796.
 2. *PREM* 1/267.
 3. Lukasiewicz, *Diplomat in Paris,* p. 122.
 4. *FO* 371/21591; *FO* 371/21592.
 5. *FO* 371/21592.
 6. *DDF,* François-Poncet to Bonnet, 12 August 1938; *Ci-devant,* p. 33.
 7. *Ibid.,* Renondeau to Daladier, 17 August 1938.
 8. *Ibid.,* François-Poncet to Bonnet, 18 August 1938.
 9. *DBFP,* II, no. 691.
10. *DDF,* Bonnet to Lacroix and Coulondre, 31 August 1938.
11. *Ibid.,* Payart to Bonnet, 2 September 1938; *New Documents on the History of Munich,* no. 26.
12. *DBFP,* II, no. 791.
13. *DDF,* 'Note for Minister', 6 September 1938 (unsigned).
14. *Ibid.,* Coulondre to Bonnet, 11 September 1938; *New Documents on the History of Munich* no. 30.
15. *DDF,* 'Conversation with M Litvinov', 11 September 1938.
16. Bonnet, *De Munich à la Guerre,* p. 116.
17. Coulondre, *op cit.,* p. 161; *DDF,* Coulondre to Bonnet, 17 September.
18. *DBFP,* II, no. 721.
19. *DGFP,* II, no. 422.
20. *DDF,* Bonnet to Lacroix, 1 September 1938.
21. *DGFP,* II, no. 440.
22. *New Documents on the History of Munich,* no. 28.
23. *DGFP,* II, no. 107.
24. Benes, *Munich,* pp. 148-9.
25. *Phipps Papers,* Phipps to Halifax, 4 September 1938.
26. *DDF,* Bonnet to Corbin, 7 September 1938.
27. *DGFP,* II, no. 422; Bonnet, *Dans la Tourmente,* pp. 49-50.
28. *DBFP,* II, no. 843 and n. 1; *ibid.,* no. 855.
29. *Ibid.,* Appendix III.
30. *DDF,* Note by Bonnet, 13 September 1938.
31. *Ibid.,* Corbin to Bonnet, 2 September 1938.
32. *Ibid.,* Corbin to Bonnet, 10 September 1938.
33. *DBFP,* II, nos. 814, 834, 842, 879; *DDF,* Corbin to Bonnet, 13 September 1938.

34. *The Moffat Papers,* ed. Nancy Harvison Hooker (Cambridge, Mass., 1956), p. 193.
35. *FRUS,* 1938, I, pp. 512-14; *DDF,* Bonnet to Saint-Quentin, 23 May 1938.
36. *DDF,* Saint-Quentin to Massigli, 17 May 1938; *FRUS,* 1938, I, pp. 500-504.
37. See Monzie, *Ci-devant,* p. 17; Bonnet, *De Munich à la Guerre,* pp. 119-24.
38. See John McVickar Haight, 'France, the United States and the Munich crisis', *Journal of Modern History,* December 1960, pp. 340-358. The article follows Bonnet's interpretation of events.
39. *The Moffat Papers,* p. 206.
40. *Dalton Diary,* note of conversation with Czechoslovak Minister of Social Welfare, Necas, (who had just visited Paris), 18 September 1938.
41. *Gamelin,* II, p. 345.
42. *DDF,* Note by Bonnet, 13 September 1938.
    It is not clear from the French archives whether Bonnet forwarded a note of this interview to the London embassy. On 14 September Masaryk, the Czechoslovak Minister in London, cabled Prague that he had from 'the most authoritative source' a report of the 'very disastrous' Phipps-Bonnet interview of 13 September. Corbin, added Masaryk, had not been informed of the talk: 'the official traffic between Paris and London is such as if these conversations did not exist, and the dispatches sent to Corbin are in a decisive and firm tone' (*GFM* 1809H/412032-3). In 1948 René Massigli, then Ambassador in London, wrote to Lacroix, formerly French Minister in Prague: 'Recently, the Department . . . asked the embassy for a series of telegrams relating to this period (*1938*). Now, out of 50 numbers requested, only a dozen were in our files. I have concluded — which does not surprise me — that everything was not communicated to the London post during the crisis . . .' (letter of 8 May 1948, *FFMA*).
43. *DBFP,* II, no. 857; *CAB* 23/95.
44. *DBFP,* II, no. 866; *CAB* 23/95; Sir David Kelly, *The Ruling Few* (London, 1952), pp. 258-9; (Phipps Papers).
45. *Ibid.,* II, no. 874.
46. *FRUS,* 1938, I, p. 595; *Bulletin of International News,* XV, 1938, p. 823.
47. *Ibid.,* 1938, I, p. 600; *DBFP,* II, no. 894.
48. Benes, *Munich,* pp. 168-9.
49. *DDF,* Bonnet to Lacroix, 15 September 1938.
50. *Ibid.,* Bonnet's note of interview with Osusky, 16 September 1938.
51. *Ibid.,* Lacroix to Bonnet, 17 September 1938; *CE, (Rapport),* II, p. 267 (Lacroix's testimony); *CE,* IX, pp. 2713-14, p. 2638 (Bonnet's testimony); *New Documents on the History of Munich,* no. 34; *DBFP,* II, nos. 888, 902, n. 2.
52. See Daladier, *Candide,* 7-14 September 1961 but J. W. Bruegel writes: 'What he *(Daladier)* alleged to have received from Blumel does not tally with the note Benes had given to Necas and which did not specify any details of the territory to be ceded' (*op cit.,* p. 268).
53. *Daladier Papers,* 'Règlement général: A propos du problème tchecoslovaque', unsigned memorandum dated 17 September 1938.
54. *CAB* 23/95.
55. Lord Templewood, *Nine Troubled Years* (London, 1954), p. 305; unless otherwise stated all other quotations are from the British record of the conference, *DBFP,* II, no. 928.
56. A. J. P. Taylor, *op cit.,* p. 220.
57. *CAB* 23/95.
58. *FRUS,* 1938, I, pp. 620-1.
59. *DDF,* 'Conversation de M Georges Bonnet le 19 Septembre 1938 avec M Osuski a 12h. 30'; *New Documents on the History of Munich,* no. 34.
60. Werth, *France and Munich,* p. 263.
61. *DDF,* Lacroix to Bonnet, 19 September 1938; Benes, *Munich,* p. 172.
62. *Ibid.,* Brunet to Bonnet, 19 September 1938.
63. Bonnet, *De Munich à la Guerre,* p. 157; *GFM* 561/412789 (French text of note left by Lacroix at Czechoslovak foreign ministry); *DDF* (Bonnet's record of instructions telephoned to Lacroix at 1.30 p.m. on 20 September 1938).
64. *DBFP,* II, no. 973, no. 975.
65. *DDF,* Lacroix to Bonnet, 20 September 1938 (received in Paris 9.45 p.m.) In his testimony to the postwar parliamentary commission of enquiry Lacroix claimed that this telegram had been doctored. He said that Hodza had first asked him 'if he was certain

that France would slip out of the alliance in the event of war'. Lacroix replied that he would seek a definite answer from Paris. The envoy alleged that Hodza's question and his own promise to seek a reply had been deleted from the text of the telegram in the Quai d'Orsay archives. But, as in the case of the telegram of 17 September which Lacroix also contended had been tampered with, the allegations are difficult to accept. Hodza, on Lacroix's own testimony, objected that to ask Paris for a definite answer would take too long: 'I admit *a priori* that France will not march' (*CE*, C Rapport), II, p. 268).

66. Benes, *Munich*, pp. 419-20, n. 149.
67. *DDF*, Bonnet to Lacroix, 21 September 1938; Bonnet's record reads: 'after having consulted M Léger I authorised M de Lacroix to give in writing the formula which we had agreed on yesterday evening . . . I had telephoned Daladier on this matter and he was in agreement' *(DDF)*. Benes alleged that the written confirmation of the démarche was more moderately phrased than the language used by the envoys during the night of 20-21 September (*Munich*, pp. 419-20, n. 149) but the texts of the confirmation and the telephoned instructions for the 2 a.m. démarche are identical. However it is possible that in telephoning instructions to Prague Bonnet encouraged Lacroix to speak as sharply as possible.
68. *CAB* 23/95.
69. Zay, *Carnets Secrets*, p. 15.
70. *DBFP*, II, no. 1093, n. 2; *FRUS*, 1938, I, pp. 646-7.
71. Quoted in Middlemas, *op cit.*, p. 385.
72. *DBFP*, II, no. 1093.
73. Templewood, *op cit.*, p. 315.
74. Middlemas, *op cit.*, p. 387; *CAB* 23/95; *Cadogan*, p. 106; *Gamelin*, II, pp. 350-1; *DBFP*, II, no. 1096, n. 1.
75. Duff Cooper, *op cit.*, p. 237.
76. According to Bullitt, Daladier showed him 'a handwritten copy' of a second letter from Chamberlain to Hitler, giving the British guarantee to France (*FRUS*, 1938, I, p. 668). This dispatch of Bullitt has been cited as a good example of the way in which more can be learnt from the American archives than from the British (see Bernadotte E. Schmitt, *American Historical Review*, January 1961, p. 308). In fact the dispatch shows how misleading the American record can be. Either Bullitt or Daladier was confused. What Daladier showed Bullitt was the written text of the verbal warning which Wilson had been authorised to give Hitler.
77. Templewood, *op cit.*, p. 315.
78. *DBFP*, II, no. 1121.
79. *Ibid.*, no. 1120.
80. *DDF*, note of interview between Charles Saint of Bonnet's *Cabinet* and a member of the British Embassy, 15 September 1938.
81. '*La France devait-elle faire la guerre pour la Tchécoslovaquie?* (Le Mans, 1938).
82. *DGFP*, II, no. 548.
83. Bonnet, *Dans la Tourmente*, p. 56; Sherwood, *op cit.*, p. 340, n. 43.
84. *DBFP*, II, no. 1106; *DGFP*, II, no. 648.
85. *Ibid.*, II, no. 1083.
86. *DDF; DBFP.*, II, nos. 1075, 1219.
87. Bonnet, *Dans la Tourmente*, pp. 57-58.
88. See chapter 9, p. 151.
89. *DDB*, V, no. 35.
90. *Lamoureux*, pp. 1786-7.
91. *Monzie*, p. 38, p. 94; Planté, *op cit.*, pp. 266-7; *Le Temps*, 29 September 1938.
92. *DDF*, Bonnet to François-Poncet, 28 September 1938; *DBFP*, II, nos. 1193, 1177.
93. For this meeting see Zay, *Carnets Secrets*, pp. 18-21; *DGFP*, II, no. 648; *DDF*, Bonnet's note of the meeting dated 27 September 1938.
94. *FRUS*, 1938, I, pp. 667-9.
95. *Ibid.*, p. 687.
96. *Ciano's Diary, 1937-38*, p. 165. Bonnet claimed that it was on France's initiative that Britain enlisted Italian mediation. (*DBFP*, II, no. 1199). And on 4 October 1938 Daladier endorsed this claim (Wheeler-Bennett, *op cit.*, p. 190). In reality British action was launched independently of France.
97. *DDF*, Francois-Poncet's memorandum: 'La journee du mercredi, 28 Septembre 1938'.

98. *Ibid.*
98a. *Ibid., DBFP,* II, no. 1158.
99. *DBFP,* II, no. 1185.
100. Bonnet, *Dans la Tourmente,* p. 64.
101. *DBFP,* II, no. 1206.
102. *DGFP,* II, no. 670; *DBFP,* II, no. 1227; *CE,* III, p. 775; *DDF,* record of conversation between Daladier and Goering, 30 September 1938.
103. Bonnet, *De Munich à la Guerre,* p. 207.

Notes to Chapter 13

1. *Gamelin,* II, p. 353.
2. *Ibid.,* I, pp. 124-5.
3. *Réponse aux chefs communistes: discours prononcé à l'Assemblée Nationale le 18 Juillet 1946* (Paris, 1946), pp. 14-15.
4. Templewood, *op cit.,* p. 289.
5. *DBFP,* III, no. 285.
6. *Daladier Papers,* 'Notes sur une action offensive pour soutenir la Tchécoslovaquie', Conseil Supérieur de la Guerre (undated note written sometime after 12 March 1938.
7. *DDF,* VIII, no. 118; *Gamelin,* I, pp. 115-121.
8. Quoted by Dr Robert Young, 'French policy and the Munich crisis of 1938: A Reappraisal', *Canadian Historical Papers* 1970, p. 194.
9. Quoted in Howard, *op cit.,* p. 119.
10. *Ibid.,* p. 119.
11. *Ibid.,* p. 118.
12. *CP* 24 (276), 11 April 1938.
13. *DBFP,* I, no. 164.
14. Slessor, *op cit.,* p. 147.
15. *DDF,* Conseil Supérieur de la Défense Nationale: Note du Secrétariat Général.
16 *DBFP,* no. 164.
17. *FRUS,* 1938, I, p. 494.
18. *DBFP,* II, no. 1093.
19. *DDF,* Conversations techniques du Général Gamelin au Cabinet Office, 26 Septembre 1938.
20. *DBFP,* II, no. 1143, n. I; *Gamelin,* II, pp. 351-2.
21. *Cadogan,* p. 107.
22. *DBFP,* II, no. 1012.
23. *Liddell Hart Papers,* memorandum of 26 September 1938.
24. *Gamelin,* II, p. 324.
25. *Ibid.,* p. 334.
26. *Ibid.,* p. 345.
27. *DBFP,* II, no. 1143.
28. *Ibid.,* no. 1202.
On 25 September the Deuxième Bureau reported: 'The Czech army . . . once its mobilisation is completed will represent a serious force of 35 divisions, with modern equipment, determined to resist and to offer battle to the invader . . . Until now it is admitted that the duration of Czech resistance could be estimated at about 1 month . . . (*Daladier Papers,* Note au sujet du memorandum présenté à M Chamberlain le 23 Septembre 1938, 25 September 1938).
29. *Cadogan,* p. 107.
30. Letter to the *Times,* 11 August 1969.
31. *DBFP,* II, no. 1148.
32. *Ibid.,* III, no. 286.
33. *DGFP,* II, no. 120.
34. *DBFP,* II, no. 807; *Gamelin,* II, p. 351; *DBFP,* III, no. 530.
35. *Ibid.,* I, no. 420.
36. Quoted in Henri Noguères, *Munich ou la drôle de Paix* (Paris, 1963), pp. 409-10.
37. *GFM.,* 1809H/412175-6.
38. *FRUS,* 1937, I, p. 97.

39. Feiling, *op cit.*, p. 334.
40. *FRUS*, 1938, I, p. 502.
41. *Ibid.*, p. 494.
42. *DDF*, Note du Département: 'Au sujet de l'URSS, Valeur de la collaboration soviétique pour la France, 24 Avril 1938'.
43. Coulondre, *op cit.*, p. 148.
44. *Ci-devant*, pp. 34-35.
45. Sir William Hayter, *The Kremlin and the Embassy* (London, 1966), p. 16.
46. Lord Strang, *Home and Abroad* (London, 1956), p. 167.
47. *DDF*, Palasse to Daladier, 26 July 1938.
48. *Ibid.*, Coulondre to Bonnet, 13 June 1938.
49. Coulondre, *op cit.*, p. 127.
50. *DDF*, VIII, no. 331.
51. *Ibid.*, Coulondre to Bonnet, 15 September 1938.
52. *Ibid.*, Coulondre to Bonnet, 24 September 1938.
53. *New Documents on the History of Munich*, no. 53; *Gamelin*, II, p. 348.
54. *DDF*, Coulondre to Bonnet, 18 April 1938.
55. *Ibid.*, Coulondre to Bonnet, 24 April 1938; *New Documents on the History of Munich*, no. 7.
56. *DBFP*, I, no. 502.
57. *DDF*, Daladier to Gamelin, 20 August 1938; Daladier to Faucher, 22 August 1938.
58. *Ibid.*, Coulondre to Bonnet, 21 September 1938.
59. *Ibid.*, Note for the Minister, 6 September 1938.
60. Quoted in Robert Young, 'French policy and the Munich crisis of 1938', p. 200.
61. *DBFP*, II, no. 1012, 1034.
62. Paul Stehlin, *Témoignage pour l'histoire* (Paris, 1964), p. 87.
63. *CE*, II, pp. 300-302; *DDF*, VIII, no. 426.
64. *Candide*, 7-14 September 1961; E. Angot and R. de Lavergne, *Une Figure Légendaire de l'aviation française: le général Vuillemin* (Paris, 1965).
65. *DDF*, François-Poncet to Bonnet, 18 August 1938.
66. *FRUS*, 1938, I, p. 70.
67. *GFM*, 621/250648-9.
68. *CE*, I, p. 33.
69. *Ci-devant*, p. 31.
70. *CE*, II, p. 313.
71. Slessor, *op cit.*, p. 218.
72. Charles A. Lindbergh, *The Wartime Journals of Charles A. Lindbergh* (New York, 1970), p. 70.
73. See Thomas Jones, *A Diary with Letters*, p. 410.
74. Slessor, *op cit.*, p. 220.
75. *The Fateful Years*, p. 192.
76. *FRUS*, 1938, I, pp. 72-3.
77. Slessor, *op cit.*, p. 220.
78. *DBFP*, II, no. 855.
79. *Ibid.*, no. 1012.
80. *Ibid.*, no. 1076.
81. *FO* 371/21596.
82. *FO* 371/21710.
83. *FO* 371/21596.
84. *DDF*, VIII, no. 343.
85. *Ibid.*, no. 426.
86. *DBFP*, II, no. 1093.
87. *Ibid.*, I, no. 164.
88. *FRUS*, I 38, I, pp. 494-5.
89. *Ibid.*, p. 601.
90. *Ibid.*, p. 501.
91. *Ibid.*, p. 712.
92. Quoted by Robert Young, *op cit.*, p. 204.
93. *DDF*, Etat-Major de l'Armée: 'Sur L'intérêt que présente pour la France, du point de vue militaire, le maintien de la Tchécoslovaquie.'

94. *DBFP*, II, no. 1034.

Notes to Chapter 14

1. W. N. Medlicott, *The Coming of War in 1939* (London, 1963), p. 20.
2. Lord Strang, *op. cit.,* p. 147
3. *FFMA*, Corbin to Bonnet, 1 October 1938.
4. *FO* 371/21592.
5. *FO* 371/21592.
6. *DBFP*, III, no. 285.
7. *DBFP*, III, no. 189; *FO* 371/21592
8. *Ibid.*, III, no. 285.
9. *Gamelin*, I, p. 130.
10. *FFMA*, Note sur la collaboration militaire franco-britannique, 23 November 1938.
11. *Ibid.*, Note concernant une collaboration éventuelle des forces franco-britanniques sur les théâtres d'opérations d'outre-mer., 13 October 1938.
12. *DBFP*, III, no. 285; no. 122 (Enclosure).
13. *Ibid.*, no. 122.
14. *Ibid.*
15. *Phipps Papers*, 969 Phipps to Halifax, 26 October 1938.
16. *Harvey*, pp. 427-8.
17. *Ibid.*
18. *CAB* 23/96.
19. See Chapter 10.
20. *CAB* 23/96, 22 November 1938.
21. *Ibid.*
22. *Ibid.,* Cabinet of 16 November 1938.
23. *Ibid.,* Cabinet of 22 November 1938.
24. Feiling, *op. cit.*, p. 389.
25. *Harvey*, p. 223.
26. *DBFP*, III, no. 325. Unless otherwise stated, all quotations are from the published British record.
27. The French army and air staffs prepared papers for the 24 November meeting. The army stated that the British Field Force should be fully equipped and disembarked in France in less than the 14 days promised. Britain should be asked to consider doubling the size of the force (*FFMA*, Note concernant les demandes à présenter au gouvernement britannique relatives à l'action militaire terrestre, 23 November 1938). French air staff submitted that in the event of a German-Italian combination France should direct the bulk of her air force against Italy, while the British air force held off German air power in north west Europe (*FFMA,* 22 November 1938).
28. Quoted in Howard, *op. cit.,* p. 126.
29. *FO* 371/21612, 12 October 1938.
30. *DBFP*, III, no. 285.
31. *FO* 371/21592, 16 November 1938.
32. *Ibid.,* memorandum by Strang, 17 November 1938.
33. *FO* 371/21597, 7 December 1938.
34. *Ibid.*
35. *FPA.*, 14 December 1938.
36. *FO* 371/21597
37. Minney, *op. cit.,* pp. 168-9.
38. *CAB* 23/97
39. *FFMA.*, Renondeau to Daladier, 10 January 1939.
40. *DBFP.*, IV, no. 44.
41. *FFMA,* 29 January 1939 (copy sent to Clapier, Daladier's *Chef de Cabinet*).
42. *Ibid,* note by Hoppenot, 30 January 1939.
43. *DBFP*, IV, no. 51, 52.
44. *Ibid,* no. 94.
45. Quoted in Howard, *op. cit.*, p. 127.

46. *DBFP*, IV, no. 129.
47. *CAB* 23/97.
48. *DBFP*, IV, no. 228.
49. *CAB* 23/97. Cabinet of 2 March 1939.
50. *DBFP*, IV, no. 94, n. 1.
51. See M. A. Reussner, *op cit.*, pp. 220-2.
52. *Gamelin*, II, pp. 400-1.
53. *Howard, op cit.*, p. 132.
54. *DBFP*, III, p. 620.
55. *FRUS*, 1938, I, p. 83.
56. Bonnet claims to have proposed Laval, Mistler or Piétri for the Rome embassy but Mussolini insisted on Poncet (*Dans la Tourmente*, p. 79).
57. *DBFP*, III, no. 329.
58. *Ibid.*, no. 288.
59. *Phipps Papers*, Phipps to Halifax, 26 October 1938.
60. This paragraph is based on a note by Bonnet dated October 1938 in *FFMA*.
61. *DBFP*, III, no. 368.
62. *Ibid.*, no. 325.
63. *Ciano's Diary, 1937-38*, p. 191.
64. *DBFP*, III, no. 484.
65. See Chapter 9.
66. Werth, *France and Munich*, p. 425.
67. *DBFP*, III, no. 405.
68. *Cadogan*, p. 127.
69. *DBFP*, III, no. 473.
70. *Ibid.*, no. 475.
71. *FFMA*, Bonnet's note of talk with Phipps, 14 December 1938.
72. *Ibid.*, note by Vuillemin for Guy la Chambre, 19 December 1938.
73. *DBFP*, III, no. 484.
74. *FFMA*, D'Ormesson to Winterton, 27 December 1938 (Winterton showed previous correspondence to Chamberlain and Halifax).
75. *Ibid.*, Bonnet to Corbin, 27 December 1938.
76. *DBFP*, III, no. 487.
77. *FFMA*, Note de la Direction des Affaires politiques, 6 January 1939.
78. *Ibid.*, Gamelin to Daladier, 7 January 1939.
79. *DBFP*, III, no. 496 (Enclosure).
80. *FFMA*, Entretiens de M Georges Bonnet et de M von Ribbentrop en présence de M Léger et du Comte Welczeck, 7 December 1938.
81. *Harvey*, p. 238.
82. *CAB* 23/96.
83. *FFMA*, Bonnet's note of talk with Phipps, 19 January 1939.
84. *Ibid.*, Note concernant le voyage de M Baudouin à Rome; Note de Monsieur Paul Baudouin: Résumé de mes entretiens avec le Comte Ciano, 5 February 1939 (copy to Daladier); *CE*, VII, pp. 2058-2060; *Haute Cour de Justice*/c. Baudouin, vol. II, pp. 12-20 *(Paris, 1947);* Paul Baudouin, 'Un Voyage à Rome', *Revue des deux mondes*, 1 May.
85. *Ciano's Diary, 1939-43*, ed. Malcolm Muggeridge (London, 1947), p. 50.
86. *C.E.*, IX, p. 2731; *Dans la Tourmente*, p. 92; *DGFP.*, IV, no. 384; *FPA*.
87. *FFMA*, Note remise à M. Georges Bonnet par M Léon Bérard sur son voyage à Burgos, 3-6 Fevrier 1939.
88. Monzie, *Ci-devant*, p. 9(; Bor.iet, *CE*, IX, p. 26660.
89. Zay, *Carnets*, p. 43.
90. *DBFP*, IV, no. 484.
91. Feiling, *op cit.*, p. 396.
92. *Harvey*, p. 250.
93. *FRUS*, 1939, III, p. 104.
94. *Gamelin*, II, pp. 389-90.
95. Orville H. Bullitt, *op cit.*, pp. 311-312.
96. *DBFP*, IV, nos. 351, 359, 365 (Enc), 362, 366, 368; Feiling, *op cit.*, p. 394.
97. *Ibid.*, no. 359.
98. *Ibid.*, no. 367.

Notes to Chapter 15

1. Coulondre, *op. cit.*, p. 163.
2. *FFMA,* Lacroix to Léger, 1 October 1938.
3. Coulondre, *op. cit.*, p. 165.
4. *FFMA,* Coulondre to Bonnet, 4 October 1938.
5. *Ibid.*, Colonel Delmas to Daladier, 3 October 1938.
6. *DBFP,* III, no. 385, n. 1.
7. Flandin, 'Le Conflit tchécoslovaque et la situation politique', *Revue de Paris*, 15 October 1938, pp. 721-42.
8. *Journal de la France, 1939-44* (Geneva, 1946), pp. 22-24.
9. *FFMA,* unsigned memorandum 'Politique extérieure de la France'.
10. *FO* 371/21612; *DBFP.*, III, no. 407, n. 1.
11. Jean Montigny, *Le Complot contre la paix, 1935-39* (Paris, 1966) p. 206.
12. This consideration is stressed by M Léon Noel in a letter of 3 July 1963 to the author.
13. Noel, *op. cit.*, p. 260.
14. *Gamelin*, I, pp. 124-130.
15. *Service historique de l'armée de l'air.*
16. *FFMA,*; *LJ.*, no. 15.
17. *DGFP,* IV, no. 12.
18. *FFMA,* François-Doncet to Bonnet, 3 October 1938.
19. *Ibid,* Bonnet to François-Poncet, 4 October 1938.
20. *Ibid.*, François-Poncet to Bonnet, 5 October 1938; *DBFP.*, III, no. 125.
21. *Ibid.*, Bonnet to François Poncet, 5 October 1938.
22. *Ibid.* François-Poncet to Bonnet, 5 October 1938.
23. For this paragraph see the British record *DBFP.*, III, no. 325.
24. *FFMA,* Entretiens de M Georges Bonnet et de M von Ribbentrop.
25. *FFMA,* Coulondre to Bonnet, 22 December 1938; *LJ.*, no. 35; Coulondre, *op. cit.*, p. 249. Bonnet claimed Coulondre was acting on instructions (*Défense,* II, p. 47) but did not repeat the claim in *De Munich à la Guerre*, p. 313.
26. *DBFP,* III, no. 441.
27. *FFMA,* Coulondre to Bonnet, 2 March 1939; *LJ.*, no. 51.
28. *Ibid.*, Corbin to Bonnet, 15 March 1939.
29. *De Munich à la Guerre,* p. 231, n. 4.
30. *DBFP,* IV, Appendix VII.
31. *Ibid.*
32. *Ibid.* Coulondre was told: 'You will avoid, however, basing your *démarche* on the consultation clause contained in the recent Franco-German declaration' (*FFMA,* Bonnet to Coulondre, 11 December 1938).
33. *Ibid.*, no. 418.
34. Noel, *op. cit.*, p. 255.
35. *FRUS,* 1938, I, p. 669.
36. Noel, *op. cit.*, p. 255.
37. *Ibid.*, p. 259.
38. *FFMA,* unsigned memorandum.
39. Lukasiewicz, *op. cit.*, p. 156.
40. *Ibid.*, p. 157.
41. Zay, *Carnets,* pp. 41-2.
42. *FFMA,* Bonnet to Coulondre, 10 October 1938.
43. *Ibid.*, Coulondre to Bonnet, 4 October 1938.
44. *Ibid.*
45. *Ibid.*, Coulondre to Bonnet, 18 October 1938.
46. *FO* 371/21600, Phipps to Halifax, 20 October 1938.
47. Bonnet, *Dans la Tourmente,* p. 84.
48. *GFM* 2469H/D517466-7 (the report is in English and came from an embassy informant).
49. Coulondre, *op. cit.*, pp. 128-9.
50. *DBFP.*, III, no. 529.
51. *FO* 371/21600, Phipps to Halifax, 20 October 1938.
52. *Ibid.*, minute by Sargent, 22 October.
53. *Ibid.*, minute by Cadogan, 24 October.

54. *Ibid.*, minute by Halifax, 25 October.
55. *DBFP*, III, no. 325.
56. *FFMA*, Bonnet's note of 28 November; *LJ.*, no. 27 (abridged version)
57. *SD*, no. 77; no. 47.
58. *Ibid.*, no. 37.
59. *Ibid.*, no. 80.
60. *FO* 371/22912, Foreign Office telegram to Dominions, 30 December 1938.
61. *FFMA*, Sur le pacte franco-soviétique, 29 December 1938.
62. *DDF*, VIII, no. 165.
63. *DBFP*, I, no. 164.
64. *FFMA*
65. *Daladier Papers*, Note sur l'intérêt diplomatique d'un renforcement de la collaboration économique franco-roumaine, 28 February 1939.
66. *Ibid.*, Note sur les pourparlers du groupe industriel francais avec le gouvernement polonais, 28 February 1939.
67. *FFMA.*, Daladier to Bonnet, 21 October 1938; Daladier to Bonnet, 24 November 1938; Note—'Etude secrète sur les commandes de matériel à effectuer en Tchécoslovaquie'; Lacroix to Bonnet, 24 December 1938; Lacroix to Bonnet, 17 January 1939.
68. *JO.*,Chambre, session ordinaire de 1939, pp. 240-49.
69. *FFMA.*, 'Etude générale faite dans le cabinet du ministre des Affaires Etrangères sur la portée du pacte franco-soviétique', January 1939.
70. *FRUS.*, 1939, I, p. 9.
71. Bonnet, *Dans la Tourmente,* pp. 103-4.
72. Lukasiewicz, *op. cit.*, p. 161.
73. *DGFP.*, IV, no. 380. Bonnet's note of this interview is at variance with Welczeck's report (*CE,* IX, p. 2664).
74. *LJ*, no. 38.
75. *DGFP.*, IV, no. 387
76. For Bonnet's record see *CE,* IX, pp. 2665-6; for Welczeck's see *DGFP.*, IV, no. 387.
77. *FFMA.*, Bonnet's record of interview with Lukasiewicz, 19 February 1939.
78. *DGFP.*, IV, no. 121; *FRUS,* 1939, II, p. 502.
80. *Ibid.*, no. 124.
81. *FFMA.*, Coulondre to Bonnet, 22 December 1938 (this passage was deleted from published *Livre jaune* version, no. 35).
82. *Ibid.*, Coulondre to Bonnet, 7 February 1939.

Notes to Chapter 16

1. Zay, *Carnets,* pp. 25-26.
2. *FFMA*, Francois-Poncet to Bonnet, 30 September 1938.
3. *Penguin Island,* (London, 1948) xi.
4. *Journals, 1889-49* (Paris, 1967), p. 318.
5. *AC Papers,* Austen Chamberlain to Lord Crewe (Paris), 20 January 1925
6. *Ibid.*, Austen Chamberlain to Lord Crewe, 24 February 1925.
7. *Ibid.*, Austen Chamberlain to Sir Eyre Crowe, 8 March 1925.
8. For the creation and work of the committee see *Akten zur Deutschen Auswärtigen Politik 1918-45,* Serie B: 1925-1933, Band I, i, 1925-26 (Göttingen 1966), nos. 10, 185, 214; Wladimir d'Ormesson, 'Une tentative de rapprochement franco-allemand entre les deux guerres', *Revue de Paris,* February 1962, pp. 18-27; Wladimir d'Ormesson, *Les Vraies Confidences* (Paris, 1962), pp. 209-10; J. Bariéty and C. Bloch, 'Une tentative de réconciliation franco-allemande et son écho, 1932-1933', *Revue d'histoire moderne et Contemporaine,* XV, July-September 1968, pp. 433-465.
9. Jacobsen, *op. cit.,* p. 150.
10. Sir Hughe Knatchbull-Hugessen, *Diplomat in Peace and War* (London 1949), p. 53.
11. Jacobsen, *op cit.,* p. 7.
12. Franz von Papen, *Der Wahrheit eine Gasse* (Munich, 1952), pp. 127-8.
13. Emile Moreau, *op cit.,* p. 452.
14. *Ibid.*, p. 453; Henry Lemery, *D'une République à l'autre: Souvenirs de la mêlée politique, 1894-44* (Paris, 1964), pp. 116-119.

15. Edward W. Bennett, *Germany and the Diplomacy of the Financial Crisis 1931,* (London, 1962), p. 94.
16. Quoted in Geoffrey Warner, *op cit.,* pp. 43-44.
17. See Bariety and Bloch, *op cit.*
18. *Ibid.*
19. J. W. Wheeler-Bennett, *op cit.,* p. 65; Marc Bloch also condemned the French middle classes for their intellectual laziness: reading *Mein Kampf* they 'could still doubt the real aims of Nazism' (*l'étrange défaîte,* p. 165).
20. *DGFP,* Series C, III, no. 399.
21. *Ibid.*
22. *André Gide, Roger Martin du Gard: Correspondance, I, 1913-34,* (Paris, 1968), pp. 586-7.
23. *DGFP,* Series D, II, no. 32.
24. *Ibid.,* Series C, III, no. 321.
25. *DBFP,* II, no. 1228.
26. *FFMA,* Francois-Poncet to Bonnet, 4 October 1938.
27. *FRUS,* 1938, I, p. 83.
28. *FFMA,* note for minister: d'une éventuelle déclaration franco-allemande, 5 October 1938 (Hoppenot Papers).
29. *DGFP,* IV, no. 337; *Ciano's Diary, 1937-38,* pp. 176-7.
30. *Ibid.,* IV, no. 337, n. I.
31. *FFMA,* François-Poncet to Bonnet, 20 October 1938; LJ., no. 18; no German record has been found but a summary of conversation is in *DGFP,* IV, no. 343; the published account in the *Livre Jaune* was edited for publication; some references, notably to a new Western pact, were omitted but the actual text was not tampered with in any way.
32. See André Scherer, 'Le Problème des "Mains Libres" à l'est', *RDDGM,* October 1958, pp. 1-25.
33. *DGFP,* IV, no. 347.
34. *FFMA,* François-Poncet to Bonnet, 20 October 1938.
35. *Ibid.*
36. *DGFP,* IV, no. 337.
37. *GFM,* 2536H/D520527.
38. *DGFP,* IV, no. 351.
39. *Ibid.,* no. 346.
40. *Ibid.,* no. 348.
41. *Ibid.,* no. 349.
42. *FFMA,* Coulondre to Bonnet, 20 November 1938; *DGFP,* IV, no. 356.
43. Zay, *Carnets,* pp. 36-38; Zay, *Souvenirs et Solitude,* pp. 168-70; Monzie, *Ci-devant,* pp. 56-57.
44. *DGFP,* IV, no. 366.
45. *DGFP,* III, no. 420.
46. For text see *LJ.,* no. 28.
47. Bonnet, *Dans la Tourmente,* pp. 87-88.
48. *Gamelin,* II, p. 380; *Herriot Papers,* note of 6 December 1938.
49. *FRUS,* 1938, I, p. 112.
50. *LJ.,* no. 163.
51. *Ibid.,* no. 168.
52. See *Défense de la Paix,* II, (p. 39) but in *De Munich à la Guerre* (p. 224) Bonnet for first time admitted that he had a second talk with Ribbentrop in afternoon of 7 December.
53. *DGFP,* IV., no. 370; According to Dr Paul Schmidt, Ribbentrop's chief interpreter, who claimed to have been present at the talk and to have drawn up the record, Bonnet was probably referring only to Czechoslovakia in using the phrase 'relations since Munich. . .' but Ribbentrop understood him to mean the whole of eastern Europe (no. 370, n. I). But it is by no means certain that Schmidt was present on 6 December. Bonnet always denied his presence and the French record does not mention him.
54. *FFMA,* 'Entretiens de M Georges Bonnet et de M von Ribbentrop en présence de M Léger et du Comte Welczeck'. The document is dated 7 December. In a letter of 21 April 1952 Léger stated that Bonnet's account of the conversation in his memoirs corresponded 'in essentials to all my recollections' (*De Munich à la Guerre,* p. 229).

55. *DDFP,* III, no. 420.
56. Otto Abetz, *Histoire d'une politique franco-allemande, 1930-50* (Paris, 1953), p. 91.
57. *DGFP,* IV, no. 370.
58. *Ibid.*
59. *FFMA.*
60. *Ibid.*
61. *Survey of International Affairs 1938,* III, ed. R.G.D. Laffan et al., (London, 1953), p. 194.
62. *Dans la Tourmente,* p. 88; *De Munich à la Guerre,* p. 224.
63. *FRUS,* 1938, I, p. 872.
64. *DDF,* Mandel to Bonnet, 25 May 1938.
65. *FRUS,* 1938, I, p. 851; *FRUS,* 1939, II, p. 127, 130, 135.
66. *FPA,* Chamber foreign affairs committee, 14 December 1938.
67. Arthur Koestler, *The Invisible Writing,* II, (London, 1954), p. 248.
68. *DGFP,* IV, no. 375.
69. *FFMA,* Coulondre to Bonnet, 15 December 1938.
70. *FFMA,* François-Poncet to Bonnet, 20 October 1938.
71. *DGFP,* IV., no. 371.
72. See Gordon Wright, *Rural Revolution in France: the Peasantry in the Twentieth Century* (London, 1964), pp. 72-74.
73. *DGFP,* IV, no. 394.
74. *Ibid.,* no. 388; letter of Coulondre to Bonnet, dated 20 February 1939 in *Dans la Tourmente,* pp. 92-93.
75. *DGFP,* IV., nos. 388, 391.
76. Orville H. Bullitt (ed), *For the President: Secret and Personal,* p. 309.
77. *DGFP,* IV, no. 388.
78. *GFM,* 5220H/E308326-7.
79. *Dans la Tourmente,* pp. 92-93; *FFMA,* 'Note pour les ministres en vue d'une prochaine réunion chez M Daladier', 20 February 1939 (Political and Commercial affairs department).
80. *FFMA,* Coulondre to Bonnet, 2 March 1939.
81. Orville H. Bullitt, *op cit.,* p. 313; Charles A Lindbergh, *op cit.,* pp. 141-2; Stehlin, *op cit.,* pp. 129-132.
82. Orville H. Bullitt, *op cit.,* p. 314.
83. *DDF,* 'Sur l'importance stratégique du Cameroun' (Note du Secrétariat Général du Conseil Supérieur de la Défense Nationale, 24 April 1938).
84. Quoted in Werth, *France and Munich,* p. 359.
85. *Bulletin of International News,* XV, part II, p. 1144.
86. *DGFP,* IV, no. 356.
87. *Unpublished Lamoureux memoirs,* pp. 1827-1837.
88. *DGFP,* IV, no. 392.
89. *GFM,* 3527H/E021455-57.
90. *Défense de la Paix,* II, p. 145.
91. *DBFP,* IV, p. 600.
92. Sir Lewis Namier, *In the Nazi Era,* p. 168.
93. Coulondre, *op cit.,* pp. 236-7.
94. *FFMA,* Coulondre to Bonnet, 23 November 1938.
95. *Ibid.,* Coulondre to Bonnet, 24 November 1938.
96. *Dans la Tourmente,* pp. 91-92.
97. *The Pillar of Fire* (London, 1951), pp. 89-90.
98. For the *Comité France-Allemagne* see Paul-Boncour, *Entre Deux Guerres,* III, p. 95; Bonnet, *Dans la Tourmente,* pp. 39-40; *Herriot Papers;* Abetz, *op cit.,* pp. 68-69; *GFM* 2620H/(Schmidt papers); *Cahiers Franco-Allemands,* 1938-39.

Notes to Chapter 17

1. Roger Parkinson, *Peace for Our Time* (London, 1971), p. 98.
2. *DBFP,* IV, no. 268; Gauche, *op cit.,* p. 85.
3. *Ibid.,* no. 234.

4. *Cadogan,* p. 156.
5. Quoted in J. W. Wheeler-Bennett, *op cit.,* p. 361, n. 2.
6. *DGFP,* IV, no. 245.
7. *Cadogan,* p. 157.
8. *DBFP,* IV, no. 276.
9. *FPA,* 15 March 1939.
10. *JO,* Chambre 1939, pp. 1026-1040; pp. 1074-1075.
11. For full text see *Les Cahiers des Droits de l'homme,* 15 March 1939, pp. 166-171.
12. Orville H. Bullitt, *op cit.,* p. 324.
13. *Ciano's Diary, 1939-43,* p. 52.
14. *FFMA,* Coulondre to Bonnet, 16 March 1939 (Bonnet's text published in *De Munich à la Guerre,* p. 322 is abridged version).
15. *DBFP,* IV, no. 418.
16. See Sidney Aster, *1939: The Making of the Second World War* (London, 1973), p. 72.
17. *DBFP,* IV, no. 402.
18. *Ibid.,* no. 405.
19. *FRUS,* 1939, I, p. 84.
20. For Bullitt's role as peacemaker see *FRUS,* 1938, I, p. 651, 692.
21. *DBFP,* IV, no. 405.
22. Feiling, *op cit.,* p. 401.
23. *DBFP,* IV, no. 506.
24. *Cadogan,* p. 161.
25. *Chips: The Diaries of Sir Henry Channon,* p. 189.
26. *DBFP,* IV, no. 458.
27. *Ibid.,* no. 484.
28. *Ibid.,* no. 507.
29. *FFMA,* de Montbas to Bressy, 21 March 1939.
30. *DBFP,* IV, no. 507. (Bonnet claims that Chamberlain promised to establish conscription, *De Munich à la Guerre,* p. 325 but there is no record of such a promise in the British papers).
31. Bonnet, *De Munich a la Guerre,* pp. 325-326.
32. *Cadogan,* p. 163.
33. *DBFP,* IV, no. 574.
34. *FFMA,* Corbin to Bonnet, 4 April 1939.
35. *Cadogan,* p. 165.
36. Earl of Birkenhead, *Halifax: The Life of Lord Halifax* (London, 1965) p. 437.
37. Quoted in Aster, *op cit.,* p. 115.
38. *J. O., Sénat:* Comité secret du 14 Mars 1940 (Paris, 1948); *Ciano's Diary, 1939-43,* p. 52; Orville H. Bullitt, *op cit.,* p. 324.
39. Paul Baudouin, 'Un voyage à Rome', *Revue des deux mondes,* May 1962, p. 82.
40. *FFMA,* Bonnet's note dated April 1939.
41. Zay, *Carnets,* p. 54.
42. *FFMA,* François-Poncet to Bonnet. 26 March 1939; *DBFP,* IV, no. 381.
43. *Daladier Papers,* Note d'Oudinot (présidence du Conseil): 'Inconvénients de négotiations avec l'Italie', 26 March 1939.
44. Zay, *Carnets,* pp. 50-53.
45. *FFMA,* memorandum by Bonnet dated April 1939.
46. Zay, *Carnets,* p. 54.
47. *FO* 371/22911, Phipps to Halifax, 27 March 1939.
48. *DBFP,* V, no. 85.
49. *Phipps Papers,* Note from Mendl to Phipps, 3 April 1939.
50. *DBFP,* V, no. 76.
51. *Ibid.,* no. 106.
52. *DGFP,* VI, no. 177.
53. *FRUS,* 1939, I, p. 120.
54. *CAB* 23/98.
55. *Gamelin,* II, pp. 403-7.
56. Zay, *Carnets,* p. 56.
57. *DBFP,* V, no. 144.
58. *Ibid. ,* no. 66.

59. *Cadogan,* p. 173.
60. For this paragraph see C. A. MacDonald, 'Britain, France and the April crisis of 1939', *Review of European Studies,* April 1972, pp. 151-169.
61. *Gamelin,* II, p. 406.
62. *SD,* no. 251.
63. *DBFP,* V, no. 186.
64. *FFMA,* Bonnet to Payart, 16 April 1939.
65. *Ibid.,* Payart to Bonnet, 16 April 1939.
66. *CAB* 23/99. Cabinet of 3 May.
67. *DBFP,* V, no. 241.
68. *Ibid.,* no. 351.
69. *Ibid.,* no. 421.
70. *Ibid.,* no. 533.
71. *Ibid.,* no. 539.
72. Aster, *op cit.,* p. 173.
73. *FFMA,* Payart to Bonnet, 8 May 1939.
74. *Ibid.*
75. *CAB* 23/98.
76. *FFMA,* Etude du problème stratégique à la date du 10 Avril 1939.
77. *CAB* 23/98.
78. *Ibid.*
79. *SD,* no. 152.
80. Orville H. Bullitt., *op cit.,* p. 325.
81. *Ibid.*
82. *DBFP,* IV, no. 458.
83. *Ibid.,* no. 608.
84. *SD,* nos. 212, 215.
85. *Ibid.,* no. 223.
86. *FO* 371/22912, Phipps to Halifax, 27 March 1939.
87. Jacques Chastenet, 'Deux Années dramatiques 1938-39', *Revue des deux mondes,* March 1973, p. 558.
88. *DBFP,* V, no. 85.
89. *Ibid.,* no. 103.
90. *CAB* 23/98.
91. *FRUS,* 1939, I, pp. 140, 143.
92. *Ibid.,* p. 140.
93. *DBFP,* V, no. 218.
94. *Ibid.,* no. 225.
95. *Ibid.,* no. 227.
96. Quoted in MacDonald, *op cit.,* p. 166.
97. *Cadogan,* p. 176.
98. *Ibid.*
99. *DBFP,* V, nos. 255, 256.
100. *Ibid.,* Appendix I, pp. 799-800.
101. *FFMA,* Bonnet's note dated 2 May 1939.
102. *Ibid.,* Francois-Poncet to Bonnet, 4 May 1939.
103. *DBFP,* V, no. 398.
104. *CAB* 23/99.
105. *DBFP,* VI, no. 48.
106. *FO* 371/22912, Phipps to Halifax, 18 March 1939.
107. *Daladier Papers,* Léger to Daladier, 15 April 1939.
108. *Ibid.,* Corbin to Daladier, 27 April 1939.
109. *SD,* no. 215.
110. Zay, *Carnets,* p. 58.
111. *DBFP,* VI, no. 317.

Notes to Chapter 18

1. *DBFP,* V, no. 249.

2. *DGFP*, VI, no. 552; *CAB* 24/287.
3. *DBFP*, V, no. 360.
4. *Ibid.*, no. 360.
5. *Ibid.*, no. 384.
6. *DGFP*, VI, no. 353; *DBFP*, V, no. 495.
7. *Ibid.*, no. 409.
8. *FFMA*, Bonnet's note of the conversation, dated 19 May.
9. *DGFP*, VI, no. 409.
10. *CAB* 24/287: 'German-Polish Dispute over Danzig', June 1939.
11. *FRUS*, 1939, I, p. 119.
12. Lukasiewicz, *Diplomat in Paris*, p. 187.
13. This paragraph is based on Lukasiewicz, *Diplomat in Paris*, pp. 187-223; L. B. Namier, *Europe in Decay* (London, 1950), pp. 308-312 (texts of letters exchanged between Bonnet and Lukasiewicz).
14. Not 17 May as stated by Bonnet (*De Munich à la Guerre*, p. 381).
15. *Europe in Decay*, p. 72.
16. *Diplomat in Paris*, pp. 192-4.
17. *Sikorski papers*.
18. *Ibid.*, No 49/7/10, Lukasiewicz to Warsaw, 22 May 1939.
19. *Ibid.*
20. *DBFP*, V, no. 569; also no. 24.
21. *FRUS*, 1939, I, p. 190.
22. Bonnet, *Dans la Tourmente*, p. 127.
23. See *Gamelin*, II, pp. 413-426.
24. *Ibid.*, p. 414.
25. *Ibid.*, p. 416.
26. *Ibid.*, p. 420.
27. *Ibid.*
28. *Ibid.*, p. 423.
29. *Diplomat in Paris*, p. 233.
30. *FRUS*, 1939, I. p. 177.
31. *Ibid.*, p. 183; *DBFP*, V, no. 418.
32. *Ibid.*
33. *Actes et Documents du Saint Siège relatifs à la seconde guerre mondiale*, 1, nos. 46, 50, 59.
34. *FPA*, Chamber Foreign Affairs Committee Minutes, 19 April 1939.
35. Stehlin, *op cit.*, pp. 375-379 (full text of his report); *LJ*, no. 123.
36. *DBFP*, V, no. 413, n. 2.
37. *CAB* 23/99.
38. *FFMA*, Payart to Bonnet, 10 May 1939.
39. *CAB* 23/99.
40. *Ibid.*
41. *Ibid.*
42. *Ibid.*
43. *FFMA*, Coulondre to Bonnet, 22 May 1939; *LJ*, no. 127; *DBFP*, V, no. 668.
44. *Ibid.*, 'Propositions franco-anglaises du 26 Mai d'un accord tripartite' (undated).
45. *CAB* 23/99.
46. *Phipps Papers*, Phipps to Wilson, 13 June 1939.
47. *DBFP*, V, no. 528.
48. *FFMA*, Bonnet's note of talk with Souritz, 26 May 1939.
49. *Ibid.*, Payart to Bonnet, 28 May 1939.
50. *Home and Abroad*, p. 173.
51. *De Munich à la Guerre*, p. 342.
52. *FRUS*, 1939, I, p. 268.
53. *De Munich à la Guerre*, pp. 356-7.
54. *DBFP*, VI, no. 358.
55. *Ibid.*, no. 378.
56. *Ibid.*, no. 414.
57. *Dans la Tourmente*, p. 138.
58. *FRUS*, 1939, I, p. 250.

59. *Ibid.,* p. 252; *DGFP,* VI, no. 603.
60. *Ibid.*
61. *DBFP,* V, no. 801.
62. *FRUS,* 1939, I, p. 180.
63. *Dalton Diary,* 10.5.39.
64. See *DBFP,* V, no. 446.
65. *La Turquie devant la guerre,* pp. 112-113.
66. See chapter 15, p. 275.
67. *FRUS,* 1939, I, p. 270.
68. *Ibid.,* pp. 193-4.
69. *DBFP,* IX, no. 125.
70. *DBFP,* IX, no. 223.
71. *FPA,* Chamber Foreign Affairs Committee Minutes, 21 June 1939.
72. *FRUS,* 1939, II, p. 504.
73. *DBFP,* V, nos. 106, 115.
74. *FFMA,* Buhrer to Gamelin, 26 July 1939.
75. *FRUS,* 1939, I, p. 271.
76. *Ibid.,* p. 378.
77. FO 800/311 (Halifax papers), Chastenet to Kenneth de Courcy, 13 June 1939; 'Deux Années dramatiques, 1938-39', *Revue des deux mondes,* March 1973, p. 559.
78. *Harvey,* p. 291.
79. *Phipps papers,* Phipps to Chamberlain, 16 June 1939.
80. See *DGFP,* VI, nos. 430, 481, 501; *GFM* 2815H/D548665-67.
81. *DGFP,* VI, no. 481.
82. Daladier to Bullitt quoted in Orville H. Bullitt, *op cit.,* pp. 350-1.
83. *FFMA,* Bonnet's note of talk with Coulondre on 24 June.
84. *Ibid.,* Coulondre to Bonnet, 29 June.
85. *DBFP,* VI, no. 186.
86. *CAB* 23/100, cabinet of 5 July.
87. *FFMA; LJ,* no. 150.
88. *DBFP,* VI, no. 212.
89. *DGFP,* VI, no. 603.
90. *LJ,* no. 168. Bonnet's reply is dated 21 July but the French original handed to Welczeck on 26 July had the date 25 July filled in by hand (*DGFP,* VI, p. 98, n. 1).
91. *LJ,* no. 162.
92. *Ibid.*
93. *DGFP,* VI, no. 658.
94. *DBFP,* VI, no. 359.
95. *Bulletin of International News,* XVI, II, p. 30.
96. FO 371/23039.
97. *Ibid.,* Campbell to London, 31 July 1939. As a result of the Aubin-Poirier affair 22 persons were arrested on charges of spying (*Daladier Papers*).
98. *FFMA,* Quai d'Orsay note of 1 June 1939.
99. *DBFP,* VI, no. 317.
100. *Ibid.,* no. 428.
101. *Ibid.,* no. 536.
102. *PREM* 1/311; *FFMA.*
103. *DBFP,* VI, no. 423.
104. Louis Planté, *op cit.,* pp. 296-8; *Piétri papers.*
105. *DBFP,* VII, no. 16.
106. *DDI,* XII, Serie 8, no. 617.

Notes to Chapter 19

1. *DBFP,* VI, no. 464.
2. *SD,* no. 395.
3. For the text of the instructions see Beauffre, *op cit.,* pp. 115-6.
4. *PREM* 1/311.
5. *DBFP,* VI, no. 520.
6. *Ibid.,* Appendix V.

7. *FFMA.*
8. General Doumenc, 'Mission à Moscou', *Carrefour,* 21 May 1947.
9. *Ibid.*
10. *FFMA,* Naggiar to Bonnet, 12 August 1939.
11. Aster, *op cit.,* p. 296.
12. *Daladier Papers;* Aster gives Beauffre as his source for the remark attributed to Daladier but Beauffre himself does not give any authority for the statement.
13. *Daladier Papers*—Rapport du Deuxième Bureau: Mission du général Doumenc en URSS du 10 août au 26 août 1939; *FFMA,* Naggiar to Bonnet, 20 August 1939.
14. *Ibid.,* Doumenc to Bonnet, 14 August 1939.
15. *Ibid.,* Doumenc to Bonnet, 15 August; Beauffre, *op cit.,* p. 142.
16. Bonnet, *De Munich à la Guerre,* p. 430.
17. *FFMA,* Naggiar to Noel, 17 August 1939.
18. Beauffre, *op cit.,* p. 145.
19. Bonnet, *De Munich à la Guerre,* p. 432.
20. *FFMA,* Naggiar to Bonnet, 20 August 1939.
21. Beauffre, *op cit.,* p. 153.
22. *DBFP,* VII, p. 609.
23. *FRUS,* 1939, I, p. 302.
24. *Ibid.,* for Bonnet's discussion of this point see *Dans la Tourmente* pp. 134-136.
25. *FFMA.*
26. Chauvel, *op cit.,* p. 59.
27. *FRUS,* 1939, I, p. 302.
28. *Ibid.,* p. 350.
29. *Ibid.*
30. *Ibid.,* p. 303.
31. For accounts of this cabinet see Zay, *Carnets,* pp. 60-64; *Herriot Papers.*
32. For the controversy surrounding this meeting see Bonnet, *De Munich à la Guerre,* pp. 450-464; Gamelin, I, pp. 23-43; Guy la Chambre 'Note sur la réunion du 23 Août' *(Guy la Chambre papers);* for record of the meeting see *CE,* II (Rapport), pp. 276-278.
33. *Gamelin,* II, pp. 443-4; Bonnet, *Dans la Tourmente,* pp. 163-165.
34. Bonnet, *Dans la Tourmente,* p. 167.
35. No formal minutes of the meeting were kept but General Decamp, who was present, made some longhand notes and a copy of these was given to Bonnet *(CE,* II (Rapport) p. 276).
36. *Survey of International Affairs, 1939-1946: The Eve of War 1939,* ed. by Arnold Toynbee and Veronica M Toynbee (London, 1958), p. 547.
37. Zay, *Carnets,* pp. 65-69; *Herriot Papers.*
38. Zay, *Carnets,* p. 69.
39. *DBFP,* VII, no. 283.
40. *Ibid.,* no. 343.
41. *LJ,* no. 261.
42. *FRUS,* 1939, I, p. 365.
43. Orville H. Bullitt, *op cit.,* pp. 315-17.
44. *Ibid.,* p. 334.
45. *Ibid.,* p. 353; Reynaud, *Mémoires,* II, p. 265.
46. *FFMA.*
47. Zay, *Carnets,* p. 74.
48. *DBFP,* VII, no. 344.
49. *De Munich à la Guerre,* p. 471.
50. Louis Planté, *op cit.,* pp. 298-9.
51. *DBFP,* VII, no. 344.
52. De Monzie, *Ci-devant,* pp. 140-1.
53. *DDI,* XIII, no. 405.
54. *DBFP,* VII, no. 496.
55. See Nicholas Bethell, *The War Hitler Won,* (London, 1972), p. 28.
56. A. J. P. Taylor, *op cit.,* p. 330.
57. *LJ,* no. 296.
58. *FFMA.*
59. See David Irving (ed), *op cit.,* pp. 115-116.

60. *FFMA*, Note of Léger, 31 August 1939; Bonnet, *Dans la Tourmente,* p. 175.
61. *Dans la Tourmente,* p. 176.
62. *DBFP,* VII, no. 604.
63. See de Monzie, *Ci-devant,* pp. 146-9; *Piétri Papers*: 'Récit de deux nuits passées dans le cabinet de M. Bonnet, *le* 31 Août et le 2 Septembre 1939' (typescript dated 14.9.39).
64. *DDI,* XIII, no. 608.
65. See Zay, *Carnets,* pp. 78-82; de Monzie, *Ci-devant,* pp. 146-148; *Herriot Papers;* Bonnet, *De Munich à la Guerre,* pp. 486-7; Coulondre, *op cit.,* p. 304, n. 2.
66. *FFMA*.
67. Coulondre *op cit.,* p. 299, n. 2.
68. *FRUS,* 1939, I, p. 398.
69. *Ci-devant,* p. 148.
70. *Le Quai d'Orsay sous Trois Républiques,* (Paris, 1961), p. 299.
71. *DDI,* XIII, no. 540.
72. *Ibid.,* nos. 543, 546, 608.
73. Bethell, *op cit.,* p. 45.
74. *LJ,* p. 431.
75. *Piétri Papers*.
76. Zay, *Carnets,* p. 84.
77. *Ci-devant,* p. 157.
78. *Ciano's Diary, 1939-43,* p. 143; *DDI,* XIII, no. 616.
79. *LJ,* no. 343.
80. *DBFP,* VII, nos. 205, 521, 528.
81. *Op cit.*
82. Bonnet, *Dans la Tourmente,* p. 183.
83. Lukasiewicz, *Diplomat in Paris,* p. 278.
84. *LJ,* no. 356.
85. Reynaud, *La France a sauvé l'Europe,* I, p. 600; Monzie, *Ci-devant,* p. 159; Suarez and Laborde, *op cit.,* p. 238, n. 2; letter of M Frot to the author, 19 June 1963 (M Frot was a member of the Committee at the time).
86. *FRUS,* 1939, I, p. 413.
87. *Ibid.*
88. *CAB* 23/100.
89. *DBFP,* VII, no. 740.
90. *Ibid.*
91. A. J. P. Taylor, *op cit.,* p. 335.
92. *Carnets,* p. 86.
93. *FFMA*.
94. Orville H. Bullitt, *op cit.,* p. 360.
95. Coulondre, *op cit.,* p. 313.
96. Bonnet, *Dans la Tourmente,* p. 196. According to Coulondre's account, he rang Paris first and the change in his instructions was notified to him. But Bonnet says he rang Coulondre first—who was just about to set off for the *Wilhelmstrasse.*
97. *DGFP,* VII, no. 563 (Enc).
98. Coulondre, *op cit.,* p. 314.
99. Monzie, *Ci-devant,* pp. 139, 152.
100. *Lamoureux unpublished memoirs,* pp. 1854-1857.
101. Montigny, *op cit.,* p. 264.
102. *Ci-devant,* p. 158.
103. *Gamelin,* II, p. 457.
104. *GFM* 456/223886; *GFM* 456/224059-60.
105. *Service historique de l'armée de l'air,* Gamelin to Vuillemin, 7 October 1939.
106. Jules Jeanneney, *Journal Politique, 1939-42* (Paris, 1972), p. 8.
107. *Phipps Papers,* Cadogan to Phipps, 6 September 1939.
108. Bonnet, *De Munich à la Guerre,* p. 529.

Notes to Conclusions

1. *DBFP,* II, no. 1093.
2. George Sakwa, 'The Franco-Polish alliance and the Remilitarization of the Rhine-

land', *The Historical Journal,* March 1973, p. 146.
3. *LJ,* no. 356.
4. See German embassy in France reports for April-September 1939 *GFM*/2796H; also Beauffre, *1940: The Fall of France* (London, 1967), p. 155.
5. *The Moffat Papers,* p. 214.
6. *DGFP,* Series D, II, no. 120.
7. *The Gathering Storm,* p. 283.

Appendix A

A NOTE ON THE FRENCH SOURCES

1. French foreign ministry archives

Sir Lewis Namier once remarked that documents, like cats, have nine lives. Would this were true of the French documents. Alas, there are major gaps in the French record which will never be filled. This may seem surprising in view of the fact that the French archives hold more documents for the period since 1914 than for the whole history of French diplomacy from Richelieu to the outbreak of the First World War.[1]

Firstly there are the inherent shortcomings of the sources. Despite the proliferation of paper from the chancelleries, many key decisions went unrecorded. A Minister or senior official communicated many decisions by voice, instead of in writing; by telephone, instead of by letter or telegram. Secondly, the French seemed reluctant to keep minutes of official meetings. The services of the *Présidence du Conseil* in the 1930s were still in a very rudimentary state and not at all comparable to those of the British Cabinet Office. The governments of the Third Republic did not keep minutes of Cabinet discussions and the historian must glean what he can from the memoirs and private papers. For military matters, the picture is more complete. Although minutes were kept of the meetings of the Permanent Committee of National Defence (*Comité permanent de la Défense nationale*) from its inception in June 1936, the deliberations of its predecessor, the *Haut Comité Militaire*, were not recorded.[2]

Thirdly an unknown quantity of papers have been lost or destroyed. The misfortunes suffered by the French diplomatic archives are probably without equal in modern history. On 16 May 1940 French officials, alarmed by the speed of the German advance, burnt many of their most secret files. With the occupation of Paris in June the Germans seized many papers left behind at the Quai d'Orsay. Some files had been evacuated for safe-keeping to Tourraine and these also fell into German hands. On the eve of the Armistice, plans were made to ship some documents to the United States. The ship carrying the records sailed from Bordeaux but was turned back by German aircraft. The ship's captain burnt some of the papers; then, the Germans carried off 4,000 to 5,000 cartons. More records were lost when a wing of the Foreign Ministry building was burnt during the liberation of Paris in August 1944. By 1945 most of the post-1929 files had disappeared. Some were later recovered in Germany and many more have since been laboriously reconstituted from the files of French missions overseas.

The pity however is that much of great importance has been irretrievably lost.[3] A few examples will quickly convey an impression of the substantial gaps. Missing are many of the memoranda of conversations held by the Foreign Minister of the day, also the minister's informal instructions and private correspondence,

397

internal Foreign Ministry minutes and secret documents not passed through the official register of correspondence. Private correspondence might include highly confidential personal exchanges between the Foreign Minister, senior officials and representatives in the field. The funeral of King George V in London on 28 January 1936 drew a host of statesmen, including the French Foreign Minister. But no record has been found of the conversations which the French Minister almost certainly had on that occasion.

The ravages of the Second World War were not entirely to blame for the deficiencies of the French record. The methods of working of the Quai d'Orsay account for some of the gaps in the archives. It was quite common in the inter-war years for a Minister or senior official to retain in his personal files, papers which should have gone to the archives. On leaving office a Minister would carry off his personal files. Also, it was not unknown for a Minister to have certain papers removed from the official record.[4] Moreover, there was no equivalent in the Quai d'Orsay of the Foreign Office practice of minuting incoming papers. Sometimes a Minister or official might annotate a telegram or report but it was not established procedure.

Amid these gaps the series *Documents Diplomatiques Français* offers a major compensation for the researcher. The French editors have drawn on material from non-diplomatic sources, notably the archives of the army, navy and air force. Unfortunately, the private papers which might have flushed out the official record have not been forthcoming in any quantity.

One possible misapprehension must be corrected. The decision of the French government in November 1970 to open its archives up to 10 July 1940 applied only to the *Archives Nationales*, not to the Ministry of Foreign Affairs or War Ministry. It is expected however that the Quai d'Orsay archives for the period 1929-45 will be open to inspection in 1976.

The Bonnet papers

When Bonnet left the Quai d'Orsay in September 1939 he retained his personal papers and it was these files which enabled him to give such an impressive documentary gloss to his memoirs. It might have been expected that Bonnet's papers would have filled some of the gaps in the official record. And certain files, labelled Dossiers Georges Bonnet, are in the archives of the Foreign Ministry. However, Bonnet's handling of his documents led one distinguished historian to conclude that 'no trust whatsoever' could be placed in 'documentary evidence' for which the former minister was 'the sole authority'.[5] The writing of this book has tended to confirm what may at the time have seemed a harsh judgement. In matters of character and motivation Bonnet may well be given the benefit of the doubt but his documents are a different matter.

Two considerations have to be kept in mind in assessing the Bonnet papers. Firstly the Bonnet papers in the possession of the Foreign Ministry are not originals or copies taken from originals in 1938-39 but copies made in 1940-41 under the Vichy government. According to Bonnet, the original manuscript notes of his talks with visitors and officials were placed in the official archives and later destroyed. Secondly, Bonnet's working methods as Foreign Minister, already examined in Chapter 9, were not such as to inspire confidence in the reliability and accuracy of the originals, even if they had survived.

When the German armies overran France in May-June 1940 Bonnet buried some of his papers in the garden of his country house at the mouth of the Gironde. Other papers were placed in the custody of the French consul at San Sebastian. After the Armistice, the Vichy government began to reconstitute the scattered records. Contact was made with Bonnet and the transcription of his papers undertaken in 1940-41. Yet the Foreign Ministry officials did not have unrestricted access to the ex-Minister's files. They worked in a hotel near Bonnet's house at

Perigueux, in the Dordogne, and copies were made of only those papers which the former Minister chose to communicate. In 1951 the Foreign Ministry informed the parliamentary commission of enquiry that it could give no assurance that the Bonnet papers in its archives were reliable and complete.

2. Livre Jaune

The French Yellow Book was a wartime propaganda publication, focussed upon the Danzig crisis of 1939, and in view of the impending publication of the French documents for 1939 it has no more than a curiosity value. That much of importance was omitted from the Yellow Book goes without saying, but the interesting question is whether the texts of the original documents were altered in any way for publication. Sir Lewis Namier noted that the Yellow Book 'was not published as originally prepared by M Girard, deputy-archivist of the Quai d'Orsay, . . . but pruned and weeded by political hands'.[6] Coulondre who was in charge of the publication affirmed that not a word of the original texts was changed.[7] In fact, some words and even passages of the originals were deleted for publication. The German Foreign Ministry carried out a study of the Livre Jaune. Comparison of eight telegrams in the Livre Jaune with the originals showed that some passages had been deleted, although the only sin of *commission* was the alteration of one word in a telegram.[8]

3. The Riom Trial

After the collapse of France the Germans urged the Vichy regime to put on trial those responsible for the French declaration of war in September 1939. But the 'Supreme Court of Justice' established at Riom by the Pétain government had far wider terms of reference than the Germans had wanted. Its mandate was to determine responsibility not only for the declaration of war but for the military defeat of 1940. Preliminary hearings were begun in 1940 but the trial itself did not start until February 1942. Léon Blum, Edouard Daladier, Guy la Chambre and General Gamelin appeared in the dock. The proceedings included depositions and documents from Bonnet and others who were never on trial. Although the Riom records in the *Archives Nationales* are still closed, the editors of *Documents Diplomatiques Français* have consulted them in the preparation of the series. Moreover, the Blum and Daladier papers at the Fondation Nationale des Sciences Politiques contain many of the depositions. In addition, the numerous published accounts of the Riom trial draw heavily on the depositions and hearings.[9]

4. The Parliamentary Commission of Enquiry

In 1946 the French National Assembly established a commission to investigate the course of events from 1933 to 1945. The creation of this commission reflected the political mood of post-Liberation France. If necessary, the commission was asked to propose political and judicial sanctions. The first meeting was held in 1947 and frequent hearings followed until 1951. Witnesses were summoned and asked to give evidence on oath. The commission's findings form a major source for the years 1933-40. Many military and diplomatic documents were published for the first time. The eleven volumes of the commission's findings comprise two volumes of a *Rapport,* by M Charles Serre, the deputy in charge of the enquiry, and nine volumes of testimonies and documents. A host of political and military leaders appeared before the commission. The second volume of the *Rapport* contains most of the documents assembled by the commission.

The work of the commission needs careful handling. It was not a dispassionate enquiry but a Riom in reverse. The members of the commission were active politicians seeking to impeach the leaders and hangers-on of two discredited regimes; Vichy and the Third Republic. Bonnet, Flandin and company accepted the challenge and retailed digests of their published memoirs. One shortcoming of the commission was that it did not make use of its power to enforce the surrender of documents. Bonnet, for example, successfully stonewalled the commission's repeated requests to see his papers. Nor was the commission consistent in the cross-examination of witnesses. Bonnet was treated to a rigorous interrogation while Daladier delivered his testimony and then found an excuse for not returning to face questions. As time went on the investigation was hampered by the reluctance of the National Assembly to provide adequate financial support. There was not enough money to send members of the commission to the United States to hear evidence from Camille Chautemps and Alexis Léger.

5. The Bonnet Memoirs

By their nature memoirs are partial and highly selective and those of Bonnet are no exception. They are a pretentious and windy farrago of half-truths and evasions, the whole salted at times by a brazen mendacity. 'A tissue of lies' was the verdict of Bullitt, American Ambassador to France.[10] To savour them fully, the memoirs must be set in the context of what may be called *Bonnetiste* writing.

The material can be divided into three periods. The first period covers Bonnet's tenure at the Quai d'Orsay. After Munich, members of the Minister's journalistic following rushed into print with the history of the crisis *ad majorem gloriam* of Bonnet. This group was led by Alfred Fabre-Luce, Pierre Dominique and Louis Thomas.[11] These authors praised the Minister's 'realist' diplomacy of conciliating Germany and retreating from eastern Europe. The Minister was eulogised as the man who had done most to save peace. Although such works may not have been directly inspired by Bonnet, they doubtless carried his *imprimatur*. The second period comprises *Bonnetiste* works published under the Vichy regime. Although Bonnet himself did not write, he is said to have inspired works by Philippe Henriot and Georges Suarez.[12] Essentially the message was the same as that of the Munich pamphleteers but now all the stops were pulled out. Bonnet was presented as the lone hero fighting for peace to the last against Communist conspiracy, Socialist obstinacy and the indecision of Daladier. The third period covers Bonnet's own literary output: memoirs, testimony to the parliamentary commission of enquiry, articles, revisions of the memoirs.

In his two volumes of memoirs, *Défense de la Paix*, published in 1946-48, Bonnet argued that he had wished to save Czechoslovakia in 1938 but France's allies all failed her. Hence Munich was inevitable. After Munich, however, he did his utmost to accelerate French rearmament and prepare for war. Forgetting that several excuses are always less convincing than one, Bonnet entangled himself in a web of contradictions. France was too weak to fight in 1938 but she would have fought but for the defection of her friends. Munich was both a device for buying time and the fatal conclusion of a series of acts of weakness towards Germany. Equally it was a victory for self-determination and the prelude to a general settlement of European problems.[13]

Although purporting to be a history of French diplomacy since 1871, much of *Le Quai d'Orsay Sous Trois Républiques* (Paris, 1961) is a rehash of the two volumes of *Défense de la Paix*. There were, however, some revealing changes of tone and treatment. In the memoirs Bonnet tried to portray himself as a friend of the Soviet Union, striving constantly for a firm Franco-Soviet pact. In *Le Quai d'Orsay Sous Trois Républiques* Stalin is shown as the great enemy, plotting unceasingly to engineer a war between Germany and the western powers. In the memoirs the Czechs were portrayed as the innocent victims of German aggression. In *Le Quai d'Orsay* it is made crystal clear that they were not worth fighting for. Germany, villain of the piece in the memoirs, has been replaced by Great Britain and the USSR.

The second volume of *Défense de la Paix* was introduced by the author as 'an objective statement of facts . . . whose width and precision have already amazed my readers'.[14] One reader who was amazed, although not in admiration, was Sir Lewis Namier. His review of the memoirs provoked a lengthy correspondence with the former Minister. It was a contest of heavyweight and lightweight. In the 1949 exchanges and a subsequent bout in 1953 Bonnet provided enough rope to hang himself. Two examples will perhaps suffice.

In the memoirs Bonnet stated that his talk with Ribbentrop of 6 December 1938 was 'the first and last I had with the German minister on political subjects'.[15] To demolish this claim Namier cited the foreign minister's own declarations to the Senate Foreign Affairs Committee, explaining that there had been official talks on 6 and 7 December. In reply Bonnet stupidly maintained his original statement that the conversation of 6 December was the only official one. The German documents reveal that the two men met for political talks on 6 and 7 December. In *Le Quai d'Orsay Sous Trois Républiques* Bonnet ignored the German record of the 7 December talk but referred to the record of 6 December as proving conclusively that he had had only the one official exchange of views with Ribbentrop.[16]

Namier also disputed Bonnet's claim to have proposed on 5 April 1939 a comprehensive Franco-Soviet military alliance. The evidence cited by Bonnet shows him to have been merely seeking Soviet aid for Poland and Rumania. In rejoinder the ex-Minister stuck to his story, adducing in support a wire of 10 April 1939 to the French Ambassador at Moscow:

I (*Bonnet*) stated most precisely that, 'as soon as the Litvinov agreement should be signed, technical conversations should immediately be undertaken'[17]

The same wire in the memoirs reads:

I think that it would be most useful for you yourself to discuss the matter with M Litvinov. Technical conversations should immediately be undertaken.[18]

What happened, one wonders, to the 'Litvinov agreement'? The minutes of the Permanent Committee of National Defence meeting on 9 April 1939 make it clear that Bonnet was only asking Moscow what assistance she would consider giving to Poland and Rumania.[19]

The searching scrutiny which Namier gave to the flood of postwar memoirs drew criticism not only from the subjects of his investigation but also from fellow historians. Namier was said to have shown too much interest in detecting 'the omissions and commissions of untrained memory', instead of elucidating the motives and dilemmas of the statesmen.[20] Whatever the general validity of the criticism, it is clear that in Bonnet's case Namier performed an essential task in dispelling the smokescreen of scholarship with which the former Minister masked his record as a statesman.

That it would be unfair to dismiss Bonnet simply for lack of historical method is not disputed. However what the Namier-Bonnet encounter revealed was that the deficiencies of the former Minister as a historian: his failure to date and identify documents, the giving of defective and incomplete transcriptions, the doctoring of quotations, pointed to much more than mere negligence or amateurishness. Bonnet the historian tailored his evidence to show that Bonnet the statesman was always right. *Défense de la Paix* was aptly titled because it was in fact a defence statement. At the time of writing Bonnet was in exile in Switzerland and risked prosecution if he returned to France. The immediate purpose of the book was to provide a plausible public defence lest Bonnet, like his colleague and friend Flandin, should be hauled before the High Court. Namier's role as prosecuting counsel was an appropriate and necessary one in the first instance.

Notes

1 See Daniel H. Thomas and Lynn M. Case, *Guide to the Diplomatic Archives of Western Europe* (Philadelphia, 1959)
2 *Servir*, II, p. 181, n. 1.
3 See *DDF.*, 2 Série, I, pp. vii-xiv.
4 For an example see Moreau, *op. cit.*, p. 385.
5 Sir Lewis Namier, *Times Literary Supplement*, 24 July 1953.
6 *Times Literary Supplement*, 1 January 1949.
7 Coulondre, *op. cit.*, p. 256, n. 1.
8 *GFM.*, M93/003194-003253; For Anglo-French discussions on the inclusion of material in the Livre Jaune see Bethell, *op. cit.*, pp. 78-79.
9 See Pierre Tissier, *The Riom Trial* (London, 1942); Maurice Ribet, *Le Procès de Riom* (Paris, 1945); James de Coquet, *Le Procès de Riom* (Paris, 1945); Paul Soupiron, *Bazaine contre Gambetta ou le Procès de Riom* (Lyon, 1944); Pierre Maze and Roger Genebrier, *Les Grandes Journées du Procès de Riom* (Paris, 1945)
10 M. Guy la Chambre to the author.
11 Alfred Fabre-Luce, *Histoire secrète de la conciliation de Munich*, (Paris, 1938); Pierre Dominique, *Après Munich, Veux-Tu Vivre ou Mourir?* (Paris, 1938); Louis Thomas, *Histoire d'un Jour; Munich 29 Septembre 1938* (Paris, 1939), Fabre-Luce had intended to entitle his book 'Histoire secrète de la capitulation de Munich' but deferred to Bonnet's suggestion of 'conciliation' (M Fabre-Luce to the author).
12 Philippe Henriot, *Comment Mourut la Paix* (Paris, 1941); Georges Suarez and Guy Laborde, *Agonie de la Paix* (Paris, 1942).
13 See chapters XIX and XX of volume I of *Defense de la Paix*. Curiously, *De Munich à la Guerre* (Paris, 1967) presented as 'a new and enlarged edition' of *Defense* does not contain chapters XIX, XX of vol. I.
14 pp. 12-13 (not reprinted in *De Munich à la Guerre*).
15 *Defense de la Paix*, II, p. 229.
16 *Le Quai d'Orsay Sous Trois Républiques*, p. 243.
17 *Times Literary Supplement*, 9 April 1949.
18 *Défense de la Paix*, II, p. 341.
19 *Servir*, II, p. 406.
20 D. C. Watt, 'Sir Lewis Namier and Contemporary History', *The Cambridge Journal*, July 1954, p. 582.

Appendix B

BIOGRAPHICAL NOTE ON FRENCH PERSONALITIES

Barthou, Louis : 1862-1934; Barrister; member of several pre-1914 Cabinets; Minister of War in Briand government (1920); Minister of Justice in Poincaré government (1922); Foreign Minister in Doumergue Cabinet (February 1934). Assassinated October 1934.

Baudouin, Paul: 1894-1964; Inspecteur des finances; Chef de Cabinet to several Ministers of Finance; Managing Director of Banque de l'Indochine; Under-Secretary of State for Foreign Affairs in Reynaud Ministry of March 1940; Foreign Minister, June-November 1940; tried by High Court and sentenced to imprisonment in 1947; released after five years and resumed active business life.

Bérard, Léon : 1876-1960; Senator for Basses-Pyrénées, 1927-44; Minister of Justice in Laval cabinets of 1931-32 and 1935-36; February, 1939 goes to Spain to discuss recognition of Franco regime; Vichy Ambassador to Holy See, 1940-44.

Bérenger, Henry : 1867-1952; Senator for Guadeloupe, 1912-45; Commissioner General for Fuel, 1918-20; journalist and writer, Director of *Paris-Midi* (1911); Member of Senate Finance Committee, 1922-36; Ambassador to Washington, 1926; negotiates Mellon-Bérenger accord; Chairman of Senate Foreign Affairs Committee, 1931-40.

Bergery, Gaston : 1892-1974; Secretary of 1918 Committee of War Reparations; served as Chef de Cabinet to Edouard Herriot in 1924-25; independent deputy for Seine and Oise; Editor of weekly *La Flèche,* 1934-39; pacifist and supporter of Munich; Member of Vichy National Council; Ambassador in Moscow in 1941 and Ankara from 1942 to 1944; acquitted in 1949 of charges of collaboration while ambassador in Ankara.

Blum, Léon: 1872-1950; elected Deputy 1919; leader of French Socialist party; formed two Popular Front governments; arrested by Vichy government and tried at Riom court of justice; imprisoned by Germans; Prime Minister December 1946-January 1947.

Bonnet, Georges : 1889-1973; held Cabinet rank from 1926; Foreign Minister April 1938-September 1939; Minister of Justice September 1939-March 1940; Deputy for the Dordogne, 1956-68.

Bressy, Pierre Gaston Prosper : 1890-   ; Counsellor at Warsaw, 1930-37; head of press and news section, Quai d'Orsay, November-December 1938; Chef de

Cabinet to Bonnet, December 1938-September 1939; Director of American section, Quai d'Orsay, 1939-40; Director of European affairs, 1940-42.

Briand, Aristide: 1862-1932; son of an innkeeper; trained as lawyer; held senior cabinet posts, 1909-11; Prime Minister and Foreign Minister 1915-17; Prime Minister, 1921-22; Foreign Minister, 1925-31; resigned to stand as candidate for Elysée and failed.

Brinon, Count Fernand de : 1885-1947; journalist; editor of *Journal des Débats* (1920-32); first French journalist to interview Hitler (1933); Chairman of France-Allemagne Committee for Franco-German Understanding; representative of Vichy government to German occupation authorities, 1941-44; tried and executed for high treason 1947.

Brunet, René: 1882-1951; Socialist Deputy for Drôme, 1928-42; junior Minister in Ministry of Finance, 1937-38; French delegate to League of Nations 1938; used by Bonnet as unofficial observer in Prague in August-September 1938; Professor of International Law, University of Alexandria, 1947.

Caillaux, Joseph : 1863-1944; Deputy for the Sarthe, 1898-1919; Senator for the Sarthe, 1925-44; four times Minister of Finance before 1914; Prime Minister in 1911 at time of Agadir crisis; 1914 Mme Caillaux shoots editor of *Figaro* and Caillaux resigns as Minister of Finance; 1918 arrested for 'intelligence with enemy' and condemned to three years imprisonment; Minister of Finance 1926; Minister of Finance 1935; Chairman of Senate Finance Committee, 1935-40.

Cambon, Roger: 1883-1971; son of Jules Cambon, French Ambassador in Berlin, and nephew of Paul Cambon, Ambassador in London from 1898-1920; Minister and Counsellor in London, 1924-40.

Champinchi, César : 1882-1941; Deputy for Corsica, 1932-41; Minister for the navy June 1937 to January 1938; Minister of Justice, January-March 1938; Minister for the Navy, April 1938-June 1940; President of Radical Socialist parliamentary group, 1936-40; arrested by Vichy government, 1940.

Chambre, Guy la : 1898-   ; held senior cabinet rank from 1934; Air Minister January 1938-March 1940; interned by Vichy and brought to trial at Riom; member of Mendès-France government, 1954-55; Mayor of St. Malo, 1947-65; Deputy 1951-58.

Chastenet, Jacques de Castaing 1893-   ; Director of *Union des mines,* 1925-30; editor of *Revue politique et parlementaire*; editor of *Le Temps* 1931-42; member of French Academy (1956); member of ORTF (1965-69); historian and businessman.

Chautemps, Camille : 1885-1963; elected Radical Socialist Deputy in 1919; served in several governments in 1920s; Prime Minister in 1930, 1933-34, 1937-38, 1938; member of Reynaud government in March-June 1940; left Pétain government on 10 July 1940 and went to United States on a semi-official mission and stayed there, returning only once to France in 1954.

Clemenceau, Georges: 1841-1929; son of a doctor; elected Deputy 1876; Minister of Interior 1906; Prime Minister, 1906-09; Prime Minister 1917-20; failed to secure election to presidency of Republic in 1920 and retired.

Comert, Pierre : 1880-1964; correspondent for *Le Temps* in Vienna, 1908-14; Director of information office of French Mission in London, 1916-18; Director of information services at League of Nations, 1919-33; head of press and information section, Quai d'Orsay, 1933-38; assistant director of American section, 1938-40;

after fall of France went to London and edited newspaper *France*; worked for *Paris-Match,* 1949- .

Corbin, Charles: 1881-1970; son of an industrialist; entered diplomatic service, 1906; Ambassador to Spain, 1929-31; to Belgium, 1931-33; to Britain, 1933-40; resigned his embassy in June 1940 and retired from diplomatic service.

Coulondre, Robert: 1885-1959; Assistant Director of Commercial Affairs, Quai d'Orsay, 1927-29; Assistant Director for Political Affairs, 1933; Ambassador to Soviet Union, 1936-October 1938; Ambassador to Germany, November 1938-September 1939; Director of Prime Minister's office with responsibility for foreign affairs, 1939-40; Ambassador to Switzerland, 1940.

Daladier, Edouard: 1884-1970; Radical Socialist deputy for Vaucluse, 1919-40 and from 1946-58; held Cabinet rank from 1924 onwards; Prime Minister in 1934; supporter of Popular Front; Prime Minister April 1938-March 1940; Foreign Minister March-May 1940; tried at Riom; deported to Germany, 1943-45; President of Radical party 1957; lost his seat in elections of November 1958.

Darlan, Jean François: 1881-1942; Vice-Admiral and Chief of Naval Staff, 1937-40; Deputy Prime Minister under Marshal Pétain, February 1941-April 1942; Commander-in-Chief French North Africa; sided with Anglo-American invasion forces in French North Africa, November 1942; assassinated, 24 December 1942.

Delbos, Yvon: 1885-1956; journalist, wrote for *La Dépêche de Toulouse*; Radical deputy for Dordogne, 1924-44; Minister of Justice 1936; Foreign Minister, June 1936-March 1938; Minister of Education, September 1939-March 1940; deported by Germans to Oranienbourg, 1943-45; re-elected deputy for Dordogne, 1946-55; Minister of Education, 1948-50; candidate for presidency of Republic in 1953.

Doriot, Jacques: 1898-1945; metal worker at Saint-Denis; secretary general of Young Communists; elected deputy (1924) and mayor of Saint-Denis; expelled from French Communist Party in 1934; founded in June 1936 *Parti Populaire Français*, having strong fascist flavour; opposed Popular Front; advocate of collaboration with Germany in 1940; fought with German forces against Soviet Union; shot on German road in 1945, possibly by fire from German aircraft.

D'Ormesson, Count Wladimir Lefevre: 1888-1973; born in St. Petersbourg; member of distinguished family of civil servants; foreign affairs editor of *Le Temps* and *Le Journal de Genève*, 1924-34; foreign editor of *Figaro,* 1934-40; Ambassador to Holy See, 1940; dismissed by Pétain; Ambassador to Argentina, 1945-48; Holy See, 1948-56; elected to French Academy, 1956; President of ORTF, 1964-68.

Flandin, Pierre-Etienne: 1889-1958; lawyer by training; elected deputy for the Yonne in 1914; member of several cabinets, 1924-34; president of Right wing *Alliance Démocratique* group; Prime Minister in 1934 and 1935; Foreign Minister at time of Rhineland *coup*, March 1936; Foreign Minister under Marshal Pétain, December 1940-February 1941; condemned in 1946 for collaboration but sentence commuted.

François-Poncet, André: 1887-; taught at Ecole Polytechnique, 1913-14; deputy for the Seine, 1924-1928; junior Minister in Cabinet of 1928-29; Under-Secretary of State to Prime Minister in 1930-31; Ambassador to Berlin, 1931-38; Ambassador to Rome, 1938-40; deported to Germany, 1943-45; French High Commissioner and then Ambassador in Germany, 1948-55; president of International Red Cross, 1949-55; elected to French Academy, 1952.

Gamelin, Maurice Gustave : 1872-1958; member of Marshal Joffre's staff, 1902-11; Chef de Cabinet to Joffre in 1914; divisional commander in 1914-18; Chief of General Staff, 1931-38; Chief of National Defence Staff and Chief of General Staff, 1938-40; replaced by Weygand in May 1940; tried at Riom and deported to Germany, 1943-45.

Géraud, André (Pertinax) : 1882-1956; London correspondent of *Echo de Paris*, 1905-14; foreign affairs editor of *Echo de Paris*, 1917-38; editor of *L'Europe nouvelle*, 1938-40; went to United States after fall of France; diplomatic correspondent of *France-Soir* after 1945.

Herriot, Edouard : 1872-1957; university teacher; Radical Socialist Deputy for the Rhône, 1919-1940; Prime Minister of 1924 *Cartel des Gauches;* Prime Minister in 1932; supporter of Popular Front; President of Chamber of Deputies, 1936-40; deported to Germany, 1943-45; President of National Assembly, 1947; Mayor of Lyons, 1905-55.

Jeanneney, Jules: 1864-1957; elected Deputy 1902; Senator 1909; Under-Secretary of State to Clemenceau, 1917-20; Vice-President of Senate, 1924; Chairman of Senate Finance Committee, 1931; President of Senate, 1932-40; Minister of State in General de Gaulle's government, 1944-45.

Laval, Pierre : 1883-1945; son of an innkeeper; barrister by profession; joined Socialist party and elected Deputy for Aubervilliers, 1914; Senator for the Seine, 1927; allied with Right wing André Tardieu; Prime Minister, 1931; Foreign Minister, 1934; Prime Minister, 1935-36; Prime Minister and foreign minister, 1942-44; tried by High Court and executed, 1945.

Lebrun, Albert: 1871-1950; mining engineer; Deputy, 1900; Senator, 1920; served in several ministries, 1911-1918; President of the Senate, 1931; President of the Republic, 1932; re-elected for second septennate in April 1939; retired from office on 10 July 1940 following National Assembly's vote of full powers to Marshal Pétain; deported to Germany, 1943.

Léger, Alexis : 1887-1975; born Guadeloupe; entered diplomatic service in 1914; secretary at Peking, 1916-20; held top-level posts in central administration of Quai d'Orsay from 1922 onwards; Secretary General with rank of Ambassador, 1933-40; went to United States after fall of France; Vichy government deprived him of French nationality; resumed literary career under pseudonym of Saint-John Perse; awarded Nobel Prize for Literature, 1960.

Mandel, Georges (Louis Rothschild): 1885-1944; chief assistant to Clemenceau in 1917; Minister of Posts under Doumergue in 1934; Minister for Colonies, April 1938 to May 1940; Minister of Interior, May-June 1940; imprisoned in France, 1940-42; deported to Germany, 1942-44; executed by Vichy Milice, July 1944.

Marchandeau, Paul: 1882-1968; lawyer; journalist; Radical Deputy for the Marne, 1926-1944; Mayor of Rheims; member of various cabinets in 1930s; Minister of Finance, April-November 1938; Minister of Justice, November 1938-September 1939.

Marin, Louis: 1871-1960; Deputy (1905-40, 1944-51); Minister of State. 1934-36, May-June 1940; leader of Right wing group in Chamber; opposed Briand's foreign policy; opposed armistice of 1940.

Massigli, René: 1888-; Assistant Director for Political Affairs, Quai d'Orsay, 1933-37; Director for Political Affairs, 1937-38; Ambassador to Ankara, October 1938-1940; joined General de Gaulle in London in 1943; Ambassador to London, 1944; Secretary General of Quai d'Orsay, 1955-56.

Mistler, Jean: 1897-; lecturer at university of Budapest, 1921-25; deputy for the Aude, 1928-40; Minister of Posts, 1933-34; President of Chamber Foreign Affairs Committee, 1936-40; after 1940 followed literary career; elected to French Academy, 1966.

Monzie, Anatole de: 1876-1947; Deputy, 1909-19; Senator, 1920-29; Deputy, 1929-40; Minister of Finance in 1925; Minister of Public Works 1925-26; Minister of Education, 1932-34; Minister of Public Works, 1938-40.

Noël, Léon: 1888-; director of the *Sûreté Générale* and Secretary General of Ministry of Interior, 1931; chief personal assistant to Laval (Prime Minister and Foreign Minister) in 1932; Minister in Prague, 1932-35; Ambassador to Poland, 1935-40; member of French armistice delegation to Germany and Italy, 1940; Deputy for the Yonne, 1951-55; President of the Conseil Constitutionel, 1959-65.

Paul-Boncour, Joseph: 1873-1972; trained as a lawyer; private secretary to Waldeck-Rousseau and Viviani, 1899-1906; elected Deputy (1909) as a moderate Socialist; member of French delegation to League of Nations; Chairman of Chamber Foreign Affairs Committee, 1927-31; Prime Minister and Foreign Minister in 1932; Foreign Minister, 13 March-10 April 1938; French representative to United Nations Assembly in London, 1946.

Pétain, Marshal Philippe: 1856-1951; after defence of Verdun in 1916 replaced Nivelle as Commander of French armies in northern France; re-established morale of troops; made a Marshal of France, 1918; sent to Morocco to suppress Abd el Krim rising, 1925-26; War Minister in Doumergue government, 1934; Member of Permanent Committee of National Defence, 1936-39; Ambassador to Spain, 1939-40; deputy Prime Minister, May-June 1940; Prime Minister, 16 June 1940; transferred government to Vichy and voted full powers by National Assembly on 10 July 1940; tried by High Court and sentenced to life imprisonment, 1945.

Piétri, François: 1878-1966; born in Corsica; Inspecteur des Finances; Deputy for Corsica, 1924-42; Minister for the Navy, 1934-36; member of Chamber Finance Committee, 1938-39; Minister for Posts, 1940; Vichy Ambassador to Spain, 1940-44.

Poincaré, Raymond: 1860-1934; held cabinet rank from 1893; Prime Minister and Foreign Minister, 1912-13; elected President of the Republic, 1913-20; refused second term of office and returned to active politics; Chairman of Reparations Commission, 1920; Prime Minister and Foreign Minister, 1922-24; Prime Minister, 1926-29.

Reynaud, Paul: 1878-1966; Right-wing deputy for Basses—Alpes, 1919-24; re-elected in 1928; member of Laval and Tardieu governments, 1930-32; after six years without office became Minister of Justice in Daladier government of April

1938; Minister of Finance November 1938-March 1940; Prime Minister, March-June 1940; arrested by Vichy authorities and given life imprisonment; deported to Germany, 1942-44; Minister of Finance, 1948; Deputy Prime Minister in Laniel government, 1953; helped in preparation of constitution of Fifth Republic in 1958; President of National Assembly, 1958.

Sarraut, Albert: 1872-1962; Radical Socialist; held office in several pre-1914 cabinets; Governor-General of Indo-China, 1911-14; Minister for colonies, 1919-24; Prime Minister in 1933 and 1936; Minister of Interior, 1938-40; deported to Germany, 1943-45; President of Assembly of French Union, 1949-58.

Thorez, Maurice: 1900-64; a miner from the age of 12; Secretary General for Communist federation of Pas de Calais, 1923; opposed action of French army in Morocco and Levant in 1920s; Secretary General of French Communist party, 1930; elected deputy for Ivry, 1932; supported Popular Front; went to Soviet Union in October 1939, returning to France in 1944; Minister of State, 1945-46.

Weygand, Maxime: 1867-1965; Chief of Staff to Foch, August, 1914; High Commissioner for Syria and Commander-in-Chief of French Forces in the Levant, 1924; Chief of the General Staff, 1930-31; Inspector General of the Army 1931-35; Commander-in-Chief in Levant, 1939; Chief of Staff of National Defence and Commander in Chief, May 1940; Delegate General in North Africa, 1940-41; imprisoned in Germany, 1943-45.

Zay, Jean: 1904-44; Radical Socialist Deputy, 1932-40; Minister for Education, June 1936-September 1939; assassinated 20 June 1944.

Appendix C

PRINCIPAL HOLDERS OF OFFICE, 1936-1939

President of the Republic	:	Albert Lebrun (May 1932-July 1940)
Prime Minister	:	Léon Blum (4 June 1936-21 June 1937)
		Camille Chautemps (22 June 1937-10 March 1938)
		Léon Blum (13 March 1938-8 April 1938)
		Edouard Daladier (10 April 1938-20 March 1940)
Minister of National Defence and War	:	Edouard Daladier (4 June 1936-18 May 1940)
Minister for Foreign Affairs:		Yvon Delbos (4 June 1936-10 March 1938)
		Joseph Paul-Boncour (13 March 1938-8 April 1938)
		Georges Bonnet (10 April 1938-13 September 1939)

Ministry of Foreign Affairs

Secretary General	:	Alexis Léger (1933-40)
Political Director	:	René Massigli (1937-38)
		Emile Charvériat (1938-40)

Armed Forces	:	
Chief of the General Staff and (from 21 January 1938) Chief of Staff of National Defence	:	Général M. G. Gamelin (1931-May 1940)
Chief of Naval Staff	:	Vice-Admiral F. Darlan (1937-40)
Chief of Air Staff	:	Général J. Vuillemin (1938-40)

Diplomatic Representatives

Ambassador at Berlin	:	André François-Poncet (1931-October 1938)
Ambassador at London	:	Charles Corbin (1933-40)
Ambassador at Moscow	:	Robert Coulondre (1936-38)
		Paul-Emile Naggiar (1938-40)
Ambassador at Rome	:	André François-Poncet (1938-40)
Ambassador at Warsaw	:	Léon Noel (1935-39)
Ambassador at Washington	:	Count René Doynel de St. Quentin (1938-40)
Minister at Prague	:	Léopold Victor de Lacroix (1936-39).
Minister at Vienna	:	Gabriel Puaux (1933-38)
Military Attache at Berlin	:	Général Renondeau (to November 1938)
		Colonel H. Didelet
Military Attaché at London	:	Géneral A. Lelong
Military Attaché at Moscow	:	Colonel Palasse
Head of French Military Mission at Prague	:	Général Eugène Faucher (1926-38)

Appendix D

FRENCH GOVERNMENTS, 1936-1939

1936 Elections

First Blum Ministry (4 June 1936-21 June 1937)
        Prime Minister: Léon Blum
        Foreign Affairs: Yvon Delbos
        Interior   :   Roger Salengro
                            (succeeded 24 November 1936 by Max Dormoy)
        Finance   :   Vincent Auriol
        Defence   :   Edouard Daladier
Third Chautemps Ministry (22 June 1937-14 January 1938)
        Prime Minister: Camille Chautemps
        Foreign Affairs: Yvon Delbos
        Interior   :   Marx Dormoy
        Finance   :   Georges Bonnet
        Defence   :   Edouard Daladier

Fourth Chautemps Ministry (18 January 1938-10 March 1938)
        Prime Minister: Camille Chautemps
        Foreign Affairs: Yvon Delbos
        Interior   :   Albert Sarraut
        Finance   :   Paul Marchandeau
        Defence   :   Edouard Daladier

Second Blum Ministry (13 March-8 April 1938)
        Prime Minister: Léon Blum
        Foreign Affairs: Joseph Paul-Boncour
        Interior   :   Marx Dormoy
        Finance   :   Léon Blum
        Defence   :   Edouard Daladier

Third Daladier Ministry (10 April 1938-20 March 1940)
        Prime Minister,
        Defence
           Minister   :   Edouard Daladier
        Deputy Prime
           Minister   :   Camille Chautemps
        Foreign Affairs: Georges Bonnet
                            (succeeded 13 September 1939 by Daladier)
        Interior   :   Albert Sarraut
        Finance   :   Paul Marchandeau
                            (succeeded 1 November 1938 by Paul Reynaud)
        Justice   :   Paul Reynaud
                            (succeeded 1 November 1938 by Paul Marchandeau)*

*Marchandeau resigned on 4 September 1939 and Bonnet succeeded him as Minister of Justice on 13 September 1939.

410

Public Works	:	L. O. Frossard (succeeded on 23 August 1938 by Anatole de Monzie)
Labour	:	Paul Ramadier (succeeded on 23 August 1938 by Charles Pomaret)
Navy	:	César Campinchi
Air	:	Guy la Chambre
Colonies	:	Georges Mandel
Ex-Servicemen and pensions	:	Auguste Champetier de Ribes
Education	:	Jean Zay (resigned on 1 September 1939, succeeded by René Besse)
Commerce	:	Fernand Gentin
Agriculture	:	Henri Queuille
Public Health	:	Marc Rucart
Merchant navy	:	Louis de Chappedelaine (resigned on 13 September 1939)
National economy	:	Raymond Patenôtre (ministry abolished, 15 September 1939)
Blockade	:	Georges Pernot (new ministry created 13 September 1939)
Armaments	:	Raoul Dautry (new ministry created 13 September 1939)
High Commissioner for the National economy	:	Daniel Serruys (15 September 1939)
Commissioner General for Information:	:	Jean Giraudoux (29 July 1939)

Appendix E

ORGANIZATION OF THE
FRENCH FOREIGN MINISTRY, 1938-1939*

Minister for Foreign Affairs
Georges Bonnet (10 April 1938-13 September 1939)

Minister's office
Chef de cabinet: Jules Henry (April-October 1938)
                  Pierre Bressy (26 December 1938-13 September 1939)
Head of administrative services: M Ripert
Assistant director   : M Charpentier
Assistant director   : M Saint
Attached   : MM Grimaldi
                               Moury
                               Demage
                               Robin

Information and press service (under Minister's office)
Director: Pierre Comert (1933-October 1938)
           Pierre Bressy (9 Nov. 1938-26 Dec. 1938)

The Secretary General: Alexis Léger (1933-May 1940)
                          Political Secretariat
                          Legislative Secretariat
                          Private Secretariat

Political and Commercial Affairs Department
Director : René Massigli (1937-October 1938)
            Emile Charvériat (October 1938-1940)

Assistant Directors : Renom de la Baume (1937-40)
                       Charles Rochat (Oct. 1938-1940)

European section: assistant director: Henri-Etienne Hoppenot
    (Preparation of instructions and collection of information on general political
    questions. Political and commercial correspondence concerning European
    countries. Questions of international law and arbitration. Contacts with Service
    attachés)

Asiatic and Oceanic section: assistant director: Jean Chauvel
    (Political and commercial contacts with Iran, Afghanistan, Muscat, Central
    and North East Asia, China, including Hongkong, Japan, Indo-China, Siam,
    Philippines, Dutch and British East Indies, Australia, New Zealand and Pacific
    islands)

*This is a skeleton plan, listing only the main departments and sections, based on the *Annuaire
Diplomatique et Consulaire de la République Française pour 1939* (Paris, Imprimerie
Nationale, 1939)

Africa and Levant section: assistant director: Ernest Lagarde
  (Tunisia, Morocco, European colonies in Africa, Egypt, Ethiopia, Liberia, Turkey,
  Levant states under French mandate, Palestine, Iraq, Arabia, Transjordan)
American section: assistant director: Pierre Comert (North, Central and South
  America, including European possessions)
Commercial affairs section: assistant director: M Delenda
League of Nations section: assistant director: M Arnal
Cultural affairs service: director: M Marx.
Cipher section
Aliens section
Legal section
Personnel and Accounts Department
Archives Department
Protocol Department

Bibliography

A. UNPUBLISHED MATERIAL

1. Official documents

(a) Czechoslovakia
German Foreign Ministry photostat records (translations of Czech documents):
Serials 1809H; 2028H; 2376 (Foreign Office Library and Public Record Office).

(b) France
Ministry of Foreign Affairs Archives (Quai d'Orsay, Paris)
Service Historique de l'Armée de l'Air (Vincennes)
Service des Archives de l'Assemblée Nationale
Mission militaire francaise aupres de la République Tchéco-Slovaque, cabinet du général, Prague le 15 Decembre 1938: *Rapport de fin de mission* (Bibliothèque de documentation internationale contemporaine, Paris, hereafter BDIC).

Rapport presenté par M. Marcel Plaisant sur les traités franco-polonais, le 9 Fevrier 1940, secret no. 18, Commission senatoriale des Affaires étrangeres (BDIC).
Haute Cour de Justice, Ministère Public c/M. Baudouin, 5 vols., Paris, 1947 (BDIC).

(c) Germany
Foreign Ministry photostat records:
State Secretary, German-French relations, Serial 121
Dienststelle Ribbentrop, Serial 314
State Secretary, Political Correspondence, Serial 387
State Secretary, War collection 1939, Serial 456
Dienststelle Ribbentrop, Confidential Reports, Serial 823
Pol. II, Political Relations, Great Britain-France, Serial 1580H
Sicherheitsdienst reports, France, Serial 1832H
Künsberg Papers, secret, Serial 2013H
German Embassy in Italy, secret, England-Russia, France-Russia, Serial 2218H.
Military affairs, 1936-43, Serial 2532H.
German Embassy in France, secret, 1939-43, Serial 2318
German Embassy in France, foreign affairs, 1938-39, Serial 2469H.
German Embassy in France, Franco-German relations, Serial 2485.
German Embassy in France, internal affairs, 1938-39, Serial 2536H.
Pol. II, France, political relations, France and Germany, Serial 2459H.
Economic Policy Department, France, Serial 3527H.
Sicherheitsdienst reports, France, 1940-44, Serial 4120H.
Press Department, secret, France, Serials 7657H; 8608H; 8685H.
Archive Commission, Serial M93.

(d) Great Britain
Prime Minister's Office files, PREM 1/311
Cabinet Conclusions, CAB 23

Cabinet documents, CAB 24
Foreign Office files, FO 371 series
Halifax Papers, FO 800/309-316.

(e) Poland

German Foreign Ministry photostat records (translations of captured Polish archives) Serial 1682H.
General Sikorski Historical Institute archives, (London)

2. Private Papers

(a) France

Léon Blum (Fondation Nationale des Sciences Politiques)
Guy La Chambre (by courtesy of M. Guy la Chambre)
Edouard Daladier (Fondation Nationale des Sciences Politiques)
Edouard Herriot (by courtesy of M Michel Soulié)
Lucien Lamoureux (by courtesy of the late M Lucien Lamoureux)
Jean Montigny (by courtesy of M Jean Montigny)
Francois Piétri (by courtesy of the late M Francois Piétri)
Albert Sarraut (by courtesy of M Henri Noguères)

(b) Great Britain

Sir Austen Chamberlain (Birmingham University)
Ist Baron Hugh Dalton (British Library of Political and Economic Science)
Sir Basil Liddell-Hart (by courtesy of Lady Liddell-Hart)
Sir Eric Phipps (by courtesy of Lady Frances Phipps)
Ist Viscount Simon (by courtesy of 2nd Viscount)
IIth Marquess of Lothian (Philip Henry Kerr) (Scottish Record Office)

B. PUBLISHED OFFICIAL DOCUMENTS

1. Belgium

Documents Diplomatiques Belges, 1920-40, vols. III-V (Académie Royale de Belgique. Commission Royale d'histoire, Brussels, 1966).

2. Czechoslovakia

Pierre Buk, *La Tragédie tchécoslovaque de septembre 1938 à mars 1939, avec des documents inédits du livre blanc tchécoslovaque* (Paris, 1939)
Fritz Berber, *Europaische Politik, 1933-39, im Spiegel der Prager Akten* (Essen, 1941).
V. F. Klochko *et al., New Documents on the History of Munich,* (Prague, 1958).

3. France

Documents Diplomatiques Français, 1932-39, 1 Serie (1932-36) (Paris, 1964-), Tomes I-VI.
Documents Diplomatiques Français, 1932-39, 2 Serie (1936-39) (Paris, 1963-), Tomes I-VII.
Le Livre Jaune Français, Documents Diplomatiques, 1939-39, Ministère des Affaires Etrangères, Paris, 1939.
Les Evénements survenus en France de 1933 à 1945. Rapport presenté par M. Charles Serre, Député, au nom de la Commission d'Enquête Parlementaire, 2 vols; *Témoignages et Documents Recueillis par la Commission d'Enquête Parlementaire,* 9 vols (Paris, 1947-51).
Débats parlementaires, Sénat, session ordinaire de 1940, Comités Secrets du 14 Mars et du 16 Avril 1940 (Paris, 1948).
Les Procès de Collaboration: Fernand de Brinon, Joseph Darnand, Jean Luchaire, compte rendu sténographique (Paris, 1948).
Ministère de la guerre, *Instruction sur l'emploi tactique des grandes unités,* Paris, Charles-Lavauzelle, 1937.

4. Germany

Documents on German Foreign Policy, 1918-45, Series C (1933-37) vols., I-V (London, 1957).

Documents on German Foreign Policy, 1918-45, Series D (1933-45) vols., I-X (London, 1949-).

Akten Zur Deutschen Auswärtigen Politik, 1918-45, Serie B, 1925-33, Band 1, 2 (Göttingen, 1968).

5. Great Britain

Documents on British Foreign Policy, 1919-39, First Series, vols., XV, XVI (London, 1968).

Documents on British Foreign Policy, 1919-39, Third Series, vols., I-IX (London, 1949-).

6. Holy See

Actes et Documents du Saint Siège Relatifs à la Seconde Guerre Mondiale, I, *Le Saint Siège et la guerre en Europe,* March 1939-August 1940 (Rome, 1965).

7. Italy

I Documenti Diplomatici Italiani, 8th Series, vols, XII-XIII; 9th Series, vol., I (Rome, 1952-).

8. Poland

The Polish White Book, Official Documents Concerning Polish-German and Polish-Soviet Relations, 1933-39 (London, 1940).

Polnische Dokumente zur Vorgeshichte des Krieges, Erste Folge, Auswärtiges Amt, Nr. 3 (Berlin, 1940).

Sprawy Miedzynarodowe, May and June 1958 (selection of reports from Polish Ambassadors in Berlin and Paris).

'Protocols of the Polish-French General Staff Conferences in Paris, May 1939', *Bellona,* no. II, 1958.

9. USSR

A. A. Gromyko *et al.,* eds., *SSR v Borbe za Mir Nakanune Vtoroi Mirovoi Voini, Sentyabr 1938g-Avgust 1939g., Dokumenti i Materiali* (The USSR in the Struggle for Peace on the Eve of the Second World War, September 1938-August 1939, Documents and Materials) Moscow 1971.

Documents and Materials Relating to the Eve of the Second World War, 2 vols., (Moscow, 1948).

'Negotiations between the Military Missions of the USSR, Britain and France in August 1939', *International Affairs* (Moscow), nos. 2-3, Feb., Mar., 1959.

10. USA

Foreign Relations of the United States, Diplomatic Papers (Washington 1943-).

1936, vol. I (Washington, 1953); 1937, vol., I (Washington, 1954); 1938 vols. I-II (Washington, 1955); 1939, vols., I-II (Washington, 1956).

C. PARLIAMENTARY DEBATES

Journal Officiel de la République Française: Débats Parlementaires, Chambre des Députés (1933-39).

Journal Officiel de la République Française: Débats Parlementaires, Sénat (1936-39).

D. PRESS

(consulted for 1938-39) *Le Temps, Le Journal, Le Figaro, L'Homme Libre, Revue des deux Mondes, Cahiers Franco-Allemands.*

E. OTHER PRIMARY SOURCES

Royal Institute of International Affairs, London, *Bulletin of International News,* 1938-39, vols. XV, XVI.

Annuaire Diplomatique et Consulaire de la République Française, volumes for 1938 and 1939 (Paris, Imprimerie Nationale).

F. MEMOIRS, DIARIES, SPEECHES

1. *Works of Georges Bonnet*

La Défense de la Paix, 2 vols., (Geneva, 1946-48).
Le Quai d'Orsay Sous Trois Républiques (Paris, 1961).
Miracle de·la France, 1870-1919 (Paris, 1965).
De Munich à la Guerre: Défense de la Paix (revised and definitive edition, Paris 1967).
Vingt Ans de Vie Politique, 1918-38 (Paris, 1969).
Dans la Tourmente, 1938-48 (Paris, 1971).
Six Mois d'Histoire: La Crise Européenne, Mai-Septembre 1938, discours prononcé par M. Georges Bonnet, Ministre des Affaires Etrangères, Au Congrès du Parti Radical et Socialiste à Marseilles, le 29 Octobre 1938
'Notes sur les Mémoires de Sir Samuel Hoare', introduction to *Neuf Années de Crises,* Paris, 1957, pp. 23-35.
Préface to Jacques Minart's *Le Drame du Désarmement français, 1918-39* (Paris, 1960), pp. i-vii.
'Les négotiations franco-russes de 1938 à 1939', in *Revue de Paris,* November 1947, pp. 93-101.
'La politique extérieure de France en 1938-39', in *Rivista di Studi Politici Internazionali,* XVI, 1949, pp. 510-530.
'Témoignage sur la période 1933-39', in *Commission internationale pour l'enseignement de l'histoire* (Brussels, 1957).
'Etats-Unis-Turquie', in *La Vie de la France sous l'Occupation, 1940-44* (Institut Hoover, Paris, 1957), II, pp. 706-7.
'Léon Bérard, diplomate', *La Revue des deux Mondes,* 15 April 1961, pp. 605-612.
Letters in *Le Monde*: 17 December 1947; 3 March 1956, 5 September 1959, 1 June 1971.
Figaro: 10 April 1964.
Letters in *Times Literary Supplement*: 19 July 1947; 19 February 1949; 9 April 1949; 30 January and 17 July 1953.

2. *Others:*

Abetz, Otto, *D'une prison* (Paris, 1950).
    Histoire d'une politique franco-allemande, 1930-50 (Paris, 1953).
Aloisi, Pompeo, *Journal, 25 Juillet 1932-14 Juin 1936* (Paris, 1957).
Amery, L. S., *My Political Life,* III (London, 1955).
Auriol, Vincent, *Hier . . . Demain,* I, (Paris, 1945)
Avon, Earl of: *Facing the Dictators* (London, 1962)

Bardoux, Jacques, *Journal d'un témoin de la troisième* (Paris, 1957)
Barman, Thomas, *Diplomatic Correspondent* (London, 1968)
Baudouin, Paul, *Neuf Mois au Gouvernment* (Paris, 1948)
    'Un voyage à Rome', *Revue des deux Mondes,* 1 May 1962, pp. 69-85.
    'Les Données du Problème Français' *Revue de Paris,* February 1938, pp. 571-594.
Beauffre, General André, *Mémoires, 1920-40-45* (Paris, 1965)
Beck, Count Joseph, *Dernier Rapport: Politique Polonaise, 1926-39,* (Neuchatel, 1951)
Benes, Edouard, *The Memoirs of Dr Benes* (London, 1954)
    Munich (Paris, 1970)
Berthelot, Jean, *Sur les Rails du Pouvoir* (Paris, 1968)
Beauvoir, Simone de, *The Prime of Life* (London, 1965)

Beuve-Méry, Hubert, *Réfléxions Politiques, 1932-51* (Paris, 1951)

Bidault, Georges, *D'une Résistance à l'Autre* (Paris, 1965)

Blondel, Jules-Francois, *Au Fil de la Carrière, 1911-38* (Paris, 1960)

Blum, John Morton, *From the Morgenthau Diaries, Years of Crisis, 1928-38* (Boston, 1959).

Blum, Robert, ed., *L'Oeuvre de Léon Blum,* vol. IV, 1937-40 (Paris, 1965)

Léon Blum, Chef de Gouvernement, 1936-37 (Fondation Nationale des Sciences Politiques, Paris, 1967).

Bois, Elie J., *Truth on the Tragedy of France* (London, 1941)

Bret, Paul-Louis, *Au Feu des Evénements: Mémoires d'un journaliste Londres-Algers, 1929-44* (Paris, 1959)

Bullitt, Orville H., ed., *For the President, Personal and Secret* (London, 1973)

Butler, Lord, *The Art of the Possible* (London, 1971)

Caillaux, Joseph, *Mes Mémoires,* 3 vols., (Paris, 1942-47)

Cambon, Paul, *Correspondance, 1870-1924,* III (Paris, 1946)

Chamberlain, Neville, *In Search of Peace: Speeches, 1937-38,* ed., Arthur Bryant (London, 1939).

Chastenet, Jacques, 'Deux Années Dramatiques, 1938-39' *Revue des Deux Mondes,* March 1973, pp. 553-563.

Chautemps, Camille, *Cahiers Secrets de l'Armistice, 1939-40* (Paris, 1963)

Chauvel, Jean, *Commentaire,* I, *De Vienne à Alger, 1938-44,* (Paris, 1971)

Churchill, Winston S., *The Second World War,* I, *The Gathering Storm,* (London, 1949)

Ciano, Galeazzo, *Ciano's Diary, 1937-38,* ed. Malcolm Muggeridge (London, 1952)
　　Ciano's Diary, 1939-43, ed. Malcolm Muggeridge, (London, 1947)
　　Ciano's Diplomatic Papers, ed. Malcolm Muggeridge (London, 1948)

Comert, Pierre, 'Lettres d'il y a trente ans sur Munich', *Politique Aujourd'hui,* January 1969.

Coote, Sir Colin, *A Companion of Honour, Walter Elliot* (London, 1965)

Coulondre, Robert, *De Staline à Hitler* (Paris, 1950)

Daladier, Edouard, *Défense du Pays* (Paris, 1939)
　　Réponse aux chefs communistes, discours prononcé à L'Assemblée Nationale, le 18 Juillet 1946, suivi de nombreux documents (Paris, 1946)
　　'Munich', *Candide,* 7, 14, 21 September 1961.

Dalton, Hugh, *Memoirs,* II, *The Fateful Years, 1931-45* (London, 1957)

Davis, Joseph E., *Mission to Moscow* (London, 1942)

Desgranges, Abbé, *Journal d'un Prêtre-Député* (Paris, 1960)

Dilks, David, ed., *The Diaries of Sir Alexander Cadogan, 1938-45* (London, 1971)

D'Ormesson, Wladimir, *Les Vraies Confidences* (Paris, 1962)
　　De Saint Petersbourg a Rome (Paris, 1969)

Doumenc, General Joseph, *Carrefour,* 21 May 1947 (account of his Moscow mission)

Duclos, Jacques, *Mémoires,* vols. I and II (Paris, 1968)

Duff Cooper, Alfred, *Old Men Forget* (London, 1953)

Fabre-Luce, Alfred, *Journal de la France, 1939-44* (definitive edition, Paris, 1969)

Fabry, Jean, *De la Place de la Concorde au Cours de l'Intendance* (Paris, 1942)

Flandin, Pierre-Etienne, *Politique Française, 1919-40* (Paris, 1947)

Francois-Poncet, André, *Souvenirs d'une ambassade à Berlin* (Paris, 1946)
　　Au Palais Farnese: Souvenirs d'une ambassade à Rome, 1938-40 (Paris, 1961).

Frossard, Ludovic-Oscar, *De Jaurès à Léon Blum: Souvenirs d'un militant* (Paris, 1943)

Gafencu, Grigore, *The Last Days of Europe* (Paris, 1947)

Gamelin, General Maurice, *Servir,* 3 vols., (Paris, 1946-47)

Gauché, General, *Le Deuxième Bureau au Travail, 1935-40* (Paris, 1953)

Gaulle, General Charles de, *Mémoires de Guerre,* I, *L'Appel, 1940-42* (Paris, 1954)

Goebbels, Joseph, *The Goebbels Diaries,* trans. and ed., Louis P. Lochner (London, 1948)

Gladwyn, Lord, *Memoirs,* (London, 1972)
Gide, André, *Journals, 1889-1949* (London, 1967)
    André Gide, Roger Martin du Gard, Correspondence, I, *1913-34* (Paris, 1968)
Guariglia, Raffaele, *Ricordi* (Naples, 1950).

Halifax, Earl of, *Fulness of Days* (London, 1957)
    Speeches on Foreign Policy (London, 1940)
Harvey, John, ed., *The Diplomatic Diaries of Oliver Harvey, 1937-40* (London, 1970)
Hayter, Sir William, *The Kremlin and the Embassy* (London, 1966)
Henderson, Sir Nevile, *Failure of a Mission,* (*Berlin, 1937-39*) (London, 1940)
Herriot, Edouard, *Jadis,* II, *D'une guerre à l'autre, 1914-39* (Paris, 1952)
Hitler, Adolf, *Mein Kampf,* new trans. with introduction by D. C. Watt (London, 1969)
    The Speeches of Adolf Hitler, 1922-39, ed. Norman H. Baynes, 2 vols., (London, 1942)
Hooker, Nancy Harvison, ed., *The Moffat Papers* (Cambridge, Mass., 1956)
Hull, Cordell, *Memoirs,* 2 vols., (London, 1948)

Ismay, General Lord, *Memoirs* (London, 1960)

James, Robert Rhodes, ed., *The Diaries of Sir Henry Channon* (London, 1967)
    Memoirs of a Conservative: J.C.C. Davidson's Memoirs and Papers, 1910-37 (London, 1969)
Jeanneney, Jean-Noel, ed., *Jules Jeanneney: Journal Politique, 1939-42* (Paris, 1972)
Jedrezejewicz, Waclaw, ed., *Diplomat in Berlin, 1933-39, Papers and Memoirs of Jozef Lipski* (London, 1968)
    Diplomat in Paris, 1936-39, Papers and Memoirs of Julius Lukasiewicz (London, 1970).
Jones, Thomas, *A Diary with Letters, 1931-50* (London, 1954)
    Whitehall Diary, ed., Keith Middlemas, I (London, 1969)

Kelly, Sir David, *The Ruling Few* (London, 1952)
Knatchbull-Hugessen, Sir Hughe, *Diplomat in Peace and War* (London, 1949)
Kirkpatrick, Sir Ivone, *The Inner Circle* (London, 1959)
Koestler, Arthur, *The Invisible Writing,* II (London, 1954)

Lagardelle, Hubert, *Mission à Rome: Mussolini* (Paris, 1955)
Lamoureux, Lucien, "Mémoires", *Le Bourbonnais Republicain* (Allier) 1952-56 (selections from unpublished memoirs)
Laroche, Jules, *Au Quai d'Orsay avec Briand et Poincaré, 1913-26* (Paris, 1957)
Lazareff, Pierre, *Deadline* (New York, 1942)
    De Munich à Vichy (New York, 1944)
Lebrun, Albert, *Témoignage* (Paris, 1946)
Leith-Ross, Sir Frederick, *Money Talks: Fifty Years of International Finance* (London, 1968).
Lémery, Henry, *D'une République à l'Autre* (Paris, 1964)
Lindbergh, Charles A. *The Wartime Journals of Charles A. Lindbergh* (New York, 1970)

Mclachlan, Donald, *In the Chair, Barrington-Ward of the Times, 1927-48* (London, 1971)
Maisky, Ivan, *Who Helped Hitler?* (London, 1964)
Maurois, André, *Choses Nues: Chroniques* (Paris, 1963)
Mantoux, Paul, *Les Délibérations du Conseil des Quatre,* II, (Paris, 1955)
Martin, Kingsley, *Editor: A Second Volume of Autobiography, 1931-45,* (London, 1968)
Massigli, René, *La Turquie devant la guerre: Mission a Ankara. 1939-40* (Paris, 1964)
Minney, R. J., ed., *The Private Papers of Hore-Belisha* (London, 1960)
Moch, Jules, *Rencontres avec . . . Léon Blum* (Paris, 1970)
Montigny, Jean, *Le Complot contre la paix, 1935-39* (Paris, 1966)
Monzie, Anatole de, *Ci-devant* (Paris, 1941)
    La saison des juges (Paris, 1943)

Moreau, Emile, *Souvenirs d'un gouverneur de la banque de France* (Paris, 1954)
Murphy, Robert, *Diplomat Among Warriors* (New York, 1964)

Nicolson, Harold, *Diaries and Letters,* I, 1930-39, ed., Nigel Nicolson (London, 1966)
Noel, Léon, *L'Aggression allemande contre la Pologne* (Paris, 1946)

Paul-Boncour, Joseph, *Entre Deux Guerres,* 3 vols., (Paris, 1945-47)
Papen, Franz von, *Memoirs* (London, 1952)
Piétri, Francois, *Mes Années d'Espagne* (Paris, 1954)
      'Souvenir de Barthou', *Revue des deux Mondes,* 1 March 1961, pp. 65-75.
Pomaret, Charles, *Le Dernier Témoin: Fin d'une guerre, fin d'une république, juin-juillet* 1940 (Paris, 1968)
      'Un destin hors-série: Anatole de Monzie', *Annales du Centre Universitaire Méditerranean,* XIV, 1961, pp. 3-18.
Puaux, Gabriel, *Mort et Transfiguration de l'Autriche* (Paris, 1966)

Reynaud, Paul, *La France a sauvé l'Europe,* 2 vols (Paris, 1947)
      Au Coeur de la Mêlée (Paris, 1951)
      Mémoires, 2 vols., (Paris, 1960-63)
Ribbentrop, Joachim von, *Memoirs,* (London, 1954)
Romains, Jules, *The Seven Mysteries of Europe* (London, 1941)
Rueff, Jacques, *Combats pour l'ordre financier* (Paris, 1972)

Salter, Lord, *Memoirs of a Public Servant* (London, 1961)
Sauerwein, Jules, *30 Ans à la Une,* (Paris, 1962)
Schacht, Hjalmar, *My First Seventy Six Years* (London, 1955)
Schmidt, Paul, *Hitler's Interpreter* (London, 1951).
Shirer, William L, *Berlin Diary* (London, 1941)
Simon, Viscount, *Retrospect* (London, 1952)
Slessor, Sir John, *The Central Blue* (London, 1956)
Spears, Major-General Sir Edward, *Assignment to Catastrophe, I, Prelude to Dunkirk* (London, 1954)
Stehlin, General Paul, *Témoignage pour l'Histoire* (London, 1964)
Strang, Lord, *Home and Abroad* (London, 1956).
Strong, Major-General Sir Kenneth, *Intelligence at the Top* (London, 1968)

Tabouis, Geneviève, *They Called Me Cassandra* (New York, 1942)
      Vingt Ans de 'suspense' diplomatique (Paris, 1958)
Templewood, Lord, *Nine Troubled Years* (London, 1954)
Tissier, Pierre, *I Worked With Laval* (London, 1942)

'Une demande d'enquête sur les responsabilités de M Georges Bonnet', *Les Cahiers des Droits de l'Homme,* 15 March 1939, pp. 166-171.

Vansittart, Lord, *The Mist Procession* (London, 1958)

Weizsäcker, Ernst von, *Erinnerungen* (Munich, 1950)
Weygand, General Maxime, *Mémoires,* III, (Paris, 1950)
Winterbotham, F. W., *Secret and Personal* (London, 1969)

Zay, Jean, *Carnets Secrets de Jean Zay,* publiés et commentés par Philippe Henriot (Paris, 1942)
      Souvenirs et Solitude (Paris, 1946)

G. SECONDARY WORKS

Abendroth, Hans-Henning, *Hitler in der Spanischen Arena* (Paderborn, 1973)
Allard, Paul, *Le Quai d'Orsay* (Paris, 1938)

Amaury, Philippe, *Les Deux Premières Expériences d'un Ministère de l'Information en France* (Paris, 1969)

Angot, E., and R. de Lavergne, *Une Figure Légendaire de l'Aviation Francaise: Le Général Vuillemin* (Paris, 1965)

Andrew, Christopher, *Theophile Delcassé and the Making of the Entente Cordiale* (London, 1968)

Ardagh, John, *The New French Revolution* (London, 1968)

Aron, Robert, *The Vichy Regime, 1940-44,* (Paris, 1958).

Aster, Sidney, *1939: The Making of the Second World War* (London, 1973)

Audry, Colette, *Léon Blum ou la politique du juste* (Paris, 1955).

Baer, George W, *The Coming of the Italo-Ethiopian War* (Cambridge, Mass., 1967)

Baillou, Jean and Pierre Pelletier, *Les Affaires Etrangères* (Paris, 1952)

Bankwitz, Philip C. F., *Maxime Weygand and Civil-Military Relations in Modern France* (Cambridge, Mass, 1967)

Barrillon, Raymond, *Le Cas Paris Soir* (Paris, 1959)

Barnett, Corelli, *The Collapse of British Power* (London, 1972)

Baumont, Maurice, *La Faillite de la Paix, 1918-39* (Paris, 1951)
  Les Origines de la Deuxième Guerre Mondiale (Paris, 1969)

Beau de Lomenie, Emmanuel, *La Mort de la Troisième République* (Paris, 1951)

Bennett, Edward W., *Germany and the Diplomacy of the Financial Crisis 1931* (Cambridge, Mass, 1962)

Berl, Emmanuel, *La Fin de la Troisième République* (Paris, 1968)

Bernanos, Georges, *Lettre aux Anglais* (Rio de Janeiro, 1943).

Bethell, Nicholas, *The War Hitler Won* (London, 1972)

Binion, Rudolph, *Defeated Leaders: The Political Fate of Caillaux, Jouvenel and Tardieu* (New York, 1960)

Birkenhead, Earl of, *Halifax, The Life of Lord Halifax* (London, 1965)

Bonnefous, Edouard and Georges, *Histoire politique de la Troisième République,* 7 vols., (Paris, 1956-67)

Bloch, Marc, *L'Etrange Défaite* (Paris, 1946)

Broustra, Jean-Claude, *Le Combat de Raymond Patenôtre* (Paris, 1969)

Bruegel, J. W., *Czechoslovakia before Munich* (London, 1973)

Bullock, Alan, *Hitler, A Study in Tyranny* (London, 1964)

Butler, J. R. M., *Lord Lothian* (London, 1960)

Cameron, Elizabeth R., *Prologue to Appeasement, A Study in French Foreign Policy* (Washington, 1942)

Carroll, Berenice, *Design for Total War: Arms and Economics in the Third Reich* (Hague, 1968)

Celovsky, Boris, *Das Münchener Abkommen von 1938,* (Stuttgart, 1958)

Challener, Richard D., *The French Theory of the Nation in Arms, 1866-1939* (New York, 1952)

Charpier, Jacques, *Saint John Perse* (Paris, 1962)

Chastenet, Jacques, *Histoire de la Troisième République,* vols., V, VI, VII, (Paris, 1960-63)

Cienciala, Anna M., *Poland and the Western Powers, 1938-39* (London, 1968)

Collier, Basil, *The Defence of the United Kingdom* (London, 1957)

Colton, Joel, *Léon Blum, Humanist in Politics* (New York, 1966)

Colville, J. R., *Man of Valour, The Life of Field-Marshal the Viscount Gort* (London, 1972)

Colvin, Ian, *Vansittart in Office* (London, 1965)
  The Chamberlain Cabinet (London, 1971)

Craig, Gordon, A., *War, Politics and Diplomacy* (London, 1966)

Craig, Gordon A and Felix Gilbert, *The Diplomats, 1919-39* (London, 1953)

Debu-Bridel, Jacques, *L'Agonie de la Troisième République* (Paris, 1949)

Desanti, Dominique, *La Banquière des Années Folles, Marthe Hanau,* (Paris, 1968)

Dilks, David N. 'Appeasement Revisited', *University of Leeds Review* XV no. 1, 1971

Dischler, Ludwig, *Der Auswärtige Dienst Frankreichs* (Hambourg, 1952)

Dominique, Pierre, *Après Munich, veux-tu vivre ou mourir?* (Paris, 1938)
D'Ormesson, Wladimir, *Nos Illusions sur L'Europe Centrale* (Paris, 1922)
Dreifort, John E. *Yvon Delbos at the Quai d'Orsay* (Kansas, 1973)
Duhamel, Georges, *Mémorial de la Guerre Blanche* (Paris, 1938)
Duroselle, J.-B., *L'Europe de 1815 à nos jours, vie politique et relations internationales* (Paris, 1964)
   La politique étrangère et ses fondements (Paris, 1954)

Einzig, Paul, *Finance and Politics* (London, 1932)
   Behind the Scenes of International Finance (London, 1932)
   World Finance, 1938-39 (London, 1939)
Eluard, Paul, *Poèmes pour tous* (Paris, 1952)
Eubank, Keith, *Munich* (Norman, Oklahoma, 1963)

Fabre-Luce, Alfred, *Histoire secrète de la conciliation de Munich* (Paris, 1938)
Farnsworth, Beatrice, *William C. Bullitt and the Soviet Union* (Bloomington, Indiana, 1967)
Feiling, Keith, *The Life of Neville Chamberlain* (London, 1946)
Felix, David, *Walther Rathenau and the Weimar Republic* (London, 1971)
Fohlen, Claude, *La France de l'entre deux guerres* (Paris, 1966)
Funke, Manfred, *Sanktionen und Kanonen: Hitler, Mussolini und der Internationale Abessinienkonflikt* (Dusseldorf, 1970)
Furnia, Arthur H., *The Diplomacy of Appeasement: Anglo-French Relations and the Prelude to World War II, 1931-38* (Washington, 1960)

Gallo, Max, *La Cinquième Colonne, 1930-40* (Paris, 1970)
Garder, Michel, *La Guerre secrète des services spéciaux français, 1935-45* (Paris, 1967)
Gatzke, H. W., ed., *European Diplomacy between two wars, 1919-39* (Chicago, 1972)
Gaulle, General Charles de, *Vers l'Armée de Métier* (Paris, 1934)
Gehl, Jurgen, *Austria, Germany and the Anschluss, 1931-38* (London, 1963)
Gicquel, Jean and Lucien Sfez, *Problèmes de la Réforme d'Etat en France depuis 1935* (Paris, 1965)
Gilbert, Martin, *The Roots of Appeasement* (London, 1966)
Godechot, Jacques, *et al.*, *Histoire Générale de la Presse Francaise*, Tome III, 1871-1940 (Paris, 1972)
Gorce, Paul Marie, *The French Army, A military and political history* (London, 1963)
Greene, Nathanael, *Crisis and Decline: The French Socialist Party in the Popular Front Era* (New York, 1969)
Griffiths, Richard, *Marshal Pétain* (London, 1970)
Grosser, Alfred, *La IV République et sa politique extérieure* (Paris, 1961)

Haight, John McVickar, *American Aid to France, 1938-40* (New York, 1970)
Halévy, Daniel, *La République des Comités* (Paris, 1934)
Hamon, Augustin and X.Y.Z., *Les Maîtres de la France*, 2 vols, (Paris, 1936-37)
Hardie, Frank, *The Abyssinian Crisis* (London, 1974)
Henriot, Philippe, *Comment Mourut la Paix* (Paris, 1941)
Hoffman, Stanley, *et al.*, *France: Change and Tradition* (London, 1963)
Honneur à Saint-John-Perse: Hommages et Témoignages Littéraires suivis d'une documentation sur Alexis Léger diplomate (Paris, 1965)
Howard, John Eldred, *Parliament and Foreign Policy in France* (London, 1948)
Howard, Michael, *The Continental Commitment* (London, 1972)
Hughes, Judith M., *To the Maginot Line: The Politics of French Military Preparation in the 1920s* (Cambridge, Mass., 1971)
Hytier, Adrienne Doris, *Two Years of French Foreign Policy, Vichy, 1940-42* (Geneva, 1958)

Irving, David, *Breach of Security* (London, 1968)

Jacobsen, Jon, *Locarno Diplomacy: Germany and the West, 1925-29* (Princeton, 1972)
Jordan, W. M., *Great Britain, France and the German Problem* (London, 1943)
Jolly, Jean (ed.), *Dictionnaire des parlementaries français: notices biographiques sur les ministres, députés et sénateurs français de 1889 à 1940* (Paris, 1960-), vols. I-VI

Kemp, Tom, *The French Economy, 1913-39* (London, 1972)
Kérillis, Henri de, *Français, voici la vérite* (New York, 1942)
Kieft, David Owen, *Belgium's Return to Neutrality* (London, 1972)
Knodel, Arthur, *Saint-John-Perse: A Study of His poetry* (Edinburgh 1966)

Laffan, R.G.D., *Survey of International Affairs 1938*, vols., II-III, (London, 1951-53)
Langer, William L and Everett Gleason, *The Challenge to Isolation, 1937-40* (New York 1952)
Lapie, Pierre Olivier, *Herriot* (Paris, 1967)
Larmour, Peter, J., *The French Radical Party in the 1930s* (Stanford, California, 1964)
Laurens, Franklin L., *France and the Italo-Ethiopian crisis* (Hague, 1967)
Lefranc, Georges, *Histoire du Front Populaire* (Paris, 1965)
Les Relations Militaires Franco-Belges, Mars 1936- 10 Mai 1940, travaux d'un colloque d'historiens belges et français (Paris, 1968)
Lévis-Mirepoix, Emmanuel de, *Le Ministère des Affaires Etrangères* (Angers, 1934)
Levy, Louis, *Vérités sur la France* (London, 1941)
Little, Roger, *Saint-John Perse* (London, 1973)

Macartney, C. A. and A. W. Palmer, *Independent Eastern Europe* (London, 1962)
Macleod, Iain, *Neville Chamberlain* (London, 1961)
Manevy, Raymond, *Histoire de la Presse, 1914-39* (Paris, 1945)
Massigli, René, *Sur Quelques Maladies de l'Etat* (Paris, 1958)
Maurois, André, *Why France fell* (London, 1941)
Medlicott, W. N., *The Coming of War in 1939* (London, 1963)
Micaud, Charles A., *The French Right and Nazi Germany 1933-39 A Study of Public Opinion* (New York, 1943)
Miquel, Pierre, *Poincaré* (Paris, 1961)
Middlemas, Keith, *Diplomacy of Illusion* (London, 1972)
Middlemas, Keith and John Barnes, *Baldwin, A Bibliography* (London, 1969)
Milza, Pierre, *L'Italie Fasciste devant l'opinion française, 1920-40* (Paris, 1967)
Montherlant, Henri de, *L'Equinoxe de Septembre* (Paris, 1938)
Minart, Jacques, *Le Drame du Désarmement Français, 1918-39* (Paris, 1959)
Montigny, Jean, *France, Libère-Toi* (Le Mans, 1939)
Morin, Edgar, *Commune en France* (Paris, 1968)

Namier, L. B., *Diplomatic Prelude, 1938-39* (London, 1948)
Europe in Decay (London, 1950)
In the Nazi Era (London, 1952)
Nevakivi, Jukka, *Britain, France and the Arab Middle East, 1914-20* (London, 1969)
Nizan, Paul, *Chronique de Septembre* (Paris, 1938)
Nobécourt, Jacques, *Une Histoire Politique de l'Armée*, I, (Paris, 1967)
Noguères, Henri, *Munich ou la drôle de paix* (Paris, 1963)

Ollé-Laprune, Jacques, *La Stabilité des Ministres sous la troisième République* (Paris, 1962)
Oprea, I. M., *Nicolas Titulescu's Diplomatic Activity* (Bucharest, 1968)
Ott, Johann, *Botschafter Sir Eric Phipps und die Deutsch-Englischen* Beziehungen (Nürnberg, 1968)

Paoli, François-André Colonel, *L'Armée Française de 1919 à 1939*, vols., I and II (1919-24) (Ministère des Armées, Service Historique, Paris, 1969-71)
Parker, R. A. C., *Europe, 1919-45* (London, 1969)
Parkinson, Roger, *Peace for Our Time* (London, 1971)
Pertinax (André Géraud), *The Gravediggers of France* (New York, 1944)

Planté, Louis, *Un Grand Seigneur de la Politique: Anatole de Monzie* (Paris, 1955)

Reibel, Charles, *Pourquoi nous avons été à deux doigts de la guerre* (Paris, 1938)
Remond, René, *La Droite en France de 1815 à nos jours* (Paris, 1954)
Renouvin, Pierre, *Histoire des Relations Internationales: Les Crises du XX Siecle,* VIII, 1929-45 (Paris, 1958)
  Mélanges Pierre Renouvin: études d'histoire des relations internationales (Paris, 1966)
Ribet, Maurice, *Le Procès de Riom* (Paris, 1945)
Robbins, Keith, *Munich 1938* (London, 1968)
Robertson, Esmonde M., *The Origins of the Second World War* (London, 1971)
Rose, N. A. *The Gentle Zionists* (Frank Cass London, 1973)
Roskill, Stephen, *Hankey: Man of Secrets,* II, 1919-31 (London, 1972)
Rossi-Landi, Guy, *La Drôle de Guerre* (Paris, 1971)
Ruby, Marcel, *La Vie et L'Oeuvre de Jean Zay* (Paris, 1969)

Sauvy, Alfred, *Histoire Economique de la France entre les deux guerres* vols., I-III (Paris, 1966-72)
Schmokel, Wolfe W., *Dream of Empire, German Colonialism, 1919-45* (Yale, 1964)
Scott, William Evans, *Alliance Against Hitler, The Origins of the Franco-Soviet Pact* (London, 1962)
Sherwood, John M., *Georges Mandel and the Third Republic* (Stanford, Calfornia, 1970)
Simone, André, *J'Accuse: The Men Who Betrayed France* (London, 1941)
Sorlin, Pierre, *La Societé Française,* II, (Paris, 1971)
Soulié, Michel, *La Vie Politiqué d'Edouard Herriot* (Paris, 1962)
Soupiron, Paul, *Bazaine contre Gambetta ou le procès de Riom* (Lyons, 1944)
Suarez, Georges and Guy Laborde, *L'Agonie de la Paix, 1935-39* (Paris, 1942)

Tarr, Francis de, *The French Radical Party from Herriot to Mendès-France* (London, 1961)
Taylor, A. J. P., *The Origins of the Second World War* (London, 1963)
Teichova, Alice, *An Economic Background to Munich* (Cambridge, 1974)
Terraine, John, *The Life and Times of Lord Louis Mountbatten* (London, 1968)
Thomas, Louis, *Histoire d'un Jour: Munich 29 Septembre 1938* (Paris, 1939)
Thomson, David, *Democracy in France, The Third and Fourth Republics* (London, 1958)
Tournoux, General P. E., *Défense des Frontières: Haut Commandement et Gouvernement, 1919-39* (Paris, 1960)
Toynbee, Arnold J., *Survey of International Affairs: The Eve of War 1939* (London, 1958)
Trevelyan, Lord, *Diplomatic Channels* (London, 1973)

Vallat, Xavier, *Le Nez de Cleopatre: Souvenirs D'un Homme de Droite* (Paris, 1957)
Vallette, Genevieve and Jacques Bouillon, *Munich 1938* (Paris, 1964)
Varenne, Francisque, *Mon Patron Georges Mandel* (Paris, 1948)

Waites, Neville, ed., *Troubled Neighbours: Franco-British Relations In the Twentieth Century* (London, 1971)
Wandycz, Piotr, *France and her eastern allies, 1919-25* (Minnesota, 1962)
Warner, Charles K., *From the Ancien Regime to the Popular Front: Essays in the History of Modern France in Honour of Shepherd B. Clough,* (London, 1969)
Warner, Geoffrey, *Pierre Laval and the Eclipse of France* (London, 1968)
Werth, Alexander, *France and Munich, Before and After the Surrender,* (London, 1939)
  France, 1940-55 (London, 1957)
  De Gaulle (London, 1965)
Weil, Simone, *Selected Essays, 1934-43* (London, 1962)
Wheeler-Bennett, J. W., *Munich, Prologue to Tragedy* (London, 1948)
Williams, Philip M., *Crisis and Compromise: Politics in the Fourth Republic* (London, 1958)

Wolf, Dieter, *Doriot* (Paris, 1969)

Watson, David Robin, *Georges Clemenceau: A Political Biography* (London, 1974)

Watt, D. C., *Personalities and Policies* (London, 1965)

Wolfers, Arnold, *Britain and France Between Two Wars: Conflicting Strategies of Peace from Versailles to World War II,* (New York, 1940)

Wrench, John Evelyn, *Geoffrey Dawson and Our Times* (London, 1955)

Wright, Gordon, *Rural Revolution in France, The Peasantry in the Twentieth Century* (London, 1964)

Young, Robert John, *Strategy and Diplomacy in France: Some Aspects of the Military factor in the Formulation of French Foreign Policy, 1934-39,* University of London, unpublished Ph.D. thesis, 1969.

Zeldin, Theodore, *France, 1848-1940* (London, 1973)

H. NOVELS

Aragon, Louis, *Les Communistes,* vol. I (Paris, 1949)

France, Anatole, *Penguin Island* (London, 1909)

Graves, Robert, *Goodbye to all that* (London, 1957)

Koestler, Arthur, *Scum of the Earth* (London, 1941)

Orwell, George, *Coming up for air* (London, 1939)

Romains, Jules, *Les Hommes de Bonne Volonté,* vol. XXVII, *Le 7 Octobre* (Paris, 1946)

Sartre, Jean-Paul, *Les Chemins de la Liberté,* vol. 2, *Le Sursis* (Paris, 1945)

I. ARTICLES

Bariéty, J., and C. Bloch, 'Une tentative de réconciliation franco-allemande et son écho, 1932-33', *Revue d'Histoire Moderne et Contemporaine,* XV, July-September 1968, pp. 433-465.

Bernstein, Serge, 'La vie du parti radical: la fédération de Saone et Loire de 1919 à 1939', *Revue Française de Science Politique,* XX, December 1970, pp. 1136-80.

Boudot, Francois, 'Sur des problèmes du financement de la défense nationale (1936-40)', *Revue d'Histoire de la Deuxième Guerre Mondiale,* XXI, January 1971, pp. 49-72.

Carlton, David, 'Eden, Blum and the Origins of Non-Intervention', *Journal of Contemporary History,* 6, 1971, pp. 40-55.

D'Hoop, J. M., 'La politique française de réarmament d'après les travaux de la commission d'enquête parlementaire', *Revue d'Histoire de la Deuxième Guerre Mondiale,* April 1954, pp. 1-26.

Fergusson, Gilbert, 'Munich, the French and British Roles', *International Affairs,* October 1968, pp. 649-665.

Haight, John McVickar (Jr)., 'France, the United States and the Munich Crisis', *Journal of Modern History,* December 1960, pp. 340-58.

Joll, James, 'The Front Populaire after thirty years', *Journal of Contemporary History,* vol. I, no. 2, 1966, pp. 27-42.

Johnson, Douglas, 'Leon Blum and the Popular Front', *History,* June 1970, pp. 199-206.

Lammers, Donald, 'From Whitehall after Munich', *Historical Journal,* XVI, 4, 1973, pp. 831-856.

Lecuir, J., 'L'Organisation de la coopération aerienne franco-britannique (1935-Mai 1940)', *Revue d'Histoire de la Deuxième Guerre Mondiale,* XIX, 1969, pp. 43-74.

MacDonald, C. A., 'Britain, France and the April Crisis of 1939', *Review of European Studies,* April 1972, pp. 151-169.

Marder, Arthur, 'The Royal Navy and the Ethiopian Crisis of 1935-36', *American Historical Review,* 1970, vol. 75, pp. 1327-56.

Michel, Henri, 'L'oeuvre de la commission parlementaire chargée d'enquêter sur les événements survenus en France de 1933 à 1945, *Revue d'Histoire de la Deuxième Guerre Mondiale,* June 1951, pp. 94-96.

Parker, R. A. C., 'Great Britain, France and the Ethiopian Crisis, 1935-36', *English Historical Review,* April 1974, pp. 293-332.

Ratliff, Ann, 'Les Relations diplomatiques entre la France et les Etats-Unis (du 29 Septembre 1938 au 16 Juin 1940)', *Revue d'Histoire de la Deuxième Guerre Mondiale,* XIX, 1969, pp. 1-40.

Sakwa, George, 'The "Renewal" of the Franco-Polish alliance in 1936 and the Rambouillet Agreement', *Polish Review,* XVI, Spring 1971, pp. 45-66.

Sakwa, George, 'The Franco-Polish alliance and the remilitarization of the Rhineland', *The Historical Journal,* March 1973, pp. 125-146.

Scherer, André, 'Le problème des "Mains Libres" à l'est', *Revue d'Histoire de la Deuxième Guerre Mondiale,* October 1958, pp. 1-26.

Stolfi, R. H. S., 'Equipment for victory in France in 1940', *History,* 55, no. 183, February 1970, pp. 1-20.

Truelle, J., 'La production aéronautique militaire française jusqu'en juin 1940', *Revue d'Histoire de la Deuxième Guerre Mondiale,* January 1969, pp. 75-109.

Vial, J., 'La défense nationale: son organisation entre les deux guerres', *Revue d'Histoire de la Deuxième Guerre Mondiale, April 1955, pp. 11-32.*

Vnuk, F., 'Munich and the Soviet Union', *Journal of Central European Affairs,* October 1961, pp. 284-304.

Wallace, William V., 'New Documents on the History of Munich: A Selection from the Soviet and Czechoslovak Archives, *International Affairs,* October 1959, pp. 447-454.

Wallace, William V., 'The Foreign Policy of President Benes in the approach to Munich', *Slavonic and East European Review,* December 1960, pp. 108-136.

Wallace, William V., 'The Making of the May Crisis of 1938', *Slavonic and East European Review,* June 1963, pp. 368-390.
    'A Reply to Mr. Watt', *Slavonic and East European Review,* July 1966, pp. 481-486.

Warner, Geoffrey, 'France and Non-Intervention in Spain, July-August 1936', *International Affairs,* April 1962, pp. 203-220.

Watt, D. C., 'Sir Lewis Namier and Contemporary European History', *Cambridge Journal,* July 1954, pp. 579-600.

Watt, D. C., 'The May Crisis of 1938: A Rejoinder to Mr. Wallace', *Slavonic and East European Review,* July 1966, pp. 475-480.

Watt, D. C., 'German Plans for the Reoccupation of the Rhineland: A Note', *Journal of Contemporary History,* October 1966, pp. 193-199.

Watt, D. C., 'Hitler's visit to Rome and the May weekend crisis a study in Hitler's response to external stimuli', *Journal of Contemporary History,* January 1974, pp. 23-28.

Young, Robert J., 'French policy and the Munich crisis of 1938: A Reappraisal', *Historical Papers* (Canadian Historical Association), 1970, pp. 186-206.
    'Preparations for Defeat: French war doctrine in the inter-war period', *Journal of European Studies,* June 1972, pp. 155-172.
    'The Aftermath of Munich: The Course of French Diplomacy, October 1938-March 1939', *French Historical Studies,* vol. VIII, no. 7, 1973.

NOTE

Because of the very long delays in the publication of this book it is necessary to point out that the text was completed in March 1974. The following books appeared after completion of the manuscript. They are studies of such importance that they must be included in any bibliography:

Les Relations Franco-Britanniques de 1935 à 1939, Communications présentés aux colloques franco-britanniques, (Paris, CNRS, 1975)

N.H. Gibbs, *Rearmament Policy,* vol. I, *Grand Strategy, History of the Second World War:* United Kingdom Military Series, ed. J. R. M. Butler (London, HMSO, 1976)

D. C. Watt, *Too Serious a Business: European Armed Forces and the Approach to the Second World War* (London, 1975)

Index

Aberdeen, Lord, 125
Abetz, Otto, 294, 299, 317, 330-2
Abyssinian crisis. *See* Ethiopia
Action Française, 10, 156
Alain (Emile Chartier), 10
Albania, 300, 308-9
Alexander, King, 32
Alphand, Hervé, 275, 297-8, 301
Alsace-Lorraine, 53
Anglo-Franco-Belgian staff conversations, 40, 70
Anglo-Franco-Turkish alliance (1939), 327
Anglo-French conversations
  29-30 Nov. 1937, 67-71; 28-29 April 1938, 179-81, 230; 18 Sept. 213-14; 25-26 Sept. 217-19, 231-2; 24 Nov. 248-50; 10 Jan. 1939, 259-60; 21-22 March, 304-5; 20 May, 315, 324-5
Anglo-French staff conversations, 40, 70-1, 86, 229-34, 246-7, 332-3
Anglo-German Declaration (1938), 270, 284
Anglo-German Naval Agreement (1935), 33, 36
Anglo-Italian Agreement (1938), 187, 255, 258
Anglo-Turkish Declaration (1939), 327
Anschluss, 63, 67, 77-81
Appeasement, 18, 59, 68-9, 80, 106-9, 22' 300, 328
Arago, Emmanuel, 116
Aragon, Louis, 137
Armistice (1918), 280
Ashton-Gwatkin, F.T.A., 298
Aster, Sidney, 336
Attolico, Bernardo, 287
Aube, L', 136, 146
Aubin, 157, 332
Auriol, Vincent, 96
Avon, Earl of. *See* Eden, Anthony

Badoglio, Marshal, 42
Bailby, Léon, 146
Baldwin, Stanley, 38

Balearic Islands, 43, 45, 69, 256
Baltic States, 272
Bank of France, 8, 14, 29, 66, 92
Banque de Paris et des Pays Bas, 144, 276
Barbusse, Henri, 281
Bardoux, Jacques, 132
Bargeton, Paul, 47, 171
Barthélemy, Joseph, 175
Barthou, Louis, 28, 31, 143, 182
Bassée, Léon, 144
Baudouin, Paul, 117, 134, 260-1, 306, 351
Baudouin-Buguet, 295
Baume, Count Renom de la, 294-5, 298
Beauffre, Captain André, 151, 167, 337-8
Beauvoir, Simone de, 60
Beck, Colonel Jozef. 89, 183-7, 271, 277, 303, 305, 319-22, 328, 337-8
Belgium, 46, 72, 161, 234
Belin, René, 351
Benes, Dr Edward, 47, 61, 79, 85, 195, 205-6, 212, 237
Béraud, Henri, 36
Bérard, Léon, 261-2
Berchtesgaden
  Agreement, 81
  Meeting, 211-12
Bérenger, Henri, 100, 131-2, 251, 293, 300, 345
Bergery, Gaston, 79, 97, 117, 133, 352
Berl, Emmanuel, 25
Berthod, Aimé, 295
Berthelot, Philippe, 137
Bethell, Nicholas, 347-8
Beuve-Méry, Hubert, 147
Bidault, Georges, 136, 146
Bloch, Marc, 148, 302
Blomberg, Field Marshal von, 67
Blondel, Jules, 81
Blum, Léon, 27, 43-4, 46, 52, 56, 84-92, 96, 112, 126, 327
Blumel, André, 52, 56, 113, 213
Bodenschatz, General, 323
Bois, Elie J., 104, 146, 277

Boisanger, Yves de, 234
Bonnet, Georges
  ambitions for premiership, 266, 277
  asked to form à government, 100
  attitudes and policies towards: Czecho-
    slovakia, 175-225; Communism, 108-9;
    eastern alliances, 265-79; Munich Con-
    ference and Agreement, 223-4, 267;
    Popular Front, 108-9; Soviet Union, 47,
    203, 273, 312; United States of America,
    99, 208-10, 222-3, 289
  Business and banking background, 110
  Career, character, 98-106
  Conversation with Bullitt,198;*with* Camp-
    bell, 334; *with* Daladier, 344; *with*
    Gamelin, 340; *with* Henderson, 333;
    with Lacroix, 194, 197; *with* Litvinov,
    183, 204, 272; *with* Lukasiewicz, 182,
    184, 186, 278, 320; *with* Osusky, 175,
    190, 198-9, 212-13, 215; *with* Phipps,
    175-6, 188, 190, 207, 210-11, 224, 241,
    253, 257, 266, 270, 300, 309, 314, 315;
    with Prunas, 187-8; *with* Ribbentrop,
    259, 269, 290-3; *with* Souritz, 274, 310,
    312-3, 326; *with* Welczeck, 188, 191,
    277, 286, 288, 301, 318
  criticisms of, 103, 302, 332
  eclipse of, 114, 327, 332
  Foreign affairs committees, 131-5
  Letter to Daladier, 221; to Ribbentrop,
    331
  Methods of working as foreign minister,
    141-3, 321; military evaluation of France
    and allies, 221, 226-44, 254; negotiations
    with Soviet Union in 1939, 327; Poland,
    319-22; Prague *coup,* 300-5; relations
    with Daladier, 109-10, 222, 331-2, 345;
    seeks British pressure on Daladier for
    negotiations with Italy, 308; war council,
    23 August 1939, 339-41; willingness to
    compromise on Danzig and Polish
    Corridor, 334-5
Bonnet, Odette, 104, 200, 332
Bonte, Florimond, 133
Boris, Georges, 277
Boulanger, General, 30
Bourret, General, 167-8
Boussac, Marcel, 221, 351
Bressy, Pierre, 146, 301, 307-8, 318, 350
Briand, Aristide, 18-19, 28, 99, 113, 138, 143,
    281-3
Brinon, Fernand de, 106, 116, 157, 261, 284,
    299
Brunet, René, 202, 215-16
Buhrer, General, 329
Buisson, Fernand, 26
Bulgaria, 275
Bullitt, William C., 48, 52, 61, 75, 100, 116-21,
    163, 176-7. 208-9, 215, 235, 243, 271, 295,

302, 312, 319, 321, 328-9, 338-9, 341-2,
    350
Bunau-Varilla, Maurice, 146
Buré, Emile, 146
Butler, R. A., 313

Cadett, Thomas, 145-6
Cadogan, Sir Alexander, 78, 80, 82, 179, 188,
    233, 274, 301, 303-4, 306, 309
Cagoule, 11, 168
Cahiers Franco-Allemands, 299
Caillaux, Joseph, 100, 108, 117, 127, 220,
    247, 256, 266, 307, 313, 352
Cambon, Roger, 91, 155, 251, 348
Cameroons, 65, 296
Campbell, R. I., 201, 343
Campe, von, 295
Campinchi, César, 123, 274-5, 307, 314, 323,
    341, 343, 345
Canard Enchaîné, Le, 156
Canary Islands, 43
Carroll, Madeleine, 188
Cartel des Gauches, 20, 30, 95
Cerruti, V., 187
Chaban-Delmas, Jacques, 7
Chadourne, Louis, 137
Chamberlain, Austen, 21, 28, 51, 281
Chamberlain, Neville, 58, 67-71, 81, 98, 130,
    162, 207, 211-25, 248-50, 258-9, 268-9,
    284, 302, 306, 315-16, 325, 333, 335,
    348-50
Chambre, Guy la, 97, 123, 289, 296, 339-40,
    341, 346
Chambrun, Count Charles de, 52
Channon, Henry, 3
Chappedelaine, Louis de, 352
Charvériat, Emile, 139, 252, 254, 311, 344
Chastenet, Jacques, 146, 313, 329
Château, 351
Chatfield, Lord, 43, 254
Chautemps, Camille, 30, 58-9, 66-71, 82-4,
    95, 123, 181, 307, 342, 345
Chauvel, Jean, 140
Chiang Kai-shek, General, 329
Chiappe, Jean, 96
Chichery, Albert, 101
China, 60, 329
Churchill, Winston, 38, 43, 90, 92, 162, 219-
    220, 228, 323, 329
Ciano, Count Galeazzo, 53, 81, 187-8, 223,
    255, 257, 314-15, 334, 344, 346-7.
Clapier, Marcel, 116
Claudel, Paul, 138
Clemenceau, Georges, 98, 121
Clerk, Sir George, 44, 53
Colonies. *See* Germany (colonial claims)
Colson, General 168
Combes, Emile, 113
Comert, Pierre, 38, 142, 148-52, 247

Comité Franco-Allemand, 281-2, 299

Comité Permanent de la Défénse Nationale (Permanent Committee of National Defence), 42, 64, 72, 169-70, 232, 242, 309-10

Confédération générale du travail (CGT), 288

Confédération générale du patronat français, 65, 295

Conscription, *See* Great Britain

Conseil Supérieur de la Défénse Nationale, 169

Conseil Supérieur de la Guerre, 170, 335

Cooper, Duff, 51, 187, 329

Corbin, Charles, 43, 67, 71, 82-3, 85, 154, 188, 207-8, 251-3, 263, 270, 301, 303, 305-6, 308-10, 320, 345

Cot, Pierre, 47, 71-2, 97, 235, 239, 341

Coulondre, Robert, 45, 48, 132, 148, 153-4, 156, 182-3, 203-4, 235-7, 261, 269-70, 287-8, 295, 298-9, 300, 302, 318, 323, 325, 330, 343-6

Crewe, Lord, 113

Crussol, Marquise de, 97, 116

Curzon, Lord, 22.

Czechoslovakia
  air force, 242
  army, 226
  British decision not to guarantee, 86
  French commitments, 23-4, 61-2, 68-70, 75-6, 84, 88, 106, 124, 175, 179, 197, 198-9, 205, 209, 212-13, 215-17
  French economic interests, 63-4, 276
  French military relations, 23-4, 40, 42, 84-5, 87-8, 227-8, 232, 234-5
  Munich Conference and Agreement 223-4
  Munich Guarantee, 268-9
  Soviet military relations, 50, 89, 237-8
  strategic significance, 226

Dahlerus, Birger, 317

Daladier, Edouard
  advisers, 115-16
  attitudes and policies towards: Britain, XV, 231, 323; Czechoslovakia, 179-80, 191, 210-11, 214, 224; eastern pacts, 266, 268, 271, 273; Germany, 106-9, 180-1, 280, 295, 328, 331; Italy, 187, 255-7, 306-8, 313-15, 328; Soviet Union, 48-9, 108-9, 325, 339; United States, 222-3, 339, 342
  Career, character, 95-8, 114-15, 180, 249
  Conversation with Bullitt, 243, 295, 310, 339; *with* Halifax, 315, 324; *with* Phipps, 210, 253, 309, 313-15, 325; *with* Welczeck 108, 191
  Domestic policy: Code Famille, 7, 358; Communist party, 96-7, 273, 357; Decree Laws, 115, 126, 129, 357; Economy, 200-1,

289, 316; Parliament, 126-36, 245, 357; Popular Front, 128-9, 201, 273
  Letter to Chamberlain, 195, 200, 333; to Hitler, 341
  message to Hitler, 295
  Relations with Bonnet, 109, 302, 327
  Stavisky scandal, 97
  war minister, 62, 84, 109

Dalton, Hugh, 51, 127, 240

Danzig, 130, 270, 303, 318-22, 328, 334-5

Darlan, Admiral François, 43, 101, 164

Dawes plan, 19

Déat, Marcel, 318, 330, 351

Debeney, General, 24

Delbos, Yvon, 42, 44-6, 66-74, 75-6, 78-84, 143, 250, 254, 284, 334

Delcassé, Théophile, 113, 143, 156

Dentz, General, 244, 246-7, 273

Deschanel, Paul, 25

Deuxième Bureau, 78, 157-8, 168, 204-5, 233, 238, 273, 300, 332, 338

Deverell, Sir Claude, 70

Dior, Christian, 221

Dirksen, Dr. H. von, 317

Disarmament, 29, 31

Djibouti, 257, 306-7

Dobler, Jean, 139

Dominique, Pierre, 25, 97, 146

Donzeau, Commandant, 236

Doriot, Jacques, 117-8

D'Ormesson, Count Wladimir, 25, 146, 258, 281

Doumergue, Gaston, 99

Dreyfus affair, 30

Duchemin, René, 281

Duhamel, Georges, 64, 281

Dupuy, Pierre, 116, 146

Eastern allies. *See* France (eastern allies)

Eastern Locarno, 31

Eden, Anthony, 28, 38, 43-4, 49, 71, 83, 143, 325, 329-30

Egypt, 308-9

Elliot, Walter, 158

Eluard, Paul, 15

Empire (French), 18, 45, 54-5, 63, 265, 291, 293, 296-7

Epoque, L', 84

Estienne, General, 166

Ethiopia, 32-6, 38

Europe Nouvelle, L', 144.

Fabre-Luce, Alfred, 25, 106, 117-8, 265

Fabry, Jean, 39, 170

Far East, 18, 48, 60, 65-6, 70, 72, 246, 328-9

Fashoda, 22

Faucher, General Eugène, 194, 234-5, 264

Faure, Paul, 12, 136, 351

Febvre, Lucien, 302

Ferry, Jules, 136
Fierlinger, Zdenek, 237, 264
Figaro, Le, 146, 258
Flandin, Pierre Etienne, 26, 39, 76, 90, 100-1, 117-18, 127, 187, 220, 265, 309, 330, 332
Fleuriau, Aimé Joseph de, 281
Foch, Marshal, 17
Fonds secrets, 144
Foreign affairs committees, 75-6, 130-6, 251, 301, 323, 329
Four Power Pact (1933), 29, 106
France
    armed forces: air force, 71-2, 88, 161-3, 239, 248-50, 258, 267, 304, 340, aircraft production, 161-3; purchase of American aircraft, 163; army, 159-161, 166-72, 226-244, 248; civilian distrust for, 30-1, 167-8; navy, 163-5
    eastern allies, 31-2, 37, 41-2, 46-50, 63-4, 75-6, 89-90, 264-79, 318-23
    economy, 4-7, 12-16, 20, 27-9, 59-60, 66, 128, 200-2, 316; overseas investments, 5, 63-4
    elections, 9, 11, 18, 125, 129-30
    Far East, *See* Far East
    French North Africa. *See* North Africa
    General Staff, 40, 42, 48, 62, 170-2, 227-8, 242-4, 266-7, 296, 311, 333, 351; war plans, 23-5, 29-30, 34, 38-40, 232, 262-3, 321-2, 340
    Germany, (1936-38), 53-6, 59, 78-9; (1938-39) 284-99; economic negotiations, 294-99; post-Prague relations, 300-1, 304-5, 308-9, 316-18, 330-2, 341, 345-6; French air mission to Germany, 238-40
    Great Britain: commitments between, 20-1, 40, 214, 218-19, 249-51, 254; French assessment of influence of Dominions on British policy, 85-6; post-1918 disunity, 21-3; relations (1935-38), 32-6, 38, 40, 43-4, 49, 51-2, 55, 66-71, 78-91, 179-81, 190-3, 195-8, 200-2, 206-8, 210-11, 213-14, 217-19, 224, 229-44; post-Munich relations, 245-63, 303-15, 324-8, 332-3, 335-6, 344-5, 347-50; attitudes towards British policies, xv, 36, 52, 54-5, 75, 82-3, 107, 211, 231, 246, 251, 268, 287, 303, 305, 309-11, 315, 323, 326
    Institutions and internal divisions, 3, 7, 9-16, 26-8, 30-1, 34-6, 45, 58-60, 65-6, 74-5, 91-2, 117-24, 125-36, 157-8, 165-6, 200-2, 245, 249, 286, 288-9, 316, 328, 334, 357;
    Italy, 31-6, 42-5, 52-3, 57, 69, 72, 80-1, 87, 90, 117, 119-20, 145, 187-9, 223, 255-7, 260-1, 306-8, 334, 343-51
    Japan, *See* Japan.
    Military measures, 39, 80, 87-8, 210, 221-2, 232, 235, 262-3, 309-10, 314, 349-51
    Pacifism, 8, 12, 25, 29, 160, 250, 294

    Parliament, 18, 34, 38, 52, 76, 80, 92, 125 36, 301-2, 342, 349, 351
    Poland. *See* Poland
    Political parties, 10-12, 14-5, 26-7, 34-5, 74-5, 79, 128-9, 136, 201, 286-7, 357; Communists, 26, 74-5, 108-9, 129, 188, 220, 273, 288, 334, 357
    Press, 18, 38, 92, 144-8, 221, 257, 299, 301, 306, 318, 357; government influence on, 144-8, 299, 318, 357
    Public opinion, 18, 37-8, 92, 124, 148, 177-8, 207, 214, 219-21, 246, 257, 286, 299, 301, 328, 357
    Rearmament, 159-66
    Soviet Union. *See* Soviet Union
France, Anatole, 280-1
Franco, General, 46, 53, 60, 259, 308, 343
Franco-German Declaration (1938), 268, 270, 274, 277, 284-94, 300, 318, 331
Franco-Soviet Pact (1935) 4, 38. *See also* Soviet Union.
François-Poncet, André, 62, 79, 152-3, 157, 195, 223-4, 255-61, 267-8, 280, 283, 285-6, 306, 308, 314-15
Frankfurter Zeitung, 66
Franklin-Bouillon, 284
Fraser, Colonel, 233
Frossard, Ludovic Oscar, 113, 120, 223, 351
Frot, Eugene, 97

Gafencu, Grigore, 317, 327
Gambetta, Léon, 136
Gamelin, General M. G., 33-4, 39, 42, 46, 50, 62, 70, 77, 87-8, 90-1, 98, 159, 167-8, 170-1, 216, 221, 225, 226-8, 231-44, 254, 259, 266-7, 271, 303, 320-2, 332, 335, 340, 348-9, 351, 355
Gamelin-Badoglio convention (1935), 33, 35, 42
Gard, Roger Martin du, 284
Gauché, Colonel, 204, 233, 238
Gaulle, Colonel Charles de, 8, 30, 39, 56, 101-2
Genebrier, Roger, 341
Gentin, Fernand, 290, 295
'Gentleman's Agreement' (1937), 53, 60
Georges, General, 168, 321
German-Soviet Non-Aggression Pact (1939), 338, 340
Germany
    air force, 161-2, 238-41
    army, 39, 161, 226-7, 232
    foreign policy: Austria, 77-80; colonial claims, 53-6, 67-8, 80, 220, 296-7, 323; Czechoslovakia, 189, 195-6, 205-6, 210-11, 217, 223-4, 276, 290-1, 300-1; Poland, 317, 380-1, 341, 342, 346; France, 37-8, 53-5, 65, 280-99, 317; intelligence and fifth column activity in France, 116, 158,

332; Paris embassy contacts with French politicians, 330.
Gerodias, General 168, 321
Gide, André, 280, 284
Gignoux, Claude-Jean, 295
Giraudoux, Jean, 25, 148
Godesberg Meeting (1938), 217
Goebbels, Dr. Josef, 132, 148, 257
Göring, Field Marshal Hermann, 156, 224, 239, 280, 285, 295
Gort, Lord, 159, 312, 332
Goy, Jean, 284
Grandi, Count Dino, 66, 81, 83
Grat, Felix, 133
Graves, Robert, 22
Great Britain
  armed forces: air force, 71-2, 161, 304; army, 5, 51, 82, 160; navy, 164; conscription, 245, 248, 251; French pressure for, 219, 245-6, 253, 313-14; defence policy and rearmament, 35-36, 70-1, 86, 164, 229-30, 248-51
  attitude towards France; 3, 21-2, 36, 51, 74, 84, 177-8, 249-51, 315; Foreign Office proposal for 'self-denying ordinance', 246; Military cooperation and staff talks with France, 5, 35-6, 40, 43, 70-1, 86, 229-44, 246-7, 332-3
  tries to influence French policy: Czechoslovakia, 86, 190, 192-4; defence, 229-34, 247, 218; domestic, 105, 247-8; Franco-Soviet Pact, 49, 51, 182, 274; Italy, 307, 313-5; Rhineland, 37-8; Spanish Civil War, 43-4; 188, 201
Greece, 309
Gringoire, 36, 148, 261
Grumbach, S, 30, 132
Guarantees, (Poland) 305; (Greece and Rumania), 308-10; (Czechoslovakia), 268-9
Guariglia, Raffaele, 343, 346
Guizot, François, 125

Haile Selassie, 34
Hainan, 262
Halifax, Lord, 65, 83, 103, 193, 206-8, 213-25, 246-7, 248-50, 260, 268-70, 274, 293, 302, 309-12, 324-7, 344-8, 352
Hankey, Colonel Sir Maurice, 21, 247
Harvey, Oliver, 103, 247-9, 260, 262
Hatay, 328
Haut Comité Militaire, 34, 39, 169-71
Havas, 144, 187
Henderson, Sir Nevile, 80, 83, 177, 296, 301, 333
Henlein, Konrad, 181, 191
Henry, Jules, 101, 141, 222, 270
Henry Haye, Gaston, 132
Herriot, Edouard, 29, 31, 47, 61, 90, 96, 119, 181, 262, 281, 283, 299, 312, 327, 351

Hesse, Prince Philip of, 285
Hitler, Adolf, 33, 65, 77, 160, 181, 195-6, 205, 210-12, 238, 221-5, 252, 284-6, 298, 313, 317, 341-2, 343
Hoare, Sir Samuel (Lord Templewood), 33, 218, 227
Hoare-Laval Plan, 33, 35, 157
Hodza, Dr. Milan, 62, 195, 217, 275
Holland, 252-3
Homme Libre, L', 144
Hoppenot, Henri, 155, 253
Hore-Belisha, Leslie, 82, 179, 251, 259, 332
Hudson, R. S., 333
Humanité, L', 11, 84, 146, 256, 260, 274

Indo-China, 60, 329
Intransigeant, L', 333
Ismay, General, 335
Italy
  air force, 160, 258
  army, 262-3
  Ethiopia, 32-6
  France, 52-3, 57, 69, 72, 80-1, 187-9, 254-9, 313-15, 344-51

Jamet, General, 335
Japan, 5, 60, 70, 72, 228-9, 329
Je Suis Partout, 121, 219
Jean-Brunhes, Georgette, 347
Jeanneney, Jules, 307, 312, 351
Jews, 287, 293
Joffre, Marshal, 167
Joliot-Curie, Fréderic, 302
Joliot-Curie, Irène, 302
Jones, Thomas, 52
Jordana, General, 256, 261-2
Jour Echo de Paris, Le, 146
Journal, Le, 146

Kasprzycki, General, 320, 322
Kayser, Jacques, 25, 73, 116, 257
Kennedy, Joseph P., 176
Kérillis, Henri de, 127, 132, 134
Keynes, John Maynard, 14, 23, 92
Kindersley, Sir Robert, 82
Krejci, General, 216
Krofta, Dr. Kamil, 41, 189
Krupps, 41.
Kundt, Dr. E., 202, 205

Lacroix, Victor de, 61, 79, 89, 142-3, 157, 175, 192, 196-99, 205-17, 235, 264, 269
Lamoureux, Lucien, 100, 117, 221, 297, 351
Lausanne
  Conference (1932), 283
  treaty (1923), 22
Lauzanne, Stéphane, 146
Laval, Pierre, 32, 33-5, 84, 90, 96, 101, 121, 128, 132, 143, 261, 283, 295, 302, 306, 330, 351

Law, A. Bonar, 22
Lazard Brothers, 82, 110
League of Nations, 17, 19, 24, 29, 34-6, 74,
    150-1, 203, 276
Lebanon, 328
Lebrun, Albert, 99, 112-13, 217, 221, 225,
    266, 302, 345
Léger, Alexis, 29, 38, 61, 67, 78, 82, 106, 124,
    137-40, 148-9, 155, 171, 223-4, 254-5,
    259, 263, 264, 270, 290, 302-3, 313-15,
    322-3, 325, 329, 339, 343-4, 350
Leith-Ross, Sir Frederick, 54-5
Lelong, General, 82, 231
Lémery, Henri, 282
Leopold, King, 342
Le Rond, General, 195-6
Levant, 22
Libya, 69, 262-3
Liddell Hart, Sir Basil, 151, 166, 168
Lindbergh, Charles A, 210, 238-42, 296
Little Entente, 23, 42, 46, 275
Litvinov, Maxim, 45, 48, 74, 121, 203-4, 237,
    272-4, 311-13, 324
Lloyd George, David, 21, 90, 306
Locarno Treaty, 38, 40
Lothian, 11th Marquess of, 51
Loustaunau Lacau, Georges, 168
Luchaire, Jean, 144
Lukasiewicz, Jules, 184-7, 271-2, 278, 303,
    306, 319-22, 337, 348-9, 351
Luxembourg, 72, 283
Lyautey, Marshal, 282

MacDonald, J. R., 98, 104, 141
MacMahon, Marshal, 30, 100
Madagascar, 293
Maginot Line, 51, 75, 161-2, 228, 248,
    312
Maisky, Ivan, 73
Majorca, 256
Malvezzi, 334
Malvy, Louis-Jean, 256, 348
Mandel, Georges, 120-2, 220, 247, 265, 274,
    288, 293, 297, 307, 329, 335, 339, 341, 350
Mann, Thomas, 287
Marchandeau, Paul, 74, 100, 119-20, 272,
    288, 307, 341, 352
Margerie, Roland de, 67, 123, 139, 142, 145
Marin, Louis, 25, 130, 133, 135, 181
Marquet, Adrien, 351
Marseilles-Matin, 92
Mason-MacFarlane, Colonel, 202, 233
Masaryk, Thomas, 62
Massigli, René, 25, 38, 67, 105, 140, 142-3,
    149-50, 247, 282, 328
Mastny, Dr. V., 224, 268
Matignon Agreements (1936), 14
Matin, Le, 146, 294
Maurin, General, 48, 170
Mayrisch, Emil, 281-2

Mediterranean, 69, 72, 227-9, 246, 256, 259,
    291-2, 308-10
Mehemet Ali crises, 22
Mein Kampf, 283-4
Memel Convention (1924), 270
Mendl, Sir Charles, 92, 145, 157, 308, 319
Michard-Pelissier, 348
Middle East, 22, 259
Milch, General, 238
Mireaux, Emile, 146, 295
Mistler, Jean, 131-2, 187, 343, 347-8
Moch, Jules, 43, 112
Moffat, Jay Pierrepont, 210
Monde, Le, 147
Monnet, Georges, 194
Monnet, Jean, 342
Montbas, Count H. Barthon de, 304
Montigny, Jean, 25, 219, 266
Monzie, Anatole de, 25, 104, 117, 120, 187,
    220, 225, 236, 239, 288, 307, 334, 339,
    343-7, 351
Morand, Paul, 138
Morocco, 160
Munich
    Agreement, 224, 267
    Conference, 223-4
    Guarantee, 268-9
    International Commission, 267-8
Murphy, Robert, 101
Mussolini, Benito, 50, 52, 57, 187-8, 223-4,
    255-60, 287, 302, 306-8, 346

Naggiar, Paul Emile, 278, 311, 327-8
Namier, Sir Lewis, 183-7, 320
Necas, Jaromir, 213
Neurath, Constantin von, 66
Newton, Basil, 61, 195, 197, 205, 215-17, 233
Nicolson, Harold, 98
Nizan, Paul, 146
Noël, Léon, 89, 142, 154, 156, 194, 266, 271,
    337, 343
North Africa, 45, 55, 65, 69, 75, 160, 256,
    262-3, 316
Notre Temps, 144
Nyon Conference (1937), 64

Oeuvre, L', 146, 318
Ordre, L', 146, 260
Osusky, Stefan, 175, 190, 198-9, 215, 269

Pabst, G. W, 299
Pact of Steel (1939), 315
Painlevé, Paul, 98-9, 112
Palasse, Colonel, 236, 273
Palewski, Gaston, 249
Papen, Franz von, 62, 282-3
Paris Peace Conference, 17, 60, 98
Paris-Soir, 146, 265
Parti populaire francais, 117-18
Patenôtre, Raymond, 123, 274-5, 332, 352

Paul-Boncour, Joseph, 30, 84-92, 104, 105, 237, 281, 299
Payart, Jean, 203, 274, 311, 324-6
Peace Ballot, 34-5
Péri, Gabriel, 76, 127, 132, 134, 146
Perrin, Jean, 302
Perth, Lord, 82, 258
Pertinax (André Géraud), 15, 97, 144-6, 274
Pétain, Marshal Philippe, 13, 84, 96, 166
Petit Parisien, Le, 104, 116, 146, 277, 307
Petitbon, Colonel, 233
Pezet, Ernest, 76, 133, 287
Peyrimhoff, Henri de, 282
Philip, Percy, 146
Phipps, Sir Eric, 32, 90, 105, 145, 177-8, 210-11, 220, 241-2, 247-8, 252-4, 266, 270, 313-15, 318, 325
Pichot, Henri, 284
Piétri, François, 31, 117, 141, 187, 221, 223, 330, 334, 346-7
Pilsudski, Marshal, 24, 29
Pivert, Marceau, 14
Poincaré, Raymond, 18-9, 113, 281
Poirier, 157, 332
Poland, 46, 89, 183-7, 236, 251, 266, 268, 271-2, 278, 303-5, 317, 319-22, 324-5, 327, 337-8, 343, 346-8
Polish Corridor, 251
Pomaret, Charles, 117, 120, 220
Populaire, Le, 260, 274
Popular Front, 44, 56-7, 79, 96, 128-9, 245, 273, 288
Portes, Countess Hélène de, 97, 123, 138
Potemkin, V. P., 50, 204, 264
Preventive war, 29-30
Proust, Marcel, 137
Prouvost, Jean, 146
Puaux, Gabriel, 81
Puricelli, 90
Pyrenees, 188, 201

Quai d'Orsay (French foreign ministry)
    Bonnet's record as foreign minister, 141-3
    criticisms of the foreign ministry, 137-40
    influence of Quai on the press, 144-8
    leakages of information, 156-7
    liaison with other ministries, 171, 321, 323
    opinions of permanent officials and representatives overseas, 148-56
    removal of officials after Munich, 247-8
Quentin, Count René Doynel de, 155, 208-9, 289
Queuille, Henri, 95, 345

Raczynski, Count Edward, 146
Radical Socialists. See France (political parties)
Radio Luxembourg, 144

Ramadier, Paul, 97, 113, 120
Rambouillet, 217
Rambouillet Agreement (1936), 46, 64, 271
Rath, vom, 287-8
Reibel, Charles, 125
Renier, Léon, 144
Renondeau, General, 223
République, La, 117, 146, 220, 333
Reynaud, Paul, 30, 39, 76, 120-4, 163, 181, 220, 249, 259, 265, 288, 307, 314, 316, 341
Rhineland, 24, 38-42
Ribes, Auguste Champetier de, 120-2, 155, 220, 307
Ribbentrop, Joachim von, 259-61, 264, 268-70, 276-9, 285-94, 290-1, 325, 327, 331, 350-1
Rochat, Charles, 140, 155, 224
Roche, Emile, 25, 100, 220
Rolland, Romain, 25
Romains, Jules, 30, 103, 137, 148, 194, 281, 342
Rome Agreements (1935), 32, 45, 158, 257
Rome-Berlin Axis, 50, 60, 255
Romier, Lucien, 282
Roosevelt, President F. D., 209, 222-3, 289, 296, 314, 339, 341-2
Rouvier, M., 136
Rucart, Marc, 194
Rueff, Jacques, 27
Ruhr, 17, 19-20, 23, 26, 29
Rumania, 89, 235-8, 242, 252, 264, 272, 275, 303-5, 308-10, 324, 327, 337-8
Runciman, Walter, 1st Viscount, 198, 202
Rydz-Smigly, Marshal, 41, 46, 156, 271

Saar, 24
Sargent, Sir Orme, 64, 66, 80, 84, 119, 201-2, 250-1, 265, 274
Sarraut, Albert, 26, 37, 41, 95, 123, 314, 343
Sarraut, Maurice, 167
Sartre, Jean-Paul, 60, 137
Sauvy, Alfred, 12
Schacht, Dr. H., 53
Schneider-Creusot, 63-4, 276
Schuschnigg, Dr. Kurt von, 41, 77-9
Schweisguth, General, 49, 166
Seeds, Sir William, 311, 325-6
Serruys, Daniel, 116
Sforza, Count, 342-3
Siam, 22
Sieburg, Friedrich, 66
Siegfried, André, 282
Siegfried Line, 234, 252, 322
Simon, Sir John, 231-2, 234
Skoda Works, 63, 276
Slessor, Group Captain J. C., 240
Socialist party. See France (political parties)
Souritz, Y. Z., 203, 274, 310, 326, 335
Soviet Union, 47-50, 73-4, 89-90, 182-3, 203-4,

235-8, 242, 272-5, 303-5, 310-13, 323-8, 335-8
Spain, 42, 188, 255-6, 261-2
Spanish Civil War, 42-5, 60, 256
Spears, Major-General Sir Edward, 219-20
Spinasse, Charles, 13
Stalin, Joseph V., 52
Stanley, Oliver, 298
Stauss, von, 282
Stavisky affair, 59, 97, 99
Stehlin, Major Paul, 323
Stern, Karl, 299
Stoyadinovitch, Dr. Milan., 47
Strang, William, 251, 325-6
Strasbourg, 38, 71, 288
Stresa Conference (1935), 33
Stresemann, Gustav, 99, 282
Stronge, Colonel, 233
Sudeten Germans, 60-1
Switzerland, 252-3
Syria, 65, 69, 160, 328

Tabouis, Geneviève, 103-4, 108, 146, 151, 274
Tardieu, André, 31, 167
Temps, Le, 76, 146, 175, 219, 255, 275, 295, 298, 318
Thierry, Adrien, 89
Thomas, Albert, 167
Thomas, Louis, 106
Thoiry, 29
Thorez, Maurice, 11, 74, 96, 181
Tientsin dispute, 329
Tilea, V. V., 303
Times, The, 145-6, 251, 258
Times Literary Supplement, 183
Titulesco, Nicholas, 41
Togoland, 65
Toussaint, Colonel, 233
Trevelyan, G. M., 65
Tukhachevsky, Marshal, 49

Turkey, 305, 309, 324, 327-8

Ukraine, 131, 251, 270, 274
Union Européenne, 276
United States of America, 4, 52, 56, 208-10, 222-3, 289
USSR. *See* Soviet Union

Valin, General, 337
Vansittart, Sir Robert, 35, 82
Vatican, 323
Versailles Treaty, 8, 17, 80, 109, 281-2, 301
Viénot, Pierre, 30, 282, 299
Villelume, Lieutenant Colonel de, 171
Voroshilov, Marshal, 49, 336-7, 341
Vuillemin, General Joseph, 49, 162, 202, 238-41, 258, 267, 321

War debts, 56, 342
Weil, Simone, 115
Weizsäcker, E. von, 223, 267-8, 278, 285-7, 301, 318, 350-1
Welczeck, Count von, 45, 53, 178-9, 191, 277-8, 286-90, 301, 317-19, 330-1, 332
Welles, Sumner, 209, 289
Werth, Alexander, 102, 103, 131
Weygand, General, 29, 31, 167-8, 247
Wiehl, E. K. J., 294
Wilson, Sir Horace, 218-9, 317, 325, 333
Windsor, Duke of, 168
Winterton, Lord, 258
Wohltat, Dr. Helmut, 317, 333

Yellow Books, 130
Young plan, 29
Yugoslavia, 275

Zay, Jean, 111, 123, 129, 147, 222, 262, 272, 288, 302, 307, 341, 345, 347, 350, 352, 362